French Provincial Cooking

Elizabeth David

French Provincial Cooking

Illustrated by Juliet Renny

Grub Street • London

This edition published in 2007 by
Grub Street
4 Rainham Close
London
SW11 6SS
Email: food@grubstreet.co.uk
Web: www.grubstreet.co.uk

Reprinted 2007

This edition is a re-issue of the original 1960 edition with the Note to 1977 edition. First published in Great Britain by Michael Joseph in 1960

Cataloguing in Publication Data for this title is available from the British Library

10 digit ISBN 1-904943-71-3
13 digit ISBN 978-1-904943-71-6
EAN 9781904943716

Printed and bound in India by Replika Press Pvt. Ltd

To
P. H.
with love

Acknowledgements

So many people have helped me in so many ways with the compiling and the production of this book—some with advice and material, others with technical assistance, typing, indexing, proof-reading—that the acknowledgements which I should like to make to all these friends would fill a number of pages.

But I have only a limited space, so I must restrict myself, first of all, to thanking Miss Audrey Withers, for so many years editor of *Vogue*, for making it possible for me to go to France on several journeys to collect material for cookery articles subsequently published in the magazine. It is these articles, with a number published in *House and Garden* between 1956 and 1959, which form the nucleus of this book.

Other material and recipes republished here first appeared in *The Sunday Times, Harper's Bazaar, The Wine and Food Society Quarterly*, Harrods *Food News* and *Wine*, edited by T. A. Layton.

M. André Simon very kindly gave me permission to reprint an article by Mrs. Belloc Lowndes which first appeared in *The Wine and Food Society Quarterly*, and Messrs. A. D. Peters to include an extract from Marcel Boulestin's *Myself, My Two Countries*, published by Cassell & Co. Messrs. Martin Secker & Warburg have also kindly allowed me to reprint a passage from Maurice Goudeket's *Close to Colette*, and Mr. Vivian Rowe has generously permitted me to reproduce an excerpt from *Return to Normandy*, published by Messrs. Evans Brothers.

Lastly, it would be ungrateful of me to miss this opportunity of thanking my friend Doreen Thornton for driving me, with much patience and care, on many rather arduous journeys around and across France in search of good food and interesting regional recipes.

Contents

Introduction

STAYING in Toulouse a few years ago, I bought a little cookery book on a stall in the *marché aux puces* held every Sunday morning in the Cathedral Square. It was a tattered little volume, and its cover attracted me. In faded pinks and blues, it depicts an enormously fat and contented-looking cook in white muslin cap, spotted blouse and blue apron, smiling smugly to herself as she scatters herbs on a *gigot* of mutton. Beside her are a great loaf of butter, a head of garlic and a wooden salt box, and in the foreground is a table laid with a white cloth and four places, a basket of bread, a cruet and two carafes of wine.

The promise of the cover was, indeed, fulfilled in the pages of this delightful little book, called *Secrets de la Bonne Table, 120 Recettes inédites recueillies dans les provinces de France*. The author, Benjamin Renaudet (date of publication not disclosed, but probably about 1900), had collected genuine recipes from country housewives, gourmet doctors, lawyers and senators, from gamekeepers and their wives, from landladies of seaside *pensions*, from the notebooks of family and friends. The dishes described are not spectacular, rich or highly flavoured, the materials are the modest ingredients you would expect to find in a country garden, a small farm, or in the market of a quiet provincial town. But it is not rustic or peasant cooking, for the directions for the blending of different vegetables in a soup, the quantity of wine in a stew, or the seasoning of the sauce for a chicken reflect great care and regard for the harmony of the finished dish. This is sober, well-balanced, middle-class French cookery, carried out with care and skill, with due regard to the quality of the materials, but without extravagance or pretension.

The book exudes an atmosphere of provincial life which appears orderly and calm whatever ferocious dramas may be seething below the surface. Here you find the lawyer's wife at work preparing her special *noisettes d'agneau* for a dinner party; a great-aunt of one of the author's friends serves the same soup her mother served to Madame Récamier when she came to dinner; the farmer's wife gathers mushrooms to garnish the chicken she is cooking for her husband when he comes in with friends from a day's shooting; a senator's cook proves to a sceptical company that an old hen can be made into a dish fit for a gourmet; the author's great-uncle at last discloses his recipe for the liqueur he makes every year and keeps locked in his linen-cupboard.

The ravages of two world wars, the astronomical rises in the cost of living, and the great changes brought about by modern methods of transport and food preservation have not destroyed those traditions of French provincial cookery. In one way indeed these circumstances have oddly combined to preserve them. After the 1914 war patriotic Frenchmen began to feel that the unprecedented influx of foreign tourists hurrying through the country in fast cars, Riviera or Biarritz bound, not caring what they ate or drank so long as they were not delayed on their way, was threatening the character of their cookery far more than had the shortages and privations of war. Soon, they felt, the old inns and country restaurants would disappear and there would be only modern hotels serving mass-produced, impersonal food which could be put before the customers at a moment's notice, devoured, paid for, and instantly forgotten. It was at this time that a number of gourmets and gastronomically-minded men of letters set about collecting and publicising the local recipes of each province in France.

At the Paris Salon d'Automne of 1924 there was, for the first time, a culinary section devoted to regional cookery. Under the direction of Edouard Rouzier, proprietor of the celebrated Rôtisserie Périgourdine, a series of regional dinners were organised and proved an immense success. Subsequently Marcel Rouff and Maurice-Edmond Sailland (who, under the pen-name of Curnonsky, came to be known throughout France as the 'Prince of Gastronomes') together published a series of guides to regional eating and drinking, not hesitating to criticise the pretentious, the dull, or the over-expensive meal when they encountered it. About the same time Count Austin de Croze compiled a book listing the products, the dishes, the cheeses and wines of every province, followed in 1929 by a closely-packed volume of recipes called *Les Plats Régionaux de France*. Before long regional cookery became fashionable. There had, of course, previously been a few restaurants in Paris specialising in the food and wines of the native province of the proprietors, but they were little known except to the habitués of the quarter and to provincials exiled in Paris. These regional restaurants now began to multiply and become smart. Today one could eat some different provincial speciality in Paris restaurants every day for weeks on end.

Country and seaside restaurateurs also began to realise the possibilities of attracting tourists by advertising some famous local dish on their menus. Often such dishes derive from peasant and farmhouse cookery and depend rather upon some typical product of the region such as a cheese or ham, mountain mutton or river fish, chestnuts, walnuts, lentils, dairy produce, rather than upon important sauces or the skill of professional chefs. But the restaurateurs do not despise them on this account. They are encouraged to serve them by the local Syndicat d'Initiative, some member of which hardworking body has probably searched the municipal archives for cookery manuscripts and persuaded members of old local families and the librarians of the great religious houses to contribute recipes.

But recipes alone are not enough. A flourishing tradition of local cookery implies also genuine local products; the cooks and the housewives must be backed up by the dairy farmers, the pig breeders and pork butchers, the market gardeners and the fruit growers, otherwise regional cookery simply retreats into the realms of folk-lore. France is still largely an agricultural country and the right conditions for the preservation of their traditions still prevail. These traditions are constantly being renewed from within; the professional cooks and the housewives adapt the old methods to changing tastes and altered conditions without thereby standardising all the food; competitions and gastronomic festivals encourage the chefs to develop new dishes based on the old ones but still using the essential ingredients; the tourist organisations work hard to foster their own local products and cookery magazines publicise them in a sane and sober way, so it is not so surprising that the regional cookery of France is a profitable and flourishing industry as well as a beneficent one.

One hears, however, and reads in the newspapers, so many bitter criticisms from English tourists about French food that a few words of warning may not be out of place. Many people who have read of the great regional specialities such as, let us say, the *Bouillabaisse* and the *Estouffat de Bœuf* of Provence, the *Cassoulet* of the Languedoc, the pike with *Beurre Blanc* of the Loire or the *Coq au Vin* of Burgundy mistakenly suppose that these dishes are cooked every day by the local housewives and the restaurateurs, and are disappointed and indignant if they are not forthcoming at a few minutes' notice. This is as absurd as if a Frenchman came here expecting to find plum pudding or Cornish lobsters at every meal and in every wayside café.

The great traditional set pieces are only made by the country people in France for feast days and holidays, wedding celebrations and other special occasions; their day-to-day food will be the simple dishes of ordinary middle-class French cookery, vegetable soups, egg dishes, beefsteaks, veal roasts, mutton ragoûts, sausages, pâtés, and salads; these may well have a regional character owing to some local tradition of seasoning or according to whether olive oil, butter, or pork fat has been used in the cooking; but they will not be the dishes advertised in the travel agencies' brochures. The restaurateurs do, of course, put these specialities quite frequently on their menus, but not every day, and very often to order only, and the fact that this is so is reassuring to anyone who prefers his food to be freshly cooked rather than dished out of a great pot kept warm over steam for several hours.

Again, there is the seasonal aspect of French cookery; to many tourists French food is known only through summer holidays, and many of the great specialities of regional cooking are then out of season. Although, yielding to a certain extent to public demand, the restaurateurs put on as many of their well-known dishes as they are able, many of these will not be at their best. High summer is not the most propitious moment for freshly made pork products and pâtés: with the best will in the world I do not think one could eat a *cassoulet toulousain*, a Provençal *chou farci* or a *gratin dauphinois* on a hot August day, even if a chef would consent to cook them. Few of the great French cheeses are in prime condition in the late summer, and the price of fresh fish and vegetables rises steeply in the tourist season.

Unfortunately, there are a few restaurateurs in France today willing to barter their birthright of taste, moderation and simplicity in cooking for the cheap publicity and quick profits of showy food served in and out of season to gullible customers with more money than sense. It is, however, perfectly easy to keep away from such pretentious and phoney places, three or four stars in the guides all too often indicate expensive décor and fussy service rather than good food; but it is equally inadvisable to go too far in the other direction. Half the complaints one hears come from people who expect to go to a humble bistro or transport café, the equivalent of which in England it would not occur to them to enter, and there to find an impeccably served and perfectly cooked meal of choice ingredients for the price of a glass of beer and a sandwich in an English public house. They will, of course, be disappointed, and the publicity recently given to the *Cafés Routiers* in this country is partly to blame. These transport cafés are places where an adequate meal, served, it is true, rather more attractively than in their English counterparts, is provided in a somewhat perfunctory manner by nimble but overworked waitresses who have not the patience to stand at your table while you deliberate upon your meal; nor has the cook the time to attend to special orders. You must take what is on the menu, unless you want sour looks and a bill out of all proportion. Occasionally you come across an exceptional establishment of this kind; if it happens to be your first experience of such a restaurant, it would be unwise to assume that it is typical; but if you are not in a hurry and if food happens to be one of your serious interests, it would probably be worth staying in the neighbourhood and making friends with the proprietor, who will almost certainly be pleased to provide special local dishes to order, particularly in the evening when there are not so many customers.

For it should be remembered by the traveller in France that in provincial towns and in the country the main meal of the day is at noon. Nowadays many summer tourists economise by having picnic lunches, and this is an admirable plan in some ways because the buying of provisions in the local shops and markets is not only itself an entertainment and an education but gives the traveller a good idea of the resources of the country; in the market you can find out for yourself which are the genuine local cheeses, what kind of sausages and hams are favoured in the district, what vegetables and fruit are in season, what is the particular characteristic of the local pâtés, and which fish have been plentiful in the market, so that even if you can't afford the really good restaurants you will at least get some idea of the region's food. On the other hand, when you arrive at your evening's destination, you may well find, at any rate in the more modest hotels and restaurants, that the specialities on the midday menu were all eaten up and you will have to make your choice from the already rather too familiar *terrine du chef*, the *truite aux amandes*, the *entrecôte garnie*, the *poulet rôti* and the *crème renversée* of the routine and relatively expensive set meal.

The cooking of these dishes would possibly make them into notable meals here in England, but in France one's expectations are higher, and one's disappointment at a dull meal consequently greater. But still, with a little forethought (one's plans all too often go astray when driving about the countryside, but I am supposing for the moment that they have not) one can nearly always get good food in France. Often it happens that a long day's drive, arduous sightseeing, or hours in the unaccustomed sunshine have made one too tired to cope with a 'menu gastronomique' of seven or eight courses even if money is no object, and in any case so much of one's enjoyment of a meal depends upon having the right food at the right moment. So as long as one arrives in good time for dinner, it is always worth explaining to the *patron* of the restaurant or the hotel what sort of meal one would like; the chances are that he will be able to provide one or two of the lesser local specialities such as some sort of *charcuterie* and perhaps a little cheese which he would not otherwise have thought of offering, because English people are generally thought only to want beefsteaks or fried eggs and chips; he will be only too pleased to find tourists interested in the genuine food of the country, and those who reject the pompous menu got up for innocent foreigners are likely to find all the more respect in his eyes.

Under such circumstances I have eaten some of the most enjoyable of French country meals; unexacting ones, ordered and served with the minimum of fuss. An omelette, perhaps, followed by the sausages which were a speciality of the local butcher, a vegetable dish and some cheese;

or perhaps snails and a homely stew, intended probably for the *patron's* own dinner but gracefully surrendered; or a vegetable soup, a slice or two of country-cured ham and a beautiful big green artichoke; and on another occasion, a *langouste* with a mayonnaise which was among the best I have ever tasted, because of the fine quality of the Provençal olive oil which had gone into it, and which was followed by a dish of tender young string beans of that intense green and delicate flavour which only southern-grown beans seem to acquire.

Surely, then, good food is there for those who look for it; bad food, too, and rather more than there used to be, but if one gets it, one very often has only oneself to blame, for arriving late and tired in some small town, for weakly going into a place obviously unsuitable, for omitting to make friends with the *patron* before ordering, for mismanagement generally. Such occasions are bound to occur, but they are the exceptions rather than the rule. And one of the great points about the cookery of France is that it is so extraordinarily varied. There seems to be an inexhaustible fund of new dishes to be discovered.

Note to 1977 Edition

It is the best part of thirty years since I started amassing the material which eventually turned into this book. It was published in 1960. Over the years, a certain amount of what I wrote about the provinces of France has inevitably passed into history. Nobody would pretend that the deep freeze isn't everywhere, or that restaurants don't sometimes serve disgraceful prefabricated sauces and inadmissible travesties of famous dishes. I'm afraid that guidebook promises have made us expect rather too much of French restaurant food.

In the markets, however, all over France incomparable produce still abounds. Buying food for picnics or to cook in holiday houses is more than ever a joy an inspiration.

When it comes to using the recipes, my inclination now is to try harder than ever for quality. A little fine olive oil, or true, clear stock, or double cream from Jersey herds, or a few fresh eggs laid by decently-fed, humanely-reared hens go a lot further than twice the amounts of third-rate makeshifts. Sybille Bedford said it all when she wrote that Escoffier's injunction *'faites simple'*, much invoked since I quoted it in these pages, 'doesn't mean *faites slapdash'*. That goes for our choice of raw materials just as much as for their preparation and cooking.

E.D.
April 1977

French Cooking in England

WHEN Curnonsky, the famous French gastronome and writer, who died in 1956 at the age of 83, describes the four distinct types of French cookery '*La Haute Cuisine, la cuisine Bourgeoise, la cuisine Régionale, et la cuisine Improvisée*' he might perhaps also have mentioned that other well-known branch of French cooking, *la cuisine À LA française*, or French food as understood and cooked by foreigners all over the world. As a Frenchman, perhaps he did not think this cooking worth consideration, but certainly he would not have sought to deny the fascination and the influence which French cookery exercises upon civilised people in all parts of the world.

With *la haute cuisine* I am not here concerned. Although at its best it is professional cooking by chefs of the very highest achievement, many sins have been committed in its name; and for financial and economic reasons it is becoming rare, even in France. The feeling of our time is for simpler food, simply presented; not that this is necessarily easier to achieve than *haute cuisine*; it demands less time and expense, but if anything a more genuine feeling for cookery and a truer taste. It is the kind of cooking which, once more, was meant by Curnonsky when he repeated, over and over again, that good cooking was achieved when 'ingredients taste of what they are.'

The principle is the one upon which English cookery also is based. Fundamentally, then, there is little in the French system which need inspire us with awe of the unknown; no basis for talk of mysterious 'secrets,' nor for easy jibes about poor materials masked with complicated sauces. There is one factor, though, that has to be remembered. A country's national food appears completely authentic only *in* that country. It is a curious fact that French dishes cooked by a Pole or a Chinaman in France are liable to seem more genuinely French than the same dishes cooked by a French cook in England, Germany, Italy, Poland or New York. The climate, the soil, the ingredients, the saucepans, the stove, even the way of arranging the food upon the serving dish, of folding the napkins and setting the table, as well as the French attitude of mind towards food, and the very smell of their kitchens while they are cooking, all play their parts.

It works both ways. A *rosbif* in Paris is not English roast beef; what the French eat and drink at *le goûter* would puzzle and infuriate an English nanny invited to tea. In France it is mildly surprising to find that any cooked ham goes by the name of *jambon d'York*, and that, all unbeknown to us, one of the most highly esteemed English cheeses is called *le Chester*. But this is quite encouraging to us, who are often mocked by the French, however amiably, for our misconceptions about their food, and scoffed at by our own catering profession, some eminent members of which are fond of claiming that English stomachs are fit only to digest roast meat, boiled vegetables, and fried fish. But then all of us nowadays, except perhaps these curiously bigoted members of the catering profession, have travelled a little, and on visits abroad have acquired tastes which, so far from disagreeing with us, have become a part of our daily lives.

Not that we all return from France so converted as the bus conductor who, a Soho shopkeeper tells me, comes in regularly once a week for two dozen snails, nor even so well informed as the barrow boy who asked me, when I was buying aubergines and peppers, if I was 'going to make a nice *ratatouille*, dear?' But when we say to friends, 'we'll just have an omelette and a salad and a piece of cheese,' what we mean is 'we won't make any fuss, but what we have will be well chosen, will make a satisfying meal and will go nicely with a glass of wine'; without our even knowing it, a little piece of French wisdom in the matter of eating has rubbed off on to ourselves.

It is when it comes to cooking of a slightly more elevated kind than the simple omelette and salad that we go astray. We get self-conscious, try too hard, and the result is perhaps a failure. Now, any woman, or man, who is capable of cooking a good English roast with potatoes, is a good enough cook, given a little encouragement, to produce something rather more imaginative. If a dish does not turn out to be quite as it was at the remembered auberge in Normandy, or at the restaurant on the banks of the Loire, is this a matter for despair? Because it is *different*, as by force of circumstance it must be, it is not necessarily *worse*. It is for us to exercise our common sense in selecting what is within our powers, in taking what suits us from the immense variety of dishes which France has to offer, and to learn how to make them our own (within limits, of course—you can't cook up a sole and a piece of hake and a couple of tomatoes and call it a *bouillabaisse*). But there is one mistake we nearly all make when first attempting French cookery. We make it too complicated. A galaxy of seasonings, oceans of wine and cream, thick sauces and a mass of garnishes are alien to the whole spirit of French cookery. Does a Paris milliner put lace trimmings on a fur hat?

Well then, here is the advice of Escoffier, one of those extremely rare great chefs whose work, although the longest and most brilliant period of his career was spent outside his own country, is as respected there as it is in England. And two of the most valuable words he ever wrote were these: *Faites Simple*.

What a Frenchman intends these words to mean may not be quite the same as what an English cook would understand by them. They mean, I think, the avoidance of all unnecessary complication and elaboration: they do *not* mean skimping the work or the basic ingredients, throwing together a dish anyhow and hoping for the best. That is the crude rather than the simple approach. To prove the point, try simplifying a recipe which calls for rather a lot of ingredients down to the barest essentials. You may well find that the dish is more pleasing in its primitive form, and then you will know that your recipe was too fanciful. If, on the other hand, the dish seems to lack savour, to be a little bleak or insipid, start building it up again. By the end of this process, you will have discovered what is essential to that dish, what are the extras which enhance it, and at what point it is spoilt by over-elaboration. This system is also useful in teaching one how to judge a recipe for oneself, instead of following it blindly from a cookery book.

The Cookery of the French Provinces

To compile a comprehensive volume of French regional recipes would take a lifetime of work and research; even then it could not be complete, because like any other lively art, or science or craft, whichever you prefer to call it, cookery is continually evolving. So all I have set myself to do in the present volume is to put together a small collection of French recipes which have pleased me and which can be reproduced in English kitchens without too much difficulty. Such a selection must naturally reflect the author's own tastes and preferences. But I have also tried to exercise a due regard for practical matters, omitting dishes which, however good, are disproportionately expensive or troublesome. But people's ideas as to what constitutes extravagance, or tediousness in the matter of preparation, naturally differ a good deal so I have tried to provide as wide a choice as my experience and space allow. I hope that readers who wish to pursue the knowledge of French cookery beyond the limited introduction contained in this volume will find the bibliography on pages 462–73 useful.

In the brief survey of the different kinds of French provincial cookery which follows I have tried to convey some idea of the variety of dishes which may be found by those who care to look. These notes are, like my choice of recipes, based on personal preferences and experiences. If I start off these impressions with a description of the food of Provence it is not necessarily because I am convinced it is the best. I have heard people with some claims to being connoisseurs assert that 'there is no cooking south of Dijon.' Preposterous though such a statement may sound, it is a question which each person must judge for himself. And if I seem to be biased in favour of the food of the South, it is perhaps because the country itself has for me such a very powerful appeal. But that is by no means to imply that I am blind to the charms of the lovely dishes of Normandy and Brittany, of Anjou and the Loire Valley, of Alsace and Lorraine and the Dauphiné, of the Languedoc and the Auvergne and Burgundy.

Provence

Provence is a country to which I am always returning, next week, next year, any day now, as soon as I can get on to a train. Here in

London it is an effort of will to believe in the existence of such a place
at all. But now and again the vision of golden tiles on a round southern
roof, or of some warm, stony, herb-scented hillside will rise out of my
kitchen pots with the smell of a piece of orange peel scenting a beef
stew. The picture flickers into focus again. Ford Madox Ford's words
come back, 'somewhere between Vienne and Valence, below Lyons on
the Rhône, the sun is shining and south of Valence Provincia Romana,
the Roman Province, lies beneath the sun. There there is no more any
evil, for there the apple will not flourish and the brussels sprout will not
grow at all.'

It is indeed certain, although the apple of discord can hardly be said
to have been absent from the history of Provence, which is a turbulent
and often ferocious one, that the sprout from Brussels, the drabness and
dreariness and stuffy smells evoked by its very name, has nothing at all
to do with southern cooking. But to regard the food of Provence as just
a release from routine, a fierce wild riot of flavour and colour, is to over-
simplify it and grossly to mistake its nature. For it is not primitive food;
it is civilised without being over-civilised. That is to say, it has natural
taste, smell, texture and much character. Often it looks beautiful, too.
What it amounts to is that it is the rational, right and proper food for
human beings to eat.

Madame Léon Daudet who, under the pen-name of Pampille, published many years ago a little collection of regional recipes called *Les
Bons Plats de France*, goes so far as to say that 'the cooking of Provence
seems to me the best of all cooking; this is not said to hurt the feelings
of other provinces, but it is the absolute truth.' Whether or not one
agrees with Madame Daudet's wonderfully sweeping statement one
should on no account be deceived by the often clumsy attempts of
London restaurateurs to reproduce Provençal dishes. To them Provence
is a name, a symbol to display to their customers; the string of garlic
hanging on the wall is something like the equivalent of an inn sign.
Nor must some ostentatious meal in a phoney Provençal 'oustalou'
whose row of medals stands for price rather than true taste or quality
be taken as representative. Provence does not consist only of the international playground of the coast. Northern and western Provence, the
departments of the Vaucluse and the Basses Alpes, are still comparatively unsophisticated, and the cooking has retained much of its traditional character, the inhabitants relying on their own plentiful resources
of vegetables, fruit, meat, game and cheese rather than on the imports
from other provinces and from Algeria which supplement the more
meagre resources of the coastal area.

Provençal food is perhaps best considered in terms of a meal such as that described, again, by Madame Daudet: 'I know of nothing more appetising,' she says, 'on a very hot day, than to sit down in the cool shade of a dining-room with drawn Venetian blinds, at a little table laid with black olives, *saucisson d'Arles*, some fine tomatoes, a slice of water melon and a pyramid of little green figs baked by the sun. One will scarcely resist the pleasure of afterwards tasting the anchovy tart or the roast of lamb cooked on the spit, its skin perfectly browned, or the dish of tender little artichokes in oil . . . but should one wish, one could make one's meal almost exclusively of the hors-d'œuvre and the fruit. In this light air, in this fortunate countryside, there is no need to warm oneself with heavy meats or dishes of lentils. The midi is essentially a region of carefully prepared little dishes.'

This was written in 1919, but these little dishes of Provence are still to be found in country restaurants where they aren't falling over backwards to provide local colour; places where you may perhaps have the routine Sunday grilled or roast chicken but with it an interesting anchovy sauce, or a mayonnaise made unmistakably with real Provençal olive oil; or a *rôti de porc* with *pommes mousseline*, the interest lying in the fact that that purée of potatoes will be good enough to serve as a separate course because the aromatic juices from the roast have been poured over it. It may be an hors-d'œuvre of anchovies and eggs, a salad of chick peas, a *pot-au-feu* or a beef stew which will be different from the *pot-au-feu* and the beef stew of other regions because of the herbs and the wine that have gone into it, even because of the pot it has cooked in. There will be vegetable dishes, too. The *haricots verts* are remarkable, although of course you won't get them on the crowded coast in August. Provence is now a great market garden centre, and from Cavaillon and Pertuis come melons, asparagus, artichokes, lettuces, courgettes, aubergines, peaches and cherries to enrich our own English markets. The little town of Le Thor supplies France with great quantities of table grapes; Carpentras is the centre of a lively trade in the local black truffles. The natural caves round about the astonishing red and ochre village of Roussillon are used for a large-scale cultivation of mushrooms; Apt provides peach jam and bitter cherry jam and most of the crystallised apricots we ourselves buy at Christmas time. It is also one of the few places hereabouts where you can still find the old traditional earthenware *gratin* dishes, saucepans and cooking pots of Provence.

Of course the inhabitants of Provence do not live upon *aïoli* and *grillades au fenouil* and *bouillabaisse*; in the hill villages of the Var and the Comtat and the Vaucluse you are lucky if you get fresh fish once a week; on the other hand nearly every village butcher makes his own sausages and pork pâtés, up in the Basses Alpes their own *pâté de grives*, too, and sometimes there will be locally cured ham, *jambon de montagne*. Once in the little town of Sault, on the lower slopes of the Mont Ventoux, I heard an old peasant lady getting very agitated because the shop assistant had inadvertently cut her a slice of ordinary commercial ham instead of the locally cured variety. The ham was for her dish of *petits pois* and that *jambon de Paris* would make it insipid, did Mademoiselle understand? Yes, Mademoiselle understood perfectly, and kept everybody in the crowded shop waiting while she cut the precise piece of ham required by the old lady.

In the season, in the villages of the Vaucluse, asparagus or wonderful broad beans will be a few francs a kilo, a basket of cherries or strawberries the same. Perhaps you may arrange for the bus driver to bring you some *brandade* of salt cod out from Cavaillon or Apt for Friday lunch; at Les Saintes Maries and Aigues Mortes and other places isolated out in the marshes the travelling market stall called the Lion of Arles sets up in the Place and sells Arles sausage, *charcuterie* and good butter. Perhaps a sheep farmer's wife will come down the hill with rabbits to sell, and the ewe's milk cheeses called *Banons*, wrapped in chestnut leaves or flavoured with the peppery herb called *poivre d'âne*, the Provençal version of savory.

Provence is not without its bleak and savage side. The inhabitants wage perpetual warfare against the ravages of the mistral; it takes a strong temperament to stand up to this ruthless wind which sweeps Provence for the greater part of the year. One winter and spring when the mistral never ceased its relentless screaming round our crumbling hill village opposite the Lubéron mountain we all seemed to come perilously near to losing our reason, although it is, of course, only fair to say that the truly awful wine of that particular district no doubt also contributed its share. It was the kind of wine which it was wisest to drink out of a tumbler so that there was room for a large proportion of water. I often wonder, when I hear people talking so enthusiastically of those fresh little wines of Provence, how they would feel about them if they had nothing else to drink. Most of them are made by the co-operative societies nowadays, and what they have lost in character they appear to have gained in fieriness. Of course there are good wines in Provence but finding them is not easy, and the situation is further aggravated by the growing habit of Provençal restaurateurs of serving all white and rosé wines so frozen that any character they may have had has become unrecognisable.

Then there was the tragic spring of 1956 when it was not so much the mistral which had struck Provence as the terrible frosts of the preceding winter. Acre upon acre of blighted, blackened olive trees made the

Provençal landscape almost unrecognisable. Hundreds of small farmers had lost their livelihood for years to come.

It does not do to regard Provence simply as Keats's tranquil land of song and mirth. The melancholy and the savagery are part of its spell.

Paris, Normandy and the Ile de France

Although I did not realise it at the time, it was by way of Norman cookery that I first learned to appreciate French food. Torn, most willingly, from an English boarding school at the age of sixteen, to live with a middle-class French family in Passy, it was only some time later that I tumbled to the fact that even for a Parisian family who owned a small farm in Normandy, the Robertots were both exceptionally greedy and exceptionally well fed. Their cook, a young woman called Léontine, was bullied from morning till night, and how she had the spirit left to produce such delicious dishes I cannot now imagine. Twice a week at dawn Madame, whose purple face was crowned with a magnificent mass of white hair, went off to do the marketing at Les Halles, the central markets, where she bought all the provisions, including flowers for the flat. I don't think any shopping at all was done locally, except for things like milk and bread. She would return at about ten o'clock, two bursting black shopping bags in each hand, puffing, panting, mopping her brow, and looking as if she was about to have a stroke. Indeed, poor Madame, after I had been in Paris about a year, her doctor told her that high blood pressure made it imperative for her to diet. Her diet consisted of cutting out meat once a week. With Friday a fish day anyway, this actually meant two days without meat. On Wednesdays, the day chosen, Madame would sit at table, the tears welling up in her eyes as she watched us helping ourselves to our *rôti de veau* or *bœuf à la cuillère*. It was soon given up, that diet. Her grown-up children, two of whom were afflicted with a tragic eye disease and were probably going blind, simply could not bear to watch her sufferings—although, of course, they were not prepared to go so far as to share in her privations. Denise, the only able-bodied daughter, was the greediest girl I had ever seen. She worked as secretary to a world-famous Parisian surgeon, and came home every day to the midday meal. Before she took off her hat and coat she would shout out to Léontine to know what was for lunch. Munching through two helpings of everything she would entertain us to gruesome details of the operations performed by her employer.

It never occurred to me at the time to wonder whether she had really

witnessed these harrowing sights or if it was just her own way of express-
ing her family's morbid preoccupation with death and disaster, which
reached its peak every Thursday. For Thursday was Madame's *jour*, and
not even the really remarkable turn-out of cakes and *petits fours*, mostly
made by Léontine, reconciled us to the fact that courtesy demanded we
put in an appearance and listen to stories of the appalling catastrophes
which had befallen during the week la cousine Anne-Marie, Tante
Berthe, her daughter Marguerite, mortally stricken with diabetes, and
about half a dozen other ladies always dressed from head to foot in
deepest black.

To make up for the ordeal of Thursday afternoon, the boarders
(there were only three of us) soon got round to finding some pretext
for not being present at Friday lunch. Ever since those days it has
remained a mystery to me how people who were so fond of good food
and who knew so much about it could endure to eat the boiled salt cod
which was the regular Friday lunch. Grey, slimy, in great hideous
flakes, it lay plonked on the dish without benefit of sauce or garnish of
any kind. At that time I had not even heard of Provençal cooking, or of
any of the excellent ways they prepare salt cod in the south, and did
not of course know how the people of Provence would scoff at the very
idea of a Norman cook producing a decent dish of *morue*. In any case, to
avoid this horror, we used to treat ourselves to lunch in a students'
restaurant near the Sorbonne, where we thought ourselves lucky to eat
egg mayonnaise and a dish of *petits pois* without being questioned by the
family as to what the morning's lectures had been about.

Another place where we enjoyed ourselves hugely was at the automatic
restaurant, in the Boulevard St. Michel I think, all shining chromium and
terribly noisy, where we got a plate of ham and an orange out of a slot
machine for a few francs. Eating here was forbidden by Madame, who
considered that neither the *ambiance* nor the food were suitable for young
girls. We used to memorise the menu posted up outside some approved
restaurant so that we should have an answer ready when she questioned
us. We seldom got away with it, of course, because we were never able
to describe the food in the detail required. What appalling *ordures* had
been in the so-called *vol-au-vent*? Were the *boulettes de viande* made from
beef or veal or lamb? Ah, tiens, *des épinards à la crème*, and did they
really contain cream or some horrible *sauce blanche*? Vous ne le savez pas?
Mais comment, chère Elisabeth, you did not notice? No, chère Elisabeth
had not noticed and did not care, for the fact was that although we
enjoyed the good food in the Rue Eugène Delacroix, we were bored
with the family's perpetual preoccupation with it, and there was little
else to talk to them about; for when they were not actually eating or

going to market, Madame and her eldest daughter were either wearing themselves out with long vigils in church or knitting for the poor. We felt stifled by the atmosphere of doom which seemed always imminent in the household, and spent more and more time in our rooms mugging up for our exams and thinking of every possible excuse for not coming in to meals.

So it was only later, after I had come home to England, that I realised in what way the family had fulfilled their task of instilling French culture into at least one of their British charges. Forgotten were the Sorbonne professors and the yards of Racine learnt by heart, the ground plans of cathedrals I had never seen, and the saga of Napoleon's last days on St. Helena. What had stuck was the taste for a kind of food quite ideally unlike anything I had known before. Ever since, I have been trying to catch up with those lost days when perhaps I should have been more profitably employed watching Léontine in her kitchen rather than trudging conscientiously round every museum and picture gallery in Paris.

* *   *

I do not think that the Robertots spent, as the French are always said to do, a disproportionate amount of their income on food. What with the bargains from Les Halles, the wine arriving in casks from Bordeaux, and cream and butter from their Norman property, their food was lovely without being rich or grand. Above all, as I see it now, it was consistent, all of a piece, and this of course was due to Madame's careful buying. There was none of that jerky feeling you get when the marketing is erratic or careless. So what emerges from those days is not the memory of elaborate sauces or sensational puddings, but rather of beautifully prepared vegetables like *salsifis à la crème*, purées of sorrel, and *pommes mousseline*. Many egg dishes, and soups delicately coloured like summer dresses, coral, ivory or pale green, a salad of rice and tomatoes, another of cold beef, and especially, of course, Léontine's chocolate and apricot soufflés. On soufflé days Denise would suddenly find she was in a fearful hurry to get back to work. This meant that the soufflé was handed to her first. She not only saw to it that she got it before it had had a chance to sink, but if there was enough for a second helping she had first go at that too.

*   *   *

Sometimes I spent part of the Easter or summer holidays with the family at their little Norman farmhouse near Caen. Here a local girl, Marie, took over the cooking, while Léontine returned to her family in the country for what must have been a well-earned rest. The only vivid memory I have of the food in this peaceful and pretty house with its old-fashioned kitchen garden is of tasting mussels for the first time. They were served in a thick creamy sauce which no doubt had cider or white wine in its composition; this seemed to me a most mysterious and extraordinary dish, something which must be quite special to the family or perhaps thought up by Marie, the little village girl, so that when a year or two later I found *moules à la crème* on the menu at Walterspiel's in Munich, at that time one of the most famous restaurants in Europe, I was quite astonished and wondered how it had found its way from that obscure little Norman village all the way to Bavaria. To this day a dish of mussels is one of the first things I ask for upon landing in Northern France, and the last thing I eat before crossing the Channel to return to England, for although since that first time I have eaten mussels served in dozens of different ways in many parts of Europe and have cooked them myself hundreds of times, they never seem to have quite the *cachet*, the particular savour, of those mussels of Normandy, so small and sweet in their shining little shells.

* * *

To the traveller as yet unacquainted with Norman cookery an impression that perhaps the inhabitants live on duck pâté and *tripes à la mode de Caen* might arouse a faint feeling of apprehension as he walks round a big Norman town such as Rouen. Every two yards there seems to be a *charcuterie*, its windows fairly bursting with all the terrines and galantines, the pâtés and *ballotines*, all made of duck; and the butchers as well as the *charcutiers* display earthenware bowls of ready-cooked tripe, very inviting looking in its savoury bronze jelly. But neither duck nor tripe, he feels, is quite the dish for every day. There is no need to worry. Take a look round the market in the morning and the spectacle is thoroughly reassuring. The fish is particularly beautiful in its pale, translucent northern way. Delicate rose pink langoustines lie next to miniature scallops in their red-brown shells; great fierce skate and sleek soles are flanked by striped iridescent mackerel, pearly little smelts, and baskets of very small, very black mussels. Here and there an angry-looking red gurnet waits for a customer near a mass of sprawling crabs and a heap of little grey shrimps. Everywhere there is ice and seaweed and a fresh sea smell.

Outside, the vegetable stalls are piled high with Breton artichokes, perfectly round with tightly closed leaves; long, clean, shining leeks; and fluffy green-white cauliflowers. At the next stall an old country woman is displaying carefully bunched salad herbs, chives, chervil, sorrel, radishes and lettuces. So far, it could well be the central market of any one of a score of French towns. But when you get to the dairy stalls, then you know you could only be in the astonishingly productive province of Normandy, where you buy the butter of Isigny and of Gournay carved off a great block, where bowls of thick white cream and the cheeses of Camembert, Livarot, Neufchâtel, Pont l'Evêque, Rouy, Isigny and a dozen other districts ooze with all the richness of the Norman pastures.

How deeply our own roots are in Normandy quickly becomes apparent to the English traveller. The churches, the old timbered houses, the quiet villages, the fruit orchards, the willows hanging over the streams, are familiar. But not the cooking (although I have heard tell of two country dishes which, in effect, must be almost identical with our own rice pudding and apple dumplings, but have never come across them). It is indeed curious that, with such similar pasture lands, we should never have taken to the manufacture of anything like the soft rich cheeses of the Normans, while they have apparently never attempted to make anything in the manner of Cheddar or Gloucester. And while we on the whole prefer to eat our butter with bread and our cream with fruit, the use of these two ingredients in Norman cooking is almost excessively lavish, both of them appearing to possess qualities which make them turn to the consistency of a sauce with very little effort on the part of the cook. When you get melted butter with a trout in Normandy it is difficult to believe that it is not cream. When a chicken or vegetables are served with a cream sauce it is most likely pure cream, unthickened with egg-yolks or flour, although it may well be enriched with Calvados, the cider brandy of Normandy. The quality of this famous Calvados varies enormously (the most reputed comes from the Vallée d'Auge, one of the chief cider districts) and it is rare to come across a really fine old Calvados except in private houses; perhaps in any case it is an acquired taste. In cooking, however, even a comparatively immature Calvados gives to sauces a characteristic flavour which cannot be imitated with any other brandy or spirit, and which I find very delicious, especially with pork and veal. Cider is of course also used in Norman cookery, although not perhaps to the extent generally supposed, and rarely in restaurants, where chefs consider that white wine gives a more delicate flavour and a better colour to the more sophisticated dishes of Norman cookery.

For the rest, the meat in Normandy is of high quality. The sheep from the salt marshes of the Cotentin yield delicious mutton and lamb; the veal is tender, the beef well nourished; the favourite local pork dishes include the *Andouille de Vire*, a lightly smoked chitterling sausage with a black skin, which is a great deal nicer than it looks, and *rillettes*, that soft, melting kind of potted pork which is to be seen in great pyramids in the *charcuteries*, and which, with the duck pâté and the *andouille*, are the mainstays of a Norman hors-d'œuvre.

Then there are the famous duck dishes made with the *Caneton Rouennais*, which is a very different bird from that of Aylesbury. A cross between a domestic and a wild duck, the breed of Rouen has a flavour, rich and gamey, all its own, due not only to breeding but to the fact that in order to retain their blood they are strangled in a manner which would not be tolerated in this country, where we treat our animals with more consideration than we do our fellow men. Mostly, Rouen ducks are partly roasted, the breast meat carved, and the carcase pressed to extract the blood, which forms an important element in the finished sauce. At Duclair, famous for a breed of duck which is a variation of that of Rouen, the Hôtel de la Poste has no fewer than fourteen ways of presenting duck, including a plain spit-roasted one as well as a very rich *canard au sang* and a *pâté de canard au porto* served in the rugged terrine in which it has cooked. It is interesting to compare these Norman duck pâtés with those of Périgord and Alsace, for they have a quite distinct and different flavour.

As for the renowned *tripes à la mode de Caen*, cooked for about twelve hours with ox feet, cider, Calvados, carrots, onions and herbs, I must confess that nowadays I quail from eating it, let alone from undertaking the cooking of such a dish. It is only at its best when prepared in copious quantities and preferably in a special earthenware pot rather the shape of a flattened-out tea pot, the small opening of which ensures the minimum of evaporation. Formerly, the pot of tripe was carried to the bakery to be cooked in the oven after the bread had been taken out, and nowadays it is more often ordered in a restaurant or bought ready cooked from the butcher or *charcutier* and heated up at home. Anyone intrepid enough to wish to attempt it at home will find a recipe in Escoffier's *Guide to Modern Cookery*.[1] His ingredients include 4 lb. of onions, 3 lb. of carrots, 2 lb. of leeks, 2 quarts of cider and ½ pint of Calvados or brandy besides the four feet and practically the whole stomach of the ox. And it is highly advisable, having eaten your *tripes à la mode*, to follow the Norman custom of drinking a *trou Normand*, or glass of Calvados, as a digestive before going on to the next course. One might think there wouldn't be a next course, but one would be mistaken. An important meal in this region, says Curnonsky in a guide to eating in Normandy, is always arranged thus: '*bouillon* and *pot-au-feu*, after which a glass of wine is taken; then tripe; then leg of mutton. Here a halt is called for the *trou Normand*. We fall to again with roast veal, then

[1] Heinemann 1956 edition.

fowl, then the desserts, coffee, and again Calvados.' This was pre-1939, and a mere snack compared with the lunch described by George Musgrave seventy years earlier in a travel book about Normandy.[1] He watched a couple (on their honeymoon, he thought) on board the river steamer at Rouen consuming a midday meal of soup, fried mackerel, beefsteak, French beans and fried potatoes, an omelette *fines herbes*, a *fricandeau* of veal with sorrel, a roast chicken garnished with mushrooms, a hock of ham served upon spinach. There followed an apricot tart, three custards, and an endive salad, which were the precursors of a small roast leg of lamb, with chopped onion and nutmeg sprinkled upon it. Then came coffee and two glasses of absinthe, and *eau dorée*, a Mignon cheese, pears, plums, grapes and cakes. Two bottles of Burgundy and one of Chablis were emptied between eleven and one o'clock.

The Île de France

A HOUSEHOLD IN THE EIGHTEEN-SEVENTIES

My own introduction to French cookery came about, as I have written in the foregoing notes on Paris household cooking, through a family of which every member appeared to be exceptionally food-conscious. That was in the nineteen-thirties. Mrs. Belloc Lowndes' quotation below from the diary of a young English girl staying with French friends in the seventies of the last century reveals that the carefully cooked and delicious food which made such an impact on myself was in precisely the same tradition as that served in a well-ordered household some sixty years previously. The kind of food, in fact, which constitutes the core of genuine French cookery, but which to us seems so remarkable because it implies that excellent ingredients and high standards are taken for granted day by day, whereas in our own kitchens the best efforts tend to be made only for parties and special occasions.

'Before August 1914, France was in very truth the land of Cocaigne. The war of 1871 had lasted less than a year, and though during the Siege of Paris the Parisians of all classes had ended by eating dogs, cats, rats and mice, the greater part of the country remained untouched by the fearful scourge; what is now called 'total war' was undreamed of. By the summer of 1872 everything connected with the preparation and serving of food, though the prices of most things had increased, had returned to normal. This was even true of a household as devastated as had been my home at La Celle St. Cloud.

'This beautiful little hamlet between Versailles and Marly-le-Roi is curiously untouched, or was the last time I was there, in the spring of 1939. Our house stands on a hill, and commands a magnificent view of the Valley of the Seine.

[1] *A Ramble through Normandy*, George M. Musgrave, 1855.

That view is bounded on the left by the Terrace of St. Germain, and on the right by the haze which always hangs over Paris.

'Where almost all my childhood and my early girlhood were spent, the head of our family, my grandmother, Madame Swanton Belloc, ruled as Queen. The household was not large, but as her friend of fifty years—Adelaide de Montgolfier, daughter of the inventor of the balloon—who always lived with her in the summer, brought her own personal maid, there were three servants, and a boy of about sixteen who ran errands, and made himself generally useful. Each of the servants could cook, and cook well, and there was none of the formality below stairs which then existed in every English household of the same type.

'In addition to a considerable circle of friends, my grandmother constantly entertained her daughters and their children, and her great-nephews and great-nieces. They were always welcome, and as there was no telephone, and the coming of a telegram would have been regarded as heralding a disaster, my aunts and my cousins frequently appeared without having given any notice. There were few days when we had not one or more guests to luncheon and dinner.

'I do not recall any discussion taking place as to food, good or otherwise, but a good deal of thought and care, and, what would have seemed to the mistress of an English country house of moderate size, a great deal of money as well, must have been spent by the even then aged mistress of the establishment, and that though there was never anything served in the way of *primeurs*.

'By an odd chance I quite lately found a diary kept by a young English cousin of my mother, during a visit to La Celle St. Cloud in 1876. She was the only daughter of a well-known London lawyer, and when at home lived in a way many English people would have thought luxurious—but she was evidently astonished and impressed by the *déjeuners* and *diners* to which she sat down each day. So much was this the case that she often took the trouble to put on record what had been served on a certain day. Her diary, which is meagre, contains little of interest apart from what I am about to quote.

'I find under the date of 19 July, the following entry:

' "Today old Monsieur Barthélemy Saint-Hilaire came to lunch (he is said to be a son of the great Napoleon, and he is very much like the famous bust of Napoleon as First Consul). Though he is quite an old man, only a little younger than Madame Swanton Belloc, for whom he evidently feels a fond affection, he did full justice to the *déjeuner* to which we sat down rather later than usual, as he had come from Paris by a way which took two hours and a half, so he must have started about nine!

' "We began with an omelette, in which was some delicious minced kidney. This omelette was so 'tasty' that I later asked Catherine, who was the cook this morning, to tell me exactly how it was made. She said two kidneys were first braised very slowly, then cut up, minced, and added to the omelette at the last moment, just before it was turned over in the pan. I told her I had heard it was a mistake to use more than two or three eggs when making an omelette. She laughed, and said that was true only if one hadn't a big omelette pan; but as she had a huge pan which is used for nothing else, it is easy for her to make an omelette for as many as five or even six people.

' "After we had eaten our omelette, we had cold salmon trout with a large silver tureenful of mayonnaise sauce. The salmon was brought from Versailles yesterday, by the housemaid who had gone there to see her sweetheart who is doing his time in the Army. It was cooked at once, as the weather is very sultry, and was far nicer than if it had been served hot. French people do not care for salmon—only for salmon trout, a fish which is seldom seen in London.

' "We then had hot roast chicken, and with it simply an endive salad. To my astonishment I learned that the chicken had been basted with the best butter for something like an hour and a half at frequent intervals. The butter was served as a sauce, in a separate sauce-boat.

' "Where the French, in my opinion, do not compare with the English is in the matter of puddings and sweets. But always, when Monsieur Saint-Hilaire is expected, there is his favourite *cœur à la crème*. This is a kind of sweet cream cheese, shaped like a heart, and with it was served a large dish of tiny, very ripe *fraises des bois* which were truly delicious. There was sugar, but without the cream which always accompanies strawberries in England.

' "Coffee was served in the drawing-room, and as I was the only girl in the party (we were five), I poured out the coffee, handed round the cups, and offered Monsieur Saint-Hilaire a choice of either brandy or a liqueur. To my astonishment Bessie told me that she thinks one reason why Madame Swanton Belloc is so vigorous, and still does so much work—she spends every morning at her writing table—is because of the good food she has always eaten during her eighty years of life. Yet I noticed that she ate much less than her old admirer. She only had a small helping of the omelette, and a little chicken and salad. Nothing else. But *he* ate everything and evidently enjoyed it all. At about three o'clock he got up and declared it was his intention to walk down to Bougival, where he would find a tram to take him to St. Germain, where he was going to spend the afternoon and dine with Monsieur Thiers." '

MRS. BELLOC LOWNDES
From an article in the Wine and Food Society Quarterly,
Summer 1945

Alsace and Lorraine

It was a late spring afternoon as, driving from the ancient city of Bar-le-Duc, we approached Nancy. It was already getting dark, and we preferred to see the capital of Lorraine for the first time in daylight. Turning back into the country, we spent the night in a seedy roadhouse on the banks of the Moselle, where the cooking was of about the same standard of artistry as the blue pottery gnomes with which the dining-room was unsparingly ornamented. It was just the sort of place in which the tourist is liable to land when too late and too tired to drive any farther, so we had only ourselves to thank for this bad beginning. In this case it was of little consequence (and it might have been worse, for we did manage to needle out some very acceptable local wine, the *vin gris* of Toul, the existence of which the landlord had done his best to conceal at the very end of a pretentious and expensive wine list) for we were all the more anxious to be up and away before breakfast, and to see the great Place Stanislas for the first time in the early morning sunlight.

The extreme elegance and aristocratic grace of the Place Stanislas, the beauty of Héré's columns and arcades, the delicacy and fantasy of Lamour's black and gilt wrought-iron balconies, and of the grilles and the gates which mark the four entrances to this square make a powerful impact when seen for the first time. As a monument to pure eighteenth-century taste the Place Stanislas must be unique in Europe. It was indeed of Nancy that Maurice Barrès, himself a native of Lorraine, wrote that 'here remains fixed the brief moment in which our society achieved its point of perfection.'

On our way from the Place Stanislas to the central food market we pass what seems, at least at breakfast time, to be an almost unbroken line of bakeries and pastry shops, wafting infinitely beguiling smells from their warm interiors. In the end, of course, we have not the strength of mind to pass another. As we go in to order our croissants, there in front of us upon the counter and all round the shop are piled hundreds of flat round orange and gilt tins, glinting and shining like little lamps in the pallid sunshine. The tops of the tins are decorated with pictures of the wrought-iron grilles of the Place Stanislas and in gilt lettering bear the words LES BERGAMOTTES DE NANCY. Upon inquiry the assistant tells me that these are little boiled sweets, scented with essence of Bergamot, and are one of the oldest specialities of Nancy. I had heard vaguely of these Bergamottes without having any precise idea as to whether they were a cake, a sweet, or perhaps some sort of candied flower petal, and as I walked away carrying my pretty little tin of childish sweets I thought how often some such trivial little discovery colours and alters in one's mind the whole aspect of a city or a countryside. On a former occasion it had been the crystallised violets of Toulouse which had caused that remarkable city of ferocious history and dignified rose and ochre buildings to show yet another side of its character; for frivolous little boxes of *violettes de Toulouse* tied up in pale mauve satin ribbons are displayed amid swirls of violet tulle in every confectioner's window.

The province of Lorraine is rich in such small associations. The first city you enter driving east from Champagne is Bar-le-Duc, ancient capital of the Dukes of Bar and Lorraine, but more familiar to me as the home of those magically translucent preserves, half-jam, half-jelly, of red currants, white currants or little strawberries, sold in miniature glass jars in luxury Paris grocery stores, and some-times served at dessert with cream or cream cheese. At the little town of Commercy originated the small, fragile, shell-shaped cakes called madeleines so beloved of French children, and which have become celebrated in French literature because it was the taste of a madeleine dipped in a cup of tea which Proust used as the starting point of his long journey into the past. (How the English madeleine, a sort of castle pudding covered with jam and coconut, with a cherry on the top, came by the same name is something of a mystery.) The name Epinal on a signpost brings back another childish memory, of primitive coloured pictures and sheets of brightly uniformed soldiers, the *images d'Epinal* which have the same primitive charm as our penny-plain twopence-coloured prints. To Lunéville, where the château was built as a replica, on a small scale, of Versailles, belongs that thick white china sprayed with stylised pink and red roses which is, to me, inseparable from the memory of café au lait in bowls, and croissants, and crisp curls of very white butter on little oval dishes. On the map of Lorraine are also to be found Contrexéville and Vittel of the mineral waters, reminders of countless restaurant cars and wagon-lits; Baccarat of the crystal decanters and wine goblets; and on all the postcard stands are crude coloured pictures of a young woman serving a great flat cartwheel of a *quiche Lorraine* to some rough peasantry seated round a scrubbed farmhouse table. The pink wine of Toul may remind collectors of insignificant in-formation that it was in that city that Claude Gelée, rather better known as le Lorrain, was apprenticed as a pastry cook before he found his real vocation as a painter. Le Lorrain is, in fact, sometimes credited with the invention of puff pastry, but this is perhaps over-enthusiastic on the part of French cookery historians, for surely it was already known to Italian cooks before Lorrain's time. (He may of course have learnt how to make it in Italy, for he worked as pastry-cook to an Italian landscape painter in Rome.)

In the great covered market place of Nancy there are new sights to be seen. Here are big bowls of pale amber-green and gold *choucroute*, and stalls bulging with sausages, the special smoked ones to go with the *choucroute*, and large, coarsely cut, but as it turns out later, most subtly flavoured sausages for boiling (our own sausage manufacturers could learn a thing or two from these Lorraine and Alsatian *charcutiers* if they cared to do so); smoked fillets and loins of pork, terrines and pâtés of pork, duck, tongue; and deep dishes in which pieces of pork lie embedded in a crystal clear jelly; this turns out to be the famous *porcelet en gelée*, an elegant brawn of sucking pig which makes a fine hors-d'œuvre; then there are trays of highly flavoured salad made from pig's head, and flat square cuts of streaky bacon smothered in chopped parsley—'to keep it fresh'—the delicious mild-cured pale pink hams of Luxeuil, strong creamy cheeses called *Géromé des Vosges*, and others studded with caraway seeds, the *Anisé* of the Lorraine farmhouses; and —but it is nearly lunchtime, and in a busy provincial town like Nancy it is as well to secure your table soon after midday, and we have already learned from the menu pinned up outside the Restaurant of the Capucin Gourmand that that famous *quiche* is cooked fresh for every customer, and we shall have to wait at least twenty minutes for it. . . .

* * *

Although it is usual to think of the provinces of Alsace and Lorraine as very similar in character, a distinct change becomes perceptible as one leaves Lorraine and drives down to the wine country of Alsace.

Lorraine, although it was an independent Duchy until it passed to the crown of France on the death of Stanislas, father-in-law of Louis XV and last Duke of Bar and Lorraine, appears to the visitor to be very French. After a few hours in Alsace one begins to feel that France is far away. The people seem to be very quiet, reserved, even wary. It is not surprising when one remembers their history. But one misses the noise, the chatter, the stuffy typical smells of France. There is something disconcertingly Swiss, or is it Austrian, about the apparent calm and neatness of the wine villages, many of them completely destroyed in the last war and now rebuilt. Those that escaped intact, such as Riquewihr, almost unchanged since the sixteenth century, have a curiously unreal air, almost as if they had been put up for a Walt Disney film. But then, as one recognises names such as Ribeauvillé, Bergheim and Mittelwihr which have long been familiar on wine labels, these places come once more into a life of their own.

The cookery here is very interesting, with a variety of traditional dishes remarkable even for a French province. This is partly due, no doubt, to the tenacity with which the people clung to their old customs during the years of German domination, partly also because of the influence of an old-established Jewish colony whose traditional dishes, brought from Poland, Austria, Russia and Germany, have become part of Alsatian cookery. Again, in spite of the devastations of the last two wars, the Alsatians have each time succeeded in rebuilding their towns and villages, re-establishing their industries, agriculture, and wine

B

production. The expansion of this wine industry and its attendant publicity being an important part of the rehabilitation policy, the restaurants in Alsatian towns, and particularly in the wine districts, tend to serve specialities very much designed to go with the local white wines.

For instance, discussions as to the best wine to serve with *foie gras* are always cropping up amongst connoisseurs and in wine and food magazines; in Alsace there is no question: a Riesling or a Traminer of the country will be placed upon the table almost before you have ordered it. The combination seems to me to be an excellent one, but whether it is the best I am in no position to pronounce. (H. Warner Allen advocates a red wine, finding a Côte Rôtie from the Rhône ideal.)

The *foie gras*, a slice or two of the whole goose liver, studded with truffles, or else a pâté or a terrine, is served very cold as an hors-d'œuvre, in solitary splendour, and is very expensive even in its home town of Strasbourg. The rest of the meal will be composed with an eye to the continued service of white Alsatian wines. In one very old-established restaurant of Strasbourg, so discreet as to be hardly recognisable as a restaurant until you get the bill, we followed our *foie gras*, on the advice of the management, with whole baby chickens grilled and coated with breadcrumbs, parsley, chopped hard-boiled egg and *noisette* butter. A little bowl of caraway seeds came with the Münster, a strong, rich, creamy textured cheese which, at the right stage of ripeness, is one of the great cheeses of France; then there were pancakes stuffed with a Kirsch-flavoured cream. The very fine Mirabelle which was our *digestif* was served in large wide goblets cooled with ice. But except for the superb *foie gras* this meal was far outclassed by the beautiful and imaginative cooking provided by M. Gaertner at the Armes de France in the rebuilt village of Ammerschwihr (it was almost totally destroyed in 1944) in the wine country.

I shall not quickly forget my first dinner at Gaertner's. An onion tart, flat as a plate but still somehow oozing with cream, preceded a subtly flavoured sausage served hot with a mild and creamy horseradish sauce as the only accompaniment, followed by *haricots verts* fairly saturated in butter; we were then beguiled into eating a sweet called a *Vacherin glacé*. This turned out to be an awe-inspiring confection of ice-cream, glacé fruits, frozen whipped cream, and meringue, which left me temporarily speechless. But coffee and a glass of very good Kirsch soon put matters right. Indeed no Alsatian meal is complete without a glass of one of the local *eaux-de-vie* made from fruit for which the country is famous. Apart from the fact that a taste for Framboise, Mirabelle, Kirsch, Quetsch, Prunelle and so on is very easy to acquire, some such *digestif* after a meal is almost as much a necessity as the wine which is drunk with it.

English visitors are apt to disregard this fact, looking upon the final liqueur as a luxury or a feminine frivolity; but these are not liqueurs at all as we understand the word; they are pure fruit spirits with a powerful bouquet (particularly the Framboise, which has such an over-powering scent of raspberries that the actual taste comes as rather an anti-climax) and a high alcoholic content without being in the least fiery or coarse. Taken in moderation, they are the best possible aids to digestion after a copious meal.

I cannot resist describing one more of the Gaertner dinners, for so often a second meal in a restaurant where the first impressions were good proves to be a disillusion. On this occasion it was the reverse. M. Gaertner's skill and his creative imagination became even more apparent. His *pâté de foie gras* and *mousse de foies de volaille*, smooth, pink, and marbled with green pistachio nuts and black truffles, served on a big, flat dish and surrounded with fine sparkling jelly, were as good and delicate as they looked. The *coq au coulis d'écrevisses*, a plainly cooked chicken with the palest of rose pink sauces of the most perfect creamy texture and subtle flavour, was accompanied by a bowl of plain, moist rice, and was the most lyrical of dishes. It would be impossible to imitate this sauce of river crayfish with any lobster or other sea fish; some restaurateurs do attempt to pass off such imitations but they are coarse and rough compared to the real thing. Not for nothing has M. Gaertner two Michelin stars; but his prices seemed relatively very moderate. Cooking of this quality is rare, and cheap at any price. The utter lack of bombast or ostentation with which it is served would also be uncommon elsewhere but is typical of Alsace. Expressions of appreciation are accepted with courteous reserve. Extravagant or indiscriminate praise would be received, one feels, with a chilling silence.

And if after these descriptions anyone still thinks that a visit to Alsace would entail the consumption of quantities of the national and somewhat formidable *choucroute garnie*, or the noodles and pastes and cakes and breads and *kugelhopf* for which Alsatian cooks are famous, I can only say that there is no necessity, so long as you don't eat at the brasseries, ever to worry about these things, although it would be a pity not to try them once at least.

Brittany and the Loire

Following the Loire from the port of Nantes in Brittany down through Anjou and Touraine to the Orléanais, the traveller in search of good food will find some of the most lovely and typical dishes in all French provincial cookery. Not extraordinary or spectacular dishes, perhaps, but, based as they are on raw materials of very fine quality and cooked in quite simple traditional ways, they make a strong appeal to English tastes. For not even the most bigoted of Englishmen could level the time-honoured taunts of 'messed-up food' or 'poor materials disguised with rich sauces' at the beautiful fish, the sole and mackerel and sardines, the mullet and the bass, the lobsters, scallops, clams, oysters, mussels and prawns of the Breton coast, at the lamb reared in the salt marshes, at the Nantais ducklings served with the tiny green peas or the baby turnips of the district. From Le Mans and La Flèche come chickens which rival those of Bresse, from the Prévalaye butter which has been famous at least since Madame de Sévigné's day, from Angers and Saumur the delicious fresh cream cheeses called *crémets* which are eaten with sugar and fresh cream, from Touraine the *rillettes de porc* which figure in every local hors-d'œuvre, and which you can see piled up in gigantic earthenware bowls and jars in all the market places and in the *charcuteries*.

At restaurants in Nantes, Tours, Angers, Vouvray, Langeais, Amboise and many other places along the banks of the Loire is to be found the unique speciality of this country, the famous *beurre blanc* which, starting off as a sauce to counteract the dryness of freshwater fish such as pike and shad, has become so popular that any excuse to eat it is good enough. Made solely from a reduction of shallots, which are to Angevin cooking what garlic is to Provence, and wine vinegar whisked up with the finest butter, the *beurre blanc* is Anjou's great contribution (although the Nantais also claim it as their own) to the regional cookery of France.

From Touraine comes another interesting recipe, a dish of pork garnished with the enormous, rich, juicy prunes which are a speciality of the Tours district.

This remarkable dish is to be found on the menus of at least two restaurants in Tours, and the recipe, given to me by one of them, is on page 362.

In Tours also, as well as in many Breton restaurants, are to be found *palourdes farcies* which are clams served in the shell with a lovely *gratiné* stuffing; then there are various versions of chicken cooked with tarragon, and a *dodine de canard* which is not the stewed duck in red wine usually associated with this name, but a very rich cold duck galantine served as a first course. Here, too, I remember wonderful wine-dark *matelotes* of eel, and a very excellent dish of *alose à l'oseille*, shad grilled and served with a sorrel sauce. It is only for a short spell during the early summer that one comes across this dish locally, for it is then that the shad—which, incidentally, is not nearly such an uncomfortably bony fish as it is advertised to be—comes up the estuary of the Loire. But on the whole I think it is less for the food, delicious as it is, than for the lovely white wines of Anjou and Touraine, particularly those of Sancerre, Pouilly and Vouvray, that one remembers meals in this part of the country. It always seems to me that while one can drink just as superb Burgundies and Bordeaux in England as in France (and, nowadays, not very much more expensively), these Loire wines have, when drunk on the spot, a lyrical quality which often seems to be missing when one drinks them in England. But the experts would probably say that this is just a question of mood and surroundings.

The Savoie

The following account, which originally appeared, in French, in a professional catering magazine, seems to me of great interest as a record both of French country-house hospitality before the 1914 war and of the impression left by this kind of cooking upon the most celebrated chef of his day.

ESCOFFIER'S SHOOTING WEEK-END FIFTY YEARS AGO

'Although it is already a good long time ago, I well remember a shooting party given by one of my friends who owned a vast property in an exquisite valley of the Haute-Savoie. My friend had chosen this domain so that he could go there to rest from time to time, far from the irritations of a too active life. It was the beginning of November, a period when the shooting offers particularly attractive sport, especially in these rather wild districts. About ten guests were assembled on the Thursday evening, and it was decided that at dawn the following morning we should all set out, dispersing as chance directed, in search of a few coveys of partridge.

'Our meal, that evening, was composed of a cream of pumpkin soup with little croûtons fried in butter, a young turkey roasted on the spit accompanied by a large country sausage and a salad of potatoes, dandelions and beetroot, and followed by a big bowl of pears cooked in red wine and served with whipped cream.

'Next morning at the agreed hour, we were all ready, and furnished with the necessary provisions and accompanied by local guides, we climbed the rocky paths, real goat tracks, without too much difficulty; and before long the fusillade began. It was those members of the party who had gone ahead who were opening the shoot by bagging two hares; the day promised to be fairly fruitful. And indeed so it turned out, since we were back at the house by about four o'clock, somewhat tired, but proud to count out: three hares, a very young chamois, eleven partridges, three capercailzies, six young rabbits and a quantity of small birds.

'After a light collation, we patiently awaited dinner contemplating the while the admirable panorama which lay before us. The game which we had shot was reserved for the next day's meals.

'Our dinner that evening consisted of a cabbage, potato and kohl-rabi soup, augmented with three young chickens, an enormous piece of lean bacon and a big farmhouse sausage. The broth, with some of the mashed vegetables, was poured over slices of toast, which made an excellent rustic soup. What remained of the vegetables were arranged on a large dish around the chickens, the bacon and the sausage; here was the wherewithal to comfort the most robust of stomachs, and each of us did due honour to this good family dish.

'To follow, we were served with a leg of mutton, tender and pink, accompanied by a purée of chestnuts. Then, a surprise—but one which was not entirely unexpected from our host, who had an excellent cook—an immense, hermetically sealed terrine, which, placed in the middle of the table, gave out, when it was uncovered, a marvellous scent of truffles, partridges, and aromatic herbs.

'This terrine contained eight young partridges, amply truffled and cased in fat bacon, a little bouquet of mountain herbs and several glasses of *fine-champagne* cognac. All had been lengthily and gently cooked in hot embers. At the same time was served a celery salad. As for the wines, we had first the excellent local white wine, then Burgundy, and finally a famous brand of champagne. The dinner ended with beautiful local fruit, and fine liqueurs.'

* * *

'The next day, Saturday, after breakfast, which consisted of boiled eggs, fresh butter from the farm and coffee with cream, we spent the morning visiting the farm and the neighbourhood. At half-past twelve we were once more gathered in the great dining-room, with two extra guests. The mayor and the village curé had been invited, an invitation which must have been all the more acceptable to them because of their rather monotonous lives in this remote part of the country.

'Luncheon was composed partly of the trophies of the previous day's shooting; the pure mountain air had advantageously taken the place of any apéritif; nor did we have any hors-d'œuvre but instead, some *ombres-cheva-liers*[1] from the lac du Bourget, cooked and left to get cold in white wine from our host's own vineyards. These were accompanied by a completely original sauce, and here is the recipe:

RECIPE: Grated horseradish, mixed with an equal quantity of skinned walnuts finely chopped; a dessertspoon of powdered sugar, a pinch of salt, the juice of two lemons, enough fresh cream to obtain a sauce neither too thick nor too liquid.

* * *

[1] The nearest English equivalent of this famous lake fish is char, which used to be fished in the Cumberland and Westmorland lakes, but is now, I believe, very rare.—E. D.

'After the *ombres-chevaliers*, we had eggs scrambled with cheese, enriched with white truffles which a shepherd had brought from the boundaries of the Savoie, close to the frontier of Piedmont.

'Then came an excellent civet of hare *à la bourgeoise*, assuredly far superior to all the fantasies known as *à la royale*; there seems no point in giving the recipe here, for it is to be found in the *Guide Culinaire*. The majestic roast consisted of the capercailzies in the centre of a great dish, surrounded by the partridges, and the small feathered game of which we had made, the day before, a hecatomb.

'A superb *pâté de foie gras*, sent direct from Nancy, was scarcely touched; on the other hand, we did considerable justice to the dessert: the season's fruits and excellent little cream cheeses.

* * *

'Having risen from table at six o'clock, we once more found ourselves there, as if by chance, three hours later, for a little cold supper; have I not already said that the air of the mountains is the best of apéritifs?

* * *

'The following day, which was Sunday, we were obliged, not without regret, to take leave of our hosts and return home. As we had two good hours of driving before arriving at the railway station, where we should not in any case have found a decent inn, we had a final lunch before our departure. It was composed of eggs and bacon, little galettes of maize flour fried in butter, a *terrine* of rabbit and cold meats.

'The chamois had been put to marinate, and would be cooked some days later for other guests.

'We all carried away with us the happiest memory of this beautiful country of Savoie and of the very hospitable welcome which we had received. For my part, I have never forgotten the sauce of horseradish and walnuts.'

A. Escoffier

Translated from 'Le Carnet d'Epicure,' January 15, 1912

Burgundy, the Lyonnais and the Bresse

La Meurette, la Pouchouse, la Gougère, le jambon persillé de Bourgogne, le jambon à la lie de vin, les porcelets à la gelée, les escargots à la Bourguignonne, le bœuf Bourguignon, le râble de lièvre à la Piron, le coq au Chambertin, la potée Bourguignonne, les petites fondues au fromage, la queue de bœuf des vignerons, les haricots au vin rouge: how the names alone of these Burgundian dishes seem to smell of the vineyard, the wine cellar, and the countryside.

Most of them are cooked with wine; others, the cheese dishes in particular, are designed to bring out the best qualities of the wines of Burgundy, whether great or humble, white or red. These dishes might, I think, be said to represent the most sumptuous kind of country cooking brought to a point of finesse beyond which it would lose its character. Here are none of the grandiose or fanciful creations of the over-zealous chef, no *filet de bœuf à la haute finance*, no *poularde farcie à l'archiduc*, no fussy fillets of sole with truffles and stuffed artichoke hearts, but rather meat and poultry, game and fish in copious helpings served on fine large dishes and surrounded by the wine-dark sauces which look so effortless, and in practice are so difficult to get precisely right. The additional garnish of cubes of salt pork or bacon, mushrooms, and glazed button onions are known, wherever French cookery is practised, as the sign of a Burgundian dish.

There is little, it will be noticed, in this full-flavoured cookery to indicate that, in the manner of the English wine connoisseur, you must eat nothing but a grilled cutlet or a mushroom on toast with your fine vintages of the Côte de Beaune and the Côte de Nuits. The menus of the Burgundian wine-growers' dinners read like something from the age when the Dukes of Burgundy feasted in royal state in the Palace of Dijon where the great vaulted kitchen was also the banqueting hall.

On January 29, 1949, for example, while we were struggling with our little bits of rationed meat and our weekly egg, the Burgundy wine potentates sat down to a meal of *boudin* and *andouillettes* (blood sausage and chitterling sausage) with real Dijon mustard; sucking pig in jelly flavoured with Meursault; the *matelote* of freshwater fish called *Pouchouse*, with pounded garlic stirred into the sauce, a haunch of wild boar with a rich *Grand Veneur* sauce and potato croquettes; roast chickens; and cheeses. The sweet was a confection called a *Biscuit Argentin* in honour of the Argentine Ambassador who was present at the banquet. The wines were a white Aligoté from Meursault, a Beaujolais or two from the previous year's vintage, two admirable wines from the Côte de Beaune, three great vintages from Nuits-Saint-Georges, Clos Vougeot and Musigny respectively, and a sparkling Burgundy from the Côte de Nuits (the chronicler of the event is reticent about this). The liqueurs were Burgundian Marc and Prunelle. To the Burgundians their wine is the most important consideration. But they are not niggardly eaters either.

* * *

The Lyonnais, their neighbours, are inclined perhaps to think more about their food than their wine; not that it could be said of them that they are niggardly drinkers, for their beloved Beaujolais flows in rivers, and it has indeed been said of Lyon that it is situated on three rivers, Rhône, Saône—and Beaujolais. But delicious and fresh as a genuine Beaujolais can be, the wines of this district do not pretend to aspire to the heights of the great wines of Burgundy, and the majority are drunk very young, the draught wine being sold locally by the 'pot,' a measure or bottle containing a little under half a litre.

Lyonnais cooking has a very great reputation. It is not, however, of a kind which I find very much to my taste. It is sometimes said that one must be a Lyonnais properly to appreciate the local cookery, and this is probably true. It would also, I think, be fair to say that the cooks of Lyon have given out so much to France, to Europe and to the Americas, that when one actually reaches this fountain-head of French provincial cookery one is conscious of a sense of anti-climax. Of the renowned *charcuterie*, only one product, the *cervelas truffé*, comes up to expectations. This is a large, lightly cured pork sausage, liberally truffled, which may be eaten sliced as an hors-d'œuvre, or poached and served with potatoes, or even used whole as a stuffing for a piece of boned and rolled meat. The ordinary everyday *cervelas* is quite a different product, a smooth sausage more like a large version of the Vienna and Frankfurter sausage, lightly smoked. Then there is the *saucisson de Lyon*, the cured sausage of the salame type (although it does not at all resemble a salame in flavour) studded with the characteristic little cubes of fat, and a big cooking sausage also lightly salted and cured; both this and the *cervelas truffé* find their apotheosis in the *cervelas* or *saucisse en brioche*, a sort of super sausage roll I suppose one might say, but the sausage does not seem to me to have the subtlety of those produced in Alsace and Lorraine, nor the robust, straightforward flavour of the *saucisse de Toulouse*, although the brioche paste in a good restaurant like that of the Mère Brezier is of the most beautiful lightness.

The pig in all its forms plays a large part in the cookery of Lyon, grilled pigs' trotters in particular appearing on every menu in almost every restaurant. At one at least of the better-known ones the proprietress is said to accept only trotters from the fore-legs, for they are smaller and more tender than those from the hind-legs. Certainly the pigs' trotters in this establishment were exceptionally good, so perhaps the story is true. But the fact is that pigs' trotters and sausages, steak and large quantities of potatoes, boiled chicken, pike *quenelles* and crayfish in one form or another soon become monotonous, however well cooked. And those pike *quenelles*, for instance—it is in fact rare to get them as they should really be. Making these *quenelles* is a lengthy and tedious business, involving much pounding and sieving of the flesh of the pike, blending it with a *panade*, cream, white of egg and so on; the paste thus obtained should be either moulded in a tablespoon or rolled into a sausage shape and gently poached, when it swells and puffs up, and should be so light that it resembles a soufflé without a soufflé case. Served in a delicately flavoured and creamy river crayfish sauce these *quenelles de brochet* can be, as I remember tasting them years ago for the first time in a Mâcon restaurant, a dish of great charm. Nowadays they are made on a commercial scale, the pounding and sieving being presumably done by machine, with a larger proportion of flour added in order to enable the *quenelles* to keep their shape when moulded, and to stand up to being set out on the counters and displayed in the windows for sale. This variety of *quenelle* tends to be stodgy, nothing much more in fact than a glorified fish-cake, poached instead of fried, so that one should be very cautious about ordering *quenelles de brochet* in any but those restaurants with the very highest reputation to maintain. Even then . . . odious though comparisons may be, I cannot help saying that anyone curious to know what a *quenelle* in all its glory is like will find it, if they happen to be travelling south, worth while making the détour from Valence across the Rhône, and forty kilometres up the winding road into the hills to Lamastre, to eat the extraordinary *pain d'écrevisses* at Madame Barattero's Hôtel du Midi, a restaurant where all the specialities are of a most remarkable finesse.

The world-wide fame of Lyonnais cooking is largely due to a whole generation of women restaurateurs who flourished during the early years of the twentieth century, of whom the most celebrated was the Mère Fillioux. The story of the Mère Fillioux is so typical of the success of so many French provincial restaurateurs that it is worth recording. In the words of Mathieu Varille, author of *La Cuisine Lyonnaise* (1928): 'In the category of restaurants *marchands de vin* that of la Mère Fillioux must be placed in the first rank. She has now entered into history through the great door of the kitchen. It is only right that her famous doings should be recounted here, to serve as an example to future generations.

'Françoise Fayolle was born, as were also her five sisters, at Cuenlhat, in the Puy de Dôme. Quite young, she found employment in the house of a general at Grenoble but was not happy there. She came to Lyon and went into the service of Gaston Eymard, director of the Insurance Company *La France*, and one of the town's greatest gastronomes. In ten years she learned all that she needed to know about the culinary arts. At this time she made the acquaintance of Louis Fillioux, whose father owned, in the rue Duquesne, a very modest apartment house, of which the ground floor was occupied by a bistro. Françoise Fayolle married Louis Fillioux; their savings were spent in buying out the owner of the bistro, which has since been much enlarged. But the beginnings were hard: "Two daughters in one year," the Mère Fillioux would recount, "and the bills to pay at the end of every month." The only customers were the builders employed upon the construction of the new quarter, and a few privileged beings whom the hostess consented to serve. You could get a copious meal for three francs fifty. With the Père Fillioux, wearing the eternal silk cap of the old silk dyers, with the faithful Mélie who waited at table, and later with her daughters, the Mère Françoise worked hard to establish the reputation of her restaurant. Little by little she unified the type of her meals, and the menu of her luncheons is now known in the four corners of the world.

'The hors-d'œuvre were composed principally of ham, sausage, and galantine; then the *volaille truffée demi-deuil*, the triumph of the house; *quenelles au gratin au beurre d'écrevisses*; *fonds d'artichauts* with truffled *foie gras*, replaced sometimes, in the season, by game; *la glace pralinée*; dessert; a capital Beaujolais throughout the meal, and a bottle of Châteauneuf-du-Pape from the Clos Saint-Patrice for the game, the artichoke hearts and the cheese.'

The Mère Fillioux always came to her customers' tables to carve the chickens; she used a little kitchen knife, and two of these knives, it is recounted, lasted her for thirty years, during which time she must have cut up some 500,000 chickens. Once some Americans offered her a thousand francs (a large sum in those days) for her knife. She refused, but after they had gone found, so powerful was the urge to possess this little talisman of good cookery, that they had stolen it.

The Mère Fillioux died in 1925; the restaurant in the rue Duquesne still goes by her name, but her legitimate successor is la Mère Brazier, proprietress of two establishments, one in the rue Royale and the other outside Lyon at the Col de la Luère. La Mère Brazier was once the cook chez la Mère Fillioux, and in her elegant, soberly decorated restaurant of the rue Royale one may eat almost the identical time-honoured menu as it was invented by the Mère Fillioux. There too one may have, unexpectedly perhaps in Lyon, what I do truly believe to be the most delicious and deliciously cooked *sole meunière* I have ever eaten. Ah, if the clients of one or two of those London restaurants specialising in fish dishes could eat a *sole meunière* as cooked at la Mère Brazier's they would certainly wonder what it was that had been served to them under the same name in London. . . . Perhaps the Lyonnais have a particular talent for cooking fish, quite apart from the renowned *quenelles*, for I also remember an especially excellent dish of skate with black butter on the menu of one of those rough and noisy but efficiently run little bistros which are typically Lyonnais. On this particular occasion we were sitting at a table next to the one at which the *patron*-cook was entertaining friends, eating his own midday meal and apparently doing the cooking at the same time. One of the great virtues of this little place in the rue Garet was that everything was served sizzling hot. The *raie au beurre noir* came to our table with the butter and the fish fairly bubbling in its own little dish; and I saw that the *patron*, having cooked his own steak, brought it to his table in a covered serving dish, ceremoniously decanted it on to his hot plate, and took the empty dish away to the kitchen before sitting down to his interrupted meal.

This aspect of service in even the humblest of French restaurants is one that I always find attractive. Everything is invariably brought on its own dish and the waiter, having served the customer, leaves the dish on the table for him to help himself to more if he wants it. It is a custom which makes the food much more appetising than does the almost universal English one of serving it straight on the plate, often with vegetables you haven't ordered and don't want mixed up with the sauce and the meat.

It was in this same little restaurant that I tasted two dishes of the Lyonnais *cuisine populaire* which, if the truth must be told, I rather preferred to most of the cooking of the high-class restaurants. These were *la salade lyonnaise* (described in the hors-d'œuvre chapter on page 147) and an oddity called *tablier de sapeur* or fireman's apron. This is an oblong slab of tripe about half an inch thick (previously cooked, of course), coated with egg and breadcrumbs, grilled to a sizzling crispness and served with a *sauce tartare*. No tripe enthusiast, I ordered it simply out of curiosity, and found it really enjoyable.

Another speciality, which appears in the brasseries rather than the restaurants proper, is the *gratinée*, a clear consommé in which a slice of bread sprinkled with cheese is browned in the oven, the whole being finally enriched with a mixture of beaten egg and port—a restorative soup of the same nature as the Parisian *soupe à l'oignon*, in this case without the onion which is generally but wrongly supposed to figure in every Lyonnais dish.

*　*　*

East of the Lyonnais and south of Burgundy lies the Bresse, a district blessed with a rich variety of high-quality raw materials, of which the *poularde de Bresse* is the most celebrated. This country is a tricky subject to write about. The town of Belley in the south-eastern corner of the Bugey district, between the Franche-Comté, the Dauphiné and the Savoie (administratively the Bugey is now part of Franche-Comté, but geographically it is inseparable from the Bresse) was the birthplace of Brillat-Savarin, and around everything to do with the author of the *Physiologie du Goût*, there hangs a kind of aureole, every chicken, every *gratin d'écrevisses*, every pâté in this district being, in the imagination of a vast number of people, automatically presented, as it were, upon a golden dish. As Maurice des Ombiaux has remarked, people seem to believe that Brillat-Savarin's recipes partook of the nature of divine revelations, whereas in reality Brillat-Savarin made no claims to being a practising cook, and his recipes, at least to modern readers, appear to be the weakest spots in his book. Apart, however, from observing that indiscriminate adulation and quotation *ad nauseam* of a few aphorisms by people who have probably never read his complete work seldom does any author's reputation much good, it is not my purpose here to discuss Brillat-Savarin's great book, which in its form as well as its content became such a landmark in the history of modern gastronomy that it set, and is still setting, the pattern for hundreds of imitators.

* * *

My first-hand knowledge of Brillat-Savarin's country is small, my only gastronomic recollection being of a very excellent but very simple meal, all the more delicious for being somewhat unexpected, in a *café routier* just outside Bourg-en-Bresse. It was in the days before these transport cafés had become well known to tourists, and stopping for petrol before going into Bourg we saw that behind the filling station was a small whitewashed farmhouse advertising accommodation and meals. We were tired after a long day's driving, and decided there and then to stay instead of battling through the traffic into Bourg.

Our dinner consisted of a small selection of hors-d'œuvre, among which the home-made pâté was unusually good; afterwards we ate a tender chicken roasted in butter, and a salad. The sweet was that wonderfully fresh and innocent-looking cream cheese dish, a *cœur à la crème*, served covered with fresh rich cream. We complimented the *patron* and his wife, a young couple who had not long set up in the restaurant–filling-station business, remarking that the *cœur à la crème* had been particularly delicious. When we came down next morning, after a night of peace and quiet as unexpected, considering we were within a few yards of the main road, as our excellent dinner, we found that the *patronne* had provided more *cœurs à la crème* for our breakfast; and on the table beside the coffee, the croissants, and the butter was a bowl of beautiful fresh wild strawberries. How she had procured them at that hour of the morning I did not ask; but she could not have had them the night before or she would have offered them to us for dinner. Perhaps a passing market van . . . but it did not matter. What mattered was that of such gestures, such imaginative little attentions, are faithful customers and good reputations made. And if that young couple are not now, somewhere in France, the prosperous owners of a successful restaurant I should be very surprised indeed.

South-Western France: The Béarnais and the Basque Country

Peppers and onions are sizzling gently in a big frying-pan, the goose dripping in which they are cooking giving off its unmistakable smell. A squat, round-bellied earthen pot, blackened with use, containing beans and salt pork and cabbage, seems to be for ever on the simmer. A string of wrinkled, dried, dark red peppers hangs from the ceiling alongside a piece of roughly cut ham; a bunch of little red sausages and a pitcher of yellow wine are on the table. The kitchen of this little peasant farm-house in the Béarn is small and smoky, by no means the ideal airy, well-ordered, well-scrubbed farmhouse kitchen of one's imagination; but the pink-washed walls are clean against the faded blue paint of the windows and shutters, and on the shelves of the little larder there are three or four tall glazed earthen jars to bear witness to the careful housekeeping of the farmer's wife. For these are the pots of *confit*, the goose and pork and duck, salted, cooked, and preserved in their own wax-white fat, which, with the ham and the sausages and the peppers, lie at the base of all the local cookery.

For here, at any rate in the deep country, butter, except for pastry-making, is considered a wretched substitute for the rich fat of the goose (Norman Douglas tells us that goose fat was held by the Greeks to be an aphrodisiac, adding, characteristically, that to him it was an emetic). So whether it is a question of frying eggs, or sausages, or a steak, of cooking a daube of beef, or the heavy thick cabbage and bean soup called *garbure*, into the pan goes the goose fat or the pork lard, to be followed by the onions, the tomatoes, the garlic and the brick red pepper called *piment basquais*. The locally cured ham, the *jambon de Bayonne* or of Orthez will add its salty tang to the mixture, along with a piece of pork either from the salting trough or from the jar of *confit*. The wines of the Béarnais and the Basque country which are drunk with these dishes are topaz or rose-coloured or rich deep red, and have curious names easy to remember but difficult to pronounce—Pacherenc de Vic

Bilh, Tadousse-Usseau, Irouléguy, Jurançon, Monein, Saint-Faust, Madiran, Chahakoa, Diusse and Rousselet de Béarn.

*   *   *

There is much talk hereabouts, too, that is to say much talk by writers and gastronomes, of Le Grand Béarnais, the hero-king, Henri IV of Navarre, who figures in all French cookery books as having expressed the pious wish that every family in the land might have a chicken in the pot every Sunday of the year. But although they have good ways of dealing with a boiling fowl in these south-western regions of France, of adding cabbage leaves filled with a savoury stuffing to the vegetables which go into the pot, and serving highly condimented sauces with the chicken, it is chiefly due to perspicacious Parisian restaurateurs that the name of Henri IV is attached to every *poule au pot* and *petite marmite* served to their customers. Neither, alas, did the hero of Arques invent or even know, the Sauce Béarnaise. It was created by a chef, whose name is not recorded, at the Pavillon Henri IV at St. Germain, round about 1830; it rapidly, and justly, became celebrated, and before long entered into the realms of *la cuisine classique*. Count Austin de Croze, the great authority on French provincial cookery and compiler of that wonderful volume of regional recipes, *Les Plats Régionaux de France*, considers, however, that the sauce is in direct descent from the local Béarnais cookery. His own recipe includes a seasoning of the pounded dried red pepper of the country.

As far as the true regional dishes are concerned, Basque and Béarnais cooking is easier to follow in manner than to the letter; when you have goose fat saved from the Christmas bird, try using it as a basis for these dishes. It gives an entirely characteristic flavour. When there is none, or if you feel as Norman Douglas did about it, then substitute pork lard or olive oil; all but the most rabid of French regionalists will tell you that there is no call to be more royalist than the king in these matters. Use the red peppers, the spiced Spanish-type sausages when they are obtainable, the salt pork, the ham, the wine, the garlic, the onions. Something of the highly individual character of this local cookery, part Spanish, part traditionally Gascon, with affinities to the cooking of Provence and even to that of parts of Italy, will still emerge. These dishes may not be for every day. But then once again it was Norman Douglas who said, 'Who wants a dish for every day?'

*   *   *

On the Basque and the Bordelais coasts there is naturally a great tradition of fish cookery, and here olive oil comes into its own again, for the oniony fish stew called Ttoro, or Tioro, for the little squid called *chipirones*, stewed with their own ink for sauce, for fresh sardines plainly fried, and prawns, langoustines, and mussels cooked with rice and peppers in the manner of the Spanish *paëlla*. Oysters, raw and ice cold, are often accompanied by sizzling hot little spicy sausages called *lou-ken-kas*, which have some resemblance to the *chorizos* of Spain. Inland, there is particularly fine river trout from the streams called *gaves* in the Béarn, and in the strange bleak country of the Landes there are ortolans and wild doves, delicious birds unknown to the English kitchen; and there are duck livers cooked with grapes, and goose liver pâtés with as great a reputation as those of the Périgord and Alsace.

South-Western France: The Bordelais

About the traditional cookery of the Bordelais, Count Austin de Croze expresses the view that it is only in England that the ancient dishes have been preserved, a circumstance due presumably to the long British occupation of this part of the country in Plantagenet times. As examples he cites the English love of 'ginger, and of rudimentary accords and discords' in their cookery.

One of the few ancient dishes still current in the Bordelais is the *tourin*, an excellent onion soup with several variations, and the custom of pouring a glass of wine into the *garbure* as the amount in your plate diminishes also still survives. The custom is known as *faire chabrot*, and is, or was, common to all Gascony and south-western France. Other old dishes cited by Count de Croze are those filling peasant maize meal cakes and galettes (maize is extensively grown in south-western France and is used among other things for cramming the geese in order to fatten their livers) called *millias* and *milliassou*, and an *estouffade de Lesparre*, a beautifully enticing name, but a dish I have never yet come across. What we now know as 'the beautiful, good, refined Bordelais cuisine,' says Count de Croze, 'dates from the time when Louis (the architect, Victor Louis) built lovely Château Margaux with its Greek temple façade, and the theatre of which Bordeaux is so justly proud. The famous—and sumptuous—*lamproie aux poireaux et au vin rouge* dates, at the earliest, from the time of Montesquieu.' Two other Bordeaux dishes universally known are *cèpes à la Bordelaise*, the rich mixture of cèpes or boletus cooked in olive oil with garlic and parsley, and *entrecôte marchand de vins* (the old Bordeaux recipes for these dishes will be found on pages 249 and 337). From what period these dishes date I do not know but properly done both have the savour and pungency of genuine country food.

The Bordelais are, no doubt, able to console themselves for their upstart cookery, dating back no farther than the end of the eighteenth century; they have the wherewithal, with the greatest wine production of any district in France, with the greatest number of classified first growths, among which are the most renowned wines in the world, with fifteen hundred châteaux of which an enormous number bear celebrated names and of which even the least-known produce good table and everyday wines.

With all this, the Bordelais can afford to play a few tricks now and again with their combinations of food and wine. As a curiosity, the menu of a dinner given at Château Margaux in 1957 in honour of a famous English wine shipper is a good example of this somewhat casual attitude. In the opinion of another highly distinguished wine merchant, to start off a meal with the very rich 1952 Château Climens was 'somewhat overdoing the salmon,' the rest of the meal was really two meals, the mixture of Burgundies and Bordeaux wines was an atrocity, and the whole arrangement was 'CHAOS.'

Here is the menu drawn up by the Académie du Vin de Bordeaux. The mixture of Burgundy and Bordeaux wines is explained by the fact that Burgundian wine growers were associated with those of the Bordelais on this occasion:

'Château Climens 1952 (Barsac), après le consommé en tasse, avec le saumon de l'Adour Aurore — La Tâche du Domaine de la Romanée-Conti 1948 — Hospices de Beaune, Volnay — Santenots, Cuvée Jehan de Massol 1929, avec le poulet Bercy — Château Canon 1945 (St. Emilion) et Château Pétrus 1945 (Pomerol), avec le Mignon de bœuf à la Neva — Château Haut-Brion 1934 (Graves) et Château Margaux 1929 (Médoc), avec le plateau des fromages — Château La Tour Blanche 1949 (Sauternes), avec la glace Napolitaine et les petits fours.'

And as a contrast here is a dinner given at Château Lafite Rothschild in 1951:

À Lafite Rothschild

Le Cornet de Jambon Lesparrain
Le Foie Gras d'Aquitaine
Le Baron de Pauillac
et les Primeurs d'Eysines
Salade Médocaine
Le Fromage du Palais Subtil
La Frangipane Pipetière
Les Fruits

Châteaux Grand Listrac 1945
Châteaux Grand Saint-Estèphe 1947
La Rose, Pauillac 1942
Château Latour 1946
Château Montbrun 1945
Château Kirwan 1943
Château Haut-Brion 1943
Château Cantemerle 1937
Château Lafite-Rothschild 1934 en Magnums

South-Western France: The Périgord

It is a remarkable fact that the two writers who have had the most profound influence upon the English attitude to food and wine in the twentieth century have both been Frenchmen writing *in English*. (I am not forgetting Escoffier, whose influence was very great, but his books were written in French and the English translations were, and remain, a good deal short of perfection.)

How M. André Simon and M. Marcel Boulestin, arriving in England as they both did, the former in 1894 and Boulestin about 1910, speaking little or no English, almost immediately settled down to assimilate them-selves into English life and before long to write and publish books in the English language is something of a phenomenon.

André Simon's work is justly famous; he has had a long and fruitful working life, but Boulestin died untimely during the 1939 war and all his books, with the exception of an anthology compiled after his death, are out of print. But the influence exercised by Boulestin, both by his books and through the restaurant which he founded, went very deep, if not sufficiently wide.

All this is not entirely irrelevant to the wonderful province of France which is the Périgord, the country of Montaigne, the country of painted caves and romanesque cathedrals, the country of black truffles and Roquefort cheese and walnut oil, of pigs and geese, and an immensely rich tradition of cookery, the country through which flow the Dordogne, the Lot and the Garonne, the country where the names of half the towns and villages end in that short, sharp yet infinitely evocative syllable *ac*—Souillac, Moissac, Capdenac, Figeac, Bergerac, Monbazillac, Montignac, Marcillac—the country which, with the Bordelais, formed the ancient territory of Guyenne which in 1154 Eleanor of Aquitaine brought as dowry to the Plantagenets and which for three hundred years remained a dominion of the English crown. And this was Marcel Boulestin's native province. His recollections of the food and the cooking pots, the kitchen and the garden of his childhood home are wonderfully evocative. Here is what he wrote in his autobiography *Myself, My Two Countries* (Cassell, 1936):

'There I lived all the daytime out of doors, and in the evening my favourite place was the kitchen. The ways of cooking were very primitive (and in many parts of the south-west of France they still are); that is to say they were perfect, and gave results which I did not appreciate enough then, and which we try now, often in vain, to imitate. The roasting was done on a spit, and the rest of the cooking on charcoal. If a dish had to be braised, it was cooked in a casserole with a hollow lid; in this warm ashes and burning charcoals were put, and the dish cooked slowly, resting on square holes. There were three or four holes in the tiled covered stand. which was a fixture. This was called a *potager*.

'If something required baking as opposed to roasting, it was sent to the baker's to be cooked after the bread had been removed. There was a baker's oven in the house at the end of the yard, but I do not remember seeing it in use.

'The grandest place was the chimney, so high and deep I could walk into it, and the dogs (which were called *landiers*) were almost as tall as I was. It was lovely to see a fat chicken or a row of partridges revolving slowly on the spit and becoming more and more golden. They were carefully basted and a subtle perfume filled the kitchen. Meanwhile, a crisp salad was being prepared with a *chapon* rubbed with garlic.

'Next to the fireplace was a large cherrywood *saloir*, where in pounds of sea-salt pieces of pork were pickled, and I can still see the unerring gesture of the cook: pushing the sliding lid out, she would put in her arm to the elbow and draw out a handful of salt, which she would throw, positively throw, in the soup, a yard away. . . .

'Some of the dishes and kitchen forks and spoons were of pewter. To my great joy I discovered one day that they melted easily. . . .

'In the store room next to the kitchen were a long table and shelves always covered with all sorts of provisions; large earthenware jars full of *confits* of pork and goose, a small barrel where vinegar slowly matured, a bowl where honey oozed out of the comb, jams, preserves of sorrel and of tomatoes, and odd bottles with grapes and cherries marinating in brandy; next to the table a weighing machine on which I used to stand at regular intervals; sacks of haricot beans, of potatoes; eggs, each one carefully dated in pencil.

'And there were the baskets of fruit, perfect small melons, late plums, under-ripe medlars waiting to soften, peaches, pears hollowed out by a bird or a wasp, figs that had fallen of their own accord, all the fruits of September

naturally ripe and sometimes still warm from the sun. Everything in pro-
fusion. It is no doubt the remembrance of these early days which makes me
despise and dislike all primeurs, the fruit artificially grown, gathered too
early and expensively sent, wrapped in cotton wool, to "smart" restaurants.

'The garden could hardly be called a garden; it was large, wild and not too
well kept. There were fruit trees amongst the flowers, here a pear tree, there
a currant bush, so that one could either smell a rose, crush a verbena or eat
a fruit; there were borders of box, but also of sorrel and chibol; and the stiff
battalion of leeks, shallots and garlic, the delicate pale-green foliage of the
carrot, the aggressive steel-grey leaves of the artichokes, the rows of lettuce
which always ran to seed too quickly.

'It was not a proud ornamental garden, but it symbolised more than anything else the French provincial life.'

South-Western France:
The Languedoc

You have decided upon your meal, and Madame, in her black dress, has
moved majestically towards the kitchen to attend to your wishes. A
bottle of cooled white wine is already in front of you, and from the big
table in the centre of the restaurant a waiter brings hors-d'œuvre, to
keep you amused and occupied while more serious dishes are being
prepared. Now, in spite of all that grave gastronomes are in the habit of
saying about the pernicious custom of starting off a meal with a lot of
little oddments and titbits, it is nevertheless a fact that the quality of a
restaurant may very largely be judged by the way in which the hors-
d'œuvre are planned and presented. At Nénette's they bring you quantities of little prawns, freshly boiled, with just the right amount of salt,
and a most stimulating smell of the sea into the bargain, heaped up in a
big yellow bowl; another bowl filled with green olives; good salty bread;
and a positive monolith of butter, towering up from a wooden board.
These things are put upon the table, and you help yourself, shelling your
prawns, biting into your olives, enjoying the first draught of your wine.
Gradually you take in your surroundings: the light and sunny dining-
room, neither too big nor too small, the comfortably worn flowered
wallpaper, the country flowers on the tables, and the shady garden
which you can see through the open window at the far end of the
dining-room.

You settle in, realising that you are in a serious restaurant, and a
serious provincial restaurant at that. You have no anxiety about the
meal to come, and you are quite right. For any international Palace
Hotel or expense-account restaurant can serve you oysters and *foie*

gras, smoked salmon and caviar, in the very pink of condition (this is a question of good buying and has nothing to do with the chefs) and still follow them up with the deadliest of dull dinners. But the eye which picked out those bowls, the taste which decreed what was to go into them, and the hand which carved that butter into its meticulously studied carelessness of shape are scarcely likely to falter when it comes to the silver sea-bass roasted over a vinewood fire, the langouste in its tomato and brandy and garlic-scented sauce, the salad dressed with the fruity olive oil of Provence. Upon this last point, however, one must not enlarge too much. For we are at Montpellier, and as Madame Nénette observed, in tones of only very mild reproof, in answer to my question about her lobster dish, 'Ah, nous ne sommes pas en Provence, Madame, ici c'est le Languedoc.' So Madame Nénette's lobster or, rather, crawfish dish is her own special version of *langouste à la sètoise* or *civet de langouste*, a dish quite remarkably similar to the famous *homard à l'américaine*. Now the port of Sète in the Languedoc was the birthplace of the chef Pierre Fraisse, who is said to have originated this famous dish, and one way and another it seems fairly obvious that, with its tomato and oil and garlic, it was adapted from the methods traditional to the fishermen of Sète and, indeed, of the whole Mediterranean coast, and never had much to do either with America or with Armorique (the old name for Brittany), where they had no oil, no tomatoes and precious little cognac; but after the 1914 war patriotic Frenchmen decided that it was absurd that a famous French dish should be attributed to America, so they came to the conclusion that the name was due to a spelling mistake, and did not stop to think of the more rational explanation that the dish was a typically Mediterranean one. Fraisse, the Sétois chef who first put the dish upon his menu in his Paris restaurant (Noël Peters in the Passage des Princes) had spent some years in America (these facts are all on record and can be read in M. Robert Courtine's book, *Le Plus Doux des Péchés*,[1]) and the whole thing seems to be explained. This comfortable theory, however, is swiftly demolished by Pierre Andrieu in *Fine Bouche* (Cassell, 1956) who says that although Fraisse may have been the originator of the name, he certainly did not create the dish, which was well known under the name of *homard Bonnefoy*, at the restaurant of that name, before 1870. He quotes Philéas Gilbert as saying that the dish was originally known as *langouste niçoise*. So we are back to the Mediterranean origin of the dish.

Whichever came first, the Sétois and Provençal versions of the dish are simply the *langouste*, or lobster, *à l'américaine*, in a rather rougher

[1] Editions Touristiques et Littéraires, 6, rue Lamartine, Bourg, 1954.

form. Nénette's variation consists in the addition of *aïoli* to the sauce, a quite common usage in Provençal and Languedoc fish cookery. Her recipe is on page 326, and it can be compared with the *américaine* version Escoffier gives in his *Guide Culinaire*, with Prosper Montagné's note on the *civet de langouste* of the Languedoc in the *Larousse Gastronomique*, and with yet another version from Pierre Huguenin's *Recettes de ma Pauvre Mère*.

From the Languedoc also come two more dishes among the most famous in the whole repertoire of French provincial cookery: the *Cassoulet* of Toulouse, with its variations from Carcassonne, Castelnaudary and Castelnau, and the *Brandade de Morue* (described on page 304), said to have originated at Nîmes.

The first, that sumptuous amalgamation of haricot beans, sausage, pork, mutton and preserved goose, aromatically spiced with garlic and herbs, is cooked at great length in an earthenware pot, emerging with a golden crust which conceals an interior of gently bubbling, creamy beans and uniquely savoury meats. A number of great cooks and restaurateurs have come out of the Languedoc, the most famous being Prosper Montagné, who had a small but world-renowned restaurant in the rue de l'Échelle in Paris between the wars. He described the *Cassoulet* over and over again in his many works on cookery (apart from the numerous books which bear his name he also compiled and edited the *Larousse Gastronomique*, a truly immense labour), and used to tell the story that in the town of Castelnaudary where he was born he went one ordinary working day to the shoemaker's and saw that the doors were locked and the shutters closed. Fearing a death in the house, he went to have a closer look. Pinned to the door was a paper bearing the notice 'FERMÉ POUR CAUSE DE CASSOULET.'

It was probably Montagné who did more than anyone else to popularise this remarkable farmhouse dish in Paris and to send it on its travels round the world, although Anatole France had already written about it in lyrical, if somewhat fanciful terms, and Auguste Colombié, also a native of the Languedoc and one of the great teaching cooks of the latter part of the nineteenth century, had also published recipes for it. It was Colombié who, to the great indignation of his professional colleagues ('Giving away professional secrets—we shall all be out of work,' they said) founded the first cookery school in Paris for 'les dames et demoiselles du monde.'

I have a crude and brightly coloured picture of him demonstrating cookery to a crowd of these elegantly hatted and plumed young women. Two of them, in flowered toques and high-boned muslin collars, lacy aprons pinned over their sweeping gowns, are gingerly stirring and chopping as M. Colombié beams indulgently from behind his primitive gas stove. It is not easy to visualise these frail and pampered-looking beauties coming to grips with a hefty, earthy dish like the cassoulet, but then one must remember that it takes more than an elegant dress and a swirl of frills and laces to come between a Frenchwoman and the enjoyment of her food.

Batterie de Cuisine

Kitchen Equipment

SINCE 1960, when this book was first published, there has come into being a new category of kitchen equipment shops catering for the needs of the serious amateur cook. The owners of these establishments are often themselves accomplished cooks. They stock good, solid, serviceable pots and pans and will take trouble to advise and inform their customers and to obtain the scarcer items of kitchen equipment. Among such shops are Scurfield's of Jesus Lane, Cambridge; Dorrie's Cook Shop at 2 Upper Bow, Lawnmarket, Edinburgh; the Kitchen, Albion Street, Leeds; Domus, 105 Clapham High Street; Habitat, 77-9 Fulham Rd., S.W.3.

Among larger provincial and Scottish stores whose kitchen departments stock serious cooking pots and tools are Edwin Jones of Southhampton, Owlby and Son of Bognor Regis, Jenners of Edinburgh, Wylie and Lockhead of Buchanan Street, Glasgow, Bainbridge & Co., Corporation Street, Newcastle upon Tyne, David Morgan, of the Hayes, Cardiff. In London Ferrari's of 60-66 Wardour Street, W.1. offer a sound selection of copper and cast-iron cooking pots, and are particularly well stocked with professional cook's knives. William Page of 87 Shaftsbury Avenue W.1., is another good source of professional equipment.

My own shop, to be opened in October 1965 at 46 Bourne Street, London S.W.1. will, I hope, be able to supply a variety of French and English earthenware, copper, aluminium, fire-proof porcelain and cast-iron cooking pots, French pastry-cooks whisks, mixing bowls, moulds, tart-tins, cook's knives, and as many of the utensils mentioned in this book as are currently available.

Madame Cadec's shop in Greek Street, for so many years the source of supply for professional and amateur cooks in search of kitchen items rare in England, has, alas, closed down.

E.D. June 1965

To know the correct type of saucepan or pot in which to cook any given dish is often as important as getting the right ingredients; and the proper knives, chopping boards, and other essential utensils make the cook's work infinitely quicker and more efficient. French has for long been the international language of cooking, and a good many of these things are still known in the trade by their French names. But during the course of time the words have become confused, corrupted and misunderstood. Not long ago I overheard a salesman blandly assuring a customer that an omelette *dish* was the same thing as an omelette *pan*. A small misunderstanding as far as the words are concerned, but a very large one when it comes to cooking the omelette. Again, even those people who read French cookery books with ease are sometimes confronted with an unfamiliar term or word not to be found in the ordinary dictionary, and the glossaries provided in cookery books are not always very helpful. They will tell you that a *bain-marie* is a Mary-bath and that a *couteau d'office* is an office knife, and it is up to you to find out for what purpose such objects could possibly be needed in the kitchen.

It is obvious that few of us possess, are in a position to acquire, or even necessarily need such things as a *poissonnière* or a *bain-marie*, or are required to make fine distinctions between a *savarin*, a *baba* and a *timbale* mould. But knowing what *should* be used to produce the best results makes it very much easier to find or to improvise a substitute.

The following brief list of French kitchen utensils, with their English equivalents, arranged in alphabetical order, gives an outline of the equipment which forms the nucleus of a well set up kitchen. I do not mean to imply that all these items are strictly necessary, but it is useful to know what they are, and for what purpose they were designed.

Bain-marie A large shallow rectangular or round pan, or bath, in which a number of narrow, tall saucepans, with handles, can be placed so that the water round them comes not more than half-way up. The

bain-marie or, more accurately, the *caisse à bain-marie*, and its several accompanying saucepans are especially designed for keeping sauces hot without danger of overheating or of their consistency altering. In small households the *bain-marie* is usually replaced with a double saucepan, or a more satisfactory method improvised from a wide shallow pan in which a small saucepan can be placed, so that there is heat all round it rather than just underneath.

Balance Scales. Buy the best you can afford, for preference the old-fashioned type with weights. An accurately-marked measuring jug also seems to me a necessity.

Bassin, Bassine (*a*) Egg bowl. A hemispheric, untinned, copper bowl for

beating whites of eggs. Professionals say that the whites cannot be so successfully beaten in any other vessel, both because of its shape and because in no other metal, or in china, can you beat the eggs so stiff without 'graining.' Undoubtedly egg-whites beaten in this special copper bowl emerge creamier and better aerated than those beaten in an ordinary mixing bowl or in an electric mixer.

(*b*) A preserving pan, for cooking jams, jellies and so on.

Bassine à friture Deep fryer.

Batte Cutlet bat.

Bocal Preserving jar, usually glass. In many ways French ones are more

practical than our own because they tend to be squat and wide instead of tall and narrow, so there is no danger of fruit or vegetables breaking when you put them in or take them out.

Bouilloire A kettle, in the present English sense of the word, for boiling water.

Braisière, Daubière Braising-pan. A deep, heavy pan, usually oval, with a tight-fitting lid and side-handles, in which meat and poultry are braised, i.e. cooked very slowly with vegetables, herbs, fat pork or bacon and a small amount of liquid. At one time these pans were made with an inset lid, upon which glowing embers were placed so that the food cooked with heat from on top as well as underneath. In household cooking, the *braisière* or *daubière* is now more generally replaced with an enamelled steel or cast-iron pan with the self-explanatory name of *fait-tout* (these also come in a round shape). Such utensils

are invaluable in any kitchen, and are now being imported from France,

Holland, Belgium and Scandinavia. The heavy French 10-pint cast-iron pot in the drawing is unlined. Such pots should be protected from rust by a film of oil or fat brushed over the interior before they are put away after use.

French cast-iron vitreous-enamelled pots, made by the famous firms of Le Creuset and André of Cousances, are now imported in quantity and in a large range of sizes and shapes. They are widely distributed. Names of stockists from the importers, Messrs. Clarbat, 302 Barrington Road, S.W.9. See also page 56.

Brise-flamme This is an asbestos or other mat which protects earthenware pots from a direct flame, enabling you to cook stews and so on very slowly on the top of the stove. A serviceable wire mat is made by the Dutch firm of Tomado. A far more satisfactory and correspondingly more expensive product is a recently invented French mat which goes by the brand name of *Mijoska*. This is heavy and durable, with a firebrick backing.

Casserole Although this word has come to mean, in English, an earthenware or other oven dish in which foods are 'casseroled,' in France a casserole is simply what we call a saucepan, with high straight sides and a handle. Technically, this kind of saucepan is called a 'casserole russe'; a shallow saucepan with straight sides is a *sautoir*, a *sauteuse*, a *casserole à sauter*, a *casserole-sauteuse*, or a *plat à sauter*; we have not even one word to describe this kind of pan, except possibly the term skillet which is beginning to come back here from the United States, where it migrated some hundreds of years ago. But in those days a skillet was an iron pan with three legs. An earthenware saucepan is a *casserole en terre*, but each variety has its own designation; e.g. a *marmite en terre*, a *cocotte en terre*, a *terrine*, a *poëlon*, a *plat à gratin*, a *casserolette*, a *ramequin* and so on. Many regional dishes also depend upon the local type of earthenware pot for their traditional manner of cooking and presentation. Among these are the *cassole* for the *cassoulet* of the Languedoc, the *tian* from Provence which has also given its name to the mixture of vegetables which is cooked in it, the *toupin* of the Béarn in which the garbure is

cooked, the *caquelon* for a cheese fondue, the unglazed porous pot called a *diable* (left) for the cooking of potatoes and chestnuts without any liquid, and the *huguenote*, an earthenware baking-pan specially designed to accommodate a large goose or other long joint, although this term is also used to describe a round stew-pot or soup-pot.

Most French—and also Spanish, Italian and Greek—earthenware cooking pots are glazed inside but not outside and can be used on the hot plates of a solid fuel or a gas stove as well as in the oven, provided that they are treated with care. They were, after all, originally designed for cooking over charcoal or wood fuels which give out just as much heat as gas or bottled gas. For safety, however, most people prefer to stand earthenware casseroles on a mat or on a raised grid between the flame and the pot, although those who are careful always to let them heat very slowly but directly over a low flame will find this method just as satisfactory. One essential precaution is to heat any liquid—wine, water, stock,—to be added to vegetables or meat already fried or frying in an earthenware pot. Cold liquid poured into a hot, all but dry, earthenware vessel will almost certainly crack it, although the occasional faulty casserole is going to crack anyway whatever precautions are taken.

English earthenware or brownware cooking pots such as the beautiful, traditional and cheap pots made by Pearsons of Chesterfield are intended only for oven cooking, although this factory has recently evolved a limited range of cooking ware unglazed on the outside and designed for use over direct heat. For this purpose I have found them perfectly successful. For electric cooking it is advisable, unless you are a very experienced cook, to use pots and pans especially designed for the purpose.

Cercle à flan Flan ring.

Chasse-noyau A little gadget for stoning olives and/or cherries. Cheap and immensely useful.

Chinois A conical sieve with a fine mesh, mostly used for the straining of sauces. One of the most useful of utensils. For a small household the stainless steel conical sieves now imported from Sweden are much to be recommended. They have no join or seam, are consequently very easy to keep clean and should last for ever. They have a hook for fixing on the side of the recipient into which the sauce is being sieved. A 6-inch diameter conical sieve is a good all-purpose size.

Cocotte (a) A deep round or oval cooking pot of varying dimensions, but always with a tight-fitting lid and handles or ears at each side; it may be made of earthenware, copper or cast iron, fireproof porcelain or glass.

(b) The small china, earthenware, or metal ramekins in which eggs (*œufs en cocotte*) are baked or steamed, and in which they are served.

Couperet Cleaver, meat chopper.

1. Norman *tripière*, for *tripes à la mode*. 2. Provençal *tian*, for vegetable and gratin dishes. 3. English brownware stew jar. Pearsons of Chesterfield. 4. *Cassole*, for the *cassoulet*. Size for one helping. (See also drawing on page 385.) 5 and 6. Earthenware *poëlons* or round casseroles much used in Provence. for vegetable dishes, stews, etc. 7. Deep *poëlon*, casserole or *caquelon*. Much used for cheese fondue. 8. Béarnais *toupin*. For bean dishes, soups, stews, etc. 9. Glazed earthenware jar for preserved goose and pork. From the Dordogne. 10. Glazed earthenware jar for *rillettes*. From the Loire.

Couteau de cuisine Cook's 6 to 8-inch knife for slicing and trimming meat and for many other jobs. Indispensable. Serious cooks still find

that carbon-steel knives are the most satisfactory and lasting for general kitchen use; their design and balance are important as well as the sharpness and flexibility of the blade. French cook's knives are recognised as the best buys. It is, of course, useful to have saw-edged stainless steel (*acier inoxydable*) knives for cutting fruit, such as oranges for salad, for slicing lemons, tomatoes, and cold cooked meat, for cutting bread and other general tasks. At the moment the French appear to be ahead of us in producing efficient and lasting stainless steel blades.

Couteau à découper Carving knife. 16-inch knife.

Couteau à désosser Boning knife. See drawing on page 334.

Couteau économe Potato parer.

Couteau à filets de sole Filleting knife.

Couteau d'office Vegetable or paring knife. Office really means the pantry where in large households certain types of kitchen work are, or were, carried out.

Couteau tranche-lard 18 to 20-inch slicing knife.

Cuiller à bouche, à soupe Tablespoon.

Cuiller à pot Small ladle.

Cuisinière Cooking stove, range.

Écumoire Skimmer. There is one shown in the drawing on page 153.

Entonnoir Funnel.

Étamine Tammy cloth. Thick cloth through which liquids are strained. In most households this is replaced by a hair sieve or rather, nowadays, a nylon one, but some sort of close-woven cloth, such as a cheese cloth, is necessary for straining consommé, aspic and fruit jellies.

Faisselle Rush basket or perforated earthenware mould for draining soft cheeses.

Fouet Whisk. The best type for the whisking of eggs is described in the chapter on egg cookery, page 200. It is shown in the drawing on page 58.

Four Oven.

Fourneau Stove, cooking range.

Fusil Steel for sharpening knives.

Glace, armoire à Ice chest. Also called *timbre à glace.*

Glacière Cold room, ice chest, refrigerator.

Glacière à sucre, Glaçoire Sugar caster, sprinkler, dredger.

Gril Grill for grilling food.

Grille Wire pastry rack. Also various patent gadgets for grilling; also frying basket.

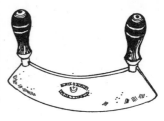

Hachinette A small solid wooden bowl complete with crescent-shaped chopping knife which is immensely useful for chopping small quantities of parsley, herbs, shallots, onions, etc.

Hachoir Chopping knife, mincing knife. Generally crescent-shaped, single, double, or multi-bladed and double-handled. For an ordinary household the single-bladed chopping knife is sufficient, although the multi-bladed chopper produces far superior minced meat to that done in the mincing machine, for it does not squeeze out the juices. But few people would care to bother with it nowadays.

Lardoire Larding needle.

Lèchefrite Dripping tin. The tin or dish placed underneath food while it is roasting, to catch the juices and fat.

Louche Soup ladle or dipper.

Mandoline An instrument consisting of a narrow rectangular wooden board on which various different cutting blades are fixed. Indispensable even in a small household for the easy, rapid and accurate

slicing of potatoes for dishes such as *pommes Anna* and *gratin dauphinois*, for cucumbers for salad, and for shredding celeriac for *céleri-rémoulade*. Also called a *Coupe-Julienne*. The English trade-name for the best-known make of this

instrument is the Universal Slicer.

Marmite A tall stock-pot or a stew-pot, usually, but not invariably, straight-sided, made of tinned copper (right), or enamelled cast-iron, or earthenware. The *pot-au-feu* and all its derivatives are cooked in a mar-

mite, the shape of the pot ensuring the minimum of evaporation. Hence, the tall earthenware or china tureens, both the large and the small individual ones, in which the consommé is served, are called *marmites*. The consommé known as *petite marmite* also gets its name from the same source. The best stock-pots for household use ever made in England were the heavy, cast-iron, enamelled round pots with flat side-handles made by Kenrick (left) and also by Izon's. They are now obsolete. The best replacement is a two-handled enamelled steel pot of Dutch origin.

Mortier Wooden or marble mortar. Although so much of the work of pounding, grinding and sieving is now done by the electric mixer, a pestle and mortar still seems to me to be a kitchen necessity.

Moule à charlotte A plain, fairly deep copper or tin mould with sloping sides (1) and sometimes with a lid.

Moule à dariole Small mould approximately the shape of a castle pudding.

Moule à douille Ring mould, cylinder mould (2). Savarin and Baba moulds are also cylinder moulds, usually fluted, and of varying depths. An Alsatian kugelhopf mould (3) is similar to a Baba mould, and is made either in copper or earthenware.

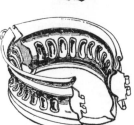

Moule à pâté A hinged round or oval open mould for pâtés cooked in a crust (4).

Mouli-légumes Vegetable mill. An excellent invention for the rapid sieving of soups, purées and so on.

Moulin à café Coffee grinder.

Moulin à poivre Pepper mill.

Mouvette Wooden spoon for stirring sauces.

Panier à friture Wire frying basket for deep frying of potatoes, fish, etc.

Panier à salade Wire salad basket for shaking lettuce and other green salad dry after washing it.

Passoire Sieve, colander.

Pilon Pestle.

Plafond A shallow rectangular baking or roasting tin or baking sheet.

Planche à découper Carving board, usually made of beechwood, with a channel or groove for catching the juices which run out when the meat is cut.

Planche à hacher A chopping board. It should be at least an inch thick with no central join. One of the most essential objects in any kitchen, however modest. It should always be kept conveniently to hand. When it has been scrubbed (butchers chopping boards are scraped, never

C

scrubbed) do not put it by the fire or in any other hot place to dry or it will warp. The board in the drawing on page 237 is a typical French one.

Planche à pâtisserie Pastry board.

Plaque à pâtisserie A baking sheet.

Plaque à rôtir Shallow copper, iron or tin baking dish in which a grid will stand, and in which joints or birds are roasted in the oven.

Plat à gratin Shallow metal, tinned copper, fireproof china, enamelled cast-iron or earthenware dish, oval or round, which exposes a large area of the food to be cooked to the top heat of the oven or grill so that a light crust is formed on the top.

Platine Small plaque (see above).

Poêle à frire Frying-pan.

Poêle à crêpes Small, very shallow iron frying-pan for pancakes.

Poêle à friture Deep-frying pan.

Poêle à œufs A small metal, fireproof china, enamelled cast-iron or earthenware dish, with side-handles or ears, in which eggs are cooked and served; e.g. *œufs sur le plat*, the French version of fried eggs. Earthenware, however rustically attractive it may look, is unsatisfactory for this purpose. The eggs stick, and the dish becomes very difficult to clean.

Poêle à omelette Omelette pan. The sloping inner sides of the pan facilitate the sliding out of the cooked omelette on to the serving dish. Although omelette pans should always be heavy with an absolutely flat base, there exists nowadays such a variety of these pans made of enamelled cast-iron, heavy aluminium, copper, etc., which can be washed and kept clean like any other pan, that they are replacing the old iron omelette pans which have to be kept greased and not washed because of the danger of rust. Many cooks, however, insist upon the old iron omelette pans, for all manner of superstitious beliefs surround the very simple process of cooking an omelette. Anyhow, it is certainly an asset to every household to possess two omelette pans, a 10-inch pan for 3- or 4-egg omelettes for two people, and a 6-inch pan for a 2-egg omelette for one person.

Poêlon A small earthenware or metal frying or sauté pan with a handle; deeper than an ordinary frying-pan, and often with rounded sides sloping to a small flat base.

Poêlon à sucre Untinned copper sugar-boiling **saucepan.**

Poissonnière Fish kettle.

 Ramequin Diminutive fireproof porcelain or glass cocotte or ramekin in which individual soufflés or cheese creams (*ramequins au fromage*) are cooked and served. See also *Cocotte* (*b*).

Ravier A shallow boat-shaped china dish for hors-d'œuvre. The most suitable dish for the serving of the simple hors-d'œuvre of French household meals, such as olives, radishes, butter, sardines, potato salad and egg mayonnaise.

Rondin A round stew-pan with two handles and a close-fitting lid. Also called a *fait-tout*.

Rouleau Rolling pin. To do its work efficiently a rolling pin should be plumb straight. French boxwood (*buis*) pins are good, and a patented French pin, ridged and on ball bearings is marvellously effective for puff and croissant pastry. This pin, called a Tutove, is horribly expensive. The price does not deter French professional pastry cooks and cookery school teachers from buying the Tutove in considerable quantities.

Saladier Salad bowl. The most characteristic French salad bowl is in plain white china, deep and round (see the drawing on page 129) or with squared corners. The enormous wooden bowls so popular here are seldom seen in France, except in rough wood for mixing bowls (called *sébilles*). When a recipe tells you to turn something into a *saladier* to set or to cool, it simply means that a large china vessel, such as a mixing bowl, should be used.

Salamandre (*a*) A round iron utensil with a long handle, also called a *fer à glacer* and a *pelle rouge*. The iron is made red hot and held close to the surface of a dish the top of which is by this means instantaneously browned, without the possibility of the main body of the dish being overheated and therefore altering in any way in consistency. These utensils are now all but obsolete, at any rate in England, and so far as I know nothing has yet been devised to replace them in the domestic kitchen.

(*b*) A grill with a very rapid action serving the same purpose as the old-fashioned salamander. Grills on household cookers do not usually, however, work in this manner, and when trying to obtain a good browned

or glazed surface on the top of a dish you simply have to allow for the fact that the rest of the contents will go on cooking.

Sauteuse A heavy and shallow straight-sided saucepan with a handle, in which small cuts of meat, vegetables, etc., are *sauté*, or tossed (or jumped as the dictionary says) in butter or other fat. The idea is that during the cooking you shake the pan to prevent the food from sticking.

Sautoir, Casserole à sauter, Plat à sauter Much the same as a *sauteuse*, except that technically the *sautoir* is supposed to have outwardly sloping sides. In fact the terms are entirely interchangeable. Few English kitchens seem to possess sauté pans, and while it is true that a good heavy frying-pan is a reasonable substitute, there are well-designed and inexpensive sauté pans in the shops, and they are most useful in any kitchen. (See also *Casserole*.)

Soupière Soup tureen.

Spatule Spatula or palette knife.

Tamis de crin A hair sieve on a wooden frame. Hair sieves are now mostly replaced, not very satisfactorily, by nylon.

Terrine Strictly speaking, an earthenware cooking pot, of varying dimensions, round or oval, without handles, but often with ears. Fairly deep, and if there is a lid this is pierced with a hole for the escape of steam during cooking. The name of the utensil has also come to mean the food cooked in it, e.g. *terrine de gibier* is a game pâté cooked in an earthenware or other fireproof dish, and a pâté *en terrine* indicates that the pâté concerned has been cooked and is served in the terrine rather than in a crust, which would properly be a pâté *en croûte*. Also, when one is told by cookery books to pour something into a ter-rine, this simply indicates that a china or glazed earthenware, rather than a metal, recipient must be used.

Timbale In terms of kitchen utensils a timbale is a round mould with straight or slightly sloping sides, sometimes fluted, made of tinned copper, tin, or fireproof china. It was originally intended to imitate the appearance and shape of a pastry crust. Once again, foods cooked in a timbale (and turned out on to the serving dish) have acquired the name of the utensil, e.g. *timbale de riz, timbale de fruits de mer*. Timbale moulds are also sometimes made with a central cylinder.

Timbale à soufflé May be in fireproof china or metal. The different dishes in which soufflés may be cooked are described in the chapter on egg cookery.

Tourtière A shallow tart tin. The most useful are made with a removable base, and the prettiest have fluted sides (1).

Fig. 2 shows a hinged cake-tin.

In former times a *tourtière* was a heavy iron or earthen-ware dish, much deeper than a tart tin, in which many things besides pastry could be cooked.

Tranchoir A trencher, or wooden carving platter.

Vasque Shallow crystal, silver, or china bowl for the elegant presentation of fruit, sweet dishes, ices, *foie gras*, and *mousses*.

Verge Metal, willow or birch-twig egg whisk.

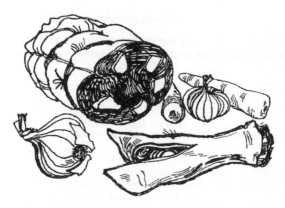

Cooking Terms and Processes

ALTHOUGH there is always plenty more to say about the processes of roasting and grilling and boiling (how many people take the trouble to put the roasting joint on a grid in the tin, or to take it out of the refrigerator several hours before cooking?), these processes are generally thought to be pretty well understood by English cooks. At least they are to be found clearly explained in cookery books. So it is upon the less familiar aspects of French cookery that I shall concentrate in this brief explanation of French cookery terms.

Once, in an English translation of a cookery book by a famous French authority, there were some highly enjoyable literal renderings. *Tomates concassées* became concussed tomatoes. *Faites tomber la sauce* meant that you were to drop it. Most of us, if we use French cookery books at all, have probably got a bit further than that stage. But there are still many confusions, due possibly to the fact that for French writers it is not necessary to explain every process every time they refer to it. *Faites déglacer* they say, and leave it at that. Or because they are professionals writing for professionals they use terms and processes not usually applicable to household cookery. To avoid the worst bewilderments, those who want to use a French cookery book would be well advised to invest in one directed at housewives rather than the restaurant chef. For this purpose Madame Saint- Ange's *Livre de Cuisine* could scarcely be bettered.

Bain-marie, Cuisson au Cooking in a *bain-marie*, or *casserole à bain-marie*, is distinct from the process of keeping something hot in the *bain-marie*.

To cook *au bain-marie* is to place the saucepan or dish in which the food is to cook in another saucepan, or tin, containing water which is kept at simmering point, or just below. The process may be carried out in the oven as well as on top of the stove, and is applied mainly to creams and sauces which would cook too fast and curdle or disintegrate if subjected to direct heat.

Blanc, Cuisson à To cook blind, i.e. to bake a pastry or flan case without its filling.

Blanc, Cuisson au To cook certain meats and vegetables in a *court-bouillon* of flour and water with a few drops of vinegar, called a *blanc*. The object is to prevent the food so cooked from discolouring. In household cooking a *blanc* is more often than not replaced simply by acidulated water. A *blanc* is not to be confused, however, with a *fonds blanc*, which is a stock made from white meat, either chicken or veal.

Bleu, Cuisson au A method of cooking fish, chiefly applied to river trout. The fish is plunged, immediately it is killed, into a *court-bouillon* of water and vinegar, and its skin thereby acquires a slightly blue tinge.

Braisage The process of braising consists of lining a heavy cooking pot, *daubière* or *braisière* with sliced onions and other flavouring vegetables, fat pork or bacon, and/or pork rinds and a calf's foot to supply a gelatinous element to the sauce. The meat or bird to be braised is laid on this bed. Cooking is started off on the top of the stove, and when some of the fats and juices from the underneath layer of ingredients have been released by the heat and a protective browning of the meat accomplished, liquid in the form of stock and/or wine is added, the pot is covered with a hermetically-sealing lid, and cooking continued by very moderate heat. Formerly this was done on top of the stove and between two fires; this was achieved with glowing coals placed on the inset lid of the braising-pan. Nowadays, after the preliminary cooking essential to a true braise, it is usually placed in the oven.

Owing to the fact that in France the secondary cuts of meat used for braising are usually boned, then rolled and tied in a long shape, braising-pans are oval. In England these cuts tend, unless you specify otherwise, to be dressed by the butcher in a round shape. In that case a round pan can be used, the important point being that it must be of a size in which the meat or bird, with all its accompanying ingredients, fits comfortably without being crowded, but not so large that the liquid will waste away leaving the meat dry and without any sauce. The whole point of a braise is that it turns a somewhat tough piece of meat or an old bird into a succulent and juicy dish that is full of flavour.

Clarification du consommé For the clarification of a consommé or an aspic jelly, two whites of eggs to between three and four pints of liquid are beaten slightly in the soup-pan; the broth to be clarified, after every

particle of fat has been removed, is then poured in cold or tepid. Heat very gently, beating with a wooden spoon. Bring to an almost imperceptible boil, and let this continue for 10 minutes. By this time the whites will have formed a sort of crust on top of the broth, to which all particles and impurities have adhered, leaving the liquid clear and limpid. Turn off the heat and leave for another 10 minutes without moving the saucepan. Place a cloth wrung out in hot water in a colander placed in a deep bowl. Very gradually pour the broth through it. Gather up the four corners of the cloth; tie with string to form a bag. Have ready on a chair another bowl, place the bag on the edge of the table so that it hangs right over the bowl, the knotted end secured to the table by a heavy weight, and let the rest of the liquid drip through without squeezing it. If you are dealing with a large quantity of broth, an improvised arrangement of two chairs, the bowl and the cloth, as shown in the sketch, serves the purpose more efficiently.

After the clarification, any necessary flavouring of wine is added. Take care not to overdo this; two tablespoons of Madeira or four of dry white wine for three pints is enough. If the broth is not clear after the first filtering, it means either that the process has been carried out too abruptly or that there were insufficient whites of egg to the quantity of broth. The whole process must be started over again with fresh whites.

At one time a quantity of lean, finely minced beef was used as well as the white to clarify clear soup and to improve its taste and colour. But if the broth has been correctly cooked in the first instance, that is to say never allowed to boil, and with the right quantity of meat, chicken or whatever it may be, the final addition of beef is not necessary. In a *pot-au-feu*, however, a piece of ox-liver is sometimes cooked, and this gives colour and flavour while clarifying at the same time.

Clarification du beurre Ideally, all butter used for frying should be clarified, as this greatly decreases the risk of the butter burning and the food sticking. To clarify butter, melt it in a *bain-marie*. Leave it to settle, then filter it through a fine cloth wrung out in warm water so that all scum is left behind. When you have no time for this, add a little olive oil to your frying butter, which will help it not to stick.

Daube, Cuisson en To cook *en daube* is much the same as to braise. Sometimes a piece of meat for a daube is larded with pork fat or salt pork as explained in the paragraph on larding, sometimes it is sliced before cooking. A daube being essentially a country dish, it is apt to be rougher than a braise, but none the worse for that. A Provençal *bœuf en daube*, for example, or *estouffat de bœuf*, has an addition of olives and tomatoes and a robust flavouring of herbs, garlic and wine.

Déglaçage Deglazing is the process of detaching the juices and all the particles which have adhered to the bottom and sides of a saucepan or sauté pan in which food has browned. This is done by adding liquid, either wine, stock, water or cream, into which these juices and particles are scraped up and incorporated to form a sauce. This is a good example of those French cookery terms which require a whole paragraph to explain in English, although some translators render *déglacer* as 'to rinse out the pan.'

Dégorger, Faire To soak meat or other food in cold water to free it of impurities; to rid it of salt; to let the blood soak out (as with brains and sweetbreads).

Dégraissage The removal of fat from a broth, a sauce. If the liquid to be cleared of fat is put into the refrigerator and left until the fat sets, it is a simple matter to remove it by lifting it up with a palette knife. Any small particles left are wiped off with a cloth wrung out in hot water. When the fat is not set, pour off as much as possible without losing the gravy or broth itself, and the rest can be quite successfully soaked up with large paper tissues. The fat removed from stock, the *pot-au-feu*, etc., is called *dégraissis*; it can be clarified and used for frying.

Dépouiller un lièvre To skin a hare.

Dépouiller une sauce To skim a sauce, to rid it of impurities by skimming them as they rise to the top during cooking.

Ébouillanter, Échauder To put or plunge something into boiling water for a few seconds. To scald. If the expression is used about fruit, it will mean to dip it into boiling water to facilitate the skinning.

Émincer To slice thinly. Term usually applied to cooked meat which is to be sliced for reheating. *Émincé* is occasionally and wrongly understood to mean minced.

Étuvée, Cuisson à l' To cook something in a hermetically sealed pot with very low heat all round, i.e. *petits pois à l'étuvée*. Some French cooking ranges have a special oven called a *fourneau à l'étuve* in which meat, poultry, vegetables and so on can be cooked in this way. It is more or less the equivalent of the coolest oven on our solid fuel stoves of the Aga and Esse types. The system can be usefully applied also to gas or electric ovens set to the lowest possible temperature. The *estouffat de bœuf à l'albigeoise* on page 342 is an example of such cooking.

Foncer, Marquer To line a stew-pan or braising-pan with fat pork, vegetables, herbs and so on before putting in the meat. *Foncer* is also a pastry term meaning to line a tin with the prepared dough.

Fouler To pound through a sieve. The word is said to be the origin of our fruit fools.

Frapper To freeze a liquid, a cream. Also to chill wine or fruit, i.e. *champagne frappé*—chilled, not frozen, champagne; *melon frappé*—iced melon.

Fricasser Literally this means to cook something in a saucepan, and although nowadays a *fricassée* is understood to mean a dish of chicken stewed in butter, the sauce thickened with egg yolks and/or cream, it formerly meant all sorts of ragoûts of meat, fish, poultry, etc. The English fricassée of left-over chicken would be called, in French, *émincés de volaille*.

Friture For deep frying, the French prefer the dripping from beef kidney fat (suet) to any other, sometimes mixing it with veal dripping. Pork lard, called *saindoux*, can also be used (see page 98). In olive-growing areas, naturally, oil is used. In times like recent years when olive oil has been very expensive, ground-nut oil (*huile d'arachides*), which is quite devoid of taste or smell, has to be substituted. But it does not produce such crisp results as olive oil. Oil, and all fats whether animal or vegetable, are improved for purposes of deep frying if simmered for the first time before using for about half an hour. The risk of frothing and boiling over is then diminished. Every time frying oil or fat has been used it is imperative to rid it of all particles and impurities by filtering it through a cloth or very fine sieve before it is put away for further use.

And since we are on the subject of frying fat, perhaps this is the place for me to beg once more of English housewives to abolish that sinister bowl of mixed fats, improperly filtered and therefore full of little specks of frizzled food and other impurities, which lurks in so many larders and refrigerators. To use these mixed fats for frying or for basting the joint is to spoil your dish from the start, for more often than not they are stale and sour, and naturally impart this horrible taste to the gravy, as well as to the meat or poultry which has been cooked in them. We all know that aftertaste of stale fat which ruins so much food in even the best restaurants. The smell as you go through the door is very often sufficient warning. In the home there is no excuse for it. By all means economise, as we were all obliged to do in the days of rationing, by saving good fat or dripping. But do not mix the fat from bacon, mutton, pork, beef, duck and so on all together in one bowl. Keep each one separate, perfectly filtered, and in a covered bowl, and do not try to keep them too long. Better to spend a few extra shillings on buying fresh lard, oil, or butter than to risk your family's health and digestions by using stale fat.

The practice of half-frying certain foods and then leaving them until meal-times before re-cooking them is common in restaurants but also not unknown in the home. It is a dangerous practice, for in the meantime the food may become infected.

Glaçage (*a*) The glazing of meat after it is cooked by anointing it with its own juices and subjecting it to fierce heat for a few seconds. The resulting varnish-like coating is for appearance' sake rather than for any flavour which the process adds to the meat.

(*b*) The painting of cold joints with melted meat glaze to give a brilliant surface.

(*c*) The freezing of any food in ice or the refrigerator (not deep freezing).

(*d*) The icing of cakes and pastries with sugar icing.

(*e*) The dusting of sweet fritters, etc., with icing sugar.

Lardage des viandes To lard a piece of meat is to introduce fat into an otherwise dry joint, such as veal, venison and second- and third-grade cuts of beef. It is done with a special larding needle (lardoire) and pieces of pork fat cut into little sticks of uniform size and shape (lardoons). These lardoons should penetrate right through the meat. Much the same results can be achieved by making deep incisions in the meat and then inserting the lardoons by hand. This is often done for a daube. The appearance of the meat is not so elegant when cut as it is if the larding has been done professionally, but the effect has been achieved. A characteristic dish in which the meat is always larded is *bœuf à la mode*. (See the drawing on page 70.)

Liaison d'une sauce The binding or thickening of a sauce. This is achieved by various methods, each one of which is clearly explained in the relevant recipes in this book. The typical sauce thickened with egg yolks is *sauce béarnaise*, page 118. For a white flour-based sauce, Béchamel on page 114 is the prototype; and for one in which the flour is browned before the addition of the liquid see the *saupiquet des Amognes*, page 231: this sauce is really a variation of *espagnole*. For a sauce made purely of butter and cream, see the recipe for the cream sauce to serve with *poule au pot à la normande*, page 403; for a cream sauce plus the butter and juices in the pan the *escalope cauchoise*, page 373, can be taken as an example. For a sauce containing flour, cream and eggs, see the cream sauce served with the *poule au riz à la crème*, page 404, from which it can be observed that when flour is present in a sauce the added egg yolks can be allowed to come to the simmering point, which would be disastrous in a sauce like Béarnaise in which there is no flour.

For a stew in which the meat is cooked in an already thickened sauce *bœuf bourguignonne*, page 343, is the best example, but such stews are not so common in French household cookery as they are in our own. They should be cooked on top of the stove rather than in the oven, because all-round heat tends to disintegrate the sauce. This misfortune may also occur, especially when it is a question of a small quantity of sauce, when something has cooked too fast on top of the stove, and you find that your meat is floating in a little clear liquid while all the nice thick juices are beginning to stick to the bottom of the pan. To remedy this, remove your meat and keep it warm; pour off the clear liquid; heat it in a separate pan, adding extra stock or water; gradually pour it back over the juices in the original pan, and cook gently, stirring all the time, for about 10 minutes, and you will find your sauce has re-integrated. It is amazing what can be done in cookery by keeping one's head and making use of a small quantity of plain water. Sometimes even a curdled cream or egg sauce can be brought back by a similar method.

The last-minute thickening of a sauce with *beurre manié*, in other words butter and flour worked together cold, is explained in the recipe for *coq au vin*, page 399. People are frightened of this method, perhaps because of the many conflicting instructions one sees in cookery books regarding the manner of its use. It is really very simple, but I think myself it is a system to which one should not have recourse too often. Flour-thickened sauces pall very easily, whereas those obtained by reduction (see the simplified recipe for meat stock and meat glaze, page 112) tend to have a much truer taste. In fact that one word *reduction* lies at the base of a really very large proportion of the most *soigné* and high-class dishes.

Thickened sauces obtained *à froid* or without cooking are emulsions of egg yolk and olive oil (mayonnaise, page 120); and the little known *sauce bretonne*, page 124, is a cross between mayonnaise and Béarnaise, being a mixture of egg yolks and barely melted butter, plus herbs, mustard and vinegar.

Beurre blanc, page 306, and *hollandaise*, page 119, are obtained by a fusion of butter with other ingredients at very low heat. The sauces of *bouillabaisse* and of *matelotes* are on the contrary obtained by the cooking of oil, water and/or wine together as fiercely and rapidly as possible. A very simple version of this system is the recipe for *moules à la marseillaise*, page 319.

There are also, of course, the straightforward sauces, of which tomato sauce is typical, and which are really purées, or *coulis*, needing no sort of extra thickenings.

Once these few different principles of sauce-making have been mastered—and, of course, many people are conversant with them without precisely knowing the reasons for what they are doing—it becomes possible to make almost any sauce without fear of failure.

Marinage des Viandes, Poissons, Gibiers To marinate is to steep meat, poultry or game in a mixture of wine, spices, aromatic herbs and vegetables for anything from an hour to several days. The objects in so doing are (*a*) to tenderise tough meat, (*b*) to give moisture to dry meat—such as an old hare or venison; for these olive oil is usually added to the marinade, (*c*) to preserve meat or game which, although *à point*, it may be more convenient to keep for a day or two. You have to use your own judgment as to the length of time to marinate a given piece of meat. In warm or stuffy weather it should obviously be for a shorter time than in the winter. When instructed to marinate fish, this will usually mean for an hour or so, in oil and lemon juice, or possibly white wine.

It is not, perhaps, imperative to go quite so far as M. Edouard Nignon, the famous *chef de cuisine* of Paillard's in Paris and at one time of Claridges in London, who in one of his books instructs his readers to prepare the string for trussing a chicken by first soaking it in cognac. . . .

Mijoter To simmer, to cook gently over low heat.

Mitonner To cook bread in broth or soup.

Panage The coating of something to be fried, or grilled, with breadcrumbs, which are made from bread dried in the oven, either until it is a pale golden colour or else removed before it has turned colour. The breadcrumbs made from the former by pounding and sieving, are called *chapelure blonde* or *brune*, and the latter *chapelure blanche*. Some writers, however, only refer to *chapelure* when they mean browned breadcrumbs to cover a gratin, and to white breadcrumbs, for coating, as *panure*. A *panade* is something different again, meaning generally a preparation of flour, breadcrumbs, butter, etc., used for binding *quenelles* and croquettes; the English panada, or basic preparation for a soufflé, is in French an *appareil à soufflé*.

Panure à l'anglaise The food to be fried, such as escalopes of veal, fish fillets, cutlets, etc., is first dipped in beaten egg, then in the breadcrumbs. (Some cooks advocate a preliminary coating of flour, but it is not really necessary.) The operation is often repeated twice, and it is essential to have very fine breadcrumbs or the final result will be that all too familiar thick and greasy blanket. Having coated the food, smooth it down with a palette knife and leave it for a little time on a grid to set. Sometimes, especially for grilling, the food is painted with melted butter instead of egg, and is then breadcrumbed. This is *panure au beurre*. If grated Parmesan is mixed with the breadcrumbs it is *panure à la milanaise*.

Papillotes Paper cases in which small items like veal cutlets or red mullet are cooked in the oven, having sometimes been already partly cooked. The object of cooking *en papillotes* is to preserve all the juices and

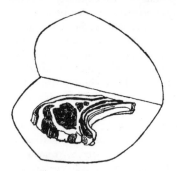

aromas intact, and the food is brought to table still in its cases. The paper should be well buttered or oiled inside before the food is wrapped in it. The illustration shows how the paper is cut and folded for a veal cutlet or other small piece of meat.

Piquage A process distinct from larding in that while in the latter case the lardoons are drawn right through the meat, in the former they are only sewn, or darned, through on the outer surface. The function of *piquage* is not to provide interior fat for the piece of meat so treated, but rather to act as a sort of elaborate barding or wrapping, to make a decorative appearance, and to add to the savour of meat such as veal. A *fricandeau de veau*, an old-fashioned dish seldom seen nowadays, and a *râble de lièvre* (saddle of hare) are two of the classic examples of piqué́d meat and game.

The household substitute for this elaborate process is to wrap your meat and game in thinly cut slices of pork fat or unsmoked bacon.

Revenir, Faire To give vegetables, meat, fish, a brief preliminary cooking in butter or other heated fat until they have taken on a very slight colour. An important process in the making of the majority of French soups, ragoûts, daubes, and in the braising of poultry and meat.

Suer, Faire Often confused with the above, this means to give a preliminary cooking to a piece of meat or a bird in butter or other fat until beads of juice start to pearl on the surface.

Tomber, Faire To cook a piece of meat very slowly without other liquid than that produced during cooking by the meat itself. The liquid is then *tombé*, or reduced, to a syrupy consistency. So when instructed to *faire tomber la sauce* it means to reduce it. *Faire tomber à glace* is an expression also used in connection with sliced or chopped onions or shallots cooked in a small amount of liquid and reduced almost to a purée or a state of glaze.

Tremper la soupe To soak slices of bread in the soup before serving it.

Vanner une sauce To make a sauce quite smooth by stirring, to prevent a skin forming. If a béchamel or other thickened sauce has to be made in advance spread the surface with little knobs of butter while it is still hot. This will form a film which prevents the formation of a skin.

WINE FOR THE KITCHEN

The technique of using wine in cookery is extremely simple, almost the only rule to remember being that the wine must be *cooked*. As with all rules, there are exceptions, and to these I will return presently, but generally speaking, wine is added to a stew right at the beginning of the cooking, and at the end of the long, slow process of simmering has become transformed into a sort of essence which, combined as it is with the meat juices, and flavoured with vegetables and herbs, forms a richly aromatic sauce. To achieve this end it is not necessary to use large quantities of wine. With the exception of two or three of the recipes in this book, no dish calls for more than one large glass of red or white wine, often less, and of course the wine used is inexpensive table wine or *vin ordinaire*; although those to whom the drinking of wine is a daily occurrence will know that a glass extracted from their bottle of respectable table wine is likely to produce better results in the flavour of the finished dish than will some thin and sour stuff reserved especially for cooking. A friend once reproached me with having withheld from her some secret in the recipe for a beef and wine stew. She had cooked it, she said, exactly as I had told her but the flavour was not as good and rich as mine had been. In a sense she was right to tax me with inaccuracy, for I had forgotten to tell her that that particular day I had used a glass of my good Rhône wine in cooking the dish, and it had made all the difference.

Since practical application is more valuable than detailed instruction in the abstract, it will be more to the point to refer the reader to recipes in which the different systems of adding wine to a dish are fully set out, than to go into lengthy explanations here.

Typical recipes in which wine gently and lengthily cooked is an essential part of the dish are *bœuf à la mode* (page 347) and the various daubes and *estouffats* of beef on pages 339 to 346, *bœuf à la bourguignonne* on page 343, and the *noix de veau à l'alsacienne*, page 371, in which the white wine of the country contributes its subtle flavour to the jellied sauce which will eventually surround the meat.

When wine is added to a quickly cooked dish such as fried steak, chops, veal escalopes or fish steaks, it is also thoroughly cooked, but much more rapidly; as soon as the meat is seized on each side, the wine is poured into the pan and the heat turned up, so that the wine bubbles and reduces, fuses with the juices already in the pan and in a matter of minutes produces a small amount of thick and syrupy sauce. Examples of this system are the *côtes de porc Vallée d'Auge*, page 361, in which cider replaces white wine, and *saumon poêlé au vin blanc*, page 311.

Even simpler are certain fish dishes, such as the grey mullet with black olives on page 289, in which the fish is baked in an open dish in the oven in a little bath of white wine, but this applies only to thick fish which take a little time to cook. If it were a question of sole, which needs only a few minutes' poaching, the wine in which it has cooked would be subsequently reduced by fast boiling over a high flame, and the resulting essence incorporated into a ready-prepared cream sauce, or thickened with egg yolks and/or cream.

Instances in which wine is *not* cooked are those occasions when Madeira (infinitely superior to sherry for this purpose) is added to a hot consommé or to a clear broth destined for aspic jelly. A very small quantity is added when the consommé is already hot, and, in the case of a jelly, after it has been clarified as explained on page 72. It is all too easy to overdo this final addition of Madeira and to spoil a beautiful consommé by pouring the Madeira straight into it from the bottle instead of measuring out a tablespoonful—and a tablespoonful, or two at the most, is enough for about six cups.

There are other dishes in which a negligible quantity of wine, uncooked, makes all the difference; one example is the *pêches au vin blanc*, page 440, which calls for a soft or sweetish white wine.

The following points with regard to the use of wine in cookery may be useful to the beginner:

(1) Many reasons are advanced for cooking with wine—that it helps the flavour of second- and third-grade cuts of meat and elderly boiling fowls, that it breaks down tough fibres and so lessens cooking time, that a wine marinade is a help in preserving meat, fish or game in warm weather or on occasions when you wish to postpone the cooking of a given dish for a day or two. All these reasons hold good but, in the last resort, the best reason for using wine in cooking is *because you like the taste it gives to the finished dish*.

(2) Experiment is always worth while. Suppose that you have no bottle of white wine and no Madeira handy but the ingredients of a Martini are in the cupboard. Then try a small quantity of vermouth; or, for that matter, Dubonnet or any of the other apéritif drinks. They are really only fortified wines treated with aromatics; sole cooked in vermouth is a well-known French chefs' dish; and there are French cooks who prefer to flame their lobster in whisky rather than brandy, presumably because whisky is much more expensive than brandy in France, so that the snob value of the dish is enhanced, and as a matter of fact once the alcohol is burnt out I doubt if many people would know the difference.

(3) This brings us to the question of the flaming, flaring, flambéing or whatever you like to call it, of brandy or other spirits. The spirit or liqueur in question should first be warmed in a soup ladle or in a very small saucepan, otherwise it may not light. Having set a match to it, pour it flaming over your dish of meat, lobster, pancakes or whatever it may be and shake and rotate the pan so that the flames spread. By the time they have died down the alcohol will have burnt away, and with it any excess of butter or trace of greasiness in the sauce will have disappeared. What is left should be a highly concentrated essence which imparts to the food a flavour which nothing else can give. Whether the operation shall be carried out in the kitchen or with a grand flourish at the table is up to everyone to decide for himself. Sometimes, of course, the flaring takes place at the beginning of the cooking, as in the *bœuf à la gardiane*, page 345, so the question does not arise. When it does, I find it preferable that the flaring process should be done in the kitchen, for personally I don't like the smell of methylated spirits normally used to heat table cookers; sometimes in London and Paris restaurants (you rarely see such a thing in serious French provincial restaurants) the

smell becomes so overwhelming that it quite ruins the more attractive but less powerful smells of your food and the bouquet of your wine.

A good example of a dish in which the liqueur, in this case Calvados, is *flambé* is the *escalope Cauchoise* on page 373, and as I have explained, whisky, strange though it may seem, can be used as a substitute for Calvados.

(4) Until you know that you can trust your judgment as to how much brandy or liqueur any given dish will take, it is wisest to stick to the amount prescribed in the recipe. Liqueurs are tricky things, and too much may well spoil a dish, while too little is simply pointless. 'A spoonful of Kirsch,' I read in a newspaper article, 'will improve your fruit salad. The contents of a whole miniature bottle will make it fit for a banquet.' If a spoonful is enough, why add more? If it is not enough, then why bother with it? Alternatively, how much fruit salad are you going to make for a banquet, and why should you put more Kirsch for a banquet than for a simple dinner party? Mystery. . . . And talking of Kirsch, it is very expensive, but if you are going to buy it, make sure to get Alsatian, Swiss or German Kirschwasser, the true fruit alcohol, rather than the sweetened variety which is just known as Kirsch, and if you ever cook *choucroute* try the recipe on page 420 and see what a really astonishing difference a small glass of Kirschwasser makes to this otherwise rather flat dish.

(5) Don't overdo the wine and liqueurs in your cooking just because you happen to have plenty to hand.

(6) If you have, say, a glass of red wine left in a bottle, pour it into a small bottle, cork it up and it will keep good for cooking for several days. But do not delay using it for too long, for it will go sour and be useless. White wine kept in the refrigerator appears to keep rather longer than red.

(7) When cooking with cider, always use an enamelled or porcelain-lined pan. Iron or tin will turn the cider black, and your sauce will have a somewhat sinister appearance.

(8) The wine to drink with wine-flavoured dishes is entirely a matter of taste, but the problem usually solves itself quite naturally, for white wine more or less automatically goes with fish (although some experts advocate a sound, but not grand, red wine such as Beaujolais, with salmon) and red wine with beef and game, even when white wine has been used in the cooking. For veal and chicken the choice is again a question of taste, the occasion, the time of year, and of what is available; personally I usually prefer white wines with both these meats, with the exception naturally of a dish like *coq au vin*, which obviously demands a red Burgundy. In France one finds that there are far fewer rules in these

matters than are laid down in England, where wine is treated with more reverence because we have less of it.

In France, as far as everyday, rather than high level, great occasion, eating and drinking is concerned, what wine is served with any given dish is largely a matter of what is grown in the district, and whether the production of red or white wines predominates. Thus, in Alsace, where scarcely any red wine is produced, one drinks white wine with all sorts of dishes, even game, usually associated with red wine. Sometimes this is successful, sometimes one begins to long for a change. In the Beaujolais and Lyon the situation is reversed; the local red wines flow more freely than the whites, and it is not uncommon to see them being drunk with those fish *quenelles* which are an inevitable item on the restaurant menus in this part of France.

Les Aromates, etc.

Herbs, spices, condiments, etc., used in French cookery

UNDER the heading of *aromates* come the herbs, flavouring vegetables such as onions, shallots, garlic, carrots and tomatoes, and the spices and sweet flavourings used in French cookery. The following brief list of such ingredients, with their French and English names, gives an idea both of the dishes for which these things are used and the manner of treating them. I have also included in this list various kinds of salt pork and ham, fats, oils, flours, wines and so on, upon the correct use of which depends much of the successful cooking of French dishes. I hope this little glossary may also be useful to those who use French cookery books but are sometimes puzzled by an obscure word or term of cookery.

Ail GARLIC The essential flavouring of the soups, meat and fish dishes, and sauces of Provençal cookery, and possibly to an even greater extent of that of all south-western France—the Béarn, the Pays Basque, the Languedoc, Bordeaux, Poitou and the Roussillon, and to a slightly lesser degree of the country dishes of Burgundy and of the Auvergne. How much garlic goes into a dish is entirely a matter of individual taste, so that while, of course, there cannot be any such thing as an *aïoli* or a *bourride* without garlic, it can, in certain dishes, be just a faint flavouring which would not, perhaps, be recognised by those not in the know but would be missed were it not present. The crushed clove of garlic included in the bouquet for certain meat dishes, such as *bœuf bourguignon*, is a good example of this technique. But garlic can play odd tricks: while a cut clove of garlic rubbed round a salad bowl does not do anything very much, the same treatment of the earthenware dish in which you are going to cook a *gratin dauphinois* (page 211) makes all the difference. The heat of the oven brings out the garlic flavour quite strongly and it communicates itself to the cream in which the potatoes are drenched. Without it, the dish is flat. Again, I have included, for the sake of interest, a recipe for a *poulet sauté dauphinois* (page 401) which calls for cloves of garlic used as if they were miniature potatoes; and a Catalan sauce (page 126) in which the amount of garlic may seem positively savage to some, while to others it would be barely sufficient. A clove of garlic, or one section of a head of garlic, is *une gousse d'ail*, while the plural of garlic heads is *aulx*.

Amidon de Blé Also known by the proprietary name of Maizena. Cornstarch, cornflour.

Anchois ANCHOVIES Salted anchovies from the barrel were formerly much used in England as well as all over the Continent, for flavouring and salting meat dishes. In certain southern dishes, the custom still survives. The anchovies most commonly used in England are the filleted variety, preserved in oil, and only mildly salted. When a recipe calls for anchovies, one should allow about four of these fillets for each anchovy specified.

Angélique ANGELICA The crystallised stalks of angelica, a member of the umbelliferae family, are well known as a flavouring and decoration for cakes and creams. In the Nivernais district of France, angelica is used in powdered form for flavouring a cream cheese tart. Fresh, the leaves are occasionally used in salads, but the stalks in their fresh state, while giving out a powerful and delicious scent, have absolutely no taste. Angelica is considered to possess strong digestive powers and is much used in the composition of liqueurs.

Anis ANISEED Used for flavouring creams, cakes and liqueurs, and a cheese called *Anisé* made in Lorraine.

Arrowroot Used for thickening soups and sauces, particularly in cookery for children or invalids.

Aulx Plural of *Ail*—garlic.

Axonge See *Saindoux*.

Badiane A variety of aniseed, also called Chinese Aniseed, used in the anisette liqueur of Bordeaux.

Basilic BASIL or SWEET BASIL A very aromatic herb not now much used in northern France but which figures in Provençal cookery, especially in the famous *Soupe au Pistou* of the Niçois country.

Bergamotte A variety of lemon, from the skin of which is extracted the oil of bergamot used in perfumery, for flavouring sweet dishes and liqueurs and in the confection of sweets such as the famous *Bergamottes de Nancy*. Bergamotte is also the name of a variety of pear.

Beurre BUTTER The uses of butter in cookery are too well known and too obvious for me to need to go into the question here. The method of clarifying butter for frying is explained on page 72.

Bigarade BITTER or SEVILLE ORANGE Important for the orange sauces which go with wild duck and other game, but for which sweet orange is often substituted.

Blé Corn.

Blé de turquie Indian corn, maize.

Bouquet garni The routine bouquet or faggot of herbs for meat dishes, soups, stews and so on, consists of a bayleaf, two or three sprigs of parsley with their stalks, and a little sprig of thyme tied together with a thread so that it can be extracted after the dish is cooked. A crushed clove of garlic is often included in the bouquet and, in Provençal cooking, a little piece of dried orange peel as well.

Bourrache BORAGE So far as I know, not used in French cookery except in the Niçois district where, in the Italian manner, it may go into the stuffing for ravioli; the leaves may be fried in batter and served as sweet fritters.

Brunoise A mixture of aromatic vegetables such as carrots, leeks, turnips and celery cut into very small dice to form the basis of a soup or a stuffing.

Camomille Used for *tisanes* or soothing herb teas.

Cannelle CINNAMON The bark of this plant of the laurel family is used both in powdered and in stick form for flavouring creams and cakes.

Câpres CAPERS The best capers in France are considered to be those which come from plants grown in the Var and the Bouches-du-Rhône departments of Provence. They are called *nonpareilles*. The flower buds are small and round and, when pickled, are still much used for sauces and flavouring in Provençal cookery.

Capucine, Graines de NASTURTIUM SEEDS Sometimes used as a substitute for capers. The leaves of nasturtiums can be used for salads and the flowers are still sometimes used for decorating a dish.

Cardomome, Graines de CARDAMOM SEEDS A highly aromatic spice which goes into curry mixtures and is much used in Arab cookery (sometimes to flavour coffee) and in that of the East Indies. The seeds are encased in hard pods which are put whole into certain Oriental dishes, while for curry powders and other spice mixtures the seeds are taken from the pods and pounded.

Cari, Kari CURRY POWDER This crops up in unexpected places in French cookery, usually in a very mild form, in dishes derived from French colonial cookery.

Carottes CARROTS One of the essential flavouring vegetables for stews, soups and many sauces and stuffings.

Carvi CARAWAY The fruit, usually referred to as the seeds, of this plant of the umbelliferae family are used, like aniseed, for flavouring cakes, creams and liqueurs, and a little bowl of caraway seeds is nearly always served as an accompaniment to the Münster cheese of Alsace.

Cassonnade Soft, unrefined sugar, either from the cane or the beet, Rarely used in modern French cookery.

Cédrat CITRON A large variety of citrus fruit with a very thick, aromatic skin, used mainly in its candied state. Grown in Provence and Corsica, where it is used to flavour a liqueur called *cédratine*.

Cerfeuil CHERVIL One of the most common herbs of French cookery, nearly always included in the mixture of *fines herbes* for omelettes, and much used for sprinkling into soups. The flavour is more delicate and elusive than that of parsley but, although it is very easy to grow, it is rare in English herb gardens. The leaves, plucked from the stem rather than chopped, are always known as *pluches de cerfeuil*. *Cerfeuil bulbeux* is turnip-rooted chervil, used as a root vegetable.

Champignons de couche CULTIVATED MUSHROOMS Used with other flavouring vegetables to make various basic mixtures such as *duxelles*, *salpicons*, and formerly *fines herbes*.

Champignons secs DRIED MUSHROOMS These are usually cèpes, or boletus, and are used for flavouring stews, soups and sauces, although less in French cookery than in Italian. A small quantity goes a long way. They should be soaked in tepid water for half an hour or so before cooking.

Chapelure Breadcrumbs for coating meat, fish, etc., to be fried, or for sprinkling over dishes to be browned in the oven or under the grill. See *Panage*, pages 77–8.

Ciboule SCALLION, WELSH ONION.

Ciboulette, Civette, Cives CHIVES Used fresh to flavour salads and sauces.

Coriandre CORIANDER The dried seeds of the coriander plant have an aromatic and slightly orangey scent, and were at one time used to flavour sweet creams, and coated with sugar were popular children's sweets or comfits. Neither the seeds nor the leaves are much used nowadays in French cookery, although both figure in the cookery of the Arab countries and of Spain.

Cornichons GHERKINS The immature fruit of the gherkin cucumbers; pickled, they appear as an accompaniment to the beef from the *pot-au-feu*, and in hors-d'œuvre, especially in northern and eastern France; and chopped gherkins always appear in any dish labelled *charcutière*, e.g. *côtelettes de porc charcutière*.

Couennes de porc FRESH PORK RINDS Much used in country daubes and stews to give richness and a gelatinous consistency to the sauce.

Crépine de porc, *Coiffe de porc* PIG'S CAUL An outer membrane which covers the intestines of the pig and to which a certain amount of fat adheres. When the greater part of this fat has been removed to be melted down for lard, the *crépine* is soaked in salt and water to cleanse it, and subsequently used for wrapping round the flat sausages which, taking their name from this covering, are called *crépinettes*. This *crépine*, *coiffe*, or *toilette* as it is sometimes called, as also that of the calf, is used a good deal in French cookery as a protective and fat wrapping for braised liver and various kinds of chopped meat mixtures. The best substitute when it cannot be obtained is a wrapping of very thin slices of back pork fat.

Cumin, *Graines de* CUMIN SEEDS A characteristic, warm and pungent flavouring of North African Arab cookery; also used occasionally in the cookery of Alsace. *Cumin des près* is wild caraway.

Curcuma TURMERIC The spice ground from the root of this plant is responsible for the yellow colour and part of the pungent flavour of curry powders.

Duxelles A preparation of chopped mushrooms, shallots and onion, melted in butter and used as a foundation for various sauces and croquette mixtures.

Échalote SHALLOT A small variety of onion which divides into two or more cloves when skinned. One of the most frequently used aromatic vegetables of the French kitchen. While its flavour is no milder than that of the onion, it is said to be easier to digest. The shallot also emulsifies to a greater extent than the onion, which no doubt accounts for its presence at the base of a number of sauces such as *bercy* and *beurre blanc*, and in basic preparations like *duxelles* and *mirepoix*.

Épeautre SPELT, GERMAN WHEAT A coarse grain which was grown a good deal at one time in Provence. It is said to be the grain from which macaroni was originally made in Italy.

Épices composées A mixture of spices and herbs used for flavouring. Carême gives the composition as follows: thyme, bayleaves, basil, sage, a little coriander and mace. All these ingredients, perfectly dried, are pounded together and sieved. Add to this mixture a third of their weight in finely ground pepper. Store them in a sealed box in a dry place.

Épices quatre, or Épices fines Another mixture of herbs and spices composed, according to the *Larousse Gastronomique*, of 700 grammes of white pepper, 300 grammes of allspice or pimento berries, 100 grammes of mace and 50 grammes each of nutmeg, cloves, cinnamon, bayleaves, sage, marjoram and rosemary, pounded and sieved as above. See also *Sel Épicé*.

Estragon TARRAGON An aromatic herb very typical of French cooking. A little goes a long way but its affinity with chicken is remarkable, and a few leaves steeped for a short while in a consommé and in clarified broth destined for aspic jelly make the whole difference to the finished dish. Tarragon is an essential flavouring in *sauce béarnaise*, *sauce verte*, and Montpellier butter and also goes into the *fines herbes* mixture for omelettes, into salads, sole dishes, and cream soups. The best tarragon vinegar, which makes all the difference to salad dressings, is made by steeping whole sprigs of the fresh herb in bottles of wine vinegar or Orléans vinegar. (The latter is also wine vinegar, the Orléans process of distilling it being somewhat different from that used for other wine vinegars.) For the tarragon vinegar of commerce, the herbs are removed after a short period of steeping, and the vinegar filtered. If made at home, leave the whole branches of tarragon in the bottles until the vinegar is all used up. The flavour will be much finer. If you are buying tarragon plants for the garden, make sure to get the variety known as True French. The kind called Russian tarragon has no scent and a rather acrid flavour.

Farigoule The Provençal name for wild thyme.

Fécule de pommes de terre POTATO FLOUR, POTATO STARCH Used for thickening soups and sauces.

Fenouil FENNEL The dried stalks and branches of the common wild fennel are used in Provençal cookery for the famous *grillade au fenouil* (page 286) and for flavouring *court-bouillons* in which fish is to be cooked. The little feathery leaves, in their fresh state, can be chopped up to flavour sauces and salads for those who like the pronounced aniseed flavour. The bulbous leaf stem of the cultivated Florentine fennel is eaten raw, like celery, or sliced up, dressed with oil, lemon and salt to make an hors-d'œuvre. It can also be cooked in much the same way as celery, partly boiled, cut in half and finished in butter with a sprinkling of cheese.

Fennel seeds, which taste very similar to caraway seeds, are used as a flavouring for sausages and stuffings in Italian cookery. The common fennel is very easy to cultivate in English gardens, although the Florentine variety (there is a drawing of it on page 129) rarely grows successfully in England.

Fines herbes Unless otherwise specified, this means a mixture of parsley, chervil, chives and tarragon, most commonly used for flavouring omelettes but also for grilled fish and chicken. At one time *fines herbes* meant mushrooms and shallots, but nowadays this mixture is called a *duxelles*.

Fournitures Salad greens and fresh herbs, which include sorrel, chervil, chives, cress, etc.

Frigolet Another Provençal name for wild thyme. Also a local liqueur.

Fromage CHEESE Swiss and French Gruyère and Emmenthal cheeses and imported Parmesan are the ones most frequently used in French cookery, although certain local dishes are naturally made with the particular cheese product of the region; there are, for example, several regional dishes in the Auvergne made from the excellent local Cantal or from *Tomme de Cantal*, which is a fresh unfermented cheese. Soft cream cheeses, of which there are scores of different varieties, are much used for sweet dishes.

Froment, Farine de Fine wheat flour. Also called *farine de gruau*.

Genièvre JUNIPER The dried berries (*baies de genièvre*) have a warm, pungent flavour and an aromatic scent, and are used in the mountainous districts of central and eastern France, in Provence and in Corsica, for flavouring the stuffings or sauces for small game birds and for pâtés; an excellent flavouring also for pork and venison. The appearance of juniper berries in a list of ingredients often puzzles English people, which is odd considering that they constitute one of the main flavouring agents of gin, which gets its name from the Latin *Ginepro* or juniper, and juniper grows wild on the hills in many parts of England. At one time juniper berries were commonly used in England in the spicing of beef and hams.

Gingembre GINGER Little used in French cookery proper, although occasionally recipes which have filtered through from the French colonies call for a flavouring of either powdered or fresh green root ginger.

Girofle, Clous de CLOVES Two or three cloves stuck into an onion are a traditional seasoning of the *pot-au-feu* and of various meat stews in France. Ground cloves are also used in the composition of mixed spices (see *Épices*).

Glace de viande MEAT GLAZE Highly concentrated extract of meat used to heighten the flavour and give body to sauces. A recipe for making it in small quantities is given on page 112.

Gousse d'ail A clove of garlic.

Graines de paradis A relative of the Cardamom family, known in England as Malagueta pepper. Cultivated and used in the French African colonies of Dahomey, the Ivory coast and French Guinea.

Graisse de rognons de bœuf, *Graisse de friture* The rendered down fat of beef kidneys, considered by many French cooks to be the best for deep frying. For the method of rendering fat, see *Saindoux*.

Graisses alimentaires, *Végétales* Vegetable fats, mixed cooking fats, synthetic fats and margarines.

Gruau, Farine de Fine wheat flour. Also called *farine de froment*.

Guimauve MARSHMALLOW, MALLOW *Pâte de Guimauve* is the equivalent of our marshmallow sweet, which however contains no mallow. See *Mauve*.

Huile d'arachides GROUNDNUT OIL Suitable for frying and for making mayonnaise for those who do not care for the flavour of olive oil.

Huile d'olive OLIVE OIL Good olive oil seems to me as essential to good cookery as is butter, but as I have gone into this question in some detail elsewhere in this book (see pages 74, 122 and 283) and also in the paragraph on *Olives* below, I will not discuss it further here.

Hysope HYSSOP A bitter herb, used at one time in savoury stuffings but mainly regarded as a medicinal herb. Used also in liqueurs.

Jambon de Bayonne A ham usually served raw, cut in fine slices, as an hors-d'œuvre; the special method of curing Bayonne hams (which are mostly made near Orthez in the Béarn) includes wine in the pickling mixture and, unlike Parma ham, Bayonne hams are usually smoked, although only very mildly. When raw ham of this type is called for in a recipe, the best English substitute is a slice of mild gammon.

Jambon blanc Boned cooked ham, also called *Jambon de Paris* and *Jambon glacé*.

Jambon du pays, *Jambon de montagne* Almost every district has its own local methods of curing hams and a slice from these is often used as an ingredient in soups, stews and so on. Two country hams with well-justified reputations are those of the Ardennes and the Auvergne.

Jambon d'York York ham is much admired in France and enormous quantities of imitations are sold, although seldom with any pretence to being the genuine article.

Lard frais The layer of hard back pork fat nearest to the skin of the animal, used mainly for lardoons (see *Lardage*, page 75). The second layer of fat, nearest the flesh, is softer in consistency and is that mainly used for rendering down, after which process it is known as *Saindoux*.

Lard fumé Cured and smoked belly or flank pork, similar to our bacon.

Lard de poitrine Fat from the belly or breast of the pig, usually salted, or salted and smoked, in which state it is similar to our streaky bacon.

Lard salé The best quality of salted pork fat comes from the top layer of fat in the back of the pig, the same as that used for lardoons (see *Lard frais* above). The second quality comes from the belly and flank; this is also known as *petit salé* and is similar to our salt or pickled pork. Both salted and smoked pork are used a good deal in braised and stewed dishes, the former rather more than the latter; so when ordinary salt pork is not available, the best alternative is unsmoked bacon.

Laurier, Feuilles de BAYLEAVES Part of the traditional *bouquet garni* and a flavouring for scores of stews and soups.

Levure YEAST.

Macis MACE The beautiful bright orange, lacy outer covering of the nutmeg. Ground mace is a valuable seasoning for many aromatic preparations, such as stuffings and pâtés, as well as for spiced cakes and breads.

Maïs, Farine de MAIZE FLOUR, POLENTA Common in the south-western provinces of France, and used to make various coarse rustic cakes and breads as well as for cramming geese which are being fattened for the sake of their livers.

Maizena A proprietary name for CORNFLOUR.

Marc, Eau de vie de A spirit made from the skins of the grapes after the juice has been pressed for wine. *Marc* is made in every wine-growing area and the quality varies enormously. The best ones seldom reach the market, as every wine-grower is allowed by law to distil only a certain very small percentage of *marc*, fixed in proportion to the amount of wine he produces. These *marcs* are, of course, used a certain amount in cookery since they are ready to hand and also much preferred by the people who make them to the brandies of Cognac and Armagnac. When a recipe specifically calls for *marc*, vodka makes a reasonable substitute.

Marinade For details of the process of marinating and for recipes, see pages 77 and 128.

Marjolaine MARJORAM An aromatic herb used to flavour stuffings and stews. More commonly used in England, especially to flavour sausages, than in France.

Mauve MALLOW I have never come across this plant in French cookery, although I believe it is still used as a vegetable, and for infusions, in country districts. In the Middle East it is the basis of a popular soup called *Melokhia*; its mucilaginous nature makes it rather an acquired taste for Europeans.

Mélisse LEMON-BALM Used in infusions and in a liqueur called *eau des Carmes*, or *eau de mélisse des Carmes*.

Menthe MINT Very little used in French cookery. Our mint sauce is considered positively barbaric by the French; *sauce paloise*, a béarnaise sauce flavoured with mint, is, however, admitted to be a good, although recent, invention.

Miel HONEY The most highly prized honey in France comes from the Narbonne district and is said to owe its distinctive aromatic flavour to the nectar of the rosemary flowers which have been sucked by the bees. Other excellent honeys come from the Gâtinais, Normandy, Burgundy, Champagne, the Savoie, Saintonge, and upper Provence. A number of spiced breads and cakes, particularly the *pain d'épice* of Dijon and other districts, are made with honey and rye flour.

Mignonnette Coarsely ground white peppercorns. According to Larousse, *mignonnette* formerly meant a mixture of allspice, nutmeg, coriander, cinnamon, ginger, and cloves enclosed in a little muslin sachet which was steeped for a few moments in a dish, in order to impart an aromatic flavour.

Mirepoix A basic preparation of chefs' cookery, composed of the red part of carrots, onions, celery and raw ham all cut into dice and stewed very gently in butter, with the addition of bayleaf and thyme. The mixture forms the basis of many sauces, including *espagnole*, and of preparations such as braised chickens, croquettes and so on.

Moutarde Mustard, one of the oldest condiments of French cookery, is mainly sold in France in the form of mustard flour mixed with verjuice, grape must or vinegar, and aromatic herbs and spices. The one most commonly used for flavouring sauces is the tarragon mustard of Dijon. The firms of Grey-Poupon and Maille are famous for the finesse of their

Dijon mustards, and that of Louit for Bordeaux mustard. This firm also puts out a mustard flavoured with the *piment* of the Pays Basque, which is excellent. It is worth spending the small extra sum for genuine Dijon or Bordeaux mustards, for the English imitations of French mustards have not the same flavour. For sauces, choose a mustard with a good yellow colour; the darker ones spoil the look of the sauce.

Moutarde de Chine The variety of mustard which, in English parlance, goes with cress.

Muscade, Noix de NUTMEG Used a good deal in French cookery, for flavouring stuffings, sauces, spiced cakes, even vegetables, particularly spinach. In Italian cookery, nutmeg goes into almost every preparation containing cheese.

Oignons, Ognons ONIONS Onions are one of the basic aromatic vegetables of all European cookery. The French grow several varieties which we lack here, chiefly the small flat ones called *grelots,* which are so much used for garnishes and which are often cooked in their fresh state, while the skins are still green and the flesh very white and strong. The mild red Spanish type of onions are grown mostly in southern France, while another popular one in the south and south-western districts is a red flat Italian onion. In the north the straw-coloured flat *oignons jaune paille des Vertus* and the orange *rouge pâle de Niort* are popular; the equivalent of our own round white onions are known as Lisbon or Portugal onions, and *oignons de Mulhouse* (Alsace) are the equivalent of our pickling or silverskin onions.

Olives Both black and green olives are, naturally, used a good deal in southern French cookery for stuffings and sauces, as well as for garnishes. Green olives are gathered immature and, after a preliminary steeping in a solution of potash, which helps to eliminate the bitter flavour, are preserved in brine. Black olives are the ripe fruit treated simply in brine, the best varieties of black olives for the table being subsequently preserved in a marinade of olive oil. Black olives make a delicious stuffing for a chicken (see page 395) and I have also come across them used as a flavouring for a duck pâté, which was quite excellent. When olives are bought loose, whether black or green, the best way to store them is to pack them into jars and cover them with olive oil. In times when olive oil is scarce, as it was during the war, its flavour can be imitated for salad dressings, to a certain extent, by steeping olives in otherwise tasteless groundnut oil. And since I have mentioned groundnut oil (*huile d'arachides*) it is as well to remark here that the people of northern France, who understand the use of butter in cookery better than that of olive oil, often express a preference for groundnut oil both for cooking and for making mayonnaise. Personally, I cannot agree with them, but on the other hand it is often difficult in the country, even in Provence, to obtain really good olive oil, for a great quantity is sent to Paris, where it fetches high prices, which means that badly seasoned salads are all too prevalent in country and provincial restaurants. To a real Provençal, however, the quality of his oil is very important and he will be able to tell you, just as a wine grower recognises the variety of grape used for any wine, from what kind of olives any given oil has been pressed. *Le Rougeon, le Redoutant, le Broutignan, la Coucourelle* are some of the different varieties of Provençal olives.

Orge perlé PEARL BARLEY.

Origan WILD MARJORAM.

Oseille SORREL The acid green leaves of wild and garden sorrel and of wood sorrel are treated as a flavouring herb for salads, omelettes and soups, as well as being cooked in the same way as spinach to make a garnish for veal and certain white fish, particularly the shad (*alose*) of the Loire and the white fish of the cod family known as *merluche* or hake. A recipe for sorrel sauce is on page 127.

Panais PARSNIP Used in very small quantities as a flavouring vegetable for the *pot-au-feu* and for soups.

Panne de porc Fat from round the kidneys of the pig. See also *Axonge* and *Saindoux.*

Paprika A mild red pepper made from dried and pounded sweet peppers. A speciality of Hungarian cookery adapted by French cooks.

Pavot, Graines de POPPY SEEDS These figure in the bread and cakes of Alsatian Jewish cookery.

Perce-Pierre SAMPHIRE Also called *Christe-marine* and *fenouil marin.*

Persil commun Single-leaved parsley.

Persil frisé CURLED PARSLEY Both varieties are used in cookery and for garnishing dishes; a sprig or two of parsley is always part of the *bouquet garni* and chopped parsley is the main component of a *fines herbes* mixture. Parsley should always be given a good rinse and then squeezed dry before it is chopped or put into any dish, for it is nearly always gritty. A third variety of parsley, *persil à grosse racine*, is cultivated for its root rather than its leaves; the flavour bears some resemblance to that of celeriac, the root being used in small quantities, like the parsnip, as a flavouring vegetable for soups and the *pot-au-feu.*

Persillade A mixture of finely chopped parsley with shallot or garlic, added as a flavouring usually during the final stages of cooking to many varieties of dishes, vegetables, fried meat dishes, stews and so on.

Petit salé See *Lard salé.*

Pignons PINE KERNELS Used occasionally in the cooking of Provence and of the Landes district. See the omelette recipe on page 195.

Piment See *Poivre.*

Piments doux, Poivrons Red or green sweet peppers, also called capsicum. The pimientos of Spain, paprika peppers of Hungary and *peperoni* of Italy.

Pimprenelle BURNET The fleshy leaves of this plant are used for salads, and formerly figured in recipes for Montpellier butter and other herb sauces.

Poireaux LEEKS One of the most important flavouring vegetables in French soup cookery. The white part only is used. To prepare leeks for cooking, cut off the root end and trim down the top leaves right to the white part. Remove the coarse outer leaves. Make a cross cut in the top of the leek and hold under a running cold tap to loosen the grit and mud. When all have been cleaned, leave them heads down in cold water for a little while and, before cooking, scrutinise each one very carefully to see that there is no sign of mud or grit. The loss of weight in leeks after trimming is very considerable, 3 lb. of untrimmed leeks being reduced to only 1 lb. when ready for cooking.

Poivre PEPPER The world's most valuable spice. While whole peppercorns (*poivre en grains*), which are the berries of the pepper tree, *piper nigrum*, retain their aroma and savour almost indefinitely, once ground, pepper rapidly deteriorates. For this reason all pepper, both for cooking and for the table, should be freshly ground in a pepper mill at the moment of use. There are very many different qualities of pepper, the most valuable and the hottest of the ordinary peppers being the white ones. White peppercorns are the inner part only of the berry gathered when fully ripe, while black ones are picked immature and retain their outer covering. While milder than white peppercorns, black ones have a more aromatic scent and flavour and are preferable for general kitchen use. One of the best qualities of black peppercorns is Malabar Black.

The peppery taste which is so overwhelming in many of the foods of commerce—English sausages in particular—is due to the fact that inferior and mixed peppers are used, and produce a hot and prickly sensation in the mouth without the proper characteristic aromatic smells and taste of good pepper. When buying peppercorns, look to see that the grains are of an even size and colour. If some are large and black and others very small and brownish looking, this means that poor quality peppercorns have been mixed with the good ones.

Poivre d'âne The Provençal name for *sarriette*, a variety of wild savory. A bitter and peppery herb which is sometimes used for flavouring the local ewe's and goat's milk cheeses in Provence.

Poivre de cayenne Very hot red pepper obtained from the dried and pounded fruit of different members of the capsicum family; *capsicum annuum, capsicum minimum.* Cayenne pepper is also known in England as Nepal pepper.

Poivre de la Jamaïque The berry of the *pimenta officinalis*, or common pimento, which has a mild warm spicy flavour and which is now more generally known in England as allspice, although formerly it was often called Jamaica pepper. Although the tree is widely cultivated in hot countries, the best variety still comes from Jamaica. It is also known in France as *toute-épice* or *quatre-épices* because its flavour has something of the clove, the nutmeg, cinnamon and pepper. The dried berries are smooth and about the size of a pea; they can also be bought in ground form and may be labelled ground pimento or ground allspice. A typical spice of Middle Eastern, Arab, Turkish and French colonial cookery, but not widely used in France.

Poivrons See *Piments doux.*

Pourpier PURSLANE Purslane leaves are used raw in salads, or cooked like spinach, or made into a sort of pickle with vinegar, in the same way in which samphire used to be used in English cookery.

Quatre-épices See *Poivre de la Jamaïque.*

Raifort HORSERADISH Delicious horseradish sauces are served in the eastern provinces of France, with beef and with sausages. Instead of the hot pungent flavour of this root being further aggravated by the addition of vinegar, as is the English custom, the horseradish sauces of Alsace and Lorraine are made with cream. When fresh horseradish is unobtainable, I recommend an excellent Swedish import—little packs of plain, very white and finely grated horseradish which makes first-class sauces. To be found in delicatessen shops. (See page 228.)

Riz RICE The long-grained rice which we call Patna is usually known in France as *riz caroline.*

Riz, Crème de RICE FLOUR or VERY FINE GROUND RICE.

D

Riz du Piémont Italian round-grained rice with a hard central core. Anti-Italian prejudice has caused a number of French cookery writers to state that this is an inferior type of rice. It is, of course, a rice of the very highest quality and the most delicious flavour.

Rocambole A member of the onion family, resembling the shallot, but also known as Spanish garlic.

Romarin ROSEMARY A beautiful plant with a powerful aromatic scent, which must be used in cooking only with the utmost care. When rosemary leaves come into contact with heat, they give out a very strong and rather acrid tasting oil, so they should never be added to any stock which is destined to become a consommé or a jelly. Sprigs of rosemary are often used to flavour roast veal and grilled fish but should always be removed before the dish is served, for they spell ruination to every other flavour if you get the spiky little leaves in your mouth.

Roquette ROCKET A plant resembling spinach, the leaves of which have a strong and peppery flavour. They are used in small quantities for salads and as a soup herb.

Safran SAFFRON The origin of the use of saffron in the *bouillabaisse* of Marseille and other Provençal dishes has been attributed to the Phoenicians, who are said to have been inordinately fond of this pungent, spicy condiment which spreads its beautiful yellow stain to the foods with which it is mixed. Saffron comes from the pistils of the autumn-flowering *crocus sativus*, and it is reckoned that 500,000 pistils, or about 170,000 flowers, go to make up one kilo of dried saffron, which goes to show why saffron is so expensive and why it has often been falsified. On the whole, it is advisable to buy it in pistil form rather than powdered, for then one can be certain that no extraneous substance has been mixed with it. However, it is not a spice which one needs very often, and an infinitesimal quantity goes quite a long way. To use saffron in pistil form, you simply pound up about half a dozen of the little threads, mix them with a couple of tablespoons of the stock from whatever dish the saffron is to flavour, or with water, and leave it to steep until the mixture is an intense bright orange. Then drain this into your rice, soup or whatever it may be and it will dye the whole dish a beautiful pale yellow. It is not a flavouring to be overdone.

Saindoux LARD Technically, *saindoux* is rendered back pork fat. The raw fat is cut into small cubes and melted extremely slowly in a deep covered saucepan with a small proportion of water, about one-eighth of a pint to a pound, in order to prevent the fat catching. When all the little pieces are swimming in their own fat, start pouring it off through a very fine strainer or thick cloth. Then put the residue back to cook again until nothing is left but the little frizzled pieces of fat, which are called *grattons* and which are used by the country people to give a savoury flavour to certain kinds of coarse bread and pastry doughs, and which are also sometimes still made into a rough sort of pâté and into *rillettes*. The fat from round the kidneys of the pig is considered to make a specially fine fat for cooking, and in its rendered state is known as *axonge*. Goose fat and beef kidney fat are rendered down in the same way. All fats should be stored in covered jars in a cool and dry place.

Salpicon May be one of a score of mixtures comprising flavouring vegetables, herbs, ham, veal, fish or meat but always cut into very small dice and bound into a thick white or brown sauce. Used as a stuffing, or as a garnish for little tartlets or *vols-au-vent*.

Sarrasin, Farine de Buckwheat flour, used especially for Breton pancakes.

Sarriette SAVORY A herb sometimes used in France in the *bouquet garni*, in sauces and in stuffings. It has a slightly bitter taste, which seems to me to detract from, rather than to enhance, the flavour of broad beans, a vegetable with which it is traditionally associated in French cookery.

Sauge SAGE Occasionally used in French cookery but never in the large quantities in which it goes into stuffings for pork and duck in English cookery. Like rosemary, it can be a most treacherous herb, overpowering and spoiling the flavour of the food with which it is cooked.

Saumure The brine in which foods are salted or pickled. It may vary in composition from a simple salt and water solution to a mixture flavoured with aromatic herbs and spices, vinegar or wine, saltpetre, peppercorns and so on.

Seigle, Farine de RYE FLOUR Used for coarse country bread and for *pain-d'épice*.

Sel-épicé Spiced salt is a composition of various ingredients, mixed and pounded together in the following proportions:

20 oz. salt	⅛ oz. cinnamon
¼ oz. cloves	½ oz. peppercorns
¼ oz. nutmeg	⅛ oz. of dried basil
6 bayleaves	⅛ oz. coriander

'After having been pounded, everything must be pressed through a silk sieve; the residue, if there is any, must be returned to the mortar and once again pounded, for the exact proportions of each ingredient contained in this seasoning, the fruit of a thousand experiments and of fifty years of experience, do not allow for any loss; sieve once again, stir the mixture so that all the ingredients are equally blended, and pack into tins, which it is essential should be hermetically closed.'—Recipe from *Le Cuisinier Durand*, 1830.

Although the decimal system of weights and measures had been in official use in France since the Revolution, many cooks evidently continued to use the old measurements of ounces and pounds, and a small measure called a *gros*, which is a little less than 4 grammes, or the eighth part of an ounce.

Sel gemme ROCK SALT

Sel gris Coarse, only partially refined, rock or sea salt used for cooking and for brines. Also called *gros sel*.

Sel marin SEA SALT One or other of the many grades of only partially refined but unadulterated salt appear to me to be essential both for cooking and for the table. If you have no salt-mill, it is easy enough to pound up a little at a time with a pestle and mortar, and the flavour it gives is so superior to that of powdered salt that, to people who have grown accustomed to pure salt, it is a deprivation to return to food flavoured with the "free-running" type of table salt, which is mixed with extraneous substances, harmless though these may be.

Sel raffiné Refined, although not necessarily adulterated salt for the table.

Semoule SEMOLINA FLOUR.

Serpolet WILD THYME.

Sucre candi CANDY SUGAR, SUGAR CRYSTALS.

Sucre crystallisé GRANULATED SUGAR.

Sucre en pain LOAF SUGAR.

Sucre en poudre, sucre semoule CASTER SUGAR.

Sucre glace ICING SUGAR, CONFECTIONERS' SUGAR.

Sucre vanillé VANILLA SUGAR This is an important flavouring for sweet dishes, syrups and creams. Vanilla-flavoured caster sugar can be bought commercially prepared but is better made at home. All that is necessary is to keep a vanilla pod or two in a well-stoppered jar of white sugar, the jar being filled up again as the sugar is used. A couple of vanilla pods kept in this way will go on giving out their flavour to the sugar almost indefinitely.

Thym THYME A sprig of thyme is one of the routine ingredients of the *bouquet garni,* and in small quantities thyme, both wild and cultivated, flavours many stuffings, stews and liqueurs.

Tilleul LIME TREE Dried lime flowers are used to make a soothing infusion or *tisane.*

Tisane A mild infusion of herbs or flowers with properties either calming, tonic or stimulating. Tea, which is much more widely drunk in France than is generally supposed, is more and more replacing the old-fashioned *tisane.*

Tomates concassées Roughly chopped tomatoes, usually skinned.

Tomates, Concentré de Concentrated tomato purée in the Italian manner.

Tomates, Confiture de Originally a semi-concentrated and sweetened tomato purée but now a term which seems to have become interchangeable with *concentré de tomates.* Also a delicious jam in the English sense.

Tomates, Fondue de A lightly cooked, or melted, sauce of fresh skinned tomatoes, seasonings and sometimes onion, garlic or other flavouring vegetable. 'Happy,' says one French cookery writer, 'is the cook who knows how to use the tomato with discretion.'

Truffes TRUFFLES Here is an interesting extract on the fascinating subject of truffles from the *Dictionnaire Encyclopédique de l'Epicerie,* by A. Seigneurie, 1904:

'Variety of parasitic mushroom which grows on the roots of certain oak and hazel-nut trees. There are a great number of varieties of the truffle, of which the only common characteristics are their interior structure, their mode of growth, the fact that they are eatable, and a certain similarity of taste; but in dimension, size, colour and shape they differ extremely one from the other. While certain varieties rarely exceed a few grammes in weight, others attain exaggerated proportions and even occasionally exceed a weight of 20 kilos.

'The truffle grows most readily in sandy or clay and chalky soils. Divers varieties are found in various climates. The most highly prized variety is, without contradiction, the truffle of the Périgord, black, with a rough skin and a penetrating scent. It is found particularly in the Charente, in the neighbourhood of Périgueux and Angoulême, also in the Gard, the Isère, the Drôme, the Ardèche, the Hérault, the Tarn, the Vaucluse, the Lozère and the

Jura. Those of the Drôme, with firm flesh and an agreeable flavour, are remarkable for their regularity of shape; they are threaded with whitish veins.

'Those of the Gard are sometimes of a softer consistency, somewhat spongy with a fairly pronounced smell of musk, for which reason they are often avoided.

'The nature of the soil has much influence upon the flavour of the truffle. Those found in Burgundy usually have a taste of resin, and those which come from Naples smell of sulphur.

'In Algeria, and in the whole of North Africa, the sand yields a truffle called *terfez*, with a smooth skin, round, and of a pure white both outside and inside. It has a delicate flavour and has been known since times of the greatest antiquity, for it figures in Roman and Punic feasts.

'The truffle is, in general, a savoury condiment with a penetrating scent. Its action stimulates the digestive organs. As for its legendary reputation,[1] it is, obviously, exaggerated.

'Recently it has been found possible to promote the artificial production of truffles either by planting or sowing so-called truffle-oaks which carry with them the spores of the truffles, or by putting on the ground, amid oak or hazel-nut plantations, a mycelium obtained from a mash of truffles in water which has been spread upon the green leaves of these trees.

'The truffle harvest, whether in natural or artificial *truffières*, is carried out in a somewhat haphazard manner, and is therefore very problematical. The search is done mainly by pigs, which have an inveterate taste for truffles, and of which the olfactory senses are very developed in this matter. The difficulties experienced in the control of these animals have led to the training of dogs, which are much more easily led.

'Fresh truffles keep no longer than a week. Preserved truffles, however well done, lose a certain part of their savour.'

The author goes on to give statistics and it is startling to find that, in the early years of the century, when his book was written, the total production of truffles in France was, according to the author, *five million kilos*, valued at 10 francs the kilo *to the producer*. Export figures were two million kilos, at an average price of 12 to 13 francs. In those days there were twenty francs to the pound sterling. The cost of truffles, although it varies a good deal from year to year and according to the quality of the truffles, is now somewhere in the region of 20,000 francs a kilo, or about £10 a pound. Although Seigneurie refers to truffles from Naples he makes no mention of the wonderful white truffles of Piedmont, which all Italians and a good many other people besides think far superior to black truffles. In fact, they are so totally different in taste and smell as to make it really impossible to compare them. Also, they are treated quite differently.

---

[1] The author means its reputation as an aphrodisiac.

Whereas black truffles are added to dishes and sauces for the sake of their powerful scent, and by the time the dish is cooked have little flavour of their own left, white truffles are rarely cooked longer than a couple of minutes and are often eaten raw, sliced paper thin on a special instrument and scattered over the top of a risotto, a cheese fondue, and so on. Although these white truffles are to be found in the French Savoie, it is perhaps again, as in the question of Piedmontese rice, the spirit of patriotism which causes the majority of French gastronomic writers to ignore their existence or to dismiss them as being unworthy of notice. On page 278 will be found various recipes and other information concerning truffles.

Vanille, Gousses de VANILLA PODS OR BEANS The fruit of the vanilla plant was first imported to Europe from Mexico, where it is said to have been enormously used, about 1510. Subsequently the vanilla was planted in many of the French colonies, notably the islands of Réunion, Bourbon and Madagascar. It is also cultivated in Mauritius and the Seychelles Islands. Apart from its chief use as a flavouring for chocolate, the dried bean also gives a pronounced scent and flavour to creams, ices and soufflés; vanilla sugar (see *Sucre vanillé*) is also much used in French and Italian household cookery for the syrups in which fruit is cooked, and for flavouring cakes and pastries. Vanilla has a particular affinity with apricots, peaches and plums. A vanilla pod used to flavour a cream or a fruit dish should be taken out, dried, and kept in a jar of sugar, for it can be used over and over again.

Vanilline This may mean either an extract of vanilla made from the essential essences of the bean which have crystallised, or frosted, on the surface, or an entirely synthetic and chemically produced essence which, because of its crude and cloying flavour, is to be avoided.

Verjus VERJUICE The juice of unripe grapes, formerly much used in cookery and as a condiment instead of vinegar. It was prepared from a quantity of juice pressed from a special variety of grape known by the same name. This juice was left for several days in shallow bowls until a scum formed on the top. This was skimmed off and salt added to the juice in order to preserve it. Alternatively, it was preserved by evaporation and a small quantity of the resulting concentrated juice used to flavour various dishes. Verjuice was, and still sometimes is, used in the preparation of mustards. A survival of the old methods of flavouring with verjuice is the Burgundian dish of oxtail cooked with grapes, for which the recipe is on page 349.

Vermouth An apéritif made on a basis of white wine in which various bitter and aromatic herbs and spices and roots are infused; the wine is then clarified and fortified with *eau de vie*. The best Vermouth in France is considered to be that of Chambéry. Vermouth may be used in cookery in the same way as other wines. (See the section on 'Wine for the Kitchen.')

Verveine VERBENA The leaves of verbena are used to flavour infusions and liqueurs, particularly the well-known *Verveine du Velay*, made in the district of Le Puy.

Vigne, Feuilles de VINE LEAVES Often used for wrapping round small game birds such as partridges, quails and thrushes for roasting, and occasionally also for fish. Vine leaves stuffed with rice are a great feature of Turkish and Balkan cookery.

Vigne, Sarments de VINE CUTTINGS Used for burning on open grills in wine-growing areas.

Vinaigre de Vin WINE VINEGAR Red or white wine vinegars, sometimes tarragon flavoured, are used in France for all cooking purposes and for salads. They vary a good deal in strength and the flavour depends both upon the wine used and upon the care with which they have been made. Many varieties of wine vinegars are to be found in England and there can be no possible reason for using the savage English malt vinegar for any purpose unless you actually prefer it to wine vinegar. Those who consider the extra expense of wine vinegar excessive could perhaps try cider vinegar, of which there are several and very inexpensive varieties now on the English market. Orléans vinegar is the name given to wine vinegar made by a special process.

Vinaigrette An oil and vinegar dressing or sauce, which may or may not also contain chopped parsley and other herbs.

Vins The use of wines for cooking is explained in the section 'Wine for the Kitchen,' pages 79–83.

Zeste de citron, d'orange LEMON AND ORANGE RIND Thinly pared, these are much used to flavour creams and ices; grated, for cakes and stuffings.

Weights and Measures

'THE dangerous person in the kitchen is the one who goes rigidly by weights, measurements, thermometers and scales.

'I would say once more that all these scientific implements are not of much use, the only exception being for making pastry and jams, where exact weights are important.' So wrote Marcel Boulestin.[1] But while I am sure he is right in so far as rigid adherence to the rules cannot in itself guarantee anything but the most routine sort of cooking, I do think that even an experienced cook needs at least an approximate guide to quantities and timing. One has to know roughly what the rules are before one can afford to disregard them.

The tradition of French cookery writers, with a few notable exceptions, is to give only rather vague directions as to quantities, oven temperatures and timing. American cookery writers are inclined to err in the other direction, specifying to the last drop and the ultimate grain the quantities of salt, sugar, powdered herbs, spices and so on, leaving absolutely nothing to the imagination or discretion of the cook. I have aimed at steering a medium course between these two systems. English cooks like to be instructed as to the quantities of the basic ingredients of a dish, so that at least they can go out shopping with a fair idea of what they should buy, but do not on the whole require to be told how many leaves of parsley or drops of lemon juice they are to add to a stew or a soup. Seasonings and flavourings are surely a question of taste; they are the elements which give individual character to each person's cookery. And then there is always the question of what happens to be available. One cook will trudge for miles to buy a sprig of thyme because the directions for a stew tell her to include a 'bouquet of thyme, parsley and bayleaf.' Another will cheerfully leave it out. A third will substitute some other herb, a fourth will abandon the whole project as being too much worry and trouble, a fifth will be careful always to have a small supply of at least the commoner herbs and spices in her store cupboard. It is not for me or anyone else to say which one is acting correctly. It is a question of temperament. And given that this matter of temperament, not to mention other unknown factors such as the varying quality of ingredients, different types of cooking utensils, ovens and so on, plays such a large part in cookery, I do not myself see that it can ever become an exact science.

[1] *What Shall We Have Today?* Heinemann, 1931.

For those who use French and American cookery books as well as English ones, there is also the question of differing units of weight and measurement. To convert kilos and grammes into pounds and ounces is simple enough, given that both French and English recipes are based on the system of weighing with scales. The American method, that of measuring everything by volume, makes the conversion of their recipes and vice versa much more difficult; and the fact that American liquid measurements are based on the 16-ounce pint instead of the English 20-ounce Imperial pint, makes for further confusion.

Some of these confusions I have tried to sort out in the following tables of approximately equivalent measurements. And please bear in mind that when I say approximate I mean that these equivalents are sufficiently accurate for the conversion of recipes but would not be accepted by a Standards Board. For that matter, neither would the majority of scales in common domestic use, and as for the cup-measuring system for solid ingredients, it appears to me even more chancy.

SOLID MEASUREMENTS

French				English
1 kilogramme	=	1,000 grammes	=	approx. 2 lb. 3 oz.
1 livre	=	500 grammes	=	approx. 1 lb. 1½ oz.
½ livre	=	250 grammes	=	approx. 9 oz.
¼ livre	=	125 grammes	=	approx. 4½ oz.
		100 grammes	=	approx. 3½ oz.
1 gros (old measurement)			=	⅛ oz.

LIQUID MEASUREMENTS

French			English
1 litre	= 1,000 grammes	=	approx. 35 fl. oz. = approx. 1¾ pints
½ litre	= 500 grammes	=	approx. 17½ fl. oz. = approx. ¾ pint plus 5 tablespoons
¼ litre	= 250 grammes	=	approx. 8¾ fl. oz. = approx. ½ pint less 2½ tablespoons
1 decilitre	= 100 grammes	=	approx. 3 fl. oz. = 6 tablespoons
1 centilitre	= 10 grammes	=	approx. ⅓ fl. oz. = 1 dessertspoon
1 setier (old measurement)		=	approx. 8 pints
1 chopine (old measurement)		=	approx. ½ pint

SOLID MEASUREMENTS

English		*American*
1 lb. butter or fat	=	approx. 2 cups solidly packed
½ lb. butter or fat	=	approx. 1 cup solidly packed
¼ lb. butter or fat	=	approx. ½ cup solidly packed
2 oz. butter or fat	=	approx. ¼ cup = 4 tablespoons
1 oz. butter or fat	=	approx. 2 tablespoons
1 lb. caster sugar	=	approx. 2⅓ cups powdered sugar
½ lb. caster sugar	=	approx. 1 cup plus 3 tablespoons
¼ lb. caster sugar	=	approx. 8 tablespoons
2 oz. caster sugar	=	approx. 4 tablespoons
1 lb. plain flour sieved	=	approx. 4½ cups sieved cake flour
¼ lb. plain flour sieved	=	approx. 1 cup plus 4 tablespoons
2 oz. plain flour sieved	=	approx. 8 tablespoons
1 oz. plain flour sieved	=	approx. 4 tablespoons
¼ oz. plain flour sieved	=	approx. 1 tablespoon
¼ lb. dry grated cheese	=	approx. 1 cup
½ lb. rice, raw	=	approx. 1 cup

LIQUID MEASUREMENTS

English		*American*
1 gallon = 4 quarts = 8 pints	=	10 pints = 1¼ gallons
1 quart = 2 pints = 40 oz.	=	2½ pints = 5 cups
1 pint = 20 oz.	=	1¼ pints = 2½ cups
½ pint = 10 oz.	=	1¼ cups
¼ pint = 5 oz. = 1 gill	=	½ cup plus 2 tablespoons
2 oz. = 4 tablespoons	=	¼ cup
1 tablespoon = ½ oz.	=	½ oz.
1 teaspoon = ¼ tablespoon	=	1 teaspoon = ⅓ tablespoon

COOKERY BOOK MEASUREMENTS

How much, I am sometimes asked, is a pinch, a dash, a drop, a suspicion, a glass? When such measurements are given in a cookery book, it is fairly obvious that a little more or a little less will make no difference, and that precise amounts of, say, salt, nutmeg, garlic or other flavourings must be left to each cook's discretion. However, for those who are worried by the vagueness of such directions, here are the interpretations, most of them as given by Philéas Gilbert in the 1931 edition of *La Cuisine de Tous Les Mois*. The table was not included in the original edition of this work, so one concludes that it was at the requests of readers that he included it in the revised edition. I do not really see of what practical use it is to know how many grains constitute a 'pinch' because few of us possess chemists' scales on which to weigh out such minute quantities. But for occasions when one might wish to calculate a recipe in large quantities, the knowledge would be useful.

LIQUID MEASUREMENTS

French		*English*
1 cuillère à bouche, à soupe	=	1 tablespoon = $\frac{1}{2}$ oz.
1 cuillère à pot	=	a small soup ladle = approx. 2 oz.
1 cuillère à café	=	a small teaspoon
1 verre = 2 décilitres	=	6 fl. oz.
1 verre à Bordeaux = 1 décilitre	=	a claret glass = approx. 3 fl. oz. or 6 tablespoons
1 verre à liqueur = 15 grammes	=	$\frac{1}{2}$ oz. or 1 tablespoon
1 tasse à café = 75 grammes	=	a coffee-cup, after-dinner size = $2\frac{1}{2}$ oz.

SOLID MEASUREMENTS

French		*English*
1 cuillère à bouche de farine	=	1 level tablespoon = $\frac{1}{2}$ oz. flour
1 cuillère à bouche de riz	=	1 level tablespoon = $\frac{1}{2}$ oz. rice
1 cuillère à bouche de sucre	=	1 level tablespoon = $\frac{5}{6}$ oz. sugar
1 cuillère à bouche de gruyère rapé	=	1 level tablespoon = $\frac{1}{3}$ oz. grated gruyère cheese

Une forte pincée de sel = 7 to 8 grammes = approx. $\frac{1}{4}$ oz. of salt
Une prise de poivre = 2 grammes = a turn of the pepper mill = $\frac{1}{15}$ oz.
Une pointe de Cayenne = $\frac{1}{2}$ gramme = a dash of cayenne = $\frac{1}{60}$ oz.
Une pointe de noix muscade = $\frac{1}{2}$ gramme = a dash of nutmeg = $\frac{1}{60}$ oz.

An average clove of garlic = 7 grammes = rather under $\frac{1}{4}$ oz.
An average onion = 100 grammes = approx. 3 oz.
An average stick of celery = 30 to 40 grammes = 1 to $1\frac{1}{3}$ oz.
An average white part of leek = 40 to 50 grammes = $1\frac{1}{3}$ to $1\frac{3}{4}$ oz.

TEMPERATURES AND TIMING

The following table should be regarded only as an approximate guide, and the temperatures given in the recipes in this book should be taken to mean those appropriate to the oven of an ordinary average-sized domestic cooker. (For cooking in very small or very large ovens, temperatures very often have to be adjusted; lowered slightly in the first case and increased in the second.) But even with tricky dishes like soufflés and the roasting of small birds, a certain margin of difference can be allowed both in temperature and timing. For large birds, roasts and stews the latitude is greater. It does not, for example, make a vast difference if you cook a stew at gas No. 1 or No. 2, or if you roast a chicken at 380 deg. or 390 deg. F. And although a certain degree of reliability has been achieved in the regulation of modern ovens, a great many people still use cookers on which the oven temperature controls bear little relation to reality. Only experience of your own oven, or alternatively the purchase of a thermometer, can be the solution in these cases. But please do bear in mind that as far as oven-cooked stews and similar dishes are concerned, timing, temperatures and quantities of liquid are calculated for cooking in earthenware, iron, or other heavy pots with properly fitting lids, so that the food will heat slowly and cook evenly with the minimum of evaporation of the liquid.

TABLE OF EQUIVALENT OVEN TEMPERATURES

Solid Fuel	Electricity	Gas
Slow	240°–310°	$\frac{1}{4}$–2
Moderate	320°–370°	3–4
Fairly Hot	380°–400°	5
Hot	410°–440°	6–7
Very Hot	450°–480°	8–9

Les Sauces

Sauces[1]

THE approach to French sauce cookery for the small household is a totally different one from that of the restaurant or the grand private establishment presided over by a professional chef. On the one hand, you have the sauces of so-called 'classic' cookery, based on large quantities of stocks and broths, essences and meat glazes, the *fonds bruns*, the *fonds blancs*, the *jus*, the *fumets* of game and of fish, all obtained by lengthy simmering, straining, reduction and all the processes which imply time, expense, a large staff, an elaborate *batterie de cuisine*, plus a very highly developed sense of taste and a devotion to his work which the cook does not always possess.

The result of all this sauce mystique, evolved in the eighteenth and

[1] See also the paragraph on the liaison of sauces, the rescue of a spoiled sauce, etc., page 76.

nineteenth centuries, when conditions were so utterly different from our own, is that today sauces have become a horribly debased branch of cookery. There now appear to be in Anglo-French cooking just two basic sauces: a thick brown one, known as *espagnole*, and a thick white one which passes for *béchamel*. The *espagnole*, made with flour and brown stock, heavily flavoured and coloured nowadays with tomato purée, is heated up over and over again and appears, flavoured with cooking port, as *sauce madère*, with shreds of orange peel as *sauce bigarade*, with diced gherkins as *sauce piquante*, with a chopped tinned truffle as *sauce Périgueux*. The near-*béchamel* becomes, with the addition of cheese, *sauce Mornay*, with a little chicken broth, *sauce velouté*, with tomato purée *sauce aurore*. The inevitable result is that every dish has the same basic flavour, and because the sauces are stale, not a very good one at that.

In simple French household cookery, because they are made freshly and in small quantities, sauces are rather different both in conception and execution. The first principle is that whenever possible the sauce for a given dish is composed of elements supplied by the main ingredient of that dish itself. That is to say, the trimmings of a joint, the giblets of a bird, the carcase and head of a fish, are simmered to make a broth or *bouillon* which will eventually supply the basis of the sauce. When no such elements are present, as in the case of grilled meat or fish, eggs, vegetables, rice, pasta and so on, then there are the egg and butter sauces of which *béarnaise* and *hollandaise* are the two most obvious, and the vegetable purée sauces such as *Soubise* (onions), tomato, mushroom. Then there are the sauces of which the juices of the meat or fish itself *after* it has cooked form the basis, with cream or wine or stock and a binding of yolks of eggs or flour and butter (*beurre manié*) being used to complete it.

Apart from all these alternatives, there is the whole repertory of cold sauces derived either from mayonnaise or more simply from vinaigrette, and all the butters flavoured with herbs and aromatics, of which *maître d'hôtel* or parsley butter is the simplest form.

So it will be seen that between the stock-pot sauces of the restaurant and the gravy browning and water of the old-fashioned English domestic cook, between the rich and complicated *coulis d'écrevisses* which is considered a fitting accompaniment to salmon in grand French cookery, and the bottled horrors of our own boarding-house tables, there is a world of delicious sauces, fresh and easily made, designed to help the food with which they are served rather than to drown it. And so long as the ingredients used are of good quality, no artificial colourings and no substitutes in the way of tinned or bottled stuff being allowed, so long as the seasoning and blending has been done with a light hand and good judgment, these simple sauces of home cookery will be more appreciated than all the grandiose confections of the now out-dated and overrated *haute cuisine*.

Anyone who can produce even the few easy sauces described in this chapter and serve them with well-cooked grills or roasts, poached or fried fish or even eggs or sausages, will soon get a reputation for that kind of unpretentious, good quality food which the French so descriptively call *une cuisine soignée*.

BOUILLON POUR LES SAUCES

STOCK FOR SAUCES

The *bouillon* from the *pot-au-feu* (see page 156) is often used in household cookery as a basis for sauces, but when you have no such meat stock available and when it is necessary to make a foundation for a sauce independently of the ingredients of the dish which it is to accompany, the following method will produce a well-flavoured clear stock without any great expense either of time or materials. It is a method simplified to the greatest possible degree for household cookery.

The ingredients are: ½ lb. each of lean stewing veal, preferably from the shin, and good quality minced beef; 2 scraped carrots, 2 halved tomatoes, 2 medium-sized onions, washed but not peeled, 2 sprigs of parsley with the stalks; no salt or pepper until a later stage.

Put all the ingredients in a small pot or saucepan which will go in the oven; cover with just over a pint of water. Cover the pot and cook in a low oven for 1½ hours. Strain through an ordinary sieve. Leave in a bowl until the fat has set. Remove the fat. Heat up the stock, strain through a muslin to get rid of any sediment. There should now be about ¾ pint of clear straw-coloured *bouillon* ready to make any sauce requiring stock.

As it has been cooked without salt, it can also be reduced to a thick syrup-like consistency, a sort of improvised meat glaze or *glace de viande*, in the following manner: put a large soup ladle of the *bouillon* into a 6-inch frying-pan or sauté pan. Let it bubble fairly gently for about 10 minutes, during which time you remove the little flecks of scum which come to the surface with a metal spoon dipped frequently in hot water. When the liquid starts to stick to the spoon and is reduced to about 2 tablespoons, it is done. The flavour is now three times as strong as it was to start with but, of course, had there been salt in it, it would have been uneatable. Pour it into a little jar, keep it covered, and when it is to be used heat it up in the jar standing in a pan of water. Although this has not the deep colour of professional meat glaze, it has the right amount of body to strengthen a sauce, plus a freshness and clarity of flavour unusual in the lengthily cooked, more elaborate confection of the chefs.

For large households the stock can be made in double quantities, and for the reduction to glaze, use a larger, 10-inch pan. For one of its best uses, see the recipe for *sauce bercy* on page 114.

TRÉSOR DE CUISINE

Under this name Mique Grandchamp, author of *Le Cuisinier à la Bonne Franquette* (1884) gives us a useful idea for conserving and making the best use of a small quantity of meat glaze.

Uncork a bottle of Madeira, pour out one wineglassful, and put the bottle in a pan of warm water; bring the water slowly to the boil and, when the wine is hot, pour in gradually a wineglass of melted meat glaze; put the cork back in the bottle and leave it in a warm place near the stove for two hours. This makes a valuable standby for adding to sauces, particularly those which are to be served with game, and for all manner of dishes where a little extra flavouring is required. The mixture can be stored almost indefinitely but, of course, a half-bottle or even less still goes quite a long way.

SAUCE BIGARADE

ORANGE SAUCE

This is to serve with wild or domestic duck. *Bigarade* is the French name for bitter oranges.

Two Seville oranges, a teacupful of veal or game stock, 1 oz. of butter, 1 tablespoon of flour, 4 lumps of sugar, salt and pepper.

Pare the rind of the oranges very thinly, cut into fine shreds, plunge them into boiling water and boil 5 minutes. Strain. Prepare a brown *roux* by melting the butter in a small saucepan, stirring in the flour and continuing to stir over a gentle flame until the mixture is quite smooth and turns café au lait colour; now add half the warmed stock, stir again, then add the other half. Cook very gently another 5 minutes. Add the seasonings, the strained juice of one of the oranges and the peel. A few drops of Madeira or port added at the last moment are an improvement and the juices which have come from the bird while roasting should also be added.

Those who prefer a milder sauce can omit the orange juice and make up the quantity with a little extra stock. In any case, this is not a sauce to be served if you are drinking a fine wine with your duck; it would overwhelm it. If it is to go with a domestic duck, the stock can be made from the giblets.

SAUCE BERCY

WHITE WINE AND SHALLOT SAUCE

A useful and excellent little hot sauce to be made when you have a small amount of natural concentrated gravy from a roast, a little jelly left over from a *bœuf mode*, or some of the meat glaze described above; or for fish, some aromatic stock made from trimmings and bones, plus sliced onion and carrot.

Chop 4 shallots very finely. Put them in a small saucepan with half a claret glass of dry white wine. Let it boil until it is reduced by half. Add 2 tablespoons of the gravy (with, naturally, all fat removed) or melted meat glaze or fish stock; season; off the fire stir in 1 oz. of good butter, a squeeze of lemon juice, and a small quantity of very finely chopped parsley.

Apart from grills of meat or fish, *sauce bercy* is delicious with eggs, fried or *sur le plat* or *en cocotte*, and with fried or grilled sausages.

SAUCE BÉCHAMEL

There are two different versions of this universally known, rather dull but useful sauce. One is a *béchamel grasse*, made with a proportion of meat or chicken stock, the other *béchamel maigre*, in which milk is the only liquid used. The latter is the one more generally useful—in fact essential—to know, for it forms the basis of many others which are infinitely more interesting.

To make a small quantity of straightforward béchamel, first put ½ pint of milk to heat in a small saucepan; melt 1½ oz. of butter in another and suitably thick saucepan. As soon as the butter starts to foam, add, off the fire, 2 level tablespoons of sieved plain flour; stir it into the butter immediately. Now add a little of the warmed milk, stirring until a thick paste is formed. Return the saucepan to a low flame and gradually add the rest of the milk. Upon this initial operation depends the success of the sauce, for once the butter, flour and milk are amalgamated and smooth, your sauce is unlikely later to turn lumpy. Having seasoned the mixture with about half a teaspoon of salt, a scrap of grated nutmeg and a little freshly milled white pepper, put a mat over the flame and let your sauce gently, very gently, simmer for a minimum of 10 minutes, stirring all the time. Half the badly made white sauces one encounters are due to the fact that they are not sufficiently cooked, and so have a crude taste of flour. Also, they are very often made too thick and pasty. A good béchamel should be of a creamy consistency.

After 10 minutes, the saucepan containing the béchamel can be placed in another larger one containing water (see drawing on page 58); this improvised *bain-marie* is a better system than cooking the sauce in the top half of a double saucepan, for by the *bain-marie* method the sauce is *surrounded* by heat instead of only cooking *over* heat, and therefore matures better and more completely.

Notes:

(1) If you have to cook your béchamel in advance, cover the surface while the sauce is still hot with minuscule knobs of butter which, in melting, create a film which prevents the formation of a skin.

(2) Always reheat the sauce by the *bain-marie* system.

(3) If the béchamel is to be served straight, without further flavouring, allow a little extra milk and simmer in it for a few minutes a little piece of onion, a bayleaf, a sprig of parsley, a slice of carrot, all tied together for easy removal when the milk is added to the sauce.

(4) If, in spite of all precautions, the sauce has turned lumpy, press it through a fine sieve into a clean saucepan. The electric liquidiser also comes to the rescue here.

(5) To make a *béchamel grasse*, for the milk substitute the same quantity, or at least a good proportion, of clear well-flavoured veal or chicken stock; to this sauce is sometimes added a proportion of cream and it becomes, in fact, a simplified version of *sauce velouté*.

SAUCE À LA CRÈME
CREAM SAUCE

This is a sauce which goes ideally with a poached chicken, but may also be used for many other dishes, including fish, eggs, and vegetables.

Start as for a béchamel, melting 1½ oz. butter in a heavy saucepan; as soon as it begins to foam stir in, off the fire, 2 tablespoons of sifted flour. When the mixture is smooth and palest yellow, start adding ½ pint of hot clear broth taken from the pot in which the chicken is cooking. (Should some other, separately made stock, or milk, be used, always have it hot before adding it to the flour mixture.) Return to a low fire and stir patiently until your sauce is thick and smooth. Now add about 8 oz. (somewhat under ½ pint) of cream and continue stirring. At this stage, the sauce looks much too thin but gradually, as you stir, it thickens. It will take about 20 minutes, over the lowest possible heat, before it is the right consistency. It need not be stirred continuously, only every now and again, in order to prevent a skin forming. Two or three minutes before serving, stir in 2 egg yolks well beaten with a little lemon juice. This addition greatly improves the sauce and gives it a final smoothness and finish. It may just be allowed to bubble once without risk of curdling, but not more. A little very finely chopped parsley and tarragon is a great improvement to the flavour.

This sauce may be poured over the carved chicken before serving, without fear of its developing the pasty looking, and tasting, quality of an ordinary white sauce.

SAUCE MORNAY

CHEESE SAUCE

To a straightforward béchamel, very lightly salted but well matured and reduced by lengthy and almost imperceptible cooking by the *bain-marie* system, add 2 heaped tablespoons of finely grated Parmesan or Gruyère cheese or, best of all, a mixture of half each. Once the cheese is added and thoroughly amalgamated with the béchamel, the sauce is ready and it is inadvisable to let it cook any further, for there is always a risk of the cheese either separating or turning lumpy. After adding the cheese, taste the sauce for seasoning, and add salt if necessary, plus a little extra freshly milled pepper and perhaps a scrap of cayenne.

Sauce mornay is always used as a sauce in which fish, vegetables, eggs and so on are reheated, usually in the oven, so it must have a certain consistency; it must not, however, be too thick (except in certain rare instances as for oysters *mornay*, described on page 316) or the finished dish will be pasty and stodgy.

BEURRE MAÎTRE D'HÔTEL

PARSLEY BUTTER

We all know how to make parsley butter. But do we always do it really well or know its many uses?

There should be about a tablespoon and a half of parsley to 2 oz. of butter and it should be very, very finely chopped. Then, in a bowl rinsed out with hot water, work your butter and parsley together with a fork, very thoroughly, adding a few drops of lemon juice, until you have an absolutely homogeneous pomade. Put it in the refrigerator or cool larder until you are ready to use it.

New potatoes or carrots with a little of this butter melting among them are exquisite. A dish of plain boiled white haricot beans, drained of their liquid and put back into a saucepan, with a lump of parsley butter added, make a lovely separate vegetable course. You just shake the pan and rotate it until the butter is at melting point. The same with those little dark green French lentils, *lentilles d'Auvergne*, for which the recipe is on page 262.

BEURRE BLANC NANTAIS
WHITE BUTTER AND SHALLOT SAUCE FOR FISH

The recipe for this wonderful butter and shallot sauce of Nantais and Angevin fish cookery is described in detail on pages 307–8.

BEURRE DE MONTPELLIER
GREEN BUTTER

Recipes for this mixture vary a good deal, as it is a sauce which has undergone a number of changes during the last hundred odd years, early versions containing no butter at all and a much larger proportion of hard-boiled egg yolks and olive oil. One current version is as follows:

Weigh approximately 4 oz. altogether of the following herbs: leaves of watercress, tarragon, parsley, chervil and spinach, in about equal proportions. If chervil is unobtainable, substitute more parsley. Burnet (*pimprenelle*), a herb with a faint taste of cucumber, is mentioned in many recipes but is seldom to be found nowadays.

Plunge all the herbs into boiling water for half a minute. Drain and squeeze as dry as possible. Pound in a mortar, adding 6 anchovy fillets, 2 tablespoons of capers, 4 miniature gherkins, the yolks of 1 raw and 3 hard-boiled eggs and lastly 4 oz. of butter. Force all this through a fine wire sieve. To the thick pomade so obtained add, slowly, 5 to 6 tablespoons of olive oil and a few drops of lemon juice. The sauce will keep some days in a covered jar in the refrigerator but should be removed some while before serving, or it will be too hard.

Montpellier butter is usually served with salmon and the chef's way of doing it is to have a fine piece of middle cut of cold salmon with the skin removed, and the fish thickly spread with the green butter.

It can also be served separately with hot salmon or any grilled fish, as one would serve parsley butter. A teaspoon of Montpellier butter added to eggs cooked *en cocotte* is also very delicious. This quantity should make sufficient to serve four to six people.

BEURRE MANIÉ

BUTTER AND FLOUR THICKENING FOR SAUCES

This is a thickening or binding for sauces, not a sauce in itself. Quantities
are 1 oz. of butter to ⅔ oz. of flour. Mix the two together very thoroughly
with a fork until you have a perfectly amalgamated paste. Divide this
mixture into little knobs and spread these on the surface of the sauce to
be thickened, which should be bubbling gently. Instead of stirring, lift
the pan from the fire, shake and rotate it and, in a few seconds, the sauce
will have thickened, taking on a shining and somewhat sticky appearance.
Thereafter, do not let the sauce boil again but serve the dish as quickly as
possible. If it has to be kept waiting, keep it barely moving over the lowest
possible heat for, while it is quite in order for the sauce in which *beurre
manié* is used to be on the boil just for a moment, further boiling is
apt to spoil the taste. A typical dish in which the sauce is thickened with
the butter and flour mixture is the *coq au vin* on page 399.

SAUCE BÉARNAISE

The origin of *sauce béarnaise* has already been explained in the introductory chapter on the cookery of south-western France. Here is the
recipe:

The yolks of 3 or 4 eggs, 4 to 5 oz. butter, half a wineglass (4 or 5
tablespoons) of white wine, 2 tablespoons of tarragon vinegar, 2 shallots,
black pepper, salt, lemon juice, a few leaves of fresh tarragon.

Put the white wine, vinegar, chopped shallots and a little ground black
pepper in a small pan and reduce it by fast boiling to about 2 tablespoons.
Strain it and add a few drops of cold water. Put this essence in the top
half of a double saucepan or in a bowl which will fit into the top of an
ordinary saucepan. This underneath saucepan should be half full of warm
water and put on to a gentle flame. To the liquid already in the top pan,
add half the butter, cut into small pieces. Let it melt quickly, then add the
rest, stirring all the time. Now add, gradually, the beaten yolks of the eggs
and stir very carefully until the sauce thickens. Add salt if necessary, which
will depend on whether the butter used is salted or unsalted, and a few
drops of lemon juice and a few of cold water. Take the sauce from the fire
and stir in the chopped tarragon, and the sauce is ready. At no time should
the water underneath the sauce boil and the sauce is not intended to be
served hot, but tepid.

Mint instead of tarragon turns *béarnaise* into *paloise*, a modern variation, useful for serving with lamb and mutton.

If you should be obliged to make your *béarnaise* in advance the least risky way of reheating it is to put the bowl which contains it inside another one containing hot water and stir it for a few seconds, but not over a flame. Never mind if the sauce is not very hot; it is better to have it cool than curdled.

SAUCE HOLLANDAISE

Here we get to a vexed question. Purists claim that the one and only true *hollandaise* sauce should consist of nothing but butter, egg yolks and lemon juice. The truth is that the basic *hollandaise* is apt to be insipid and many cooks have discovered that the addition of a preliminary reduction of white wine or vinegar, as in a *béarnaise*, makes a better flavoured sauce. This was the alternative method suggested by Prosper Montagné, and by Madame Saint-Ange in her *Livre de Cuissne*.

In a small pan put 3 tablespoons of wine vinegar (I prefer to use white wine if I happen to have a bottle open) and 2 tablespoons of cold water. Reduce it by boiling to one scant tablespoon. Add half a tablespoon of cold water. Have ready beaten in a bowl the yolks of 3 large eggs and, on a warmed plate, between 6 and 7 oz. of the finest unsalted butter, divided into 6 or 7 portions.

Into the top half of a double saucepan or into a china or glass bowl which will equally fit into the bottom half of the double saucepan which contains the hot water, put the cooled reduction of vinegar or wine. Add the yolks. Stir thoroughly. Set the whole apparatus over the heat. Add one portion of butter. Stir until it starts to thicken before adding the next portion, and so on until all is used up. Do not allow the water underneath the saucepan to boil and, if you see that the sauce is thickening too quickly, add a few drops of cold water. The finished sauce should coat the back of the spoon. Season with salt and a few drops of lemon juice.

If all precautions fail and the sauce disintegrates, put another egg yolk into a clean bowl. To this add your failed sauce a little at a time, replace it over the hot water and proceed with greater circumspection this time until it has once more thickened. I should add, perhaps, that this only works if the sauce has *separated*. If the eggs have got so hot that they have granulated, what you have is scrambled eggs.

A *sauce hollandaise* is served with asparagus, artichoke hearts, broccoli, poached salmon, sole and all white fish, chicken, and poached or *mollet* eggs.

These quantities will serve four to six people.

SAUCE MOUSSELINE

This is *sauce hollandaise* with, for the above amount, about 2 tablespoons of whipped cream folded in at the very last moment before serving. Allowing for the cream, a little extra seasoning may be necessary for the sauce.

SAUCE NIVERNAISE

WHITE WINE, BUTTER AND GARLIC SAUCE

A quarter-bottle of dry white wine, 2 or 3 shallots, herbs, parsley, garlic, lemon juice, 2 oz. butter, the yolks of 2 or 3 eggs, salt, pepper.

First prepare a snail butter with 2 tablespoons of chopped parsley and 1 or 2 finely chopped cloves of garlic mashed up with 2 oz. of butter. Season with a little salt, lemon juice and pepper.

Now put the white wine into a pan with the shallots, another clove of garlic, a faggot of herbs and a little ground black pepper. Reduce by rapid boiling to half its original quantity. Strain, put into the top half of a double saucepan over hot, but not boiling, water. Stir in the beaten yolks of eggs. When thick, add the snail butter, about a quarter at a time. Whisk until amalgamated.

For anyone who likes garlic in strong doses this sauce can be served with a number of dishes—roast mutton, grilled chops, steak, grilled or poached fish (but not delicate fish like trout), eggs, raw vegetables such as celery, fennel and cauliflower, or with boiled or grilled chicken.

SAUCE MAYONNAISE

In 1956, French cooks celebrated the two hundredth anniversary of the creation of mayonnaise. The legend that the sauce was invented by the cook of the Duc de Richelieu in 1756, while the French under his command were besieging the English at Port Mahon in Minorca, is probably no more reliable than other legends of the kind, usually thought up by imaginative cookery historians at a later date. There are indeed various other and older versions of the origin of mayonnaise, one of them being that the name came from the word *manier*, to manipulate; another attributes it to *moyeu*, an old French name for a yolk of egg. It certainly seems likely that by the 1750's the sauce was already known in Spain and in Provence and it is an interesting point that the Spaniards are the only people who, so far as I know, have a special and traditional utensil for pouring the oil for mayonnaise. This is a teapot-shaped can with a long straight spout from which the oil comes out drop by drop; it is sold in all sizes in Spanish hardware shops. Similar oil pourers in glass or plastic are also commonly to be found in Spanish kitchens.

What, however, is more to the point than the origin of mayonnaise is the fact that it is one of the best and most useful sauces in existence, but because it is not cooked at all the making of it seems to represent to the uninitiated something in the nature of magic, or at least of a successful conjuring trick, although the mystery has been somewhat diminished by the advent of electric mixers and the fact that a beautiful thick mayonnaise can be produced from the liquidiser in a matter of a minute or two. But although I regard this machine with the utmost gratitude, since it is a mechanical kitchen-maid rather than a gadget, I do not care, unless I am in a great hurry, to let it deprive me of the pleasure and satisfaction to be obtained from sitting down quietly with bowl and spoon, eggs and oil, to the peaceful kitchen task of concocting the beautiful shining golden ointment which is mayonnaise.

(1) Proportions, to make it really easy, and for six plentiful helpings, are 3 egg yolks (although you can easily make do with 2 when you have a little experience) to about half a pint of olive oil. Half a teaspoon of salt, a few drops of tarragon or wine vinegar or the juice of half a lemon at most.

(2) If the oil has become congealed in cold weather, stand the bottle in a warm room to thaw very gradually and do not use it until it is once more quite limpid and clear. Frozen oil will curdle the sauce as sure as fate. But also it must not be too warm. In tropical climates the oil has to be cooled on ice before a mayonnaise is made.

(3) Stand the bowl in which the mayonnaise is to be made on a damp cloth or newspaper to prevent its sliding about. Use a wooden spoon for stirring.

(4) Whisk or stir the yolks pretty thoroughly before starting to add the oil, which is best poured out into a measuring jug, so that you can see just how much you are using.

(5) Add salt, then the oil, drop by drop at first, but with 3 yolks the drops can quickly be turned into a slow, thin stream. It is only, with this quantity of eggs, when about a third of the oil has gone in that the mayonnaise starts coming to life and acquiring its characteristic solidity. After this it should, if a spoonful is lifted up and dropped back into the bowl, fall from the spoon with a satisfying *plop*, and retain its shape, like a thick jelly.

(6) Add the vinegar from time to time from a dropper or a teaspoon, not straight from the bottle, or you risk ruining the whole thing by adding more than you intended.

(7) If it is more convenient to make the mayonnaise a day, or even two or three days beforehand, stir in at the very last 2 tablespoons of boiling water. The mayonnaise will then neither separate nor turn oily on the surface. Keep it in a cool place but *not* in the refrigerator.

(8) Groundnut oil (*huile d'arachides*) at about a third of the price is usually substituted for olive oil in such restaurants as do take the trouble to serve proper mayonnaise. Although, to me, nothing can replace the flavour and aroma of a genuine, mildly fruity olive oil (but not too strong, for in mayonnaise its flavour is accentuated), this is expensive and none too easy to obtain, so it should be said that a great many people both here and in the non-olive-growing parts of France prefer to use groundnut oil not only because of its cheapness but because they are not accustomed to the flavour of olive oil. Groundnut oil makes quite passable mayonnaise and could certainly be used for practising but, as it is absolutely devoid of taste, it is necessary to add flavour in the form of a little extra lemon juice and perhaps mustard. If this is used, it should be stirred, in powder form, into the eggs before the oil is added.

SAUCE VINAIGRETTE À L'ŒUF
VINAIGRETTE AND EGG SAUCE (1)

Chop very finely a small shallot or a little piece of onion with a tablespoon of parsley, add salt and freshly milled pepper, stir in 3 tablespoons of olive oil, a little vinegar or lemon juice and, when available, a few chives, cut with scissors. Boil an egg for 3 minutes, scoop out the yolk into the sauce, give it a stir, add the chopped white. This sauce is excellent with a boiled chicken, or with fish.

SAUCE GRIBICHE
VINAIGRETTE AND EGG SAUCE (2)

Much the same as above but with the addition of chopped gherkins, a scrap of chopped lemon peel, and hard-boiled instead of soft-boiled egg.

SAUCE RÉMOULADE

Pound the yolks of 2 hard-boiled eggs to a paste with a drop of vinegar. Stir in a raw yolk, a teaspoonful of French mustard, salt, pepper. Add olive oil (about ⅛ pint) as for a mayonnaise. Flavour with chopped tarragon, chives and capers, allowing about one teaspoonful of each. This makes a sauce of a creamier consistency and less rich than a mayonnaise.

SAUCE PROVENÇALE POUR LES SAUMONS
PROVENÇAL SAUCE FOR SALMON

Bertrand de Guégan[1] quotes this recipe as being from the hand of Maneille, *chef des cuisines* of the famous restaurant of the Trois Frères Provençaux, which flourished in Paris in the days of the First Empire, and the proprietors of which are said to have been responsible for introducing the *brandade de morue* to Parisians and to have invented *poulet à la Marengo* for the benefit of Napoleon's generals, returned victorious from Italy. It is a more likely theory than that which attributes the invention to Napoleon's cook upon the battlefield. Maneille's version, incidentally, is made without tomatoes.

Here is the Provençal sauce for salmon; it is, as anyone can see, very little different from what we now call a *sauce rémoulade*, but it is an excellent version which can be followed in every detail.

'Take a medium-sized onion, 50 grammes (approximately 1½ oz.) of capers and a substantial pinch of parsley; chop all together, after having washed the onion and parsley and wrung all three ingredients dry in the corner of a cloth. Take 2 anchovies (which you rinse well before pounding), 2 cooked yolks of eggs and 1 raw one. Beat all together and incorporate, little by little, ½ lb.[2] of olive oil, smelling of the fruit, and the juice of a lemon. Your preparation, being well worked, can be kept for at least three days without being retouched. This sauce needs a great deal of care to be made without failure.'

I must say it does not seem at all difficult to me—much more reliable than a straightforward mayonnaise. But I find a tablespoon of capers and 3 or 4 anchovy *fillets* rather than 2 whole anchovies provide a sufficiently strong flavouring.

SAUCE RAVIGOTE

Chop very finely a big bunch of mixed parsley, tarragon, and watercress, with chervil and chives when they are available (about 2 oz. altogether), plus 3 anchovy fillets, a tablespoon of capers and 2 or 3 little gherkins or a small pickled cucumber. Stir in about 4 tablespoons of olive oil, a very little tarragon vinegar, and a thread of lemon juice. The sauce should be

---

[1] *La Fleur de la Cuisine Française*, Vol. II.
[2] Approximately 8 fluid ounces.

pretty thick, and can also be further seasoned by the addition of a little mustard. Good with boiled beef and chicken as well as with fish. Enough to serve four to six people.

SAUCE VERTE

This is, I think, one of the great achievements of the simpler French cooking, but when I say simple I mean simple in conception rather than in execution, for it is hard work to make in any quantity, and so far as I know there is no short cut.

First prepare a very thick mayonnaise with 2 or even 3 egg yolks, ⅓ to ½ pint of best olive oil, and a few drops of wine or tarragon vinegar. The other ingredients are 10 fine spinach leaves, 10 sprigs of watercress, 4 of tarragon, 4 of parsley. Pick the leaves of the watercress, tarragon and parsley from the stalks. Put all these leaves with the spinach into boiling water for 2 or 3 minutes. Strain, squeeze them quite dry, pound them and put the resulting paste through a fine sieve. It should emerge a compact and dry purée. Stir it gradually into the mayonnaise but leave this final operation as late as possible before the sauce is to be served.

To the salmon of the summer months, lacking the exquisite curdy flesh of the early part of the year, *sauce verte* supplies the interest which might otherwise be lacking, but it need not be confined to fish. An hors-d'œuvre of hard-boiled eggs with this green sauce is just that much grander than an ordinary egg mayonnaise. It never fails to please.

SAUCE MOUTARDE AUX ŒUFS OR SAUCE BRETONNE
EGG, BUTTER AND MUSTARD SAUCE

This is an egg and butter sauce reduced to its greatest possible simplicity. It has no relation to the *sauce bretonne* of the chefs.

Stir the yolks of 2 eggs in a bowl; add a pinch of salt and pepper and a teaspoon of yellow French mustard; then a few drops of tarragon vinegar; then a heaped teaspoon of fresh herbs finely chopped. These can be chosen according to what dish the sauce is to go with; fennel and parsley for fish; tarragon and chervil for steak; mint for grilled lamb cutlets, and so on. Have ready 2 oz. of unsalted butter just barely melted over hot water, and not at all hot. Add this gradually to the eggs and stop stirring as soon as it has reached the consistency of a mayonnaise.

Sometimes, if the sauce is made in advance, it goes grainy as the butter coagulates. The remedy is to stand the bowl inside another containing a little hot water; stir until the sauce is smooth again.

This, although so little known, is an immensley useful sauce for those with little time to spare, for it can take the place of *hollandaise* or *béarnaise* to serve with steak, fish, grilled chicken and so on, and for those who cannot eat olive oil it can even do duty instead of mayonnaise. It has not, however, the body which these sauces have, so it should always be served separately in a sauce-boat, not used as a *coating* sauce.

SAUCE SOUBISE
ONION SAUCE

One of the nicest of the old-fashioned sauces, seldom met with now-adays. It can be made in two ways, with stock or with milk. The first method makes the better sauce, if you have some veal and beef *bouillon* available.

Slice $\frac{1}{2}$ lb. onions, weighed when peeled, very thin. Soften them in $1\frac{1}{2}$ oz. of butter, letting them just turn pale yellow. This takes about 7 minutes. Stir in one dessertspoon of sieved flour; add a seasoning of salt, pepper and nutmeg, then just over $\frac{1}{4}$ pint of warmed, clear stock or milk. Simmer gently for 15 minutes. Sieve. If the resulting purée is too thick, thin it with a few drops of the stock. If too thin, let it simmer again until it has reduced.

Serve hot as a background to poached or fried eggs and fried bread, or with roast pork, chicken or mutton.

Sauce Robert is made in much the same manner, with the addition of a fairly strong seasoning of French mustard stirred in while the sauce is being heated up for serving.

SAUCE TOMATE OR COULIS DE TOMATES
FRESH TOMATO SAUCE (1)

Although it is so well known, I find that many amateur cooks are uncertain about how to make a good tomato sauce from the fresh fruit. It is very useful and very easy but, all the same, demands a certain care in the seasoning, and judgment as to the length of the cooking time. Here it is, in its simplest form, without stock, wine, thickening or meat.

Ingredients are 1 small onion, $1\frac{1}{4}$ to $1\frac{1}{2}$ lb. of very ripe tomatoes, $\frac{1}{2}$ oz. of butter, 1 tablespoon of olive oil, 1 teaspoon salt, a lump of sugar, a teaspoon of chopped celery leaves or parsley, a clove of garlic, a couple of fresh or dried basil leaves if available.

Melt the butter and olive oil in a shallow wide pan and in this cook the finely sliced onion very gently until it turns yellow. Add the chopped tomatoes and all the other ingredients. Simmer over a moderate fire for 15 to 20 minutes. Put through the food mill. If it is at all watery, put it back into the rinsed-out pan and set it over a gentle flame until it has dried out a little. Taste for seasoning, as some tomatoes need more sugar than others.

As well as being the traditional accompaniment of spaghetti dishes, a tomato sauce goes well with fried chicken, with all manner of croquettes, with fried steak and with fried eggs.

COULIS DE TOMATES À LA PROVENÇALE
FRESH TOMATO SAUCE (2)

Put 1 lb. of chopped tomatoes in a thick pan with a tablespoon of olive oil, a chopped onion, a clove of garlic, a chopped carrot, some parsley stalks, a little fresh or dried marjoram or basil, a little salt and freshly ground pepper. Simmer until the moisture has reduced and the tomatoes are a thick pulp. Sieve, and taste for seasoning.

SAUCE CATALANE
TOMATO, GARLIC AND ORANGE SAUCE

From the Perpignan district, to the west of the Languedoc, where the cookery has a distinct Spanish influence, comes this sauce which in its native region goes particularly with partridges and with pork. But it is good with other things from chicken and mutton to fried eggs or slices of baked gammon.

Heat two tablespoons of olive oil in a sauté pan. Put in several whole cloves of garlic and add immediately about 1 lb. of ripe, peeled tomatoes, roughly cut up. Season with a little salt, pepper and a lump of sugar, and cook for 10 minutes. Now add half a dozen slices of Seville or bitter orange, pips, but not rind, removed. Cook uncovered for another 20 minutes, until the sauce is thick. Remove the garlic before serving. (In the Roussillon they like a colossal quantity of garlic and do not, of course, take it out; but then they are accustomed to these large amounts of garlic, whereas here we are not.) The bitter orange slices give a curious and interesting flavour to the sauce but do not let them cook it in more than 20 minutes or they will be *too* bitter.

PURÉE D'OSEILLE

SORREL SAUCE

Wash and chop very finely a small handful of sorrel leaves, not much more than ¼ lb. Melt it gently in ½ oz. of butter. Stir in, bit by bit, ¼ pint of cream previously boiled (this is important, for sorrel is very acid and there is a risk of the cream curdling when the two come into contact) and then thin it with a tablespoon or two of the stock from the dish the sauce is to accompany—usually veal or fish. A very excellent little sauce, which also makes, in larger quantities, a good accompaniment to poached eggs.

It may be hard to believe, but a purée of green gooseberries, barely sweetened, with the same additions of cream and stock, is almost indistinguishable from a sorrel purée.

SAUCE RAIFORT AUX NOIX

WALNUT AND HORSERADISH SAUCE

On page 38 I have quoted Escoffier's recipe for this sauce as he noted it down after a visit to the Haute Savoie. The sauce was served, he records, with an *ombre-chevalier*, the excellent freshwater fish from the Lac du Bourget, cooked in white wine from his host's vineyards and left to cool in its cooking liquid. But it is so original and delicious that it seems a pity to confine it to partnership with a rare fish. I have often served it with cold salmon trout and have come to the conclusion that it is an even better sauce for this lovely and delicate fish than the more usual *sauce verte*.

To make the sauce for three or four people, use 2 oz. shelled and skinned walnuts and 2 tablespoons of freshly and finely grated horseradish (see page 97), a teaspoon of sugar, a little salt, the juice of half a lemon, and ¼ pint of thick cream.

To skin the walnuts, pour boiling water over them and rub off the skins as soon as they are cool enough to handle. It is a tedious operation but, having compared the sauce made with unskinned walnuts to the original version, there is no question but that the latter is very much finer. It is an example of how a short cut in cooking can be taken only to the detriment of the final result.

Having skinned the walnuts, then, chop them finely. Stir them very lightly into the cream and add the horseradish. Add the seasonings, and lastly the lemon juice.

SAUCE RAIFORT À LA CRÈME
HORSERADISH AND CREAM SAUCE

This is the delicious, mild, creamy horseradish sauce which one finds in Alsace, served with a plain poached sausage. The recipe is on page 228.

MARINADE POUR LES GIBIERS
A MARINADE FOR GAME

A coffee-cup, after-dinner size, of olive oil (to provide lubrication for the dry meat), ⅓ of a bottle of red wine, a sliced onion, 2 teaspoons of crushed coriander seeds for venison, or 1 of juniper berries for hare, a crushed clove of garlic, a sprig of thyme or marjoram, a little ground black pepper. Pour over the venison or hare in a deep china bowl and cover. Leave for 12 hours for a hare, 24 to 36 hours for a 3 lb. piece of venison. Inexpensive port can be used instead of red wine, in which case add a tablespoon of wine or cider vinegar. Dry the meat well before starting to cook it and if it is to stew in its marinade, strain off the herbs, vegetables and spices and add fresh ones.

This is a marinade which is particularly useful for venison or for an old hare, but there are many alternative mixtures. See, for example, the recipes for pork to taste like wild boar on page 364, for the *civet de lièvre* on page 424 and the stewed venison on page 429.

Les Hors-d'œuvre et les Salades

Hors-d'œuvre and salads

FROM the luxurious pâté of truffled goose or duck liver of Alsace to the homely household *terrine de campagne*, from the *assiette de fruits de mer* of the expensive sea-food restaurant to the simple little selection of olives, radishes, butter, sliced sausage and egg mayonnaise of the *café routier*, an hors-d'œuvre is the almost invariable start to the French midday meal. The English visitor to France cannot fail to observe that the artistry with which the French present their food is nowhere more apparent than in the service of the hors-d'œuvre. So far from appearing contrived, or zealously worked on, each dish looks as if it had been freshly imagined, prepared for the first time, especially for you.

E

Now, since the main object of an hors-d'œuvre is to provide something beautifully fresh-looking which will at the same time arouse your appetite and put you in good spirits, this point is very important and nothing could be less calculated to have the right effect than the appearance of the little bits of straggling greenery, blobs of mayonnaise and wrinkled radishes which show all too clearly that the food has been over-handled and that it has been standing about for some hours before it was time to serve it. And the place for wilted lettuce leaves is the dustbin, not the hors-d'œuvre dish. What is the matter with a plain, straight-forward half avocado pear, a mound of freshly boiled prawns, a few slices of good fresh salame, that they must be arranged on top of these eternal lettuce leaves? I swear I am not exaggerating when I say that in London restaurants I have even had *pâté de foie gras* served on that weary prop lettuce leaf. . . .

Now here are one or two ideas from France which have struck me as being particularly attractive for the service of an hors-d'œuvre.

To start with the north, where the ingredients obtainable are not so very different from our own, I remember the big airy first floor dining-room of the Hôtel de la Poste at Duclair. At a table overlooking the Seine we sat with a bottle of Muscadet while waiting for luncheon. Presently a rugged earthenware terrine, worn with the patina of years, containing the typical duck pâté of the country, was put upon the table, and with it a mound of *rillettes de porc*; to be followed at a suitable interval with a number of little dishes containing plain boiled *langoustines* (we used to know them as Dublin Bay prawns before they turned into Venetian *scampi*), shrimps also freshly boiled with exactly the right amount of salt; winkles, a cork stuck with pins to extract them from their shells; sardines and anchovies both in their deep square tins to show that they were high-class brands. Then a variety of little salads each with a different seasoning, and forming, in white-lined brown dishes, a wonderfully imaginative-looking array, although in fact there was nothing very startling.

There were thinly sliced cucumbers, little mushrooms in a red-gold sauce, tomatoes, cauliflower vinaigrette, carrots grated almost to a purée (delicious, this one), herring fillets. The colours were skilfully blended but sober. The pale rose-pinks of the *langoustines*, the pebbly black of the winkles, the different browns of the anchovies and herrings and the dishes themselves, the muted greens of the cucumber and cauliflower, the creams and greys of shrimps and mushrooms contrasted with the splash of red tomatoes, the glowing orange of the carrots, and yellow mayonnaise shining in a separate bowl. Each of these things was differently, and very sparingly, seasoned. Each had its own taste and was firm and fresh. The shrimps and the *langoustines* smelt of the sea. And with the exception of the duck pâté there was nothing in the least complicated. It was all a question of taste, care, and the watchful supervision of the proprietor. And although there was such a large selection, larger probably than one would want to serve at home, it had no resemblance at all to one of those trolleys loaded with a tray of sixty dishes which may look very varied but in fact all taste the same, and which almost certainly indicate that the rest of your meal is going to be indifferent.

This is what food connoisseurs condemn when they say that a mixed hors-d'œuvre is not only unnecessary but positively detrimental to the enjoyment of a good meal; on the other hand a nicely presented and well-composed hors-d'œuvre does much to reassure the guests as to the quality of the rest of the cooking, and to put them in the right frame of mind to enjoy it.

I vividly remember, for instance, the occasion when, having stopped for petrol at a filling station at Remoulins near the Pont du Gard, we decided to go into the café attached to it, and have a glass of wine. It was only eleven o'clock in the morning but for some reason we were very hungry. The place was empty, but we asked if we could have some bread, butter and sausage. Seeing that we were English, the old lady in charge tried to give us a ham sandwich, and when we politely but firmly declined this treat she went in search of the *patron* to ask what she should give us.

He was an intelligent and alert young man who understood at once what we wanted. In a few minutes he reappeared and set before us a big rectangular platter in the centre of which were thick slices of home-made pork and liver pâté, and on either side fine slices of the local raw ham and sausage; these were flanked with black olives, green olives, freshly washed radishes still retaining some of their green leaves, and butter.

By the time we had consumed these things, with wine and good fresh bread, we realised that this was no ordinary *café routier*. The patron was pleased when we complimented him on his pâté and told us that many of his customers came to him specially for it. It was now nearly midday and the place was fast filling up with these customers. They were lorry drivers, on their way from Sète, on the coast, up through France with their immense tanker lorries loaded with Algerian wine. The noise and bustle and friendly atmosphere soon made us realise that this must be the most popular place in the neighbourhood. We stayed, of course, for lunch. Chance having brought us there it would have been absurd to stick to our original plans of driving on to some star restaurant or other where we probably wouldn't have eaten so well (my travels in France are studded with memories of the places to which I have taken a fancy but where I could not stop—the café at Silléry where the still champagne was so good, the restaurant at Bray-sur-Seine where we had a late breakfast of raw country ham, beautiful butter and fresh thin *baguettes* of bread, and longed to stay for lunch—inflexible planning is the enemy of good eating). But here at Remoulins we stayed, and enjoyed a good sound lunch, unusually well-presented for a *café routier*.

We came back the next night for a specially ordered dinner of Provençal dishes, for the proprietor was a Marseillais and his wife the daughter of the owners of the house, which had been converted from a farm to a restaurant–filling station. The young man was a cook of rare quality, and the dinner he prepared to order put to shame the world-famous Provençal three-star establishment where we had dined a day or two previously. But had it not been for the appearance of the delicious hors-d'œuvre, which was so exactly the right food at the right moment, we should have had our drink and paid our bill and gone on our way not knowing. . . .

Even simpler in composition was another hors-d'œuvre which was served us at a hotel at Les Saintes-Maries-de-la-Mer. It consisted simply of a very large round dish, quite flat, completely covered with over-lapping circles of thinly sliced *saucisson d'Arles*; in the centre was a cluster of shining little black olives. Nothing much, indeed, but the visual appeal of that plate of fresh country produce was so potent that we felt we were seeing, and tasting, Arles sausage and black olives for the very first time.

So you see one does not need caviar and oysters or truffled *foie gras* and smoked salmon or even pâtés and terrines and lobster cocktails to make a beautiful first course. One needs imagination and taste and a sense of moderation; one must be able to resist the temptation to overdo it and unbalance the whole meal by offering such a spread that the dishes to follow don't stand a chance; one must remember that eggs and vegetables with oil and mayonnaise drâtessings, and pés with their strong flavours and fat content and their accompaniments of bread or toast are very filling but not quite satisfactory to make a meal off; so the different components of an hors-d'œuvre must be chosen with great care if they are to fulfil their function of serving as appetisers rather than appetite killers.

To translate all this into practical terms I would say that a well composed mixed hors-d'œuvre consists, approximately, of something raw, something salt, something dry or meaty, something gentle and smooth and possibly something in the way of fresh fish. Simplified though it is, a choice based roughly on these lines won't be far wrong. Then, apart from the selection of these things described in more detail below, there are a few French hors-d'œuvre which are nearly always served on their own, such things as poached or *mollet* eggs in a tarragon-flavoured aspic jelly, a salad made from the sliced boiled beef of the *pot-au-feu*, *crevettes bouquet* (large freshly boiled prawns served plain with lemon and salt), *salade niçoise* and *artichauts vinaigrette*.

LES CRUDITÉS

RAW VEGETABLES

These are for the raw, crisp element of an hors-d'œuvre. They consist of sliced very firm raw tomatoes, dressed with the minimum of oil, lemon and seasoning, sprinkled with finely chopped parsley. Cucumber sliced very thin and dressed in the same way. Radishes, washed, trimmed of excess greenery but left otherwise as God made them, rather than disguised as water lilies. Raw Florentine fennel, the outer leaves removed, the heart cut into quarters, and sprinkled with plenty of lemon juice to prevent it turning brown. Or alternatively cut into fine strips and dressed with oil, salt, lemon. Celery treated the same way. Very young raw broad beans piled on a dish in their pods, to be eaten *à la croque au sel*, i.e. simply with salt. Raw red or green peppers, cut into the thinnest of rounds, all seeds and core carefully removed, dressed with oil; prepared in advance and perhaps mixed with a few black olives.

Raw carrots (*carottes râpées*) very finely grated, the red part only, the yellow core being discarded; the resulting preparation almost a purée, is mixed with a very small amount of finely chopped shallot, a little oil, lemon juice, salt and a pinch of sugar if necessary, depending on the quality of the carrots.

Céleri-rave rémoulade, peeled and washed raw celeriac, shredded on the special crinkled blade of the mandoline into match-size strips, put straight into a bowl of acidulated water to preserve its colour; blanched a few seconds in boiling salted water, drained very dry, mixed with a thick mayonnaise very highly seasoned with salt, mustard and a good deal more vinegar than is ordinarily allowed.

One would not, of course, have all these things at the same time, the choice depending a good deal upon the time of year; only very small quantities of each should be served, so that nobody will be tempted to eat too much before the main course.

With a *plat de crudités* is usually served either a slice or two of *pâté de campagne*, salame sausage or raw ham; in the south, olives and anchovies, or tunny fish in oil; in the north, pickled gherkins and sardines or fillets of mackerel in white wine; and if there is no other rich sauce, possibly an egg mayonnaise.

LA CHARCUTERIE

PORK PRODUCTS AND COOKED MEATS

Under this heading come all pork products such as the cured salame type of sausage, hams raw and cooked, galantines and the like. A *charcutier*, or pork butcher, also sells various other foods in the form of cooked or cured meats, pâtés, ready prepared dishes, and sausages for cooking; but for the moment we are only concerned with those which are served as cold hors-d'œuvre.

Nearly every province in France produces its own special variety of ham, the most renowned being that of Bayonne, which is in fact produced in the Orthez district of the Béarn; the hams of the Auvergne and of that part of Burgundy known as the Morvan, of Alsace and of Lorraine are equally prized, and one comes across any amount of locally cured hams all over the country, many of which are very good, although none, I think, has quite such a fine flavour as the famous Italian hams of Parma. The only French ham which ever appears in England is that of Bayonne, and it can be served with figs or melon, or just with butter, in the same way as the *prosciutto di Parma*. But look out for imitations with little or no merit. The so-called Bayonne ham from Denmark, heavily smoked, has no relation to the original article, for real Bayonne ham is very lightly smoked, sometimes not at all. (It is a common misconception that all hams eaten raw, including that of Parma, are smoked. It is not the case.)

Very little in the way of French *charcuterie* is at present exported to England, but instead of the cured sausage of Arles or Lyon or other country districts (a particularly good one called the *rosette* is to be found in the Ardèche, and another with the curious name of *Judru* is a speciality of the little town of Chagny in the Côte d'Or) we can buy Italian salame which is at least as good, if not better.

When buying it make sure that it is the genuine Italian variety, very fresh, of a deep rose colour, and the fat very white. If the fat is yellow, or the sausage dry and cracked, it is not worth buying. If you serve salame often, it is an economy to buy a whole sausage, or at least a half one; keep it hanging up in the larder or some other airy place in a net or string bag, and slice it as it is needed. Cut it very thin, and serve it as described above, in overlapping rows on a flat round or oval dish, with perhaps a few olives in the centre, but never messed up on a plate with salads or any other hors-d'œuvre with a sauce.

Among the commonest and cheapest hors-d'œuvre in France, to be bought at every cooked meat shop and on the market stalls, are the salads of *museau de bœuf* and *museau de porc*, ox muzzle or pig's snout; these are sold ready seasoned with a good deal of chopped shallot, parsley and a vinaigrette dressing. To prepare them at home is a lengthy process, for the meat must be first salted for a day or so, then simmered very gently for about four hours until quite tender, then sliced and seasoned. The same sort of salad can be made from any gelatinous meat such as brisket, ox cheek, calf's and pig's head, shin and so on. It should be cut thinly into small rectangular slices and seasoned, if possible, while still warm. A recipe for making one of these salads on a large scale, for a party, is on page 147. Recipes for pâtés and terrines will be found on pages 217–21.

LES SALAISONS

SALT FISH, OLIVES, ETC.

The salt element in the hors-d'œuvre is nearly always supplied by olives, anchovies or salt herrings. Whenever possible, buy loose olives, choosing the smaller varieties, the bigger ones being more suitable for cooking. Store them in jars, covered with oil, and they will keep well and always be to hand when needed. The little Spanish green olives stuffed with anchovies or hazel nuts which are imported in tins are delicious. Unless you consume a vast quantity of anchovies it is best to buy the little 2 oz. tins of anchovy fillets in oil rather than the big tins, which soon go stale after they are opened. Herrings in brine vary so much in quality that it is impossible to give any specific instructions, but if they are too salt they should be steeped in half milk, half water, drained, and then dressed with a vinaigrette, with a little chopped hard-boiled egg and a few capers as a garnish.

LÉGUMES EN SALADE

VEGETABLE SALADS

A salad of cooked vegetables supplies the soft element of an hors-d'œuvre; it may be potato salad, white haricot beans, beetroot, leeks, french beans. Boil them, in the case of potatoes and beetroots, in their skins. Keep them firm; drain them carefully. Always skin and season them while still hot with a dressing of oil, vinegar or lemon, salt, pepper; a little mustard if you like. According to taste add a little chopped shallot or garlic; parsley, chives or tarragon. Recipes for various vegetable salads are given below. See also the chapter on vegetables.

A rice salad, mixed with a few little prawns or strips of sweet pepper, comes into the same category; again, keep the rice on the firm side; season while hot, not forgetting a little nutmeg and tarragon vinegar as well as oil, salt and pepper. The detailed recipe for rice salad is on page 151.

LÉGUMES À LA GRECQUE

VEGETABLES COOKED IN OIL FOR HORS-D'ŒUVRE

In spite of the name, this method of preparing vegetables to be served cold is typically French, and also provides the soft, emollient element in a mixed hors-d'œuvre. Leaf artichokes, celery, mushrooms, courgettes, fennel, small onions, leeks can all be served in this manner. Recipes are on pages 138 and 139.

CONCOMBRES EN SALADE

CUCUMBER SALAD

To slice cucumber really thinly you need the instrument called a mandoline (see page 64). In France the cucumber is nearly always peeled (use a potato parer) and is best prepared a little time ahead. Slice it almost paper thin on the mandoline, sprinkle it with salt, put in a colander with a plate pressed down over it and leave to drain. After a minimum of half an hour press it dry and dress with oil, a few drops of vinegar, a pinch of sugar. Sprinkle with chopped chives, chervil or parsley.

The gherkin cucumbers, short and fat, which are used for pickling and which come into the shops in August, can be treated in the same fashion, and it is essential to peel them as their skins are apt to be bitter; then cut them in half lengthways and discard the coarse seeds before slicing them, and be rather more generous with the sugar in the dressing.

As the season advances, ordinary cucumbers become full of seed and watery, and they too should have the seeds removed in the same way as the *cornichon* cucumbers.

SALADE DE .POMMES DE TERRE

POTATO SALAD

It is far from easy to make a good potato salad without the right variety of potatoes, and it is a curious fact that in England, where the potato is considered such an essential daily food, it is next to impossible to find those long kidney-shaped waxy potatoes which are grown on the Continent and which are the only ones which do not collapse in the cooking. When asked if they could not put these potatoes on the market the growers give the usual stonewalling reply, 'there would be no market for them.' How do they know there would be no market for them until they try? Was there, one cannot help wondering, a 'market' for avocado pears, passion fruit, Chinese gooseberries, mangoes, for leaf artichokes at five shillings apiece, for aubergines, sweet peppers and suchlike until someone thought of creating that market? As a matter of fact, from time to time some enterprising grower produces potatoes of the Kipfler or other kidney varieties, and because they are such rarities the luxury shops are able to sell them for something like three shillings and sixpence a pound—which makes a potato salad a rather costly dish.

Anyhow, to make a good potato salad, at least choose new potatoes or one of the firm-fleshed varieties such as Majestic or King Edward. Scrub them, and boil them in their skins, keeping a watchful eye upon them to see that they do not overcook. Drain them, and peel them as soon as they can be handled. Slice them, and season them while they are still warm (this is essential) with salt, pepper, plenty of good olive oil and a little tarragon or wine or cider vinegar. Add a generous sprinkling of finely chopped parsley or chives.

An alternative dressing is a home-made mayonnaise, thinned to the consistency of cream with a little warm water. A hot potato salad is the frequent accompaniment of a hot poached country sausage, and a very delicious combination it is. The recipe is on page 228.

PIMENTS DOUX EN SALADE

SWEET PEPPER SALADS

Sweet red or green peppers can be served in two ways for an hors-d'œuvre. First raw, in which case you cut off the stalk end, extract the core and the seeds, rinse the pepper under the cold tap to make sure no seeds remain, then slice it in the thinnest possible rounds. Dress with oil and salt and add a few black olives.

The second method is to skin the peppers by impaling them on a long fork or skewer and holding them over the gas flame, turning them round and round, until all the skin is charred quite black. It will then rub off quite easily, with the aid of a little running cold water. Every scrap of burnt skin must be removed, likewise the seeds and cores. Cut the peppers into lengthwise strips, season with salt, olive oil, a little chopped garlic if you like, and parsley.

SALADE DE POIS CHICHES

SALAD OF CHICK PEAS

For the method of cooking chick peas see the *soupe aux pois chiches* (page 164). While the peas are still warm they can be very easily slipped out of their skins, although this is a tedious business and not strictly necessary. Season the peas well with salt if they need it, pepper and olive oil, and if you like a little finely sliced onion.

TOPINAMBOURS EN SALADE
SALAD OF JERUSALEM ARTICHOKES

Put the peeled and washed artichokes in cold salted water, simmer rather than boil them, and keep a wary eye on them after the first 10 minutes, testing them with a skewer and extracting each from the pan as soon as it is ready. For salad they should remain a little resistant. While still warm, slice them as you would potatoes, season with salt, pepper, plenty of olive oil and a little wine vinegar, or lemon juice. For 2 lb. of artichokes mix in a heart of raw celery cut in thin strips, parsley, garlic if you like. Cover the bowl until the salad is to be served. A layer of chopped ham on top of the salad makes a nice addition.

COURGETTES À LA GRECQUE
LITTLE MARROWS STEWED IN OIL

Wash 1 lb. of courgettes, or small marrows, and pare off any damaged part of the skin; otherwise do not peel them. Remove the two ends, slice them into inch-long pieces, put them in a colander, sprinkle them with salt and leave them to drain for an hour or so.

Prepare the following mixture: a coffee-cupful (after-dinner size) of olive oil, the juice of a lemon, ½ pint of water, a bayleaf, a sprig of thyme, a few crushed peppercorns and coriander seeds and a little salt. Bring this to the boil; put in 3 skinned and chopped tomatoes and the courgettes. Cook fairly fast for 20 to 25 minutes. Serve cold. The coriander seeds and tomatoes are optional, and garlic can be added by those who like it.

Enough for four.

ARTICHAUTS À LA GRECQUE
ARTICHOKE HEARTS STEWED IN OIL

Except for those who grow their own (there have been increasing numbers of English artichokes on the market in recent years) these are a very expensive vegetable, but treated *à la grecque* as an hors-d'œuvre they are comparatively economical. To prepare them for cooking in this way, and for all recipes in which the hearts only are used, proceed as follows: Have ready a bowl of water acidulated with lemon juice. Draw your sharpest knife through a lemon, and rub the artichoke also with lemon. Cut off the stalk and the hard leaves on the underside, then slice through the leaf part right down to the tip of the last but one row of leaves nearest the stalk. Holding the artichoke in your left hand rotate it while with the knife held slanting towards you in your right hand you slice off the hard outer leaves until only the little tender pale green ones remain. Scoop out the choke (*le foin*, the hay) with a little silver spoon. As each artichoke is ready throw it into the prepared bowl of water. Although it takes so long to describe, it is only really a matter of a minute, especially after a little practice.

The *fonds* or hearts are now ready to be boiled, stewed, *sauté* in butter, stuffed, etc. To cook them *à la grecque*, first prepare a mixture of ½ pint of water, a small coffee-cup of olive oil, a sprig of thyme and a bayleaf, about 10 coriander seeds, a little salt and pepper, and the juice of half a small lemon. Bring this to the boil in a small saucepan, tall rather than wide. Put in the prepared artichoke hearts (4 for this quantity of liquid), and let them simmer steadily for 15 minutes. Leave them to cool in the liquid. Cut them in quarters when cold and serve them in a shallow hors-d'œuvre dish with some of their liquid.

As part of quite a small mixed hors-d'œuvre this is enough for six people, and is really quite as good as the miniature whole artichokes in oil which one gets in France and Italy. I don't recommend tinned or bottled artichokes; they are flabby, and through overcooking have lost their curious and refreshing delicacy of flavour.

CHAMPIGNONS À LA GRECQUE
MUSHROOMS STEWED IN OIL

The addition of a little tomato to the usual *à la grecque* manner of preparing mushrooms makes the dish more interesting. Put 3 table-spoons of olive oil, 3 of water, 2 skinned and chopped tomatoes, 3 or 4 crushed peppercorns, half a dozen coriander seeds, a bayleaf, a sprig of thyme and a little salt into a small saucepan. Bring this to the boil, let it simmer 2 or 3 minutes, then add ½ lb. of very small button mushrooms washed, drained and rubbed with lemon juice. Cook gently about 5 minutes. Take out the mushrooms, put them in a small shallow oval serving dish; continue cooking the sauce a few more minutes until it is thick and somewhat reduced. Pour over the mushrooms. Serve cold. If very small button mushrooms are unobtainable, larger ones cut into quarters, stalks included, can be used, but they must be of the closed-up variety. This quantity will be enough for four if it is part of a mixed hors-d'œuvre.

FILETS DE MAQUEREAUX AU VIN BLANC
MACKEREL FILLETS IN WHITE WINE

One of the standard hors-d'œuvre in the north of France, these mackerel fillets can be bought there in tins as commonly as sardines; perhaps one of these days our own fish-canning industry will get around to the idea; how much better, for example, would be our Cornish pilchards prepared in a similar way rather than in a slushy tomato sauce.

For part of an hors-d'œuvre for four, 1 large mackerel or 2 little ones will be enough. Prepare a very aromatic *court-bouillon* by cooking together a large glass each of dry white wine (dry cider also serves the purpose admirably) and water, with a sliced onion, a branch of fennel, a little strip of lemon peel, 4 or 5 whole peppercorns, a bayleaf, a little salt. Let this mixture simmer for 10 minutes. Leave to cool. Strain. Poach the mackerel, which for convenience' sake can have been boned by the fishmonger, in this liquid. They must cook very gently indeed, the liquid not even simmering but merely shuddering. They will take 10 to 15 minutes. When the fish are no longer pink in the centre they are done. Leave to cool a little; lift them out and gently ease off every trace of skin. When quite cold, divide into fillets and remove all bones. Mix about half the cooking liquid, again strained, with a little french mustard and chopped parsley, and pour over the fillets.

If you happen to have obtained mackerel with soft roes, which are very good, poach the roes separately after the mackerel have cooked, for a minute or two only.

CÉLERIS AUX ANCHOIS
CELERY WITH ANCHOVY SAUCE

Pound the contents of a 2 oz. tin of anchovy fillets in oil, to the resulting paste add a little pepper, olive oil and vinegar. Serve in a bowl accompanied by celery hearts cut into short lengths and left to get crisp in iced water for an hour.

MOULES EN SALADE
MUSSEL SALAD

Mussels, cooked and shelled, are dressed with a straightforward oil and vinegar or lemon dressing, or with any of the cold oil-based sauces described in the chapter on sauces. They can also be mixed with rice cooked and seasoned as for the rice and tomato salad on page 151.

CREVETTES COURCHAMPS

Serve plain cooked prawns with the same sauce as the one described for lobster on page 325, pounding a couple of prawns into the sauce instead of the lobster coral.

PLATEAU DE FRUITS DE MER

A big dish of assorted shellfish, some cooked, some raw, all arranged on a bed of cracked ice and seaweed with halves of lemons is one of the best of all hors-d'œuvre, but comes very much into the luxury class nowadays. But if we cannot afford oysters and cannot obtain the various kinds of exquisite little clams, the *praires*, the *palourdes* and the *clovisses* which one gets in France and Italy, there is nothing much wrong with a dish of freshly boiled shrimps, a few Dublin Bay prawns, a few cockles or winkles, and mussels cooked as for *moules marinière*, with the addition of a little oil. The giant Pacific prawns now available at a very reasonable price retain more of their flavour after freezing than the Dublin Bays or ordinary prawns; if bought uncooked, simmered in an aromatic *court-bouillon* for a few minutes and served piled up, still in their shells, with a mayonnaise separately, they make a very good hors-d'œuvre. They are very filling, and 2 to 4 per person should be enough, although it depends rather on what is to follow.

ŒUFS DURS MAYONNAISE

EGG MAYONNAISE

It may seem superfluous to give a recipe for so basic a dish as egg mayonnaise, but sometimes, in the search for originality, the most obvious dishes are forgotten. No one need ever be ashamed to offer their guests a well-made dish of egg mayonnaise, for it is always appreciated.

Having prepared a generous amount of really good thick mayonnaise according to the recipe on page 120, arrange it spoonful by spoonful on a flat oval or round dish. On top go the shelled hard-boiled eggs, cut in half lengthways and placed cut side down. Then the smallest possible sprinkling of very finely chopped parsley and absolutely nothing else whatever.

This is a filling dish, and 3 eggs for every two people should be more than enough.

ŒUFS DURS EN TAPÉNADE

An interesting Provençal hors-d'œuvre.

To make the *tapénade*, called after the capers (*tapéno* in Provençal) which go into it, the ingredients are 24 stoned black olives, 8 anchovy fillets, 2 heaped tablespoons of capers, 2 oz. of tunny fish, olive oil, lemon juice.

Pound all the solid ingredients together into a thick purée. Add the olive oil (about a coffee-cupful, after-dinner size) gradually, as for a mayonnaise, then squeeze in a little lemon juice. It is an improvement also to add a few drops of cognac or other spirit, and sometimes a little mustard is included in the seasoning. No salt, of course.

Spread the prepared sauce in a little flat hors-d'œuvre dish, and put 6 to 7 hard-boiled eggs, sliced in half lengthways, on the top. The curious thing about this sauce is that it has a kind of ancient, powerful flavour about it, as if it were something which might perhaps have been eaten by the Romans. Well, it was invented less than a hundred years ago by the chef at the Maison Dorée in Marseille, although it must certainly have been based on some already existing sauce. The original method was to stuff the eggs with the *tapénade*, plus the pounded yolks. At la Mère Germaine's beautiful restaurant[1] at Châteauneuf du Pape the *tapénade* is served pressed down into little deep yellow earthenware pots, like a pâté, and comes as part of the mixed hors-d'œuvre.

TOMATES AUX ŒUFS DURS ET À LA MAYONNAISE
TOMATOES WITH HARD-BOILED EGGS AND MAYONNAISE

A decorative little hors-d'œuvre, very easy to prepare, which I first came across in Lyon.

Rather large ripe tomatoes are essential, and for each tomato you need 1 hard-boiled egg. Slice the tomatoes from the rounded top down towards the stalk end, cutting slightly on the bias, but not right through, so that the tomato can be opened out like a miniature concertina. Between each tomato slice slip a slice of hard-boiled egg, cut crossways. On top put a spoonful or two of very thick mayonnaise, and sprinkle with a little parsley.

ŒUFS EN GELÉE À L'ESTRAGON
EGGS IN TARRAGON-FLAVOURED JELLY

This is not at all so easy a dish to get right as might be supposed. It is not common to find it well done even in a good restaurant. But when perfect,

[1] This restaurant has now changed hands. Of the new owners or of the present state of the cooking I know nothing.

the egg yolk just soft enough to run when you break into it, the jelly firm and clear and delicately flavoured, it is an exquisite dish. Making the jelly for the sole purpose of preparing these eggs would be considered rather a performance in most households, but although during the time of rationing, when there were no meat or calves' feet to make aspic, it was understandable that the jelly had to be made with gelatine, it is not really a satisfactory solution, gelatine aspic being too sticky and gluey, and lacking of course the delicate flavour of jelly made from beef and veal. So I suggest that when there happens to be home-made aspic jelly in the larder, prepared for jellied consommé, jellied chicken or beef or from boiled pigs' trotters as described on page 224, a little can be saved to make jellied eggs. It should be clarified, as described on page 72, and when this is done, allowing a coffee-cupful, after-dinner size, of the liquefied jelly for each egg, heat it up gently and add a teaspoon of Madeira per ½ pint; add also 4 or 5 fresh tarragon leaves and let them infuse in the warmed jelly for a time.

The eggs can be either poached or *mollet*, which is to say cooked 5 or 6 minutes in boiling water, according to size. For each egg have a thin slice of mild, tender, cooked ham. Trim off all the fat; cut each slice to the size and shape of your little oval or round china egg ramekins. Place the ham at the bottom. Put your shelled egg on the top. (To shell *mollet* eggs easily see page 183). When your jelly is quite cold but before it begins to set, pour it gently over the egg, which should be quite covered. Decorate with a couple of tarragon leaves dipped in the liquid jelly. Serve very cold, preferably in their own little dishes, and with a spoon.

Sometimes jellied eggs are turned out, but this is a tricky business, because either the jelly or the egg or both tend to break, and then the dish is spoilt. Special hinged oval moulds are in fact made especially for jellied eggs, but they are really just as nice in their little china pots.

The jelly from *bœuf à la mode*, clarified, makes delicious jellied eggs.

ARTICHAUTS VINAIGRETTE

GLOBE OR LEAF ARTICHOKES WITH VINAIGRETTE SAUCE

Allow 1 large leaf artichoke per person. Rinse them in cold water and, holding them upside down, shake them so that any grit may fall out. Cut off the stalks level with the heads, so that they will stand up nicely on the plate when they are served. Put them into a very large saucepan of boiling salted water with half a lemon. Cook for 25 to 40 minutes, until one of the outer leaves will come away easily when you pull it.

Serve cold with the vinaigrette sauce separately. But make it with only a minimum of vinegar, or better still, lemon juice instead of vinegar.

PAIN GRILLÉ AUX ANCHOIS *or* ANCHOÏADE

Pound 2 cloves of garlic in a mortar, then add the contents of two 2 oz. tins of flat anchovies in olive oil, and pound them to a rough paste. Thin with olive oil, about a tablespoon, added gradually, and a few drops of vinegar. Toast 8 rather thick slices of bread on one side only. While it is still hot spread the anchovy paste on the untoasted side with a fork, pressing it well down into the bread. Heat in a fast oven for 3 or 4 minutes. This is not so much an hors-d'œuvre as the sort of thing to get ready quickly any time when you are hungry and want something to go with a glass of wine (after you have eaten it you may no longer be hungry, but you will certainly be thirsty).

There are many versions of *anchoïade*, and all sorts of things can be added, such as black olives, a few drops of cognac, a pounded tomato or a little concentrated tomato paste. (If whole anchovies in brine are being used, allow 6 oz. Skin and bone them, divide them into fillets and de-salt them in warm water for half an hour.) It is by no means an everyday dish, but like so many dishes which one forgets about for months at a time, when one wants it one feels that nothing else will quite do. Rustic and coarse though it is, *anchoïade* was not disdained by the famous Caramello who presided over the kitchens of the Réserve at Beaulieu, for years the best known restaurant on the coast, and then went to the Réserve at Monte Carlo. Expensive, solid, elegant in an old-fashioned way, the comfortable restaurant of this hotel used to provide unusually good food on a lavish scale. The *anchoïade* here was outstandingly good and I remember, in spite of the immense portions served, ordering, much to the amusement of the head waiter, a second helping. When I returned to the restaurant a few days later, he was ready with my double portion of *anchoïade* before I had even asked for it.

CERISES À L'AIGRE-DOUX
SWEET-SOUR CHERRIES

For each pound of morello cherries (the bright red bitter cherries which come into season in August) use 6 oz. of white sugar, 12 fl. oz. of wine vinegar and 6 whole cloves. Leave an inch or so of stalk on the cherries, discard any that are at all damaged or bruised and pack the rest into wide preserving jars, filling them about three-quarters full.

Boil the vinegar, sugar and cloves together for 10 minutes. Leave until cold and then pour over the cherries. Screw down the tops, and leave for a month before opening.

Served like olives, these sweet-sour cherries are delicious as part of a mixed hors-d'œuvre, and are obviously a useful standby, for they will keep for a year.

Although not, one would think, a typical French recipe, I first came across these cherries served as an hors-d'œuvre at la Mère Germaine's[1] at Châteauneuf du Pape. The hors-d'œuvre are beautifully served here, in small oval *raviers* of glowing deep yellow Provençal pottery. Brought on a basket tray which was left on the table so that we could help ourselves, they consisted only of olives, marinaded mushrooms, a rice and prawn salad, anchovies, these pickled cherries and the *tapénade* already described on page 142. But the visual effect had been skilfully thought out, and against the yellow background these few simple things made a dazzling display of colour.

LE SAUSSOUN, *or* SAUCE AUX AMANDES DU VAR

From Roquebrune in the Var comes this curious sauce which, served as an hors-d'œuvre to be spread on bread, or in sandwiches for tea, has a cool, fresh and original taste.

Pound 4 fresh mint leaves to a paste, then add 4 anchovy fillets. Have ready 2 oz. of finely ground almonds, about 2 oz. of olive oil, and half a coffee-cup (after-dinner size) of water. Stir in these three ingredients alternately, a little of each at a time, until all are used up. The result should be a thick mass, in consistency something like a very solid mayonnaise. Season with a little salt if necessary, and a drop of lemon juice.

SALADE NIÇOISE (1)

This is always served as an hors-d'œuvre. The ingredients depend upon the season and what is available. But hard-boiled eggs, anchovy fillets, black olives and tomatoes, with garlic in the dressing, are pretty well constant elements in what should be a rough country salad, rather than a fussy chef's concoction.

Arrange a quartered lettuce in your salad bowl. Add 2 hard-boiled eggs, cut in half, 2 very firm quartered tomatoes, not more than half a dozen anchovy fillets and 8 or 10 black olives, and if you like them, a few capers. Only when the salad is about to be eaten, mix it with the dressing, made from the best fruity olive oil you can lay hands on, tarragon vinegar, salt,

[1] See page 142.

pepper, a crushed clove of garlic. It is up to you to choose the other ingredients: tunny fish, cooked french beans, raw sliced red peppers, beetroot, potatoes, artichoke hearts. It depends what is to come afterwards.

SALADE NIÇOISE (2)

Tunny fish in oil, the flesh of tomatoes, diced anchovy fillets. Seasoning of tarragon, chervil and chopped chives, with or without mustard.

ESCOFFIER'S version

SALADE NIÇOISE (3)

Ingredients: Young artichoke hearts in quarters, black olives, raw sweet peppers, quartered tomatoes, anchovy fillets.

Seasoning: Olive oil, vinegar, salt, pepper, mustard, *fines herbes.*

HEYRAUD: *La Cuisine à Nice*

SALADE NIÇOISE (4)

Escudier[1] has yet another version. This salad, he says, which is a delicious summer hors-d'œuvre, is not served in a salad bowl, but in a flat round or oval dish.

Cut very firm tomatoes in slices and take out the seeds. Salt lightly. Arrange the slices in a dish. On top of the tomatoes lay some anchovy fillets. Strew with little lozenges of sweet green pepper and with black olives. Moisten with olive oil and vinegar, and pepper lightly. You can also sprinkle the salad with chopped basil leaves and decorate the border of the dish with slices of hard-boiled egg.

PIMENTS FARÇIS

MARINADED AND STUFFED PEPPERS

'Choose very small green sweet peppers, no larger than a thumb, make an incision in the side, extract the seeds, and put them to soak in vinegar for 20 days. At the end of this time, take them out, dry them, and through the incision stuff them with the following mixture:

An onion finely chopped with stoned black olives, a few anchovy fillets

[1] *La Véritable Cuisine Provençale et Niçoise.*

and a handful of capers. The proportions are 5 parts of olives to 1 of capers, 1 of anchovies, and 1 medium-sized onion.

Arrange the little stuffed peppers in a jar and cover them with oil.'

HEYRAUD: *La Cuisine à Nice*

LA SALADE LYONNAISE

This purely local Lyonnais hors-d'œuvre consists of several different meats each seasoned with an oil, vinegar, shallot and parsley dressing and served in separate dishes or bowls. The composition may vary slightly but the various components will be chosen from the following: pigs' and sheep's trotters cut into chunks, thinly sliced calf's head, ox muzzle and boiled beef; there may also be some *cervelas* sausage, sliced and served with a mayonnaise. There are two distinct types of *cervelas* sausage, as I have explained elsewhere in this volume, and the one served with the *salade lyonnaise* is that variety which is lightly smoked and rather resembles a frankfurter in texture, although it is a much larger sausage.

Although not exactly what one might call a refined dish, the *salade lyonnaise* is excellent food of a rough kind, and very cheap if prepared in quantity. I would welcome it myself if it were occasionally to be offered in English restaurants as an alternative to the everlasting potted shrimps and indifferently made *pâté maison*.

BŒUF EN SALADE

BEEF SALAD

Here is a recipe for a very simple cold dish made on a large scale, sufficient for a dish at a buffet supper party for about twenty people. It is only an extension of the salad made regularly in French households with the boiled beef from the *pot-au-feu*, but it makes very good party food. It looks attractive, the meat is in manageable pieces, the sauce makes it sufficiently moist without being too runny, and it has plenty of character without being outlandish.

Ingredients are about 4 lb. of stewing beef, a piece of knuckle of veal weighing about 3 lb. including bone, 4 carrots, 2 onions, a bouquet of herbs, seasoning. The correct piece of beef is really ox muzzle or cheek, but this is not always obtainable, and shin or top rump can be used instead. Flank is also good but rather fat, and an extra pound is needed to allow for the waste when the fat is trimmed off after cooking. If possible have the meat, whatever it is, cut in one large piece, and tied into a good shape so that it will be easy to cut when cooked. For the sauce: 8 to 10 shallots, 2 oz. capers, 3 or 4 medium-sized pickled cucumbers, a little mustard, a very large bunch of parsley, ½ pint of olive oil, tarragon vinegar, 2 tomatoes.

Put the beef and veal into a deep pan with the onions, carrots and bouquet of herbs. Add 1 tablespoon of salt, cover with 7 to 8 pints of water, cook with the lid on the pan either in a very low oven or on top of the stove over a very gentle heat for 3½ to 5 hours, depending upon the cut of meat (ox cheek takes the longest) until the meat is quite tender. Remove both veal and beef, sprinkle them with salt and olive oil and leave until next day. Keep the stock for soup. To make the salad, cut the meat when quite cold into thin slices, narrow and neat, a little smaller than a visiting card. Mix the veal and the beef together.

The sauce takes time to prepare. The shallots must be chopped exceedingly fine with the parsley, which must be first washed in cold water and squeezed dry; when both shallots and parsley are chopped almost to a pulp stir in a little French mustard, salt, pepper, the chopped pickled cucumber and the capers. Add the olive oil gradually, and a very little tarragon vinegar. Mix the sauce very thoroughly with the meat. Lastly add the roughly chopped tomatoes, which are there mainly for appearance' sake. Leave for several hours before serving. Arrange in shallow dishes with a little extra chopped parsley on the top. There should be enough parsley in the sauce to make it quite thick and quite green.

This recipe can be applied to almost any kind of boiled meat or to fish and chicken, the quantities for the sauce being reduced in proportion to the amount of meat.

SALADE SIMPLE, SALADE DE SAISON

GREEN SALAD

This is a plain lettuce or other green salad dressed only with oil, vinegar, salt and pepper, and served either with or after the meat, poultry or other main course.

The generally accepted formula for a so-called French dressing, for which, so far as I know, there is no French translation, is 3 tablespoons of oil to 1 of vinegar. This is much too vinegary even with a mild vinegar. Six to one is nearer the mark, although, naturally, this must remain a question of individual taste. Red or white wine vinegar, tarragon or Orléans vinegar are the ones to go for. The dressing should, however, taste predominantly of olive oil; when the salad has been turned gently over and over and over in the dressing (the best way to do it is with your hands), so that every leaf is coated with its film of oil, serve it at once, fresh, green and shining.

More than once I have heard English people express astonishment and disapproval of the fact that all they get in France when they ask for a green salad is 'plain lettuce with oil and vinegar.' But to a Frenchman that is what a green salad means; and it is served with or after the roast. The English type of mixed salad, with tomato and beetroot and cucumber added, would be served, if at all, as an hors-d'œuvre, like the *salade niçoise*. And it would still be dressed with oil and vinegar, not mayonnaise or salad cream.

In south-western France walnut oil, although it is now becoming rather rare, is often used instead of olive oil; it has a rather powerful and strange flavour and is not to everybody's taste, but those who like it like it very much indeed. Walnut oil (*huile de noix*) is occasionally to be found at Roche, the French shop in Old Compton Street, Soho, but it is even more expensive than the best olive oil.

SALADE AU CHAPON

For those who like a garlic-flavoured salad without actually having to swallow whole hunks of the bulb, this is a good method. The *chapon* is a large piece of bread or toast well rubbed on both sides with a cut clove of garlic, and sprinkled with oil. This is placed in the bowl underneath the lettuce and mixed into the salad with the dressing at the last minute. When everyone has helped himself to salad, the *chapon* is divided up and served to the more avid garlic eaters.

SALADE DE PISSENLITS

DANDELION SALAD

In France dandelion is specially cultivated under cover for picking in winter and spring. Occasionally both winter and summer varieties can be found in shops such as Roche in Old Compton Street, specialising in French vegetables. One of the best ways of eating it is to fry a few little cubes of streaky bacon until the fat runs, pour this hot over the prepared dandelion (1 lb. is ample for four or five people) in the salad bowl, quickly add 2 or 3 tablespoons of wine vinegar to the fat in the frying pan, let it bubble, then pour this, too, over the salad. Mix well and eat it quickly. This is a good country way of dealing with any rather tough-leaved and bitter salad such as curly and Batavian endives, called *endive frisée* and *scarole* respectively.

SALADE VERTE À L'ANGEVINE
GREEN SALAD WITH GRUYÈRE CHEESE

This salad was chosen by Curnonsky one year when several of the contributors of *Cuisine et Vins de France*, the magazine which he founded, chose their ideal Christmas Eve menu. Curnonsky's chosen dishes were *pâté de foie gras de Strasbourg en croûte*, Belon oysters, a truffled goose with chestnut stuffing, the *angevin* salad, cheeses and fruit.

The salad consists simply of a few leaves of green stuff (lettuce or curly endive or dandelion) and little cubes of Gruyère cheese, the salad seasoned with savory and dressed with olive oil and no more than a suspicion of vinegar.

It is simple, interesting and good.

ENDIVES EN SALADE
BELGIAN ENDIVE SALAD

Having discarded the outside leaves of the long smooth Belgian endives, also sometimes called chicory or witloof, wipe the endives clean with a cloth (do not wash them), cut the root end off with a silver knife, then cut the endives across into half-inch chunks. Mix them well with a dressing of olive oil, salt, pepper and lemon juice.

A few thin rounds of red or green sweet pepper or some well-seasoned beetroot both go well with endive, the latter being almost a routine French winter salad.

SALADE DE CÉLERIS ET DE BETTERAVES
CELERY AND BEETROOT SALAD

An admirable winter salad to serve either after a chicken or meat dish or at Christmas with your turkey. The diced beetroot is dressed with a highly seasoned oil and vinegar dressing, a scrap of garlic, chopped parsley. The celery, cut into julienne strips, is separately seasoned with oil, salt and lemon, and piled lightly on top of the beetroot just before serving.

SALADE DE RIZ AUX TOMATES
RICE AND TOMATO SALAD

The success of this dish lies in the cooking of the rice to the right degree and in the seasoning, which must be done while it is still hot.

For four people cook 8 oz. of good quality rice, whether round or long-grained is not of great importance, in plenty of boiling salted water. Add a piece of lemon, which helps to keep the rice snow white. For most rice 12 minutes after the water comes back to the boil will be enough, but this is impossible to say exactly, because rice differs so very much in quality, and there are the factors of the amount of water, the size of the saucepan and so on to take into consideration. At any rate, the rice should not be very soft, rather it should have a bite to it. Drain it in a colander, and immediately mix with it any extra salt needed, quite a generous grating of nutmeg, about 4 tablespoons of olive oil and 2 teaspoons of tarragon vinegar.

The tomatoes should be prepared beforehand: 4 or 5 large, ripe, red ones should be skinned (to do this dip them in boiling water), sliced into rounds, and left on a plate sprinkled with salt and pepper. Place them on top of the rice. Over them sprinkle some very finely chopped chives or tarragon or, when neither of these is available, parsley. Sometimes, when they are in season, some thin rounds of raw green peppers may appear in the salad. It goes beautifully with cold veal or chicken or with hard-boiled eggs for an improvised meal, but in the Paris household of which I have written in the introductory chapters we always had it by itself, instead of a vegetable course.

Since those days I have learnt that this is a speciality of Poitou, but why this should be so I do not quite know, unless it is a legacy from the Spaniards. In fact, rice salad is not a common dish in France, although one does sometimes come across it in the south, where it is liable to contain shell fish or olives and sweet peppers as well as tomatoes. Whatever its origin it has always seemed to me a first-class salad.

FONDS D'ARTICHAUTS EN SALADE
SALAD OF ARTICHOKE HEARTS AND LETTUCE

I have already told the story of la Mère Fillioux and the dishes which made her restaurant famous in Lyon and all over the world. One of these dishes consisted of *fonds d'artichauts* with *foie gras*, and is also served as one of the specialities at la Mère Brazier's in Lyon. (Madame Brazier was once the cook at la Mère Fillioux'.) So when I saw a dish of artichoke hearts listed on the menu at la Mère Brazier's I supposed that it would be the renowned *foie gras* affair. Coming towards the end of an already copious menu consisting of *saucisson en brioche, sole meunière* and *poularde demi-deuil* I was wondering how on earth I could manage an artichoke heart topped with a slice of *foie gras*, a combination which, famous though it may be, does not seem to me an altogether happy one. But when the dish came it proved to be a perfectly simple and straightforward salad, exactly what was needed to refresh the palate after the meal we had had. In fact it was one of the most delicious salads I have ever eaten, and one of the best possible ways of appreciating the subtle, elusive flavour of the globe artichoke.

One fine large artichoke must be allowed for each person. The artichokes are prepared as explained on page 138–9, but it is easier to leave the chokes and scoop them out after cooking, in boiling, salted and slightly acidulated water for 25 to 40 minutes; while still warm season them with a dressing of olive oil, salt, and a little lemon juice or very good tarragon vinegar. The artichokes thus prepared are placed on top of a salad of lettuce hearts, mixed at the last moment with the same dressing and arranged on a flat dish rather than in a salad bowl.

SALADE CAUCHOISE

SALAD OF POTATOES, CELERY AND HAM

Cook about 1½ lb. of waxy potatoes in their skins, keeping them firm. Cut a large celery heart into julienne strips, and keep them in cold water until they are needed. Peel the potatoes while they are still warm, cut also into strips, and mix them in a bowl with the drained celery. Season plentifully with salt, freshly ground pepper, and not more than 2 tablespoons of very good white wine vinegar. Shortly before serving whip about 6 oz. of very fresh cream, adding gradually the juice of half a lemon; if the cream thickens too quickly add a few drops of milk. Season with salt and pepper and fold the cream lightly into the salad. Over the top sprinkle about 4 oz. of cooked ham cut in little strips and mixed with a little chopped parsley. This salad was at one time a speciality of the Hôtel de la Couronne in Rouen (*cauchoise* means that it is called after the district of Caux in Normandy), and a truffle or two would be chopped with the ham to enrich the dish. It is a salad to serve after something light, such as an omelette or a grilled sole, but if the cream is omitted and the mixture dressed with oil instead, it makes a good hors-d'œuvre

Les Potages

Soups

'The making of a good soup is quite an art, and many otherwise clever cooks do not possess the *tour de main* necessary to its successful preparation. Either they over-complicate the composition of the dish, or they attach only minor importance to it, reserving their talents for the meal itself, and so it frequently happens that the soup does not correspond in quality to the rest of the dishes; nevertheless, the quality of the soup should foretell that of the entire meal.'

Madame Seignobos, who wrote these words some fifty years ago in a book called *Comment on Forme une Cuisinière*, was probably referring to trained cooks, and does not mention those other happy-go-lucky ones who tell you, not without pride, 'of course I never follow a recipe, I just improvise as I go along. A little bit of this, a spoonful of that . . . it's much more fun really.' Well, it may be more fun for the cook, but is seldom so diverting for the people who have to eat his products, because those people who have a sure enough touch to invent successfully in the kitchen without years of experience behind them are very rare indeed. The fortunate ones gifted with that touch are those who will also probably have the restraint to leave well alone when they *have* hit on something good; the ones who can't resist a different little piece of embroidery every time they cook a dish will end by inducing a mood of gloomy apprehension in their families and guests. The domain of soup-making is one which comes in for more than its fair share of attention from the 'creative' cook, a saucepan of innocent-looking soup being a natural magnet to the inventive, and to those who pride themselves on their gifts for inspired improvisation.

I remember when I was very young being advised by the gastronomic authority among my contemporaries to take pretty well everything in the larder, including the remains of the salad (if I remember rightly some left-over soused herring was also included), tip it into a pan, add some water, and in due course, he said, some soup would emerge. I very soon learnt, from the results obtained by this method, that the soup-pot cannot be treated as though it were a dustbin. That lesson was elementary enough. The ones that are harder to assimilate are, first, in regard to the wisdom or otherwise of mixing too many ingredients, however good, to make one soup; the likelihood is that they will cancel each other out, so that although your soup may be a concentrated essence of good and nourishing ingredients it will not taste of anything in particular. Secondly, one has to learn in the end that the creative urge in the matter of embellishments is best kept under control. If your soup is already very good of its kind, possessed of its own true taste, will it not perhaps be spoilt by the addition of a few chopped olives, of a little piece of diced sausage, of a spoonful of paprika pepper? These are matters which everyone must decide for himself.

I know that many people think that their guests will find a simple vegetable soup dull, and so attempt to dress it up in some 'original' way. I don't think myself that a well-made vegetable soup, tasting fresh and buttery, and properly seasoned, is ever dull (I am talking about home-made soups).

In her beautiful book about Mexico *The Sudden View*,[1] Sybille Bedford mentions 'a cream of vegetable soup which would have done honour to a household in the French Provinces before the war of 1870.' The phrase reminded me of the lovely soups made by Léontine, the cook of whose

[1] Collins 1953. Re-issued 1960 as *A visit to Don Otavío*.

food I have already written in the pages about Paris household cookery in the introductory chapters to this book. These soups were anything but dull. They certainly were not complicated or expensive either: they belonged neither to *haute cuisine* nor to robust peasant cooking. They were, as befitted the household of a middle-class Norman family, in the direct line of French bourgeois and provincial cookery. Of course I did not know this at the time and did not think about it, I just enjoyed Léontine's delicious vegetable purées without the faintest idea why they were so good, but looking back now I remember how delicate and fresh they were, and I think they must have been the kind of soups Sybille Bedford had in mind when she wrote those lines.

Again, I remember the ordinary everyday soup of a provincial restaurant which has been famous for thirty years for its half-dozen rather grand specialities. These were, and are, beautiful dishes cooked and served to perfection, but the vegetable soups, made for the staff as well as for the customers, had just as much finesse in a different way. Composed of cheap vegetables such as carrots, potatoes and leeks, enriched with good butter and cream and faintly flavoured with parsley or chervil, made into purées of about the consistency of thin cream (I think we often make our cream soups too thick, too porridgy, in England, although I have heard people complain that French soups are too thin), they were soups which embodied so much of the charm, the flavours and scents of a country house kitchen garden that every evening while I stayed in that little hotel it was a struggle not to accept second or even third helpings of soup and so risk having no appetite left for the dishes to follow.

This is one of the dangers of a good soup. No doubt because the tin and the package have become so universal, people are astonished by the true flavours of a well-balanced home-made soup and demand more helpings if only to make sure that their noses and palates are not deceiving them. So it is always best to announce, as soon as the soup is served, what dishes are to follow, and not to go in for any false modesty in this respect. 'But there's nothing, absolutely nothing else coming' means, to the initiated, that there are going to be five courses of rather filling food. But it is kinder to guests to say so in a rather more direct manner.

The soup recipes in this book are mainly of the simple variety I have described. They are, on the whole, the kind most suitable to conditions in England. The ingredients are easily found; they are neither complicated nor costly. For those which require stock, I have described in detail how the best kind of meat broth, that from the *pot-au-feu*, is made. Not that one has to go through this performance every time one wants a little stock; but I do think it is essential that the principle should be understood. Once anybody has got the idea of a properly made broth into their heads, it is unlikely they will ever again resort to the hit and miss methods of the 'bundle it all into the stock-pot' school.

As far as the peasant and farmhouse soups, the *garbures* and the *potées* of traditional regional cookery go, I have only included one or two of these. In their way they are admirable, but heavy mixtures of pork and cabbage, beans and sausages and bread, constitute almost a whole meal in themselves, to be enjoyed by people who work hard all day in the open air; and I hope readers will excuse me for referring them to another volume, *French Country Cooking*,[1] for recipes for this type of soup.

One more point. Although it is not necessary to know a great number of soups, it is highly desirable to have at least one well-tried recipe for every season of the year, and then one will not be led into the expense of buying out of season vegetables or into the error of unnecessary substitution. For example, the potato and tomato soup on page 167, which is one of my favourites, also demands leeks. On several occasions I have tried, when leeks were out of season, using onions instead. Those who had not already eaten it cooked with leeks were probably unaware that anything was wrong, but I was myself quite conscious of the fact that the soup was not absolutely as it should have been. So I have given up trying to make the soup in the summer when no leeks are to be had; and serve instead a cream of fresh green peas, or the delicious *potage Crécy*, or the very light tomato soup described on page 173. If one is going to the trouble of preparing home-made soups one might as well have each one as good as possible of its kind.

POT-AU-FEU

No mystery attaches to the making of a *pot-au-feu* so long as it is understood that it is two dishes, first a beef broth which may be thickened with rice or pasta or served as a clear consommé and, secondly, the boiled beef which has itself contributed the major part of its savour to the broth. Most cooks and housewives know that the making of a good broth entails care both in the selection of meat and vegetables and in the very slow cooking, but often suppose that the French *pot-au-feu* holds some other special secret which eludes them. This is understandable, because recipes for *pot-au-feu* are apt to make such heavy weather out of a very simple process. Lengthy explanations in chemical terms and paragraphs of quotation from Brillat Savarin jumbled up with romantic folklore about generations of French housewives conjuring magic out of their venerable earthenware pots cause the English reader, who tends to be more

[1] Penguin, 3s. 6d.

interested in the hows than the whys of cookery, to abandon the whole mystery and revert to his own methods, right or wrong.

Another possible reason for the rejection of the French method is that when in England we wish to eat boiled beef, the preference goes to salted silverside or brisket which, properly prepared and cooked, is after all one of our best culinary assets, and superior in many ways to an ordinary piece of beef boiled in the *pot-au-feu*. On the other hand it is obvious that stock from salt beef is no use for consommés or sauces, whereas in the case of the *pot-au-feu* the broth, apart from its qualities as a soup, plays an important part in enriching the dishes and sauces of French household cookery, giving them savour and body and taking the place of that indeterminate liquid from the stock-pot, the making of which at one time was thought to be the height of good management in an English kitchen. The editors of the 1891 *Mrs. Beeton* (not Mrs. Beeton herself) told their readers that 'everything in the way of meat, bones, gravies and flavourings that would otherwise be wasted should go into the stock-pot, 'shankbone of mutton, gravy left when the half-eaten leg was moved to another dish, trimmings of beefsteak that went into a pie, remains of gravies, bacon rinds and bones, poultry giblets, bones of roast meat, scraps of vegetables . . . nothing is too insignificant to be useful . . . such a pot in most houses should be always on the fire.' Such instruction was the absolute negation of the principles of good cookery. All these miscellaneous leavings could not produce a stock with a true, fresh flavour, nor could it ever be clear and limpid because all the bacon bones and thickened gravies would cloud it, even if the cook were to stand all day over the pot skimming it; twice-cooked vegetables contribute nothing to a stock; nor would it have any strength because there is no raw, fresh meat to give out its juices and flavour. The gospel of the everlasting stock-pot (with a tap like a tea urn so that you could draw off the requisite amount of the fluid when required) is, I think, no longer preached or believed—many of us found out during rationing what a thankless task it was trying to coax stock out of skin and bone and scraps—and in fact I have only referred to it in order to highlight the difference between this fictional, or dustbin method, and the proper system of obtaining good broth.

The Choice of Meat for the Pot-au-feu

Briefly, the cuts of meat which are most satisfactory from the points of view of both *bouillon* and *bouilli*, as the beef is called in its cooked state, are the forequarter flank (*plat de côtes*)[1] which is relatively cheap, a good shape, and emerges reasonably moist even after lengthy cooking, and if this is considered too fat, then a cut from the thick flank called in French

[1] The cut shown in the drawing on page 153.

the *tranche grasse* which corresponds to top rump in English terms; alternatively, a piece of silverside (*gîte à la noix*), or a cut from the shoulder near the blade-bone, known in French as the *paleron*, but of which there is no precise English equivalent. Shin, because of its gelatinous qualities, is good for the *bouillon* but produces an indifferent *bouilli* and is in any case not sufficient in itself alone to produce a good *bouillon* Some cooks advocate the use of equal proportions of two different cuts, such as silverside and shin, which is a good plan for a big *pot-au-feu*, but less successful for a modest family one, because a piece of meat weighing anything less than 2 lb. will cook too quickly and will hardly emerge in a presentable condition.

In addition to the main piece of meat the *pot-au-feu* is improved by a piece of knuckle of veal, both meat and bone, to give body and a gelatinous quality; a beef marrow bone to provide marrow to spread on the baked bread which is served with the broth; the giblets of one or two fowls for flavour; and a piece of ox liver to promote clarity in the broth. Some families like to enrich their *pot-au-feu* with an ox-tail, which can be used later for another meal.

The Vegetables for the Pot-au-feu

Onions, leeks, carrots, a very small proportion of turnip, celery and parsnip, plus grilled tomatoes and, when they are available, a few pea-pods dried in the oven to give colour. The usual bouquet. Cabbage in the *pot-au-feu* is frequently encountered in France, but in my opinion utterly wrecks it. If cabbage is to be served with the meat, then extract some of the broth when the time comes and cook the cabbage in it separately.

The Saucepan for the Pot-au-feu

The pot, or marmite, is usually a tall straight-sided or slightly bulbous stock-pot made of earthenware, copper, enamelled iron, or heavy aluminium. Having had occasion to use all four, as well as an English 'round pot' or stock-pot made of cast iron lined with vitreous enamel, I cannot say that any one produces a better *pot-au-feu* than the other, although the enamelled ones are the easiest to clean. Many English households do not possess even one pot of the requisite capacity (ideally, two gallons) so it does not seem relevant to lay down rules as to which it should be. French cooks disagree fiercely on the subject, conservative housewives swearing by the efficacy of their earthenware marmites, and professional cooks advocating copper (so long as the tin lining is in mint condition) and condemning earthenware on the grounds that eventually it acquires an ineradicable smell of stale fat which communicates itself to the broth cooked in it. (See the drawings of stock-pots on pages 64 and 153.)

Quantities

4 lb. of forequarter flank of beef or of one of the other cuts mentioned above, or alternatively 2 lb. of one of these and 2 lb. of shin, or even of ox cheek, which is a bargain as prices go nowadays, and can be turned into delicious salad. A piece of knuckle of veal weighing about 2 lb. including bone. Optionally, a beef marrow bone, sawn into short lengths, chicken giblets, and 6 oz. of ox liver in one piece; and possibly an ox-tail cut into the usual lengths.

4 large leeks, 4 large carrots, 2 large onions, a very small turnip, a little piece of parsnip, 1 stalk of celery with its leaves, 2 tomatoes, 4 to 6 dried pea-pods if available, a bouquet consisting of 2 bayleaves, 2 or 3 sprigs of parsley and thyme, 1 tablespoon of coarse salt. The proportion of water is 2 pints per pound of meat, so for this quantity allow 8 pints. Some cooks allow extra for the bones, but the result is rather too thin a broth.

Preparation of the Ingredients

Tie the meat into a good shape. Wrap the pieces of marrow bone tightly in a muslin and tie with string so that the marrow cannot fall out. If ox-tail is being used, steep it in cold water for a couple of hours to let the blood soak out. Trim and wash the leeks and tie them in a bundle, with the stick of celery. Scrub the carrots. Peel the turnip and parsnip. Cut the tomatoes in halves and grill them. Wash the onions, but do not peel them unless they look gritty, because the skins help to colour the broth. The traditional clove stuck in the onions does not seem to me to be necessary. Prepare the bouquet and tie up the dried pea-pods with it.

The cooking

Put the beef and veal, and the giblets if they are being used, into the pot. Pour over the water. Bring extremely slowly to simmering point; when the scum starts rising skim it off. Presently it will get much thicker, and will go on rising for about 15 minutes while the water simmers gently. It is important to remove all this scum as long as it is a brownish-grey colour and thick, otherwise the broth will never be clear. When the scum turns to a thin white foam it can be left, as this will disperse of its own accord. Now put in the vegetables, the bouquet and the salt. Put the lid on the pot, but tilt it so that steam can escape. Allow to barely simmer, to tremble or shudder rather, in the centre of the pot only, for $3\frac{1}{2}$ hours, keeping the heat absolutely regular. Now put in the parcelled-up marrow bone and the piece of liver and cook for another 30 minutes to an hour.

The serving

Turn off the heat and lift out all the solids. If the beef is to be served hot
put it in a covered dish and keep it warm. Spread a wet cloth in a colander
and strain the broth through it into a large bowl or soup tureen. Extract
the marrow from the marrow bone and spread it on pieces of French
bread baked golden in the oven. Remove as much fat as possible from the
broth by means of absorbent kitchen paper or thick paper tissues laid
on top and gathered up as soon as each has become saturated with
the grease. Taste the broth and see if it needs more salt; if so, add it
only to that portion of the broth which is now to be served; the rest,
if needed for stock or sauces, may have to be reduced, and must not
therefore be made any more salt. The leeks and carrots from the
pot-au-feu are sometimes chopped and handed separately with the
soup, as there will not be enough to go with the beef, for which fresh
ones, including potatoes, should have been cooked separately. With the
beef serve also pickled gherkins, coarse salt, horseradish sauce, capers,
mustard, a vinaigrette dressing or any of the usual accompaniments
of beef.

Alternatively, and the better method perhaps when the *pot-au-feu*
is an occasional dish rather than a weekly occurrence, time the cooking
so that the beef will be ready by lunch or dinner-time, but leave the
strained broth to get cold until next day, so that all fat can be very easily
removed. (Keep it, for it is good for sauté potatoes or fried bread.) Also
remove the meat from the veal bone, season it with oil and salt, and next
day cut it in strips and dress it with a well-seasoned sauce of chopped
shallots, parsley, capers, oil and vinegar and serve it as an hors-d'œuvre.
The ox liver is pussy's share of the *pot-au-feu*, at any rate in my house.

To use up the Beef from the Pot-au-feu

Salad from the boiled beef is, I think, one of the most delicious of dishes;
sometimes called *salade parisienne*, it is thinly sliced beef arranged in
alternate layers with boiled potatoes, each layer well soaked in a highly
flavoured dressing of oil, vinegar, mustard, salt, pepper, chopped capers,
shallots, pickled cucumber and a large quantity of parsley. The shallots
and parsley should be very, very finely chopped, so that the finished
result is more like a thick sauce than a salad dressing. The salad is
garnished with hard-boiled eggs and sometimes tomatoes, and is served
on its own as an hors-d'œuvre.

The *bouilli* is also used in France to make the rissoles which they call
boulettes de viande (French rissoles being minced meat enclosed in pastry),
the croquettes, the hashed beef and potatoes familiar to our own kitchens,
as well as the famous *bœuf miroton* in which the sliced beef is heated up

with sliced onions, very slowly, in a little of the thickened broth. One way of using ox-tail cooked in the *pot-au-feu* is to coat the pieces with bread-crumbs and grill them as described on page 350.

To store the Broth

If to be kept, the broth should be brought to the boil every day in hot weather, every two days in winter, returned to a clean bowl, and covered when it is cold, not before. Vegetables left in any stock will make it turn sour very rapidly, and so will the system of leaving it in a saucepan over the stove while the oven is on or on the side of the range overnight. If the stock is kept in a refrigerator be sure that it is covered, or it may freeze solid like a water-ice and be ruined.

Provençal Variation of the Pot-au-feu

There are any amount of regional variations of the *pot-au-feu*, the chief differences being in the kind of meat used. One of the best is the old Provençal recipe, in which a piece of lamb or mutton replaces a proportion of the beef and in which the seasonings include garlic, juniper berries and a small proportion of white wine. The meat, I need hardly add, is served with olives and capers, and traditionally, a salad of chick peas, the making of which is described on page 137.

Cold, next day, an *aïoli* may go with it, while the lamb makes good stuffing for aubergines and tomatoes. This Provençal *pot-au-feu* is excellent, but not everybody cares for the taste of mutton in the broth, which also restricts its uses from the point of view of stocks and sauces.

BOUILLON POUR POTAGES
STOCK FOR SOUP

It is not often, in a small household, that stock is made especially for soups. It is rather for occasions when stock, perhaps from boiled beef, veal bones, a duck, chicken or turkey carcase, happens to be available that one wants to know how to use it to the best advantage. Three or four of the soups in this chapter do need stock, but for the majority of vegetable soups it is not necessary. When it is essential, and none is available, it is safe enough to use a chicken *bouillon* cube, always remembering that these are already salted. They add, of course, nothing to the consistency of the soup, only to the flavour, and if the use of them becomes a habit then your soups will inevitably begin to taste monotonous. Most of us remember how every stock or soup, stew and sauce during

F

the days of rationing tended to have the same background taste because bacon bones and bacon rinds were the mainstay of stock-making.

When making stock from chicken or turkey carcases upon which little meat is left, there are two points to be made. First, use them quickly, without waiting for them to get dried up and stale. Second, it is a mistake to cook them too long, or a strong and unpleasant flavour of bone will result (this is what makes pressure-cooked stocks so horrible) and they will be cloudy. Whenever possible it is a great improvement to add a small proportion of raw veal or beef to such stocks.

For occasions when stock has to be made specially for a soup, here is a recipe for a small quantity.

Put ½ lb. of chopped stewing veal, a small carrot, a small unpeeled onion, a clove of garlic, a chopped tomato, a bouquet of herbs and a little salt into a saucepan, with 1¾ pints of water. Bring to simmering point, skim, then transfer the pot to a low oven for about an hour. Strain through a fine sieve. There should be 1½ pints of clear stock, which will add body and richness to soups but will not overwhelm other flavours.

CONSOMMÉ DE GIBIER

GAME CONSOMMÉ

One stewing partridge, ½ lb. stewing veal, carrots, onions, celery, a tomato, pork or bacon dripping, parsley.

Fry a sliced onion in a little melted pork or bacon fat. When browned, add the roughly chopped veal, and let it brown slightly. Add salt, pepper, 3 or 4 carrots, a whole small unpeeled onion, a chopped tomato, a small piece of celery, some parsley stalks. On top put the partridge, pour over 2 pints of cold water, simmer extremely gently for 3½ to 4 hours. Strain off the liquid and leave it to get quite cold, when it will be easy to skim off the fat. There will be a strong clear consommé which should not need clarifying, and which has only to be reheated. A stewing pheasant or a couple of pigeons can also be used for this consommé.

Use the bird or birds which have been cooked in the soup to make a little cold dish. Cut them in half, put them in a small earthenware terrine; in a saucepan heat 2 tablespoons of the consommé, season it well, stir in 2 oz. of butter, and when it has melted pour it over the partridge and serve very cold, garnished with sliced hard-boiled eggs and watercress.

LA SOUPE AU LARD, OR POTÉE LORRAINE

This is a rough kind of *pot-au-feu*, in which either bacon or salt pork, depending upon which part of the province you are in, replaces the usual beef. Personally, I prefer to use salt pork or unsmoked bacon. The smoked variety gives the broth too powerful a flavour.

Having obtained a 2–2½ lb. square-cut piece of breast of salt pork, and soaked it in cold water for two or three hours, cover it with fresh water and bring gently to the boil. After 5 minutes' boiling, throw away this first lot of water, put back the bacon in the saucepan with 10–12 carrots, the same number of potatoes, 2 onions and 2 leeks tied together with a sprig of parsley, a bayleaf, thyme, a piece of celery and a piece of garlic. Season with pepper, and cover with about 4 pints of water. Bring very gradually to an almost imperceptible boil. Skim. Continue cooking very gently for 1½ hours; 30 minutes before serving add the heart of a small white cabbage, cut in half and previously blanched for 5 minutes in boiling water; 10 minutes later add a cupful of shelled broad beans and the same of green peas.

Remove the pork and strain off the vegetables. The liquid, with bread soaked in it, plus a small quantity of the vegetables, chopped, and if you like fried a minute or two in lard, is served as a soup. The pork and the rest of the vegetables are kept warm for the second course.

A boiling sausage and a piece of knuckle or belly of fresh pork can also be added to the *potée* to supplement the salt pork, and in the winter when there are no fresh green vegetables, ½ lb. of dried white haricot beans, previously soaked and partly boiled, are added at the same time as the potatoes and carrots.

The meats and sausage will also be good cold, with the vegetables made into a salad. If you decide to serve it in this way, keep your cabbage rather undercooked and cut it into fine strips as for a raw cabbage salad; mix it with the potatoes and carrots and to an oil and vinegar dressing add 4 or 5 crushed juniper berries, a teaspoon of sugar, and 4 or 5 tablespoons of cream.

TOURIN BORDELAIS

The onion soup generally regarded as 'French,' with sodden bread, strings of cheese and half-cooked onion floating about in it seems to me a good deal overrated, and rather indigestible. But certainly onions make warming and comforting soups for cold nights, and are admirable when one is suffering from fatigue or a bad cold. This country recipe makes a soup which is very acceptable under such circumstances. It requires no stock, but is enriched with egg yolks.

Slice 3 large mild onions into the thinnest possible rounds. In a heavy saucepan heat 2 large tablespoons of pure pork dripping, and cook the onions in this, stirring until they begin to soften. Then season with salt, cover the pan and leave to cook very gently for about 30 minutes. The onions should be reduced almost to pulp, but should still be of a creamy yellow colour. Pour over 2 pints of cold water, bring slowly to the boil, simmer 10 minutes. Beat 2 egg yolks in a bowl with a few drops of vinegar and some of the hot soup, return this mixture to the pan and stir until very hot, but on no account boiling. Slices of French bread baked in the oven should be put into each soup plate and the soup poured over.

LA SOUPE AUX POIS CHICHES
CHICK PEA SOUP

Chick peas, the pale corn-coloured round peas which look rather like nasturtium seeds, are the *garbanzos* and the *ceci* of Spanish and Italian cooking respectively. They are also (although less so now than a few years ago) grown a good deal in Provence. They are very hard and need lengthy soaking and cooking, but the following method, indicated by Austin de Croze in *Les Plats Régionaux de France*, although it sounds rather a performance, does shorten the cooking time from about 4 or 5 hours to rather less than $2\frac{1}{2}$, and results in them being very well cooked and tender. One thing about chick peas which is encouraging to the forgetful cook is that it is virtually impossible to *overcook* them.

Suppose you are going to cook 1 lb. of chick peas (half of which can be made into soup, the other half into a salad or vegetable dish). Put them to soak overnight in tepid water into which you have put a handful of coarse salt and 2 tablespoons of flour. Next day, boil the water in which they have soaked, adding a good pinch of bicarbonate of soda; the water having boiled, leave it to get cold; put in the rinsed chick peas, bring to the boil, then leave them to simmer gently for an hour. Strain, discard the original liquid and throw the peas into a large saucepan containing about 6 pints of boiling, lightly salted water, and cook until they are quite tender and the skins begin to loosen. Now remove about half the peas and while they are still warm season them, add olive oil, and set them aside for a salad or other dish.

Strain the remainder, reserving the liquid. Heat a couple of tablespoons of olive oil in a saucepan and in this melt a sliced onion and the chopped white parts of 2 leeks. Add a large skinned and chopped tomato; put in the chick peas and cover with the reserved liquid. Add salt if necessary and a little pepper. Simmer until the peas are soft enough to sieve. Heat up the resulting purée, adding more water, or stock, if it is too thick. Serve with croûtons of bread fried in olive oil. Enough for six good helpings.

This makes an interesting soup, although I suppose that the curious flavour of chick peas would not be to everybody's taste.

LA SOUPE AU PISTOU

A famous Niçois soup of which there are many versions, the essential ingredient being the basil with which the soup is flavoured, and which, pounded to a paste with olive oil, cheese and pine nuts makes the sauce called *pesto* so beloved of the Genoese. The Niçois have borrowed this sauce from their neighbours, adapted it to suit their own tastes, and called it, in the local dialect, *pistou*. It is the addition of this sauce to the soup which gives it its name and its individuality. Without it, the soup would simply be a variation of *minestrone*.

Here is the recipe given in *Mets de Provence* by Eugène Blancard (1926), a most interesting little collection of old Provençal recipes.

In a little olive oil, let a sliced onion take colour; add 2 skinned and chopped tomatoes. When they have melted pour in 1¾ pints of water. Season. When the water boils throw in ½ lb. of green French beans cut into inch lengths, 4 oz. of white haricot beans (these should be fresh, but in England dried ones must do, previously soaked, and cooked apart, but left slightly underdone), a medium-sized courgette unpeeled and cut in dice, 2 or 3 potatoes, peeled and diced. When available, add also a few chopped celery leaves, and a chopped leek or two. After 10 minutes add 2 oz. of large vermicelli in short lengths.

In the meantime prepare the following mixture: in a mortar pound 3 cloves of garlic with the leaves of about 10 sprigs of very fresh basil. When they are in a paste, start adding 2 or 3 tablespoons of olive oil, drop by drop. Add this mixture to the soup at the last minute, off the fire. Serve grated Parmesan or Gruyère with it. Enough for four.

CRÈME À · LA VIERGE
CREAM OF TURNIP SOUP

This soup, and the one which follows, come from the little book called *Les Secrets de la Bonne Table*, about which I have already written in the introduction to this book. Both have the detailed instructions and that carefully studied quality of the cookery of an age when attention to detail was not considered a waste of time. It is worth following the recipes exactly; both produce very delicious soups.

'I collected this recipe at Mondoubleau in Loir-et-Cher. Not everyone likes turnips, so before preparing it, make sure that it is to the taste of the guests. The variety of turnips known as *Vertus* (the long carrot-shaped ones) are preferable to any others, but in any case do not use hard or hollow turnips or those kept for the winter which usually have a strong taste; with new turnips, and a little care, the rather special taste of this vegetable will not be accentuated.

'Put a large saucepan of water on to boil. Peel a dozen new turnips, cut them in rounds, and throw them into the boiling water. Cover the saucepan and remove it from the fire; it must not boil again. After five minutes, strain the turnips, rinse them in abundant cold water, and drain them in a teacloth. Put 2 oz. of butter in a saucepan and heat the turnips in this without allowing them to turn golden, then add about 2 pints of milk, salt, a pinch of mixed spice and a pinch of white pepper. Cover the pan.

'When the turnips are cooked press them through a fine sieve with a wooden pestle.

'If the purée is too thick, thin it with milk, and then stir in 2 oz. of butter. From this moment the soup should be kept very hot, but without boiling. Cut some bread into slices as thin as possible, arrange them in the soup tureen and pour the soup over them.' Plenty for four.

CRÈME DE LA GRAND' TANTE
CREAM OF CAULIFLOWER SOUP

'When I was young,' says M. Renaudet, 'we gave this name to a soup which was the triumph of the great-aunt of one of my friends. She rarely omitted to tell us on these occasions how her own mother, an intimate friend of Madame Récamier and Monsieur de Châteaubriand, served it to them when they came to sit at her table, and that they complained whenever this soup was replaced by another. It does not, however, call for any complicated ingredients, nor for any difficult process in its preparation.

'For six people you need a cauliflower, 1¾ pints of *bouillon*, a glass of milk, 4 oz. of butter, 4 yolks of eggs, salt, no pepper.

'Take off the outside leaves of the cauliflower, separate it into branches, wash it, and cook in very lightly salted water. When it is absolutely soft, drain it, pound it to a purée with a wooden pestle, and pass it through a fine sieve.

'Add this purée to the *bouillon* and bring it to the boil very gradually over a low fire. Let it simmer a quarter of an hour. Draw the saucepan to the side of the stove and add a glass (about ¼ pint) of milk. Taste to see if the soup is neither too much nor too little salted; if too much, add a little more milk. Add the butter, stirring as it melts. To finish, beat the yolks with half a glass of water, and add them to the soup, heating it gently but without letting it boil, so that the yolks thicken the soup into a cream.'

Disliking cauliflower cooked in its more ordinary ways, I find this soup a very satisfactory method of dealing with this vegetable, its normal coarse flavour and soggy texture being transformed into a delicate and smooth cream.

POTAGE CRÈME DE TOMATES ET DE POMMES DE TERRE
CREAM OF TOMATO AND POTATO SOUP

The white part of 2 leeks, ½ lb. tomatoes, ¾ lb. of potatoes, 1½ oz. butter, a little cream, chervil or parsley.

Melt the butter in a heavy saucepan; before it has bubbled put in the finely sliced leeks; let them just soften in the butter. Half the success of the soup depends upon this first operation. If the butter burns or the leeks brown instead of just melting the flavour will be spoilt.

Add the roughly chopped tomatoes; again let them cook until they start to give out their juice. Add the peeled and diced potato, a seasoning of salt and two lumps of sugar. Cover with 1¼ pints of water. After the soup comes to the boil let it simmer steadily but not too fast for 25 minutes. Put it through the food mill, twice if necessary. Return the purée to the rinsed-out saucepan. When it is hot, add about 4 oz. of cream. In warm weather it is advisable to first bring this to the boil, as if it is not quite fresh it is liable to curdle when it makes contact with the acid of the tomatoes. Immediately before serving stir in a little chervil or very finely chopped parsley. Enough for four good helpings.

For all its simplicity and cheapness this is a lovely soup, in which you taste butter, cream and each vegetable, and personally I think it would be a mistake to add anything to it in the way of individual fantasies. It should not, however, be thicker than thin cream, and if it has come out too solid the addition of a little milk or water will do no harm.

The chef's soup known as *potage Solférino* is based on this purée of tomatoes, leeks and potatoes but is complicated, needlessly to my mind, with a final addition of little pieces of french beans and tiny marbles of potatoes scooped from large ones with a special implement.

POTAGE CRESSONNIÈRE À LA CRÈME
CREAM OF WATERCRESS AND POTATO SOUP

A richer version of the potato and watercress soups found in household cookery all over France.

Peel 1 lb. of potatoes and cut them into even sizes but not too small, or they will become watery. Even so elementary a dish as potato soup is all the better for attention to the small details. Boil them in 2½ pints of salted water, adding the stalks of a bunch of watercress. Keep the leaves for later. As soon as the potatoes are quite soft, after about 25 minutes, sieve the whole contents of the pan through the food mill, using the medium mesh.Mix a tablespoon of rice flour (*crème de riz*) or potato flour (*fécule*) to a paste with a little of the soup; add this to the rest, heat gently, and simmer for 25 minutes; sieve again, this time through the fine mesh. The result should be quite a smooth cream, more cohered than the usual potato soup in which the potatoes always tend to separate from the liquid. Before serving add a pinch of nutmeg, about 2 table-spoons of the finely chopped watercress leaves and a good measure of cream, say about ¼ pint. The result is a soup of the delicate colouring and creamy texture of so many of the dishes which charmed me when I first experienced French cooking with a Norman family. Plenty for four.

POTAGE CRÉCY

CARROT SOUP (1)

¾ lb. carrots, 1 large potato, 1 shallot or half a small onion, 1 oz. butter, 1 pint veal, chicken or vegetable stock, or water if no stock is available, seasoning, parsley and chervil if possible.

Scrape the carrots, shred them on a coarse grater, put them together with the chopped shallot and the peeled and diced potato in a thick pan with the melted butter. Season with salt, pepper, a scrap of sugar. Cover the pan, and leave over a very low flame for about 15 minutes, until the carrots have almost melted to a purée. Pour over the stock, and simmer another 15 minutes. Sieve, return the purée to the pan, see that the seasoning is correct, add a little chopped parsley and some leaves of chervil. Enough for three.

Sometimes boiled rice is served separately with Crécy soup, which makes it pretty substantial. Fried breadcrumbs or small dice of fried potatoes are alternatives.

POTAGE CRÉCY

CARROT SOUP (2)

This is a slight variation of the above recipe, and made in a larger quantity.

Prepare 1 lb. of carrots, 4 medium-sized potatoes and 2 chopped shallots as for the previous soup, and stew them in 1½ oz. butter in the same way. Add salt and 2 small lumps of sugar. Add 2 pints of stock, or half stock and half water. Cook until carrots and potatoes are quite soft and then sieve them or purée them in the blender. Do not make too smooth a purée; there should be perceptible little pieces of vegetable in the soup.

Return the soup to the saucepan, heat it up, and if it is too thick add more stock or water; taste for seasoning; stir in a good large lump of butter (its very buttery flavour is part of the charm of this soup) and some very, very finely chopped parsley. This will serve six people.

For both these soups it is of course important to have very good quality carrots, and both the taste and the colour of the soup will depend on this, and will vary accordingly. Young carrots will give a clear bright orange colour and a sweet flavour; later in the season the full-grown carrots will give a yellow soup and will probably need more sugar in the seasoning. The little stumpy French carrots called *carottes nantaises demi-longues* have an intense flavour all their own; but when carrots are old and cracked and woody in the centre they will not make a good soup at all, so it is not worth spending the time and the trouble on it.

The consistency of the soup depends to a certain extent upon the quality of the potatoes, which makes it almost impossible to give an exact quantity for the stock.

POTAGE BONNE FEMME

This old-fashioned French soup is the cheapest and one of the nicest of all vegetable soups.

1 lb. potatoes, 3 carrots, 2 large leeks, 1½ oz. butter, 2 pints water, seasoning. To finish the soup, a little cream, parsley, or chervil when available.

Melt the butter in your soup pan, put in the cleaned and finely sliced leeks and the diced carrots. Let them get thoroughly hot and saturated with the butter; add the peeled and diced potatoes, the water, a little salt, a lump or two of sugar. Cook steadily but not at a gallop for 25 to 30 minutes. Sieve through the finest mesh of the *mouli*, twice if necessary. Taste for seasoning, and when ready to serve add the cream, and parsley or chervil chopped very, very finely. Enough for four.

The carrots are not essential to the soup, but they add a little extra flavour and colour.

CRÈME FLAMANDE

CREAM OF ONION AND POTATO SOUP

½ lb. potatoes, 1 large leek, 2 large onions, a few sprigs of parsley, 3 oz. of single cream, butter.

Cut all the vegetables except one of the large onions into large pieces and simmer them in 2 pints of water with seasonings, until quite soft. Sieve them, and return to the pan. Slice the second onion very finely, and melt it in butter. Don't let it brown; when it is pale yellow and quite soft, add it to the soup, with its butter, and simmer 10 minutes. Add the boiling cream.

This soup may not sound much, but it is extraordinarily good, and makes five or six helpings.

POTAGE AUX HARICOTS BLANCS ET À L'OSEILLE
HARICOT BEAN AND SORREL SOUP

$\frac{1}{4}$ lb. sorrel, 6 lettuce leaves, 1 oz. butter, $\frac{1}{2}$ pint chicken or vegetable stock, $\frac{1}{4}$ lb. dried white haricot beans, 4 tablespoons cream, salt.

Cook the previously soaked beans in $2\frac{1}{2}$ pints water until they are quite soft. Meanwhile melt the washed sorrel and lettuce leaves in butter, and cover the pan until they are soft. Add the stock and simmer 10 minutes.

When the haricot beans are ready, drain and sieve them with the sorrel mixture. Add to the purée enough of the liquid from the beans to thin the soup to the right consistency, and stock or more water if it is still too thick. When it is hot and ready to serve stir in, very cautiously, the cream, previously boiled and slightly reduced. Ample helpings for four.

Watercress makes an admirable alternative to sorrel, so rarely obtainable in England. A small bunch will be enough, for stalks as well as leaves can be used. It will, of course, produce a soup of a rather different flavour, peppery instead of acid, but many people will prefer this.

POTAGE DE LENTILLES A L'OSEILLE
LENTIL AND SORREL SOUP

Cook $\frac{1}{4}$ lb. of previously soaked green or brown lentils in $2\frac{1}{2}$ pints of water until the lentils are quite tender, adding salt only towards the end. Add about $\frac{1}{4}$ lb. of sorrel, washed, chopped and cooked in butter; sieve the whole mixture. Heat up, and if too thick add more water or, better, a little meat stock; taste for seasoning—a little sugar may be necessary. Stir in a good lump of butter before serving. Enough for four.

As with the haricot and lentil soup, watercress may quite successfully be used instead of the sorrel.

POTAGE AUX CHAMPIGNONS À LA BRESSANE

MUSHROOM SOUP

This is an old-fashioned way of making mushroom soup in which bread rather than flour is used for the slight amount of thickening needed. It is a soup with a very fine flavour, but it does need some sort of mild chicken, veal or beef stock.

For ¾ lb. of mushrooms the other ingredients are 2 oz. of butter, garlic, parsley, nutmeg, a thick slice of bread, 1¾ pints of stock, 3 to 4 oz. of cream, seasonings.

Rinse the mushrooms in cold water and wipe them dry and free of grit with a soft damp cloth. Do not peel them or remove the stalks. Cut them in small pieces. Melt the butter in a heavy soup saucepan, put in the mushrooms and let them soften; when the moisture starts to run add a very small piece of chopped garlic, a tablespoon of chopped parsley, a little salt, freshly milled pepper, grated nutmeg or mace, and let the mushrooms continue to stew in the butter for several minutes.

A thick slice of crustless white bread should have been soaked in a little of the stock while the mushrooms were being prepared. Now squeeze out the moisture and add the bread to the mushrooms. Stir until the bread amalgamates with the mushrooms. Now add the stock, and cook for about 15 minutes until the mushrooms are quite soft. Put the soup through the coarse mesh of the *mouli*, then through the next finest one. Or better still, sidestep these two operations by blending the soup in the electric liquidiser. You will not get the thick or smooth purée usually associated with mushroom soup, but rather a mixture of the consistency of thin cream broken by all the minuscule particles of the mushrooms. Return it to the rinsed-out saucepan and when it is reheated add the boiling cream and another tablespoon of parsley, this time chopped very fine indeed. These quantities should make enough for four.

POTAGE DE CÈPES

DRIED MUSHROOM SOUP

A useful stand-by soup. Stock is needed, and if necessary this can be from either a meat or chicken *bouillon* cube, but the ideal is stock made from the carcase and giblets of a duck. For each pint of stock the other ingredients are ½ oz. of dried cèpes (usually called dried mushrooms; Italian are the best), a tomato and a crushed clove of garlic. Cream or eggs or Parmesan cheese or parsley and ham.

Soak the dried cèpes in cold water to cover for 10–15 minutes; drain them, put them with the garlic and chopped tomato into the stock, cover the saucepan and simmer very gently, preferably in the oven, which will cause less evaporation of the liquid than direct heat, for about an hour, until the cèpes are absolutely soft. Strain the soup and discard the cèpes; their flavour has all gone into the stock.

The soup can now be enriched with three or four tablespoons of cream or with grated Parmesan cheese stirred into it just before serving, or with a thickening of egg yolks beaten with a little lemon juice. Or it can be served as it is with the addition of a little finely chopped ham and parsley.

POTAGE DE MARRONS DAUPHINOIS

CHESTNUT SOUP

To skin and peel chestnuts, score them across on the rounded side, and put them in a baking tin in a gentle oven (gas No. 3, 330 deg. F.) for 15 to 20 minutes, or else drop them in boiling water and boil them for about 8 minutes. Extract a few at a time, so that the rest do not get cool, for then they become difficult to peel. Squeeze each chestnut so that the shell cracks, and then with the aid of a small knife it is quite easy to remove both skins. For this soup you need 1 lb. of chestnuts.

Prepare a vegetable broth from 2 carrots, 2 leeks, a small head of celery with the leaves, 1 onion, 2 or 3 sprigs of parsley, all cleaned, sliced and melted in 1½ oz. of butter in a heavy saucepan. When the vegetables soften and begin to look transparent pour in 2 pints of cold water, season with salt, cover the pan, and simmer very gently for one hour. Now pour off half the liquid, and in this stew the shelled and skinned chestnuts until they are quite soft. Sieve, then thin the resulting purée with the rest of the strained vegetable broth. When heating up add a teacupful of hot milk, and see that the seasoning is correct. Serves four.

Although all this may sound a lot of fuss to make a chestnut soup, it is well worth the trouble.

The vegetables cooked for the stock should not be wasted. Sieved and thinned with milk, a lump of butter and some chopped parsley added immediately before serving, they make an excellent soup for next day.

POTAGE MOUSSELINE DE CÉLERIS

MOUSSELINE OF CELERY SOUP

Make a chicken broth in the usual way with a chicken carcase, the feet and giblets, an onion, a carrot and a heart of celery cut into small pieces.

Simmer very gently with water to cover for about an hour. Strain. Measure the broth, and allow 1 egg yolk to each ½ pint. Beat the yolks very well in a bowl, with a few drops of lemon juice. Pour a little of the heated broth over the eggs, whisking all the time with a fork. Return this to the rest of the hot broth in the saucepan and heat again, stirring all the time until the soup is hot and slightly thickened, but do not let it boil.

Those who like the aniseed flavour of fennel will find that Florentine fennel instead of the celery makes a most delicious and unusual soup.

POTAGE CRÈME DE CÉLERI-RAVE

Scrub a celeriac weighing ½ to ¾ lb. and boil it until tender (about 45 minutes: test with a skewer, which should go in easily). When cool, peel and sieve it, mix it thoroughly with a purée made from ½ lb. of potatoes cooked in 2 pints of salted water and sieved with their liquid. Heat up, thin with a cupful of milk, season well, add either a good lump of butter or a little cream before serving. Enough for four.

SUMMER SOUPS

In France, after the 14th of July, a great many people take advantage of their holidays to give their livers, about which the French are so obsessed, a little rest. The watering places are filled with people taking cures and in seaside, mountain and country establishments the meals, at any rate the evening meals, are apt to be composed of light and refreshing soups, plainly cooked meat or fish, and only a moderate amount of salads and fruit; and just before bedtime a tisane or infusion of lime flowers or some other scented, calming herb.

The two following recipes are typical of the sort of soups which one might get under these circumstances. The habit of serving soup iced, except for consommé, has not really spread to the country places of France. But even in hot weather a hot soup, so long as it is not too substantial, can be quite refreshing.

POTAGE DE TOMATES ESTIVAL
LIGHT TOMATO SOUP

Slice 2 lb. of ripe juicy tomatoes into a saucepan; add half an onion finely sliced and 2 teaspoons of salt. Cook with the lid on the pan, but without any liquid or butter, for 10 to 15 minutes, until the tomatoes are quite soft. Put through the food mill. In a bowl dilute 1 tablespoon of ground rice with a little cold milk. Stir this into the purée. Heat gently, and gradually add about 1½ pints of hot milk, or half milk and half light chicken or veal broth. Cook very gently, stirring often, for about 15 minutes until all traces of the little white globules formed by the ground rice have disappeared. It should be quite smooth, but if it is not, press it once more through a fine sieve. Stir in some very finely chopped parsley or chervil. Properly made, this very simple soup is most refreshing and delicate, but it can, if you prefer, be enriched with a little cream or a lump of butter stirred in before it is served, though it should remain on the thin side. Makes four to six helpings.

POTAGE DU PÈRE TRANQUILLE
LETTUCE SOUP

The Père Tranquille seems to have been a somewhat mysterious Capuchin monk, but the name of this soup is also a reference to the supposed soporific effects of lettuce. It is a trouble to make but useful for those who have more lettuces in their gardens than they can eat as salads. Ordinary round or cabbage lettuces are the best ones to use.

Two large whole lettuces, or the outside leaves of 3, about 1 pint of mild chicken or veal broth and 1 pint of milk, seasonings, a little butter or cream.

Cut the carefully washed lettuce leaves into fine ribbons; put them in the saucepan with just enough broth to cover them. Let them simmer gently, adding a little more liquid, until they are quite soft. Sieve them, or purée them in the electric blender. Return the purée to the pan, gradually add the rest of the broth and enough milk to make a thin cream. Season with salt if necessary, a lump or two of sugar and a scrap of nutmeg. Before serving stir in either a small lump of butter or a little thick fresh cream. Makes five or six helpings.

Both these soups can be, and usually are, poured over thin slices of French bread baked pale golden in the oven, but personally I prefer them without. To make a smoother soup, sieve it again after the liquid has been added.

CRÈME VICHYSSOISE GLACÈE
ICED POTATO AND LEEK SOUP

It is interesting to follow the way French recipes develop as they are carried round the world by French cooks, emigrants and all those thousands of people who have enjoyed French cooking in its native land and who on returning home have reproduced various dishes with the modifications suitable to the climate, the conditions and the local products of another country.

As I have already observed, it is rare to come across iced soups of the vegetable purée variety in France, and *crème vichyssoise* is, as is well known, an American soup. But it was evolved by a Frenchman, Louis Diat, for forty-one years *chef des cuisines* at the Ritz-Carlton in New York. Based on the ancient formula for *potage bonne femme*, the leek and potato soup known to every French housewife, the iced *vichyssoise* was served for the first time by Louis Diat at the Ritz-Carlton in the summer of 1917, and has since become famous all over the United States. Diat's recipe makes a delicious soup, its sole disadvantage to English readers being that it is almost impossible to obtain leeks in the summer months, the time when one would most naturally think of serving iced soups. But I expect it won't be long before leeks, like celery, are grown at seasons of the year other than those we have come to expect, so here is the recipe:

'Finely slice the white part of 4 leeks and 1 medium onion and brown very slightly in 2 ounces of sweet butter. Then add 5 medium potatoes, also sliced finely.

'Add one quart of water or chicken broth and one tablespoon of salt and boil from 35 to 40 minutes. Crush and rub through a fine strainer.

'When the soup is cold add 1 cup of heavy cream. Chill thoroughly before serving, at which time finely chopped chives may be added. This quantity is sufficient for eight people.'

NOTE: The American quart is 32 oz., or a little under 1¾ English pints; and the American measuring cup contains 8 oz., or half the American pint. In American kitchen terms sweet butter means unsalted butter.

In spite of it seeming, under the circumstances, rather impertinent to criticise M. Diat's recipe, I cannot help remarking that the soup seems better to me without the onion, so I substitute another couple of leeks instead. Also I use an extra ¼ pint of water to cook the soup and correspondingly less cream, for to my taste 8 oz. makes the soup too cloying.

POTAGE CRÉME DE PETITS POIS
CREAM OF GREEN PEA SOUP

This is one of the nicest, freshest and simplest of summer soups. Those who claim not to be able to taste the difference between frozen and fresh peas will perhaps find it instructive to try this dish. Not that a very excellent soup cannot be made with frozen peas, but when fresh peas are at the height of their season, full grown but still young and sweet, the difference in intensity of flavour and of scent is very marked indeed.

Quantities are 1¾ lb. of peas, the heart of a cabbage lettuce, ¼ lb. (yes, ¼ lb.) of butter, 1¾ pints of water, salt and sugar.

Melt the butter in your soup saucepan; put in the lettuce heart washed and cut up into fine strips with a silver knife; add the shelled peas, 2 teaspoons of salt and a lump or two of sugar. Cover the pan; cook gently for 10 minutes until the peas are thoroughly soaked in the butter. Add the water; cook at a moderate pace until the peas are quite tender. Sieve them, or purée them in the electric liquidiser. Return to the pan and heat up. A little extra seasoning may be necessary but nothing else at all. Enough for four ample helpings.

Fish Soups

SOUPE DE POISSONS DE MARSEILLE
MARSEILLAIS FISH SOUP

This is a typical Provençal fish soup made from all sorts of the little shining red, pink, brown, yellow and silver-striped fish which one can buy by the basketful from the market stalls in the Vieux Port (although much of the Vieux Port quarter was destroyed by the Germans in the last war the fish stalls are still there). I don't think it is possible to make the soup without all these odd little Mediterranean fish, which are too bony to be used for anything except *la soupe*, and I have not attempted to cook it since I lived on the Mediterranean shores, but still the method, which was shouted above the hubbub of the market to me many years ago by the fishwife at a market stall, is worth recording.

For six people you buy rather over 2 lb. of fish[1] and a couple of dozen of the very small spider crabs they call *favouilles*. In your earthenware or copper soup-pot you heat a few tablespoons of olive oil, and in this you melt the sliced white part of 2 leeks or an onion, adding a couple of chopped, large, ripe tomatoes, 2 cloves of garlic, a sprig or two of fennel and of parsley. Then you put in all your fish and let them take colour before adding a good 3½ pints of water, a seasoning of salt and pepper, and a good pinch of saffron. Let all this cook together about 15 minutes, then put the whole thing through a fine sieve lined with a muslin or cheese-cloth, so that none of the little bones can get through into the

[1] These should include miniature *rascasses*, too small to be of use for the *bouillabaisse*, little rock fish called *rouquiers* and *girelles* and a piece of sea-eel.

broth. Pound the fish a little with a wooden pestle so that the very essence gets through into the broth. Return the broth to the saucepan, see that the seasoning is right (the soup should be rather highly spiced) and in it cook some short, chunky pasta, about ¼ lb.

As soon as the pasta is cooked, serve your soup very hot, with grated Parmesan or Gruyère cheese separately if you like.

POTAGE DE POISSONS À LA NÎMOISE
NÎMOIS FISH SOUP

Durand, the famous Nîmois chef, gives the formula for this soup in his book *Le Cuisinier Durand*, published in 1830. It is enriched with eggs and, at the last minute, with a mixture of *aïoli*, the garlic mayonnaise of Provence—in fact it is a Languedoc version of the Provençal *bourride*.

Ask your fishmonger for 2 or 3 cod or halibut heads; he will probably sell them for quite a small sum, and they are good value, containing plenty of white flesh, and their gelatinous quality gives body to the broth. Other ingredients are an onion, a carrot, and a couple of large leeks, 2 large tomatoes, a clove of garlic, parsley and whatever other herbs you happen to have available—tarragon, fennel, lemon thyme, plus olive oil and seasonings. For the thickening of the soup you need egg yolks, garlic, lemon juice and olive oil.

Slice the cleaned vegetables and melt them in 2 tablespoons of olive oil in a large soup-pot. When all the vegetables, including the tomatoes, have softened, put in the fish heads, and the herbs tied together in a bunch. Cover with 3 to 3½ pints of water. Add a tablespoon of salt. Bring slowly to the boil, and thereafter simmer for 30 to 40 minutes. Strain the broth, and separate as much flesh from the heads and bones as possible. There will be about 2 good cupfuls, and this is set aside for another dish.

For 3 pints of broth, which will amply serve six people, beat 6 egg yolks—these are Durand's quantities; I find 3 or 4 quite sufficient—with a little lemon juice and a ladle of the hot broth. Add this mixture to the broth in the saucepan and stir until the soup is quite hot and has thickened, but do not let it actually boil. Off the fire, stir in 3 or 4 tablespoons of *aïoli*, which is prepared by pounding a clove or two of garlic in a mortar, stirring an egg yolk with it, and then adding 4 or 5 tablespoons of olive oil, exactly as for a mayonnaise. Serve your soup as soon as the *aïoli* is added.

I commend this soup without reservation to anyone who likes garlic. For those who do not, the alternative is to cook 2 or 3 tablespoons of rice in the strained broth, then add the egg yolks as above, and a good deal of extra lemon juice. This makes a soup similar to the well-known Greek *avgolémono* (egg and lemon), usually made on a basis of chicken broth.

LA SOUPE AUX MOULES

MUSSEL SOUP

Having scraped and cleaned about 4 pints of mussels, put them in a saucepan with a couple of chopped shallots, a little garlic and chopped parsley and ½ pint of water or ¼ pint each of white wine and water. As soon as the mussels have opened take them out, shell them, and filter the liquid which comes from them, together with that left in the saucepan, through a cloth.

Heat a little olive oil or butter in your soup saucepan and in this melt the white part of 2 leeks, a couple of skinned tomatoes and a little piece of garlic, all finely chopped. Make up the filtered mussel liquid to 1¾ pints with water. Add this to the vegetables in the saucepan. When it comes to the boil throw in 2 tablespoons of rice and boil gently until the rice is cooked. Sieve half the soup or purée it in the electric blender. Mix this with the rest. Heat up, add the mussels, taste for seasoning, and simmer gently for 5 more minutes until the mussels are hot. Enough for four.

POTAGE CRÈME NORMANDE

NORMAN CREAM OF FISH SOUP

A 6 to 8 oz. slice of cod or other white fish, ½ pint of boiled, unshelled prawns or a small crawfish (*langouste*) tail, a carrot, an onion, a tomato, a small piece of celery, a clove of garlic, a small glass of cider or white wine, 2 heaped dessertspoons of soft white breadcrumbs, herbs and seasonings, nutmeg or mace, ¼ pint of cream.

Shell the prawns, put the white fish, the shells of the prawns, the vegetables, garlic, fresh or dried herbs (fennel, marjoram, parsley), and cider or wine in a saucepan with salt, pepper and 2 pints of water. Simmer for 25 minutes or so. Strain, pressing the fish and vegetables against the sides of the sieve so as to extract the maximum of juice. Into the saucepan put the prawns and breadcrumbs pounded together to a paste with two or three spoonfuls of the stock; gradually add the rest of the stock, and simmer for 15 minutes or so, stirring frequently. Season with pepper and nutmeg, and more salt if necessary. At this stage the soup still looks rather unpromising; but when the cream, boiled a minute or two in a separate pan, is added, all will be well. Before serving, stir in a little very finely cut parsley. Those who like a thicker, more substantial soup, can add the yolks of 2 eggs, as for the celery soup on page 172. Or the water in which rice has boiled can be used instead of plain water to make the stock.

POTAGE CRÈME DE POTIRON AUX CREVETTES
CREAM OF PUMPKIN AND SHRIMP SOUP

Peel a 2 lb. slice of pumpkin, throw away the seeds and the cottony centre, cut the flesh into small pieces, salt and pepper them, and put them into a thick saucepan with a stick of celery cut in pieces. Cover them with 1½ pints of milk previously boiled, and 1 pint of mild stock or water, and simmer until the pumpkin is quite soft, about 30 minutes. Sieve the mixture; return the purée to a clean pan. Mash or pound in a mortar 4 oz. of peeled prawns or shrimps (buttered shrimps will do), adding a few drops of lemon juice. Dilute with a little of the pumpkin purée, add this mixture to the soup, simmer gently for 10 minutes or so, sieve again if the soup is not quite smooth, taste for seasoning and, when reheating, thin with a little more hot milk or stock if necessary. Immediately before serving stir in a good lump of butter. Ample for six.

Pumpkin is a vegetable which tends to go sour very quickly, so this soup should be used up on the day, or day after, it is made.

Les Œufs, et les Hors-d'œuvre Chauds

Eggs, cheese dishes and hot hors-d'œuvre

'THEY reckon 685 ways of dressing eggs in the French kitchen; we hope our half-dozen recipes give sufficient variety for the English kitchen.' Doctor William Kitchiner, who wrote these words in *The Cook's Oracle*, round about 1821, therewith betrays himself as a pretty smug fellow.

For the life of me I cannot see why, if our neighbours 21 miles across the Channel have 685 ways of cooking eggs, we should have to make do with six. Six recipes would no more than cover the basic ways of egg-cookery common to all countries, but Dr. Kitchiner was certainly right in so far as it is important to understand these methods thoroughly before embarking on the 679 remaining variations.

'Have ready twelve freshly poached eggs,' says the cookery book, and with a shudder you turn over the page, knowing that, allowing for disasters, those twelve eggs will probably turn into twenty and that your kitchen will be a charnel house of eggshells and a shambles of running egg yolks. Or 'shell eight *œufs mollets*,' they say, 'lay each in a puff pastry case and mask with an hollandaise sauce. Pour a cordon of melted meat glaze round each egg and brown with a salamander.' And one begins to agree with old Dr. Kitchiner. For elaborate dishes of this sort are not really to be recommended for household cookery. Leave them to the restaurant kitchens where there is a *chef-pâtissier* to prepare the pastry cases, a larder cook to provide the meat glaze, a sauce cook ready with the hollandaise, and half a dozen kitchen boys to clear away, to say nothing of the waiters ready to rush it from the kitchen to the tables.

There are still plenty of lovely egg dishes of a much simpler kind to be made at home; with constant practice and given the time, it is perfectly possible to poach a few eggs successfully; an omelette is very easily made, in spite of all the talk about light hands and heavy frying pans; and once you know the trick, the shelling of *œufs mollets* is quite easy, provided you have a steady hand.

I shall try to explain these things, and others connected with the successful manipulation of eggs, for they are well worth the practice needed and the time and money you must spend. From unsuccessful attempts there is much to be learnt, so one must count an occasional wasted egg or failed soufflé as profit rather than loss. Egg dishes have a kind of elegance, a freshness, an allure, which sets them quite apart from any other kind of food, so that it becomes a great pleasure to be able to cook them properly and to serve them in just the right condition.

Eggs in their own right, as well as all those allied dishes such as the onion tarts of Alsace, the cream and bacon *quiches* of Lorraine and all the various cheese and egg, potato and cream, and hot pastry confections of the different provinces of France which come under the heading of hot hors-d'œuvre make the best possible dishes to serve as a first course at luncheon on the occasions when something hot is required. But it cannot be claimed that these are particularly *light* dishes. Eggs, and especially eggs with cheese or cream, are very filling. So if you are starting with a soufflé, or an onion tart, or a *pipérade*, it is best to make the second course something not too rich, and certainly not one requiring an egg or cream sauce.

ŒUFS À LA COQUE

BOILED EGGS

Although eggs are cooked in such a variety of exquisite ways by French cooks, the ordinary boiled egg is not their strong point. One would be

lucky, I think, to get boiled eggs as good as those described by Henry
James after a luncheon at Bourg-en-Bresse, which was composed entirely
of boiled eggs and bread and butter. 'They were so good that I am ashamed
to say how many of them I consumed.' An *œuf à la coque* in fact usually
means, in France, an egg plunged in boiling water, taken out again,
and there you are. But Madame St. Ange, thorough in this matter as in
all others, gives no less than five different methods of boiling an egg in
her incomparable *Livre de Cuisine*, starting off her chapter on eggs with
the remark that a 'true boiled egg must have been laid the day it is to be
eaten.' Not an easy rule to observe, but certainly few people will quarrel
with the rule that an egg more than three days old had better be cooked
some other way.

Here are the Saint-Ange methods, summarised:

(1) Allowing ¾ pint of water for 2 eggs, bring it to the boil in a fairly
deep saucepan. Off the fire, lower the eggs into the water in a tablespoon.
Cover the pan and cook 4 minutes without further boiling.

(2) Put the eggs into a saucepan; cover them plentifully with cold
water. When the water reaches a full boil, the eggs are cooked. Remove
them at once.

(3) Bring a saucepan of water to the boil; remove from the fire to
put in the eggs. Cover the pan. Put back on the fire. From the moment
the water comes to the boil again allow 3 minutes. If the eggs are very
large leave them a further minute off the fire.

(4) Plunge the eggs into the pan of boiling water. Taking it immediately from the fire, keep it closely covered for 10 minutes.

(5) Plunge the eggs into boiling water. Cover; leave *one* minute
over the fire. Remove from the fire and leave 5 minutes.

From all these alternatives everyone should surely be able to choose
that which suits them best. Personally, I prefer systems No. 4 or 5,
which produce boiled eggs with nice creamy whites. With the first
method they are insufficiently cooked for my taste, and methods No. 2
and 3 are useful if you are in a hurry but do not produce such lovely
whites.

ŒUFS MOLLET

There seems to be no really adequate translation of the word *mollet* in
this context. Soft eggs mean to us soft-boiled breakfast eggs; 'tender
eggs,' as I have seen them translated, is explanatory enough but somehow
sounds odd. Perhaps it is best just to leave them in the French. They are
cooked in boiling water until they are of a consistency midway between a

soft-boiled and a hard-boiled egg; that is to say that the whites are quite set, the yolks still just runny. For the average egg 5 minutes is the exact time to allow from the moment the eggs are plunged into boiling water; as soon as they are taken out cool them under the running cold tap to prevent further cooking. For very small or very large eggs the timing must obviously be slightly adjusted. Owing to the time lag between the lowering of the first egg and, say, the fifth or sixth into the water, it is perhaps easier to pour the boiling water over the eggs in the saucepan, allowing for a few extra seconds' cooking while the water comes back to the boil. Alternatively, there exists a useful utensil, usually obtainable at Woolworths as well as at good kitchen stores, in which 4 to 6 eggs are placed, the whole gadget being lowered into a deep pan of boiling water, so that the risk of the eggs cracking is minimised, and the timing greatly facilitated.

Once shelled as described below, the eggs can be kept ready, if they are to be served with a hot sauce, in a bowl of warm water. *Œufs mollets* are suitable, in fact preferable in many ways, for most dishes in which poached eggs are generally used, especially for eggs in aspic jelly.

To shell hard-boiled or *mollet* eggs, they should be plunged immediately they are cooked into cold water, to arrest the cooking, and to make them cool enough to handle. If it is not convenient to shell them at once they can be left until they are quite cold, but on the whole it is easier to shell them while they are still warm. Many people find this quite a difficult operation, particularly with *mollet* eggs.

The best way to set about it is to tap the egg gently all over, as soon as it can be handled, with the back of a knife, until the whole egg is mapped over with fine cracks. Hold the egg in the palm of one hand, and with the other start peeling, and both inner skin and shell should come off quite easily as you turn the egg carefully over. Of course, in the case of *mollet* eggs caution must be exercised or they may break, so do not try to do this operation in a hurry. Take your time over it, doing it with care and deliberation.

If there are little particles of shell adhering to the egg, it is easier to remove them by dipping the egg in cold water rather than picking them off by hand.

ŒUFS MOLLETS À LA CRÉCY

Scrape and shred 5 large carrots, melt a good lump of butter in a heavy pan and in this stew the carrots, covered, until they are quite soft. The flame must be kept very low or the carrots will burn. In the meantime prepare ¼ pint of thick béchamel sauce and cook 4 *mollet* eggs—that is, eggs boiled exactly 5 minutes, cooled, and shelled. Or, if you prefer, poach the eggs.

Season the carrots, place a spoonful in the bottom of each individual small egg dish, put the egg on the top and cover with the béchamel. Sprinkle very lightly with breadcrumbs and a little melted butter. Put the egg dishes on a baking sheet at the top of a very hot oven for 4 to 5 minutes.

LES ŒUFS DURS

HARD-BOILED EGGS

On the whole, the most satisfactory and the simplest way to hard-boil eggs is to put them in a saucepan in which they just about fit (you don't want two eggs rattling about in a huge saucepan), cover them completely with cold water, bring them gently to the boil and then cook them 7 to 10 minutes. Drain off the hot water and run plenty of cold water over them so that they stop cooking at once. By this method the yolks should emerge yellow and not too crumbly and without that sinister ring of grey round the edge.

Stuffed hard-boiled eggs, however carefully and subtly made the stuffing, nearly always finish up by being dull. I have tried many sound French and other recipes for such dishes, and invariably found them lacking in charm; with a sauce they become stodgy; without one, dry. If it is a question of improvising in an emergency, I think it is preferable to serve hard-boiled eggs quite plain as a salad, with a vinaigrette dressing, with mayonnaise, or perhaps heated up in a tomato sauce, thereby dispensing with the fiddling jobs of mashing up sardines or anchovies, taking the yolks out of the eggs, putting them back again, decorating the dish and all the rest of it.

Recipes for *œufs mayonnaise* and other cold egg dishes will be found in the hors-d'œuvre chapter.

ŒUFS À LA TRIPE

(*Also called Œufs à la Lyonnaise*)

In a thick frying pan, stew ½ lb. very finely sliced mild onions in 1½ oz. butter until they turn pale yellow; season them with salt, pepper and nutmeg, stir in a dessertspoon of flour and, when it has amalgamated, pour in ½ pint of milk. Cook gently for 15 to 20 minutes. If the sauce becomes too thick, add a little more milk or cream. Carefully incorporate 4 thickly sliced hard-boiled eggs and shake the pan without stirring until the eggs are hot. At the last minute add a good lump of butter cut into little pieces and, when it has melted, transfer to a hot serving dish. A silver entrée dish, it used to be, until such things were replaced with fireproof glass, for this dish was at one time immensely popular in England as a first course at luncheon. It was also known under the name of Convent Eggs, the other alternative name of *œufs à la lyonnaise* being due to the presence of the onions in the sauce, since onions are associated by popular tradition with the cookery of Lyon.

ŒUFS DURS SOUBISE

HARD-BOILED EGGS WITH ONION AND CREAM SAUCE

Quite often in cookery one comes across two or more dishes containing almost identical ingredients and seasonings, but which yet turn out to be quite different in taste and appearance. *Œufs à la tripe* and *œufs durs soubise* provide one such example, the latter having, to my mind, greater charm and finesse.

For the sauce: ½ lb. onions weighed when peeled, 1½ oz. butter, ¼ pint of veal or chicken stock or milk, 1 scant dessertspoon of flour, salt, freshly ground white pepper, nutmeg and 2 or 3 tablespoons of cream.

Melt the finely sliced onions in the butter; when they are transparent and very pale yellow, after about 7 minutes, stir in the flour; add the warmed stock or milk and seasoning. Simmer gently for 15 minutes until the onions are quite soft. Sieve. Return the purée to the saucepan and if it is too thick add a little more stock; if too thin, let it reduce a little. If you like, it can be flavoured with a teaspoon of French mustard.

Hard boil 4 eggs, shell them while still warm, cut them in quarters lengthways, arrange them in circles in a round shallow fireproof egg dish in which they just fit. Over them pour the hot sauce, on top trickle the cream and then add a small sprinkling of very fine breadcrumbs. Put on the top shelf of a very hot oven for 5 minutes.

If you have an electric blender in which to purée the sauce, it can be made without the thickening of flour, and is all the better and lighter.

ŒUFS SUR LE PLAT, AU PLAT, AU MIROIR (1)

Œufs sur le plat are fried eggs served in the dishes in which they have cooked, shallow metal, earthenware or other fireproof utensils with a little handle at each side; butter is melted in the dishes, and the eggs, usually 2 per person, previously broken into a plate, are slid gently in.

Cover the pans, so that the eggs acquire their characteristic mirrored appearance without the business of spoonnig the whites over the yolks. Cook either on top of the stove over a low flame or in a moderate oven until the whites are set. About 4 minutes in a moderate oven should be enough, but timing depends as much upon the dish itself as upon the degree of heat. Some, such as the heavy enamel or porcelain-lined cast-iron ones, retain the heat more than thin metal ones, and the eggs continue cooking to an alarming degree after they have been taken from the fire, so this must be allowed for.

The great advantage of eggs cooked in this way is that you are always sure of getting your eggs hot; also the risk of the eggs breaking as they are transferred from pan to dish and from dish to plate is eliminated.

ŒUFS SUR LE PLAT (2)

In that beguiling book *Cooking in Ten Minutes*,[1] Dr. Edouard de Pomiane suggests a dish which is a happy compromise between *œufs sur le plat* and our own eggs and bacon, a dish much admired in France 'Take two very thin slices of bacon. Melt some butter in the fireproof dish. Lower the gas. Lay the 2 slices of bacon on the butter, cut in two so as to cover the bottom of the dish. When the fat is transparent break two eggs into the dish. Turn up the gas. The white sets immediately. Break it here and there so that the surface white also cooks. Whatever happens do not touch the yolk. As soon as the white is cooked put the dish on a plate. Salt very lightly. Pepper with discretion.'

ŒUFS SUR LE PLAT (3)

This recipe should prove very useful to those whose kitchens lack a proper supply of fireproof egg dishes, and the method certainly produces, as the author says, very good results.

'To obtain perfect *œufs sur le plat*, they must be cooked over steam. If you have a stew or some vegetables cooking, replace the lid of the saucepan with a plate, or a china dish, according to how many eggs you have to cook. Put to melt in this dish, over the steam from the saucepan, a piece of fresh butter. When it is melted, break your eggs one by one into a saucer, taking care not to break the yolks. When all the eggs are broken, slide them gently into the butter in the dish and put the saucepan lid over them. They will cook evenly, the underneath of the plate being

[1] Bruno Cassirer, Oxford. Translated by Peggie Benton.

heated by the steam, and the yolks will be covered with a transparent white veil. Salt lightly, without letting the salt fall on to the yolks.'

B. Renaudet:
Les Secrets de la Bonne Table

ŒUFS SUR LE PLAT BERCY

Two eggs per person cooked in butter in flat fireproof egg dishes, each dish garnished with 2 little fried chipolata sausages and a ring of tomato sauce made from skinned and chopped tomatoes cooked almost to a purée —3 tomatoes making ample sauce for two people. A very good and simple little dish, but all the same not so easy because of the problem of cooking the three different ingredients separately, all at the same time; so it is best to cook the sausages and the sauce first and keep them hot in the oven while you cook the eggs; and be sure to keep these covered while they are cooking so that the yolks come out with a nicely veiled appearance instead of having a hard yellow skin.

ŒUFS FRITS

By fried eggs the French usually understand eggs fried in deep fat or oil, one at a time; they puff up like fritters, are taken out with a perforated spoon and laid on a folded cloth to drain. The operation requires a little practice and dexterity, but fried like this the eggs are delicious served on a bed of spinach, potato or sorrel purée, with sausages, or with fried bread and a tomato sauce. Here are the directions given by the famous *Cuisinier Durand* of Nîmes, published in 1830.

'Break an egg into a plate; season it with salt and pepper, and put it into the frying-pan in boiling butter or oil; during the cooking tilt the handle of the frying-pan, so that the oil, flowing all to one side, completely surrounds the egg; have a care to sprinkle it with the same oil so that the white envelops the yolk, after which you remove the egg; do likewise with all the eggs you wish to fry, and when they are done, pour from the pan part of the oil; leave only enough to make a sauce; put into it a well-chopped shallot, season with salt, pepper and a thread of vinegar and pour it over the eggs.'

ŒUFS FRITS AU BEURRE NOIR

This is one of the most delicious and simple of egg dishes, but not usually practical to do for more than two or three people, for the eggs must come straight from stove to table without being kept waiting.

Fry your eggs gently in a little butter, keeping them covered. Transfer them to a very hot fireproof serving dish. Into the clean frying-pan put a dessertspoon of butter for every 2 eggs. Let it melt and when it is foaming and just turning colour, pour it over the eggs. Quickly pour a tablespoon of vinegar into the pan and let it boil. Pour this, too, over the eggs. Serve instantly.

It is important to note that any butter left in the pan in which the eggs have fried should be discarded before the fresh butter is put in (alternatively, use two pans). And in spite of its name, the second lot of butter is not cooked until it is black, but only until it is just turning a little darker brown than the shell of a hazel-nut.

LES ŒUFS POCHÉS

POACHED EGGS

Whatever foolproof instructions are given in cookery books for the poaching of eggs, most people find it a tricky task, and cannot do more than one at a time. The egg-poaching moulds which produce a sort of egg cake are not at all a satisfactory solution. After years of practice I find the two following methods the most reliable:

(1) First dip each egg in a saucepan of boiling water while you count 30 seconds. This process coagulates a thin outer layer of white nearest the shell, and when the egg is subsequently poached the rest of the white tends to spread and fly about less than when the raw egg is put straight into the water. Having carried out this first operation, boil a fresh pan of water (a sauté pan or deep frying-pan is better than a saucepan) acidulated with a few drops of vinegar. Break each egg into a saucer. When the water boils make a whirlpool in the centre by whizzing the water round with a wooden spoon. Into this slide your egg. Keep the water whirling round until it boils again. Remove the pan from the heat, cover it, and leave $2\frac{1}{2}$ to 3 minutes.

(2) Break the eggs into saucers. When the water is just at boiling point, slide in the egg. As the white starts to set, quickly, with a metal spoon roll your egg over, at least twice, so that it acquires a neat oval shape, the white wrapped round the yolk. It is not such a dangerous operation as it sounds. Then remove the pan from the heat, cover it, and leave $3\frac{1}{2}$ to 4 minutes. With this system 2 eggs can be done at once. Whatever cookery books say, it is almost impossible for amateurs to poach 6 eggs at a time by any method except that of the egg-poaching moulds.

When the eggs are ready, take them from the pan with a perforated spoon and lay them to drain on a folded cloth. Any trimming of white necessary to give the eggs an elegant appearance is done at this stage. They can be kept warm in a bowl of warm water. Although some cooks advocate the use of 'eggs of the day' for poaching, I prefer them two or three days old. The whites of true new laid eggs fly about too much. Old eggs, however, are quite useless for poaching, as the whites go tough and ropy or separate completely from the yolks, which also tend to break. As William Verral says in his *Cooks Paradise*, 1759: 'From the experience I have had, I am sure it is not in the power of the best cook in the kingdom to poach stale ones handsome, notwithstanding they may come whole out of the shell.'

The vinegar in the water helps to coagulate the white, but cooks disagree violently as to whether or not salt should be added. Which probably goes to show it does not greatly matter. I never add it myself.

ŒUFS POCHÉS À LA CRÈME ET AU GRATIN
POACHED EGGS WITH CREAM SAUCE

For the sauce, heat 1 oz. of butter in a heavy saucepan; stir in 2 dessert-spoons of flour; when this mixture is smooth add gradually a little under $\frac{1}{2}$ pint of milk; stir until you have a smooth thick sauce, season with a very little salt, pepper and nutmeg, and cook a good 10 minutes over a very low flame. Now add from 4 to 6 tablespoons of thick cream, and stir for 2 or 3 more minutes, before stirring in 3 to 4 tablespoons of grated Parmesan cheese and a good teaspoon of yellow Dijon mustard (Grey Poupon is the one I always use). Taste for seasoning; more salt may be necessary, depending upon the saltiness of the cheese.

When the sauce is ready, poach 4 eggs. While they are cooking, pour a little of the hot sauce into each of 4 little china egg ramekins. Put an egg on top; cover each completely with more sauce, to fill the ramekins. Sprinkle lightly with breadcrumbs. Put under a hot grill for about half a minute and serve immediately, bubbling hot.

LES ŒUFS DU PÊCHEUR
POACHED EGGS WITH MUSSEL STOCK

Poach your eggs in the liquor saved from *moules marinière*. Put a slice of fried bread in each buttered egg dish, put the poached eggs, one or two to each dish, on the bread, cover them with hot cream, then with grated Gruyère. Cook in a hot oven for about 3 minutes, so that the cheese, which protects the yolks of the eggs from the heat, melts without the eggs hardening.

This delicious recipe is by the famous dressmaker, Paul Poiret, from his book, *En Habillant l'Époque.*

ŒUFS POCHÉS À L'HUGUENOTE
POACHED EGGS WITH MEAT SAUCE

This is just one version of a dish once popular throughout France; it is made when there is some sort of rich juice or wine-flavoured sauce left from a *bœuf mode,* a *daube* or the Médocain recipe described on page 385.

Poached eggs are arranged on slices of bread fried in butter, olive oil or pork fat. The juice or gravy is simmered until it is reduced a little then poured round the eggs. It is an excellent dish and the same system can be used for *œufs sur le plat,* the juice being poured round the eggs when they have set.

LES ŒUFS EN COCOTTE

Eggs *en cocotte* are a cross between a poached egg and an egg *sur le plat.* They are cooked and presented in little round or oval china ramekins or *cocottes,* each large enough to hold one egg. They may be cooked on top of the stove or in the oven. On the whole, the former is the easier way. You place your little *cocottes* in water in a heavy frying-pan or sauté pan, and put a little knob of butter in each. When the water boils and the butter is melted, you slide a very fresh egg into each *cocotte,* cover the pan and cook 3 to 4 minutes. The yolks of eggs *en cocotte* should be quite soft and the whites well set.

In a London hotel where a good deal of fuss is made about the food, I once ordered eggs *en cocotte.* When they arrived, after a long wait, they were as hard as rocks. My host called for the *maître-d'hôtel* and irritably observed that a chisel rather than a spoon would have been the right implement with which to eat them. 'How were they cooked?' I asked the *maître-d'hôtel.* 'Oh, it is rather complicated,' he replied, in imitation broken English. 'First they are steamed and then they are baked.' 'I always thought *œufs en cocotte* were soft.' 'Oh no, madame; of course, you can order them soft, but properly they are hard.'

By such fake expertise are we poor English bedevilled into believing reams of rubbish about French cookery.

LES ŒUFS EN COCOTTE À LA CRÈME

Proceed exactly as above, and when the whites of the eggs have started to set, pour a tablespoon of thick cream into each little ramekin. Cover the pan again and finish cooking. This is one of the most delicious egg dishes ever invented, but it is rare to get it properly done.

LES ŒUFS EN COCOTTE AU JUS

When you have a little delicious natural gravy left from a roast, a bird or a rich stew, cook your eggs as above and pour a little of this gravy on top of the eggs, taking care not to cover the yolks.

ŒUFS EN COCOTTE PASCAL

For 4 eggs prepare a sauce as follows: chop very finely indeed a little bunch of parsley, leaves only, with, if available, a few tarragon leaves and chives. There should be about 3 good tablespoons altogether when the herbs are chopped. Stir in 2 teaspoons of rather strong French mustard, a seasoning of salt and freshly milled pepper, then 4 tablespoons of thick fresh cream. Heat the sauce and pour it bubbling over the eggs which have been cooked in 4 little buttered ramekins standing in a pan of simmering water, covered, for 3 to 4 minutes. Serve quickly.

OMELETTES

As everybody knows, there is only one infallible recipe for the perfect omelette: your own. Reasonably enough; a successful dish is often achieved by quite different methods from those advocated in the cookery books or by the professional chefs, but over this question of omelette making professional and amateur cooks alike are particularly unyielding. Argument has never been known to convert anybody to a different method, so if you have your own, stick to it and let others go their cranky ways, mistaken, stubborn and ignorant to the end.

It is therefore to anyone still in the experimental stage that I submit the few following points which I fancy are often responsible for failure when that ancient iron omelette pan, for twenty years untouched by water, is brought out of the cupboard.

First, the eggs are very often beaten too savagely. In fact, they should not really be beaten at all, but stirred, and a few firm turns with two forks do the trick. Secondly, the simplicity and freshness evoked by the delicious word 'omelette' will be achieved only if it is remembered that it is the *eggs* which are the essential part of the dish; the filling, being of secondary importance, should be in very small proportion to the eggs. Lying lightly in the centre of the finished omelette, rather than bursting exuberantly out of the seams, it should supply the second of two different tastes and textures; the pure egg and cooked butter taste of the outside and ends of the omelette, then the soft, slightly runny interior, with its second flavouring of cheese or ham, mushrooms or fresh herbs.

As far as the pan is concerned, I have already given a few notes about this in the chapter on kitchen equipment (page 66), so it will be sufficient to say here that a 10-inch omelette pan will make an omelette of 3 or 4 eggs. Beat them only immediately before you make the omelette, lightly as described above, with two forks, adding a light mild seasoning of salt and pepper. Allow about ½ oz. of butter. Warm your pan, don't make it red hot. Then turn the burner as high as it will go. Put in the butter and when it has melted and is on the point of turning colour, pour in the eggs. Add the filling, and see that it is well embedded in the eggs. Tip the pan towards you and with a fork or spatula gather up a little of the mixture from the far side. Now tip the pan away from you so that the unset eggs run into the space you have made for them.

When a little of the unset part remains on the surface the omelette is done. Fold it in three with your fork or palette knife, hold the pan at an angle and slip the omelette out on to the waiting dish. This should be warmed, but only a little, or the omelette will go on cooking.

An omelette is nothing to make a fuss about. The chief mistakes are putting in too much of the filling and making this too elaborate. Such rich things as *foie gras* or lobster in cream sauce are inappropriate. In fact, moderation in every aspect is the best advice where omelettes are concerned. Sauces and other trimmings are superfluous, a little extra butter melted in the warm omelette dish or placed on top of the omelette as you serve it being the only addition which is not out of place.

L'omelette de la Mère Poulard

As everyone knows, the Hôtel Poulard, formerly the Auberge de Saint-Michel Tête d'Or, at Mont St. Michel, became famous for the omelettes made by the proprietress. Many writers have attempted to account for the wonderful flavour of la Mère Poulard's omelettes, explaining that her 'secret' lay in adding this, that, or the other ingredient. Here is a letter, dated June 6, 1922, which she wrote to M .Robert Viel, a celebrated Paris restaurateur and collector of a famous library of cookery books:

'Monsieur Viel,

'Voici la recette de l'omelette: je casse de bons œufs dans une terrine, je les bats bien, je mets un bon morceau de beurre dans la poêle, j'y jette les œufs et je remue constamment. Je suis heureuse, monsieur, si cette recette vous fait plaisir.

'ANNETTE POULARD.'

Madame Poulard died in 1931, at the age of 80, but she and her husband had retired from the hotel many years before. Her menu, which before the 1914 war cost 2.50 fr., including cider, and butter on the table, was always the same. It consisted of the famous omelette, ham, a fried sole, *pré-salé* lamb cutlets with potatoes, a roast chicken and salad, and dessert.

Now, over fifty years later, there are, I believe, two restaurants at the Mont St. Michel which both claim to be the successors of the original Mère Poulard, and who are still making fortunes out of serving their customers with the one and only true 'omelette Poulard.' But what of the rest of the menu?

OMELETTE FINES HERBES

Prepare 1 tablespoon of mixed finely chopped parsley, tarragon, chives and, if possible, chervil. Mix half of this, with salt and pepper, in the bowl with the eggs, and the other half when the eggs are in the pan. If you like, put a little knob of butter on top of the omelette as it is brought to the table.

OMELETTE À LA TOMATE
TOMATO OMELETTE

One tomato, skinned and chopped small, cooked hardly more than a minute in butter, with salt and pepper, is added to the eggs already in the pan.

OMELETTE AU LARD
BACON OMELETTE

Add a tablespoon of finely chopped bacon softened a minute or so in its own fat, to the eggs already in the pan; take care not to salt the eggs too much.

G

OMELETTE AU JAMBON

HAM OMELETTE

Add a heaped tablespoon of cooked ham, finely chopped and mixed with a little parsley, but not previously heated at all, to the eggs already in the pan. Again, take into account the saltiness of the ham when seasoning the eggs. A little extra butter melting on top of the omelette is a good addition, for there is none with the filling.

OMELETTE AUX CHAMPIGNONS

MUSHROOM OMELETTE

Not very complicated, you might think, but how often does one get a really good mushroom omelette? The answer is that the mushrooms should be in the form of a creamy little sauce, very well seasoned. A quarter of a pound of small white mushrooms or mushroom stalks is enough for two 3-egg omelettes. Chop the cleaned mushrooms very finely, melt them in butter in a small pan, season with salt, pepper, nutmeg or mace, stir in just a pinch of flour, then 2 tablespoons of cream. The mixture, very hot, is added to the omelette when it is already in the pan.

OMELETTE MOLIÈRE

CHEESE OMELETTE

This delicious omelette is called after a little restaurant in Avignon where I used often to eat very cheap and simple meals. This was one of my favourite dishes there.

Beat 1 tablespoon of finely grated Parmesan with 3 eggs. When the omelette is in the pan, add 1 tablespoon of very fresh Gruyère cheese cut into minuscule dice, and 1 tablespoon of thick fresh cream. In a few seconds the Gruyère starts to melt and your omelette is ready. Fold it over, serve and eat it without delay.

OMELETTE BASQUAISE

(1) A tablespoon or so of Pipérade mixture (see page 198) added to a 3-egg omelette when the eggs are in the pan. Serve folded over in the ordinary way.

(2) A mixture of finely chopped shallot, garlic, raw ham or gammon,

and sweet pepper with a few cubes of spiced sausage, gently cooked in butter or olive oil, added to the eggs already in the pan; oil instead of butter is used for cooking this omelette, which is made rather thick and served flat.

OMELETTE LANDAISE
OMELETTE WITH PINE-NUTS

Three or four tablespoons of pine-nuts are very gently heated in butter in the omelette pan until they just barely begin to turn colour. Take care, because they burn in a twinkling, and they have to go on cooking after the eggs, beaten with salt and pepper, are poured into the pan and the omelette made in the usual way. This is a rather odd dish, but not without charm.

There are great stretches of pine-woods in the Landes country, and to extract the nuts the cones are warmed in the oven or near the fire, and when they open the little kernels are shaken out. Sometimes sugar instead of salt is added to the eggs, and the omelette served as a sweet.

OMELETTE BRAYAUDE
PORK AND POTATO OMELETTE

A dish from Riom in the Auvergne.

Cut a slice of salt pork or a rather thick rasher of fat, unsmoked bacon and a large potato into small dice. Melt the bacon in an omelette pan. When the fat begins to run, put in the potato and cook gently until it is soft. Shake the pan now and again so that the potatoes do not stick and, if necessary, add a little more fat or butter.

Beat 2 or 3 eggs, season with salt and pepper, turn up the heat under the pan and add a small piece of butter; pour in the eggs; let them nearly set, as for an ordinary omelette; pour a little hot fresh cream on the top and slide the omelette out flat on to a hot plate. Sprinkle, if you like, with a little grated cheese.

Enough for two or three people, for it is rather a filling dish.

OMELETTE AU BOUDIN DE NANCY
OMELETTE WITH BLACK PUDDING

The blood sausages, or black puddings, of Nancy in Lorraine, are renowned. The usual variety to be bought in England are rather insipid, but for those who make their own or can buy them at Harrods or in Soho (where there is a butcher who makes them properly flavoured with onions) here is a very excellent recipe.

About 6 oz. of blood sausage is cut into thickish slices which are fried lightly in butter. Chop very finely a couple of shallots and some parsley. Melt this mixture in butter; add it to 6 eggs and beat them lightly with salt and pepper. Using half the eggs make an omelette, turn it out flat on to a hot round dish. On top place the slices of *boudin*. Make another flat omelette with the rest of the eggs, turn it out on top of the sausage, and serve instantly.

In other parts of France I have come across an *omelette campagnarde*, a very similar omelette to the above, made with ordinary pork sausage of the coarsely-cut Toulouse type. It makes a very good lunch dish for two people. The sausage used can be either a cooked or uncooked one; if it is already cooked, skin and slice it and just heat the slices very gently in butter for a few seconds, and proceed as for the *omelette au boudin*.

An ordinary folded omelette can also, of course, be made with sausage but, in this case, cut the sausage into rather small cubes.

OMELETTE AUX MOULES
MUSSEL OMELETTE

Scrub, beard and thoroughly clean 1 pint of mussels—small ones when possible. Reject any which are gaping open or broken. Put them in a saucepan with just a little water, and cook over a fast flame until they open, which takes 5 to 7 minutes. Remove each from the pan as soon as it is properly open.

In a mixture of butter and oil melt the finely chopped white part of 1 fairly big leek; add 2 skinned, roughly chopped tomatoes and seasonings of freshly milled pepper, a little salt, a scrap of garlic if you like. Let all this cook until it is quite thick. Put in the shelled mussels and moisten with a few drops of their stock, filtered through a fine cloth. Add plenty of chopped parsley. This filling is added to the omelette when the eggs are already in the pan, and makes enough for two, or even three, 2-egg omelettes.

OMELETTE AU THON
TUNNY-FISH OMELETTE

First prepare a *beurre maître-d'hôtel* by working together a tablespoon of butter, a little chopped parsley, salt and lemon juice. Then in a small saucepan heat for a minute or two, in butter, a heaped tablespoon of tunny fish drained from its oil and mixed with a scrap of garlic, about half a chopped shallot, and freshly-ground pepper. While butter to cook the omelette is heating in the omelette pan, put the *beurre maître-d'hôtel* on to a warmed omelette dish. As soon as the eggs are in the pan add to them the tunny preparation. Turn the completed omelette out on top of the *maître-d'hôtel* butter, which should by now be just melting, and eat it at once. Proportions for a 3- or 4-egg omelette.

What, it may be asked, is to be done with the rest of the tin of tunny fish? The omelette is so good that perhaps it will be wanted to make another next day; or it can be pounded up and stirred into a mayonnaise for hard-boiled eggs; or added to a rice stuffing for peppers, or to a risotto; but don't spoil the omelette by adding another ha'porth of tunny fish just to finish it up.

OMELETTE À L'OSEILLE
SORREL OMELETTE

Wash a few sorrel leaves, not more than a handful. Chop them very fine. Melt them in butter; add a little salt; cook 4 or 5 minutes. Add this mixture to the omelette when it is already in the pan. One of the nicest of omelettes.

OMELETTE AUX TRUFFES

Périgord truffles are more highly prized than those of the Vaucluse, for they have a more powerful scent. There is, however, quite an important truffle market in the Vaucluse, of which the highly interesting little town of Carpentras is the centre.

In a village not far from Carpentras the local truffle hunter (he used a trained dog to sniff them out, not pigs as they do in the Périgord) who used occasionally to sell me two or three imperfect truffles for what amounted to a pittance compared to what he got on the Carpentras market for good specimens, told me that the proper way to make a truffle omelette is first to break your eggs into a bowl, then add your truffle, neither peeled nor cooked, but well scrubbed, and cut into fine rounds; cover the bowl and leave for several hours. By the time you come to beat up the eggs and make your omelette the eggs are beautifully scented with the truffle, and the minute or so which they spend in the pan with the eggs is quite sufficient to cook them.

Although in England the exact method of cooking a truffle omelette is not of very great moment, since we cannot buy fresh truffles, the truffle hunter's system is all the same of some interest because I have never seen it mentioned in any cookery book, and the omelettes made in this way have a much better flavour than those one usually gets in restaurants. Like many such small culinary details, it is a question of putting one's observations to practical use. For the truffle, from the moment it is dug out of the ground, starts giving off its powerful scent, which slowly loses its potency. Eggs, on the other hand, have a unique capacity for absorbing scents; therefore lose no time in putting your truffles and your eggs together, and the result will be a truffle omelette made under the best possible auspices.

LES ŒUFS BROUILLÉS

SCRAMBLED EGGS

For scrambled eggs, unlike those for an omelette, the eggs should be very well beaten, and it is an improvement to extract 1 white in every 4. For the rest, everybody has his own method, which is invariably the only right and proper one. Mine is to melt a very large lump of butter in a thick non-sticking saucepan, add the well-seasoned and beaten eggs, and stir over a low flame until they start to thicken. At this stage, add another lump of butter, and take the saucepan from the fire as soon as the first characteristic granules begin to appear. Go on stirring, because the eggs will continue to cook simply with the heat from the saucepan. Scrambled eggs should be evenly creamy and granulated, not half liquid and half set. Of course, they must be served at once, in a very hot dish. And eggs for scrambling must be of the most absolute freshness.

As far as French dishes of scrambled eggs are concerned, although one finds quite a variety given in cookery books, the only ones I remember ever having eaten in France (except in houses belonging to English people) were both in the Béarnais country. One was a dish of artichoke hearts filled with very creamy scrambled eggs and surrounded with a freshly made tomato sauce, the other the famous *pipérade*, for which the recipe follows.

LA PIPÉRADE

Because this concoction of eggs and peppers from the Basque country is one of the most widely travelled of all French regional dishes, it is also one which is frequently misinterpreted. Here is the very simple recipe.

Heat a generous tablespoon of goose or pork dripping or olive oil in a large frying-pan, and in this cook a finely sliced onion until it begins to turn yellow. Add 6 green peppers, core and seeds removed and cut into quite large strips. Cook about 15 minutes before adding 2 lb. of tomatoes, skinned and roughly chopped. Add a little chopped garlic if you like, a pinch of dried basil, salt, and pepper if the mixture needs it. Cook until the tomatoes are almost in a pulp. Add 4 well-beaten eggs. Stir until they begin to thicken, like scrambled eggs, but take the pan from the fire before they have solidified. Serve on a heated omelette dish, with a slice of grilled or fried ham (in the Béarn this would be *jambon de Bayonne*, and here gammon rashers from the middle or corner cut make a very respectable substitute) per person on the top. Or if something less substantial is needed simply surround the *pipérade* with a few croûtons of fried bread. The strips of green pepper should still retain something of their crispness, and be clearly distinguishable from the main mass. When green peppers are out of season they are sometimes replaced in the Béarn by peppers pickled in vinegar.

SOUFFLÉS

To some cooks the making of a soufflé appears to be perfectly effortless, to others a matter of careful measuring, clock watching and nervous anxiety. Those in the first category have certainly, perhaps even without knowing it, mastered the beating of the whites of the eggs to the precise point, and know how to fold them into the main mixture with speed and a light hand, for it is at this point that many a soufflé is foredoomed. The proceeding is as follows:

(1) Failing the special copper bowl which the professionals use for the purpose, at least one large china mixing bowl should be in every kitchen for the beating of egg whites.

(2) Any fat substance present in the whites will prevent them rising, so to start with the bowl itself and the whisk must be scrupulously clean and dry. Then if any of the yolk has slipped into the whites during the separation of the eggs, it must be carefully extracted, using a half-shell as a scoop.

(3) The whites need not be spanking fresh, so that if, say, the yolks have been used for a sauce the whites can be kept in a covered bowl in a larder for 2 or 3 days or in the refrigerator for as long as 5 or 6 days before they are used. But it is not at all advisable to keep them longer than this.

(4) Some cookery books tell you that the whites should be brought into a warm room half an hour before they are to be whipped. I find the exact opposite to be the case. They come up much better if put in the refrigerator for 20 to 30 minutes previous to beating.

(5) For a small quantity of whites, say up to 4 or 5, I find a small spiral wire whisk the most satisfactory implement. For a larger quantity a fairly large double-looped wire whisk is better. These implements produce properly aerated whites rather than the too compact mass achieved by many patent whisks and by the electric mixer.

(6) The moment to stop beating is when the eggs are sufficiently stiff and creamy to stand in peaks, and to remain adhering in a point on the top of the whisk when this is held upright. If they are beaten too long they will break when you start folding them into the main mixture and the result will be a soufflé insufficiently risen and grainy in the centre.

(7) Once the whites are ready, fold them without delay into the main mixture. If they are left waiting about there is a risk that they will sink and go watery.

(8) To fold in the whites the process is as follows: The whites, half at a time if the quantity is four or more, are tipped on to the basic mixture, which should be cool or tepid, for if it is very hot the whites will start coagulating before the soufflé gets into the oven. With the left hand rotate the bowl slowly while, with a knife, palette knife or wooden spatula, the whites are gradually incorporated into the main mass, being lifted, folded, lifted and folded again, care being taken that the mixing implement reaches right to the bottom and sides of the mixture. The process should be carried out with speed and thoroughness but with as light a touch as possible. When the folding in has been completed, the whole mixture should have a spongy, almost frothy appearance.

(9) Immediately, before it has time to lose this sponginess, turn the mixture into the utensil in which it is to be cooked; this must instantly be transferred to the preheated oven so that cooking starts without delay. It is a great help, with soufflés, to stand the dish on a baking sheet which has been standing in the oven so that it is already hot. In this way cooking starts from the bottom as well as the top, and the over-liquid layer which sometimes remains at the bottom of an otherwise well-cooked soufflé is avoided. On the other hand a good soufflé should retain a slightly creamy liquidity at its centre, which supplies the soufflé with, as it were, its own sauce.

(10) Although it is now considered essential to have special straight-sided fireproof china or glass dishes for soufflés, this was not always the case. They were formerly cooked in oval metal utensils which, when taken from the oven, were slipped inside a larger more ornamental dish with handles, in which they were brought to table. So, if called upon to do so, it should be quite easy to improvise a soufflé even in a pie dish or any other fireproof utensil.

SOUFFLÉ AU FROMAGE
CHEESE SOUFFLÉ

Prepare the basic mixture by stirring one generous tablespoon of flour into 1 oz. of butter melted in a heavy saucepan. Gradually add just under ½ pint of warmed milk, stirring until your mixture is quite smooth. Let this sauce cook very gently over an asbestos mat, stirring frequently, for close on 10 minutes. Now stir in 2 oz. of finely grated Parmesan cheese (or if you prefer, 1 oz. each of Parmesan and Gruyère) and then the very thoroughly beaten yolks of 4 large eggs. Remove the mixture from the fire, and continue stirring for a few seconds. Now add a seasoning of salt (always to be added *after* the cheese) and quite a generous amount of freshly-ground pepper, plus, if you like, a scrap of cayenne. This basic mixture can be made well in advance.

When the time comes to make the soufflé, preheat the oven to Gas No. 6, 400 deg. F. Have the shelf placed fairly low in the oven, and a baking sheet on the shelf. Butter a 1½-pint soufflé dish (the size is important).

Whisk the whites of the eggs, plus one extra, in a large, scrupulously dry and clean bowl, until they will stand in peaks on the whisk and look very creamy. Tip half the whites on top of the basic mixture. With a palette knife cut them into it, slowly rotating the bowl with your left hand, lifting rather than stirring the whole mass. Add the remainder of the whites in the same way. All this should take only a few seconds and as you pour the whole mixture, without delay, into the dish, it should look very bubbly and spongy, but if the whites have been over-beaten or rammed into the main mixture with a heavy hand, it will already begin to look flat. With the palette knife, mark a deep circle an inch or so from the edge, so that the soufflé will come out with a cottage-loaf look to the top. Put it instantly into the oven.

As to timing, it depends so much upon the size and type of both the oven and the dish that it is misleading to give precise details. I can only say, as a general guide, that in the oven of a representative domestic gas cooker, this soufflé is perfectly cooked at No. 6 in 23 to 25 minutes.

PETITS SOUFFLÉS AUX COURGETTES
MINIATURE COURGETTE SOUFFLÉS

1 lb. courgettes, 2 whole eggs and 2 extra whites, 5 tablespoons of grated Gruyère cheese (1½ to 2 oz.), a béchamel sauce made from 1 oz.

butter, 2 tablespoons of flour and a scant ¼ pint of warmed milk, the whole well seasoned with pepper but not too much salt until after the cheese has been added.

Prepare the courgettes as explained on page 253, and when they have been salted and drained, cook them in a heavy saucepan with a ladle of water until they are quite soft and the liquid evaporated. If they dry up before they are soft add more water, but only a very little, because the object of this operation is to extract the moisture from the vegetables, not to add more. Sieve them and stir the resulting purée into the prepared béchamel. Add the cheese; then, off the fire, the well-beaten yolks. Leave to cool before folding in the whites, beaten until they stand in peaks. Turn into miniature buttered soufflé dishes, filling them within half an inch of the top. Stand them in a baking tin containing water, cook in a pre-heated, moderate oven, Gas No. 4, 355 deg. F., for approximately 25 minutes. They should be well risen but still creamy in the centre. These quantities fill 6 little dishes of about 4 oz. capacity.

I first had these little soufflés at a lorry drivers' restaurant about three miles from the Pont du Gard. They came after cooked ham and cold vegetables served with a powerful *aïoli*, and were followed by a *bœuf à la gardiane* garnished with heart-shaped croûtons of fried bread. Then came a home-made ice with home-made almond *tuiles*. After which the local *marc* from Châteauneuf du Pape was a welcome digestive. It was not, I must add, the set meal of the café, but had been specially prepared for us by the proprietor, a Marseillais, at quite short notice. He had, I think, invented these delicious little soufflés himself.

SOUFFLÉ .AUX COURGETTES

COURGETTE SOUFFLÉ

To make a courgette soufflé in one large dish instead of several miniature ones, prepare the mixture as described above. Turn into a buttered soufflé dish of 1¼ to 1½ pints capacity. The dish should be full almost to the top. Stand it in a baking tin filled with water, sprinkle the top with grated cheese, and cook in the centre of a preheated oven, Gas No. 4, 355 deg. F., for 40 to 45 minutes. Alternative timing is 30 minutes at gas No. 7, 440 deg. F.

Three people can easily dispose of this size soufflé. For six, double all the quantities exactly and make two soufflés rather than one huge one.

PETITES FONDUES À LA BOURGUIGNONNE

Except for the fact that it contains cheese, this has very little in common with the well-known Swiss fondue. The recipe is from an old collection of Burgundian recipes and came from the Restaurant de la Cloche in Dijon. I give it in half quantities though, for the final operation of cooking and frying the little fondues is a tricky one at first and it is best to get it right in a small amount to start with. It makes a first course luncheon dish of great charm.

The ingredients are 2 oz. each of butter and flour, ½ pint of milk, 1½ oz. each of grated Gruyère and Parmesan, the yolks of 3 eggs, salt, pepper, nutmeg. For the final operation, a whole egg, approximately 2½ oz. of breadcrumbs and a mixture of butter and oil for frying.

First make a thick basic sauce by melting the butter in a heavy sauce-pan, then stir in the flour. When the two have amalgamated, add, about a third at a time, the heated milk, and stir thoroughly until smooth, thick, and coming away from the sides of the pan. Now add the grated cheese, salt, a plentiful seasoning of freshly-milled pepper and a grating of nutmeg. The mixture should be rather highly seasoned. Lastly, add the beaten yolks and stir, away from the fire, until the mixture is quite smooth. Turn it into a small baking tin, very lightly oiled, in a layer about half an inch thick. Put in a cold place and leave until next day.

With a knife dipped in cold water, mark out the mixture into rectangles about 1½ × 2½ inches. There will be sixteen pieces. Cut them through, then separate them with a palette knife. Have ready on one large plate the beaten egg and on another the very fine, pale golden breadcrumbs. Coat each square first with the egg and then with the breadcrumbs, taking care to cover sides as well as top and bottom. Use a palette knife for the coating operations which can all be done a little time before the meal. When the time comes to cook them, heat about 2 oz. of butter (clarified if possible) and 2 tablespoons of oil. Fry half the little fondues in this, turn-ing them over once or twice until they are golden and you see the mixture just beginning to spread at the sides. Take them out with a slice, keep them hot in a gentle oven while the second batch is fried, then serve quickly. This quantity will be enough for three. To make clarified butter, see page 72.

LA GOUGÈRE

With the exception of the delicious cheese of Époisses, in Upper Burgundy, there is no notable Burgundian cheese, but the Burgundians are great cheese eaters for the obvious reason that cheese is one of the best accompaniments for wine. Cheese dishes may be served as a first course or as a savoury; in this case it will come after the cheeses themselves, to go with the last glass of wine, before the sweet. The gougère, a kind of cheese pastry made with choux paste similar to that used for éclairs, is the great cheese dish of the country. It is rather tricky to make, so if it doesn't come right the first time one just has to persevere.

To make a gougère for six people, the ingredients are ½ pint of milk, ¼ lb. of flour, 2 oz. of butter, 4 eggs, 3 oz. of Gruyère cheese, salt and pepper.

The paste is made as follows: bring the milk to the boil and then let it get quite cold. Strain it. Put in the butter cut in small pieces, and a teaspoon of salt and a little freshly-ground pepper, and bring rapidly to the boil so that the butter and milk amalgamate. Pour in, all at one go, the sifted flour. Stir until a thick smooth paste is obtained; it will come away clean from the sides and bottom of the pan.

Off the fire stir in the eggs one at a time, each egg to be thoroughly incorporated before the next is added. When the paste is shiny and smooth add the cheese, cut into very small dice, reserving 1 dessertspoon of the little cubes. Leave to cool a little.

Lightly butter a baking sheet. Take tablespoons of the mixture and arrange them, like so many half eggs, in a circle about 7 inches across, the space in the middle being about 2½ inches. When you have made one circle, put the remaining spoonfuls on top of the first, so that you have quite a high wall round the central well. Pat into an even shape with a palette knife. Place the little pieces of reserved cheese on top and all round. Brush with milk. Cook in the centre of a preheated oven at a moderately hot temperature, Gas No. 5, 375 deg. F., for about 45 minutes.

Although the gougère begins to smell cooked after the first 20 minutes, do not be taken in; it will have swelled up and turned golden brown, but it is not ready. If you can resist, do not open the oven, because of the risk of the mixture collapsing. If you feel you have to look, open and shut the door of the oven very gently. To test when the gougère is done press lightly with a finger in the centre of the cake; it should be firm to the touch. If it is too soft it will fall the instant you take it from the oven into a sad flat pancake.

If you are going to serve the gougère hot (it makes a good first dish at luncheon) transfer it for 5 minutes to a warm place such as the plate drawer before transferring it to the serving dish, or if you cook by gas, turn the oven off and leave it 5 more minutes. If to be served cold, ease the cake off the baking sheet on to a wire cake rack so that there is air all round it, but keep it away from sudden draughts.

TARTE À L'OIGNON, *or* ZEWELWAÏ

ONION AND CREAM TART

This is the famous Alsatian speciality. It makes a truly lovely first course.

For the pastry: 4 oz. plain flour, 2 oz. butter or 1 oz. each of butter and meat dripping, 1 egg, salt, water.

For the filling: 1½ lb. onions, the yolks of 3 eggs, a good ¼ pint of thick cream, seasonings including nutmeg and plenty of freshly-milled pepper, butter and oil for cooking the onions.

Make a well in the sieved flour, put the butter cut in small pieces, the egg and a good pinch of salt in the middle. Blend quickly and lightly but thoroughly, with the fingertips. Add a very little water, just enough to make the dough moist, but it should come cleanly away from the bowl or board. Place the ball of dough on a floured board and with the heel of your palm gradually stretch the paste out, bit by bit, until it is a flat but rather ragged-looking sheet. Gather it up again, and repeat the process. It should all be done lightly and expeditiously, and is extremely simple although it sounds complicated written down. Roll it into a ball, wrap it in greaseproof paper and leave it to rest in a cold larder or refrigerator for a minimum of 2 hours, so that it loses all elasticity and will not shrink or lose its shape during the baking. This is one version of the *pâte brisée* or *pâte à foncer* used for most open tarts in French cookery. Without being as rich or as complicated as puff pastry, it is light and crisp. But those who already have a satisfactory method for tart and flan pastries may prefer to stick to their own. In spite of all the cookery rules, the making of pastry remains a very personal matter. I find myself that the easiest and most generally successful tart pastry is the one described for the cheese dish in the next recipe.

For the filling, peel and slice the onions as finely as possible, taking care to discard the fibrous parts at the root of the onions. Melt 2 oz. of butter and a little oil in a heavy frying-pan. In this cook the onions, covered, until they are quite soft and pale golden. They must not fry, and they should be stirred from time to time to make sure they are not sticking. They will take about ½ hour. Season with salt, nutmeg and pepper. Stir in the very well-beaten yolks and the cream, and leave until the time comes to cook the tart.

Oil an 8-inch tart or flan tin. Roll out your pastry as thinly as possible (the great thing about this dish, as also the *quiches* of Lorraine, is that there should be a lot of creamy filling on very little pastry). Line the tin with the pastry, pressing it gently into position with your knuckle. Pour in the filling, cook in the centre of a fairly hot oven, with the tin standing on a baking sheet at Gas No. 6, 400 deg. F., for 30 minutes. Serve very hot.

TARTE AU FROMAGE
CHEESE TART

Line an 8- to 9-inch flat pie or flan tin with a crumbly pastry made from 6 oz. plain flour, 3 oz. butter, half a teaspoon of salt and 2 to 4 tablespoons of iced water. Simply crumble the butter into the sieved flour and salt, add the iced water, and form into a ball. Do not knead or roll it or leave it to rest, but spread it directly into the tin with your hands, pressing it lightly into place with your knuckles. Prick the flat surface evenly with a fork, fill with dry beans, and bake in a hot oven, Gas No. 6, 400 deg. F., for 20 minutes.

Have ready the following mixture: a stiff béchamel made with 1 oz. butter, 2 tablespoons of flour, ¼ pint of warmed milk. Season with freshly ground black pepper, cayenne pepper, a scrap of nutmeg. When well cooked and reduced, stir in 2 oz. of grated Gruyère cheese and ½ oz. of grated Parmesan; then, off the fire, 2 very well-beaten yolks of eggs. When cool fold in, as for a soufflé, the 2 stiffly whipped whites. Pour immediately into the partly cooked pastry case, if you like brush the edges of the pastry with cream or milk, sprinkle the top with grated cheese, return to the oven at the same heat and cook for 12 to 15 minutes until the filling is risen and golden brown, but still a little creamy inside.

LA QUICHE LORRAINE
CREAM AND BACON TART

As in all regional dishes of ancient origin which have eventually become national as well as purely local property, there have been various evolutions in the composition of a *quiche*. Also called, in different parts of the province, *galette, fiouse, tourte, flon* and *flan*, a *quiche* is a flat open tart, and originally it was made of bread dough just like the Provençal *pissaladière* and the Neapolitan *pizza*. Gradually the bread dough came to be replaced with pastry while the fillings, of course, vary enormously, from sweet purple quetsch plums or golden mirabelles to savoury mixtures of onion, of chopped pork and veal, of cream flavoured with poppy seeds, of cream and eggs and bacon, of cream and cream cheese. According to its filling the tart will be called a *quiche aux pruneaux*, *quiche à l'oignon*, and so on. The one universally known as the *quiche*

Lorraine contains smoked bacon, cream and eggs. Parisian, and English, cooks often add Gruyère cheese, but Lorrainers will tell you that this is not the true *quiche Lorraine*, whose history goes back at least as far as the sixteenth century.

There is, however, a time-honoured version containing a proportion of fresh white cream cheese as well as the cream, and it is perhaps this recipe which has caused the confusion. No doubt it is all largely a matter of taste, and for myself I find that whereas the combination of the mild flavour of white cream cheese with the smoked bacon of Alsace and Lorraine (which much resembles our own at its best) is quite attractive, that of Gruyère cheese with the same smoked bacon tends to be rather coarse and heavy. At any rate, here is a recipe for the plain cream and egg and bacon variety.

For the pastry the ingredients are 4 oz. of plain flour, 2 oz. of butter, 1 egg, salt, a little water. Cut the butter into little pieces and crumble it thoroughly with the sieved flour, adding a good pinch of salt. Break in the egg and mix the dough with your hands. Add enough water (2 to 4 tablespoons) to make the dough soft, but it should still be firm enough to come away clean from the bowl or board. Simply knead it into a ball, wrap it in greaseproof paper and leave it for a minimum of 2 hours. When the time comes to use it, roll it out very thin and line an 8-inch flan tin with it, and with a fork prick the surface.

For the filling cut 6 thin rashers of streaky bacon into inch-wide strips. Cook them in a frying-pan for a minute so that some of the fat runs. Arrange them in circles on the pastry. Have ready ½ pint of double cream mixed with the very well-beaten yolks of 3 eggs plus 1 whole egg, and well-seasoned with freshly-ground pepper and a little salt (taking into account the saltiness of the bacon). Pour this mixture over the bacon and transfer immediately to a pre-heated oven, Gas No. 6, 400 deg. F. Leave it for 20 minutes, then cook for another 10 minutes at a lowered temperature, Gas No. 4, 350 deg. F. By this time the filling should be puffed up almost like a soufflé, and golden brown. Let it rest a minute or two after you take it from the oven, to make it easier to cut, but don't wait until it has fallen before serving it.

QUICHE AU FROMAGE BLANC
CREAM CHEESE AND BACON TART

For this version, well worth a trial, the filling consists of ¼ lb. of fresh, unsalted, or slightly salted, cream cheese, beaten together with ¼ pint of thick cream, the yolks of 3 eggs and 1 whole egg, plenty of freshly milled pepper, a little salt, and 6 thin rashers of smoked streaky bacon. The pastry is made, the mixture is poured over the lightly fried bacon, and the *quiche* is cooked, all as in the foregoing recipe.

To get a smooth mixture it is usually necessary to sieve the cream cheese.

PISSALADIÈRE

PROVENÇAL ONION PIE

The *pissaladière* is a substantial dish of bread dough spread with onions, anchovies, black olives and sometimes tomatoes, baked in the oven on large heavy baking trays, and sold by the slice in bakers' shops or straight from the baking trays by street vendors. It is not so common nowadays as it was before the war, when it could be bought hot from the oven in the early morning at every street corner in the old quarters of Marseille and Toulon. Not so long ago, however, having spotted some in a bakery in Avignon, I went in and asked for 'une tranche de Pissaladière.' The shopkeeper did not know what I meant. 'What, then, is that?' I asked. 'Ça, Madame, c'est du Pizza Provençal,' was the surprising reply. Odd how that Neapolitan *pizza* has captured people's imaginations, even in Provence, where they have their own traditional version of it, the great difference being that the Provençal variety is made without the top dressing of chewy cheese characteristic of the Neapolitan *pizza*. In fact, the Provençal one more nearly resembles the traditional Roman *pizza*, and it is, I suppose, possible that it was introduced by Roman cooks during the reign of the Popes in Avignon.

Truthfully it must be admitted that both the Italian *pizza* and the Provençal *pissaladière* lie somewhat heavy upon the stomach, because of the bread dough which is the basis. The version made with pastry which is sometimes served in restaurants and private houses and may be bought ready made at *pâtisseries* is often an improvement. It is the filling which, if you happen to like the aromatic mixture of onions, olive oil, anchovies and olives, is important. The following recipe makes a splendid first course at luncheon, so long as it is followed by something not too substantial—a fine grilled fish, for instance, or a little best end of neck of lamb nicely roasted.

PISSALADIÈRE À LA MÉNAGÈRE

PROVENÇAL ONION PIE WITH YEAST PASTRY

5 oz. plain flour, 1½ oz. butter, 1 egg, ½ oz. yeast, salt, a little water. Cut the butter in little pieces and rub it into the flour. Add a good pinch

of salt. Make a well in the centre; put in the egg and the yeast dissolved in about 2 tablespoons of barely tepid water. Mix and knead until the dough comes away clean from the sides of the bowl. Shape into a ball, make a deep cross-cut on the top, put on a floured plate, cover with a floured cloth and leave in a warm place to rise for 2 hours.

For the filling: 1¼ lb. onions, 2 tomatoes, a dozen anchovy fillets, a dozen small, stoned black olives, pepper, salt and olive oil.

Heat 3 or 4 tablespoons of olive oil in a heavy frying pan. Put in the thinly sliced onions and cook them very gently, with the cover on the pan, until they are quite soft and pale golden. They must not fry or turn brown. Add the skinned tomatoes and the seasonings (plus garlic if you like). Continue cooking until tomatoes and onions are amalgamated, and the water from the tomatoes evaporated.

When the dough has risen, sprinkle it with flour and break it down again. Knead once more into a ball, which you place in the centre of an oiled, 8-inch tart tin. With your knuckles press it gently but quickly outwards until it is spread right over the tin and all round the sides. Put in the filling. Make a criss-cross pattern all over the top with the anchovies, then fill in with the olives. Leave to rise another 15 minutes. Then bake in the centre of a pre-heated oven, with the tin standing on a baking sheet, at 400 degrees, Gas No. 6, for 20 minutes, then turn down to 350 deg., Gas No. 4, and cook another 20 minutes.

TARTELETTES À LA PROVENÇALE

A delicious derivation of the *pissaladière* was once, and perhaps still is, a speciality of a small hotel in the dusty, sleepy little town of St. Rémy, in Provence. It consisted of little open pastry cases with three different varieties of fillings; an onion and black olive mixture like the one described above, one with mushrooms and tomatoes, and the third with prawns and green olives. Those who sometimes feel tempted to put everything from the larder into a *pizza* or *pissaladière* may care to take a hint from this. Each of these little tartlets was delicious in its way, but I much doubt if they would have been so good if all the ingredients had been jumbled up together to make one mixture.

FLAN DE POIREAUX À LA BERRICHONNE
CREAM AND LEEK PIE

Line an 8-inch pie tin with crumbly pastry, as for the *tarté au fromage*, p. 206. Chop the white part of 2 lb. of leeks and let them melt in butter. Add 2 oz. of lean ham cut into dice. Spread this mixture on the pastry.

Beat together 3 egg yolks and ½ pint of cream; season with salt and pepper. Pour this mixture over the leeks, put a few small pieces of butter on the top, and cook in a medium hot oven for 30 to 40 minutes.

Under the name of *flamiche* or *flamique* a very similar dish is made in Picardy and other parts of northern France, but does not usually include the ham, more leeks (3 lb.) and less cream (¼ pint) being used for the filling. Sometimes a bread dough or yeast pastry is used and sometimes the *flamiche* is covered over with a lid of pastry so that it becomes more like a pasty.

BOULETTES DE SEMOULE, *or* PFLÜTTEN
SEMOLINA AND POTATO GNOCCHI

These are a cross, as it were, of semolina and potato gnocchi, the final cooking being more like that of potato croquettes. It is rather a good combination, lighter in texture than either kind of gnocchi, and quite easy to make.

First prepare a purée from 1 lb. of potatoes, boiled in their skins, then peeled, and mashed while still warm. Season them liberally, adding grated nutmeg as well as salt and pepper. Add, a little at a time, ¾ pint of milk. When this purée is amalgamated put it in a saucepan and, stirring all the time, bring just to simmering point. Pour in 3 oz. of fine semolina, and stir with a wooden spoon until the mixture is very stiff and coming away from the sides of the pan. Remove from the fire and stir in 2 whole well-beaten eggs. Have ready a buttered tin, pour in the mixture in a layer nearly an inch thick. Leave until next day.

For the final cooking, cut squares of the mixture, roll these in your floured hands into little croquette shapes. Fry them in a mixture of oil and butter until they are firm and golden. They can be served dry, as a first course, or as an accompaniment to meat, or they can be put in a fireproof dish with melted butter and grated cheese and left in the oven until the cheese has melted.

Although it is not traditional, a little grated Gruyère or Parmesan, about an ounce, added to the original mixture at the same time as the eggs, is an improvement. And since the frying of this quantity of croquettes is heavy on butter and rather tricky to do all at one time, they can be cooked and served like Italian potato gnocchi. That is, instead of forming the mixture into croquettes, roll them lightly into small round or cork shapes. Drop them into very gently boiling salted water, and take them out with a perforated spoon when they float to the top, which takes 3 or 4 minutes. Put them in a buttered gratin dish, sprinkle with grated cheese and a little more butter and leave in a moderate oven for a few minutes. They are very light done like this.

L'ALIGOT

The French have invented dozens of excellent potato dishes, but many of them turn out less successfully here than in France because we can rarely get the right varieties of kidney or waxy potatoes. Here is one which is suitable to English potatoes. It is a purely local country dish which I came across at Entraygues, a little town on the confluence of two rivers, the Lot and the Truyère, in south-western France. It was described to me by a very ancient lady in the shop where I was buying local cooking pots, and the proprietress of the hotel where we were staying obligingly cooked it for us.

2 lb. floury potatoes, 10 oz. cheese, 2 oz. butter, 4–5 oz. cream, salt, garlic.

The cheese used for this dish is the soft white unfermented *tomme de Cantal* (not to be confused with Cantal proper, which somewhat resembles English cheeses in consistency) but I find that Caerphilly, a mild cheese which melts easily, serves the purpose very well. A mild and unmatured Lancashire would also be suitable but, being stronger flavoured, 2 oz. less would be sufficient.

Cook the potatoes in their skins, peel and sieve them to a dry purée, and add seasoning. Heat the butter and cream in a heavy pan, put in the purée, stir until hot and amalgamated, add a very little crushed garlic, then the cheese, cut into small squares, all at once, and stir until it is all melted and quite smooth. Serve quickly before the mixture starts getting grainy.

As will be perceived from the list of ingredients, this is scarcely a light dish. It was served to us quite on its own, as a first course, but I think myself a few small slices of bread fried in butter provide a good accompaniment—something crisp to contrast with the softness of the potatoes.

If there is some left over, it makes most excellent potato cakes. Simply form the mixture into small flat cakes, roll them lightly in flour and fry them gently to a light golden colour.

GRATIN DAUPHINOIS

Dauphine and *dauphinois*, similar though they sound, are two very different preparations of potatoes, both most excellent in their ways.

pommes dauphine (the recipe is on page 273) make an ideal accompaniment to steaks and small roasts, for those who are not daunted by last-minute deep frying. *Gratin dauphinois* is a rich and filling regional dish from the Dauphiné. Some recipes, Escoffier's and Austin de Croze's among them, include cheese and eggs, making it very similar to a *gratin savoyard*: but other regional authorities declare that the authentic *gratin dauphinois* is made only with potatoes and thick fresh cream. I give the second version which is, I think, the better one; it is also the easier. And if it seems to the thrifty-minded outrageously extravagant to use half a pint of cream to one pound of potatoes, I can only say that to me it seems a more satisfactory way of enjoying cream than pouring it over tinned peaches or chocolate mousse.

Peel 1 lb. of yellow potatoes, and slice them in even rounds no thicker than a penny; this operation is very easy with the aid of the mandoline (see page 64). Rinse them thoroughly in cold water—this is most important—then shake them dry in a cloth. Put them in layers in a shallow *earthenware* dish which has been rubbed with garlic and well buttered. Season with pepper and salt. Pour ½ pint of thick cream over them; strew with little pieces of butter; cook them for 1½ hours in a low oven, Gas No. 2, 310 deg. F. During the last 10 minutes turn the oven up fairly high to get a fine golden crust on the potatoes. Serve in the dish in which they have cooked; it is not easy to say how many people this will serve; two, or three, or four, according to their capacity, and what there is to follow.

Much depends also upon the quality of the potatoes used. Firm waxy varieties such as the *kipfler* and the Fir-apple Pink which appear occasionally on the London market make a gratin lighter and also more authentic than that made with routine commercial King Edwards or Majestics which are in every respect second best.

Two more points concerning the proportions of a *gratin dauphinois:* as the quantity of potatoes is increased the proportion of cream may be slightly diminished. Thus, for 3lb. of potatoes, 1¼ pints of cream will be amply sufficient; and the choice of cooking dish (for the appropriate shape see the *tian*, Fig. 2, page 61. is also important, for the potatoes and cream should, always, fill the dish to within approximately three quarters of an inch of the top.

The best way, in my view, of appreciating the charm of a *gratin dauphinois* is to present the dish entirely on its own, as a first course. It can precede grilled or plain roast meat or poultry, or a cold joint to be eaten with a simple green salad.

La Charcuterie

Pâtés and terrines, sausages, ham dishes and other pork products

A GREAT deal is said and written about the innate cooking skill of every French housewife and every *patron-chef* of every other auberge, restaurant and transport café in the land. While not wishing in any way to belittle the culinary talents so lavishly bestowed by Providence upon the French, and so brilliantly cultivated by them, it should be observed that both housewife and restaurateur frequently lean heavily upon their local *charcutiers* and *pâtissiers*. If a housewife has but little time for cooking, she is able to rely upon the terrines and pâtés, the sausages, the hams and all the miscellaneous pork products of the *charcutier*, to make a quick midday meal for her family or a first course for her lunch party. If the talents of her cook do not lie in the direction of pastry-making, she can with perfect confidence order a *vol-au-vent* to fill with a rich creamy sea-food mixture, or a cake, a handsome fruit flan or a *savarin* to serve as dessert, while she and her cook concentrate upon the meat, the fish and the vegetables.

The reputation of many a small restaurateur has been built upon the products of the local *charcutier*. A careful look at the details of restaurant specialities given in the Michelin and other guides shows that not a few of them owe their star to some kind of sausage, or pâté, *andouillette* or *pieds de porc truffés*. Ten to one you will find that not far away from that restaurant is a first-class pork butcher. Or it may be that the pork butcher himself has gone into the restaurant business as an outlet for his products. In fact, this is partly the reason that the English tourist often finds that the one-star restaurant is a disappointment, for the rest of the cooking is not always up to the standard of the *charcuterie*.

I cannot say that Lamastre in the Ardèche is typical of any small French provincial town, for it has been made famous throughout France by Madame Barattero and the lovely food she has been serving there for thirty years at the Hôtel du Midi. Neither can it be suggested that Madame Barattero relies upon the local *charcutier*, for, first by her husband and, after he died, by her chef, the same few beautiful and high-class dishes have been produced almost every day of those thirty years. But the first-class *charcutier* is there all right and works in co-operation with the hotel, supplying it with at least one of its renowned specialities, a sausage which the Barattero chef cooks and presents wrapped in the lightest and most melting of puff pastries. . . .

Into Montagne's beautiful blue and cream tiled shop, hidden away in a narrow, unprepossessing street in Lamastre, I strolled, therefore, one Whitsunday morning to see what might be going on while all the housewives and restaurateurs in the town would be busy preparing their Sunday midday feast.

Besides the sausages and the hams, the pâtés and the local Ardéchois specialities called *jambonnettes*, *cayettes* and *rosettes* (unexpectedly, this is a salame type of sausage also popular in Lyon but better made here, I thought—it is identifiable by the coarse-meshed net in which it is presented for sale), there were all sorts of special things for the fêtes. There were trays of snails, their shells almost bursting with fresh-looking parsley butter, and Sunday hors-d'œuvre of cones of raw ham alternating with little chicken liver pâtés moulded in sparkling aspic jelly, all arranged by Madame Montagne herself on long narrow-plated dishes and ready to take away. There was a huge supply of *quenelles de brochet* (you can't get away from them in these parts) and in the magnificent butcher's block of smooth scrubbed wood was a tank-sized two-handled pan of pale orange-coloured sauce full of chopped olives, to serve with the *quenelles*. Beside it was one of those monolithic loaves of butter which never fail to have their effect upon English eyes accustomed to seeing only little half-pound slabs in paper wrappings.

There was a steady stream of customers making last-minute purchases for their Sunday lunches. One woman came in with her saucepan and took away her sauce in it, all ready to put upon the stove and to serve with her *quenelles*. For another, Madame Montagne swiftly cut half a pound of *jambon du pays* in the requisite postcard-thin slices. (The French don't always take sufficient care about this point. I have seen the otherwise excellent *jambon d'Auvergne* absolutely murdered by being slashed into doorsteps.) A small boy had been sent by his mother to buy an extra chicken to roast. There was none left. What about some sausages instead? The cooking sausages from chez Montagne are the very ones which go into the *feuilletage* at Barattero's, and, as we were to discover presently, made those of Lyon appear very coarse in comparison. And in between serving her customers, Madame Montagne told me how the *jambonnettes* are cut from the knuckle end of a ham, boned, stuffed with fresh pork meat and sewn up into a fat little cushion shape, how the *rosette* is called after the particular kind of sausage skin in which it is encased, a thick and fat skin which, during the curing process, nourishes the meat inside and gives it its characteristically fresh and moist quality; how a mixture of leg and shoulder meat is used for this kind of sausage and how it is the favourite *charcuterie* speciality of the Ardèche, so that out of every four pigs killed the legs of two only are made into hams, the others, and the shoulders, being used for *rosettes*; how the fresh dry air up here at Lamastre is more propitious for the manufacture of sausages than the notorious fog and damp of Lyon; how they do not care here for that ancient traditional *saucisse aux herbes* which is still made down on the Rhône, but how the same sort of mixture of pork with cabbage, spinach and *blettes* is made into *cayettes*. These resemble rather large rissoles, cooked in the oven, all browned and very appetising-looking in serried rows on their baking trays. Madame Montagne said she didn't think I'd like them, but they have a not unattractive, coarse flavour which collectors of genuinely rustic dishes would appreciate.

Another speciality, Madame Montagne told me, her green almond eyes curious that I should want to know all these things, was the pâté made largely with *grattons*, the little browned scraps which are the residue after the pork fat has been melted down, and which were also the original ingredient of the renowned *rillettes de Tours*.

And the interesting decoration of the shop? Who had created it? It was designed twenty-five years ago by M. Montagne's grandfather; the lapis-coloured tiles were really to discourage flies, for it is well known that blue repels them but, using the blue as his starting point, old M. Reymond achieved a most original and oddly beautiful combination, a kind of mosaic of sea colours which turns the *charcuterie* into a cool and orderly grotto, if such a thing can be imagined, with the rows of hanging sausages and hams for stalactites. The young Montagnes are very go-ahead (the family have been in the *charcuterie* business for some eighty years) and would like to install a large refrigerated cabinet—but it would mean destroying some of *grandpère*'s work and that would break the old man's heart. And I hope that even after he is dead the young couple will leave his shop intact, for it is the work of a man who was an artist in design as well as in *charcuterie*.

Madame Montagne told me that many foreign customers who come to Lamastre to eat Madame Barattero's food also come and buy the *charcuterie* products (once again, the link between the restaurant and the local shopkeepers), Germans, Belgians, Swiss, even Italians. She did not, I think, realise what a compliment this is, for it is not common to find sausages anywhere in Europe as good as those of Italy. And all these visitors would surely be sorry to see the old decoration and the elegant little façade of the shop replaced with gleaming glass and chromium.

Here in England we have nothing quite comparable with the French *charcuterie*. In the Midlands and the North it is true that there are excellent pork butchers who sell ready-cooked pigs' trotters, stuffed chines of bacon for slicing cold, a kind of pâté made from pork scraps, very similar to the *grattons* of French country *charcutiers*, and cooked shoulder gammon. The majority of us, however, must rely upon the commercial liver pâtés sold in the delicatessen shops, rather bleak cold cuts of beef, ham and pork, central European type boiling sausages made in this country, very expensive imported salame sausages and our own commercial frying or grilling sausages. It is, incidentally, a curious anomaly that while we are willing to pay something like twelve shillings a pound for imported salame sausages, we are unable to face the fact that if we want pure pork sausages for cooking they will cost up to seven shillings a pound, and this makes it difficult to reproduce many of the hot sausage dishes which are such a feature of French cookery and which provide such an excellent solution to the problem of what to serve as a rather substantial hot first course when the rest of the meal is to be comparatively light. Nevertheless there are signs that a renaissance of the English sausage is at hand and so I do not feel that it is quite useless to include in this chapter a few recipes for hot sausage dishes, together with such things as grilled pigs' trotters, ham in a cream sauce, and other little dishes which, strictly speaking, are meat dishes but which, in French cookery, nearly always precede the main dish, whether it be chicken, fish, game or another meat course. Most of these dishes can naturally be adapted to form the chief dish at the midday meal.

As for pâtés and terrines, with the exception of the incomparable *pâté de foie gras*, bought pâtés in England are seldom very satisfactory, and it is not difficult to make your own. If you have no earthenware or fireproof porcelain terrines in which to cook them, this need be no deterrent. For a very small cost enamelled baking tins in all sizes, fireproof glass dishes, or even oblong loaf tins can be bought, and these serve just as well. They don't look quite so nice on the table, but the pâtés can be turned out on to a dish and sliced for serving.

There is a tendency among English restaurant cooks to put far too much bacon in their pâtés. No doubt this is a legacy of the days of rationing, when bacon was easier to come by than fresh pork. Nowadays there is no need and no reason for it.

TERRINE DE CAMPAGNE
PORK AND LIVER PÂTÉ

This is the sort of pâté you get in French restaurants under the alternative names of *pâté maison* or *terrine du chef*.

The ingredients are 1 lb. each of fat pork (belly) and lean veal, ½ lb. of pig's liver, an after-dinner coffee-cup of dry white wine, 2 tablespoons of brandy, a clove of garlic, half a dozen each of black peppercorns and juniper berries, a ¼ teaspoon of ground mace, 4 oz. of fat bacon or, better still, if your butcher will provide it, of either flare fat, or back fat, which is the pork fat often used for wrapping round birds for roasting.

An obliging butcher will usually mince for you the pork, veal and liver, provided he is given due notice. It saves a great deal of time, and I always believe in making my dealers work for me if they will.

To the minced meats, all thoroughly blended, add 2 oz. of the fat bacon or pork fat cut in thin, irregular little dice, the seasonings chopped and blended (half a dessertspoon of salt will be sufficient), and the wine and brandy. Mix very thoroughly and, if there is time, leave to stand for an hour or two before cooking, so that the flavours penetrate the meat. Turn into one large 2-pint capacity terrine, or into 2 or 3 smaller ones, about 2 to 2½ inches deep. Cut the remaining fat or bacon into thin strips and arrange it across the top of the pâté. Place the terrines in a baking tin filled with water and cook, uncovered, in a slow oven, Gas No. 2, 310 deg. F. for 1¼ to 1½ hours. The pâtés are cooked when they begin to come away from the sides of the dish.

Take them from the oven, being careful not to spill any of the fat, and leave them to cool. They will cut better if, when the fat has all but set, they are weighted. To do this, cover with greaseproof paper and a board or plate which fits inside the terrine and put a weight on top. However, if this proves impractical, it is not of very great importance. If the terrines are to be kept longer than a week, cover them completely, once they are cold, with a sealing layer of just-melted pure pork lard.

When cooking the pâtés remember that it is the *depth* of the terrine rather than its surface area which determines the cooking time. The seasonings of garlic and juniper berries are optional.

Serve these pâtés as a first course, with toast or French bread. Some people like butter as well, although they are quite rich enough without.

Lastly, the proportions of meat, liver and seasonings making up the pâtés can be altered to suit individual tastes, but always with due regard to the finished texture of the product. A good pâté is moist and fat without being greasy, and it should be faintly pink inside, not grey or brown. A dry pâté is either the result of overcooking, or of too small a proportion of fat meat having been used. And ideally all the meat for pâtés should be cut up by hand rather than put through the mincing machine, which squeezes and dries the meat. But this is a counsel of perfection which few people nowadays would care to follow.

Alternative proportions for those who like more liver and less meat

1 lb. 2 oz. pig's liver, 1¼ lb. belly of pork, ½ lb. lean veal, a coffee-cup of dry white wine, 2 tablespoons brandy, 2 cloves garlic, 6 to 8 juniper berries (optional), 1 dessertspoon salt, 4 black peppercorns, mace, 4 oz. of back pork fat or 4 rashers of fat bacon.

The procedure is exactly as in the first recipe.

TERRÍNE DE GIBIER
GAME PÂTÉ

A wild duck (mallard), 1½ lb. of fat pork, ¼ lb. fat, mild bacon, seasonings and white wine as above.

The orthodox way to make a game pâté is to strip all the flesh off the bird in its raw state. It is a tedious, wasteful process until you have done it many times, so it is permissible to half roast the bird, let it cool, and then remove and mince or chop the meat.

Put your duck, therefore, to roast for 20 minutes or so in a medium hot oven. When cool remove all the meat and discard the skin, but be careful to preserve as much as possible of the juices which run out during the process. Chop or mince the meat, coarsely. Blend it thoroughly with the minced pork and 2 oz. of the fat bacon, cut into little cubes, and which supply the squares of fat characteristic in these home-made pâtés. Add the seasonings and the wine exactly as for the pork and liver pâté, and cook in the same way.

Any game birds can be turned into pâté in this way, allowing approximately the equivalent weight in pork of the uncooked weight of the bird. So instead of one mallard you would need three teal, or two stewing partridges, or two large pigeons, which make a cheap and excellent pâté. A domestic duck, being so fat, needs only a small proportion of pork, or a mixture of pork and veal.

For a *terrine de lièvre* or hare pâté, also allow equal proportions of fat pork, or even a little more, for hare is very dry, and the flavour too needs softening to make a successful terrine.

TERRINE DE PORC ET DE GIBIER
PORK AND GAME PÂTÉ

Here is a pâté on a somewhat larger scale, suitable for a party or for a buffet supper. It will be sufficient for twenty to twenty-five people, and is all the better for being made three or four days in advance.

Quantities are, 2 lb. each of belly of pork and leg of veal (the pieces sold by some butchers as pie veal will do, as these are usually oddments of good quality trimmed from escalopes and so on), $\frac{1}{2}$ lb. of back pork fat and 1 wild duck or pheasant. For the seasoning you need 2 teacups of dry white wine, 1 tablespoon of salt, 8 to 10 juniper berries, 1 large clove of garlic, 10 peppercorns, 2 tablespoons of stock made from the duck carcase with a little extra white wine or Madeira.

Mince the pork and the veal together, or to save time get the butcher to do this for you. Partly roast the duck or pheasant, take all the flesh from the bones, chop fairly small and mix with the pork and veal. Add 5 oz. of the fat cut into little pieces, the garlic, juniper berries and peppercorns all chopped together, the salt. Pour in the white wine, amalgamate thoroughly and leave in a cold place while you cook the duck carcase and the trimmings in a little water and wine with seasonings to make the stock. Strain it, reduce to 2 good tablespoons, and add to the mixture (if it is necessary to expedite matters, this part of the preparation can be dispensed with altogether; it is to add a little extra gamy flavour to the pâté).

Turn into a 3-pint terrine; cover the top with a criss-cross pattern of the rest of the pork fat cut into little strips. Cover with foil. Stand in a baking tin containing water, and cook in a low oven, Gas No. 3, 330 deg. F.

for 2 hours. During the last 15 minutes remove the paper, and the top of the pâté will cook to a beautiful golden brown.

One wild duck or pheasant to 4 lb. of meat sounds a very small proportion for a game pâté, but will give a sufficiently strong flavour for most tastes. Also the seasonings of garlic, pepper and juniper berries are kept in very moderate proportions when the pâté is for people who may not be accustomed to these rather strong flavours, and with whose tastes one may not be familiar.

To serve a large pâté for a party the best plan is to slice it down just before the party, but leaving it in the terrine in its original shape. In this way the appearance will not be spoilt, but the slices will be quite easy to lift out.

PÂTÉ DE CANARD LUCULLUS
TRUFFLED PÂTÉ OF DUCK

At the restaurant Barattero at Lamastre is served just about the best duck pâté, or galantine, which I have ever eaten. It is not at all too rich, and its flavour is most delicate. It is quite a complicated dish to make and even if you can afford all the ingredients and have an obliging poultry dealer who will bone the duck for you, there is still a good deal of work to be done on it. Even then the chances are that the result will not be quite as it is at Barattero's, but this would not be a disgrace, for the chef there has been serving it, along with the four or five other specialities of the house, every day for a considerable number of years, so it is not altogether surprising that he should have brought it to a point of perfection which even the most talented amateur cook could hardly be expected to reach. All the same, such a dish represents something of a challenge; for those who care to take it up, here is the recipe which Madame Barattero has given me permission to publish:

'Take a good white Bresse duck, weighing about 3½ lb.; open it right along the back, taking care not to pierce the skin, and completely remove all the flesh. Take care to preserve the feet intact; bone the carcase completely and set aside the liver.

'Take 2 lb. 2 oz. of good white fillet of pork, with fat and sinews removed; mince it in the finest blade of the mincer with the flesh of the duck.

'Pound this minced mixture in the mortar and season it with ⅓ oz. of salt, 1/10 oz. of pepper, a pinch of mixed spice, incorporate into it 2 whole eggs, some truffle essence, 2 oz. of cognac, and then stir into the whole mixture just under 2 oz. of *foie gras*.

'Lay the skin of the duck out flat, spread it with the stuffing and in the centre put the liver of the duck, a little more *foie gras* and some slices of truffle. Draw the edges of the skin together, and sew them up with a trussing needle.

'This operation complete, the duck will look like a long fat sausage with the feet of the duck sticking out at the end. Wrap it up in fine slices of back pork fat, and cover the whole with greaseproof paper. Cook 50 minutes in a fairly hot oven, basting it frequently with its own juices.'

This pâté is served as an hors-d'œuvre, quite alone of course, no salad or anything else whatever.

RILLETTES DE PORC
POTTED PORK

As an alternative to a home-made pâté, *rillettes*, which might be described as a kind of potted pork, are quite easy to make at home, and as they keep well, can be made in a fair quantity and stored.

Get the butcher to remove the rind and the bones of approximately 2 lb. of belly or neck of pork and 1 lb. of back pork fat. Rub the meat well with salt and leave it to stand for 4 to 6 hours in summer, overnight in winter. Cut it in thick strips along the grooves from where the bones were taken out, then again into little strips rather shorter than a match and about twice as thick. Put all these into an earthenware or other oven dish, with the pork fat also cut into small pieces; bury a crushed clove of garlic and a bouquet of herbs in the centre, season with a little pepper, add a soup ladle of water, put on the lid of the pan and cook in a very low oven, Gas No. 1, 290 deg. F. for about 4 hours.

By this time the meat should be very soft and swimming in its own limpid fat. Taste to see if more salt or pepper are needed. *Rillettes* are insipid if not properly seasoned.

Turn the contents of the pan into a wire sieve standing over a big bowl, so that the fat drips through. When well drained, partly pound and then with two forks pull the *rillettes* until they are in fine shreds rather than a paste. Pile lightly into a glazed earthenware or china jar or two or three little ones. Pour the fat over the top of the *rillettes*, leaving behind any sediment and juices, and completely filling the jars. Cover with foil. *Rillettes* should be of a soft texture, so if they have to be stored in a refrigerator, the jars should be removed several hours before serving time.

As I have described in the introductory chapter dealing with the food of the Loire valley, *rillettes* and another version of the same dish, called *rillons,* in which the pieces of pork are much larger, are to be bought in every *charcuterie* and are served in every restaurant. Nowadays the final shredding of *rillettes* is often done by machine, but the good *charcutiers* will tell you that this is not satisfactory, for it reduces them to too purée-like a consistency.

RILLETTES D'OIE

POTTED GOOSE AND PORK

Few people nowadays would want to cut up a goose simply to make *rillettes,* but when you have, say, a leg of roast goose and some good pieces of the carcase meat left over at Christmas time, this is an excellent dish in which to use it up.

Cut the goose meat from the bones and cook it with 1½ to 2 lb. of fat pork and seasonings exactly as described above, plus about 4 tablespoons of the fat saved from the goose when it was roasted.

The timing and finishing of the dish are also as for the pork rillettes.

RILLETTES DE LAPIN

POTTED RABBIT AND PORK

About ½ lb. of rabbit meat, weighed uncooked and cut from the bone, to 1½ lb. of fat pork, the whole cooked exactly as described for the pork *rillettes,* make an excellent little hors-d'œuvre.

GALANTINE DE PORC AU VIN BLANC

GALANTINE OF PORK WITH WHITE WINE

For this galantine the ideal cut is a hand of pork, an inexpensive joint comprising both a good proportion of lean meat and the trotter which, together with the rind of the meat, supply the necessary gelatinous elements.

An average hand of pork will weigh about 5 lb. Get the butcher to remove the rind and bone and tie the joint. Other ingredients are 2 wineglasses of dry white wine, 4 or 5 little onions and the same number of carrots, 2 cloves of garlic, a tomato, a bouquet consisting of a stick of celery, a leek, 2 bay leaves, several sprigs of parsley and a little piece of lemon peel; seasonings are a scant dessertspoon of salt, 4 crushed juniper berries, 6 peppercorns.

Split the trotter. Put it together with the rind of the pork cut into strips, and the bones from the joint, into a big saucepan in which all the ingredients will fit without leaving too much space. Add the vegetables, the bouquet, the seasonings, and the meat tied into a sausage shape. Put in the wine and enough water to just about cover the whole contents of the pan, bring very gently to the boil, skim, cover the pan, and cook extremely slowly for about 2 to 2½ hours. Remove the meat, which by now should be very tender. Continue cooking the rest for another hour, then strain the liquid into a bowl and leave it to set. (With the debris a second stock can be made for some other dish.)

Chop the meat and at least half of the rind roughly, not too small. Pack it into a fairly deep terrine or bowl of about 4-pint capacity so that it is about three-quarters full. See that it is well seasoned. Pour in about one soup ladle of the warm stock and leave the galantine to set. All this must be done while the meat and stock are still warm or the mixture will not coagulate.

This, in principle, makes the ordinary galantine, which can be sliced like a pâté. If it is for a special occasion, put the meat into an oblong tin or terrine so that it can be cut into elegant-looking slices. The jelly, which in the ordinary way is reserved for some other purpose, can accompany it. Proceed as follows:

Remove every speck of fat from the jelly when it has set. Beat the whites of 2 eggs just until they begin to froth. Put them into a saucepan with the jelly, bring very gradually to simmering point and leave over the lowest possible flame so that the liquid is only just moving, for 7 to 10 minutes. Turn off the heat and leave another 10 minutes. Strain through a cloth wrung out in warm water. The liquid should now be absolutely clear, and a pale straw colour. Leave it to set again.

To serve the galantine, slice it and arrange it in the centre of a long, flat dish. Surround it with the chopped jelly, which will be beautifully flavoured and as clear as glass.

This recipe is based on one used in Lorraine for making one of their traditional feast day dishes—a galantine for which a whole sucking pig is cut up. The wine, the vegetables, the herbs and spices, all combine to make it one of the best dishes of its type I have yet tasted; but pork galantine is not a long-keeping dish so don't choose to make it in exceptionally hot or thundery weather.

GALANTINE DE PORC À LA BOURGUIGNONNE
GALANTINE OF PORK WITH PARSLEY AND GARLIC

Make your galantine as above (it can, of course, be made in smaller or larger quantities) and when the meat is ready chopped to go into the terrines, mix with it 3 or 4 tablespoons of parsley very finely chopped with a clove or two of garlic. This makes a particularly charming looking galantine, reminiscent in appearance of the famous Burgundian ham galantine, the *jambon persillé*, which is one of the great specialities of Burgundy, always served at Easter, and for which a whole, uncooked ham is simmered with pigs' feet and white wine. The jelly, mixed with parsley and garlic, is poured over the ham, which is cut in fairly large pieces and pressed down into a big white salad bowl. But, unless you have your own home-cured hams or want to cook a whole one, this is not a practical proposition for English kitchens, for it is difficult to buy half or quarter of a cured, uncooked ham; and gammon, even unsmoked, does not quite do instead.

PIEDS DE PORC PANÉS OR STE. MÉNÉHOULD
GRILLED PIGS' TROTTERS

Pigs' trotters are considered quite a delicacy in France and can usually be bought ready-cooked and breadcrumbed in the *charcuteries*, so that all you have to do is to heat them up under the grill. *Pieds de porc truffés* have made the reputation of many a *charcutier* and restaurateur, and provide a good example of the way the humblest kind of plebeian dish can be transformed into a luxury; the cooked trotters are boned, stuffed with chopped pork or sausage meat and truffles, wrapped in *crépine*[1] and grilled. But quite apart from the expense of the truffles, this is rather a performance to attempt at home and even penny-plain pigs' trotters simply boiled, breadcrumbed and grilled make an excellent hot hors-d'œuvre for those who do not despise cheap foods.

The method is as follows: for 4 pigs' trotters the other ingredients are an onion, a couple of carrots, a big bouquet of parsley, bayleaf, a stick or two of celery and a strip of lemon peel tied together, seasonings and water. For the final operation, breadcrumbs, melted butter and, to serve with the trotters, a *sauce tartare*.

If possible, buy the trotters a day in advance, sprinkle them with coarse salt and leave them in a cool place until the time comes to cook them. Then rinse them, put them in a large saucepan with the vegetables, herbs and a little salt, and cover them completely with cold water. Bring to simmering point, take off the scum and cover the pan, tilting the lid so that steam can escape. Let them simmer for about 3½ hours until you see that the skin and meat are coming loose from the bones. Take them out and leave in a dish to cool a little. Strain the stock and keep it. Cooked again with some minced beef it will make a fine jelly.

[1] See page 88.

While the trotters are still warm, coat them with barely melted butter
and then with dried breadcrumbs. One coating will be sufficient but it
should be a very thick one and should be well pressed down. About 1½ oz.
each of breadcrumbs and butter should be enough for this operation.

Now the theory is that the trotters should be put straight under the
grill and cooked until the outside is brown and crunchy but, in practice,
this does not work very well because, under the grill of a domestic
cooker, the outer coating will be cooked before the trotters are really hot,
so the best system is to put them in a flat fireproof dish or in the grill
pan, pour a little more melted butter over them and let them get
thoroughly hot in a moderate oven for about 15 minutes. Then transfer
the dish to the grill and let the outer coating get thoroughly browned and
crisp. Trotters must be served absolutely sizzling hot on sizzling hot
plates; the *sauce tartare*, or *rémoulade*, should be rather highly
flavoured, and there should be plenty of it.

SAUCISSON EN BRIOCHE À LA LYONNAISE

SAUSAGE BAKED IN BRIOCHE DOUGH

The sausage used in Lyon, where this dish is a renowned speciality, may
be one of three kinds; it may be one of the routine cooking sausages, very
coarsely cut and interlarded with large cubes of fat; it may be a *cervelas*,
a close-textured sausage, very lightly smoked; or it may be a *cervelas
truffé*, an unsmoked sausage of coarsely-cut pork generously truffled and
spiced. Whichever it is, it will weigh in the region of 12 to 14 oz. and
be about 1½ inches in diameter, and because the pork for these sausages
(as indeed for the majority of fresh or partly cured French sausages) is
either brined for a night and a day or has saltpetre added to the mixture
before the skins are filled, the colour of the finished sausage is a good
red instead of the pinkish-grey characteristic of our own sausages.

Randall & Aubin, in Brewer Street, Soho, sell a coarsely-cut garlic-
flavoured sausage which is not unlike the Lyon sausage, and the Italian
shops of Soho supply *cotechino*, the Modena boiling sausage which is also
suitable for this dish; and at Harrods' butchery counter there is a special
pure pork luncheon sausage, English in character, which is admirable
for this dish and for the two which follow, for I see no reason why we
should not adapt these splendid French dishes using the ingredients
which are available to us here. And no doubt many readers will be able
to persuade their own local butchers to obtain the right casings for these
large sausages and to fill them with their own favourite sausage mixture.
But it should be borne in mind that if you are going to wrap a sausage

H

in a brioche dough or even a flaky pastry, as for our own sausage rolls, it is really preferable to have a pure meat sausage. If you use a sausage containing the usual English mixture of 35 per cent bread or rusk, it means you are going to eat a rather doughy dish.

Now for the recipe.

It must be given in some detail and will take up a good deal of space, but I trust that its rather formidable length will not deter readers from trying it, for in many ways it makes the almost perfect hot first course dish, the majority of the work being done well in advance and the timing of the final cooking such that it can be put in the oven a few moments before your guests are expected and, in half an hour, is ready to emerge, a beautiful, golden roll of brioche enclosing the delicious savoury sausage. The procedure is as follows:

(1) If the sausage is to be served at lunch, the brioche dough is made the previous night; if for dinner, in the early morning of the same day. It is extremely easy, for this is a simplified brioche dough. First you mix to a paste a scant $\frac{1}{2}$ oz. of baker's yeast and 2 tablespoons of barely tepid milk. In a bowl you then put 6 oz. of plain flour, a half teaspoon of salt and 1 of sugar. Make a well in the centre. Into this break 2 whole eggs, and add the yeast mixture. Fold the flour over the eggs and yeast and knead all together until the mixture is smooth. Now beat in with your hands 4 oz. of the best butter, softened but not melted. Knead again and shape it into a ball. Put it in a clean bowl, a wooden one for preference, in which you have sprinkled some flour. Make a deep crosswise incision across the top of the ball of dough with a knife. Cover it with a clean, folded muslin. Put the bowl in a warm place, such as a heated linen cupboard or near the boiler, or in the plate drawer of the cooker with the oven turned on to a very low temperature. Leave it for 2 hours, by which time it should have risen to at least twice its original volume and will look and feel light and spongy. Break it down, knead it lightly once more into a ball, cover it again, and this time put the bowl in a cool larder and leave it until next day, or until the evening.

(2) Put your large sausage (the quantity of dough is enough for a 12 to 14 oz. sausage) into a pan in which it will lie flat. Cover completely with cold water. Bring very gently to simmering point and thereafter let it cook with the water barely moving for 45 minutes to an hour. Take it out and put it on a board or dish until it is cool enough to handle. Now remove the skin, very carefully.

(3) Allowing yourself half an hour the first few times you do this dish (afterwards it will be much quicker) make the final preparations. Very lightly rub a baking sheet with butter. Put your dough on this, sprinkle

it with flour, and with your hands spread and pat it out into a rectangular shape on the baking sheet. Turn it over (by this time you can, or should be able to, handle the dough as easily as if it were a piece of material). Put your skinned sausage, still warm, in the centre. Gather up the edges of the dough and, having dipped your fingers in cold water, pinch the edges lightly together, along the top and at the ends, so that the whole thing looks rather like a small bolster. Now dip a pastry brush in cream and paint the whole of the exposed surface with it (cream makes the best glaze for these sorts of dishes—not so shiny as egg and smoother than milk). With the back of a knife lightly mark a few criss-cross lines on the dough. The sausage and its brioche can now be left for 15 to 20 minutes, ready on its baking sheet, before it goes into the centre of a pre-heated oven at Gas No. 5, 375–380 deg. F., to bake for 30 minutes. When you take it from the oven, leave the brioche standing for 5 minutes before transferring it, with the aid of a flat fish slice, to a serving dish, and carving it deftly into thickish slices, starting in the middle and working outwards. It will be ample for four.

One should not perhaps expect this dish to come exactly right the first time, except for those accustomed to working with yeast doughs. But although it may sound complicated, after one or two tries it becomes a matter of timing rather than of any special knowledge, and you get a splendid-looking delicious dish with absurdly little trouble. It is mainly a question of assembling all your ingredients and utensils before each of the two main operations—the original mixing of the dough and the final wrapping of the sausage in it. Points to observe carefully are:

(1) Brioche dough is very much more liquid than bread dough, but if after the initial mixing it is really too soft to handle, it may be because you have added a little too much milk to the yeast, or because the eggs were unusually large, or because you are using a soft flour. A little more flour sprinkled in will put matters right.

(2) The sausage is to be put into the dough while it is still warm, because if it is left to get quite cold it will separate from the brioche when it is cut; but if it is too hot the fat running from it will make your dough liquid and difficult to handle.

(3) Be sure to join the edges of the dough well together round the sausage without drawing it too tightly or the sausage will burst through during the baking. This does not detract from the taste of the dish, but rather spoils its appearance.

(4) It is essential that the sausage be cooked right through to start with; once inside its casing of brioche, it will heat but will scarcely cook any more.

SAUCISSON CHAUD À LA LYONNAISE

POACHED SAUSAGE WITH HOT POTATO SALAD

This is an exceedingly simple, almost primitive, dish which is very popular in Lyon and in many country districts of central France. It consists of a large pork sausage, the seasoning and exact composition of which varies according to local tradition, simply poached very slowly (a 12 to 16 oz. sausage takes about 1 hour) in plenty of water to cover, and served on a long dish surrounded by a hot potato salad.

This is made by slicing boiled waxy potatoes into thick rounds while they are still hot, and seasoning them with a little oil, vinegar, salt and pepper dressing. The dish is usually served as a first course, or hot hors-d'œuvre, although it can well make a main luncheon dish. Given a good sausage and well-seasoned potatoes, it is a most delicious dish, which will not be despised by the most fastidious.

Francis Amunatégui, a distinguished French gastronome and journalist, writes of this Lyonnais sausage in deeply emotional terms: 'The appearance,' he says, 'of a hot sausage with its salad of potatoes in oil can leave nobody indifferent . . . it is pure, it precludes all sentimentality, it is the Truth.'

SAUCISSON CHAUD À L'ALSACIENNE

POACHED SAUSAGE WITH HORSERADISH SAUCE

Again, a large poached sausage served plain as a first course and accompanied only by a mild and creamy horseradish sauce. To make this you need either freshly grated horseradish or the kind imported from Sweden and sold in $1\frac{1}{4}$ oz. cartons at Harrods and other delicatessen counters. The brand name is Winborg, and the importers are Trustin Foods, 55 Chalk Farm Road, N.W.1.

About 1 tablespoon of this horseradish is stirred into $\frac{1}{4}$ pint of thick cream; season with salt and squeeze in a little lemon juice. You then add a few drops of olive oil; this stabilises the sauce, which should be thick and quite smooth.

It may well be asked, what is to be served after these sausage dishes? Almost anything, except pork, beef with Yorkshire pudding, or any other dish containing dough or pastry after the brioche, and, of course, no horseradish sauce with beef after the Alsace dish, and no dish requiring potatoes after the Lyonnais one.

A fine salmon trout, either hot or cold, is what I usually choose in the summer season, or sometimes a cold lobster with the sauce described on page 325, and then a vegetable dish or salad. This sounds odd after a meat dish, but in France they seem to have fewer inhibitions about planning the menu than we have here, and on at least three occasions I remember being served with fish, not specially ordered but on the menu of the day, after sausage dishes: after the brioche sausage, it was *sole meunière*; after sausage in flaky pastry, fish *quenelles*; and skate with black butter followed the sausage with hot potato salad. In Alsace, the hot sausage with horseradish sauce was followed by an open, creamy, onion tart. But a roast or grilled chicken with salad, a cold chicken in a cream sauce, a veal roast, escalopes, a duckling, pheasant or partridge, according to what suits the occasion, would all make a lovely meal. For a simple lunch, one of the sausage dishes followed by a hot vegetable, cheese, and some little creamy sweet or fruit in wine would be perfect.

SAUCISSES EN CHEMISE

This is a charming, light-hearted dish but shouldn't be taken too seriously. It involves rather lengthy preparation for such trifles as miniature chipolata sausages, but it is a dish which always has a great success, especially with young people, so it's worth it if you have the time and the aptitude for this sort of entertainment.

Having bought a pound of the miniature chipolata sausages sold as cocktail sausages (about twenty-five to the pound), poach them very gently in stock for a few minutes only. Prepare a *choux* paste as follows: put a full teacupful of water into a thick pan with 4 oz. of butter and bring to a fast boil. When the butter has fused with the water and is foaming, pour in, all at one go, 4 oz. of sieved flour. Stir, lifting the batter up and round, until you have a smooth mass which comes away from the sides of the pan. This takes only a minute or two. Now add, away from the fire, and one at a time, 4 whole eggs. Each egg must be thoroughly incorporated into the paste before the next is added. The paste should have something of the appearance of a very thick custard but with a slightly elastic spring in it. Spread it on a flat dish and, with a palette knife, coat each little sausage, well drained, so that it is completely encased. This is finicky work, but no worse than icing a cake. It can be done in advance.

Finally, the prepared sausages are plunged into a large, wide pan of very hot oil, a few at a time so as to leave room for them to swell. When they are golden and beautifully puffed up, drain on large sheets of crumpled kitchen paper or on paper towels ready near the stove. Pile them up on a very hot dish, fry a few sprays of parsley to garnish them with and serve as soon as possible, as a first course, or with drinks before dinner. No sauce is necessary but have some mustard to hand.

Large peeled prawns are highly successful cooked *en chemise* in this fashion, and should be accompanied by halves of lemon.

SAUCISSES À LA NAVARRAISE

SAUSAGES WITH SWEET PEPPERS AND WINE

Gently fry 1 lb. of *chorizo* or other coarse-cut, spiced, pork sausages in goose or pork fat or olive oil. When they have turned colour, transfer them to a fireproof dish with a little stock or water and finish cooking them in the oven, while in the same fat in which they have browned you cook a mixture similar to the one described for the wild duck recipe on page 422, but minus the carrot, i.e. 2 or 3 finely chopped shallots, a slice of ham or gammon, half a sweet red or green pepper cut in small pieces. When the shallots start to take colour, add a glass of medium sweet white wine, or dry white wine with the addition of a little Madeira. Let this bubble and reduce, then simmer very gently until the sausages are ready. Fry some triangles of bread in oil, or goose or pork fat. Put the sauce in the serving dish, the sausages on the top and the fried bread all round.

The best *chorizo* sausages, which are highly spiced with red pepper, are to be bought in the Spanish shops of Soho, and are the nearest equivalent we can obtain here to the Basque spiced sausages. Passable imitations are sold in most of the more enterprising delicatessens. This recipe also offers a good way of dressing up our own ordinary pork sausages.

SAUCISSES DE TOULOUSE

TOULOUSE SAUSAGES

These are fresh, pure pork sausages, coarsely cut and with a fairly large proportion of fat. Apart from their use in *cassoulets* and other such substantial dishes, they are often fried or grilled and served with a purée of potatoes, with stewed haricot beans or with apples. If the sausages are to be fried or grilled, it is advisable first to stiffen them by dipping them for a few moments in boiling water. Fried gently in butter, then transferred to an oven dish and baked at moderate heat for about 20 minutes, while half a dozen sweet dessert apples, peeled, cored and sliced are fried in the same butter, they make an attractive first-course dish, or they can equally well be served with a hot potato salad, as for the Lyonnais recipe on page 228. If for a first course, one sausage per person will usually be enough, for they are very rich and fat.

BOUDIN GRILLÉ AUX POMMES

GRILLED BLACK PUDDING WITH APPLES

Boudin, black pudding, or blood pudding which, in France, is nearly always heavily flavoured with onion and so much less insipid than the kind usually to be found in England, is cut into lengths of about 5 inches, painted with olive oil or pork fat and grilled about 5 minutes on each side. Serve it on a bed of peeled, cored and sliced sweet apples, six to a pound of sausage, gently fried in pork fat.

An old-fashioned way of serving these blood sausages was on a bed of onions similarly fried in pork fat, with the addition of little pieces of pig's liver and heart; the onions were then removed and kept warm while the sausage was fried in the same fat. This makes good rough food for those who like such things, but it is not exactly easy on the digestion.

LE SAUPIQUET DES AMOGNES

HAM WITH PIQUANT CREAM SAUCE

Saupiquet consists of a *sauce piquante à la crème* served with slices of ham fried in butter. It is a modernised version of a famous and very old speciality of the Nivernais and the Morvan districts of Burgundy.

To make the sauce, which is one well worth knowing, a clear well-flavoured meat stock, preferably made from veal and beef, is a necessity. To 1½ teacups (about 8 fl. oz.) of this stock the other ingredients are 2 tablespoons each of butter and flour, about 4 shallots, 6 tablespoons of wine vinegar, 2 or 3 crushed juniper berries, 6 tablespoons of white wine, ⅓ pint of very fresh thick cream, and a little extra butter with which to finish the sauce.

First of all chop the shallots very finely and put them with the juniper berries in a small saucepan with the vinegar. Bring to the boil and cook until the vinegar has all but dried up and only the shallots are left.

In another saucepan melt the butter, stir in the flour, continue stirring until the mixture is quite smooth and turns pale coffee colour; pour in the heated stock, rather gradually. Keep on stirring until the mixture thickens; add the white wine and then the shallot mixture; cook gently for some time longer, about half an hour, until all taste of flour has disappeared, and removing any scum which comes to the surface; then sieve the sauce. Return it to a clean pan, reheat it, taste for seasoning, stir in the bubbling cream and a small lump of butter. Keep the sauce hot in a *bain-marie* until it is wanted. It should be a beautiful pale coffee-cream colour, smooth, but not very thick.

Have ready 2 or 3 large slices of uncooked ham or gammon weighing about 6 oz. each, steeped in water for half an hour or so. Fry them gently in butter on both sides; transfer to the serving dish; pour your hot sauce over them. Enough for three.

I also quite often make this dish with about ½ lb. of cold cooked ham or gammon cut into thinnish slices. Instead of frying them, simply arrange them, overlapping, in a big shallow baking dish, pour the hot sauce over, and heat very gently, uncovered, in the oven, for 10 to 15 minutes.

JAMBON À LA CRÈME

HAM WITH CREAM SAUCE

This is another version of the foregoing dish, a whole boiled ham served hot with the same piquant cream sauce. It is usually made with a ham from the Morvan, a district of Burgundy where the mild cured hams have a great reputation. The dish is in fact often called *jambon à la morvandelle*.

However, it is not often nowadays that one wants to cook a whole ham to serve hot for it is rather extravagant in the carving and since, in England, uncooked hams are usually only sold whole, the same dish can be made with a piece of gammon.

It should perhaps be explained that whereas a ham proper is cut from the pig as soon as it is killed and the salting, curing and maturing carried out slowly over a period of several weeks, or even months, a gammon is a leg ham quick-cured by the bacon method on the whole side of the pig. The texture and flavour of a gammon, which may be smoked or unsmoked, is therefore somewhat different from that of a ham, but a whole leg of gammon or a piece of one is cooked in very much the same way. So although there is not, so far as I know, any precise equivalent of our gammon produced by French pork curers, I see no reason why we should not adapt some of the French recipes for ham to this excellent and relatively cheap product of our own.

In recent years we have taken to the American system of serving pineapple, peaches, apples and oranges with our hams and gammons. The Burgundian cream sauce makes a welcome change.

Now here is the method of cooking the gammon. It could hardly be simpler.

Buy a piece of middle gammon, which is the easiest to carve, weighing 4 to 4½ lb. Soak it in cold water, changed at least once, for 12 to 24 hours. To cook it, cover it completely with fresh cold water, and bring it very, very slowly to a bare simmering point. Calculate half an hour to the pound from the time you put it on to cook, and throughout the whole process keep the water just murmuring, not boiling. If you are going to use this water for soup stock add carrots, onions and a bouquet of herbs.

Start off the cooking in sufficient time before dinner to allow you to leave the gammon in its pan of water for about 20 minutes after cooking time is finished. This slight cooling will give the joint time to get a little firmer and make it much easier both to skin and to carve.

In the meantime, while the gammon was cooking you will have made your sauce, as in the foregoing recipe, but in double quantities to serve, say, six to eight people.

Take the gammon from the pan, put it on a board, run a sharp little knife down between the fat and the skin and then peel the skin off. It should come away very easily in one whole piece.

Carve two fairly thin slices of the gammon per person and arrange them in a shallow metal dish. Pour some of the hot sauce over them, put the dish over a low flame for a few seconds just to give the ham time to heat up again, and serve at once.

The rest of the ham can be kept warm in a low oven, and more carved for second helpings.

Although vegetables are not usually served with this dish, you can, if you like, have a few plain boiled potatoes. A straightforward green salad afterwards will be welcome.

JAMBON À LA CRÈME AU GRATIN

HAM WITH CREAM AND CHEESE SAUCE

Make a cream sauce with 1½ oz. of butter, 2 tablespoons of flour and, when these have amalgamated, 4 tablespoons of warmed white wine. Then add ½ pint of warmed milk. Season with a little salt and a generous amount of freshly milled pepper. Simmer this sauce, very gently, stirring frequently, for 15 minutes. Now transfer the saucepan in which it is cooking into another large and shallow one containing hot water (or, of course, a proper *bain-marie* if you happen to possess such a thing) and add 4 or 5 tablespoons of fresh thick cream. Stir again. Lastly, add 2 tablespoons of grated Gruyère or Parmesan cheese. The cheese must not dominate the sauce but is there to give it pungency, as a condiment. Add more salt if necessary, always taking into consideration the saltiness of the ham. Of this you need ½ lb., cooked, and cut in thin even slices. Into a shallow *gratin* dish, pour a little of the cream sauce. On top put the ham, in one layer, with the slices overlapping each other. Cover completely with the rest of the sauce. Add some minuscule little knobs of butter. Place in a hot

234 *French Provincial Cooking*

oven, near the top, for 5 to 10 minutes. Finish under a hot grill for a minute or two and serve immediately, when the surface is blistering and bubbling.

JAMBON À LA CORSOISE

HAM WITH TOMATO AND GARLIC SAUCE

This is a dish I remember from my first visit to Corsica, which now seems a very long time ago. In the little town of Piana of the red rocks, I took a room in the house of a very humble family. There were a large number of children in their teens. Their mother was a great big brawny woman with a robust sense of humour. Amid a tremendous clatter we would all sit down to meals at one big table. Madame's cooking was of the same nature as her own: rough, generous, full of character and colour. There were great dishes of ham and tomatoes, eggs and olives, plenty of salads and oil, huge hunks of bread and great bowls of bursting ripe figs. In all the years since then I have never quite forgotten the very special savour of that food. The ham dish was made with thick slices of the Corsican version of *prosciutto*, or raw ham, fried and served on top of a tomato sauce freshly cooked in oil and well spiced with garlic, pepper and herbs. Nowadays I sometimes make it with gammon rashers, but cooked in a baking tin, just covered in water, in the oven, then drained and just barely browned in olive oil. Served on a big round earthenware dish, surrounded by the tomato sauce, flavoured with plenty of dried basil as well as garlic, and with some croûtons of bread fried in oil, this makes a splendid quickly cooked dish for lunch or supper.

JAMBON AU FOIN

The old-fashioned French farmhouse way of cooking a ham was to tie it in a cloth, place it on a bed of sweet hay, completely surround it with more hay, then cover it with water and boil it in the usual way. The hay is said to give a particularly fragrant flavour to the ham.

A purée of dried split peas would often be the accompaniment to hot boiled ham.

LE JAMBONNEAU

CURED KNUCKLE OF PORK

A *jambonneau* is a little knuckle of pork, cut and cured separately from the ham, being simply salted for about 6 to 8 days. It is then simmered for about 2 hours in stock with carrots, onions, a clove or two, and a bouquet of herbs, including a bay leaf.

It is left to cool in the broth, but before it is quite cold the skin is removed and the exposed surface breadcrumbed in the same way as a ham. The meat is pressed down a little from the top, exposing the bone, which is then garnished with a little cutlet frill so that the whole thing looks like a miniature ham. A *jambonneau* may also be served without the skin being taken off, in which case it is brushed with butter and coated with breadcrumbs while still warm. (See the drawing on page 213.)

Saltpetre is usually included with the curing salt, so that the *jambonneau* has a good pink colour. Alternatively, 20 grammes (i.e. ⅔ oz.) of saltpetre can be added to the cooking liquid.

Jambonneaux are to be bought ready prepared in most French *charcuteries* but are not to be confused with *jambonnettes*, the Ardéchois speciality described in the introduction to this chapter and which is a boned and stuffed knuckle, formed into a little fat cushion shape.

SOUFFLÉ GLACÉ AU JAMBON
ICED HAM MOUSSE

This is a useful dish for using up a piece of cooked ham. Ingredients are ½ lb. of cooked lean mild ham, ¼ lb. of cooked salt tongue, 3 leaves of gelatine, 2 whites of egg, ½ pint of double cream. First of all prepare the gelatine. Cut the leaves into small pieces, put them into the top half of a double saucepan, pour over them ¼ pint of hot, not boiling, water and steam gently over hot water until the gelatine is quite dissolved, and you have a perfectly clear liquid. Leave to cool.

Now chop the ham finely and then pound it to a paste in a mortar or in the electric blender. Cut the tongue into little dice, and mix the two together. Pour in the cooled gelatine, through a strainer. Mix very thoroughly. Now fold in the cream, whipped until it is light and frothy. Season with a little freshly-milled pepper but no salt. Turn into a bowl and leave in the refrigerator or a cold larder for about an hour. It should be firm but not quite set. Whip the whites stiffly; fold them into the mixture with great care and thoroughness. Put into a soufflé dish or other mould which can be brought to table, of 1 pint capacity. Pile it up so that the mixture comes about 1½ inches above the top and when it is served it will look like a risen soufflé. Put in the refrigerator to set. If the weather is very warm, it may be necessary to pin a band of oiled paper round the outside of the dish to enclose the mousse, but in normal weather this can be dispensed with. Alternatively, an extra leaf of gelatine can be used, but the charm of this mousse is its delicate creamy taste and texture, which is spoilt if it is too rock-like.

Serve it as a first course instead of a pâté. This quantity is enough for four to six people according to what else is to be served. The same dish made on a large scale makes a handsome appearance on a buffet lunch or supper table.

Les Légumes

Vegetables

WHAT, I am sometimes asked, is the difference between fresh and frozen vegetables; surely they are exactly the same? Astonishing though such a question may seem to anyone who knows what is really meant by fresh vegetables, I think the explanation is that to a great many English people vegetables mean simply an accompaniment to meat. Gravy and horse-radish, mustard and mint, to say nothing of the meat itself, distract attention from second-rate or inadequately cooked vegetables. Eaten for themselves alone, as a separate dish, vegetables take on a very different significance. Both their charms and their defects become more apparent.

Apart from cauliflower cheese, we haven't much tradition in the way of vegetable dishes which stand on their own. But we have plenty of vegetables, and often it is the commonplace ones like onions and beetroot, carrots and spinach and leeks which make the most delicious dishes.

True, we cannot often obtain those little round flat onions which, golden and glazed, appear so frequently in French cookery, although mostly as a garnish to meat dishes. And potatoes. When, oh when will some enterprising grower supply us with the right firm-fleshed varieties such as *Kipfler* or *Belle de Juillet*, which make such infinitely superior salads and chips, not to mention sauté and soufflé potatoes? And how nice if, just for a change, we could buy the little non-wrinkling peas to make *petits pois à la française*. Is it too fanciful to hope that in the near future we shall be able to obtain these things? It is in the matter of vegetables and fruit that a country's eating habits evolve most rapidly.

There was a time, after all, when there were no potatoes in England, when the tomato was new to Italy, when *petits pois* were first brought to France (and caused a furore at the Court of Louis XIV), when bananas, grape fruit, and the cultivated mushrooms we now take for granted were exciting novelties. Before the war you had to go to Soho to buy a piece of garlic, whereas now it is to be found at every greengrocer's shop. Not so long ago French beans meant only coarse scarlet runners, but now we can buy several varieties of string beans and dwarf beans. Exotic vegetables and fruit, such as aubergines, sweet peppers and avocado pears have become commonplace in our shops. Enterprising English growers are supplying us with little courgettes as an alternative to gigantic vegetable marrows.

So, I wonder if, eventually, we shall not come round to the habit, taken for granted in French cookery, of regarding vegetable dishes as an important part of the meal rather than simply as an adjunct to the roast. If we do, we shall surely find that we enjoy the meat course more as well as the vegetables, for both must, when required to stand on their own, be more carefully bought and more meticulously cooked.

As for the deep freeze, I have no doubt that we shall come to treat its benefits with a sense of proportion. We shall make use of it when it is expedient to do so, but I fancy that the very rapidity of its development, particularly in regard to the conservation of vegetables, is at the same time creating a demand for food which is genuinely fresh in the old sense of the word.

LES ARTICHAUTS

LEAF ARTICHOKES

Globe or leaf artichokes are a kind of thistle. There are a great many varieties; the enormous round ones which look like water lilies when they are cooked and opened out a little are called *Camus de Bretagne*, and are grown mostly in northern France; these are the kind most suitable for serving plain boiled, to be eaten leaf by leaf, with melted butter, *sauce hollandaise* or *vinaigrette*. They take about 25 to 40 minutes' cooking, in plenty of salted, acidulated water.

Artichoke hearts, or *fonds*, are used a good deal in French cookery as a garnish for rather ceremonial meat dishes, and are also served as a separate dish, usually with some rather rich stuffing or creamy sauce. In a country where artichokes are plentiful and cheap, it is natural that a large variety of such dishes should have been created but, truth to tell, I think that elaborate or luxurious concoctions, rich creamy sauces and *foie gras* stuffings cannot but detract from the delicate and unique flavour of the artichoke. One of the most delicious ways of serving them is in the salad given on page 151, and the method of preparing the hearts for cooking is described on page 139. Those who grow their own artichokes may find the following recipe useful.

ARTICHAUTS À LA BARIGOULE

LEAF ARTICHOKES STEWED IN OIL

This method of cooking artichokes seems to be one of the oldest of Provençal dishes. There are many versions, and in the course of time it has been elaborated to include all sorts of extra ingredients, but Provençal cooks mostly agree that it is best in its primitive form. The result is not unlike the famous *carciofi alla giudia* of Roman taverns, although the method is different.

Rather small young artichokes (the long violet-leaved variety are the most common in Provence) in which the choke has not yet formed should be used. Rub the artichokes all over with lemon; cut off the stalks, leaving about ½ inch. Then cut off about ¾ inch from the top end of the artichokes, and remove about two layers of the outer leaves. Put them in a saucepan or sauté pan or deep frying-pan. Pour in olive oil to come half-way up. Then cover with water. Turn the heat as high as possible so that the oil and the water come rapidly to a fast boil (it is the same method as that used for a *bouillabaisse*) and amalgamate. Let it continue boiling, spluttering and crackling (uncovered) for the whole cooking time, which is from 15 to 20 minutes, according to the size of the artichokes. Towards the end, you can see that the artichokes have turned golden brown and crisp and the outer leaves have spread out. Finally, the liquid will stop spluttering because all the water has evaporated leaving only the oil. Take out the artichokes, and arrange them, stalks in the air, on a hot dish, so that they look like beautiful little bronzed flowers, with the crisped petals spreading out. Sprinkle over a little of their cooking liquid and some salt. Allow two artichokes per person if they are small.

LES ASPERGES DE CAVAILLON

CAVAILLON ASPARAGUS

The following recipe was given on the wrapping paper of asparagus exported to England from Cavaillon in the Vaucluse. Apart from those of Lauris and Argenteuil, the Cavaillon asparagus are supposed to be the best in France.

'Rake each asparagus with an office knife[1] and throw them one after the other in a large earthenpan full of cold water: wash them carefully, fasten them in bunches of 10 or 12 asparagus, according to their size, put them in slightly salted boiling water, and maintain boiling during 10 to 12 minutes on a lively fire. The asparagus are cooked when they melt under the finger's pressure. To avoid that the soft part of the asparagus will not break in cooking, it is preferable to put the asparagus upright with the heads out of the water; this part of the asparagus being more tender than the rest; the water which recovers them in boiling suffices to make them well done.'

Personally, I do not go out of my way to pay huge sums for asparagus, either in or out of season. When I stayed in the Cavaillon neighbourhood, we used to buy the local asparagus for a few francs a bundle, but with all the trouble they were to prepare and cook (they had to be arranged flat in a roasting tin on top of the Butagaz cooker, as there was no suitable saucepan included in the *batterie de cuisine* of that house), I thought the fresh young broad beans, the exquisite *haricots verts* and the beautiful violet-leaved artichokes more worth while. In any case, asparagus are always best served in a straightforward way, with melted butter or *hollandaise* sauce, and the Cavaillon recipe, peculiar though the English is, is perfectly sound, although 10 to 12 minutes is very much on the scanty side for any but freshly picked and rather thin green asparagus.

A small quantity of cooked asparagus tips, particularly the small thin ones which are often sold very cheaply, make a first-class garnish for eggs *en cocotte* with cream.

ASPERGES À LA MAYONNAISE

ASPARAGUS WITH MAYONNAISE

If you find yourself landed with those enormous fat white asparagus which, although rather expensive, have nothing like the flavour of the thin green ones, boil them (they may take as long as 30 minutes) and serve them cold with a mayonnaise flavoured with lemon juice rather than vinegar.

[1] i.e. a sharp paring knife, to scrape the gritty stalks.

LES AUBERGINES

The English name of this vegetable, egg plant, is presumably due to the fact that there is a variety which produces white fruit almost exactly the shape and size of an egg. The other two main varieties are deep violet, one long like a fat sausage, the other round. There is also a violet and white striped variety, *Zébrine*, now being grown in France as well as in the Near and Far Eastern countries. Except for certain purées and salads, aubergines should not be peeled. The skin provides flavour as well as holding them together. Before cooking they are sliced, either lengthwise into thinnish long strips, or crosswise into rounds, or into small cubes. Put them in a colander, sprinkle with salt, press a plate down on top and leave them an hour or two so that excess moisture and the bitter juices drain off. Dry them carefully and always use oil for cooking them.

Some of the world's most renowned vegetable dishes are made with aubergines—the Balkan *moussaka*, in which minced beef or mutton also figures, the Provençal *ratatouille*, a stew of aubergines, tomatoes, onions and peppers, the Sicilian *caponata*, a wonderful cold dish with a sweet-sour tomato sauce, the salad or purée of highly-seasoned aubergines which is sometimes rather idiotically called *aubergine caviar* and, best of all, the Turkish *imam bayeldi*, a rich and marvellous mixture of onions, tomatoes, spices and aubergines cooked in oil and eaten cold.

A convenient aspect of stewed aubergine dishes is that, provided they have not been overcooked in the first place, they nearly always improve with reheating and are also, with the exception, of course, of fritters and other dishes in which they are quick-fried, just as good cold as hot, and sometimes even better.

BROUILLADE D'AUBERGINES

STEWED AUBERGINES WITH TOMATOES

A Provençal recipe.

Cut 3 medium-sized unpeeled aubergines into small squares. Salt them, leave them to drain for an hour and dry them in a cloth. Heat a coffee-cupful (after-dinner size) of olive oil in a thick frying-pan, and in this cook the aubergines, but not too quickly or the skins will burn. When they are getting soft, drain off any excess of oil and add about 1 lb. skinned and chopped tomatoes; continue cooking until they are reduced almost to a pulp. Stir in a little chopped parsley and garlic, and add salt if necessary. Can be eaten hot or cold. Enough for four.

AUBERGINES AU GRATIN

AUBERGINES BAKED WITH TOMATOES

A dish for those who may find the amount of oil normally used in cooking aubergines excessive.

Slice 2 unpeeled aubergines obliquely and about ½ inch thick. Plunge into boiling salted water and cook for 3 minutes. Leave in a colander to drain very thoroughly. Arrange in a large, flat, lightly oiled baking dish. Spread each slice thickly with a *coulis* of tomatoes, made as in the recipe below, sprinkle with breadcrumbs and chopped parsley, pour a few drops of oil on each slice, cook uncovered in a slow oven for about an hour. Like most aubergine dishes, this one can be eaten hot or cold.

If you have no suitable dish, the aubergine slices can be cooked on a baking sheet.

COULIS DE TOMATES

THICK TOMATO SAUCE

Melt a finely chopped shallot or small onion in a mixture of oil and butter; add 1 lb. of roughly chopped ripe tomatoes; season with salt, a lump of sugar, a little freshly-ground pepper, some chopped parsley and celery leaves or dried basil. Simmer until the tomatoes are soft and thick. Sieve through the food mill. If too liquid, return to the pan and let the sauce dry out a little over gentle heat.

RATATOUILLE NIÇOISE

AUBERGINES, TOMATOES, ONIONS AND PEPPERS STEWED IN OIL

There are any amount of versions of this dish, the variations being mainly in the proportions of each vegetable employed, the vegetables themselves being nearly always the same ones: aubergines, sweet peppers, onions, tomatoes, with courgettes sometimes being added and occasionally potatoes as well. Some people add mushrooms, but this is a rather pointless addition because they get completely lost in the mass of other vegetables. Garlic is optional, but the cooking medium must be olive oil.

To make a dish of *ratatouille* sufficient for about eight people, the ingredients are 3 medium-sized onions, 3 large aubergines, 3 large sweet red peppers, 3 courgettes, 4 large tomatoes, 2 cloves of garlic, a few coriander seeds, fresh or dried basil if available, or parsley, 2 coffee-cups (after-dinner size) of olive oil.

Prepare the vegetables by slicing the onions thinly and cutting the unpeeled aubergines and courgettes into $\frac{1}{4}$ inch thick rounds and then into cubes. The aubergines, and the courgettes if they are being used, should be sprinkled with salt and put into a colander with a plate and a weight on the top, so that excess moisture is pressed out. This will take an hour or so. Cut the peppers in half, remove the core and all the seeds, wash them, and slice them in thin strips. Skin the tomatoes.

Heat the olive oil in a wide, heavy and shallow pan. Put in the onions and, when they are soft—but not brown—add the aubergines, courgettes, peppers and chopped garlic. Cover the pan and cook gently for 40 minutes. Now add the chopped and skinned tomatoes, a teaspoon or so of pounded coriander seeds, and taste for seasoning. Cook another 30 minutes until all the vegetables are quite soft, but not too mushy. Stir in the basil or parsley and serve hot as a separate dish, or cold as an hors-d'œuvre. *Ratatouille* is a dish which takes kindly to reheating but, of course, it can be made in smaller quantities. Also, it can perfectly well accompany a joint of lamb or veal, grilled chops, steaks or sausages.

AUBERGINES EN PERSILLADE
AUBERGINES WITH PARSLEY AND GARLIC

Slice the unpeeled aubergines thinly and in bias cut rounds. Salt them and leave in a colander for an hour. Dry very carefully. Fry them slowly in plenty of hot, but not too hot, oil, turning them over from time to time. When quite soft take them out; drain them; put them in a warmed dish. In the remaining oil fry for a few seconds only a handful of parsley chopped with 2 cloves of garlic; pour this over the aubergines and serve hot. If other herbs such as marjoram or basil are available add some to the parsley mixture.

AUBERGINES À LA TURQUE
AUBERGINES BAKED WITH ONIONS AND TOMATOES

Since aubergines were originally an import to southern France from the Orient, it is natural that the French should have accepted some of the methods of cooking them in their native countries. The two following recipes are examples of such dishes.

Cut three unpeeled aubergines—the round variety are best for this dish—into slices about $\frac{1}{3}$ inch thick. Salt and leave to drain in a colander for an hour. Shake them dry in a cloth; fry them in moderately hot olive oil until both sides are golden. Remove them from the pan, and in the same oil cook 3 thinly-sliced large onions until soft and pale yellow; add

5 skinned and chopped tomatoes and a chopped clove or two of garlic. Season with salt, a teaspoonful of ground allspice and a pinch of sugar. Cook until the sauce is thick. Lay the aubergine slices on an oiled baking sheet, or shallow dish, put a tablespoon of the sauce on each slice, bake in a moderate oven for 40 to 50 minutes.

A dish which could well precede the roast as an hors-d'œuvre (it is excellent cold) or go with it, hot, as a vegetable.

AUBERGINES IMAM BAYELDI
AUBERGINES STEWED IN OIL WITH TOMATOES AND SPICES

This is a French version given in the *Larousse Gastronomique*, and probably worked out by Prosper Montagné, of the famous Turkish dish for which there are many recipes, and which gets its name (which means 'satiated or exhausted Imam') from the legend that the first time it was made and put before a certain Imam, he over-indulged in the rich and aromatic confection.

4 aubergines, 4 tomatoes, 4 medium-sized onions, about 2 oz. currants, salt, pepper, ground allspice, parsley, olive oil, a clove of garlic, a bay leaf.

Remove the stalks from the aubergines, but do not skin them. Make four or five lengthways incisions in each aubergine, from end to end, but without cutting right through. Salt them and leave to drain while the stuffing is prepared.

Fry the finely chopped onions in olive oil until they turn colour. Add the skinned and chopped tomatoes, salt, pepper, about half a teaspoon of allspice and a tablespoon of chopped parsley. Fry gently until the tomatoes and onions are amalgamated almost into a purée. Add the currants which have been previously soaked a few minutes in water. Cook 2 or 3 more minutes, until the oil is all absorbed and the mixture fairly dry. Leave to cool a little and then, with a small spoon, stuff the mixture into the slits in the aubergines, putting in as much as they will hold. Put them in a fireproof dish in which they will fit comfortably and pour olive oil over them to come half-way up. Add a clove of garlic and a bayleaf.

Cover the pan and cook very slowly either on top of the stove or in a low oven for about an hour, until the aubergines are quite soft, and there is a slightly sticky residue at the bottom of the pan. If they are cooked too fast the skins will be tough and the dish spoilt.

Leave them to cool in the oil, and serve them cold next day, with most of the oil poured off, and make the rest of the meal light and plain.

BEIGNETS D'AUBERGINES
AUBERGINE FRITTERS

Cut unpeeled aubergines into long, thin slices. Salt and leave them to drain. Dip them in frying batter (see below) and cook them 2 or 3 minutes, until they are crisp and golden, in a deep pan of very hot oil. Drain them on kitchen paper and serve them piled up on a hot dish with lemon.

PÂTE À FRIRE
FRYING BATTER

Sieve ¼ lb. of flour; stir in 3 tablespoons of olive oil and a pinch of salt; gradually add approximately ¼ pint of tepid water. Stir to a smooth cream. Leave to stand 2 hours.

Before using, fold in the stiffly whipped white of 1 small egg.

This is the frying batter I have always used in preference to any other. It is one which is light and crisp and makes only a thin coating for the food to be fried, rather than a heavy greasy blanket.

LES BETTERAVES
BEETROOT

During the summer, young beetroots, simply scrubbed, boiled 20 to 40 minutes according to size, then peeled, sliced and served with parsley butter, make a delicious vegetable dish.

In the winter, much more use could be made of the large cooked beetroots to be bought at the greengrocers. Of course, they must be chosen from a greengrocer who cooks them carefully, which is none too common. Sliced and dressed with oil and vinegar and a touch of garlic, or garlic vinegar, with chopped parsley and strips of raw celery mixed in at the last moment, they make a good salad. Or sliced and heated very gently with a little butter, a peeled chopped tomato or two and a little parsley, they make a nice hot vegetable to go with pork chops or a steak, especially useful for people in a hurry.

On page 427 is an excellent recipe for hare served with beetroot.

BETTERAVES EN ROBE DES CHAMPS
BEETROOTS BAKED IN THEIR SKINS

Medium to large beetroots are scrubbed but not peeled, and cooked in a baking tin in the oven in much the same way as baked potatoes. They take a good deal longer, about 3 hours in a slow oven for medium-sized beets, so this is a vegetable to cook when the oven is already in use for some other long and slow-cooked dish.

Peel them and serve them hot with salt and butter, or slice them and season them while still warm for salad. Baked in this manner, the flavour is infinitely superior to that of boiled beets.

BLETTES À LA CRÈME
CHARD WITH CREAM SAUCE

The large fleshy-stalked green leaves called *blettes* are occasionally to be found in England and are known as Swiss chard. They have not a great deal of flavour and the best way to serve them is in a creamy sauce.

Wash the leaves, remove the hardest part of the stalks and leaf centres, and cook them in a little water in the same way as spinach. Drain them, press them as dry as possible and chop them.

Prepare, for 1 lb. of chard, a béchamel as described on page 114, and enrich it with $\frac{1}{4}$ pint of cream. Cover the bottom of a wide gratin dish with a thin layer of the sauce, put the chopped chard on the top and cover it completely with the rest of the sauce. Put a few little knobs of butter on the top and cook in a moderate oven—Gas No. 3 or 4, 330 to 355 deg. F.— for 20 to 25 minutes, until the surface is barely beginning to turn pale gold. Enough for two, as a separate course.

This is also an excellent way of serving coarse-leaved spinach and beet spinach.

CAROTTES VICHY

This is one of the best known vegetable dishes of French cookery. It is exceedingly simple, and makes a particularly welcome dish in the spring before the new peas and beans have arrived.

New carrots are scraped, and sliced into bias-cut rounds about $\frac{1}{4}$ inch thick. Put them into a heavy pan with 1oz of butter, a pinch of salt, 2 lumps of sugar, and $\frac{3}{4}$ pint of water per pound of carrots. Cook uncovered for 20 to 25 minutes until nearly all the water has evaporated and the carrots are tender. Add another lump of butter and shake the pan so that the carrots do not stick. Add a little finely-chopped parsley before serving.

The water of the Vichy region is non-chalky and is therefore said to be particularly satisfactory for the cooking of vegetables, and it is this circumstance which no doubt gives the dish its name. A pinch of bicarbonate of soda in the water helps to produce the same effect.

Carottes Vichy can be served as a garnish to meat or as a separate dish.

CAROTTES À LA CRÈME
CARROTS WITH CREAM SAUCE

Cook the carrots as above and, instead of the final addition of butter, pour a little boiling cream into the saucepan and shake it over the flame until it has slightly thickened.

CAROTTES GLACÉES
GLAZED CARROTS

Glazed carrots are cooked in much the same way as *Carottes Vichy* but are usually cut in quarters or thick chunks instead of in slices, and a larger proportion of water is needed to cook them. Take care not to put more than a pinch of salt in the water or, when it has evaporated, the carrots will be too salt. Add about a teaspoon of soft sugar with the final lump of butter, and let this mixture cook until it has formed a little thick syrup which coats the carrots, but don't let it turn to toffee.

CAROTTES À LA NIVERNAISE
GLAZED CARROTS AND ONIONS

Whenever a meat dish is described in a menu as *à la nivernaise*, it means there are glazed carrots and onions as a garnish.

Cook the carrots as for *carottes glacées*, adding if possible a little good, clear stock or meat glaze when the water has evaporated. Little glazed onions cooked as described on page 265 are then mixed with the carrots and these vegetables are arranged round a joint of beef or lamb.

SAUTÉ DE CAROTTES ET DE POMMES DE TERRE
SAUTÉ OF CARROTS AND POTATOES

This is a delicious and simple vegetable dish which goes equally well with a roast of lamb, a chicken, or a beef stew.

To 1 lb. of rather large new potatoes, you need $\frac{1}{4}$ lb. of carrots, 2 or 3 shallots or little onions, parsley, seasonings, and about 2 oz. of butter. Boil the scraped potatoes and carrots separately in salted water until they are only two-thirds cooked. Drain them and cut the potatoes into inch squares and the carrots into thick strips. Chop the peeled shallots or onions, mix all together, and finish cooking them in a frying-pan in the foaming butter, turning the vegetables over and over, and shaking the pan until they are all buttery and beginning to turn crisp. Then lower the heat and cook gently until the potatoes and carrots are tender. Stir in a little chopped parsley just before they are served.

CÉLERIS ÉTUVÉS AU BEURRE

CELERY STEWED IN BUTTER

The old way of preparing whole celery hearts, blanched, then stewed in butter and finally enriched with meat glaze has become a rather costly dish, since at least one heart must be allowed for each person, and celery is now an expensive vegetable.

A more economical way is as follows: having trimmed and washed the celery very thoroughly, cut all except the very coarse outside sticks (but even these can be used if you take the trouble to scrape the strings off with a sharp knife) into chunks about ½ inch long. Melt a large lump of butter and a few drops of olive oil in a thick frying-pan and in this let the celery stew gently, covered, with a very little seasoning of salt, for about 15 minutes. If you have a little good clear meat, chicken or game stock, add a spoonful or two and let it reduce so that it forms a little syrupy sauce.

This dish makes a splendid accompaniment for pheasant and other game dishes, as well as for lamb, pork and fried or baked sausages.

ÉTUVÉ DE CÉLERI-RAVE

CELERIAC STEWED IN BUTTER

Celeriac, or celery-root, is appearing in increasing quantities in the shops and makes most delicious winter salads and vegetable dishes as well as soups.

Peel a celeriac, rinse it, and shred it into fine strips. If you possess a mandoline (see page 64), it is a matter of moments to do this on the fluted blade. Cook the celeriac in butter in a frying-pan for about 10 minutes, turning it over and over; towards the end of the cooking time, add salt, pepper, a teaspoon of French mustard, a dash of tarragon or wine vinegar and a little finely chopped parsley. The celeriac should retain some of its crispness and bite.

PUREE DE CÉLERI-RAVE ET POMMES DE TERRE

CELERIAC AND POTATO PURÉE

Scrub the celeriac and cook it unpeeled in plenty of water until it is quite tender. When it is cool enough to handle, peel and sieve it, then mix it with a purée of potatoes made separately. Season rather highly. Heat up in a double saucepan, with a good lump of butter and 2 or 3 tablespoons of cream.

Proportions are $\frac{1}{2}$ lb. of potatoes to a celeriac weighing $\frac{1}{2}$ to $\frac{3}{4}$ lb.

This purée is particularly nice with fried or grilled cutlets and with game dishes. As an alternative to the celeriac, Jerusalem artichokes can be used.

CÈPES À LA BORDELAISE

CÈPES (BOLETUS EDULIS) STEWED IN OIL WITH PARSLEY AND GARLIC

Of this famous dish, Alcide Bontou, author of the *Traité de Cuisine Bourgeoise Bordelaise* (1929), says: 'The cèpe was little known in Paris forty years ago, and was not listed on restaurant menus; I was the first to have them brought specially to the Café Anglais. Parisians could not accustom themselves to the oil and to the seasoning of garlic; we tried to cook them in butter, but the only way to prepare them is in the Bordelais way.'

Here is his recipe:

'Choose 12 firm cèpes, small rather than large, and with dark heads; remove the stalks and peel them, but only wipe the heads; make incisions on the underside of the heads with the point of a knife. Put a glass of olive oil in a frying-pan; when it is hot, put in the heads of the cèpes; turn them over when they have browned on one side. Season with salt and pepper.

'Chop the stalks with 4 cloves of garlic and some parsley. Throw this mixture over the cèpes. Let them all *sauter* in the pan for 3 or 4 minutes.

'You may add a tablespoon of soft white breadcrumbs. Serve.'

LES CHAMPIGNONS DE COUCHE

CULTIVATED MUSHROOMS

About ten kilometres from the little town of Apt, in the Vaucluse department of Provence, the curious village of Roussillon stands on the side of a steep hill. Its orange and saffron and terracotta-coloured houses look as if they are about to come crashing down the cliffs. Its steep narrow streets are barely negotiable by car; and about Easter-time the lilac trees and the wistaria come into flower, so that a backdrop of mauves and pinks and greens against the ochre rocks makes the whole place look highly theatrical. Apart from ochre-mining, these rocks provide the district with a flourishing little subsidiary industry, for they are honeycombed with caves which are used for the cultivation of mushrooms.

While we were staying in a neighbouring village some years ago, the local mushrooms proved to be our most valuable resource in the way of vegetables during the very early spring, for most of the root vegetables were finished and the *primeurs* had not yet started. No deep freeze, of course, and the vegetables imported from North Africa seldom penetrated as far as these hill villages. Our kitchen was not conspicuous for planned comfort or modern amenities; most of our cooking had to be of the quick and simple variety, and the mushrooms were a blessing in this respect. But these local mushrooms, as with most French cultivated ones, required very meticulous cleaning and washing, for they are grown in very sandy, gritty soil.

English ones are rather easier to deal with. They can simply be wiped with a soft damp cloth, or given a brief rinse in cold water, if they look at all gritty. They can be rubbed with a cut lemon to preserve their whiteness, but neither peel nor stalks should be removed.

The three following dishes are among those we used to cook with the little cultivated mushrooms, and there are more recipes in the hors-d'œuvre chapter, and an excellent soup on page 171.

CHAMPIGNONS À LA CRÈME
MUSHROOMS WITH CREAM

For $\frac{1}{2}$ lb. of mushrooms, cleaned as above, heat about 1 oz. of butter in a frying-pan and add a tablespoon of olive oil. Slice the mushrooms fairly thin and cook them at a moderate pace for a minute before adding salt, pepper, a scrap of nutmeg and a tablespoon or so of finely chopped parsley and shallot. Shake the pan so that the mushrooms do not stick. Stir in 3 or 4 tablespoons of thick cream. It will thicken naturally: 5 minutes' cooking altogether is enough—when people complain that cultivated mushrooms are insipid, it is nearly always because they have been overcooked.

The dish goes well with steak, veal and chicken; with little triangles of fried bread it makes a good dish on its own; to go with sausages and bacon it is better without the final addition of cream. Enough for two.

CHAMPIGNONS FINES HERBES
MUSHROOMS WITH HERBS AND BUTTER

Cut $\frac{1}{2}$ lb. of small mushrooms, already cleaned in the usual way, into quarters. Cook them in butter with a little scrap of garlic, salt, pepper and nutmeg. When the juice is running, after 5 or 6 minutes' cooking, take the pan from the fire and add about 1 oz. of parsley butter (page 116) to which you have added, if possible, a little chopped tarragon. Shake the pan *over* the flame but not directly on it, so that the butter spreads, melts and forms a little sauce without actually cooking.

A good vegetable to go with a steak or to serve by itself. Enough for two.

CHAMPIGNONS À LA BORDELAISE

MUSHROOMS STEWED IN OIL WITH PARSLEY AND GARLIC

The large flat mushrooms or the shaggy brown ones or, of course, the now rare field mushrooms, are best for this method.

Having cleaned and sliced them as usual, pour a little oil over them, with salt and pepper. Leave them to marinate for an hour or so. Drain them; sauté them in fresh oil in a small heavy pan. The preliminary marinading will prevent the mushrooms from catching on the bottom of the pan, which ordinarily they are apt to do in the first few moments of cooking, before they start giving out moisture. After 5 minutes' gentle cooking, add, for ½ lb. of mushrooms, 2 tablespoons of parsley chopped with a little garlic, or shallot if you prefer it, and 2 tablespoons of breadcrumbs. When this mixture has absorbed the oil in the pan, the mushrooms are ready to serve. Enough for two.

LES CHANTERELLES

These lovely apricot-coloured fungi rarely reach the shops or markets in England as they do in France (where they are also called *girolles*) and, indeed, all over the Continent, but they grow quite commonly in the British Isles.

To prepare *chanterelles* for cooking, cut off and discard the muddy ends of the stalks and wash the *chanterelles* very thoroughly in plenty of cold running water, and then examine them carefully to see that there are no little pockets of grit left. If the *chanterelles* are large, slice them lengthways into strips. Cook them in a mixture of butter and oil, with a little salt, in a covered frying-pan for about 10 minutes, and then add either a sprinkling of parsley chopped with, if you like, a little piece of garlic, or else some thick fresh cream; in this case, shake the pan over the flame until the cream thickens.

CHANTERELLES MAÎTRE D'HÔTEL

CHANTERELLES WITH PARSLEY BUTTER

Cook the washed and sliced *chanterelles* in butter in a covered frying-pan, then add salt and a very little pepper. When they are tender, add a lump of parsley butter cut into little pieces and, if possible, a tablespoon or two of good clear chicken or veal stock. Shake the pan until the butter has melted and, with the stock, formed a little sauce. This is, perhaps, the best way of serving *chanterelles*.

CHOU FARÇI AUX MARRONS

CABBAGE STUFFED WITH CHESTNUTS

A warming winter dish of Alsatian origin.

The ingredients are a white cabbage, ½ lb. of chestnuts, 6 oz. of salt pork or bacon bought in the piece, ½ to ¾ pint of clear stock.

Blanch the cabbage in boiling salted water for 10 minutes, and drain it carefully. Shell and skin the chestnuts as described on page 263 (½ lb. looks rather a small amount but they swell a good deal in the cooking) and cut the pork or bacon into squares. Remove the outer leaves of the blanched cabbage, put it on a board, open it out carefully and cut out the hard inside stalk and centre. Season with pepper, a scrap of nutmeg, and a very little salt, and then pack in the chestnuts and bacon. Reshape the leaves round the stuffing, tie the cabbage into its original shape with tape, and put into an earthenware or enamel-lined pot in which it will just fit. Over the top lay the outside leaves which have been removed, and which will prevent the top of the cabbage drying up. Pour over the stock, cover the pan and cook in a very slow oven for 5 hours. To serve, extract it very carefully from the pot and put it in the serving dish before removing the tape. Pour the juice over it. Enough for four.

CHOU ROUGE À L'AIGRE-DOUX

SWEET-SOUR RED CABBAGE

A small red cabbage (about 2 lb.), 2 medium-sized onions, 2 cooking apples, 2 tablespoons sugar, 2 tablespoons each of port or other dessert wine and wine vinegar, a bouquet of parsley, thyme and bayleaf, salt, pepper.

Remove the outer leaves of the cabbage, cut off the stalk, cut the cabbage in quarters and cut out the hard white stalk. Slice the cabbage fairly thinly.

Arrange in layers in a deep earthenware pot alternately with the sliced onions and peeled, cored and sliced apples. Season as you go with the sugar, salt and pepper. Put the bouquet, tied with thread, in the middle. When all ingredients are packed into the pot, pour over the wine and vinegar. Cover the pot; cook for about 3 hours in a low oven, Gas No. 2, 310 deg. F.

This amount is enough for four if served as an accompanying vegetable, and can very well be prepared a day in advance, as it improves, if anything, with reheating. This goes well with roast hare and with sausages, goose and pork.

LES COURGETTES

These are very small marrows, grown from varieties of which the fruit can be picked while immature. Courgettes vary in size from about 2 inches to 8 inches long. Their initial preparation is much the same as that of aubergines; they are left unpeeled, or if they are rather large the rough ridge parts are pared off, leaving the courgettes with a striped appearance. They are sliced, salted and left to drain, then dried and *sauté* in oil or butter. When properly treated courgettes are most delicate and make one of the best soufflés in existence, for which the recipe is on page 202.

Courgettes, however, are versatile as well as delicate. They can be stewed in oil with tomatoes and/or onions and served hot or cold; they can be fried in butter; or cut into long thin slices, dipped in batter and deep-fried to make delicious fritters; they can be cut into miniature chips and deep-fried as the Italians like them; they can be stuffed with rice, or puréed and mixed with cheese to make a *gratin*; they can be plainly boiled, sliced and mixed with oil and lemon for a salad; halved lengthways, the flesh scooped out and the shells fried; the larger ones can even be stuffed with a Lobster Mornay mixture to make a charming and original dish like the one John Stais serves at the White Tower Restaurant in Charlotte Street.

COURGETTES FINES HERBES
COURGETTES WITH FRESH HERBS

Wash but do not peel the little courgettes. Slice them into thin bias-cut rounds. Sprinkle with salt; leave in a colander with a plate and a weight on top for an hour so that excess moisture drains off. Put them in a saucepan with a ladle of water and cook gently for 10 minutes. Drain. For 1 lb. of courgettes heat 1 oz. of butter in a frying-pan and let the courgettes finish cooking in this quite gently. Turn them over once or twice and shake the pan so that they do not stick. When they are tender, stir in a tablespoon of finely-chopped parsley, chervil or chives and a squeeze of lemon juice. Enough for two or three.

Good with veal, chicken, steak and lamb, and as a separate vegetable dish.

COURGETTES AUX TOMATES
COURGETTES WITH TOMATOES

1 lb. small courgettes, $\frac{1}{2}$ lb. tomatoes, olive oil, garlic, salt, pepper.

If the courgettes are very small, simply wash them and leave them unpeeled. If they are the larger, coarser variety, pare off the rough ridge parts of the skin, so that the courgettes present a striped appearance. It is a pity to peel them entirely, for there is flavour in the skins. Slice them across on the bias, about $\frac{1}{4}$ inch thick. Sprinkle with salt, put in a colander and leave for an hour or two until the excess moisture has drained out. Shake them in a cloth to dry them. Heat 2 tablespoons of olive oil in a heavy frying-pan or sauté pan and put in the courgettes. Add a crushed clove of garlic. Let them cook, not too fast, until they have softened, turning them over with a palette knife and shaking the pan from time to time so that they do not stick. Now add the skinned and roughly chopped tomatoes and, when these have softened and turned almost to a sauce, season with a little freshly-milled pepper and turn on to a serving dish. Enough for two or three.

Nice as a separate vegetable, as an accompaniment to veal or lamb, or cold as an hors-d'œuvre.

COURGETTES À LA NIÇOISE
COURGETTES WITH TOMATOES AND BLACK OLIVES

Cook the courgettes exactly as in the above recipe, and when they are ready add about half a dozen stoned and halved black olives and a sprinkling of parsley.

GRATIN DE COURGETTES ET DE TOMATES
BAKED COURGETTES AND TOMATOES

For this recipe the courgettes are peeled and butter only is used in the dish, which is an unusually delicate one. Its disadvantages are the time it takes to prepare and the fact that, if it is served as a first course, two people can quite easily consume the whole lot. But it also makes a very good accompaniment to lamb, in which case it should be enough for four people.

3 oz. butter, 2 lb. courgettes, 1 lb. tomatoes, parsley, 1 small clove of garlic; salt and pepper. Breadcrumbs.

Pare the courgettes very thinly, leaving just a few strips of the green skin; slice them into even rounds about $\frac{1}{4}$ inch thick. This can be done on the mandoline or Universal Slicer. Put the courgettes in a colander, salt them lightly and leave them to drain. Skin the tomatoes; chop them roughly. Chop about 2 tablespoons of parsley with the garlic.

Shake the courgettes as dry as possible in a thick tea cloth. Heat 1 oz. of the butter in a frying-pan and put in half the courgettes (unless you have a very large frying-pan they won't all go in at once). Do not let the butter burn or even turn brown. Let the courgettes cook gently until they are soft and transparent looking; transfer them to a gratin dish and cook the rest in the same way in another ounce of butter. Having transferred these also to the gratin dish, melt another half-ounce of butter in the pan and in this cook the tomatoes and the parsley and garlic mixture with a seasoning of salt and pepper until the tomatoes have lost the greater part, but not all, of their moisture; they should be in a thickish purée but not too dry. Amalgamate this mixture with the courgettes. It should completely fill the dish. Smooth down the top; strew with a light layer of pale golden breadcrumbs. Divide the remaining half-ounce of butter into little pieces and put them on the top. Put the dish on the top shelf of a hot oven, Gas No. 7, 425 deg. F., for 25 to 30 minutes, and serve sizzling hot when the top surface is deep golden and bubbling.

Simple though this dish appears it is not easy to get it quite right at the first attempt; it is mainly a question of getting the tomatoes to the right consistency so that the finished dish is neither too liquid nor too dry, and this provides a useful demonstration of the treatment of tomatoes to go into any *gratin* or other oven dish. If they are put in raw they will give out so much moisture in the cooking that the result will be a thin and watery dish with a sadly amateurish air about it, whereas the preliminary cooking gets rid of excess moisture and also concentrates the flavour.

LES ENDIVES BELGES

BELGIAN ENDIVES

Belgian endives, chicory or *witloof* make first-class winter vegetable dishes as well as salads. It is a mistake to wash them or to give them a preliminary cooking in boiling water; all that is necessary is to cut off the tough part of the root end, to remove any outside leaves which are wilted and brown and to wipe the endives with a soft cloth. Use a silver or stainless knife for cutting them.

ENDIVES AU BEURRE (1)
ENDIVES STEWED IN BUTTER

Allowing 2 whole endives, prepared as above, for each person, put them in a thickly buttered fireproof dish in which they will just about fit. Arrange the endives in one or two layers, interspersing them with a plentiful amount of butter cut into little knobs, with more on the top, altogether about 2 oz. of butter for 2 lb. of endives. Cover the dish with buttered paper or foil and, if possible, a lid as well. Cook them in a low oven, Gas No. 3, 330 deg. F., for about 1½ hours. By the time they are ready they will be golden brown and, of course, very much shrunk, so for appearance' sake transfer them to another serving dish, with all their buttery juices. Now, and not before, sprinkle them with salt and lemon juice.

ENDIVES AU BEURRE (2)
ENDIVES STEWED IN BUTTER

Allow 1½ to 2 endives per person. Peel off any brown outside leaves; wipe the endives with a soft cloth. With a fruit knife cut each into half-inch lengths. Melt a good lump of butter in a frying-pan. Put in the vegetables; let them cook a few seconds, turning them about with a wooden spoon, before adding salt, turning down the heat and covering the pan. By this method they will be sufficiently cooked in about 10 minutes (as opposed to over an hour when they are cooked whole) but uncover them and shake the pan from time to time to make sure the endives are not sticking. Before serving add a squeeze of lemon juice.

A variation is to add a few little cubes of bacon or ham. Leeks are excellent prepared and cooked in the same way.

ENDIVES AU LARD
ENDIVES WITH BACON OR HAM

Prepare and cook the endives exactly as for *endives au beurre* (1) and, 15 minutes before they are to be served, add 2 oz. of mild bacon previously fried a minute or two, or cooked salt pork or ham cut into little strips. Add a squeeze of lemon juice before serving, but no salt.

ÉPINARDS AU NATUREL
SPINACH WITH BUTTER

To prepare spinach for cooking, first swirl it round in a big basin of cold water, then pick out all the weeds, discard any badly wilted leaves and break off the coarse ends of the stalks. Remove all the spinach to a colander, rinse out the basin, refill it with cold water and plunge the spinach back into it, again swirling it round. This operation usually has to be repeated three or four times, especially with English spinach, which comes to market in a much muddier condition than French spinach, which is consequently worth its slightly higher price.

To cook the spinach, pack it into a saucepan, either with just the water left in from its washing or, which is perhaps preferable, just a small amount of boiling water. Add salt when the spinach has shrunk somewhat and stir with a wooden spoon to eliminate the danger of the underneath layer sticking to the saucepan: 7 to 10 minutes' steady cooking is enough. Turn it into a colander, press a plate down on top of it and on this put a weight. Leave it 3 or 4 minutes, then with the edge of the plate (don't use a valuable one) and with the spinach still in the colander, make a few chopping movements so that the leaves are roughly divided and more liquid flows out. Return the spinach to a clean pan in which a lump of butter has been melted and heat for a few seconds. This is *épinards en branches* or *épinards au naturel*. Allow 1 lb. of spinach for two people.

ÉPINARDS EN PURÉE

If the spinach is to be served as a purée, it can be left to drain until quite cool, then squeezed dry with the hands and either sieved or, better still, very finely chopped. It is then heated up in a double saucepan with rather a lot of butter. In fact, there is scarcely any limit to the amount of butter which spinach will absorb.

ÉPINARDS À LA CRÈME
SPINACH WITH FRESH CREAM

Thoroughly wash 3 lb. of spinach in several waters. Only the coarse stalks should be removed. Cook in the usual way, in a large saucepan containing a small amount of already boiling water or, if you prefer the English system, with only the water left on the leaves after washing. Add salt only when the spinach has boiled down. Drain, and when cool squeeze as dry as possible, then sieve or chop finely. In a fireproof

I

porcelain or enamel-lined saucepan, melt 2 oz. butter; stir in the spinach; when warm, add pepper, salt if necessary and a pinch of sugar. Stir in gradually about 4 oz. of boiling cream (use, if possible, double cream for this dish) and, if not to be served at once, cover the pan, put an asbestos mat underneath and turn the flame as low as possible to prevent the spinach from sticking to the pan. Served as a separate course, as it should be, this will serve four or five people. It is, I think, one of the most delicious vegetable dishes in the whole of French cookery. Any left over (but there seldom is any) can be reheated in a double boiler. A scrap of grated nutmeg can be included in the seasonings.

FÈVES AU BEURRE

BROAD BEANS WITH BUTTER

Cook very young broad beans exactly as for *haricots verts au beurre*, page 261, and serve them either as a separate dish or with a plain roast chicken. When they are fully grown, skin them after they are boiled and before heating them up in butter. In France, it is traditional to flavour broad beans with savory (*sarriette*), but this is a herb which is both peppery and bitter and, to my mind, spoils the flavour of the beans.

PURÉE DE FÈVES

PURÉE OF BROAD BEANS

The tender pods of very young broad beans make an excellent purée. Top and tail the pods, break them into chunks and cook them in boiling salted water, with a couple of diced potatoes. Strain off the liquid (which can be used for making a potato soup) and put the vegetables twice through the *mouli*. Heat up in a double saucepan with a lump of butter, seasonings and a scrap of sugar. Stir in a tablespoon or two of cream before serving.

This makes a good background to fried or poached eggs or to lamb cutlets.

FÈVES AU JAMBON

BROAD BEANS WITH HAM

Boil 2 lb. of shelled broad beans and strain them, keeping a little of the water in which they have cooked.

Make a béchamel sauce according to the recipe on page 114, using the reserved liquid instead of part of the milk. Enrich the sauce with 3 to 4 oz. of cream, and when it is ready stir in 2 oz. of cooked ham or of unsmoked gammon cut into small strips. Add the beans (skinned, if they are old ones). Let them get thoroughly hot; stir in a little chopped parsley.

This is a slightly more refined version of the well-known *fèves au lard*, in which salt pork or bacon is used instead of the ham. If either of these are to be used, the pork must first be boiled and the bacon fried until the fat starts to run.

LES HARICOTS BLANCS SECS
DRIED WHITE HARICOT BEANS

The dried white beans commonly sold in English grocers' shops as haricot beans are small and of variable quality; they must be carefully chosen, preferably from a shop which has a large turnover so that there is little risk of their having been in stock for too long a period. Haricot beans should not be more than a year old, or they will be impossibly dry and hard. In a friend's house in the country I was once asked to cook some haricot beans; after two days and two nights in the oven of the Aga they were still like little stones. I then thought to ask my hostess how long the beans had been in her store cupboard. 'Oh, only about four years, I think,' was the reply.

The new season's beans come into the shops about October or November, and a variety sold under the brand name of 'Trophy' is one I have found reliable, but the best are the medium-sized oval ones called *Soissons*, which can be found in Soho shops, and these are the ones most commonly used in France for *cassoulets* and all haricot bean dishes. A variety called *Arpajon*, very small and round, are rather more like the kind known to us as haricot beans.

Early in the season 6 to 8 hours is sufficiently long to soak haricot beans; later 10 to 12 hours will be necessary, but if for some reason they have to be left longer, take care to change the water or the beans may start to ferment. Allow 2 to 3 oz. of beans per person.

HARICOTS À LA CRÈME
HARICOT BEANS WITH CREAM SAUCE

Having soaked the beans, drain them, put them in a saucepan amply covered with fresh water, add a bouquet; cook steadily for about 1¼ hours after the water has come to the boil. Add salt only during the final 10 minutes. Drain, reserving the liquid for soup. Remove the bouquet.

For ½ lb. of beans, fry a couple of rashers of streaky bacon cut into little pieces, in a little extra fat or butter. Put in the beans with 2 tablespoons of meat stock or of the cooking liquid; heat gently; add 2 or 3 tablespoons of thick cream and a tablespoon of finely chopped parsley, and continue cooking until the sauce has thickened, shaking the pan rather than stirring, so as not to break the beans.

If you have a little left over roast lamb or pork, it can be used instead of the bacon

HARICOTS BLANCS MAÎTRE D'HÔTEL
DRIED HARICOT BEANS WITH PARSLEY BUTTER

Soak the beans overnight in plenty of cold water. Drain them, put them in a saucepan and completely cover them with fresh cold water by about 2 inches.

For ½ lb. beans, add a piece of salt breast of pork or streaky bacon weighing about ¼ lb. Put in a bayleaf and a sprig of thyme and, if you like, a crushed clove of garlic, tied together. Bring slowly to the boil and cook steadily, but not at a gallop, for 1½ hours. Strain through a colander, reserving the cooking liquid. Remove the rind from the pork; cut it into small strips. Return the beans and pork to the saucepan and add just enough of their cooking liquid, or better still, if you have it, good meat stock, to keep them from sticking. About ¼ pint is enough. Heat them gently. When they are bubbling, stir in a tablespoon of parsley butter (butter worked with very finely chopped parsley and flavoured with lemon juice). Turn off the heat and shake the pan until the butter has melted and amalgamated with the sauce.

Serve either as a dish on its own or with sausages.

Half a pound of beans is enough for three people, but it is worth cooking rather more than one needs for one meal. The beans left over, sieved, and heated up with the rest of the cooking liquid, and possibly a little stock added, make a good soup.

HARICOTS À LA BRETONNE
DRIED HARICOT BEANS WITH ONIONS AND TOMATOES

This way of cooking beans makes a dish which is a good background for eggs as well as a useful vegetable to serve with all kinds of meat and sausages.

Half a pound of medium-sized dried white beans, previously soaked, are cooked in water to cover by about 2 inches, with the addition of an onion stuck with a clove, a carrot, a small piece of celery, a bouquet of thyme, parsley and bayleaf. Add salt only at the end. When they are tender, drain them, reserving the liquid. Chop the onion which has cooked with them and fry it in butter; add 2 peeled and chopped tomatoes, fry 2 minutes, dilute with a little of the reserved liquid. Add to the beans; reheat them gently, adding, if available, a little juice from a roast, or meat glaze.

HARICOTS AU VIN ROUGE
DRIED HARICOT BEANS WITH RED WINE

Soak ½ lb. of white haricot beans, preferably the long kidney-shaped ones called *Soissons*, in cold water for 12 hours. Put them on to cook in about 1½ pints of fresh cold water with a piece of salt pork or streaky bacon weighing about 6 oz., or if you like 3 oz. each of pork and bacon. Add a bouquet of bayleaf, thyme and a crushed clove of garlic. Cook at a moderate pace for 1½ to 1¾ hours. Take out the pork; drain the beans, reserving the liquid. In a mixture of butter and olive oil, fry a finely-sliced onion, then add the pork cut into little cubes. After a minute or so pour in half a tumbler of red wine. Let it bubble fast for half a minute. Put in the beans, stir them round and add a little of the cooking liquid. Cook gently about 10 minutes. Before serving stir in a little lump of butter.

An excellent way of serving haricot beans, preferably as a dish on their own.

HARICOTS VERTS AU BEURRE
FRENCH BEANS WITH BUTTER

When you can get young and tender little French or string beans, of the variety which need only topping and tailing, they make one of the most beautiful vegetable dishes imaginable, and should always be served as a separate course, when their exquisite flavour can be appreciated.

Simply cook them in a small amount of boiling water, lightly salted, for about 15 minutes. Drain them. In the saucepan melt a large lump of butter, at least 1 oz. per pound of beans, put back the drained beans, shake the pan over the flame until the butter has melted, and serve instantly. One pound of string beans should serve four people.

HARICOTS VERTS À LA PROVENÇALE
FRENCH BEANS WITH TOMATOES

For this dish coarse French beans or scarlet runners can be used.

Top and tail the beans, slice off the strings, break the beans into chunks, blanch them 10 minutes in boiling salted water and drain them. In a frying-pan heat 2 tablespoons of olive oil; put in the drained beans and 2 or 3 skinned and roughly chopped tomatoes and a clove of garlic. Cook gently for 10 minutes until the tomatoes have turned almost to a purée. Shake the pan from time to time so that the beans do not stick. Remove the garlic, add a little parsley and turn into a hot serving dish.

LES LENTILLES

LENTILS

In French cookery there are two kinds of lentils; *lentilles blondes*, which are the kind we know as brown or German lentils, and *lentilles du Puy*, which are smaller and a mixture of beautiful dark green and slate colours which, however, turn brown when they are cooked. The red and yellow lentils which are the ones most commonly found in English shops I have never seen in France. They are good for soups and purées but useless for either of the following vegetable recipes, as they turn to a fibrous mush after half an hour's cooking and must be sieved.

Brown lentils can be found at Harrods and other large stores as well as in Soho shops, and are excellent, although their flavour is less fine than that of the green lentils of Le Puy, which can be bought at Roche's in Old Compton Street—at a price.

It is not strictly necessary to soak either of these varieties of lentils, but it shortens the cooking time to do so. And although nowadays lentils are very carefully picked over before they are packed, it is still advisable to spread them out on a dish to make sure there are no little stones or pieces of grit. Allow 2 to 3 oz. of lentils per person.

LENTILLES MAÎTRE D'HÔTEL

LENTILS WITH PARSLEY BUTTER

For ½ lb. of either brown or green lentils, the other ingredients are a teacup of chicken or veal or beef stock, 1½ oz. of *maître d'hôtel* butter (see page 116), water and salt.

Put the lentils on a plate and pick out any pieces of grit. Cover them with cold water and leave them to soak for an hour or so. Drain them. Put them in a saucepan with 2½ pints of fresh cold water. Bring to the boil and then simmer them at a moderate pace for 1¼ hours, by which time all the water will be evaporated and the lentils tender without being mushy. If they are not yet sufficiently cooked, add more water, which should be boiling. If there is any excess of water by the time the lentils are ready, drain it off.

To the cooked lentils add the cup of stock and simmer again for a few minutes until it is absorbed. Put in the parsley butter, turn off the heat, and shake the saucepan until the butter is just barely melted and has formed a little sauce which binds the lentils. Serve at once in a hot dish.

As a separate vegetable dish this is hard to beat, especially in winter when there are no fresh green vegetables. It is also delicious with pheasant, venison, pork and sausages.

LENTILLES AU PETIT SALÉ

LENTILS WITH SALT PORK

Put ½ lb. of brown or green lentils to soak in cold water for an hour. Cover a 6 to 8 oz. piece of breast of salt pork with cold water and bring it to the boil. Let it cook 5 minutes and drain it.

In a heavy saucepan heat ½ oz. butter; in this melt a small onion thinly sliced; add the drained lentils. Give them a stir, pour in 2½ pints of hot water, add the piece of salt pork and a bouquet of bayleaf, parsley, and a crushed clove of garlic, tied with a thread. Simmer for 1¼ to 1½ hours uncovered. By this time the liquid should all be absorbed and the lentils quite tender. Remove the pork, taste the lentils for seasoning and add salt if necessary; turn into a shallow serving dish; squeeze in a little lemon juice; cut the pork into squares or strips and put them on top of the lentils. Strew with a little parsley and serve hot.

LES MARRONS

CHESTNUTS

A tremendous fuss is made about the difficulty of shelling and skinning chestnuts. It is really very easy but people who are not accustomed to cooking and, consequently, to handling food when it is hot, are better advised to leave the job to more experienced cooks and housewives. It is all a question of how much heat your hands can stand, and it is well known that women are better at this than men. The procedure is as follows:

Score the chestnuts across on the rounded side and put them in a baking tin in a gentle oven, Gas No. 3, 330 deg. F., for 15 to 20 minutes, or else drop them in boiling water and boil them for about 8 minutes. Extract a few at a time so that the rest do not get cool, for then they become difficult to peel. Squeeze each chestnut so that the shell cracks and then, with the aid of a small knife, it is quite easy to remove both skins and shell. The chestnuts are now ready to be simmered gently in water to cover, until they are quite soft.

MARRONS EN PURÉE
CHESTNUT PURÉE

For four people, 1 lb. of chestnuts makes an ample amount.

Prepare the chestnuts as explained above. When they are shelled and skinned, put them in a saucepan and cover them completely with half milk and half water or stock. Simmer very gently indeed for about an hour until they are very soft and only a little of the liquid is left. Sieve them, or purée them in the electric blender, with the liquid. The resulting purée should be rather liquid. To heat it up, put it into the top half of a double saucepan with a small piece of butter and light seasoning of salt. Cook over gently boiling water, stirring frequently. Chestnut purée very easily dries up and becomes stodgy but, done in this way, it should remain creamy and rather liquid. Before serving, stir in a tablespoon or two of the sauce or juice of the bird, meat or game which it is to accompany. A good chestnut purée should be café au lait colour rather than dark brown.

MARRONS À LA DIABLE
DEVILLED CHESTNUTS

Cook shelled and skinned chestnuts in stock or water to cover, very gently, until tender. Extract them with a perforated spoon rather than by tipping them into a colander, and put them in a sieve to drain. Sprinkle them with salt and a little cayenne pepper. Fry them very gently in a little olive oil, for a minute or two only.

Nice with bacon or grilled gammon rashers, or with a roast saddle of hare.

NAVETS AU JAMBON
TURNIPS WITH HAM

Pare 2 lb. of very small turnips. Throw them into boiling salted water and cook for 10 minutes. Drain, cut them in halves or quarters, put them in a sauté pan in which $1\frac{1}{2}$ oz. of butter has been heated, cover the pan and cook gently till the turnips are tender (about 15 minutes), shaking the pan from time to time to make sure they do not stick. Now add $\frac{1}{4}$ lb. ham cut into thick strips; just let it heat through and serve the turnips with a sprinkling of chives on the top. Enough for four.

NAVETS À LA BORDELAISE
TURNIPS WITH PARSLEY AND BREADCRUMBS

Give the turnips a preliminary cooking as above, and the second cooking in olive oil instead of butter. When they are all but done, add 3 table-spoons of breadcrumbs mixed with chopped parsley, and a chopped shallot. By the time the olive oil has been absorbed by the breadcrumbs the vegetables should be ready. The contrast of the crisp breadcrumbs with the soft turnips is particularly pleasing.

NAVETS GLACÉS
GLAZED TURNIPS

There are two or three ways of cooking this dish, of which the simplest is the same method as that used for *carottes glacées*, page 247. The turnips should be very young and tender ones, peeled and cut into quarters or eighths, according to their size. If they are large and beginning to get tough and strong in flavour, they should, when peeled and quartered, be given a preliminary blanching for 10 minutes in boiling salted water.

Glazed turnips make an excellent garnish for mutton and lamb dishes and for duck.

OIGNONS GLACÉS
GLAZED ONIONS

To make glazed onions use the small silverskin pickling onions when they are available, or new white onions, or the French ones called *grelots*. They should be all the same size. Peel them; sauté them gently in butter until they acquire a very pale golden colour. Sprinkle them with sugar, cover with stock or water and simmer until the liquid has almost evaporated and the onions are beginning to be caramelised.

OIGNONS À L'ÉTUVÉE
ONIONS STEWED IN WINE

This is a dish to make when you have a glass of wine, red, white, rosé, sweet, dry or aromatic (i.e. some sort of Vermouth) to spare and also, perhaps, when you have been bullied or cajoled by one of the Breton onion boys into buying far more onions than you know what to do with. You peel 6 to 8 rather large onions, all the same size. You put them with a tablespoon of olive oil in a thick pan in which they just fit comfortably. You start them off over a moderate flame and, when the oil is beginning to sizzle, you pour in a small glass of your wine. Let it boil fiercely a few seconds. Add water to come half-way up the onions. Transfer to a low oven and cook uncovered for about 1½ hours. Put back on top of the stove over a fast flame for 2 or 3 minutes, until the wine sauce is thick and syrupy. Season. Serve as a separate vegetable, or round a roast.

OIGNONS RÔTIS AU FOUR

ROAST ONIONS

Medium-sized whole onions, unpeeled, are cooked in a baking tin in a slow oven, Gas No. 3, 330 deg. F., for 1½ to 2 hours. Serve them hot with salt and butter, or cold with a *vinaigrette* dressing.

This is one of the best possible ways of cooking onions in the winter when the oven is, in any case, turned on for the cooking of a stew or some other long-cooked dish. The onions can be served as a first course, or as a separate vegetable after the meat. Red Spanish onions will take a good deal longer to cook than the mild white kind.

L'OSEILLE

SORREL

In principle, sorrel is cleaned and cooked in exactly the same way as spinach but, as it is of a rather different consistency, melting and softening much more quickly, it can be cooked simply in butter without any water at all, and then chopped or sieved to make a purée. Or if there is only a small quantity, it can be cut into the thinnest of ribbons (*chiffonnade*) before cooking.

Most people prefer the acid flavour softened with cream or eggs (it makes a delicious filling for an omelette) and a small proportion of sorrel added to a lentil or potato or haricot bean soup makes an admirable mixture. In fact sorrel enters into a very large number of refreshing French country soups, giving a flavour for which there is no quite satisfactory substitute, although watercress can very successfully be used as an *alternative* in many soups and sauces in which sorrel appears.

A purée of sorrel is also the old-fashioned accompaniment of a *frican-deau* and other veal dishes, and of one or two fishes, notably shad (*alose*) and hake (*colin*). Allow ½ lb. sorrel per person.

PURÉE D'OSEILLE À LA CRÈME
CREAMED SORREL

For 1 lb. of sorrel, washed and drained, melt 1½ oz. of butter in a thick saucepan; cook the sorrel in this with a little salt until it is soft. Sieve it or chop it finely. Return it to the saucepan and let it dry out a little over very gentle heat. Stir in 3 or 4 tablespoons of creamy béchamel, or *sauce à la crème* (page 115).

Fresh thick cream can be used instead of the cream sauce, but the acid in the sorrel tends to curdle the cream so it is wisest to stir a teaspoon of flour into it and to heat it up until it boils, and then stir it into the purée. Beaten yolks of egg can also be used to bind a sorrel purée.

Excellent with veal and with white fish.

PETITS POIS AU BEURRE
GREEN PEAS STEWED IN BUTTER

The great difference between the way peas are served in French and English cookery respectively is that while we cook ours so that each pea is, so to speak, separate (and very often a separate bullet), the French cook them so that they are bound together with a sauce, although that sauce usually consists only of butter.

But to cook English peas *à la française*, that is to say, entirely in butter with lettuce heart and tiny onions, is only possible when the youngest, smallest, tenderest, garden peas are available. When they are full grown, although still young, a compromise between the English and French methods produces excellent results.

For 3 lb. of peas, freshly shelled, shred 1 small cabbage lettuce heart; put this with the peas, a little salt and a lump of sugar, in sufficient boiling water just to cover the peas. Cook uncovered until they are barely tender. Drain them. Return them to the rinsed saucepan with a large lump of butter—¼ lb. is by no means too much—and let the peas and lettuce stew gently in this butter for a few minutes. The result will be a dish of peas with the most delicate flavour and a sauce of an almost creamy consistency. It is, of course, a dish to be served on its own, so you need about 3 lb. of peas for four people.

PETITS POIS DE CONSERVE

TINNED PETITS POIS

French and Belgian tinned *petits pois* are excellent when fresh ones
cannot be obtained. They were, I believe, one of the first vegetables
ever to be preserved by the tinning method and those made by a firm at
Nantes in Britanny very quickly became famous. No green colouring
matter is ever put with French or Belgian tinned peas, for if it were
nobody would buy them. In England, I am told by grocers and the
canning firms, people would not buy them without the green colouring.
But judging by the number of people willing to pay high prices for the
French and Belgian varieties, there should surely be a market, even if a
limited one, for home-grown peas preserved without colouring matter.

Probably the best way to serve tinned *petits pois* is to drain off all but a
small amount of the existing liquid, heat the peas in what is left and,
when it has evaporated, add a large lump of butter, shaking the pan
until it has melted. Some brands of tinned peas need extra seasoning in
the way of sugar and salt; others are already sufficiently seasoned.

LES POIREAUX

LEEKS

Leeks are tiresome to clean, but once ready they seldom need more than
10 minutes' cooking. Trim off all the coarse green part of the leaves, the
outside covering of the white part and the root. Cut all the leeks to
approximately the same length. Make a cross-cut on the top of each.
Hold them under a running cold tap for a few seconds, then turn them
upside down and shake them. Leave them, heads downward, in a jug
or saucepan of fresh cold water for half an hour before cooking them.
Any grit left in the leeks will by then have seeped out or become apparent
in little dark patches under the outer leaves. If it is difficult to get at,
make a little slit along the leek and rinse it again.

On page 209 is a recipe for a leek pie, and three soups in which leeks
are the characteristic and indispensable flavouring are in the soup chapter.
For vegetable dishes allow a minimum of ½ lb. leeks per person.

POIREAUX À LA NIÇOISE

LEEKS STEWED IN OIL WITH TOMATOES

2 lb. leeks, 2 tomatoes, 2 cloves of garlic, parsley, olive oil, lemon
juice, salt, cayenne pepper.

In a frying-pan warm about 4 tablespoons of olive oil. Put in the cleaned leeks, laying them side by side. As soon as the oil starts bubbling turn the leeks over. Sprinkle with salt and cayenne pepper. Cook half a minute, then turn down the flame, cover the pan and cook slowly for about 7 minutes for small leeks, 9 or 10 for large ones. Test by putting a skewer into the root end of the leek, which is the toughest part. Take out the leeks and put them in a long dish. Into the oil in the pan throw the 2 tomatoes, skinned and chopped, the chopped garlic (more or less according to taste) and a little chopped parsley. Cook fairly fast for about 2 minutes but don't let the oil burn. Pour this mixture over the leeks, squeeze a little lemon juice over and serve hot.

Cooked in this way the leeks, instead of having that seaweed-like look and texture which they acquire from being overcooked in water, retain a certain crispness and all their flavour. Served cold, this dish also makes a good hors-d'œuvre.

POIREAUX AU VIN ROUGE
LEEKS WITH RED WINE

Unexpectedly, perhaps, when wine is to be used in the cooking of leeks, the French always use red rather than white wine.

Choose small leeks, all of a size. Having cut them down almost to the white part and cleaned them thoroughly, put them side by side in a frying-pan in which you have heated 3 or 4 tablespoons of olive oil. As soon as they have taken colour on one side, turn them over. Season with very little salt. Pour over them, for 1 lb. of leeks, a wineglass of red wine (look out for the spluttering), let it bubble, add 2 tablespoons of good meat stock, or water if no stock is available, cover the pan and cook at a moderate pace for 7 to 10 minutes, turning the leeks over once during the process. They are done when a skewer pierces the root end quite easily. Put the leeks on a shallow oval dish, cook the sauce another few seconds until reduced and pour it over the leeks.

Serve hot as a separate vegetable course, or cold as an hors-d'œuvre. This is an example of a dish for which one would not buy wine specially, but which is delicious if you happen to have a glass to spare. It is a dish of particularly beautiful appearance, with the green of the leeks and the dark purple of the wine sauce.

PIMENTS DOUX FARCIS AU RIZ
SWEET PEPPERS STUFFED WITH RICE

Stuffed sweet peppers, whether in France, Italy, England or anywhere else, very often become a very heavy and stodgy dish. The common mistake is to cram the peppers too full with too solid and rich a mixture.

This recipe, said to be of Corsican origin, makes a good dish to serve as a hot first course, and shows how small a quantity of stuffing is necessary for peppers.

Ingredients are 4 large red or green sweet peppers, 1 teacup of rice, olive oil, lemon juice, 2 to 3 tablespoons of finely-chopped parsley mixed with a little marjoram or wild thyme, salt and freshly-milled pepper. Boil the rice, keeping it a little undercooked. Drain and season it; stir in the parsley mixture, some lemon juice and a little olive oil. Cut the peppers in half lengthways. Remove all the core and seeds and rinse the peppers under running cold water to make sure that no single seed is left. Put 2 tablespoons of the rice mixture into each half pepper; pour a film of olive oil into a shallow baking dish, put in the stuffed peppers, cover them and cook in a gentle oven, Gas No. 3, 330 deg. F., for about an hour. From time to time baste the peppers with the oil in the dish, adding more if necessary. The rice should remain moist, and no hard crust should form on the top. There should be ample for four.

The dish is usually served hot but is also good cold as an hors-d'œuvre.

POIVRONS À LA CORSOISE
SWEET PEPPERS STEWED WITH TOMATOES

Cut a slice from the stalk ends of two sweet red or green peppers; extract the cores and seeds. Rinse the peppers to get rid of any lurking seeds; cut them in narrow strips; fry them gently in a little olive oil in a covered pan for 10 minutes; add a sliced clove of garlic, 1½ lb. of skinned and chopped tomatoes, several dried basil leaves, salt and pepper. Cook until the whole mixture is a fairly thick purée. Enough for three or four.

Serve with sausages, fried chicken or eggs.

Poivrons is the alternative French name for sweet peppers.

LES POIS CHICHES
CHICK PEAS

The method of cooking dried chick peas is described in the soup recipe on page 164.

For those who have a taste for their slightly odd flavour, chick peas, once boiled and drained, can be finished in the same ways as haricot beans (see pages 259–61) and go well with lamb dishes, or while still warm they can be mixed with an *aïoli* (see page 302), and served as a vegetable with a beef stew. This dish, into which other vegetables such as haricot beans, cooked artichoke hearts, French beans and potatoes can be mixed, is a Provençal one, called *aïgroissade*.

LES POMMES DE TERRE
POTATOES

From all the scores of interesting potato dishes invented by French cooks, I can include here only some half-dozen, each one representative of a particular method. It is not good potato recipes we lack in England, it is good potatoes. Because we do not grow any of the true varieties of firm and waxy potatoes which do not disintegrate in the cooking, many French dishes can only be made when new potatoes are in season; on the other hand, the old-fashioned floury potatoes are equally hard to come by. English potatoes are neither one thing nor the other. They need extreme care in the cooking and timing and, for this reason, as well as because they are fattening, I personally rarely serve potatoes with the meat course.

One of the most delectable of all French potato dishes is the *gratin dauphinois*, for which the recipe is on page 211, but this should be served on its own, not with the meat, and it is scarcely kind to offer such a dish to people who are thinking about their weight.

POMMES FONDANTES
POTATOES COOKED IN BUTTER

This is a good example of the method by which potatoes are cooked in butter without first being boiled.

Choose small new potatoes all of a size and, to cook them in, a heavy pan in which they will all fit in one layer. In this pan heat one ounce of butter for each pound of potatoes, put in the potatoes, cover the pan and leave over a very gentle flame, simply shaking the pan from time to time to make sure they don't stick. After 15 minutes, turn them over very carefully, cook another 5 to 10 minutes and test with a skewer to see that they are done. Salt them before serving.

POMMES DE TERRE À LA BARIGOULE
POTATOES COOKED IN OLIVE OIL

Whole, medium-sized firm potatoes are cooked in olive oil the same way as *artichauts à la Barigoule* (page 239).

Choose new potatoes all of a size, scrape them and put them in a thick pan with olive oil to come half-way up. Just cover with water. Set them over a flame so that the oil and water come to a rapid boil and amalgamate. Let them cook in this manner for 15 to 20 minutes, until the water has all evaporated and the potatoes are tender and turning a rich golden brown. Take care they do not stick to the saucepan at this stage, for the remaining oil will quickly dry up.

Serve them with roast or grilled meat or chicken. A typically southern method of cooking potatoes.

POMMES PURÉE *or* POMMES MOUSSELINE
POTATO PURÉE

Cook 2 lb. of good quality potatoes in their skins, either in the oven or in a small amount of water. It makes a great difference to the ultimate consistency of the purée if the potatoes are quite dry when cooked. If they become water-logged to start with, it is impossible to obtain a good purée.

Having skinned the potatoes as soon as they can be handled, either sieve them through a *mouli* or mash them with a wooden masher or a heavy wire whisk. Gradually add half a cupful of very hot milk, whisking with great thoroughness; season; beat in 2 oz. of softened butter and whisk and whisk until your arm aches. Only in this manner can you get a really light purée, but the whole operation should also be done with as much speed as possible.

Many French cooks have remarked upon the difference between the English and French methods of making a potato purée, stressing the fact that whereas the French like theirs to be very creamy and on the runny side, the English one is a much more solid affair. Carême, whether by accident or design one cannot quite be sure, calls English potato purée *mass*-potatoes.

Some French cooks like to use stock or broth instead of milk when making their purée, which certainly makes it a little lighter, although it then loses its creamy whiteness.

Ideally, potato purée should be served as soon as it is ready, but for the best method of keeping it hot see the following recipe.

POMMES MOUSSELINE FAÇON PROVENÇALE
POTATO PURÉE WITH MEAT JUICE

A purée, made as above, is put in a hot dish, some of the juices from a garlic and herb-flavoured roast of pork or veal is poured round the purée, and it is served first, as a separate course, before the meat. Sometimes the hot potato purée will be followed by the meat served cold. We should probably prefer the potatoes and meat together. So if the purée has to be kept hot, put it in a saucepan in a *bain-marie* and pour a little melted butter over and round the potatoes to prevent a crust forming, and cover the saucepan. When the time comes to serve them, mix the butter in with them before pouring in the meat juice.

POMMES DE TERRE DAUPHINE

This is one of the very nicest ways of serving potatoes to go with a steak, or a roast bird, but their final cooking in hot oil or fat is a last-minute operation, so they are better not attempted when the cook's attention is likely to be distracted elsewhere.

Cook 4 medium-sized potatoes (about ¾ lb.) until they are quite soft; drain them very well and put them through a sieve. In a thick saucepan melt 1 oz. of butter and pour on it half a tumbler of water; let this boil a minute or two and then add, through a sieve, 1½ oz. of flour; stir it very rapidly until it thickens; now lower the flame and go on stirring until you have a smooth mixture, which should be in 2 or 3 minutes. Next, add, off the fire, and slowly, 2 beaten eggs, stirring all the time, and when they have amalgamated with the flour mixture, start stirring in the potato purée, a little at a time. When the mixture is perfectly smooth and thick, season it with salt, pepper, a scraping of nutmeg and a tablespoon of grated cheese. This preparation can be made beforehand.

When the time comes to cook the potatoes, heat a deep panful of olive oil or pure beef dripping and, when it is very hot, but not absolutely boiling, drop in small spoonfuls of the mixture, cooking about half a dozen at a time, and leaving room for them to swell. They should be about the size of large walnuts. Turn them over very gently once with a palette knife; as soon as they are golden, lift them out with a perforated spoon on to a piece of kitchen paper. When they are all cooked, pile them up in a hot dish and serve at once. Enough for four.

POMMES DE TERRE SAUTÉES À LA LYONNAISE
SAUTÉ POTATOES WITH ONIONS

This is a well-known dish, but so seldom properly cooked that it may be worth while giving the correct recipe.

Firm potatoes, boiled in their skins, are peeled and sliced about $\frac{1}{4}$ inch thick and seasoned with salt. They are gently fried in a capacious heavy frying-pan until they are golden brown on both sides. When they are all but ready, some onion, sliced very thin and fried until pale gold in a *separate frying-pan*, is mixed in with the potatoes, and the dish is ready to serve.

It bears little resemblance, as can be seen, to the greasy mixture of unevenly browned potatoes and frizzled onions which usually passes for *pommes lyonnaises*.

Proportions are 1 medium-sized onion to each pound of potatoes and, for cooking each vegetable, 1 oz. of butter or pure beef dripping.

The potatoes take about 15 minutes to cook, the onions up to 10 minutes.

POMMES DE TERRE À L'ARDENNAISE
POTATOES WITH JUNIPER BERRIES

This is a curious recipe but extremely good if you like the pungent flavour of juniper berries.

Peel a pound or so of potatoes and shred them as fine as matches, on the fluted blade of the mandoline, or alternatively on a coarse grater. Put them in a sieve or colander and rinse them thoroughly under running cold water to get rid of the starch. Shake them dry in a cloth. Heat a couple of ounces of butter and a spoonful of olive oil (to prevent the butter burning) in a heavy frying-pan. Put in your potatoes and let them stew rather than fry in the butter. Add a seasoning of salt, freshly-milled pepper and half a dozen crushed or chopped juniper berries. Turn the potatoes over from time to time. When they have amalgamated into a mass and are quite tender, turn them on to a hot flat dish and, on top, put whatever meat or poultry they are to accompany—veal cutlets, a roast, fried or grilled chicken, grilled pork chops.

SAUCISSES DE POMMES DE TERRE
POTATO SAUSAGES

Here is an admirable cheap little recipe, and quite an old one (it appears with variations in several early nineteenth-century French books) for using up left-over meat or chicken.

Suppose you have just a very small amount, say 3 or 4 tablespoons, of cooked and finely-chopped meat, calf's head, brains, kidney, chicken or turkey. Then in a small quantity of butter, about $\frac{1}{2}$ oz., melt a couple of chopped shallots and a little parsley; stir in your meat and add 2 or 3 tablespoons of stock or broth, then stir in about a teaspoon of flour or potato flour; let it reduce; add seasonings and then 2 well-beaten whole eggs. Stir until the mixture starts to thicken, and then take quickly from the fire before it turns to scrambled eggs.

You have ready, or you now prepare, a purée from 4 large potatoes boiled in their skins, peeled and mashed very smooth with a little butter, salt and pepper, but no milk. Into this purée incorporate your meat mixture, and beat again until it is all well amalgamated.

Spread thickly on a lightly-buttered plate and leave to get quite cold, preferably until next day. You then take little spoonfuls of the mixture and, on a well-floured board, you roll them and shape them into little sausages no larger than small chipolatas or cocktail sausages. You fry them, not too fast, in good clear beef dripping or clarified butter, turning them over once or twice until they are golden and crisp on each side. Take them out, as they are done, with a perforated spoon.

Serve them very hot as a first course with, if you like, a freshly-made tomato sauce, but they are also excellent on their own.

POMMES DE TERRE BRAYAUDE
POTATOES BAKED IN THE OVEN

Boil 2 lb. of potatoes in their skins, keeping them a little undercooked. Peel them, cut them into thick slices or rough cubes and season them. Melt a couple of tablespoons of pork or goose dripping or olive oil in a large shallow earthenware baking dish. Put in the potatoes. Cook them uncovered in a moderate oven, Gas No. 4, 350 deg. F., for about 45 minutes, turning them from time to time in the fat. By the end of the cooking time, each piece of potato should be shining and very slightly crisp on the outside. Add some parsley before serving.

SALSIFIS SAUTÉS AU BEURRE
SALSIFY COOKED IN BUTTER

Salsify is a very considerable trouble to clean, so it is really only worth cooking if you are sure that those who are to eat it will appreciate its delicate and subtle flavour.

The salsify root must be very thoroughly scraped clean of all its black skin and each one, as it is ready, put into a bowl of acidulated water. When all are done, cut them in half, then cut the thick ends in half lengthways.

Plunge them into fast boiling salted water and cook them for 20 to 25 minutes. (Most cooks say 40 minutes: it is too long.) Drain them and then let them cook gently for a few minutes in a frying-pan with a little butter, so that they just turn a pale gold. Serve them with a little lemon juice squeezed over and a dusting of parsley.

BEIGNETS DE SALSIFIS

SALSIFY FRITTERS

Prepare and cook the salsify as above, keeping them slightly under-cooked. Drain them well, steep them for an hour or so in oil and lemon juice, dip them in frying batter (page 245) and fry them crisp in a deep pan of olive oil.

TOMATES À LA LANGUEDOCIENNE

TOMATOES STUFFED WITH BREADCRUMBS AND PARSLEY

A dish similar to *tomates provençales* but milder in flavour. It is to be made when large, sprawling, ripe tomatoes are available, and for 4 of these—one per person—the other ingredients are 2 slices of white bread, parsley, garlic and olive oil, salt and pepper.

Cut the tomatoes in half, score the cut surface with a sharp little knife, press in some salt and, when it has dissolved, turn the tomatoes upside down on a plate and leave them an hour or two. At the same time prepare the bread by cutting off the crusts, rubbing the crumb on both sides with a cut clove of garlic, sprinkling it with olive oil and leaving it to soften. Chop quite a lot of parsley—enough to make two good table-spoons, and then chop the softened bread with it, adding a seasoning of salt and pepper. Squeeze out the surplus juice and pulp from the tomatoes and press in the bread and parsley mixture. Sprinkle with more olive oil and cook the tomatoes in a fireproof gratin dish under the grill, slowly at first, then closer to the flame so that the surface browns.

LES TOPINAMBOURS

JERUSALEM ARTICHOKES

Two snags about Jerusalem artichokes prevent them from being cooked more frequently than they are. They are tiresome to peel and they are apt to cook unevenly. There are, however, varieties now being cultivated which are much smoother than the old knobbly kind and which are scarcely more trouble to deal with than potatoes.

The Legumex, that admirable gadget which makes the skinning of potatoes, particularly new ones, so very easy, is also quite effective for Jerusalem artichokes. Some people skin the artichokes after they have been boiled; others tell me that they find it more satisfactory to part boil them, drain and skin them, and then finish cooking them. It is all a question of what you are used to. Personally, I prefer to get all the cleaning over before embarking on the cooking. As for the difficulty of timing them, they *can* be steamed in a potato steamer, but this is rather a long job and perhaps the best way out of the difficulty is to bring them to the boil on the top of the stove and then transfer the pan, covered, to a fairly fast oven. In about 15 to 20 minutes they should be cooked, and more evenly than when they are boiled over direct heat. Allow ½ lb. per person.

TOPINAMBOURS À LA PROVENÇALE
JERUSALEM ARTICHOKES WITH TOMATOES AND HERBS

Simmer your artichokes in salted water until they are almost, but not quite, cooked. Strain them. Cut each in two. Heat a little olive oil in a heavy pan, put in the artichokes and, for each pound, add 2 skinned and chopped tomatoes, and a seasoning of dried basil or marjoram chopped with a little scrap of garlic, salt and freshly-milled pepper. By the time the tomatoes have melted to form a sauce, the artichokes should be quite tender and the dish ready to serve, either by itself or as an accompaniment to lamb, pork or sausages. This is a dish which also goes remarkably well with goose.

TOPINAMBOURS À LA CRÈME
JERUSALEM ARTICHOKES WITH CREAM

Choose large artichokes for this dish, allowing ½ lb. per person, and, having peeled them, slice them as evenly as possible, about ⅛ inch thick. In a thick frying-pan, melt a little butter, put in the artichokes, rinsed and drained, and let them absorb the butter. Season, just cover with water, and cook steadily in the open pan until nearly all the liquid is evaporated and the artichokes tender. For 1 lb. of artichokes pour in 3 tablespoons of cream, a scrap of nutmeg, some chopped parsley, cook another minute and squeeze in a few drops of lemon.

TOPINAMBOURS AU JUS

JERUSALEM ARTICHOKES STEWED WITH STOCK

Prepare and cook as above, using chicken or meat stock instead of water, and when there is just enough left to form a sauce, add another lump of butter and a squeeze of lemon juice. Shake the pan so that the butter melts quickly.

LES TRUFFES

TRUFFLES

'I have little to say about this expensive luxury. If you have only a few truffles, use them to stuff a chicken or flavour an egg dish. If you have a quantity, cook them in port and serve them with meat.'

EDOUARD DE POMIANE: *Le Code de la Bonne Chère*, 1930

'The *réveillon* took place at the Marquise's flat, just a quiet, greedy supper with pounds of beautiful truffles quite plain, cooked under the ashes, of which Colette and myself ate an enormous amount. Willy was not feeling well, ate none and drank Vittel water. I particularly remember this meal as it was very different, conversation and all, from our previous suppers; quite like a simple family gathering, but with a kind of "atmosphere"—also the truffles were perfection.'

MARCEL BOULESTIN: *Myself, My Two Countries*, Cassell, 1936

'Once a year at home we had truffle-day. But that could only take place if the bank account allowed, for Colette used to say: "If I can't have too many truffles, I'll do without truffles," and she declared they should be eaten like potatoes. We waited until, with the coming of the frost, Périgord should send the finest of its mushrooms. It appears that cleaning them is an art and Colette would not entrust the responsibility for this to anyone else. You put half a bottle of dry champagne in a black stew-pan, with some bits of bacon fat lightly browned, salt and pepper. When this mixture boils you throw in the truffles. A divine and slightly suspect odour, like everything that smells really good, floats through the house. Under no pretext must the truffles leave the stew-pan, the scented sauce is served separately, hot in port glasses, and anyone who does not declare himself ready to leave Paradise or Hell for such a treat is not worthy to be born again.'

MAURICE GOUDEKET: *Close to Colette*

A recipe for a truffle omelette is on page 197, and one for a lovely dish of pork studded with truffles on pages 365–6. Some notes on truffles are on pages 101–3.

Le Poisson

Fish

PROBABLY some of everyone's most dismal nursery memories are connected with food. One might come to accept the stewed prunes, the hateful greens, even the tapioca pudding, as part of Nannie's mysterious lore as to what it was necessary to eat in order to survive the perils of childhood. The miseries of fish days were harder to overcome because the food looked so terrifying even before it was on your plate. Egg sauce didn't do much to compensate for the black skin and monstrous head of boiled cod; fish pudding, a few spiteful bones inevitably lying in wait in that viscous mass, and whitings biting their own tails, were frightening dishes for children, and often painful too. Later came schoolday experiences of limp fried plaice, followed by tinned apricots and custard; of the boiled salt cod which on Fridays so unnervingly replaced the normally delicious food eaten by the family with whom I lived in Paris; of fried eel nauseatingly flavoured with sage and regarded as a treat in a Munich household. None of these dishes did anything to allay the suspicion which I fancy is shared by a good many English people when 'fish for dinner today' is announced.

Under the circumstances, it is hardly surprising that lobster *à l'américaine*, or fillets of sole in some rich cream sauce, represent to many Englishmen the very height of sophisticated cookery; with such a dish you know you are safe from lurking bones, from black mackintosh skin, from the empty eye-socket and accusing stare; nothing is there to recall the nursery, the schoolroom or the railway dining-car.

It was not, I think, until my first visit to the Mediterranean that I began to suspect that there might be better ways of eating fish than in these disguised fashions, and to appreciate the beauty of red mullet, bass or sardines brought straight from the sea to the grill and served crackling and golden with no garnish but a lemon. Since those days I have nearly always preferred grilled sole, trout, salmon, mullet, herring or mackerel to any subtle concoction of sole, lobster or turbot with cream, wine, or mushrooms.

So in the recipes in this fish chapter I have concentrated on rather simple dishes. Do not expect to find recipes for chefs' concoctions of sole with sophisticated cream sauces and complicated garnishes. Such dishes are indeed often delectable, and they make fine backgrounds for the lovely white wines of Burgundy or the Loire but, because they entail last-minute finishing touches which can all too easily go wrong, but without which they would be incomplete and pointless, few of them are suitable for home cookery. Into the question of one or two famous regional fish dishes such as the *bouillabaisse*, the *brandade de morue* and the lobster *à l'américaine* I have gone in some detail, because these are dishes in which many people are interested in spite of the fact that they are unsuited to English domestic cookery.

On the whole, though, dishes which are very simple in execution are those which also best preserve the natural tastes of the fish and at the same time present well. In no branch of cookery, I think, is the presentation of more importance than where fish dishes are concerned. It is so easy to be put off by a ragged-looking fish steak, a herring broken in the grilling or a clumsily fried trout. And a garnish of brightly coloured vegetables does little to redeem matters. Even a beautiful, and beautifully cooked, salmon trout will fail to arouse interest if it comes to table with its head and tail lolling over the ends of the dish and a sea of cucumber surging all round it. As to the last point, I cannot help wondering how long it will be before the various associations for the promotion of fish cookery in this country turn their attention to the utter lack of dishes suitable to the service of large fish.

What we need are long, narrow dishes especially designed to hold a whole fish and its juices, and, preferably, these dishes should be in plain white china, which seems to me to make the best background for fish. If the dishes were fireproof so much the better, and they should be available in three different sizes. Such dishes (although they were not fireproof) used to be made by English china manufacturers. I have some, and very nice they are; but they are no longer made, and one must search the second-hand shops and the market stalls for them. In a country in which the fishing industry is of the greatest importance this is, to say the least, odd.

LES POISSONS GRILLÉS

GRILLED FISH

Fish suitable for grilling under modern gas and electric grills are mackerel, herring, red mullet, grey mullet, sea-bream and sea-bass provided they are not too large, trout, sole; and salmon, eel and white fish cut into steaks.

For whole fish cleaned and scaled, make two or three slantwise incisions on each side, so that in cooking the heat will penetrate without the skins bursting, paint the fish with olive oil, rub them with salt, add a sprinkling of fresh herbs if you like, and cook them close to the grill to start with, then farther away once the skin has become crisp. There should be no necessity to turn them over more than once, but they will need a little basting with more oil during the cooking. They are done when you can see that the flesh is white right down to the bone.

Sole for grilling should be skinned on both sides, and should be grilled rather more gently than the fat type of fish. To make them less liable to dry up during cooking, they can be marinated for 30 minutes to an hour in a little olive oil and lemon juice, and then lightly coated with bread-crumbs, in which case no incisions should be made in the flesh. How sole is grilled in the majority of restaurants remains something of a mystery. It appears to be first steamed, then popped under a grill for a moment. Not a very satisfactory procedure.

Fish steaks for grilling should be well coated with oil and not cooked too close to the heat or the outer surfaces will become charred and dry; to minimise the risk of breakage, they should be turned only once during the cooking.

The cookers with capacious eye-level grills, introduced in recent years, are a blessing to those who feel that grilling is the best way to cook fish, and who have hitherto been hampered by a grill large enough for only two small fish at a time. There are also any number of separate grilling units, gas and electric, which can be installed independently of the cooker proper, and in the past three or four years many people have rediscovered the merits of the primitive charcoal-burning grill. This, however, needs a properly ventilated kitchen, or at least a table standing by an open window, or you will be suffocated by the fumes. The technique of charcoal grilling also requires a certain amount of practice and skill as, for that matter, does any other form of grilling, but at least with gas and electricity it is mainly the food you have to attend to, not the fire as well. It is not quite enough to set down your steak or your fish on a wire grid over a charcoal fire and thereafter leave it to look after itself. Certain of the new London bistro type of restaurants are crowded with people drawn in by the magic words 'charcoal grilling' but, unfortunately, this too often proves to be just one more variation on the theme of good materials wrecked by the cook. Make no mistake, tending a charcoal fire is as much an art as cooking on it and those unpractised in this art will find that their food, so far from being deliciously scented with an elusive aroma of smoke, is partly burnt to a cinder and partly raw, abominably permeated with the taste of burnt fat into the bargain.

In all the wine-growing districts of France there still exists the method of grilling over vine cuttings and this, when well done, does truly give a uniquely aromatic flavour to the food so cooked. But it is not really a method one can import into one's own kitchen, even were the vine cuttings available.

POISSONS À GRANDE FRITURE
DEEP FRIED FISH

Under the names of *friture de la Loire, du Rhône, de Seine, du golfe, du lac*, or mixed fried river, sea, lake fish, etc., French restaurants serve a mixture of small fried fish quite often unidentifiable, the varieties depending upon what the day's catch has brought forth. When it is a question of the *friture du golfe*, in other words local sea or rock fish, these can be, when very fresh, barely dusted with flour and crisply fried in olive oil, very delicious. They are served with a garnish of lemon, nothing else.

About the small freshwater fish from the rivers and lakes, I am not quite so sure; they can be very bony and rather tasteless.

Having mentioned olive oil I cannot help but repeat once more that

for the deep frying of fish there is no other fat to compare with it.
Nothing else makes it so crisp and crackling; and never, with olive oil,
will you get that after-taste of stale fat which mars the best fried sole
in even the most expensive of our restaurants. For this reason, you will
nearly always find that an Italian, a Jewish or a Provençal cook will
serve you with beautifully fried fish, because, traditionally, these people
all use olive oil for their frying.

As already explained on page 74, groundnut oil is a cheap and fair
substitute for olive oil. Whichever you are using see that it is completely
free of any sediment from previous frying. Heat it until it gives off the
faintest blue haze. The proper deep-frying temperature is 356 deg. F.,
but you can test it by dropping in a little cube of bread. It should fry
golden in barely one minute.

POISSONS À LA MEUNIÈRE

FISH FRIED IN BUTTER

I am always rather surprised when I read in books and articles that to
cook fish *à la meunière* is one of the simplest of achievements. Simple in
conception certainly; but in execution, no. This is a confusion of two
distinct aspects of cookery into which it is very easy to fall. As we all
know, there is a big difference between theory and practice, and the
theory of a *sole meunière* is that the fish, fried in butter, is transferred to
a serving dish and over it is poured a quantity of *freshly cooked*, hissing,
foaming butter. A squeeze of lemon juice, a scrap of parsley, and the
dish is ready. But do they think to tell you, the instructors of the nothing-
is-simpler school, that the butter in which you fry your sole must be
clarified butter, that you must watch your fish like a hawk to see that
it does not stick and burn, that to turn it without breaking it is a tricky
business, that you should discard the remains of the butter in which
your fish was cooked, and that you must start again with a clean pan and
a quantity of *fresh* butter, *not clarified*, and that this butter must be
brought just exactly to the right point when it turns a pale hazel-nut
colour, no more and no less, that it must be poured instantly over the
waiting fish which must with equal immediacy be set in front of those
who are to eat it? Do they even tell you, the optimists who have seen the
dish being cooked without doing it themselves, or the professionals who
have special pans at their disposal, that in the ordinary 10-inch frying-
pan to be found in most households there will not be room to cook more
than one not very large sole?

Few small households possess the large oval pans especially designed for the shallow frying of fish, and one must be realistic about this point. What is the use of instructing the housewife to cook *sole meunière* for six, or even four people, in one small pan? By the time the second and third batches have been cooked, the first will be cold and sodden. In a restaurant or hotel the cooks can perhaps get away with this sort of thing —they are not paying for spoiled materials. The housewife with a critical family, or guests accustomed to good cooking, cannot take the risk of wasting fine quality and expensive ingredients. So, unless your kitchen is supplied with a suitable pan, it is best not to try to cook *sole meunière* or similar dishes for more than two people.

COLIN SAUCE RÉMOULADE
HAKE WITH RÉMOULADE SAUCE

Colin is the French fishmonger's name for hake, which, when salted and dried, becomes *merluche*. *Colin à l'oseille* used to be a common Friday dish in French restaurants but one rarely comes across it nowadays. This may be because people have come to appreciate the excellence of fresh hake and it no longer comes into the category of cheap fish, either in France or England.

Hake can be poached or baked or fried, but is at its best cut into steaks, grilled, and served with a rather highly flavoured sauce such as *rémoulade* (pages 122 and 123) or, if you like a more delicate sauce, an *hollandaise* (page 119).

Steaks weighing about 6 oz. each are generously coated with olive oil and seasoned with a little lemon juice, salt and pepper. They take 12 to 15 minutes to grill, not too close to the flame, being turned once or twice.

If you can lay hands on some sorrel, the purée described on pages 127 and 267 makes an excellent sauce for hake and also for cod and other white fish.

DAURADE AUX MOULES
SEA-BREAM WITH MUSSELS

Sea-bream, occasionally to be found in English fishmongers' shops, is a broad, rather thick, red and silver fish, smaller than the Mediterranean *daurade* but similar in appearance (in fact it is more the equivalent of the Provençal *pagel*) and makes excellent eating.

For a bream weighing about 2 lb. before cleaning, other ingredients are 1 quart of mussels, 3 tomatoes, 1 leek, a large bunch of parsley, olive oil, fennel leaves when available, a clove of garlic, seasonings, a claret glass of dry white wine.

First, clean and scrub the mussels, small ones when obtainable. Put them in a wide pan with the white wine, and let them open over a fairly fast flame. Remove them from the pan as soon as they open. When all are open, filter the stock left in the pan through a muslin, and take the mussels from their shells.

Next, put 2 tablespoons of olive oil (or a mixture of olive oil and butter if preferred) in a small frying-pan. In this melt the finely sliced white part of the leek, then add the tomatoes roughly chopped, then about 3 tablespoons of chopped parsley, the chopped garlic (which is optional), seasoning and a few fennel leaves if these are being used; when the mixture begins to look like a purée thin it with a little of the strained mussel stock. Then, off the fire, add the mussels.

Now spread a sheet of aluminium foil, or greaseproof paper, with a film of olive oil. Lay the cleaned and decapitated bream on this. Surround with the prepared sauce; wrap the foil or paper round, twisting the edges so that no juices can run out. Put on a baking dish and cook in a slow oven, Gas No. 3, 330 deg. F., for 35 to 40 minutes. To serve, turn out on to a heated dish with the sauce and juices all round. Add lemon quarters. Grey mullet and John Dory can be cooked in the same way.

ÉPERLANS FRITS

FRIED SMELTS

Smelts are one of the nicest small fish for frying, although to fry them on a skewer, as one is always instructed to do, is a trickier business than it sounds. As served by the *patronne* at the Hôtel du Louvre at Pont-Audemer, a dish of these skewer-fried smelts is nicely described by George Musgrave in *A Ramble Through Normandy*, 1855.

'She had an extraordinarily expeditious way of frying smelts. I had bespoken a score and a half (after having seen some in the market) and they were dished as they were fried, with two skewers; fifteen on each skewer—the slender pin passing through the heads, and the ring at its extremity serving to turn them in the pan, all at once, for the more even frying.'

It is not often that one comes across smelts at the fishmonger's, but the easiest way to cook them when they are available is to dredge flour over them and fry them in deep oil in the usual way, draining them on kitchen paper and serving them with halves of lemon. Alternatively, they can be shallow-fried in butter.

GRILLADE AU FENOUIL
SEA-BASS OR RED MULLET GRILLED WITH FENNEL

There are two or three slightly varying versions in the presentation of this dish, but the main elements are red mullet or sea-bass (the Mediterranean *loup de mer*, sometimes translated as sea-perch, the ordinary French name for sea-bass being *bar*) and dried fennel stalks.

Get the fishmonger to clean the fish, but in the case of red mullet leave in the liver, which is considered a delicacy. Make two deep crosswise incisions on each side of the fish. Stick two or three short pieces of fennel in the incision through which the intestines of the fish were removed. Paint the fish all over with oil, and grill on each side for about 7 minutes, turning them over once only. On a long fireproof serving-dish arrange a bed of dried fennel stalks, remove the grid with the fish on it from under the grill and place it over the fennel. In a soup ladle or small saucepan warm a small glass of Armagnac or brandy; set light to it; pour it flaming into the dish. The fennel catches alight and burns, giving out a strong scent which flavours the dish.

The fennel-burning performance can either be carried out in the kitchen or at the table under the noses of the guests. In either case it is advisable to have a second hot dish in readiness to receive the fish and its strained juices, for when it comes to serving the fish nobody wants little pieces of burnt fennel on his plate.

GRONDIN AU FROMAGE
RED GURNET WITH CHEESE SAUCE

The red gurnet or gurnard (also sometimes called *rouget-grondin* in French, but not to be confused with the *rouget* proper, which is red mullet), is a rather ugly fish with a large head, which is likely to be a bargain when it appears on the fishmonger's slab.

Poach a whole gurnard in cold water to cover, with a sliced onion, a bouquet, 2 tablespoons of vinegar and salt. When it is cooked, remove the skin and all bones. Put the fillets in a buttered fireproof dish.

Prepare a sauce exactly as for *raie gratinée au fromage*, page 291, and then bake the fillets of gurnard in the same way. The flesh of gurnard has some resemblance to that of the turbot.

HARENGS GRILLÉS, SAUCE À LA MOUTARDE
GRILLED HERRINGS WITH MUSTARD SAUCE

'Put your cleaned herrings into a china dish and pour a little oil over them. Sprinkle them with a little salt, add some sprigs of parsley, and turn them round in this seasoning. A quarter of an hour before they are to be served, grill the herrings; when they are done arrange them in the serving dish and pour over them a white butter sauce, into which you have stirred a tablespoon of mustard, and take care not to let the sauce boil.'

This recipe comes from the *Dictionnaire Général de la Cuisine Française*, 1866. The following is a simple method of making a butter and mustard sauce; there is no risk of it boiling, for it is not cooked over the fire.

Sauce à la moutarde

Put 2 teaspoons of yellow Dijon mustard into a sauce-boat or bowl. Stir in a tablespoon of chopped parsley, then 3 oz. of just barely melted butter. Stir gently until it is smooth and add a good squeeze of lemon juice. This makes enough sauce for four people.

LAITANCES EN SABOTS
SOFT ROES IN BAKED POTATOES

Bake some very large potatoes in their jackets. Cut them in half lengthways, scoop out the centres, replace each with 2 soft herring roes previously cooked $\frac{1}{2}$ minute in butter; add seasoning, melted butter, and breadcrumbs, and return to the hot oven for 2 or 3 minutes until browned. Serve with more melted butter. A quarter-pound of roes will be sufficient for 2 large potatoes.

MAQUEREAUX À LA FAÇON DE QUIMPER
MACKEREL WITH EGG, BUTTER AND HERB SAUCE

The fish dishes of the Breton coast have the charm of very good quality ingredients very simply cooked. *Maquereaux à la façon de Quimper* are notable for the excellence of the sauce, which is so easy and quick to make that it is a most useful one to know, for it can be used for many other fish, for hard-boiled eggs, even for steak instead of *béarnaise* when one happens to be in a hurry.

Break the yolks of 2 eggs into a bowl, stir in a large teaspoon of yellow Dijon mustard, salt, freshly-ground pepper, a few drops of vinegar. Add a good tablespoon of chopped parsley and any other herbs which may be available, such as chervil, chives, tarragon or fennel. Now pour in slowly 2 oz. of just barely melted butter, stirring all the time. The sauce is ready and should be of the consistency of a thin mayonnaise. As it is not a very solid sauce and is inclined to sink into the fish or whatever it is poured over, it is best either to add it at the last minute or serve it separately in a bowl.

Mackerel in the Quimper way are poached in a highly seasoned *court-bouillon*, skinned and filleted when cool, arranged in a circle in a flat dish, garnished with a sprinkling of parsley and slices of lemon, with the sauce in the centre of the dish.

FILETS DE MAQUEREAUX À LA TOMATE

FILLETS OF MACKEREL WITH POTATOES AND FRESH TOMATO SAUCE

Coat the fillets of mackerel lightly with flour. Fry them in olive oil or in clarified butter. On the serving dish arrange a circle of hot sliced potatoes, seasoned with olive oil, pepper, salt and a little vinegar. In the centre put the fried mackerel fillets. Serve separately a freshly made *coulis* of tomatoes as described on pages 126 and 242.

MAYONNAISE DE POISSON

FISH MAYONNAISE

When a respectable quantity of a baked or poached fish is left from one meal, about the two best ways to use it up are either cold with a mayonnaise or hot with a creamy cheese sauce, as described for *raie gratinée au fromage*. To make a fish mayonnaise with, say, a large breakfast cup of cold salmon, turbot, bass or other white fish meticulously freed of skin, and flaked, make a mayonnaise with one or two egg yolks and about ⅓ pint of olive oil. Season it with lemon juice rather than vinegar. Separate it into two equal parts. Into one mix the flaked fish. Arrange this in a mound on an oval or round dish, leaving a space all round to put some diced fresh or pickled cucumber, stoned green olives, a few slices of hard-boiled egg, strips of sweet pepper, a few capers, some peeled prawns—not all these things, of course: just two or three, enough to make a fresh and interesting looking dish. Cover the fish only with the reserved half of the mayonnaise and sprinkle chopped parsley or other fresh herbs lightly over the whole dish.

MERLAN EN RAYTE
WHITING WITH RED WINE SAUCE

'Cut a large whiting into good slices 2 centimetres thick. Roll them in
flour, put them into a frying-pan in which you have heated a few
tablespoons of olive oil. Cook them briskly, and when they are golden
on one side, turn them and fry the other side. Drain them, and then
let them simmer gently for 8 to 10 minutes in a sauce made exactly as
explained for the *morue en rayte* (page 306), only in smaller quantities.
Add also a few capers, and serve in the same way.'

REBOUL: *La Cuisinière Provençale*

MULET AUX OLIVES ET AU VIN BLANC
GREY MULLET WITH OLIVES AND WHITE WINE

A very simple and effective recipe which can be applied to many sorts of
fish, including red mullet, sea-bream, sea-bass, whiting and mackerel;
I have chosen grey mullet as an example because for some reason it is
sold in this country at prices far below its true value, and represents
something of a bargain.

For 2 medium-sized fish, each weighing approximately 1 lb. gross
weight, the other ingredients are a coffee-cupful (after-dinner size) of
olive oil, 2 or 3 tablespoons of white wine, a dozen stoned black olives,
some slices of orange or lemon, and, if possible, a little piece of fennel—
otherwise a sprig of thyme or a bayleaf.

Put the cleaned fish into a shallow oval fireproof dish, pour the oil
over them, add your herbs, a sprinkling of salt and pepper and the white
wine. Bake, uncovered, for 15 to 20 minutes in a medium oven, Gas
No. 4, 350 deg. F.

Now add the stoned black olives and cook another 5 minutes. The
mullet can be served in the dish in which they have cooked, or be transferred to a flat serving dish, in either case with their own juice and slices
of orange or lemon arranged along each fish. May be served hot or cold.

RAIE AU BEURRE NOIR
SKATE WITH BLACK BUTTER

Skate, that spectacular fish which looks like some fantastic kite, has,
when cooked in ideal conditions, a very fine flavour. It is one of the rare
fish which is better kept for an interval of two to three days after it has

K

been caught rather than eaten fresh from the sea but, since the circumstance of having too fresh a skate is scarcely likely to arise in most people's lives, it is more important to know that the creature should reach the kitchen as soon as possible after the requisite wait of two or three days, for stale skate can be disastrous, and because of the powerful ammoniac smell which it gives out some fishmongers do not care to buy it. In England a good deal is sold to the fried fish shops, but poached and served with browned foaming butter according to the well-known French recipe, it can be a real treat.

The common skate, *raie batis*, and the thornback, *raie bouclée*, are the two varieties of skate most often to be found in French markets and here, and these fish are extraordinarily voracious. M. Donies, author of a manual called *Les Poissons de Mer*, asserts that in the stomach of one monster specimen of the common skate were found two large plaice, a lobster, two mackerel, a thornback nearly half a metre long and a salmon. A well-nourished fish, in short.

Supposing that you have a piece of wing of skate, weighing 1¼ to 1½ lb., the other ingredients are an onion, a few sprigs of parsley, vinegar and butter. You also need a pan sufficiently wide for the piece of skate to lie flat while cooking. Into this pan you put the skate, cover it completely with cold water, add a sliced onion, a couple of sprigs of parsley, a little salt and 2 tablespoons of vinegar. Bring gently to the boil, with the pan uncovered. Thereafter let it barely simmer for 15 to 20 minutes. Lift it out and put it on a dish or board so that you can remove the skin and the large cartilaginous pieces of bone and divide the fish into 2 or 3 portions. This has to be done with some care, or the appearance of the fish will be spoiled. Transfer it to a fireproof serving dish, sprinkle it with chopped parsley, and keep it hot over a low flame while the black butter is prepared.

For this you put 2 oz. of fresh butter into a small frying-pan and heat it over a fast flame until it foams and begins to turn brown. At this precise moment, not sooner nor later, take the pan from the fire, for in a split second the butter will take on the deep hazel-nut colour which is *beurre noir*. (It should be only a little darker than *beurre noisette*, which is light hazel-nut colour.) Pour it instantly over the fish. Into the pan in which the butter has cooked, and which you have replaced on the fire, pour 2 tablespoons of wine vinegar, which will almost instantly boil and bubble. Pour this, too, over the fish, and bring at once to table; for, like all dishes in which *beurre noir* figures, the ideal is only attained when the dish is set before those who are to eat it with the sauce absolutely sizzling.

In one of those noisy, busy, cheerful Lyon bistros renowned for very simple, rather rough but well-cooked food, in copious quantities, I had skate with black butter beautifully served. We were sitting within a yard of the kitchen but even so the *patron* almost ran from the stove to our table with the little covered dish containing the skate and its hissing, bubbling sauce, to which a few capers, cooked with the vinegar, had been added.

RAIE GRATINÉE AU FROMAGE
SKATE WITH CHEESE SAUCE

Skate with black butter is so good that it seems unnecessary to go looking for other or more recherché methods of cooking it but, if you have some left over, or choose to cook an extra piece to serve next day, or find the black butter method impossible because of the last-minute cooking involved, it is excellent done with a creamy cheese sauce and augmented, if necessary, with a few potatoes, cooked and sliced into rounds.

Line a gratin dish with a layer of your prepared sauce, put in the skate, freed of all skin and bone, and put a ring of sliced potatoes round the edge. Pour the rest of the sauce over the top, covering the potatoes as well as the fish. Strew with breadcrumbs and a few little nuts of butter and bake in a fairly hot oven, Gas No. 7, 420 deg. F., for about 15 minutes. Finish for a minute under the grill.

To make the sauce

Heat 1 oz. of butter; stir in one good tablespoon of flour. When it is smooth add a scant $\frac{1}{4}$ pint each of the strained cooking liquid from the fish and creamy milk; the stock should go in first, and both should be warmed. Stir until the sauce is creamy, season lightly with freshly-milled pepper, salt and nutmeg. Leave to simmer very gently with a mat under the saucepan for 15 minutes, stirring at frequent intervals. Stir in 2 tablespoons of grated Parmesan or Gruyère.

These quantities are enough for a good large cup of cooked skate.

ROUGETS À LA MEUNIÈRE
RED MULLET FRIED IN BUTTER

By name, sole or other fish fried *à la meunière* are known to everyone who frequents restaurants either here or in France. In fact, it is rare to get it in precisely the correct condition because it is essentially a frying-pan-to-plate dish. The butter poured over the fried fish immediately it is cooked should still be foaming as it comes to table. Once the butter has cooled the dish is no longer the same; it has started to become greasy. The supposition that French cooking is greasy is largely due to dishes such as these being not so much imperfectly cooked as served in the wrong condition.

I give the recipe here in quantities for two people only. For 2 moderate-sized red mullet weighing, say, about ½ lb. each, first clarify a minimum of 2 oz. of butter. (Butter for frying fish is always best clarified—that is, gently melted over hot water, then filtered through a damp muslin; the risk of the fish sticking to the pan is then greatly diminished.) While this clarified butter is heating in the frying-pan, coat your fish very lightly in seasoned flour. Do not do this in advance, or the coating will turn soggy.

When the butter is hot, but not too hot, put in your fish and let it get quite crisp on one side before you lower the heat and gently turn the fish over: 10 minutes altogether of quite slow cooking, the fish having been turned once more during this time, will be sufficient. Remove the fish to a very hot dish. Quickly pour off the used butter (not down the sink, it will make a spluttering and a smell), wipe the pan clean, and into it put 2 oz. of fresh butter—not clarified this time—and when it is foaming pour it over the mullet, sprinkling a dusting of fine parsley over it and adding a squeeze of lemon as you bring it to table.

ROUGET GRILLÉ EN CHEMISE

'Scale a red mullet, make an incision just by the liver, season with salt and freshly-milled pepper, and leave to marinate in a little olive oil for about an hour. Cook it a minute or two, until it has stiffened, in the oil from the marinade. Drain it, sprinkle it while still hot, with fennel (the leaves) and *serpolet* (wild thyme), without overdoing it. Wrap it in 1 or 2 vine leaves, according to its size, tie it up not too tightly and finish cooking slowly on the grill, basting frequently with olive oil. Take care that it does not catch. Untie carefully, without damaging the vine leaves, and serve with a bowl of butter, melted but not clarified.'

Recipe from La Bonne Auberge at Saint-Étienne-les-Orgues

ROUGET GRILLÉ AUX OLIVES
GRILLED RED MULLET WITH OLIVES

It is probably not so often in England that one can get either the vine leaves with which to cook mullet as in the foregoing recipe, or the dried fennel branches for the one on page 286, and then, when one or other of these ingredients is to hand, where is the mullet? So here is another and very simple way of grilling this delicious fish which, in England, you buy when you see it, for it is rarely to be had when you are counting on it.

Having gutted the mullets but left the liver intact in the fish, score them across twice on both sides, and marinate them for an hour or so in a little olive oil and 2 or 3 tablespoons of wine (either red or white, for mullet is one of the few fish which can be successfully cooked in red wine) and sprinkle the fish with salt, wild thyme and some chopped fennel leaves if you have them.

A large red mullet weighing 1 to 1¼ lb. will take about 10 to 15 minutes to grill, being started off close to the heat. Turn over once and, when the second side is crackling and crisp, move the grilling pan farther away from the heat.

When the fish is cooked, remove it carefully to the serving dish, put the pan with the juices and a dozen or so stoned black olives over a fast flame for a few seconds, pour over the fish and garnish with slices of orange or lemon.

This dish is also good cold.

FILETS DE ST. PIERRE À LA DEAUVILLAISE
FILLETS OF JOHN DORY WITH ONION AND CREAM SAUCE

St. Pierre is the large fierce-headed fish which we call John Dory. Like the haddock, it has the 'thumb-marks of St. Peter' on its back and its flesh is firm, white and with an excellent flavour, not unlike that of the turbot.

It is preferable to have the fish filleted; off each fish you get 2 rather large thick triangular fillets. Poach the fillets, allowing about 15 minutes, and finish them with the onion sauce as described for *sole à la deauvillaise*, (page 296) Madame Seignobos, in an interesting book of pre-1914 cookery, called *Comment on Forme une Cuisinière*, says that in some parts of France the St. Pierre is known as *l'horrible*, which seems rather unfair to the poor St. Pierre, for, while certainly no beauty, it has an expression of melancholy about its great head rather than anything savage or horrible.

SOLE DIEPPOISE

'During the stroll along the streets and the quays, the aroma of Dieppe makes itself remarked for its diversity and richness. All ports have a compounded smell of fish and tar and seaweed and alcohol and all the ordinary odours of closely-packed humanity, but that of Dieppe is peculiar to itself. I always feel that it is due to a lingering memory of the more exotic smells of Africa, ghostly scents from the days when the seafarers of Dieppe opened up the trade with West Africa and held for long a practical monopoly of ivory carving in Europe. (If you do visit the castle, there is a fine collection of ivories in its museum.)

'But richest of all the constituents will be the appetising whiff of your own *sole dieppoise* as you approach your chosen restaurant, where your dish should now be ready.

'This is what will have been going on in your absence. The chef will have taken a large sole, prepared it, placed it in a fireproof dish with salt, pepper, butter and a glass of white wine; he will then have placed it in the oven to poach. He will have prepared prawns and mussels, separately; the water in which they were cooked, together with the wine and butter used for the sole, will have been reduced and then mixed with more butter, flour and fresh cream. The sauce will have been cooked slowly until reaching the consistency of cream, and then sieved over the sole through a muslin. The prawns and mussels will have been added at the last moment, and no king will ever have had a finer dish set before him. And now you know why you have to order it an hour or more before your meal time.

'This magnificent dish is not to be ruined by drinking cider with it. Every traveller, every guide-book, will tell you that cider is the drink of Normandy; that when in Rome you should do as the Romans, that you should always drink the drink of the country you are in. In a sense, cider is the drink of Normandy, but there is never traveller or guide-book to tell you when it is to be drunk. Certainly it is not to be drunk with fine dishes; honest wine is cheap all over France, and Normandy is no exception to that rule, even though the vine does not flourish there.

'No, cider is to be drunk when you are thirsty, after a long walk or ride along a dusty road. Its pleasant sharpness drives away thirst, its deceptively imperceptible strength overcomes fatigue, the natural virtue of the fruit restores the elasticity of tired muscles. It is a splendid refresher between meals, but makes a deplorable *mésalliance* with delicate foods. It is sold in two forms, corked (*bouché*) or uncorked; the only difference I have ever been able to find between the two, save for a slight variation in price in favour of the latter, is that the uncorked has its sediment at top and bottom, and the corked, if any, at the bottom only.

'You will meet, as I have done, the Englishman who turns up his nose at Norman cider as thin sour stuff not worth the trouble of drinking, then you will know that he has been brought up on the fabricated, gassy stuff, all but tasteless and non-alcoholic, which all too often goes by the name of cider in England and which appeals to the palates of those who have never passed beyond a teen-age appreciation of sugared and aerated liquids prepared by commercial laboratories. Be tactful with him, for he errs from ignorance. Do not laugh him to scorn or hold him up to contempt, but rather lead him quietly to a more mature appreciation. By doing so, you will probably add years to his life and greatly increase the pleasure he derives from it.'

VIVIAN ROWE: *Return to Normandy*, 1951

SOLE EN MATELOTE À LA NORMANDE
SOLE STEWED IN CIDER WITH MUSSELS

This is not the elaborate restaurant dish called *sole à la normande*, but rather the primitive version from which, no doubt, the more luxurious concoction derived.

As a matter of fact, although the *sole normande* is now to be found in many of the restaurants of Normandy, it was originally a creation of Paris chefs. Carême (a Parisian) is thought to have invented the first version, which was simplified by Langlais, chef at the Rocher de Cancale, a restaurant famous in the early decades of the last century. Since then the dish has undergone many changes, and nearly every chef has his own version of the one and only true *sole normande*.

For the simple matelote the ingredients are a fine fat sole weighing about 1 lb., 2 pints of mussels (small ones when available), a wineglass of dry cider, 1 large onion, seasoning, a tablespoon of butter and a tablespoon of parsley butter. First slice the onion finely and melt it in the butter, stewing it very gently until it is quite soft but still pale yellow. Meanwhile, put the cleaned mussels in a saucepan with the cider, set them over a fast flame and extract them as soon as they open.

Put the onion mixture, well seasoned, into a long shallow fireproof dish. On top put the sole, skinned on both sides. Through a muslin pour into it enough stock from the mussels barely to cover it. Cover the dish, and cook in a moderate oven for 15 minutes. Put the shelled mussels round the fish, and the parsley butter on top of it. Return to the oven for 5 minutes, just sufficient time to allow the mussels to heat through. Serve in the same dish.

Be sure to use a porcelain or enamel-lined dish; tin or unlined cast-iron will turn the cider black.

A small whole turbot, a sea-bream, a piece of skate, or fillets of John Dory (St. Pierre) can be cooked in the same way.

FILETS DE SOLE DEAUVILLAISE

FILLETS OF SOLE WITH CREAM AND ONION SAUCE

Sole cooked *à la deauvillaise* is a curious combination, perhaps, but one much liked by those who share the Norman fondness for onions.

For four people the ingredients are 2 fine soles, filleted, 6 oz. onion, $\frac{1}{3}$ pint cream, butter, cider or white wine, nutmeg, French mustard, lemon, seasonings, breadcrumbs.

Weigh the onions after they have been peeled; chop them. Melt $1\frac{1}{2}$ oz. of butter in a thick pan; in this cook the onions very gently, so that they turn transparent and yellow but not brown. In the meantime make a little fish stock by cooking the carcase of the sole for 10 minutes with $\frac{1}{4}$ pint of cider or white wine, $\frac{1}{2}$ pint of water, a slice of lemon and a little salt. Strain. Sieve the onions to a purée, add about 2 tablespoons of the prepared stock and the cream; stir till smooth and fairly thick. Season with grated nutmeg, a little freshly-ground pepper, salt if necessary and a scant teaspoon of French mustard. All this can be done in advance. When the time comes to cook the fish, poach the fillets in the remainder of the stock. About 5 minutes is enough. Remove them to a heated oval *gratin* dish. Cover them with the sauce, gently reheated. Sprinkle breadcrumbs on the top, and add a few little pieces of butter. Put under the grill for about 3 minutes and serve at once, with little triangles of bread fried in butter arranged round the dish.

Fillets of John Dory, sea-bream, whiting or even plaice can be prepared in this way.

SOLE BERCY

SOLE WITH SHALLOTS AND WHITE WINE

Put not much more than a teaspoon each of finely chopped shallot and parsley into a well-buttered oval gratin dish. Add 2 tablespoons of white wine. Put in the oven for 5 to 7 minutes, so that the shallot and wine cook a little and amalgamate. Now put in your sole, skinned on both sides and seasoned with salt and pepper. On top put a tablespoon of butter in small pieces. Cover with buttered paper. Cook in a low oven, Gas No. 3, 330 deg. F., for 15 minutes, for a medium-sized sole weighing about $\frac{3}{4}$ lb. Spread some of the shallot and juices on top of the sole and put the dish under the hot grill for 2 minutes so that it acquires a light glaze. Serve in the same dish.

It is quite possible to use dry vermouth instead of white wine for this dish.

SOLE SUR LE PLAT

PLAIN BAKED SOLE

This is an even simpler way of cooking sole than the Bercy method.

Make a little concentrated fish stock by just covering the skin, taken from both sides of the sole, with water. Add seasoning (but only a very little salt) and a sprig or two of parsley. Simmer until there is only about 2 tablespoons of liquid.

Put your seasoned sole in a well-buttered fireproof dish, pour over the strained liquid, cook in the oven and finish under the grill exactly as in the Bercy recipe above. Put a little *maître d'hôtel* butter (page 116) on top of the fish before serving.

TURBOT SAUCE MESSINE

TURBOT WITH CREAM AND HERB SAUCE

For those who can lay hands on tarragon and chervil, a herb and cream mixture called *sauce messine*, from Lorraine, is one of the most delicious of summer sauces to serve with fish.

Buy a piece of turbot weighing a little over 2 lb. (the bones are very large, so this is not too much for four people), put it in a baking dish and cover it completely with half water and half milk. Cut turbot is much apt to dry up during cooking, and so should have plenty of moisture. Add salt and a sprig of fresh tarragon and parsley.

Bake, covered with a buttered paper, in a fairly slow oven (Gas No. 3, 330 deg. F.) for about 55 minutes, until you see that the flesh comes easily away from the bones. One side of the turbot is thicker than the other, so the timing depends a little bit on whether you have a thick or thin piece. Lift out the fish on to a hot serving dish, and have the sauce ready to be served separately.

The sauce

First chop together the leaves of half a dozen sprigs of tarragon, the same of parsley and chervil and 2 small shallots. Then work together 2 oz. of butter and a teaspoon of flour, add a teaspoon of French mustard, the beaten yolks of 2 eggs and ½ pint of thin cream. Blend with the herb and shallot mixture, season, and put all in a small saucepan. Heat with the saucepan standing in hot water, stirring all the time until the sauce thickens. Do not let it boil. Immediately before serving, squeeze in the juice of a small lemon.

LA BOUILLABAISSE (1)

A whole chapter could be devoted to the bouillabaisse. Every French gastronomic writer and cook for the past hundred years (and some before that) have expounded their theories upon the dish so beloved of the Marseillais, and each one of them gives his own recipe—the only authentic one. And, however many Marseillais, Toulonnais, Antibois or other natives of Provence you ask for the correct recipe, you will never get the same instructions twice.

There is no authentic bouillabaisse without white wine, you are told; it is a heresy of the most deadly kind to add white wine; the best bouillabaisse includes a *langouste* and mussels; *langouste* and mussels are only added in Paris because they haven't the other requisite fish; you *must* rub the croûtons with garlic; you must on no account rub the croûtons with garlic, and so on and so on.

I would not myself think it a great deprivation if I were told that I could never again eat a bouillabaisse. I have had good ones and bad ones, but to be quite truthful I have also eaten far superior dishes of the same sort, call it a soup or a stew or what you like, in Italy, notably on the Adriatic coast (and I hope no Marseillais will ever see these words, for the consequences might be serious).

However, for those who are interested in both the theory and the practice of the cooking of a bouillabaisse, a few constant factors emerge from all the confusion. They are as follows:

(1) It is useless attempting to make a bouillabaisse away from the shores of the Mediterranean. All sorts of variations can be and are devised in other parts of the world, but it would be foolish to pretend that these have more than a remote relationship to the true bouillabaisse.

(2) The fish must be spanking fresh from the sea, and of diverse kinds. The *rascasse* is essential, and the fish is always served with its head. If *langouste* is included, this is cut in half lengthways and served in its shell. Mussels, if part of the bouillabaisse, are likewise left in their shells.

(3) Olive oil and saffron are equally essential.

(4) Furious boiling, so that the olive oil and water (or wine if you are a heretic) amalgamate, is another absolute essential of the success of the dish.

(6) The Toulonnais sometimes add potatoes (a practice which appals a Marseillais). The potatoes are best cut (raw) into thin rounds and added at the same time as the soft fish.

(7) A bouillabaisse is not intended to be a *soup*. There should merely be enough of the broth, fused with the olive oil by the very rapid boiling, to produce a generous amount of moistening for the slices of bread.

From all the writers who have poured out such eloquent words (very often in verse) on the subject of the bouillabaisse, I have chosen two descriptions to quote and both of these include splendid recipes. But what, I cannot help wondering, would be the consequences if any of these people should chance to see what I with my own eyes have seen—tins, yes, *tins*, ½ pint tins of something called Danish bouillabaisse actually on sale, proudly displayed in our most expensive food stores. What unhappy man can have had such a terrible, sad idea? Who are the people who can be induced to buy such concentrated effrontery?

LA BOUILLABAISSE (2)

Austin de Croze, who gives the following recipe in *Les Plats Régionaux de France*, says he considers it the best there is. It was contributed by a Marseillais, M. Etienne Fauché, one-time Mayor of Cassis, and subsequently President of the Syndicat d'Initiative of La Sainte Baume, in the Var.

'The secret of a successful bouillabaisse may be summed up as follows: live fish in large variety; good olive oil and top quality saffron. The only difficulty in executing the dish consists in bringing it to the boil rapidly and fiercely.

'Every locality in Provence has, of course, its claim to the genuine bouillabaisse. But the true one comes from Marseille. For is it not in the waters of the beautiful bay of Marseille that all the requisite varieties of brilliant-hued rock fish, which go to make up the excellence of a bouillabaisse, are to be found?

'Those who have attempted to complicate the simple recipe for a bouillabaisse have succeeded only in spoiling its character; it is a mistake to cook the fish in a previously prepared broth of small fry; it is a culinary heresy to add white wine to a bouillabaisse (although it is indispensable on the table with it). It is superfluous to thicken the sauce, even with a purée of sea-urchins. All such elaborations are simply a fashion of disguising the poverty or lack of freshness of the fish. Bearing these considerations in mind, here is the recipe for bouillabaisse, in its simplicity and integrity.

'For ten people, take about 5 lb. of different fish, comprising *rascasse*,[1] angler fish [*baudroie*], weaver [*vive*], John Dory [*St. Pierre*], sea-hen [*galinette*],[2] whiting and two crawfish [*langoustes*]. Scale, gut and wash these fish, in sea-water if possible, and cut them in slices.

---

[1] A spiky, spiny rock-fish sometimes called a sea-scorpion.
[2] A fish of the same family as the gurnard.

'In a heavy pan, wider than it is high, put 2 onions, 4 tomatoes and 4 cloves of garlic, all coarsely chopped; moisten with a decilitre (3 oz.) of best quality olive oil, add 2 sprigs of fennel leaves, a bay leaf and a good pinch of powdered saffron; season with $\frac{1}{2}$ oz. of coarse salt and $\frac{1}{4}$ oz. of pepper. Mix all well together, and add the firm fish, keeping the soft ones (*galinette*, John Dory and whiting) to add 5 minutes later. Pour over boiling water to cover the fish, taking into account those which are to be added. Put the pan over a very fierce flame and give it 12 to 15 minutes at a very rapid boil. It is upon this fast boiling that success depends.

'In the meantime, cut a long loaf into slices; dry them a few seconds in the oven but without letting them take colour.

'When the bouillabaisse is ready, arrange the slices of fish carefully in a dish, and through a sieve pour the *bouillon* over the bread arranged in a deep vegetable dish. Sprinkle with parsley.

'The bouillabaisse should be served when the guests are at table. Which is to say that it must not wait, but be waited for.

'In a well-cooked bouillabaisse, the particular flavour of each fish should be distinct. The pepper should be slightly dominant; the broth should be naturally thickened by the violent boiling.

'I should advise that the heads of the fish, with the exception of those of the *rascasses*, should be sacrificed to the broth. Cut them in several pieces and, when the fish has been removed to its serving dish, it will do no harm to the broth to let it boil fiercely another five minutes before straining it over the bread.'

LA BOUILLABAISSE DES PÊCHEURS

'I was a child of ten. He was called Bauzan, my fisherman at Canet, our fishing rendezvous on the banks of the *étang de Berre*. And before eating his bouillabaisse, I used to savour the delights of watching him fish for it.

'Hardly had my grandfather's creaking but reliable old wagon, dusty from having carried us so far through the scrub, come to a standstill than I, with what alacrity, leap to the ground, and into the arms of my friend the old sea-wolf.

' "Quick, let's get off."

' "The mistral is blowing; we shall dance about a bit."

' "Oh, how lovely—."

'The more the little cockleshell danced in the waves, the happier I was. Actually, there was no danger. Bauzan, who had been round the world five times, took the helm, and the "sailor," his third son (the two eldest were serving in the squadron at Toulon), was at the oars. How I should always have liked to have been "sailor's" mate—if only my parents had let me have my way!

'Already, a league out, Bauzan's still piercing eyes had caught sight of the little indicator buoy. Stop! Sailor pulled towards the buoy. We dropped anchor. Now, round a pulley and across the boat the long rope was coiled in, two metres at a time, and the baskets came out of the waves. After we had drained off the water there was a gurgling inside— sometimes, however, there was nothing.

'It was I who had the excitement of undoing the catch which closed the lid. And there, in the bottom of the boat, multicoloured and sparkling and smelling good, lay the bouillabaisse; *rascasses* and *canadelles*, red mullet and gurnard and *muggions* [grey mullet] and other rock-fish whose names I no longer remember, but not forgetting the exquisite little *favouilles* [crabs] nor the eels, those viscous and slippery sea-serpents which Bauzan had taught me to catch with three fingers.

'We returned by sail, in ten minutes, for we were hungry. On the shore, in the wind, Madame Bauzan had lit a great wood fire upon which, in a huge cauldron, a litre of olive oil was coming to the boil, with four sliced onions, as many cloves of garlic with, of course, salt, pepper and saffron, with a few tomatoes in the season, and two or three potatoes, not forgetting, for Parisians, a handful of flour mixed with a glass of water.

'The mob of little Bauzans and their mother wasted no time in jumping on board, cleaning the fish and throwing it, all fresh as it was, into the saucepan, where the poor eels, cut in slices, went on wriggling in the boiling liquid. No more than a quarter of an hour's cooking and the divine golden yellow *bouillon* was poured through a strainer over a mountain of large slices of bread, and the fish served separately. And then, my children, our stomachs hollow from the sea-voyage, we stuffed ourselves up to the neck!

'Nowadays, I still feast sometimes on bouillabaisse—Parisian bouillabaisse. But in Paris, alas, the little crabs have to be replaced by mussels, the *rascasses* and the *canadelles* with a modest *langouste*, and so on. A makeshift, in fact. And it is a long time since I was ten years old, and Canet no longer belongs to us, and what has become of my friend Bauzan?'

PAUL ALEXIS:
Quoted in *L'Art du Bien Manger* by Edmond Richardin, 1913

AÏOLI

'Provençal *aïoli*—dish of the farmhouse and the *cabanon*[1]—triumph of the Provençal kitchen, is composed of a garlic mayonnaise and an assortment, as varied as possible, of fresh vegetables cooked in salted water, white fish cooked in *court-bouillon* and cold meats.'

EUGÈNE BLANCARD: *Mets de Provence*, 1926

Aïoli is indeed one of the most famous and most beloved of all Provençal dishes. The magnificent shining golden ointment which is the sauce is often affectionately referred to as the 'butter of Provence.' With this wonderful sauce are served boiled salt cod, potatoes, beetroot, sweet peppers, either raw or cooked, carrots, a fine boiled fish such as a bream or mullet, hard-boiled eggs, sometimes little inkfish or octopus, French beans, globe artichokes, even little snails and perhaps a salad of chick peas.

The *aïoli garni* is, in fact, a Friday dish as well as one of the traditional Christmas Eve dishes; on non-fasting days the beef from the *pot-au-feu* or even a boiled chicken may form part of the dish: it then becomes *le grand aïoli*. It will be seen, then, that with all these different accompaniments, the *aïoli garni* is essentially a dish for a large family or a party of intimate friends, although personally I could quite well dispense with all the rest provided there were a large bowl of potatoes boiled in their skins and perhaps some raw peppers and celery to go with the *aïoli*. In a small country restaurant in Provence where I once asked, at short notice, if it were possible to produce an *aïoli garni* for dinner, it was too late for the *patron* to go out and buy anything specially, but he produced a handsome dish of ham accompanied by potatoes and the vegetables in season, with the *aïoli* in a bowl in the centre of the dish. It was an excellent demonstration of the sort of impromptu *aïoli* which can be produced with ingredients to hand.

To make the *aïoli* sauce:

Allow roughly 2 large cloves of garlic per person and, for eight people, the yolks of 3 eggs and nearly a pint of very good quality olive oil—failing Provençal olive oil, the best Italian or Spanish will do. Crush the peeled garlic in a mortar until it is reduced absolutely to pulp. Add the yolks and a pinch of salt. Stir with a wooden spoon. When the eggs and garlic are well amalgamated, start adding the oil, very slowly at first, drop by drop, until the *aïoli* begins to thicken. This takes longer than with a straightforward mayonnaise because the garlic has thinned the yolks to a certain extent. When about half the oil has been used, the

[1] *Cabanons* are the huts of the *gardians* of the Camargue.

aïoli should be a very thick mass, and the oil can now be added in a slow but steady stream. The sauce gets thicker and thicker, and this is as it should be; a good *aïoli* is practically solid. Add a very little lemon juice at the end, and serve the sauce either in the kitchen mortar in which you have made it or piled up in a small salad bowl. Should the *aïoli* separate through the oil having been added too fast, put a fresh yolk into another bowl and gradually add the curdled mixture to it. The *aïoli* then comes back to life.

Now as to the amount of garlic: you can, of course, use less but you are likely to find that the mass of eggs and oil is then too heavy and rich. A true *aïoli* is a remarkable mixture of the smooth mayonnaise combined with the powerful garlic flavour which tingles in your throat as you swallow it. One Provençal writer suggests that those who find the *aïoli* indigestible should take a *trou* or *coup du milieu* in the form of a little glass of *marc* in the middle of the meal.

LA BOURRIDE DE CHARLES BÉROT

Bourride is one of the great dishes of Provence. There are various different ways of presenting it but the essential characteristic is that *aïoli* or garlic flavoured mayonnaise is added to the stock in which the fish has cooked to make a beautiful smooth pale yellow sauce—and of this there must be plenty for it is the main point of the dish.

M. Bérot, once *chef des cuisines* on the *Île de France*—a liner celebrated for its good cooking—served us his own version of this dish at the Escale, a hospitable and charming restaurant at Carry-le-Rouet, a little seaside place west of Marseille.

The ingredients you need for four people are 4 fine thick fillets of a rather fleshy white fish. M. Bérot uses *baudroie* or angler fish, but at home I have made the dish with fillets of John Dory, of turbot, of brill (*barbue*).

In any case, whatever fish you choose, be sure to get the head and the carcase with your fillets. Apart from these you need a couple of leeks, a lemon, a tablespoon of wine vinegar, at least 4 cloves of garlic, 2 or 3 egg yolks, about one-third of a pint of olive oil, a couple of tablespoons of cream, and seasonings. To accompany the *bourride* you need plain boiled new potatoes and slices of French bread fried in oil.

First make your stock by putting the head and carcase of the fish into a saucepan with a sliced leek, a few parsley stalks, a teaspoon of salt, a slice of lemon, the wine vinegar and about $1\frac{1}{4}$ pints of water. Let all this simmer gently for 25 to 30 minutes. Then strain it.

While it is cooking make your *aïoli* with the egg yolks, 3 cloves of garlic and olive oil as explained on page 302.

Now put a tablespoon of olive oil and the white of the second leek, finely sliced, into the largest shallow metal or other fireproof pan you have; let it heat, add the spare clove of garlic, crushed; put in the lightly seasoned fillets; cover with the stock; let them gently poach for 15 to 25 minutes, according to how thick they are.

Have ready warming a big serving dish; take the fillets from the pan with a fish slice and lay them in the dish; cover them and put them in a low oven to keep warm.

Reduce the stock in your pan by letting it boil as fast as possible until there is only about a third of the original quantity left. Now stir in the cream and let it bubble a few seconds.

Have your *aïoli* ready in a big bowl or a jug over which you can fit a conical or other sauce sieve. Through this pour your hot sauce; quickly stir and amalgamate it with the *aïoli*. It should all turn out about the consistency of thick cream. Pour it over your fish fillets. On top strew a little chopped parsley and the dish is ready.

I know that all this sounds a tremendous performance, and indeed I wouldn't recommend *bourride* for days when you have the kind of guests who make you nervous; but as a matter of fact when you have cooked it once (try it in half quantities, just for two) it all seems quite easy, and it's a very satisfactory dish to be able to make.

Incidentally, I usually cook the potatoes and fry the bread while the fish is poaching; both can be kept warm in the oven, and then at the last minute you can give your undivided attention to the sauce.

LA BRANDADE DE MORUE
CREAM OF SALT COD

This is not really a dish to be made at home and, indeed, nowadays, the majority of housewives in the Languedoc and in Provence buy it ready made for Friday lunch at cooked food shops which specialise in it. There is one such shop in Nîmes, Raymond, 43 rue d'Avignon, from whence it is sent all over France. It is one of those dishes which you either like or detest. Personally, I find it delicious, although even then a little goes a long way.

Briefly, you must soak 2 lb. of salt cod in cold water for 12 hours at least. Drain and rinse it, put it into a pan of fresh cold water and bring it very gently to the boil, then remove it at once from the fire. Take out all the bones, flake the fish, add a crushed clove or two of garlic, and place over a low flame. In separate small saucepans have some olive oil and some milk. Keep all three saucepans over a flame so low that the contents never get more than tepid. Crushing the fish with a wooden spoon you add, gradually and alternately, a little milk and a little olive oil, until all is used up and the cod has attained the consistency of a thick cream. All this, however, is quicker said than done. It requires great patience and also considerable energy (the famous chef Durand, of Nîmes, who has a recipe in his book, published in 1830, specifies that two people are needed to make the *brandade*, one to pour, the other to stir and rotate the pan), and if you own a pestle and mortar, it is better to crush the fish first in this. It can be done in an electric mixer, which I believe is nowadays used by the people who make the *brandade* on a commercial scale. In south and south-western France, the *brandade* is usually to be found at the restaurants and in the cooked food shops on a Friday, but rarely on other days.

The *brandade* is served warm, surrounded by triangles of fried bread or pastry.

One of the nicest subsidiary dishes to be made with this creamed salt cod is *œufs Bénédictine*, poached eggs placed on top of the *brandade* and covered with *sauce hollandaise*.

Note: Salt cod should always be soaked and cooked in porcelain, glazed earthenware or enamelled vessels. Metal tends to discolour it. And if your *brandade* has oiled or separated, the remedy is to mix in a small quantity of smooth potato purée.

MORUE AUX TOMATES
SALT COD WITH TOMATOES

'Skin 5 or 6 large tomatoes; remove the pips as much as possible; chop the tomatoes small. Melt a chopped onion in warmed olive oil; add the tomatoes and stir until most of their moisture has evaporated, add a tablespoon of flour, moisten with ¾ pint of stock or water; add a bouquet of herbs, 2 cloves of garlic, salt and pepper, and continue cooking while the salt cod is prepared.

'Take your soaked cod,[1] scale it, cut into square pieces, roll them in flour and fry them in a deep pan of olive oil. When they are golden on both sides, remove and drain them on paper. Put them into the tomato sauce; simmer another 10 minutes before serving.'

[1] See the recipe for *brandade* above.

MORUE EN RAYTE

SALT COD IN RED WINE SAUCE

One of the oldest dishes of Provence, traditional for Christmas Eve.

'In a saucepan heat a few spoonfuls of olive oil; in this cook a finely chopped onion until it turns pale golden; add a good tablespoon of flour, stir it a few moments; add ½ litre[1] each of red wine and boiling water. Stir well and let it bubble; season with pepper, a little salt, add 2 cloves of garlic, a bay leaf, thyme and parsley tied in a bouquet, a tablespoon of concentrated tomato purée and cook until the sauce is fairly thick.

'Having prepared your salt cod as explained in the preceding recipe, put the pieces in the sauce with 2 tablespoons of capers and cook another 10 minutes before serving.'

This and the preceding recipe are from Reboul's *La Cuisinière Provençale*.

MORUE À LA PROVENÇALE

'1 lb. of salt cod, plenty of shallots, garlic, parsley, onions, 2 lemons, 2 tablespoons of olive oil, 1 oz. of butter, breadcrumbs, pepper.

'The salt cod, soaked, cooked and drained, is arranged in a fireproof baking dish between two thick layers of chopped parsley, garlic, onion and shallots, with slices of peeled lemon, pepper, oil and butter. Cover with dried breadcrumbs; strew with little nuts of butter. Cook in the oven for an hour. Serve in the same dish.'

SOLANDRÉ: *Six Cents Bonnes Recettes de Cuisine Bourgeoise*

This is an excellent way of dealing not only with salt cod but with any coarse white fish, and with smoked cod fillets.

LE POISSON AU BEURRE BLANC

FISH WITH WHITE BUTTER SAUCE

Curnonsky, renowned throughout France as a gastronome, man of letters, writer on all culinary subjects, founder of a monthly food and wine magazine and perhaps more than any other one man responsible for the great revival of interest in regional food after the 1914 war, was himself a native of Anjou (his real name was Maurice-Edmond Sailland). This is what he says in one of his books, *A l'Infortune du Pot*, 1946, about the *beurre blanc*:

[1] About ¾ pint.

'The high priestess of the *beurre blanc* was la Mère Clémence, Madame Lefeuvre Prault, who kept an auberge at Saint-Julien-de-Concelles, on the left bank of the Loire, five kilometres from Nantes. She vanished some years ago but the tradition of the *beurre blanc* has not been lost; and you can still taste it all over Anjou.

'It is a sauce of exquisite finesse and lightness, discreetly seasoned with Angevin shallots; it wonderfully accompanies the pike and the shad of the Loire, and even some salt-water fish such as bass and whiting. . . .

'Remember that the shallot must be, so to speak, volatilised in the vinegar, and that it should be no more than a remote presence. . . . Many gastronomes hold that there is a sort of sleight of hand in making this sauce, given only to Angevin *cordons bleus*—try and see if you can give them the lie.'

Well, first a suitable fish must be chosen as a vehicle for your sauce. Pike and shad don't come our way often in England, but even in its own country they serve instead certain sea-fish—bass or whiting, as Curnonsky suggests, or turbot or sole; I have had it with Loire salmon at Tours and have heard of it being served with *quenelles*, with trout and even with lobster.

Whatever fish is chosen, it is nearly always poached in a white wine *court-bouillon*. The reduction of shallots and vinegar for the sauce can be prepared while the fish is cooking, but the addition of the butter must be left until the fish is actually ready and keeping hot on a covered serving dish.

Quantities for four people are as follows: 3 shallots, 3 tablespoons of white wine vinegar, 3 tablespoons of dry white wine, 6 oz. of finest quality butter, unsalted for preference.

Chop the shallots until they are almost a purée. Put them in a small saucepan with the wine and vinegar and cook until the shallots are completely soft and the liquid all but dried up. When this mixture has cooled, start adding the butter, about 1 oz. at a time. Keep over a very low flame and whisk for a few seconds. As soon as the butter looks like getting soft and melting, remove the pan from the fire, because at no time during the cooking must the butter completely melt. It must finish up the colour and the consistency of thick cream. It only takes a minute or so. If it goes wrong the first time, don't be unduly discouraged. At the next try you know that you probably made the mistake of letting the sauce get too hot, and take your precautions accordingly.

Charles Gay, whose sumptuously produced book *Vieux Pots, Saulces et Rosts Mémorables*, contains many Angevin recipes, says that it is only after making it fifteen times that the great chefs allow that you can produce a really perfect *beurre blanc*. But Curnonsky was more encouraging, for he considered it as essentially a dish, not of chefs, but of that *cuisine de femme* which he always praised so highly. Charles Gay, incidentally, adds a little thick cream to his *sauce au beurre blanc*, which is delicious but considered by purists to be a grave heresy.

The wine to go with this dish is a Muscadet from the Côteaux de la Loire or from the Sèvre-et-Maine district, situated respectively on the left and right banks of the river below Nantes. These attractive dry wines, which go so admirably with fish and shellfish dishes, and with hors-d'œuvre of all kinds, are made from a Burgundian vine, the *Melon*, transplanted to the Nantes district. They acquire their special qualities from the pebbly soil of the region. A good Muscadet has quite a strong bouquet, and as the catalogues say, 'a delicate fragrance.'

TERRINE D'ANGUILLE À LA MARTÉGALE
EEL BAKED WITH LEEKS AND BLACK OLIVES

'This was the traditional dish served at Martigues for the *gros souper* on Christmas Eve. This excellent recipe is worth recording—and cooking.

'Cover the bottom of a gratin dish with finely sliced leeks, so that they make a thick bed. Strew with chopped parsley and garlic. Add a good handful of black olives (stoned) and moisten with a good glass of dry white wine. On this bed lay a large skinned eel. Cover with breadcrumbs and cook in the oven for about 1½ hours, the precise time depending on the size of the eel.'

ESCUDIER: *La Véritable Cuisine Provençale et Niçoise*

ÉCREVISSES À LA NAGE
FRESH-WATER CRAYFISH IN COURT-BOUILLON

Fresh-water crayfish rarely come our way in England; they do exist in our rivers but nobody bothers to catch them. In France, a number of restaurateurs who specialise in crayfish dishes keep a tank or *vivier* for these little creatures, whose flavour is so remarkably much finer than that of the large sea-crayfish and the lobster; they were evidently well-known to our ancestors, for many eighteenth- and nineteenth-century English cookery books give recipes for them. La Chapelle (1773) has one for pigeons or chickens with a *coulis* of crayfish, which must have been very similar to the dish still made by accomplished French chefs.

The basic way of cooking and serving crayfish is *à la nage*, in other words simply simmered in a *court-bouillon*. One way of making this is as follows: slice a carrot in a dozen very thin rounds; cut 4 small onions and 2 shallots also in fine slices; shred an ounce of the white part of a celery heart and put all these ingredients into a saucepan with ¾ pint of white wine half that quantity of water, 3 tablespoons of cognac, some parsley stalks, a scrap of dried thyme and bayleaf, ⅓ oz. of salt. Simmer this mixture until the carrot and the onion are quite tender.

The crayfish, which are always cooked live, must also have the intestinal gut removed, particularly at the spawning period, for it is liable to make the crayfish bitter. The end of this little black gut is at the opening under the central flange of the tail; it is pulled out with the aid of a little knife, gently, so as not to break the fish.

The crayfish, 2 or 3 per person, are put into the hot *court-bouillon* and boiled steadily for about 12 minutes. To serve them hot, remove them to a bowl or deep serving dish; reduce the *court-bouillon* to half its original quantity; add a dash of cayenne pepper and somewhat under 1 oz. of butter; pour this mixture, vegetables and all, over the crayfish and strew with a little cut parsley. To serve them cold, the procedure is the same, but leave out the final addition of butter. Pour the reduced *court-bouillon* over the crayfish and leave them to cool.

CARPE À LA JUIVE

SWEET-SOUR CARP IN THE JEWISH FASHION

Unless carp is exceedingly fresh it is scarcely worth cooking.

Here is a recipe from *La Cuisine Messine*, a collection of recipes from Lorraine with special emphasis on the old dishes of the Metz district, written by Auricoste de Lazarque in the nineteen-hundreds. This, he says, is the genuine formula for the *carpe à la juive* as cooked in Lorraine.

'In a deep pan, or if you are going to cook the fish whole, in a fish kettle, heat nearly ½ pint of olive oil. When it is hot, throw in a quantity of small onions. As soon as they have turned golden stir in a little flour and a little soft white sugar; stir and do not let the flour and sugar brown. Add as much water as you will need to allow the fish to swim in it, a spoonful of wine vinegar, a little more sugar, some Malaga raisins and ¼ lb. of skinned and sliced almonds. Bring to the boil, and add a pinch of salt. Put in your fish, either whole or cut into steaks.

'When the fish is tender, remove it to a fairly deep serving dish. Over it pour the cooking liquid and all its contents, arranging the almonds and the raisins round the fish.

'To be served cold in the sauce, which turns to a jelly.'

A 2 lb. fish needs only half the quantities given above and takes about 30 minutes to cook. But I think myself that the dish is an acquired taste.

POCHOUSE SEURROISE

BURGUNDIAN FISH STEW

Never having had the opportunity to cook or to eat the famous Burgundian stew of fresh-water fish called *pochouse*, I cannot judge of its merits. Some speak of it with reverence and affection, others with fear and horror. Here is a recipe contributed by Henri Racouchot, former proprietor of the Trois Faisans (this famous restaurant is now incorporated with the Pré aux Clercs) at Dijon, to a collection of Burgundian recipes called *Les Meilleures Recettes de ma Pauvre Mère*, by Pierre Huguenin, published in 1936.

'Brown in butter, without letting them fry, 150 grammes (about 5 oz.) of fat bacon cut into slivers and previously blanched; add 18 little onions already three-quarters cooked in salted water to which a little flour has been added. On top place your sliced fish (tench, eel, perch, pike and carp); 6 crushed cloves of garlic, salt, pepper and sufficient very dry white wine to cover the whole mixture. When it boils, add a Bordeaux glass of Burgundian *fine*, set light to it and then cook for 18 to 20 minutes, then add, little by little, 2½ oz. of *beurre manié*, shaking your pan so that the butter mixture amalgamates with the sauce and binds it; but take care, for the sauce must not become too thick. Finally, add another lump of butter, and serve with croûtons of bread fried in butter, and rubbed with garlic.

'Some people finish their *pochouse* with a binding of egg yolks and cream, but I do not see the necessity for this and it is contrary to the precepts of the original recipes.'

Alfred Contour in *Le Cuisinier Bourguignon* gives a very similar recipe but calls it *pauchouse* and omits the flaming with brandy; Charles Blandin in *Cuisine et Chasses de Bourgogne et d'Ailleurs* spells it *pochouze*, and says that the sauce, highly flavoured with garlic, should be sieved and then poured over the fish and the croûtons already in the serving dish.

A *meurette* of fresh-water fish is again very similar, but red wine instead of white is used, as in the *matelotes* of the Rhône and of the Seine.

At Tours I have eaten a *matelote d'anguilles*, which consisted of eels stewed in red wine, with *pruneaux de Tours*, the sauce thick and rich and very dark. It was a dish which had a kind of ancient grandeur and allure but I would not want to eat it often. The same might be said of the Provençal *catigau d'anguilles*, a saffron-coloured stew of eels served with very fiery *sauce rouille*, which is a speciality of a charming restaurant at the Pont de Gau in the Camargue.

SAUMON POÊLÉ AU VIN BLANC DE LA LOIRE
SALMON STEAKS WITH WHITE WINE

French cooks tend to be rather fanciful in their treatment of salmon. Crayfish or mushroom sauces and all sorts of rather elaborate garnishes may appear with it. These seem to me to be unnecessary, if not detrimental, to a fish already so rich, but this little recipe from the Loire is excellent and provides a quick and easy way of making the best of the late season's salmon.

For 4 salmon steaks weighing about 6 oz. each, melt 1 oz. of butter in a thick frying-pan. Put in the seasoned salmon slices, cook rapidly on each side, pour over a wine-glass of dry white wine (Muscadet or a dry Anjou), let it bubble, reduce the heat and cook gently for about 7 more minutes. There should be only a small amount of reduced sauce. Serve the salmon with a few small plain boiled potatoes and sliced cucumber.

SAUMON GRILLÉ DIABLE
GRILLED SALMON WITH DEVIL SAUCE

Have your salmon cut in steaks each weighing 5 to 6 oz. Season them with salt and pepper, paint them with olive oil and grill them, not too fast, for about 7 minutes, turning them once and moistening them during the cooking with a little more oil. Transfer them to a hot serving dish and on top of each steak put some of the following mixture: 2 oz. of butter worked with a coffee spoon of yellow Dijon mustard, the juice of half a lemon, a scrap of Cayenne pepper and a little finely-chopped parsley. Keep this butter very cold until the salmon is ready.

DARNE DE SAUMON BEURRE DE MONTPELLIER
MIDDLE CUT OF SALMON WITH GREEN BUTTER

For this dish, see the recipe for Montpellier butter on page 117. A *darne* of salmon is a fine thick piece from the middle of the fish, in this case poached and served cold. An alternative to the Montpellier butter, which is something of a labour of love to make, is a simple *sauce ravigote*, which, while containing similar ingredients, is very quickly made. It lacks the subtlety and elegance of the beautiful green butter, but is still a very attractive sauce in its own right. The old Provençal sauce for salmon on page 123 is another excellent alternative.

Instead of poaching the salmon in water or a *court-bouillon* it is more satisfactory to wrap it in oiled or buttered foil and bake it in a slow oven as explained in the following recipe for salmon trout. In this way texture, flavour and the natural creaminess of salmon are preserved intact.

A thick piece, weighing 2 to 2½ lb., will take 1 hour at Gas No. 1, 290 deg. F.

TRUITE SAUMONÉE AU FOUR

BAKED SALMON TROUT

Few of us now possess fish kettles in which a large whole fish can be poached, but the system of wrapping the fish in greaseproof paper or foil and cooking it in the oven produces, if anything, better results.

Cut a piece of aluminium foil about 6 inches longer than your fish. Butter it copiously, or if the fish is to be served cold, paint it with oil. Lay the fish in the middle, gather up the edges and twist them together, so that no juices can escape. Also twist the two ends very securely taking particular care that the paper touching the tail and the head is well buttered or oiled, as these are the parts which stick easily.

Have your oven already heated for 10 minutes at a very low temperature, Gas No. 1, 290 deg. F. Place your wrapped fish on a baking sheet and leave it severely alone for the whole cooking time—1 hour for a 2 lb. fish. All you have to do when it is cooked is to lay it on the warmed serving dish, unwrap the paper and slide the fish and all its juices off the paper on to the dish. A hot salmon trout does not really need any sauce other than its own juices and a little bowl of fresh melted butter. If it is to be served cold, have with it a *sauce verte* or Montpellier butter or, best of all, I think, Escoffier's horseradish and walnut-flavoured sauce, for which the recipe is on page 127. It also makes serving easier if the skin is removed while the fish is still warm; this is not difficult so long as the fish has not been overcooked but, of course, it must be done gently and patiently.

There is one more point. A cold salmon trout eaten a couple of hours after it is cooked is infinitely superior to one cooked and kept until the following day.

Sea-bass (*loup de mer*) is excellent cooked in the same way.

LA TRUITE
TROUT

'Never with butter, never with almonds; that is not cooking, it is packaging. (It is, of course, understood that my recipes are not for all comers.) With the exception of *truite au bleu* nobody knows how to cook a trout. It is the most unfortunate fish on earth. If an atomic bomb destroyed the world tomorrow, the human race would vanish without ever having known the taste of a trout. Of course, I am no more talking of tank-bred trout than I would give a recipe for cooking a dog or a cat.

'So, a fine fat, or several fine fat, trout from the river, fresh (that goes without saying), gutted, scaled, etc.

'A frying-pan previously rinsed out with flaming wine vinegar. Make this empty pan very hot. Into this very hot pan, a mixture of water and virgin olive oil (a claret glass of olive oil to 3 of water). Let it boil fast. Add a bouquet of thyme and nothing else whatever except 2 crushed juniper berries and some pepper.

'Reduce the mixture, and when there is nothing but a centimetre of fast boiling liquid left in the pan, put your fine fat, or several fine fat, trout gently into the liquid. Do not turn the fish over. Cover the pan and boil 1 minute, then 3 minutes very gently, and serve.'

JEAN GIONO: in the number of *La France à Table* devoted to Haute Provence

Jean Giono is surely right about trout with almonds—it is a dish which seems to me rather pointless; but I would not condemn the cooking of trout with butter in quite so sweeping a way. As far as tank or reservoir trout are concerned, and one rarely gets any other kind either in French or English restaurants or fishmongers' shops, cooking them *à la meunière* (see the recipe for *rougets à la meunière* on page 291) or grilling them are about the two best systems. But I must admit I would never go out of my way either to buy these fish or to order them in a restaurant.

LES TRUITES À LA MANIÈRE ALSACIENNE
TROUT IN COURT-BOUILLON

'A trout, when it is a fairly large one, I prefer cooked *au bleu*, with the sole accompaniment of a few little curls of butter; but when chance—a happy chance—has filled your fishing basket with only a score or so of small trout, you can make an exquisite dish of them by cooking them in a *court-bouillon* in which white wine, butter, onion, salt, pepper, parsley, a clove and a little good stock have prepared, for your little fishes, a marvellously aromatic bath.

'Then, when they are cooked, which does not take very long, you simply sprinkle them with butter in which you have cooked a few breadcrumbs until they are golden.

'Here is an exquisite dish, even a naïf dish, but one in every way worthy of the learned gastronome.'

GASTON THIERRY: *La Table*, 1932

Les Coquillages et les Crustacés
Shell-fish and crustacea

COQUILLES ST. JACQUES À LA BRETONNE
SCALLOPS WITH BUTTER AND BREADCRUMBS

Allow 2, 3 or 4 scallops per person, according to size. Remove the little strip of skin and thick muscle on the outside of the white part. Rinse the white part and the red coral and drain well. Cut into small cubes. Allow 1 oz. of butter and 1 heaped tablespoon of very fine, pale golden breadcrumbs per person. Butter the deep scallop shells with half the butter, then add half the breadcrumbs. Lay the scallops on top. Season them lightly with salt and pepper. Cover with the rest of the breadcrumbs, and the remaining butter cut in very small dice. Cook uncovered in a very low oven for 20 minutes. By the time the scallops are done the breadcrumbs have soaked up all the butter; they should be golden and just beginning to turn crisp, but still moist. Obviously, the breadcrumbs soak up a lot of butter, and if too little has been used, the dish will be dry. For those who like it, a scrap of finely-chopped garlic or shallot and a little parsley can be mixed in with the breadcrumbs.

COQUILLES ST. JACQUES AU VIN BLANC
SCALLOPS WITH WHITE WINE

For 4 large scallops the other ingredients are 2 oz. of streaky salt pork or unsmoked bacon, a shallot or two, butter, flour, a small glass of dry white wine, parsley.

Melt 1 oz. of butter in a frying-pan, put in the finely-chopped shallots and the pork or bacon cut into tiny cubes. Cut the cleaned scallops into larger cubes, season them with pepper but no salt, sprinkle them with flour and put them in the pan when the shallots have turned pale yellow and the pork is beginning to frizzle. Let them cook very gently for 5 to 7 minutes. Take them out of the pan and put them in the serving dish. Pour the white wine into the pan and let it bubble fiercely, stirring so that it amalgamates with the juices and all the little bits left behind in the pan. When it has thickened to a syrupy consistency, add a very little finely-chopped parsley and pour the sauce over the scallops.

The mixture of pork or bacon with the fish sounds odd, but it is an old-fashioned and delicious one, although the amount must not be overdone.

COQUILLES ST. JACQUES À LA PROVENÇALE
FRIED SCALLOPS WITH GARLIC AND PARSLEY

The scallops which come from the Mediterranean are very much smaller than those from the Atlantic, but this method of cooking them can be applied just as well to the large variety. Slice the cleaned white part of the scallops into two rounds, season them with salt, pepper and lemon juice; immediately before cooking them, sprinkle them very lightly with flour, fry them pale golden on each side in a mixture of butter and olive oil. Put in the red parts, add a generous sprinkling of finely-chopped garlic and parsley and shake the pan so that the mixture spreads evenly amongst the scallops. Five minutes' cooking altogether will be enough.

HUÎTRES MORNAY
OYSTERS MORNAY

This is one of the best of cooked oyster dishes, but it is tricky to get the sauce to exactly the right consistency and attention to detail is important.

First prepare a very thick *sauce mornay*. This is started off in the same way as béchamel. Melt 1 oz. of butter, stir in 2 tablespoons of flour, when it has amalgamated with the butter, stir in gradually ¼ pint of hot milk. Cook slowly and stir constantly until the sauce is thick. Season with a very little salt, some freshly-ground white pepper, a little cayenne. Stir in 1 tablespoon of thick cream and 2 heaped tablespoons of grated Parmesan cheese (Gruyère is the usual cheese for *mornay sauce*, but for oysters I prefer Parmesan). Reduce your sauce by slow cooking until it is about twice as thick as the usual béchamel, and really sticks to the spoon.

Now take 2 dozen small oysters, or 18 large ones, from their shells; with their juice put them in the smallest pan you have and simmer them gently for about half a minute. This operation is necessary to extract moisture which would otherwise come out of them when they are cooked with the sauce, making the sauce too runny. Now strain the juice through a muslin into the sauce; there won't be very much, but enough to give a flavour. If necessary, simmer the sauce again for a minute or two.

The dish can be completed in two ways. One way is to put each oyster into its deep half-shell and cover with the sauce. But unless large oysters are being used, I find it better to put them into very small egg ramekins or fireproof china shells or even scallop shells, either six or a dozen in each. Cover them completely with the hot sauce. Pour a little melted butter on top. Put the little dishes or the shells on a baking tray and put them at the very top of a very hot, and preheated, oven for about 5 minutes, until the tops are golden and just bubbling.

All this sounds a formidable operation, but it is described in such detail in order that those who may be attempting a hot oyster dish for the first time may be spared disillusion.

Enough for two or three.

LES HUÎTRES OU LES PALOURDES FARCIES
STUFFED OYSTERS OR CLAMS

In Brittany and Touraine this dish is usually made with *palourdes*, the delicate little clams of the Atlantic coast. In England, Cornish oysters make an admirable alternative.

For 18 small oysters prepare the sauce as follows: chop 1 small shallot very finely with a teaspoon of parsley. Cook this in a little butter in a small frying-pan until the shallot is just beginning to turn yellow. Into the pan pour $\frac{1}{4}$ pint of double cream. Let it boil for a minute, add a heaped dessertspoon of finely-grated Gruyère cheese, then a teaspoon of fine golden breadcrumbs. In a few seconds the cream will be quite thick. Season with freshly-milled pepper and a scrap of salt.

Rinse the oysters and their half shells rapidly in cold water; it is necessary to do this with the small Cornish oysters because their shells seem to chip so easily when they are opened, and little bits of shell and grit in the finished dish must be avoided. Put them back on the half shell and arrange them in a flat fireproof dish. Cover each completely with the sauce. Sprinkle very lightly with more breadcrumbs and put under a hot grill for 2 minutes. This is essentially a stove-to-table dish. It cannot be prepared in advance, it cannot be kept waiting, and if it is cooked too long the oysters underneath their sauce will be uneatably tough.

Enough for two or three.

NETTOYAGE ET CUISSON DES MOULES
THE CLEANING AND COOKING OF MUSSELS

Put the mussels into a large bowl of cold water as soon as they arrive in the kitchen. If they are not to be used until next day, cover the bowl with a cloth and sprinkle salt on top. Keep them in a cool place. When it comes to cleaning them, discard all broken ones, any that are gaping open and any in which the two shells can be slid against each other:

these last will be full of mud or sand, and will make all the others gritty. With a knife remove the beard, or seaweed-like bits protruding from the shell, scrape off any barnacles or limpets adhering to the mussels, scrub the shells and wash them in several waters until, at the final washing, the water comes out quite free from grit. Keep them in cold water during the whole process. Allow approximately 1½ pints of mussels per person.

To cook, put them in a large wide pan with a large glass of dry cider or white wine to every quart, cook fairly fast until the mussels open and remove them as soon as they do so to a warmed tureen or bowl. When all are ready, strain the remaining stock through a muslin, return to the pan, heat it up again, pour over the mussels and add chopped parsley. Serve as quickly as possible, providing plenty of bread, deep plates, forks to extract the mussels from their shells, soup spoons for the juice and a bowl for the empty shells. This is the most primitive version of *moules marinière* and is only really successful with the small and tender mussels which are none too easy to find in towns.

MOULES À LA NORMANDE
MUSSELS WITH CREAM SAUCE

A grander version of *moules marinière*.

Melt 1 oz. of butter in a wide pan, add a shallot, parsley and a few celery leaves all coarsely chopped, then a large glass of dry cider or dry white wine. Add 3 quarts of cleaned mussels, cover the pan for the first few minutes, then remove the lid and take out the mussels as they open and transfer them to a warmed dish or tureen. Strain the remaining stock through muslin, return it to the pan and let it reduce by about half. Put about ⅓ pint of double cream to boil in a small pan, so that it reduces and thickens, and meantime remove the empty half shells from the cooked mussels.

Add the boiling cream to the mussel stock, and off the fire stir in a good lump of butter. Pour bubbling hot over the mussels, add chopped parsley and serve quickly. For four people. One of the best wines to drink with mussels is a fresh clean Muscadet from the Loire.

MOULES EN BROCHETTES
MUSSELS ON SKEWERS

When very large mussels are available, try them cooked by the excellent method used at la Mère Nénette's restaurant in Montpellier where this dish is one of the specialities; the *brochettes* are quite a bit of trouble to prepare, so I give quantities for two people only. You will need a dozen large mussels per person, so buy at least 30, or about 3 pints, to allow for any which may be useless.

Clean and cook them as explained above. Remove from the shells, thread them on skewers, alternating each mussel with a little square of bacon. Sprinkle with flour, then roll the *brochettes* in beaten egg, then in very fine breadcrumbs. All these preparations can be done in advance.

When the time comes to cook them, heat a wide pan of oil to smoking point, plunge in the brochettes; about a minute will cook them.

Serve as quickly as possible. La Mère Nénette serves a few little *gaufrette* potatoes and a *béarnaise* sauce with the *brochettes*. The potatoes could, I think, be dispensed with, and alternatives to the *béarnaise* sauce are mayonnaise or even vinaigrette.

MOULES À L'ARMORICAINE
MUSSELS WITH ONION AND TOMATO

For a quart of small mussels, the other ingredients are a medium-sized onion, 2 large tomatoes, butter.

In a heavy frying-pan melt the butter; put in the roughly chopped onion and let it turn golden. Add the skinned and chopped tomatoes. Then put in the cleaned and scrubbed mussels, without any other liquid. Turn up the flame and cook until the mussels are open, shaking the pan from time to time so that the sauce gets evenly distributed among the mussels. Serve boiling hot immediately the mussels are open. Add freshly-milled pepper as you bring them to table.

Enough for two.

MOULES À LA MARSEILLAISE
MUSSELS WITH SHALLOTS AND OLIVE OIL

Put a couple of finely-chopped shallots in a saucepan with half a claret glass of water and 3 or 4 tablespoons of very good olive oil. Bring it very quickly to an absolutely galloping boil (this is the principle also applied to the cooking of a *bouillabaisse*—it is essential that the oil and water be rapidly amalgamated). Put in a quart of cleaned mussels and cook fast until they open. Sprinkle with roughly-chopped parsley and serve in very hot soup plates with all their juice. Enough for two.

MOULES À LA PROVENÇALE

'Wash the mussels well several times, changing the water so as to cleanse them thoroughly; put them dry in a saucepan over a hot fire, till the shells open. Take off one valve of the shell only. Put into a saucepan half a glass of oil, parsley, chives, mushrooms, truffles, half a clove of garlic, all chopped very fine. Put it on the fire. Moisten it with a glass of white wine, a spoonful of broth and half the quantity of liquor from the mussels. Boil this sauce, and when it is nearly reduced to half, add the mussels, with a spoonful of gravy; let the whole boil a few minutes; then add a spoonful of lemon juice, pepper and grated nutmeg, then serve.'

Dictionnaire Général de la Cuisine Française Ancienne et Moderne,
1866 edition

MOULES AU RIZ À LA BASQUAISE
MUSSELS WITH SPICED RICE

1½ teacups of long-grained Patna rice, 2½ teacups of light chicken, veal or fish stock and ¼ teacup of olive oil, half a raw red or green sweet pepper, 3 to 4 oz. of *chorizo* sausage (or other coarsely-cut pork sausage of the type to be bought in delicatessens), 2 pints of mussels, a few prawns, paprika pepper.

Boil the rice for 7 minutes in plenty of water, without salt. Drain it, and hold the colander under the running cold tap until all starch is washed away.

Put it in an earthenware or other oven dish with the stock, the olive oil, the sausage cut into little cubes, the pepper, freed of all seeds and core, sliced into thin rounds, and a teaspoon of paprika pepper, which is the nearest we can get to the *piment basquais*—it is not so very different. Bring to simmering point on top of the stove. Cover with a folded cloth, a lid, and put in a moderate oven, Gas No. 4, 350 deg. F. In 20 to 25 minutes the rice will have absorbed all the liquid and be beautifully cooked and well spiced. Turn on to a hot shallow dish, add the mussels which have been opened over a hot flame with just a little water, and left in their shells, and the prawns gently fried in a little oil. Garnish with quarters of lemon. There should be enough for four.

In small quantities this dish is also excellent cold, as an hors d'œuvre, and in larger quantities makes a nice party dish. The quantity of liquid is always twice that of the volume of rice—i.e. 4 cups of stock, including the olive oil, to 2 cups of rice.

CREVETTES SAUTÉES À LA CRÈME
PRAWNS WITH CREAM AND BRANDY SAUCE

A very simple little dish which, requiring the minimum of preparation, does nicely for a first course at dinner or lunch when time rather than money is lacking.

About 5 to 6 oz. of cooked and shelled prawns for two people, 1½ oz. of butter, rather under ¼ pint of thick cream and a small glass of brandy, plus seasonings of pepper, lemon juice, nutmeg and parsley. A teacup of Patna rice.

Heat the butter in a frying-pan and sauté the well-seasoned prawns gently for a couple of minutes. Warm the brandy in a soup ladle, pour it flaming over the prawns and shake the pan so that the flames spread. When they have gone out, turn the heat low and leave a minute or two; then turn up the heat and add the cream. Let it bubble until it starts to thicken, again shaking the pan and spooning the cream up and round. Stir in a little finely chopped parsley and serve the prawns on top of the plain boiled rice, which has been keeping warm in the oven.

HOMARD À L'AMÉRICAINE (1)

This is the version Escoffier gives in *Ma Cuisine*:

'The essential condition is to have the lobster alive. Split it down the centre; remove the bag near the head, for this is generally gritty. On a plate set aside the greenish-creamy parts which are found next to the bag: thoroughly mix with them, mashing with a fork, a tablespoon of butter. Sever the claws from the body; crack them to facilitate the removal of the flesh after cooking. Slice each half lobster into 3 or 4 pieces; season them with salt and pepper.

'For a lobster weighing approximately a kilo (2 lb. 2 oz.), thoroughly heat 4 tablespoons of olive oil and 2 of butter in a sauté pan; throw in the pieces of lobster and *sauté* them until they have turned bright red. Moisten with 4 to 5 tablespoons of cognac and 1½ decilitres (approximately 5 oz.) of dry white wine; add 2 chopped shallots, 6 fine tomatoes, peeled, seeded and finely chopped, a little scrap of garlic, a pinch of cut parsley, a dash of Cayenne pepper, 4 or 5 tablespoons of melted meat glaze and an equal quantity of half-glaze. Cover the pan and give the lobster 18 to 20 minutes' cooking over a good heat.

'Arrange the pieces of lobster in a deep dish; using a small egg whisk, incorporate into the cooking liquor the reserved creamy parts of the lobster; cook a few seconds and finish the sauce, off the fire, with 100

L

grammes (3⅓ oz.) of butter divided into little morsels, and the juice of half a lemon; pour over the pieces of lobster and sprinkle with a pinch of chopped parsley.

'*Nota:* The lobster should be put shell side down on the dish so that the flesh is covered with the sauce.

'Serve at the same time some pilaff rice.'

HOMARD À L'AMÉRICAINE (2)

Another theory, another version. Pierre Huguenin, author of *Les Meilleures Recettes de ma Pauvre Mère* (1936) gives the following recipe, noting that it was given to his mother *by its inventor*, the chef Pascal at the café Brébant in 1877.

'For twelve people. In a sauté pan put 1 lb. of very good butter to melt. When the butter is hot, put into it a medium-sized bowl of *mirepoix* (grated shallots and carrots) and ½ litre (nearly a pint) of white Meursault or Chablis, a bouquet of parsley, onion, a *head* of garlic; thyme and bay leaf; 6 tablespoons of tomato and 6 of olive oil, 3 of cream, 3 of concentrated meat juice, abundant pepper, a scrap of saffron and curry powder; leave all to boil for three-quarters of an hour.

'Cut your lobsters, either in pieces or in halves according to their size, put them to cook in the sauce the necessary time (half an hour) and then serve them in a *timbale*, adding a few little pieces of fresh butter worked with a little chopped parsley. Pour in ¼ litre (9 oz.) of good cognac, set light to it and serve when the flames have gone out.'

Well, let the cooks and the historians go on arguing about the origin and the proper composition of the *homard à l'américaine*. These matters are interesting but not, to most of us, very vital. Let Édouard de Pomiane have the last word for now. Dr. de Pomiane is a learned, high-spirited, infinitely stimulating mixture of *grand seigneur* and *enfant terrible* of the gastronomic world. Many must be the grave pontiffs of that world whom he has successfully deflated, for his irreverence is backed by a profound knowledge and understanding of every aspect of his subject. The *langouste à l'américaine*, then, says Dr. de Pomiane, is a 'gastronomic cacophony' . . . the tomato sauce, the cayenne pepper, the shallots—they confer upon the mixture a dominant note which is not that of the *langouste*. . . . And the book in which he drops this little firecracker has a title with which none but he could get away. It is called *Vingt Plats qui Donnent la Goutte*. Twenty dishes which give you the gout. . . . You are to prevent the onset of this painful complaint, I should add, not by the avoidance of these twenty delectable dishes, but by means of a glass of a patent medicine taken the evening after eating any of these dishes and again next morning. It bears the name of *Pipérazine Midy*.

HOMARD À LA CHARENTAISE
LOBSTER WITH VERMOUTH AND CREAM SAUCE

This is similar to the recipe for *langouste à la crème* on page 326 and, although lobster instead of crawfish is used, the two are interchangeable as far as these dishes are concerned.

For four people, get 2 freshly-boiled lobsters, not too large. Other ingredients are 1 oz. of butter, a shallot, 2 teaspoons of flour, ½ pint of cream, a teaspoon of Louit's Pimento mustard or, failing that, of Grey Poupon yellow Dijon mustard, a tablespoon of grated Parmesan or Gruyère, 4 tablespoons of Pineau des Charentes or of dry white vermouth, salt, freshly-milled pepper, nutmeg and breadcrumbs.

Heat the butter in a thick saucepan; in this melt the finely-chopped shallot, but do not let it fry. Pour in the Pineau (this is a white wine and brandy apéritif drink made in the Charente district; it can be obtained in England but any good dry white vermouth will do as well) and let it bubble fast for a minute or two. Lower the heat and stir in the flour. When it has thickened, start adding the cream rather slowly, stirring all the time. Season with a little salt, pepper and nutmeg. Put the saucepan on a mat and let the sauce barely simmer for 15 to 20 minutes, stirring it at frequent intervals. Stir in the mustard and the grated cheese.

Remove all the flesh from the claws and tails of the split lobsters. Slice it into neat little rounds. Pour a little of the sauce into each shell. Arrange the slices of lobster meat tidily on top. Cover with the sauce. Strew breadcrumbs over the top and add a few very small knobs of butter. Put the lobsters thus prepared in fireproof gratin dishes. Heat very slowly in the oven, covered if possible, for 15 minutes. Then put under the hot grill until the surface is golden and bubbling.

HOMARD OU LANGOUSTE À LA MAYONNAISE
LOBSTER OR CRAWFISH WITH MAYONNAISE

When all is said and done, plain freshly-boiled lobster or crawfish served either hot or cold is infinitely superior to all the fancy and showy dishes such as Newburg, *à l'américaine* and the rest. In towns, lobsters are seldom sold alive, nor would one wish to have to carry them home, struggling and clacking their claws in the most alarming way. Having done this job in seaside villages in Cornwall and in the west of Scotland, in Greece and in Provence, having manœuvred them into cauldrons of cold water, brought them gradually to the boil in the way recommended by the R.S.P.C.A. and eaten them in the freshest possible condition, I think I would still rather buy them ready cooked from a reliable fishmonger, who will choose good ones, split them, crack the claws and send them more or less ready to serve. Medium-sized or small ones are the best, very large ones often being old and tough. If you can get hen lobsters or crawfish, so much the better. The red coral part inside can be pounded up and mixed into your mayonnaise, and gives it a most delicious flavour.

MAYONNAISE DE HOMARD OU DE LANGOUSTE
LOBSTER OR CRAWFISH MAYONNAISE

This is really a way of making your lobster go rather further than it normally would; it can be an excellent dish but rather overwhelming and is best, perhaps, served in small quantities as a first course rather than as a main dish.

It is made in the same way as any *mayonnaise de poisson* (page 288), with the lobster flesh cut into neat escalopes, the creamy parts rubbed through a sieve into the mayonnaise, the whole piled up in a pyramid in a shallow dish and the coral, if any, sprinkled over the top as a garnish. Crisp little lettuce hearts should be arranged round the base of the pyramid. The tails of *langoustines* or Dublin Bay prawns, freshly boiled (personally I do not think frozen ones worth buying) can be served in the same way.

HOMARD COURCHAMPS

While looking up references to the *homard à l'américaine*, it occurred to me that it would be interesting to know how the lobster and the *langouste* were served by French cooks before the *américaine* dish became so fashionable. Among the rather scarce earlier recipes was a spit-roasted one with truffles and champagne in the sauce, another with the juice of a Seville orange squeezed over it; several cold lobster dishes with varying forms of *ravigote* or *rémoulade* sauce, and one which appears, with slight variations, in three well-known cookery books: first in the *Dictionnaire Général de la Cuisine Française*, 1866, originally published in 1834 under the title *Néo-Physiologie du Goût*; in Dumas the Elder's *Grand Dictionnaire de Cuisine*, 1873; and in the *366 Menus de Baron Brisse*, 1875 edition (first published 1867) which also, incidentally, contains a recipe for *homards à la bordelaise* which is suspiciously like our friend the *américaine* again. The Baron Brisse calls the dish *homard au court-bouillon*. Neither of the other authors provides it with a name, and I have called it after the Comte de Courchamps, author of the *Néo-Physiologie du Goût*. Here is the recipe.

The lobster is boiled in the usual way but with the addition of a 'full goblet' of Madeira wine, a large lump of butter, a bunch of parsley, a red pepper and the white part of 2 or 3 leeks to the salted water, and the lobster is left to cool in its broth.

The sauce is made as follows: 'all the creamy parts, and the red coral if it is a hen lobster, are mixed with fruity olive oil, a full spoonful of good mustard, 10 to 12 drops of Chinese soy sauce, a good pinch of chopped *fines herbes*, 2 crushed shallots, a fair quantity of mignonette pepper and finally a half-glass of *anisette de Bordeaux*, or simply of aniseed ratafia. When all these ingredients are well amalgamated, you add the juice of 2 or 3 lemons according to the size of the lobster and you serve the sauce "à proximité de ce plat d'entremets." '

The recipe rather implies that the flesh of the lobster is served on a dish without the shell, for the instructions are to 'detach all the white flesh with the end of a sharpened quill.'

It sounds, to say the least, outlandish, but I never believe in condemning recipes simply because they sound unorthodox or because they happen to have escaped the attention of the great professional masters of the past. (The three authors mentioned above were all amateurs.)

A certain degree of curiosity is surely necessary to a cook. And curiosity nagged at me until I finally went out and bought a bottle of Chinese soy sauce, some Marie Brizard *anisette* liqueur and a nice, freshly-boiled hen lobster. It would have to do without its bath of Madeira, butter and herbs, for as none of the cooking liquid is used for the sauce this really does seem rather wasteful, although of course it should make the basis of a pretty high-class soup.

To make the sauce I used, apart from the exact quantities of shallot, soy and the cream and coral from the lobster as specified, a teaspoon of chopped tarragon and parsley, 1 of yellow Dijon mustard, not much more than 2 teaspoons of *anisette*, 4 tablespoons of fruity olive oil and the juice of one small lemon (lemons are said to be much larger nowadays than they were when these recipes were written).

Whoever invented that sauce knew what he was doing. It is remarkably well constructed, it has bones, guts and balance; its flavour is certainly original, but it is stimulating without being discordant, and one way and another this is the sauce I have adopted for cold lobster in preference to any other.

LANGOUSTE COMME CHEZ NÉNETTE

This is the variation of *langouste à la sètoise*, in its turn a variation of *homard à l'américaine*, about which I have written in the introductory notes concerning the specialities of the Languedoc on pages 53–4 of this book

'Cut a live crawfish into not too large pieces; put them at once into a wide and shallow pan containing a little smoking olive oil, add salt and pepper and cook until the shell turns red. Add some finely chopped shallots and a clove or two of garlic, crushed and first cooked separately in a little oil.

'Pour in a small glass of good cognac and set light to it; when the flames have gone out, add a half bottle of still champagne or chablis, and a spoonful of tomato purée. Cover the pan and cook over a steady fire for about 20 minutes. Remove the pieces of crawfish, which are now cooked, and keep them hot.

"Press the sauce through a very fine sieve, let it boil up again, season with a scrap of cayenne and, at the last minute, add 3 good spoonfuls of *aïoli*.

'Pour the sauce over the crawfish and sprinkle a little finely-chopped parsley over the dish.'

CIVET DE LANGOUSTE

'The *langouste* (crawfish), divided in pieces, is treated as described for *langouste à l'américaine*, the quantity of tomato being increased and a strong flavouring of garlic added.'

This note is given by Prosper Montagné in the *Larousse Gastronomique*, and he also observes that the dish belongs to the *Cuisine Catalane et du Languedoc*.

LANGOUSTE À LA CRÈME AU GRATIN

CRAWFISH OR ROCK LOBSTER WITH CREAM AND WHITE WINE SAUCE

Quantities for two people: 1 medium-sized hen crawfish, about 3 oz. of double cream, 1 teaspoon flour, 4 tablespoons dry white wine, 1 teaspoon brandy, 1 heaped teaspoon of French mustard, butter, dried or fresh tarragon, breadcrumbs, seasonings.

Have the cooked crawfish split in half and the claws cracked by the fishmonger. Scoop out all the coral and the creamy meat and set aside. Take the flesh from the tail, cut into neat scallops, return to the half shells, and put these in an oval gratin dish.

Prepare the sauce by melting about ½ oz. of butter in a thick saucepan. Stir in the flour; when it is smooth add the white wine; let this bubble quite fast for half a minute; stir in the mustard, then the cream (reserving one tablespoon), and when it is thick, the brandy (because it is not in this case flamed, a teaspoon is enough; more would overpower the other flavours). Season with a very little salt, freshly-ground pepper, a scrap of Cayenne, and half a teaspoon of chopped fresh or dried tarragon. Leave over a low flame while you pound the coral with the reserved cream. Stir this into the sauce, giving it a turn or two over the fire. Spoon it over the crawfish so that all the meat is quite covered. Sprinkle with bread-crumbs; pour over a little melted butter. Put in a low oven for 10 minutes, covered, so that it heats through gently, then finish under the hot grill until the surface starts to blister and bubble.

LANGOUSTINES EN BROCHETTES
GRILLED DUBLIN BAY PRAWNS

For each person have half a dozen tails of freshly-boiled Dublin Bay prawns. Take them from the shells without breaking them, season them with pepper and lemon juice, paint them with just melted butter, thread them on to small skewers, putting a whole mushroom head, also seasoned and buttered, between each. Grill them gently, turning the skewers round once or twice.

Serve either on a bed of rice cooked as for the mussel dish on page 320, or by themselves with a *sauce béarnaise, hollandaise* or *bretonne.* You can, of course, use frozen Dublin Bay prawns, or scampi as they are now called, but personally I would not, for immensely popular though they are, I cannot help but think that Dublin Bay prawns are one of the least successful of all frozen fish products, such flavour as they have being faintly unpleasant and in no way comparable to that of the fresh fish. Why this should be so I do not know, and perhaps those who have never tasted them as they are when freshly caught and boiled might not be aware of the difference.

LES CALMARS, SEICHES, ENCORNETS
INKFISH, SQUID, CUTTLEFISH

Both on the Mediterranean and Atlantic coasts of France (where they go by the name of *chipirones*), squid are a popular dish. They can be stewed, stuffed, fried, grilled, added to fish soups and to rice dishes. They have a rich, slightly sweet flavour, and although they are not to everyone's taste, there are many people who regard them as the poor man's lobster.

At one time the only places one could buy squid in England were two fishmongers' shops in Soho. Recently, fishmongers in other areas where there are foreign customers have started to supply them. I would not say squid is a fish one would want to eat every day, but if you know how to clean and cook them they make an occasional excellent and cheap dish.

To clean them, put them in a bowl of water and pull out the tentacles and head to which are attached the intestines; these you detach and throw away, as also the transparent spine bone. Rub off the purplish outside skin, which comes away very easily. From each side of the head remove the ink bags, and also the little horny bit in the centre of the tentacles. Turn the pocket-like part of the fish inside out and rinse it free of grit under running cold water. By the time this cleaning operation, which is very quickly done, is finished, the inkfish is a beautiful milky-white colour and does not look at all frightening or unappetising.

CALMARS À L'ÉTUVÉE

STEWED INKFISH

Having cleaned 4 medium-sized inkfish as above, cut the body part into $\frac{1}{4}$ inch rounds and slice the tentacles. Heat 4 tablespoons of olive oil in an earthenware or other stew-pan, and in this melt a couple of large sliced onions and a clove or two of garlic. Put in the inkfish and, after a minute or two, add a glass (4 oz.) of red, white or rosé wine, let it bubble a minute, then turn the flame low. Season with salt and pepper; put in a bouquet of herbs which should include, if possible, a sprig of fresh or dried fennel. Cover the pan, and cook very slowly indeed for an hour to an hour and a half, either on top of the stove or in the oven.

Just before serving, cook 4 or 5 skinned and chopped tomatoes in a little olive oil in a separate pan; when they have turned almost to a purée, season them rather highly and add them to the inkfish mixture. After another minute or two of cooking, the dish is ready. It is best served with plainly cooked rice. Enough for three or four.

One or two small inkfish cooked in this way can be added to the mussel and rice dish described on page 320, and give it a very rich flavour.

Rounds of stewed inkfish are also excellent dipped in frying batter (see page 245) and fried in a deep pan of oil.

POULPE

OCTOPUS

'In France, *Octopus vulgaris* is highly prized for bait, and is also considered very good as food; and in *Life in Normandy*, Vol. I, is the following recipe for cooking it:

'A dish of cuttlefish is divided in the centre by a slice of toast; on one side of the toast is a mass of cuttlefish stewed with a white sauce; and on the other a pile of them beautifully fried, of a clear even colour, without the slightest appearance of grease. The flour of haricot beans, very finely ground, and which is as good as breadcrumbs, is added.'

M. S. LOVELL: *Edible Mollusks*, 1867

Lovell seems to be confusing octopus with cuttlefish but then there are those tiny cephalopods called *suppions* which, crisply fried in olive oil, make delicious and quite tender little morsels. Although often referred to as octopus, I think they are, in fact, technically a variety of squid.

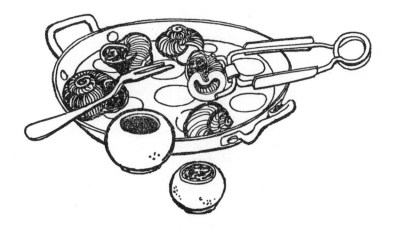

LES ESCARGOTS

SNAILS

Here are the instructions for the preparation of snails, given by Madame Millet-Robinet in *Maison Rustique des Dames*, a book which was enormously popular in the mid-nineteenth century and which, judging from the manner of its arrangement and content, may well have had some influence on our own Mrs. Beeton.

'The first essential is to leave the snails to starve for at least one month, enclosed in some kind of vessel, left in a cool but not damp place. There are cases of accidents having occurred when this precaution has not been taken: the snails, having fed on noxious plants, have caused food poisoning. At the end of this time, the snails are thrown into a cauldron filled with boiling water (to which some add wood ash) and they are cooked for 20 minutes. This done, they are taken from their shells; the little intestine is removed; they are washed in several waters; they are put again into fresh water, salted and boiled for a few minutes, and then they are drained.

'The snails are then put into a saucepan with butter and a large spoonful of flour; stir them, moisten them with stock, water or white wine; add thyme, bay leaves, salt, pepper, mushrooms if possible, and leave to cook until the snails are tender. You then add the egg yolks, to which a little verjuice (the juice of unripe grapes), lemon juice or vinegar can be added.'

ESCARGOTS FARCIS

STUFFED SNAILS

'The snails are prepared and cooked and drained as above; the shells are carefully cleaned; a stuffing is made as follows: mushrooms, parsley, shallots and garlic are all very finely chopped, seasoned with salt and pepper and mixed with a little breadcrumbs and a sufficient quantity of butter; a little of the stuffing is put into each shell, then the snail, and the shell is filled up with the stuffing; put the snails in a fireproof dish into which a half glass of white wine has been poured, and the dish is put in the oven for a quarter of an hour.'

MADAME MILLET-ROBINET: *Maison Rustique des Dames*

ESCARGOTS DE CONSERVE À LA BOURGUIGNONNE

TINNED SNAILS WITH PARSLEY AND GARLIC BUTTER

Tinned snails of the specially reared variety known as *helix pomatia* or *hélices vigneronnes*, apple or vine snails, consumed and exported by the French in millions, can be served with the stuffing described by Madame Millet-Robinet (pounded walnuts are sometimes added to this kind of stuffing), or in the well-known Burgundian manner with parsley and garlic butter. This is made as follows: chop very finely indeed a handful of the freshest parsley, rinsed and squeezed dry, and the stalks discarded, with a shallot or two. Add a finely pounded clove of garlic, or two if you like. Work this mixture into approximately 7 oz. of very fine unsalted butter, season with pepper, nutmeg and only the smallest pinch of salt, because tinned snails are usually already quite sufficiently salted.

These quantities are enough for 4 dozen snails, and the butter should be made only on the day it is needed, for the garlic and shallots will quickly turn the butter sour. For this reason, snails bought ready filled, although they may be excellent the day they arrive from France, will not be too good if they have been hanging about in the shop.

Put a little knob of the butter in each shell, then the snail, then fill up with more butter, pressing it in so that each shell is crammed as full as it can be. Put the filled shells, open end uppermost, in the dishes specially designed for the purpose (see the drawing on page 329), cover each dish with a buttered paper or piece of foil and put them in a fairly hot oven for 7 to 10 minutes. Take great care, when getting the dishes out of the oven, not to let the snails slip over on their sides, for the hot melted butter will drip out and the snails will be spoilt.

A recently invented system which does away with the necessity for special dishes and tongs is to have minuscule pots, one for each snail, made of coarse brown or grey stoneware. The French name for these little pots is *godets*. They are shown in the drawing on page 329, as are also the special dishes and implements normally required. All can be bought in England. (For shops see page 69.)

The following information about various old country methods of cooking snails comes from M. S. Lovell's *Edible Mollusks*, already quoted above.

'The inhabitants of Central France use several sauces for snails, and the four principal are the following, according to Dr. Ebrard:

'*L'ayoli*, or *ail-y-oli*, of Languedoc; a paste made with olive oil and pounded garlic.

'*L'aillada*, of Gascony; a most complicated sauce of garlic, onions, chives, leeks, parsley, etc., with spices, cloves and nutmeg, the whole thickened with oil.

'*La limassade* of Provence, called *la vinaigrette* in Paris.

'*La cacalaousada* of Montpellier, composed of flour, ham, sugar, etc. At Bordeaux the *aillada* is softened with a mixture of bread, flour and yolk of egg, boiled with milk.

'Stuffed snails are also considered very good. A fine stuffing is made with snails previously cooked, fillets of anchovies, nutmeg, spice, fine herbs, and a liaison of yolks of eggs. The snail shells are filled with this stuffing, then placed before the fire, and served *very* hot. In some countries Blainville states that snails are eaten smoked and dried.'

LES PETITS GRIS

These are the small snails which the country people go out and gather by the basketful after the spring showers. Lovell quotes Dr. Ebrard as saying that this variety, the *helix aspersa*, 'has a variety of names in France, and in the north it is called *colimaçon, jardinière* and *aspergille*; at Montpellier, *caraguolo*; in Bordelais, *cagouille, limaou* and *limat*; in Provence, *escargot escourgol*; at Avignon, *caragaou* and *contar*; *banarut* at Arles; and *bajaina* at Grasse.'

LES CUISSES DE GRENOUILLES
FROGS' LEGS

It is odd that frogs' legs, which are such delicate little morsels that surely even the most fastidious could not object to them, should inspire such horror in England. Only the green frogs with black markings are considered edible, and the back legs are the only parts ever served. However, it is not much use giving directions as to their cooking, since they are unobtainable in this country (although I see tinned frogs' legs are being imported). The systems of cooking are, in fact, extremely simple, the frogs' legs being usually simply floured and *sauté* in butter. They take about 10 to 12 minutes to cook. With the addition of chopped parsley, garlic and lemon juice, they become *grenouilles à la provençale*, and a particularly delicious dish of frogs which I ate at a restaurant in Chagny in the Côte d'Or was called *grenouilles à la bressane*; they were in a butter and cream sauce with a quantity of finely-chopped parsley and a little tarragon.

Les Viandes

Meat

FRENCH cooks, it is sometimes alleged, have perfected their particular brand of magic with second-class materials because they have no first-class ones. This, of course, is nonsensical. French cooks hold good-quality materials in the highest esteem, and certainly have plenty to work with. But the attitude of a French cook or housewife is extremely realistic. Appreciating the fact that not every fish that comes out of the sea is a sole, and that not even carefully nurtured animals are entirely constructed of prime steaks and cutlets, they have made it their business to know how to present coarser fish, elderly birds and second or third-grade cuts of meat with the identical skill and ceremony accorded to luxury roasts and show-pieces. Thus a number of cheap delicacies have become famous, and have acquired a considerable snob value wherever French cooking is known. Such things as *andouilles* and *andouillettes* (tripe sausages) are notable examples; *bœuf gros sel* which is boiled beef from the *pot-au-feu* with coarse salt, pigs' trotters *à la Ste. Ménéhould, blanquette de veau, tendrons de veau,* oxtail stews and calf's head *vinaigrette* have become specialities of sophisticated restaurants.

Also, a good French butcher takes as much trouble over the cutting, trimming and presentation of his cheap cuts as with the prime joints. Such things as shoulder and breast of lamb, shoulder cuts, skirt and briskets of beef, shins of veal and belly of pork are so neatly prepared that when the housewife buys them she knows exactly what she is getting; there will be no trimming or boning for her to do at home and so no waste, of either time or materials. Beef for braising or for *bœuf mode, bœuf bourguignon* or the *pot-au-feu* will be on display at the butcher's without her having to order it specially, to have it larded or to explain what is to be done. And this is where we come up against a difficulty when we want to cook French meat dishes in England, for it is not only the meticulous cutting and seaming, trimming and larding and tying which is differently approached in France, but the separation of the carcases into their various cuts is done on a different system, particularly in regard to beef and veal, so that it is not easy to get, in England, the precise equivalent of a French shoulder cut of beef for a *pot-au-feu,* of a leg cut for a *daube,* of a *noix* of veal for roasting, or escalopes for frying.

In the meat recipes, therefore, I have tried wherever possible to indicate English equivalents or alternatives to the French cuts.

This, perhaps, is the place to add that although I have included a good many recipes for the cheaper cuts of meat, since I believe that these are the kind of dishes most needed by English housewives today, I have kept recipes for liver, kidneys, sweetbreads and brains down to a minimum. Once cheap delicacies, these things are now almost in the luxury category and, at least as far as sweetbreads and brains are concerned, the fact that they are also tedious to prepare seems to put them rather out of the good value class.

LE BŒUF
BEEF

One of the worst stumbling blocks to the buying of meat in England is the insistence upon cuts which can be quickly prepared and cooked. Butchers are inundated with demands for roasting and grilling cuts, of which, after all, there is only a limited quantity in each animal.

To satisfy customers, butchers bone, trim and tie up secondary cuts of meat in a more or less rough and ready manner and sell them at a small amount less than, say, sirloin or prime ribs. The inexperienced housewife puts them in a hot oven to roast and hopes for the best. Ten to one the joint will emerge tough, dry (dryness is the main defect to combat in the cooking of second-class cuts) and impossible to carve. This is partly because the joint is too small for the kind of baking which we call roasting, and partly because the meat has been too hastily cut and dressed.

A skilful, experienced butcher treats his meat almost as a tailor does his cloth. If it is stretched out of shape, if there are seams in the wrong places, if he has to make up a respectable-looking joint by adding a piece here, skewering in some fat there, he knows that as soon as the meat is exposed to violent heat it will contract; unnaturally stretched muscles will spring back into place; it will cook unevenly; it will end up looking like a parcel damaged in the Christmas mails. No wonder people say that the cheaper cuts are a false economy. But if that same piece of meat had been stripped of membrane, sinew and gristle before it was rolled and tied, it would be a compact little joint which would keep its shape during cooking and which could be quite successfully roasted.

This is the French method even with what might be termed first-class secondary joints such as topside and the equivalent of our aitchbone, which are used for such delicious dishes as *bœuf mode* and *bœuf bourguignon*. But only in rare instances are these methods practised in England. Even so, the English cook can still make the best of the secondary English joints, such as rolled top rib or a piece of top rump, by cooking them gently, with a little extra liquid to moisten them, and with aromatic vegetables and seasonings to help the flavour, in a closely-covered pot so that all possible moisture is retained; and if they are not so elegant in appearance as the French cuts they will still emerge tender, juicy and well flavoured.

RÔTI DE CONTREFILET

ROAST UPPER FILLET OF BEEF

A piece of that cut of beef known as the eye of the sirloin or upper fillet and which the French call *contrefilet* or *faux filet*, bone and all gristle and sinew removed, tied in a compact rectangular shape, weighing between 2¼ and 3 lb., makes an ideal *small* roasting joint. Expensive, of course, but still cheaper than fillet, and most people would, I think, agree, finer in flavour. (It is shown in the drawing opposite.)

Simply brush the cut surfaces of the meat with olive oil, stand the joint on a grid in a baking tin, put it in the centre of the oven preheated to Gas No. 7, 420 deg. F. After 10 minutes lower the heat to Gas No. 5, 375 deg. F., and cook altogether for just about an hour, basting from time to time with its own fat. Those who like beef very underdone will probably find 45 minutes sufficient.

Potatoes, already all but cooked, can be put in the tin underneath the meat as soon as sufficient fat has run. They will roast beautifully. If any sauce is required apart from the natural juices which run from the beef as it is carved, something very simple, like *maître d'hôtel* butter, to which a little tarragon has been added, is the best solution, unless you like to serve a *sauce béarnaise*, which is the alternative to the more usual Madeira sauce served in France.

A larger piece of meat does not need very much more cooking; the joint will be longer but not thicker, and it is the thickness which counts.

CHÂTEAUBRIAND SAUCE BÉARNAISE
DOUBLE FILLET STEAK WITH BÉARNAISE SAUCE

A *châteaubriand* steak is a cut from the centre and thickest part of the fillet, weighing about 12 oz., and enough for two people. It is too thick to be grilled on an ordinary domestic cooker, as the meat will be too near the flame and will dry up before it is sufficiently cooked. The best solution is, having painted the meat with olive oil and sprinkled it with a little coarsely-ground pepper, to give it about a minute on each side close to the hot grill and then to transfer it, standing on a rack, in a baking tin to a very hot oven, Gas No. 8, 445 deg. F., and roast it for about 12 to 15 minutes.

Serve it with *pommes fondantes* (page 271) and a *sauce béarnaise.*

Sometimes a much larger piece of fillet weighing up to about 1½ lb. is described as a Châteaubriand.

ENTRECÔTE GRILLÉE
GRILLED RIB STEAK

An *entrecôte*[1] is, properly speaking, and as its name implies, a piece of meat cut from between two ribs, from the part of the back known in English as wing-ribs and in French as *train-de-côte*.

Slices of meat from the boned *contrefilet*, in English the upper fillet or eye of the sirloin, or from the back ribs, are also frequently sold as *entrecôtes* and, in French restaurants, a slice of rump steak or, indeed,

[1] See the right-hand drawing on page 334.

any other slice of beef nicely cut and trimmed to look like a 'bifteck' are presented on the menu as *entrecôte*. On the whole, it is a dish to be avoided in France except in high-class restaurants. It is not that the quality of the beef in France is not often excellent and just as good as our own; but like our own it is variable and, again, as in England, restaurateurs are not always conscientious about these matters.

When buying *entrecôtes* to cook at home, one usually allows a steak of a good ½-inch thickness, weighing 7 to 8 oz., for each person; the steaks should be seasoned with freshly-milled pepper, lightly coated with oil, and grilled, not too near the flame, for about 4 minutes on each side, salt being added as each side is browned. Do not be misled by the name *entrecôte minute*, often used in connection with these steaks, into thinking that they should be so thin that they are cooked in a minute. It is just a manner of speaking and a thin, flat, *entrecôte* makes a poor, dry steak.

ENTRECÔTE À LA BORDELAISE
RIB STEAK WITH SHALLOTS AND MARROW

'The *entrecôte* should be cut 2 fingers thick. Marinate it in a tablespoon of oil, salt and pepper. Prepare a fire of glowing charcoal and put the meat on the grill. Chop together 4 shallots, a good, firm piece of beef marrow and a little handful of parsley. Turn your steak. On the upper surface spread this mixture, and from time to time press it with the heated blade of the knife, so that the marrow softens. When the *entrecôte* is cooked, put it on the serving dish, taking care not to upset the shallot and marrow mixture which is on the top.

'This is the old way of cooking the *entrecôte à la bordelaise*. In times gone by gourmets did not disdain an invitation to go down into the wine cellars and eat an *entrecôte* with the cellar master and the *tonnelier*, who had a reputation for preparing it well. They made their fire with hoops of chestnut wood from old barrels, and claimed that this gave a particularly good flavour to the meat.

'Paris restaurateurs serve their *entrecôte à la bordelaise* with a red wine sauce; it does not at all resemble the traditional *entrecôte* of Bordeaux.'

ALCIDE BONTOU: *Traité de Cuisine Bourgeoise Bordelaise*

To cook and extract the marrow from the beef bones, proceed as follows: have a marrow bone sawn in about 3-inch lengths. If possible buy it the day before you need it and soak it for 12 to 24 hours in cold water, changed several times. This process makes the marrow a much better colour, a pale creamy pink, whereas if cooked straight away it tends to be a rather unappetising grey. Put the bones in cold water to cover, bring slowly to the boil and allow to barely simmer for about 20 minutes. Scoop the marrow out with the handle of a small spoon.

ENTRECÔTE À LA BRETONNE
RIB STEAK WITH PARSLEY BUTTER

For 2 thick *entrecôtes* (see recipe for grilled *entrecôte*) chop 1 shallot very fine; work it with 2 oz. of butter, a teaspoon of chopped parsley, a drop of lemon juice and a scrap of freshly-milled pepper. While your steaks, previously coated with oil, seasoned with freshly-milled pepper and, at the last minute, with salt, are grilling, get a fireproof serving dish really hot. Place it over a saucepan of boiling water. When the steaks are ready, and rather underdone, put your prepared butter in the dish. Put the steaks on the top. Cover them. Leave for 3 or 4 minutes. Then spoon the just melted butter over the steaks and serve them at once, with a purée of potatoes to help mop up the delicious butter sauce. *Tournedos* or fillet steaks can be done in the same way.

TOURNEDOS AU VIN BLANC
TOURNEDOS WITH WHITE WINE

Have the *tournedos* cut from the fillet or undercut, about an inch thick and weighing in the region of 6 oz. each. An hour or so before cooking them, paint them with olive oil and rub a little coarsely-milled pepper on both sides.

Heat a thick frying-pan and put in your steaks without adding any extra fat. Let them sizzle on each side; pour in, for 2 steaks, a claret glass (about 4 oz.) of white wine. It will at once bubble fiercely because of the heat of the pan. After a few seconds turn the heat low and let the steaks simmer for about 4 minutes. Remove them to a hot serving dish. Turn up the heat again and reduce the sauce to the consistency of a syrup. Off the fire, add 2 oz. of butter cut into little pieces. Shake and rotate the pan *over* the flame but not *on* it until the butter has amalgamated with the wine and thickened it. Quickly add a little finely-chopped parsley or tarragon. Pour the sauce over and round the steaks and serve at once, with potatoes if you like, or a few mushrooms.

BIFTECKS À LA MODE DU PAYS DE VAUX
FILLET STEAKS WITH BUTTER AND HERBS

This recipe is given by Edmond Richardin in *L'Art du Bien Manger* (1913 edition), one of the most imaginative and attractive cookery books in the French language. Richardin, himself a native of Lorraine, was the owner of a celebrated restaurant in Nancy. The Vaux is in western Lorraine, not far from Verdun:

'Take some fillet steaks, grill them and season them; chop some hard-boiled eggs, one for each steak. Mix them with some chopped *fines herbes*, moisten with lemon juice, add salt and pepper. Spread this mixture on a well-heated fireproof serving dish; place the steaks on top, put some good fresh butter on top of each steak. Heat over a gentle fire before serving.'

LES DAUBES[1]

'O, scent of the daubes of my childhood!

'During the holidays, at Gemeaux, in the month of August, when we arrived in my grandmother's dark kitchen on Sunday after Vespers, it was lit by a ray of sunshine in which the dust and the flies were dancing, and there was a sound like a little bubbling spring. It was a daube, which since midday had been murmuring gently on the stove, giving out sweet smells which brought tears to your eyes. Thyme, rosemary, bay leaves, spices, the wine of the marinade and the *fumet* of the meat were becoming transformed under the magic wand which is the fire, into a delicious whole, which was served about seven o'clock in the evening, so well cooked and so tender that it was carved with a spoon.'

PIERRE HUGUENIN: *Les Meilleures Recettes de ma Pauvre Mère*, 1936

LA DAUBE DE BŒUF PROVENÇALE
PROVENÇAL MEAT AND WINE STEW

There must be scores of different recipes for daubes in Provence alone, as well as all those which have been borrowed from Provence by other regions, for a daube of beef is essentially a country housewife's dish. In some daubes the meat is cut up, in others it is cooked in the piece; what goes in apart from the meat is largely a matter of what is available, and the way it is served is again a question of local taste.

[1] See page 73.

This is an easy recipe, but it has all the rich savour of these slowly-cooked wine-flavoured stews. The pot to cook it in may be earthenware, cast iron, or a copper or aluminium oven pot of about 2 pints capacity, wide rather than deep.

The ingredients are 2 lb. of top rump of beef, about 6 oz. of unsmoked streaky bacon or salt pork, about 3 oz. of fresh pork rinds, 2 onions, 2 carrots, 2 tomatoes, 2 cloves of garlic, a bouquet of thyme, bayleaf, parsley and a little strip of orange peel, 2 tablespoons of olive oil, a glass (4 fl. oz.) of red wine, seasoning.

Have the meat cut into squares about the size of half a postcard and about ⅛ inch thick. Buy the bacon or salt pork in the piece and cut it into small cubes.

Scrape and slice the carrots on the cross; peel and slice the onions. Cut the rinds, which should have scarcely any fat adhering to them and are there to give body as well as savour to the stew, into little squares. Skin and slice the tomatoes.

In the bottom of the pot put the olive oil, then the bacon, then the vegetables and half the pork rinds. Arrange the meat carefully on top, the slices overlapping each other. Bury the garlic cloves, flattened with a knife, and the bouquet, in the centre. Cover with the rest of the pork rinds. With the pan uncovered, start the cooking on a moderate heat on top of the stove.

After about 10 minutes, put the wine into another saucepan; bring it to a fast boil; set light to it; rotate the pan so that the flames spread. When they have died down pour the wine bubbling over the meat. Cover the pot with greaseproof paper or foil, and a well-fitting lid. Transfer to a very slow oven, Gas No. 1, 290 deg. F., and leave for 2½ hours.

To serve, arrange the meat with the bacon and the little pieces of rind on a hot dish; pour off some of the fat from the sauce, extract the bouquet, and pour the sauce round the meat. If you can, keep the dish hot over a spirit lamp after it is brought to table. At the serving stage, a *persillade* of finely-chopped garlic and parsley, with perhaps an anchovy and a few capers, can be sprinkled over the top. Or stoned black olives can be added to the stew half an hour before the end of the cooking time.

Although in Italy pasta is never served with a meat dish, in Provence it quite often is. The cooked and drained noodles, or whatever pasta you have chosen, are mixed with some of the gravy from the stew, and in this case the fat is not removed from the gravy, because it lubricates the pasta. Sometimes this *macaronade*, as it is called, is served first, to be followed by the meat.

Nowadays, since rice has been successfully cultivated in the reclaimed areas of the Camargue, it is also quite usual to find a dish of rice, often flavoured with saffron, served with a meat stew.

This daube is a useful dish for those who have to get a dinner ready when they get home from the office. It can be cooked for $1\frac{1}{2}$ hours the previous evening and finished on the night itself. Provided they have not been overcooked to start with, these beef and wine stews are all the better for a second or even third heating up. The amounts I have given are the smallest quantities in which it is worth cooking such a stew, and will serve four or five people, but of course they can be doubled or even trebled for a large party; if the meat is piled up in layers in a deep pan it will naturally need longer cooking than if it is spread out in a shallow one.

DAUBE DE BŒUF CRÉOLE

NEW ORLEANS DAUBE OF BEEF

From a little book of New Orleans cookery published under the name of Madame Bégué, who many years ago had a restaurant in that city of traditional good cooking, comes an interesting variation on the Provençal daube of beef, adapted by the Creole cooks to accord with the ingredients available locally. The meat is studded with olives and cooked with rum instead of wine; and the curious point is that although the result is a very rich-tasting dish I think few people would be able to detect the presence of the rum, or to say in what precise way the stew differs from the French original.

$2\frac{1}{2}$ to 3 lb. topside or round of beef in one piece, a dozen pimento-stuffed olives, $\frac{3}{4}$ lb. of salt streaky pork or bacon, a large onion, 4 or 5 tomatoes, bouquet of herbs, butter or dripping, half a teacup of rum, salt and pepper, garlic.

Trim excess fat from the meat, and make a double row of deep incisions on each side; in these stick the olives, each one cut in half lengthways. Tie the meat into a good oblong shape. Slice the onion and let it take colour in a little butter or dripping heated in an earthenware or other stewing-pot of about 2 pints capacity. Put in the salt pork cut in cubes, and when the fat from this starts to run put in the meat and let it brown a little on each side. Now heat the rum, set light to it and pour it flaming over the meat. Shake and rotate the pan until the flames die down, then add the tomatoes, skinned and roughly chopped, a clove or two of garlic crushed with a knife, the bouquet of herbs (bayleaf, fresh parsley, a sprig of thyme and dried basil if you have it) tied with a thread, a very little salt and quite a lot of freshly-milled pepper. Cover with a sheet of greaseproof paper or foil and a lid. Cook in a very slow oven, Gas No. 1, 290 deg. F., for about 3 hours.

Remove the bouquet before serving and crush the tomatoes into the sauce with a wooden spoon. The sauce will be rather rich and highly flavoured, and the best accompaniment is either a dish of plain rice or, in the Provençal fashion, some plainly boiled noodles mixed with a little of the juice from the meat.

In the original recipe, which I have adapted somewhat because of its vagueness as to cooking methods, the meat is larded with the salt pork as well as the olives, but to my taste this tends to make the meat over-salted.

Although at a first glance readers may find it curious that this recipe, and two or three others which do not belong strictly to metropolitan France, should be included in this book, these recipes seem to me to be of great interest as showing the way in which French cooks develop their dishes in different countries. At home they tend to be extremely con-servative and would very likely be horrified at the idea of using rum instead of wine in a stew or of serving a leek and potato soup iced with cream as did Louis Diat when he turned *potage bonne femme* into *vichyssoise glacée*; but when they settle abroad they soon realise that if they are going to be well fed they must also be flexible in the matter of adapting local ingredients new to them. Wherever the French have settled or French chefs have been employed one finds interesting varia-tions on the old regional dishes of France itself.

ESTOFAT DE BŒUF ALBIGEOIS
BEEF STEW WITH RED WINE AND BRANDY

A fine large piece of topside or top rump of beef is required for this dish, and it is not worth attempting with less than 4 to 5 lb. The other in-gredients are a little pork or goose dripping or oil, carrots, onions, garlic, half a bottle of red wine, brandy if possible, a big faggot of aromatic herbs including bay leaves, thyme and parsley, about 1 lb. of streaky salt pork and 2 pigs' trotters.

Have your beef rolled and tied in a good shape; melt the dripping in a heavy pot which has a well-fitting lid; put in the meat, surround it with 2 large sliced onions, 4 or 5 carrots, a couple of cloves of garlic. Start off over a gentle flame for 15 minutes, and when the fat is running and the onions beginning to colour, pour in 4 oz. (8 tablespoons) of brandy; let it bubble; add the wine; put in the salt pork, the trotters (split) and the

bouquet, and a very little salt. Cover the pot, transfer to the lowest possible oven, and there leave it for about 7 or 8 hours.

The result of this lengthy, almost imperceptible cooking is a beautifully tender piece of meat and a rich, aromatic, but rather fat sauce; to counteract this, serve with it plenty of plain boiled or purée potatoes or rice if you prefer. The dish is also delicious cold, and resembles a *bœuf mode*, except that the meat is not larded, and the jellied sauce is thicker and darker. The vegetables must be strained off, and the fat removed when the sauce has set. The trotters, from which the bones will have almost fallen out, can be coated with melted butter and breadcrumbs, gently grilled and, with a *sauce tartare*, make a little hot hors-d'œuvre.

BŒUF À LA BOURGUIGNONNE
BEEF STEW WITH RED WINE, ONIONS AND MUSHROOMS

This is a favourite among those carefully composed, slowly cooked dishes which are the domain of French housewives and owner-cooks of modest restaurants rather than of professional chefs. Generally supposed to be of Burgundian origin (although Alfred Contour's *Cuisinier Bourguignon* gives no recipe for it) *bœuf à la bourguignonne* has long been a nationally popular French dish, and is often referred to, or written down on menus, simply as '*bourguignon.*' Such dishes do not, of course, have a rigid formula, each cook interpreting it according to her taste, and the following recipe is just one version. Incidentally, when I helped in a soup kitchen in France many years ago, this was the dish for feast-days and holidays.

2 lb. of topside of beef, 4 oz. of salt pork or streaky bacon (unsmoked for preference), a large onion, thyme, parsley and bayleaves, $\frac{1}{4}$ pint of red wine, 2 tablespoons of olive oil, $\frac{1}{2}$ pint of meat stock, preferably veal, a clove of garlic, 1 tablespoon flour, meat dripping. For the garnish, $\frac{1}{2}$ lb. of small mushrooms, a dozen or so small whole onions.

Cut the meat into slices about $2\frac{1}{2}$ inches square and $\frac{1}{4}$ inch thick. Put them into a china or earthenware dish, seasoned with salt and pepper, covered with the large sliced onion, herbs, olive oil and red wine. Leave to marinate from 3 to 6 hours.

Put a good tablespoon of beef dripping into a heavy stewing-pan of about 4 pints capacity. In this melt the salt pork or bacon, cut into $\frac{1}{4}$ inch thick match-length strips. Add the whole peeled small onions, and let them brown, turning them over frequently and keeping the heat low. Take out the bacon when its fat becomes transparent, and remove the onions when they are nicely coloured. Set them aside with the bacon. Now put into the fat the drained and dried pieces of meat and brown them quickly on each side. Sprinkle them with the flour, shaking the pan so that the flour amalgamates with the fat and absorbs it. Pour over the strained marinade. Let it bubble half a minute; add the stock. Put in a clove of garlic and a bouquet of thyme, parsley and bayleaf tied with a thread. Cover the pan with a close-fitting lid and let it barely simmer on top of the stove for about 2 hours.

Now add the bacon and onions, and the whole mushrooms washed but not peeled and already cooked in butter or dripping for a minute or so to rid them of some of their moisture. Cook the stew another half-hour. Remove the bouquet and garlic before serving.

There should be enough for four to six people.

If more convenient, the first 2 hours' cooking can be done in advance, the stew left to cool and the fat removed; it can then be reheated gently with the bacon, mushrooms and onions added. There are those who maintain that the dish is improved by being heated up a second time; the meat has time to mature, as it were, in the sauce.

To make a cheaper dish, chuck (shoulder) beef may be used instead of topside, and an extra 45 minutes' cooking time allowed. And when really small onions are not available it is best simply to cook a chopped onion or two with the stew, and to leave onions out of the garnish, because large ones are not suitable for the purpose.

For formal occasions a boned joint of beef may be cooked whole and served with a similar sauce and garnish, and then becomes *pièce de bœuf à la bourguignonne*.

BŒUF À LA GARDIANE

BEEF AND WINE STEW WITH BLACK OLIVES

A dish from western Provence and the Camargue demonstrating the stewing of a tough piece of meat in red wine without the addition of any stock or thickening for the sauce.

Ingredients for four people are 2 lb. of top rump of beef, 4 tablespoons of brandy, 1 large glass (6 oz.) of red wine, a bouquet of thyme, parsley and bayleaf, plus a little strip of orange peel and a crushed clove of garlic, butter and olive oil; and about 6 oz. of stoned black olives.

The meat should be cut into small neat cubes, not more than an inch square. Brown them in a mixture of olive oil and butter. Warm the brandy in a soup ladle, pour it over the meat, set light to it, shake the pan until the flames go out. Add the red wine; let it bubble fast for about half a minute. Season with only very little salt and pepper, put in the bouquet tied with thread, turn the flame as low as possible, cover the pan with at least two layers of greaseproof paper or foil and the lid.

Cook as gently as possible, on top of the stove, with a mat underneath the pan, for about 3½ hours. Ten minutes before serving remove the bouquet and put in the stoned black olives. Taste for seasoning before serving. A dish of plain boiled rice can be served separately.

The flaming with brandy, although not absolutely essential, burns up the excess fat and makes quite a difference to the flavour of the finished sauce, which will be a short one, most of the liquid having been absorbed by the meat. The old Nîmoise cook who showed me how to make this particular version of the dish used Châteauneuf du Pape to cook it in (we were in the district, so it wasn't so extravagant as it sounds, and it most definitely pays to use a decent and full-bodied wine for these beef stews) and she garnished the dish with heart-shaped croûtons of fried bread instead of rice.

LA DAUBE DU BÉARN

BEEF AND WINE STEW WITH HAM AND TOMATOES

This does not differ substantially from the Provençal and other daubes already described, but variations upon these kinds of dishes are always useful to know.

For this one the ingredients are approximately 2 lb. of topside or leg of beef cut into slices about ½ inch thick and about half the size of an ordinary postcard, 6 to 8 oz. of salt, streaky pork, a slice of raw ham (or gammon from the middle or corner cut) weighing about ¼ lb., 2 carrots, a large onion, 3 or 4 tomatoes, a claret glass of red wine, a bouquet of herbs and a piece of dried red pepper, and if you have it, a couple of tablespoons of rich goose or beef stock.

Cut the pork, rind included, into cubes, and the ham or gammon into strips. Slice the onion and carrots. Arrange all these ingredients in a braising-pan or earthen pot (in the Béarn they use a fat round pot narrowing towards the top, called a *toupin*),[1] and set over a low flame. When the fat starts to run put in the meat arranged in overlapping layers, with the bouquet in the centre. No salt. Cover the pan and cook gently about 10 minutes. Pour over the wine, bubbling hot. Cook another 15 minutes or so on top of the stove, and then transfer to a very low oven. If the lid of the pan is not a well-fitting one, seal the pot with a piece of foil or greaseproof paper.

Cook very slowly, Gas No. 1 or 2, 290 to 310 deg. F., for 4 to 5 hours; about half an hour before serving, put in the tomatoes, roughly chopped, and the goose or beef stock, and cover the pan again.

A purée of potatoes, or rice, goes with the daube, which is even better when heated up again next day. Enough for four.

JARRET DE BŒUF EN DAUBE
SHIN OF BEEF STEWED IN WINE

Cut 4 to 6 oz. of fat bacon or salt pork into little cubes and put them, with a tablespoon of olive oil, into a heavy and fairly wide iron or earthenware pot; when the bacon fat runs add a large sliced onion. On top, arrange about 3 lb. of shin of beef, off the bone, skin and excess fat removed, and cut lengthways into thick pieces. Add a clove or two of garlic, and a big bunch of parsley, thyme and bayleaf, all tied with a thread. Pour in a large glass (6 to 8 fl. oz.) of red wine, previously heated. Let it come to a fast boil and leave 3 or 4 minutes. Add an equal quantity of hot water, or stock should you chance to have it, and allow to boil again. Season with 2 teaspoons of salt.

Cover the pot with paper or foil and a well-fitting lid. Transfer to a very slow oven, Gas No. 1, 290 deg. F., and in about 3 hours it will be cooked. Or you can half-cook it one day and finish the process just as slowly the next, for, as explained in many of the recipes in this chapter, wine stews improve and mature with reheating. The sauce is to be neither thickened nor reduced; it is to be mopped up with plenty of bread, rice or potatoes. And if your oven is too small for your cooking pot, then it can simmer extremely gently on top of the stove. There should be enough for six people.

[1] See the drawing on page 61.

BŒUF À LA MODE

COLD BEEF IN JELLY

Recipes for this dish vary quite a bit, every cook having his own idea as to the seasonings and herbs, but the essentials are always the same. They are a large piece of a secondary cut of beef such as topside, top rump, or even sometimes a shoulder cut, plus calf's feet, carrots and wine. The dish can be served either hot or cold, but is at its best cold when the juices have set to a beautiful soft, limpid jelly, but although this aspect of the dish seems to make it an ideal one for summer, beware of making it in sultry or thundery weather, for the jelly easily goes sour under such conditions.

Ingredients are a 4 to 5 lb. piece of roll of silverside, top rump or topside, 4 oz. of strips of back pork fat, 2 onions, a bouquet of herbs, 2 lb. of carrots, 2 calf's feet, ½ pint of red or white wine, a small glass of brandy, meat stock or water, butter, oil or lard, and seasonings.

The meat must be boned, and preferably, although not essentially, tied in a large sausage shape. It should also be larded lengthways with little strips of back pork fat as explained on page 75, and if you do this yourself, season the pieces of fat with a little salt, pepper, chopped herbs and, if you like, garlic; if the butcher has already done the larding, simply rub the meat well with the seasonings.

Slice the onions and let them take colour in a little fat; put in the meat and let it brown on the outside. Pour in the warmed brandy and flame it. Then add the wine. Let it bubble a minute or two. Add the calf's feet, split and rinsed in cold water, a little more salt, 2 carrots, a big bouquet of parsley, bayleaf, thyme (sometimes a little piece of orange peel is included in the bouquet), and a crushed clove of garlic. Pour in enough stock (veal stock is ideal) or water to just cover the meat. Seal the pot with a couple of layers of greaseproof paper or foil, then a well-fitting lid.

The beef must now simmer extremely slowly for 3½ to 5 hours, either on top of the stove or in the oven. When the dish is to be served cold, it can be cooked a little longer than when it is to be served hot, because even though the meat appears to be very tender indeed it will still harden up a little when it is cold. It should, in fact, be tender enough to cut with a spoon, hence the alternative name of *bœuf à la cuiller* sometimes given to *bœuf mode*.

The time taken for the beef to cook depends very much upon the cut and quality of the meat; but should it appear to be cooked in too short a time, that is to say in less than 3½ hours, it probably means it has been cooked at too high a heat or that your piece of meat is rather small. What you do then is to remove the meat and let the rest of the ingredients go on cooking slowly, to make sure that the gelatine from the calf's feet is thoroughly extracted, otherwise the sauce will not set to a good jelly.

The final operations are the tricky ones. The usual instructions are that, having untied the string from your meat, you arrange the rest of the carrots, separately boiled, all round it, and pour over the hot strained stock, leaving it to set and taking off the fat when it has done so. The dish is then ready to serve.

A more satisfactory method from the point of view of final results is to pour your strained stock into a separate bowl and leave it overnight to set. You then clear it completely of the fat. This process is explained on page 73. The meat itself can be sliced for serving (although this is only to be recommended to those who have a sure hand in operations of this kind), reconstituted into its original shape and placed in the serving dish, which should be a deep and capacious one, with the carrots all round. The jelly, heated until it is just melted, should be poured over the meat when it is quite cold but before it starts to re-set. If you pour it warm over the meat, more fat will be released, and when the jelly is set the surface will be once more studded with little particles of fat. This does not really matter, but detracts slightly from the beautiful limpid appearance of the finished dish; it can be remedied, however, to a certain extent by wringing out a cloth in hot water and with this carefully removing the little fat globules. 'What are you doing?' a guest once asked me as he saw me at this task. 'Polishing the beef?' Which I suppose is what it really amounts to.

All that is needed to go with the *bœuf mode* is a plain salad. Do not, I beg and beseech, subscribe to the English custom of serving hot vegetables with cold meat. In the first place their presence on the plate will melt the jelly and nullify the whole idea of the dish, and in the second place they are totally out of keeping. You already have meat, carrots and a wine-flavoured jelly; a dish in fact quite complete in itself; nothing else is needed.

The calf's feet are sometimes cut up and minus their bones arranged round the beef with the carrots; sometimes they are coated with bread-crumbs and melted butter and grilled to make a little hot hors-d'œuvre for another meal, sometimes they are cooked again with fresh vegetables, herbs and seasonings plus perhaps some meat to make a second lot of jellied stock. And, incidentally, when calf's feet are unobtainable, as they quite frequently are in this country, at any rate in London, pigs' trotters will do instead, but remember that they are much smaller, so you will need three or four instead of two. Or two plus some strips of pork rind, which are also valuable for their gelatinous qualities.

Whether you use red wine or white is really a matter of taste or of what is available. Red wine makes a darker, more sumptuous-looking jelly; white produces a somewhat milder, lighter flavour.

QUEUE DE BŒUF AUX OLIVES NOIRES
STEWED OXTAIL WITH BLACK OLIVES

For 2 oxtails the other ingredients are olive oil, brandy, white wine, stock or water, a big bouquet of bayleaves, thyme, parsley, orange peel and crushed garlic cloves, about ½ lb. of stoned black olives.

Have the oxtails cut into the usual pieces by the butcher. Put them to steep in cold water for a couple of hours so that the blood soaks out. Take them out and drain them. Heat 2 or 3 tablespoons of olive oil in a big heavy stew-pan or *daubière*. Put in the pieces of oxtail and let them sizzle gently a few minutes. Pour over 4 to 6 tablespoons of warmed brandy and set light to it. When the flames have died down, add a large glass, about 6 to 8 ounces, of white wine. Let it bubble fiercely a minute or so. Add just enough stock or water to come level with the pieces of oxtail. Bury the bouquet in the centre. Cover the pan. Transfer to a very slow oven, Gas No. 1, 290 deg. F. Cook for about 3 hours. Pour off all the liquid and leave until next day. Remove the fat. Heat the remaining stock; pour it back over the oxtail. Add the stoned olives. Cook for another hour or so on top of the stove, until the oxtail is bubbling hot and the meat coming away from the bones. Serve with a dish of plain boiled rice.

This dish can, of course, be cooked all in one operation but, for those who don't like very fat rich food, the system of getting rid of most of the fat from the sauce makes a better dish. The flaming with brandy also does much to strengthen the flavour of the sauce, but it can be left out if it seems a rather extravagant ingredient in a dish which should really be a cheap one.

These quantities should make plenty for six people, but the dish is one which can very well be made with one oxtail only.

For a good way of using up left-over oxtail see the recipe on page 350.

LA QUEUE DE BŒUF DES VIGNERONS
OXTAIL STEWED WITH WHITE GRAPES

Oxtail 'as cooked by the winegrowers' is a lovely dish made out of what should be inexpensive ingredients, but as in England grapes are not to be had just for the picking, one should perhaps only attempt it when imported grapes are plentiful and cheap. To make the lengthy cooking worth while buy at least 2 oxtails, cut into the usual 2-inch lengths by the butcher. The other ingredients are 3 to 4 oz. of salt pork or of a cheap cut of fat unsmoked bacon bought in one piece, 2 large onions, 4 large carrots and 2 lb. of white grapes. Seasonings include, besides salt and freshly-milled pepper, a little mace or allspice, a bouquet of 2 bay-leaves, parsley, thyme and 2 crushed cloves of garlic tied in a little bunch.

Steep the oxtail in cold water for a minimum of 2 hours, so that the blood soaks out.

Cut the bacon, without the rind, into little cubes. Chop the onions and dice the carrots. At the bottom of a heavy cooking pot put the bacon with the vegetables on top. Start off on a low flame and cook 10 minutes until the fat from the bacon is running. Now put in the pieces of oxtail, and put the bouquet in the centre. Season the meat. Cover the pot and cook gently for 20 minutes. Now add the grapes, which you have picked off their stalks and crushed slightly in a bowl. Cover the pot with 2 sheets of grease-proof paper and the lid. Transfer to a very slow oven, Gas No. 1, 290 deg. F., and cook for a minimum of 3½ hours. Oxtail varies very much in quality, and sometimes takes a good deal longer, and unless the meat is so soft and tender it is almost falling from the bones it will not be good. Once cooked, quickly transfer the pieces of oxtail and a few of the little bits of bacon to another terrine or to a serving dish, and keep them hot while you sieve all the rest of the ingredients through the finest mesh of the *mouli-légumes*. Pour the resulting sauce over the oxtail. A dish of potatoes boiled in their skins, or a potato purée, should accompany the dish.

An alternative method is to cook the dish for half an hour less, take out the oxtail, and leave the sieved sauce separately so that excess fat can be removed from the top when it is cold. Having done this, pour the sauce, warmed, over the meat and heat on top of the stove rather than in the oven, because all-round heat tends to make the sauce oily, whereas with direct heat it will retain its consistency. The dish can, as a matter of fact, be reheated two or three times without damage.

Two oxtails should make six to eight ample helpings.

QUEUE DE BŒUF PANÉE
GRILLED OXTAIL

Oxtail cooked in the *pot-au-feu* (see page 156) or left over from a stew makes a good and useful hot hors-d'œuvre or luncheon dish. Paint the pieces with softened butter, coat them with breadcrumbs and bake them in the oven, finishing them under the grill as explained for pigs' trotters, page 224. Serve with a *vinaigrette* or, if there is any left, some of the sauce which went with the original dish.

ROGNONS DE BŒUF À LA CHARENTAISE
OX KIDNEY STEWED IN WINE WITH MUSHROOMS

Cooked in this way the toughest ox kidney will become tender and have a most excellent flavour. Ingredients are ½ lb. ox kidney, 2 oz. mushrooms, 2 oz. cream, brandy, white wine, butter, meat stock.

Soak the skinned kidney in warm, salted water for a couple of hours. Slice into pieces about ½ inch thick. Heat a little butter in a frying-pan and turn the kidneys over and over in this for a minute or so. Add salt and pepper, and the chopped mushrooms. Pour over 2 tablespoons of brandy warmed in a soup ladle, set light to it and shake the pan until the flames go out. Pour a small glass of white wine into the pan, let it bubble, then add about a coffee-cupful (after-dinner size) of very good meat stock. Turn the kidneys and their juice into a small earthenware casserole, cover and put into a low oven for 30 to 40 minutes. Boil the cream in a small, wide pan; pour in the sauce from the kidneys. Stir, and cook quickly until the sauce is thick. Pour back over the kidneys; serve with croûtons of fried bread. Enough for two or three.

One way of making the sauce for this dish less expensive is to cook it when you have some rich gravy left over from any of the meat stews already described. The wine can then be omitted, for the gravy is already flavoured with it.

L'AGNEAU ET LE MOUTON
LAMB AND MUTTON

French methods of cutting up lamb and mutton are substantially the same as our own, except that the shoulder is very often boned, and sometimes tied into a round shape, when it is described as a *ballotine d'agneau*. The saddle is cut shorter than in England, and the leg often has the central bone removed while retaining the shank bone. The *carré* or row of best end of neck cutlets is trimmed right down to the bones, which are cut short, making it into a very elegant and manageable little joint, which can equally well be cooked on top of the stove or in the oven. If it is from very small tender lamb it can be grilled.

For breast of lamb, which is really, apart from the scrag end of neck, the only cut which could fairly be described as cheap, the French method

of two separate and distinct processes of cooking is probably one of the very best. According to this system, usually known as *à la Ste. Ménéhould* and applied to pigs' and sheep's trotters, as well as to breast of veal and lamb, the meat is first slowly braised, left to cool, boned (if this has not already been done prior to cooking), divided into strips, coated with breadcrumbs and grilled, so that you get a dry crisp outer covering for your fat and gelatinous meat inside.

Small quantities of already cooked breast of lamb can also very successfully be used to make a pilaff or risotto, and to stuff tomatoes and aubergines.

GIGOT À LA BRETONNE

LEG OF MUTTON OR LAMB WITH HARICOT BEANS

Not many of the legs of lamb and mutton served daily in Paris restaurants under this name come from animals pastured in the salt meadows of Brittany; and, indeed, unless they figure on the menu as *gigot de pré-salé* there is no reason to assume that they are anything of the kind. It is the invariable garnish of haricot beans which is characteristically Breton.

The joint, a clove or two of garlic pushed in near the bone, is roasted in the routine way, being basted from time to time with a little stock. The beans, soaked overnight, are prepared as explained in the following recipe, but, of course, for a whole leg of lamb you need more beans than for a small joint like the best end of neck. Allow 1 lb. or even more, for if any are left over they can always be heated up a second time.

It is as well to bear in mind, when ordering roast lamb in a French restaurant, that the French like this meat rather underdone—sometimes uneatably so to English tastes—so that it is advisable to inquire as to this point before giving your order.

CARRÉ D'AGNEAU AUX HARICOTS
BEST END OF NECK OF LAMB WITH HARICOT BEANS

The *carré* (see the drawing opposite) is the French butcher's term for the best end of neck joint, consisting of eight cutlets. It is trimmed exactly as the cutlets would be if they were to be cut separately for grilling, with the chine bone and most of the fat removed, so that only the actual cutlets with their bones are left. Neatly tied, it makes a compact little joint, very easy to cook and carve, and suitable for a small party when a leg or saddle would be too much. It should make ample helpings for four.

First of all, prepare a stock from the bones and trimmings, with an onion, garlic, carrot and seasoning, and water barely to cover. Simmer for an hour or so, strain, leave to cool and skim off the fat. This stock is for basting the joint, so only about a breakfast cup is needed.

To cook the joint, butter the roasting tin, lay the joint in it fat side up, and cover with a thickly-buttered greaseproof paper or aluminium foil. Put a lid on the roasting-pan, and put in the centre of a preheated oven at Gas No. 5, 380 deg. F. After about 20 minutes remove the paper and baste the meat with the juices in the pan and some of the prepared stock, heated. Altogether, the joint will take about 50 minutes to cook and should be basted three or four times, being left uncovered for the last 10 minutes so that the outer coating of fat browns. Red wine instead of stock can, if preferred, be used for basting. In this case, pour a large glass of red wine into a saucepan, add either a couple of chopped shallots or 3 or 4 whole cloves of garlic, and boil until the wine is reduced by half. Use in the same way as the stock.

When the meat is cooked, keep it hot in a large shallow serving dish. Put the rest of your stock or wine into the roasting-pan, scrape up all the juices, let it bubble a minute and add a little of it to the prepared haricot beans and serve the rest separately.

The dried haricot beans are cooked *à la bretonne*: 12 oz. of medium-sized and long, rather than round, white haricot beans are soaked overnight if for lunch, or for 6–8 hours (which is quite long enough provided the beans are those of the current season and not a couple of years old) if for dinner. Drain them, simmer them in water to cover by 2 inches, with a carrot, an onion, a bouquet of herbs and a piece of celery. According to

M

the quality of the beans they may take anything from 1½ to 3 hours. So it is best, if you don't know your beans, to prepare them in advance. They have to be reheated anyhow. When they are tender, but not broken, drain them, reserving the liquid, and season them well with salt. Extract the carrot and the herbs and throw them away. Chop the onion and fry it in butter. Add 3 or 4 skinned and chopped tomatoes and cook till soft, thinning with a little of the reserved cooking liquid. The beans are gently reheated in this mixture, the juice from the roast being added when they are ready. The beans are then turned into the serving dish round the meat or, if preferred, served in a separate dish. Little paper frills are slipped on to the end of the bones, and the joint is carved straight down into cutlets.

If you like, a *béarnaise* sauce can be served with the lamb; in which case you wouldn't really need the gravy as well, except a little to mix with the beans.

The ordinary English cut of best end of neck can, of course, be cooked in the same way, allowing a little longer cooking time.

CARRÉ D'AGNEAU LORRAIN

BEST END OF NECK OF LAMB WITH CARROTS, LEEKS AND TOMATOES

Cut 3 or 4 carrots and the white part of 3 or 4 leeks into small dice; chop 2 shallots and a little piece of garlic; skin and chop 3 or 4 tomatoes; in a shallow fireproof dish or frying-pan heat a mixture of olive oil and butter, and in this melt the shallots and 2 rashers of streaky bacon cut into small pieces; add the leeks and carrots. When the vegetables start to take colour put in your little joint—a piece of best end of neck comprising 6 to 8 cutlets, preferably trimmed, partly boned and tied in the French way, as described in the preceding recipe. Let it brown very lightly on each side. Add the tomatoes and salt and pepper (the sauce should be rather highly seasoned) and a bouquet of thyme and parsley. Pour in a teacup of stock previously prepared from the trimmings of the joint, and let it bubble. If a frying-pan has been used for this preliminary cooking, the joint and sauce are now all to be transferred to an oven dish, covered with a buttered paper or foil, and cooked for just about 1 hour in a moderate oven, Gas No. 4, 350 deg. F.: 10 minutes before the end of this time, remove the paper, cut the string from the joint, sprinkle the fat side with breadcrumbs and finely-chopped parsley, and let it brown.

To serve, put the joint on a hot serving dish, pour off excess juice and fat from the sauce, give the residue a quick stir over the fire, and pour it round the meat. A purée of white haricot beans is served at the same time.

Other joints of lamb can be cooked in the same way; in fact, when I had this dish in Nancy it was made with a shoulder of baby lamb, so small that each joint provided portions for only two people—that is to say two people expected still to have very respectable appetites after consuming their fair share of a *quiche.*

FILET D'AGNEAU AU FOUR

ROAST FILLET OF LAMB

This way of presenting roast lamb makes an attractive dinner-party dish. The fillet is a piece of loin, boned, rolled in a sausage shape and tied. A good butcher will do it with much less waste than you can manage at home; it is initially an expensive joint, but there is no waste. A 2 lb. piece (before boning) should be enough for four people, and lamb is not at its best cold, so there is little point in buying more than you need in this case. Ask for the bones to be put in with the meat.

Season your meat, sprinkle it with a little thyme, and for those who like the flavour of garlic with lamb and mutton put a clove or two underneath the meat in the roasting-pan, where it will flavour both meat and gravy without being overwhelming. Put the bones round the meat and add 2 soup ladles of water, or meat stock if you have it, and cook uncovered in a medium oven, Gas No. 5, 380 deg. F., for about 45 minutes to an hour, or even a little more, depending on the thickness of the meat. Remove the bones, pour off the juice into a saucepan and leave the meat to brown in the uncovered pan. Pour the fat off the gravy, reduce what is left to a good consistency by fast boiling and serve it separately.

SELLE D'AGNEAU AU FOUR

ROAST SADDLE OF LAMB

The average weight of an English or New Zealand saddle of lamb is about 6 lb. and should serve at least eight people. Preheat the oven to Gas No. 5, 380 deg. F. Wrap up the joint in plentifully buttered foil, and stand it on a grid over a baking tin. Cook it in the centre of the oven for 1¼ hours. Unwrap it, turn the oven down to No. 3, or 330 deg. F., and cook it another ½ hour. Have ready a large cupful of good strong stock made from trimmings and bones of lamb. During the final cooking baste the joint with this. This, and the juices from the meat itself, will then form the gravy. Carve the joint in long thin bias-cut fillets, then turn it over and carve from the undercut. Reconstitute the joint as nearly as possible in its original shape, and serve it surrounded by little potatoes, baby carrots and tender little string beans, all cooked separately and well buttered.

French butchers cut a saddle of lamb shorter than is the custom in England, which makes it more manageable. But this makes little difference to the cooking time, as it is the thickness of the joint rather than the length which has to be taken into consideration.

CARBONNADE NÎMOISE
LAMB OR MUTTON BAKED WITH POTATOES

Carbonnade is a name usually associated with a Flemish dish of beef cooked in the local Belgian beer. A *carbonnade* of mutton is also a traditional dish from Nîmes in the Languedoc, home also of the famous *brandade de morue*, the Friday dish of salt cod found all over southern France. The Nîmois *carbonnade* is one of those slow-cooked dishes of meat and vegetables which is still, in places where household ovens are rare, sent to cook at the local bakery. Put in as soon as the bread is taken out, while the oven is still very hot, it is left 3 or 4 hours and, by the time the oven is cool, the meat is so tender that it could be eaten with a spoon. This form of cookery is obviously most convenient for people who have Aga or similar cookers, or for anybody who wants to leave the food to look after itself while they are out.

The ingredients for a *carbonnade nîmoise* for four people are 2 slices of mutton or lamb cut from the leg, each about ⅓ inch thick and weighing about ¾ lb., ¼ lb. bacon, 2 lb. potatoes, garlic, herbs, olive oil.

Lard the meat with little spikes of bacon and garlic. Heat a little olive oil in a large baking dish, put in the rest of the bacon cut in strips, put the meat on top, sprinkle it with salt, pepper and thyme or marjoram, surround it with the potatoes, peeled and cut into small squares, and put the dish, uncovered, into a hot oven for 20 minutes. Then turn the oven very low, Gas No. 2 or 3, 310 to 330 deg. F., cover the pan, and leave for 3½ to 4 hours. By the time it is cooked most of the fat will have been absorbed by the potatoes, and the whole dish will have a typical southern flavour and smell. Sometimes other vegetables: onions, artichoke hearts, a tomato or two, fennel cut in quarters, carrots or aubergines, unpeeled, but cut into small squares, are added with the potatoes.

TRANCHES DE MOUTON À LA POITEVINE
MUTTON STEWED WITH BRANDY AND GARLIC

Have two thick slices cut from a leg of mutton, with the bone, weighing about ¾ lb. each. Brown them in butter in a heavy shallow pan with a well-fitting lid. Salt and pepper them; pour over about 4 fl. oz. of brandy or *marc* (see page 92) and the same amount of water. Add a dozen peeled cloves of garlic. Cover with paper and the lid, lower the flame, and cook as slowly as possible for about 2½ hours. There will only be a little concentrated juice when the dish is ready, but the mutton will be very tender with a highly aromatic flavour. You can, of course, use less garlic if you like, but some there must be. Almost any root or dried vegetables go well with this dish, either braised or plain boiled, or in a purée.

Slices of shoulder of lamb can be stewed in the same way, allowing 1¾ to 2 hours' cooking time. There should be enough for four.

ÉPAULE D'AGNEAU BOULANGÈRE
SHOULDER OF LAMB BAKED WITH POTATOES

'She was a capital cook; and her method of boning and rolling up a shoulder of mutton like a large Bologna sausage was a mystery which cost me a considerably long post-prandial lucubration to penetrate.'

> GEORGE MUSGRAVE, writing of the Hôtel du Louvre at
> Pont-Audemer in *A Ramble Through Normandy*, 1855

The boning and rolling of a shoulder of lamb or mutton is not really such a mystery as it seemed to George Musgrave; any decent butcher will do it for you, and the system certainly does make the joint very simple to carve. This particular way of cooking a boned shoulder owes its name to the fact that, like the *carbonnade nîmoise*, it was a dish which would be prepared at home and carried to the bakery to be cooked in the oven after the bread was baked. It makes an excellent and quite economical dish for a large household.

The boned shoulder will weigh about 4 lb. Press salt, pepper, chopped fresh thyme or marjoram, and for those who like it, garlic, into the inside of the rolled meat. People who like the flavour of garlic without wishing to find it in the meat might try putting a clove or two under the joint in the pan while it is cooking. In this way it will flavour the gravy and the potatoes, but will scarcely be perceptible in the meat itself. Personally, I find a little garlic with lamb as indispensable as others find mint sauce.

Melt an ounce of butter and a tablespoon of oil in a large pan; brown the seasoned meat in it. Transfer it to an oven dish; put in the garlic and 2 lb. of whole new potatoes. In the same fat fry a sliced onion until it turns golden; pour over 2 teacups of meat *bouillon* or stock, which can have been made from the bones of the joint, cook a minute or so and pour over the meat and potatoes. Cover with a buttered greaseproof paper and the lid of the dish. Cook in a slow oven, Gas No. 3, 330 deg. F., for 2 hours or a little under if you like the meat faintly pink. Before serving salt the potatoes and sprinkle with more fresh herbs. The stock, reduced a little by fast boiling, will serve as a sauce.

POITRINE D'AGNEAU SAINTE MÉNÉHOULD
BRAISED AND GRILLED BREAST OF LAMB

A very economical meat dish which is, or used to be, popular at the midday meal in French restaurants; it is served as a hot hors-d'œuvre rather than as a main course.

Ingredients for four to six helpings are a breast of lamb, a large onion, a bouquet of herbs, 2 carrots, and optionally 3 oz. of a cheap cut of boiling bacon bought in the piece. For the second cooking: mustard, a large egg, 2 oz. of fine breadcrumbs per side of breast of lamb, melted butter.

Arrange the sliced vegetables and the bacon and the bouquet in a shallow baking dish; on top lay the breast of lamb, neatly divided in two by the butcher. Season it, add 2 soup ladles of water (or meat stock if available). Cover with oiled paper or foil and a lid.

Cook in a very slow oven, Gas No. 2, 310 deg. F., for 3 hours. Remove the meat and leave until cool enough to handle. Pour the stock through a strainer into a bowl. Remove the bones from the meat. Most of them will slip out quite easily and the rest can be eased out with the help of a small, sharp knife. Put the meat on a flat dish, cover with paper and a weighted board. When absolutely cold, slice the meat into bias-cut strips about an inch wide. Spread them with mustard. Coat them with egg and then with bread-crumbs. Leave on a wire grid for this coating to dry and set. When the time comes to cook them put them in the grilling-pan, pour over them a little melted butter and put them in a moderate oven until they are quite hot, then place them under the grill, or better still, on one of those iron grill plates which are heated directly over a gas burner or electric hot-plate. Let them brown rapidly, turning them very carefully. Once should be sufficient. The egg and breadcrumb coating should be dry, crisp, and even here and there slightly scorched with the characteristic black grill marks characteristic of French grilled food. Serve them on a hot dish with watercress, wedges of lemon and, if you like, a *sauce tartare* or vinaigrette.

Breast of lamb prepared in this way is a wonderfully cheap delicacy for those prepared to take the trouble, admittedly considerable, of preparing it. It is sometimes called *épigrammes d'agneau*, but *épigrammes* should really include fried lamb cutlets alternating in the dish with the pieces of breast.

CERVELLES D'AGNEAU AU BEURRE NOIR
BRAINS WITH BLACK BUTTER

To prepare the brains for cooking, first put them to steep in plenty of cold water for a minimum of two hours, the water being changed three or four times. After this preliminary steeping, during which most of the blood will have soaked out of the brains, every scrap of the thin skin covering the brains must be removed, and the brains put back to soak in tepid water, so that the rest of the blood will dissolve and seep out.

For 6 sheep's brains, prepare a *court-bouillon* of 1¾ pints of water, a teaspoon of salt, an onion, 2 tablespoons of wine vinegar and a bouquet of herbs, all simmered together for ½ hour. Leave to cool, and strain. In this liquid poach the brains very gently for 15 minutes. Drain them carefully, put them in a hot serving dish, sprinkle them with parsley, and over them pour 3 oz. of butter cooked in a saucepan or small frying-pan until it is turning deep hazel-nut colour; in the same pan quickly boil a couple of tablespoons of vinegar and pour this, too, sizzling over the brains. This is a better way of presenting *cervelles au beurre noir* than the more usual system of having the brains ready cooked, and then frying them.

Calf's brains are prepared in precisely the same way but need 20 to 25 minutes' poaching. They can be sliced into neat scallops for serving.

LE PORC FRAIS
FRESH PORK

While the main defect of the cheaper cuts of beef is their tendency to dryness the very opposite might be said of the second- and third-grade cuts of the pig. An excess of fat on the fore-end, the blade-bone, spare rib and belly of pork makes these cuts appreciably cheaper than leg and loin, which are the prime roasting and grilling pieces. Much depends, of course, on the breed and the feeding of the pig, and in these days of

aversion to fat meat a good deal has been done to ensure the maximum of lean, even on the fat cuts. For instance, belly of pork now tends to contain much more lean in proportion to fat than would have been the case on a similar cut some thirty or forty years ago.

In the old recipes the fat cuts of pork, usually salted, are generally eked out with enormous quantities of dried peas, potatoes, barley, rice and so on, to make thick soups or stews further thickened with quantities of flour—dishes which nowadays we should find horribly stodgy.

The principle on which these recipes were based, however, that of pulses or starchy vegetables absorbing excess fat from the meat and thereby themselves acquiring the lubrication they need to make them palatable, still applies in modern recipes, at least as far as pork is concerned.

Fat belly of pork is also used a good deal in the making of the pâtés and terrines, and for the *rillettes* described in the section on pork products.

Remember also that the rind of fresh pork is valuable for the gelatinous quality it gives to stock; and in French cookery enormous use is made of the rind of either salt or fresh pork to lubricate and enrich beef stews and bean dishes—notably the cassoulet of Toulouse. But use it sparingly, for it is rather rich for those not accustomed to such food.

The prime cuts of pork, from the leg and loin, also offer first-class value, and as will be seen from the recipes in this section, some really beautiful dishes can be made from them, many of these being at their best cold, as is so often the case with a fat meat. And, personally, plebeian though it may be considered, I find a well-seasoned pork chop properly grilled a good deal more interesting than the everlasting and often overrated beefsteak.

CARRÉ DE PORC PROVENÇAL
ROAST LOIN OF PORK WITH WINE AND HERBS

Carré of pork is the part of the loin comprising seven or eight neck cutlets. Half the joint can be cooked if the whole one is too big, but it is so good cold that I usually cook more than is needed for one meal.

Ask the butcher to pare off the rind without removing any of the fat, unless the joint happens to be a very fat one, and to chine the bones. Insert a few little slivers of garlic close to the bones. Rub the meat well with salt. Pour a large glass of white or red wine over it, add 2 or 3 sprigs of fresh thyme and leave to steep for a couple of hours.

Put the meat and its marinade into a baking tin, cover with greased paper or foil and cook, fat side up, with the rind underneath to enrich the sauce, in a moderate oven, Gas No. 4, 355 deg. F., for approximately 1¼ hours. If the liquid dries up, add a little water.

Have ready half a cupful of chopped parsley mixed with fine breadcrumbs. Remove the paper from the meat, and spread the parsley mixture over the fat side, pressing it gently down with a knife. Lower the oven to No. 2, 310 deg. F., and cook for another 35 to 50 minutes, basting the meat now and again with its own liquid so that the breadcrumbs and parsley form a nice golden coating.

Serve with the *pommes mousseline façon provençale*, as described on page 272. Ample for four.

CÔTES DE PORC VALLÉE D'AUGE
GRILLED PORK CHOPS WITH CIDER SAUCE

Chop 3 or 4 shallots very finely with parsley; season with salt and pepper; score 4 pork chops lightly on each side and spread with the shallot mixture. Moisten with melted butter or olive oil, and grill. Have ready a glass of cider heated in a small pan and when the chops are cooked transfer the grilling pan to the top of the stove; pour in the cider; let it bubble over a very fast flame until it has amalgamated with the juices from the meat and formed a sauce, which will take 2 or 3 minutes. If Calvados is available, add a small quantity after the cider has been poured into the pan. It cuts the richness of the pork. Straw potatoes, or a purée, or simply a plain green salad go with the pork chops. For four people.

NOISETTES DE PORC AUX PRUNEAUX

PORK NOISETTES WITH PRUNES AND CREAM SAUCE

This dish, a speciality of Tours, is a sumptuous one, rich and handsome in appearance as well as in its flavours. But it is not one to try out for the first time on guests, unless you can be sure of ten minutes or so uninterrupted in the kitchen while you make the sauce. Neither is the dish exactly a light one, and is perhaps best eaten, as pork dishes are always supposed to be, at midday rather than in the evening.

Ingredients are 6 to 8 *noisettes* cut from the boned and skinned chump end of the loin of pork, each one weighing about 3 oz.; 1 lb. of very fine large juicy prunes (there should be approximately 2 dozen, and the best Californian prunes are perfect for the dish); a half-bottle of wine, which should, by rights, be white Vouvray, a tablespoon of red-currant jelly, approximately $\frac{1}{2}$ pint of thick cream (you may not use it all but it is as well to have this quantity, as I will explain presently); 2 oz. of butter, a little flour, seasonings.

Both the utensil for cooking the pork and the dish to serve it in are important. The first should be a shallow and heavy pan to go on top of the stove, either a sauté pan or the kind of dish in which a whole flat fish is poached; failing this the meat will first have to be browned in a frying-pan and then transferred to an oven dish. The serving dish should be a big oval one, preferably one which can go for a few minutes into the oven without risk.

First, put the prunes to steep in a bowl covered with $\frac{1}{2}$ pint of the wine; this is supposed to be done overnight, but with good prunes a half-day will be sufficient. After which, cover them and put them in a very low oven to cook. They can stay there an hour or more, the longer the better, so long as the wine does not dry up.

Season the pork very well with freshly-milled pepper and salt and sprinkle each *noisette* with flour. Melt the butter in the pan; put in the meat; let it gently take colour on one side and turn it. Keep the heat low, because the butter must not brown. After 10 minutes pour in the remaining 2 tablespoons or so of the white wine. Cover the pan. Cook very gently, covered, on top of the stove, or in the oven if necessary, for approximately 45 minutes to an hour, but the timing must depend upon the quality of the meat. Test it with a skewer to see if it is tender.

When it is nearly ready (but it will not, being pork, come to harm if left a bit longer even after it is tender), pour the juice from the prunes over the meat—this, of course, must be done over direct heat on top of the stove—and keep the prunes themselves hot in the oven. When the juice has bubbled and reduced a little, transfer the meat to the serving dish and keep it hot.

To the sauce in the pan add the red-currant jelly and stir until it has dissolved. Now pour in some of the cream; if the pan is wide enough it will almost instantly start bubbling and thickening; stir it, shake the pan and add a little more cream, and when the sauce is just beginning to get shiny and really thick, pour it over the meat, arrange the prunes all round and serve it quickly. The amount of cream you use depends both on how much juice there was from the prunes and how quickly the sauce has thickened; sometimes it gets too thick too quickly, and a little more cream must be added. In any case there should be enough sauce to cover the meat, but not, of course, the prunes. These are served as they are, not 'boned,' as the French cooks say.

On the whole, I think it is better to drink red wine than white with this dish. And, of course, you do not serve any vegetables with it. Even with light first and last-course dishes, 8 *noisettes* should be enough for four people.

CÔTES DE PORC EN SANGLIER
PORK CHOPS TO TASTE LIKE WILD BOAR

Pork chops can be marinated and cooked in the same way as the leg of pork described on page 364. Cut the rind from 4 thick loin chops, and reduce the quantities of the marinade by half; leave them for 2 to 4 days.

Cook them in the same way for about 45 minutes. Alternatively, shake flour over the chops when you take them from the marinade, brown them lightly in butter; add the heated and strained marinade plus a ¼ pint of good stock, or, in default, water. When the meat is tender, put it on the serving dish and keep it hot while you stir a tablespoon of red-currant jelly into the sauce and thicken it a little by letting it boil, stirring and lifting it so that it does not stick. Pour it over the meat, and serve with stewed celery (page 248) or prunes cooked as in the foregoing recipe for *noisettes de porc aux pruneaux*, or a potato purée.

This is a useful recipe to know for those occasions when it may be necessary to buy one's meat in advance or, alternatively, when one has a small quantity of wine to use up for cooking.

TERRINÉE DE PORC
PORK CHOPS BAKED WITH POTATOES

4 pork chops, 1½ lb. of potatoes, a small glass of white wine, 1 onion, 2 or 3 cloves of garlic, a few juniper berries, parsley, 4 oz. of ham or bacon.

Peel the potatoes and slice them evenly and very thinly. Arrange half of them, and half the sliced onion, in an earthenware casserole.

Near the bone of each pork chop put a small clove of garlic and a couple of juniper berries. Brown them on each side in a little pork dripping. Put them on top of the potatoes. Cover them with the remaining half of the potatoes and onion; season with salt and pepper. Cover with the bacon or ham in slices. Pour over the white wine. Put two or three layers of paper over the pot, then the lid. Cook in a very slow oven for about 3 hours. Before serving, pour off some of the abundant fat which will have come out of the meat, and garnish the dish with a little parsley. This is heavy, rustic food, but the flavour is delicious, and for lunch on a cold day it is a fine dish for three or four hungry people.

Cider can be used instead of wine.

CUISSOT DE PORC FRAIS EN SANGLIER
LEG OF PORK MARINATED IN WINE

This is a method of making domestic pig taste like wild boar. For those who happen to like this taste, it is remarkably successful. I don't say it is a dish which one would want to eat very often but it is interesting to try once in a way, and also useful for those who have their own pigs and would like to vary the cooking of their pork from time to time.

For a half leg of fresh pork, weighing between 5 and 6 lb., the ingredients for the marinade are as follows: ½ pint of red wine, 4 tablespoons of vinegar, 2 carrots, 1 onion, 2 shallots, 2 cloves of garlic, 3 bayleaves, half a dozen or so parsley stalks, several sprigs each of wild thyme and marjoram, a dozen whole peppercorns, a half-dozen juniper berries, 2 teaspoons of salt.

Slice the carrots, onions and shallots, put all the ingredients into a saucepan, bring to the boil and simmer 5 minutes. Leave to cool.

Have the skin removed from the meat, which can be either boned or not, as you please; it is, of course, easier to deal with if it is boned, for a half leg is always an awkward piece to carve. Also score the fat lightly across the top, so that the marinade has more chance to sink in. Put the meat in a deep china bowl and pour the cooled marinade over it. Leave it to steep for 4 days, turning it once a day in the liquid.

Make a pint or so of well-seasoned stock from the skin of the pork, plus the bones if the meat has been boned, or some veal bones if it has not, vegetables and herbs. Strain, cool and remove the fat. To cook the meat you will need 2 tablespoons of olive oil or pork lard, 2 tablespoons of flour, the stock and the strained marinade.

Take the meat out of the marinade, remove any pieces of vegetables and herbs which may be adhering to it, wipe it dry, and let it brown on both sides in a heavy braising pan in which the oil or lard has been heated. Take it out of the pan. Bring the marinade, with all its vegetables, to the boil in a separate saucepan. Stir the flour into the fat in the pan; gradually add the marinade through a strainer; stir until it is smooth; add sufficient of the prepared stock to make the sauce about the consistency of a thin béchamel. Put back the meat. Cover the pan. Transfer to a low oven, Gas No. 3, 330 deg. F., and cook for 2½ to 3 hours, by which time the pork should be quite tender and coming away from the bone. Transfer it to a hot serving dish. Leave the sauce to settle for a few minutes, then pour off as much of the excess fat as possible. Pour the rest of the sauce into a small saucepan, let it come to the boil and reduce a little. Taste for seasoning. Serve it separately in a sauce-boat.

The accompanying vegetable can be a very creamy purée of chestnuts, lentils, or celeriac and potatoes, into which is incorporated a little of the sauce from the meat. Red-currant jelly can also be served with it. There should be enough for about ten people, but the dish is also excellent cold.

At one time such dishes as this were often made in imitation of wild boar, while haunches of mutton would be treated in similar ways to imitate venison. Probably the method was evolved as much to preserve meat when there were no refrigerators as to gratify a desire for game out of season.

ENCHAUD DE PORC À LA PÉRIGOURDINE
LOIN OF PORK STUFFED WITH TRUFFLES

For those who like pork, this is one of the loveliest dishes in the whole repertoire of south-western French cookery. It cannot very often be made in England in its full beauty because the pork should be studded with black truffles. Occasionally, though, when one feels like a little extra extravagance, even quite a small tin of truffles is sufficient to give the right flavour to the meat. It is one of the dishes which I like to make at Christmas as an alternative to the turkey, or to serve as a cold dish for a large lunch party. It is shown in the drawing on page 360.

Have a fine piece, about 4 lb. or more, of loin of pork, boned and with the rind removed. Lay the meat on a board, salt and pepper it, cut 2 or 3 truffles into thick little pieces and lay them at intervals along the meat. Add a few little spikes of garlic and some salt and pepper as well. Roll the meat up and tie it round with string so that it is the shape of a long, narrow bolster. Put in a baking dish with the bones, the rind cut into strips and all the trimmings. Let it cook about 30 minutes in a low oven, Gas No. 3, 330 deg. F. When the meat has turned golden, pour in about a pint of clear hot meat stock or $\frac{3}{4}$ pint of water and $\frac{1}{4}$ pint of white wine. plus the liquid from the tin of truffles. Now cover the dish and leave the meat to cook another 2 to $2\frac{1}{2}$ hours.

Pour off the sauce and remove the fat when it has set. Chop the jelly which remains beneath the fat and arrange it round the cold pork in the serving dish. Enough for about ten people.

The beautifully flavoured fat from this pork dish can be spread on slices of toasted French bread and makes a treat for the children at tea-time, as used to be our own toast and beef dripping.

Without the truffles, this pork dish is sometimes cooked at the time of the grape harvest, and La Mazille, author of *La Bonne Cuisine en Périgord*, says that slices of bread spread with the dripping and a piece of the cold pork topped with a pickled gherkin are distributed to the harvesters for their collation.

Remember, also, that this beautifully flavoured pork dripping is a wonderful fat in which to fry bread or little whole potatoes.

ROULADE DE PORC À LA GELÉE
ROLLED LEG OF PORK IN JELLY

This is really a more everyday version of the *enchaud de porc* described above.

Have a half leg of pork weighing about 5 lb. boned, the rind removed, and tied into a fat sausage shape.

Make two rows of incisions along the meat and into these press chopped fresh herbs and, if you like, little spikes of garlic, rolled in pepper and salt. Put the meat in a roasting pan with the bones, trimmings, skin cut into strips, and a pig's foot split in two. Add water to come about half-way up the meat; cover the pan. Put in a slow oven, Gas No. 3, 330 deg. F., and cook for about $3\frac{1}{4}$ hours. Remove the meat; strain the liquid into a bowl. Leave both to cool.

Next day remove the fat from the stock, which should have set to a jelly; to serve the meat, remove string, carve into thin slices; turn out the jellied stock; chop it finely and arrange round the meat.

Serve with a potato salad, or a straightforward green salad. There should be enough for ten people.

If you happen to have a little white wine to spare, use it instead of a proportion of water.

COCHON DE LAIT RÔTI AU FOUR
ROAST SUCKING PIG

For the stuffing for a sucking pig weighing within the region of 12 lb., mix together ½ lb. of fine dry breadcrumbs, a big bunch of parsley (about 2 oz.) finely chopped with 2 or 3 shallots, and a clove or two of garlic; add the grated peel of a whole large lemon and of 1 orange; add the juices of both. Mix in 6 oz. of softened butter, about a teaspoon of salt, plenty of freshly-milled pepper and a little grated nutmeg. Finally stir in 3 whole eggs well beaten. Taste to see if there is sufficient lemon, for sucking pig is a rich meat and the stuffing for it should provide a mildly acid counteracting flavour; for this reason sausage meat, chestnuts, prunes, and other such rather cloying ingredients are not so suitable for stuffings as the simple *fines herbes* and lemon mixture.

Having stuffed your pig, give it a generous coating of olive oil, and if possible cook it, lying on its side, on a rack placed in the baking dish so that the underside does not stew in its own juices. Put it in a moderate, preheated oven at Gas No. 4, 350 deg. F., for 2 to 2½ hours altogether. From time to time baste it with its own juices, or with more olive oil, and at half-time turn the animal over with great care so as not to damage the crackling. When it is ready to serve transfer it to a hot dish and keep it in a low oven while you pour off from the baking tin as much as possible of the fat, transferring the gravy to a small pan. To this add a little glass of white wine and, if you have it, an equal quantity of clear veal or beef stock. Give it a quick boil and serve it separately.

Many modern domestic ovens are too small to take a whole sucking pig, although the length of the animal depends, of course, upon the breed of the pig. Should it be found that the piglet has to be cooked in two pieces, the best plan is to get the butcher to divide it in two and to roast the whole of the back and the hindquarters, the head and neck being kept for a separate dish such as the galantine described on page 222. In this case about half the quantities of stuffing will be sufficient.

ROGNONS DE PORC AU VIN BLANC
PIG'S KIDNEYS IN WHITE WINE

Pig's kidneys are cheaper than those of lamb or veal and are quite good provided they are given a preliminary soaking and blanching to rid them of their rather acrid smell.

Remove the skin of 2 kidneys, therefore, and soak them in warm salted water for a couple of hours. Cut them transversally in slices about

½ inch thick. Put them in a saucepan covered with cold water and bring slowly to the boil. Let the water boil not more than a minute and then drain it off. In a clean frying-pan melt an ounce of butter for 2 kidneys. Add a little fat bacon cut in very small dice—2 small rashers is enough. Put in the kidneys. Let them cook gently for a minute. Add 3 or 4 mushrooms cut in quarters, then a small glass, about 4 tablespoons, of white wine. Let it bubble. Turn the flame low, put in a little bouquet of parsley, bayleaf and thyme, season with salt and pepper, add 4 tablespoons of good meat stock and simmer gently with the cover on the pan for 10 to 15 minutes. Serve sprinkled with parsley and accompanied by little triangles of bread fried in butter, or a *mousseline* of potatoes (page 272). Enough for two.

If it happens to be more convenient, use red wine, vermouth or cider instead of white wine for this dish.

LE VEAU

VEAL

One of the most difficult cuts of meat to get a butcher to supply in perfection is an escalope of veal. It should be cut on the bias, in clean,

even slices from the topside of the leg of veal, or from the boned loin or
fillet without seam, gristle or skin, and weighing a little over 3 oz. each.
They should be thin enough not to need the whacking out with a heavy
bat with which the majority of butchers finally remove all life and hope
from the clumsily hacked lumps of meat which they sell as escalopes.
Now, before any of my good and kind friends among London's butchers
rush at me with their steak-beaters, let me add that I am quite well aware
that this question of cutting veal escalopes is deeply involved with the
economics of butchering. Very briefly, the situation is that the English
method of cutting up a leg of veal, crosswise into joints for roasting,
precludes the possibility of cutting proper escalopes, because of the seams
which run through the meat, whereas the Continental method of
separating the leg, lengthways as it were, into the several joints into
which it naturally falls produces at least four compact, self-contained
cuts, each of which can be used whole as a roasting joint or from which
escalopes can be cut. But even this method is still wasteful, because, if
the escalopes are properly cut on the bias, there will always be end-pieces
too small to do anything much with and which therefore have to be
sold with various other bits and pieces as 'pie veal' or mince, at a much
reduced price. Italian housewives are in the habit of buying these
oddments from their butchers and making all sorts of little dishes out of
them, and since Italian butchers know that they have a sale for these
pieces they are always willing to cut their escalopes in the proper way.
In France this can be almost as much of a struggle as it is here, but it is a
struggle in which the housewife usually wins, for she knows the penalties
of bad cutting.

What has happened here in England is that our demand for cuts of
meat which are rapidly prepared and cooked has run ahead of our
knowledge of the material with which we are dealing, and the butchers
are really no more to blame than the customers who cheerfully pay
fantastic prices for meat so ill-cut that however thin and flat it appears
after its beating will buckle back to its original shape as soon as it comes
into contact with the heat, will consequently cook unevenly and present
a most lamentable appearance when it comes to table. To attempt to
circumvent this difficulty by having slices of meat cut $\frac{1}{2}$ inch thick and
weighing in the region of $\frac{1}{2}$ lb., as I have seen done in restaurants, is
again a misunderstanding of the raw material, for these leg cuts of veal
are too dry and fatless to be presented like a steak, and although they
look nice are stodgy when you come to eat them.

It is for this reason that the French system of larding or piquéing
with pork fat thick cuts of veal, such as the *fricandeau*, a cushion-shaped
piece from the leg, or the little steaks called *grenadins*, also from a leg

cut, has arisen. Such cuts are not, of course, for frying-pan cookery, and if frying-pan cookery you must have then it seems to me more satisfactory to call a truce with your butcher over the sore point of escalopes and to buy instead, if he will provide it, a solid piece of that little joint from the leg which is rather the shape of a sausage, which corresponds to the roll of the silverside or *gîte à la noix* in beef, and which is sometimes, although incorrectly, called the fillet. From this little joint it is easy to cut your own slices of meat into whatever thicknesses you please. Cut very thin and slightly flattened out they constitute the dish which the Italians call *scaloppine* or *frittura piccata*, miniature escalopes in fact, which are cooked in a minute or two. Cut about $\frac{1}{2}$ inch thick, like minuscule fillet steaks, they become *médaillons*, which after a preliminary cooking on each side in butter are simmered gently for about 25 minutes. In either case the garnish and sauces, the cream, wine, mushrooms and so on given in recipes for escalopes can be adapted to these cuts, so long as the cooking times are adjusted.

Loin chops also offer good value; they are not very satisfactory for grilling, but once seized on each side and some sort of moistening in the way of stock or wine added, they can be transferred to the oven and thereafter more or less look after themselves.

Veal roasts such as the joints known to French butchers as the *noix*, the *sous-noix*, the *noix-patissière* (which are those which provide escalopes), the above-mentioned fillet, the *longe* or *rognonnade*, which is the equivalent of a saddle including the kidneys, but in the case of veal usually boned out, the *filet* proper which comes from the middle and back loin, the *carré*, which is the row of best end of neck cutlets on the bone, are all luxury cuts which contain plenty of good tender meat but which need sauces to enhance the somewhat insipid flavour, although the loin and the best end of neck or *carré* are much less dry than the leg cuts. *Quasi de veau*, rump end of loin, is a favourite French cut for a slow roast or a daube, and boned and rolled shoulder is another good slow-cooked oven dish.

Reasonable bargains for anyone not deterred by the necessity for lengthy cooking are shin (to my mind one of the best of all veal cuts), rolled and stuffed breast, and the strips of cartilaginous meat cut from between the end of the ribs next the flank which are called *tendrons* or sometimes *côtelettes parisiennes*.

Curiously enough, French cookery does not seem to provide any equivalent of the best of all cheap veal dishes, the Lombard *ossi buchi*, shin of very young veal sawn into short chunks and stewed with tomato and white wine, although there is a Provençal dish called *aïllade de jarret de veau* in which the shin meat is cut from the bone in solid strips, and stewed with tomato, which seems to have a natural affinity with veal, with the addition of garlic and parsley. *Blanquette de veau*, made alternatively from a mixture of breast and shoulder, or shoulder only, is famous, but to my taste this dish with its creamy white sauce is rather insipid, and I find that the same cuts stewed in the Marengo fashion, with oil, tomato and white wine, have a good deal more character.

In the recipes in this section I have tried to show methods, some of them purely local, of cooking veal which are not normally to be found in cookery books; and once one has understood the type of meat with which one is dealing it is very easy to devise one's own recipes, for veal is a meat which makes a good background for quite a variety of flavourings and sauces.

Whatever one may feel about the desirability or otherwise of the expensive cuts and those roasts with little clumps of vegetables called *jardinière, printanière* and the rest which become so monotonous on Continental hotel menus, particularly in Switzerland, it must be remembered that veal is an immensely useful, indeed almost essential ingredient in good cookery. This is mainly because of the gelatinous quality but neutral flavour imparted to stocks and broths and sauces by the bones, trimmings, feet, shin and head; and the close texture and mild flavour of lean, minced veal makes it an indispensable ingredient in numbers of pies and pâtés, galantines, and stuffings for game and poultry.

NOIX DE VEAU À L'ALSACIENNE
VEAL IN WHITE WINE JELLY

A perfect summer dish, which owes its characteristic flavour to the white Alsatian wine in which the meat is cooked.

Ingredients are a *noix* of veal, the cut approximating to the topside of the leg in beef, weighing 2½ to 3 lb., trimmed of all fat and tied into a sausage shape; a large onion and a large carrot, 2 thickish rashers of very fat smoked bacon, a wine-glass of dry white Alsatian wine (Hugels Flambeau d'Alsace is ideal) and approximately the same quantity of clear, well-flavoured stock made from shin of veal so that it will set when the dish is cold; parsley and tarragon; butter.

Cut each rasher of bacon into three strips lengthwise; roll these in salt and pepper; if you have no larding needle make three deep incisions lengthwise in the meat from both ends, and push the strips as far in as possible with a knife, so that, working from both ends, the meat will be larded right through. Cut the carrot into small cubes and chop the onion. In an oval earthenware or iron pot in which the meat will just about fit, melt a good lump of butter. Let the vegetables stew in this until they start to turn golden. Put in the veal and let it brown a little. Heat the wine and pour it over. Let it bubble and reduce a little. Add a good soup ladle of the stock. Cover the pot with foil or greaseproof paper, then the lid. Put in a slow oven, Gas No. 2, 310 deg. F., and cook for 2 hours or a little over. Remove the meat and the vegetables and leave them to cool. Pour the juice into another bowl and leave it to set, so that the fat can be easily removed. Heat the jelly in a saucepan until just melted, stir in a tablespoon each of very finely chopped tarragon and parsley, and taste for seasoning. Having cut the string from the meat and put it in a shallow bowl with the onions and carrot round it, pour the liquefied jelly over it. There will not be enough jelly to cover it but just sufficient to make a little sauce. Natural aspic jelly does not keep well in hot weather so it is useless to make a great deal. If preferred the jelly can be clarified by the usual process, with white of egg, the chopped herbs naturally being added afterwards, but although it will look more elegant, it will lose some of its flavour, and also diminish somewhat in volume. There should be plenty of meat for six people.

A salad of lettuce hearts with a mild dressing is the best accompaniment. And if the butcher cannot cut a *noix* of veal, a boned and rolled shoulder can be used.

DAUBE DE VEAU À L'ESTRAGON

VEAL STEWED WITH WHITE WINE AND TARRAGON

Buy about 3 lb. of the chump end of loin of veal (*quasi de veau* in French butchers' terms) and have it boned and tied in a sausage shape. The other ingredients are a calf's foot, split in two, a wine-glass of white wine and a small glass of brandy if possible, 2 tomatoes, an onion, 1 lb. of carrots, garlic and tarragon. If possible buy also from the butcher half a dozen strips of pork rind, which, as I have already explained in several recipes, are much used in these sort of dishes to give an extra gelatinous quality to the sauce.

Spike the meat with little pieces of garlic rolled in salt, pepper and chopped tarragon. Brown it in a mixture of oil and pork dripping; put it in an earthen or iron pot lined with the strips of pork rind. Add the sliced onion, also browned in dripping, 2 carrots, the tomatoes cut in half, a sprig of tarragon and the calf's foot. Salt and pepper. Pour over the brandy and the wine and an equal quantity of water. Cover with two layers of greaseproof paper and the lid. Set in a low oven, Gas No. 2,

310 deg. F., and leave for at least 3 hours until the veal is absolutely tender.

Take out the meat and leave it to cool before removing the string. Put it in a deep dish, surround it with the whole carrots cooked separately (cooked in the daube they give too strong a carroty flavour to the sauce) and cool the strained sauce separately. When it has set to a jelly next day remove all traces of fat, melt it sufficiently to pour over the veal and leave to set again, incorporating a few fresh tarragon leaves for decoration. English veal does very well for this dish and there should be enough for six.

A plain lettuce and hard-boiled egg salad goes well with it.

ESCALOPES DE VEAU CAUCHOISE
ESCALOPES OF VEAL WITH CREAM, CALVADOS AND APPLE

I usually avoid escalopes of veal in French provincial restaurants, partly because there are usually more interesting dishes on the menu and partly because it seems to me that the French have a hard job of it to beat the Italian methods of combining veal with Parma ham and Parma cheese, but I was tempted by the description of this dish at the Beffroy restaurant in Rouen, and it proved excellent and original.

Quantities for two people, apart from two fine escalopes, cut slightly on the bias from the wide part of the leg and without seams, but not beaten out too flat, are half a sweet apple, ¼ pint of thick cream, butter, seasonings, Calvados.

Cut the peeled half apple into little cubes; season the meat plentifully with salt, pepper and lemon juice. Melt about 1½ oz. of butter in a thick frying-pan. When it starts to foam, put in the meat, let it take colour rapidly on each side; add the apple cubes. Heat a liqueur glass (about 2 tablespoons) of Calvados in a little pan; set light to it. Pour it flaming over the meat, at the same time turning up the heat under the pan. Rotate the pan until the flames die down. Pour in the cream. Lower the heat. Cook gently another 2 minutes or so, stirring the sauce and scraping up the juices all the time. As soon as the cream has thickened, transfer the meat to the serving dish, arrange the apple cubes on top of each escalope and pour the sauce all round.

Cognac, Armagnac, *marc*, or even whisky, which, curiously enough, is the best substitute, can be used instead of Calvados, but then, of course, it is no longer quite the dish of the Pays de Caux.

Although triangles of bread fried in butter would not be out of place as a garnish, vegetables should be kept until afterwards, as always with these creamy dishes, for one doesn't want them floating about the plate and getting mixed up with the sauce. Also, however tempted one may be to cook the whole apple just for the sake of using it up, it would be a mistake to do so. It is just that little hint of a sweet taste and contrasting texture that gives the dish its originality. More would be heavy-handed.

ESCALOPES À LA SAVOYARDE (1)

ESCALOPES OF VEAL WITH VERMOUTH AND CREAM SAUCE

For two escalopes cut from the topside or thick flank of veal, each weighing approximately $3\frac{1}{2}$ oz., the other ingredients are 1 oz. of butter, $\frac{1}{4}$ pint of thick cream, 4 or 5 tablespoons of dry white vermouth (in the Savoie they use the local Chambéry vermouth), and seasonings.

Season your escalopes with salt, pepper and lemon juice. Cook them rapidly on each side in the foaming butter; pour in the vermouth; let it bubble. Moderate the heat. Add the cream. Shake the pan so that the cream and wine amalgamate; now lower the heat again and simmer another 3 or 4 minutes, until the cream has thickened.

ESCALOPES À LA SAVOYARDE (2)

ESCALOPES OF VEAL WITH VERMOUTH AND CREAM SAUCE

Miniature escalopes cut either from the *filet mignon* or from the narrow end of one of the larger leg cuts can be treated in the same way. Allow two to four per person according to size (these miniature escalopes are not necessarily cheaper than the large ones, but as I have already explained in the introductory note they often represent better value). Instead of partially lowering the heat when the cream is added, leave it as high as possible. The cream will start to thicken almost immediately. Shake the pan, spooning the cream up and over the meat, and serve the minute the sauce is thick. It comes out a beautiful pale coffee colour.

It is always difficult to decide what vegetables, if any, should go with these creamy veal dishes. On the whole it is best simply to serve a few little croûtons fried in butter, or some small plain boiled potatoes as a garnish, and to keep green vegetables for a separate course.

CÔTES DE VEAU À L'ARDENNAISE

VEAL CHOPS BAKED IN THE OVEN

Have four very thick veal chops cut from the loin, each weighing about 6 oz., or, better still, get slices weighing about 4 oz. each from the boned and rolled loin; prepare a seasoning of a dozen dried and crushed juniper berries, salt, freshly-milled black pepper, and dried marjoram or thyme; squeeze lemon juice over the meat and then rub the seasoning well in.

Chop a small onion and dice 3 carrots; melt a good lump of butter in a shallow flame-proof dish; put in your onion and carrots and when they start to turn pale golden add the meat; let it brown lightly on each side; pour in a small glass of white wine or vermouth; let it bubble and reduce; add the same quantity of water; on top of each chop or slice of veal place a dessertspoon of chopped cooked ham; cover with a mixture of breadcrumbs and chopped parsley; put a little piece of butter on top of each piece of meat; transfer the dish to a low oven, Gas No. 2, 310 deg. F., and cook uncovered for 1¼ hours.

Serve bubbling hot in the same dish. The juice should be somewhat reduced, the meat tender and juicy, the top nicely browned. A few potatoes go well with it. Enough for four.

If you have no suitable flame-proof dish, the preliminary cooking can be done in a frying-pan, the sauce and meat being transferred to a baking dish before the addition of the ham and breadcrumbs.

BRÉZOLLES LORRAINES

SLICED VEAL BAKED IN THE OVEN

Brézolles are slices of veal cut from that inside part of the leg known as the *noix patissière*, or the *rouelle*, although this latter term may also mean slices from the knuckle end of the leg, cut right across with the bone.

The brézolles should be cut rather thicker than escalopes, should weigh 3 to 4 oz. each and should not be flattened out. For two of these slices the other ingredients are a shallot, a slice of cooked ham, a little parsley, butter, a very little white wine, breadcrumbs.

In a frying-pan heat a good lump of butter. Into this put your shallot and parsley, both finely chopped. Let them cook a few seconds, then add the chopped ham. After another few moments put in your slices of meat, previously seasoned. Let them take colour on each side. Pour in 2 or 3 tablespoons of white wine or vermouth and let it bubble. Then lower the heat and cover the pan for 2 minutes. Transfer the meat and sauce to a lightly buttered, shallow, fireproof serving dish. Strew the meat with fine breadcrumbs and add a few small nuts of butter. Finish cooking for 20 to 25 minutes, uncovered, in a moderate oven.

ÉPAULE DE VEAU BOULANGÈRE

SHOULDER OF VEAL BAKED WITH POTATOES

Rub the boned and rolled shoulder with salt, pepper and chopped herbs. Heat 1 oz. of dripping or butter in a roasting tin or earthenware baking dish. Put in the meat; let it cook at the top of a hot oven for 10 minutes. Now add 2½ to 3 lb. of potatoes, peeled and sliced about ⅛ inch thick, and arranged underneath and all round the joint. Season with a little salt; if liked put 2 whole cloves of garlic underneath the joint to flavour both potatoes and meat. Add a soup ladle of meat stock or water. Cover with greased aluminium foil and a lid, or another roasting tin inverted. Cook in the centre of the oven at Gas No. 3, 330 deg. F., for just under 2 hours. During the last 15 minutes remove the lid, the foil and the protective slice of fat which has been tied round the meat by the butcher, strew the top surface with breadcrumbs and leave the dish uncovered so that the top will brown.

Before serving ladle off some of the excess liquid, and let the meat stand a few minutes before carving. Enough for eight people. Veal cooked by this method but without the potatoes is also excellent cold.

MÉDAILLONS DE VEAU AU VIN BLANC

MINIATURE VEAL STEAKS WITH WHITE WINE

For four *médaillons* (see page 370) peel 16 very small pickling onions; cook these gently in a frying-pan in a mixture of 1 oz. of butter and a little olive oil to prevent burning. When golden, remove the onions and keep warm. Slightly flatten out the *médaillons*, season with salt and pepper; brown them lightly on both sides in the butter from the onions. Pour a good glass of white wine into the pan, let it bubble a few moments, turn the flame low; return the onions to the pan with the meat, add 4 oz. diced lean cooked ham. Cover the pan and simmer very gently about 20 minutes. Serve on a hot dish, with the sauce from the pan poured round. Enough for four. These little cuts of veal (shown in the drawing on page 368) are, in kitchen terms, alternatively called *noisettes*; when flattened out to an oval shape and *piquéd* all over with pork lard to resemble a miniature *fricandeau* they become *grenadins*.

PAUPIETTES DE VEAU BOURBONNAISE

STUFFED ESCALOPES OF VEAL

Paupiettes, or *alouettes sans tête*, are to be found everywhere in France and, indeed, in Belgium and Italy as well, but every cook has a different recipe for them.

They are primarily designed to use up small quantities of cooked meat which go into the stuffing, although this does not by any means imply a makeshift dish; with good veal and a nicely blended and seasoned stuffing they often make a 'speciality of the house' in France, and at restaurants there is a great demand for them when the *patron's* recipe is known to be a good one.

For this particular version the ingredients are 6 slices of veal cut as for small escalopes, beaten out thin, and weighing between 2 and 3 oz. each. For the stuffing about 2 oz. of unsmoked bacon and the same quantity of cold boiled beef or chicken or a mixture of both, parsley, a small clove of garlic or a shallot, 2 tablespoons of fine breadcrumbs, 1 egg, seasoning, a few drops of cognac if possible. To cook the paupiettes, 1 oz. of butter, a small glass of red or white wine, a small onion, a little stock or broth.

Chop all the ingredients for the stuffing quite small (mincing them makes too close-textured a mixture), season with salt and pepper, add the breadcrumbs, the beaten egg and the cognac. There should be enough stuffing to fill a teacup, closely packed. Spread the veal slices out flat; season them with salt, pepper and lemon juice. Divide the stuffing into six portions and put one on each slice of veal. Roll them up, tuck in the ends to prevent the stuffing escaping, tie each round with two circles of string. In a sauté pan melt the butter, put in the finely-sliced onion; as soon as it turns very pale yellow put in the paupiettes; leave them over a moderate flame a minute or two; pour over the wine, let it bubble, then add the stock. Transfer the dish to the oven, and cook gently, uncovered, for just under an hour, Gas No. 3, 330 deg. F. The sauce should be fairly reduced and does not need any thickening. Simply transfer the paupiettes, minus their string, to a heated serving dish and pour the sauce over them; add a very little chopped parsley. Enough for three.

The same dish can be made with beef (very thin slices of topside or skirt steak) and, of course, the stuffing can be varied according to what is available, but don't resort to sausage meat, which makes too heavy a stuffing. If you like, a very light purée of potatoes can go with the *paupiettes*, or triangles of fried bread.

The preliminary preparation of onions in butter which forms the basis of the sauce is, I think, particular to this recipe from a Bourbonnais cook.

POITRINE DE VEAU FARCIE AUX OLIVES
BREAST OF VEAL STUFFED WITH OLIVES

For a piece of breast of veal weighing about 4 lb. before boning, the ingredients for the stuffing are ¼ lb. of minced lean pork, a thick slice of white bread without the crust, a little milk, 8 to 10 stoned black olives, a big bunch of parsley, a clove or two of garlic, basil, pepper, nutmeg and 1 egg. Other ingredients are an onion, 2 tomatoes, 1 teacup each of white wine and water or alternatively 2 teacups of good meat broth, a little olive oil.

Soak the bread in milk until it is soft, then squeeze it dry. Chop it together with the garlic and parsley and a leaf or two of basil, either fresh or dried; add the minced pork and the roughly-chopped black olives. Season with freshly-milled pepper and grated nutmeg. Add the well-beaten egg. Spread this stuffing over the boned and flattened out breast of veal. Roll it up into a large sausage and tie securely.

Heat 2 tablespoons of olive oil in a wide shallow pan or baking dish. In this cook the sliced onion until it is pale yellow, adding some sliced garlic if you like. Put in the meat and let it brown very lightly. Add the skinned and chopped tomatoes. Pour over the wine and let it reduce a little. Add the water, a little salt and the bones from the meat. Cover with oiled paper or foil, and the lid. Transfer to a low oven, Gas No. 3, 330 deg. F., and cook for about 3 hours.

Personally, I think this dish is best eaten cold, and is certainly more economical that way. Cut in the finest possible slices and served with a salad it should be enough for three meals for four people. The sauce should be strained and left to set to a jelly. Remove the fat from the top and put the chopped jelly round the meat. This dish should not cost more than ten shillings,[1] including the wine and the ingredients for the stuffing, and provides a good demonstration of how a little extra trouble with a cheap cut of meat is amply repaid.

TENDRONS DE VEAU MARENGO
BREAST OF VEAL STEWED WITH TOMATOES

The Marengo fashion of cooking veal calls for ingredients and methods very similar to those of the famous Milanese *ossi buchi*. Allow two tendrons, or *côtelettes parisiennes*; cut as explained on page 370 (they are also shown, in the dish, in the drawing on page 368), weighing about 6 oz. each, for each person. A sliced onion and a clove of garlic are first gently cooked in 2 tablespoons of olive oil, then removed while the meat is browned on each side. For four tendrons a coffee-cupful of white wine and 2 tablespoons of stock are then added, plus 1 lb. of tomatoes chopped but unskinned, the onion and garlic returned to the pan, seasonings and a bouquet put in, the pan covered and the whole cooked 1½ to 2 hours.

[1] Those were 1960 prices. Now (1965) it will cost about three shillings more.

The meat is then kept hot in the serving dish while the sauce is sieved and reheated. Pour it round the meat and serve very hot.

The dish is much improved by an unorthodox addition of finely-chopped parsley, lemon peel and garlic sprinkled over it before serving. Rice can be served with it, although small glazed onions, mushrooms and triangles of bread fried in oil are the traditional garnishes. Tendrons must always be very well cooked indeed; the meat and sauce should have that slightly sticky quality characteristic of stewed veal.

AÏLLADE DE JARRET DE VEAU
SHIN OF VEAL STEWED WITH TOMATOES AND GARLIC

For four people buy 1½ lb. of shin of veal cut lengthways from the bone in strips weighing about 3 oz. each. First prepare a sauce from ½ lb. of skinned and chopped tomatoes stewed down to a pulp without the addition of any other liquid, but well seasoned with salt, pepper, sugar and dried basil or marjoram. Now brown the veal in a good tablespoon of meat dripping or olive oil; season it, add the tomato sauce and a little under ¼ pint of meat stock. Simmer uncovered on top of the stove for 15 minutes, then put in a very low oven for an hour, with the lid on the pan. When the veal is tender, strew on the top 3 tablespoons of breadcrumbs mixed with a finely-chopped clove of garlic, a scrap of lemon peel and a tablespoon of parsley. Leave uncovered in the oven for another 10 to 15 minutes. There should be only a small amount of thickish sauce, and, as in the preceding recipe, the meat should have that sticky quality peculiar to stewed veal.

Serve with rice.

VEAU SAUMONÉ ANGOÛMOIS
SALTED AND MARINATED LEG OF VEAL

Buy a piece of boned and rolled leg of veal weighing 2½ to 3 lb. Rub the meat all over with a mixture of 1 large tablespoon of coarse salt and half a teaspoon of saltpetre (to be bought from the chemist) which will give the finished dish a good pink colour. Put it in a bowl or earthenware casserole and add 3 sliced onions, 2 bayleaves, half a dozen each of peppercorns and juniper berries, half a lemon cut in slices, a branch of thyme and tarragon if possible, and pour over about half a tumbler of wine vinegar. Cover the bowl, and leave for 4 days, turning the meat every day. To cook it, put it in a saucepan with its brine, and all the onions, herbs, etc., cover with cold water and simmer, covered, extremely gently for 4 hours. Take the meat from the pan, put it in a bowl, cover with paper and a plate and weight it.

Next day it can be carved into slices as thin as ham. The original dish is served with two sauces, a thick paste of $\frac{1}{4}$ lb. anchovy fillets pounded with capers, shallots and parsley, which is spread over the meat, and a mayonnaise served separately. The powerful anchovy flavour would be too much for most people and a better solution is a thick *ravigote* sauce compounded of chopped parsley, tarragon, capers, a little shallot, 3 or 4 anchovy fillets, a scrap of lemon peel, olive oil and lemon juice. This may be either spread over the meat or served separately.

With a cucumber salad *veau saumoné* makes a good and original cold supper dish which will be enough for six people. It should, according to the old recipe, be decorated with bunches of parsley and nasturtium flowers.

If needed for a larger party, the amount can of course be doubled, and extra cooking time allowed.

On no account throw away the liquid in which the meat was cooked; with its somewhat acid flavour it makes the basis of an excellent beetroot consommé. Strain off the onions, herbs, etc., skim the fat, and into the liquid put about 1 lb. of peeled, diced, raw beetroots. Simmer gently for about 30 minutes, strain without pressing the beetroots, and the result is a beautifully flavoured deep red consommé which can be served hot or cold.

FOIE DE VEAU CAMPAGNARDE

CALF'S LIVER WITH HERBS AND MUSHROOMS

A very simple, excellent, but not generally known way of serving liver. For two people you need 4 to 6 thin and evenly cut slices of calf's liver, 4 medium-sized mushrooms and a little parsley, some chives and tarragon when available, a little piece of shallot or garlic, flour and seasonings, oil.

Chop the cleaned mushrooms very finely with the parsley, the shallot or garlic and the herbs.

Season the liver; dust it with flour. Heat about 1 oz. of butter in a frying-pan with a teaspoon of olive oil. Let the liver take colour quickly on each side, put in the herb and mushroom mixture and cook another 3 minutes or so over a gentle flame, shaking the pan so that the liver does not stick. Turn into a hot serving dish; squeeze over a little lemon.

The mushroom and herb mixture is the old-fashioned version of *fines herbes*.

Lamb's liver can be cooked in the same way.

RIS DE VEAU

VEAL SWEETBREADS

Veal sweetbreads are considered a great delicacy but, like calf's liver and lamb's kidneys, now fetch such a high price that it seems doubtful whether they are worth it; they also require lengthy and meticulous preparation which cannot be skimped if they are to become the really delicate morsels they should be.

There are both throat and heart sweetbreads, the latter being the more highly prized. They are rounder and more regularly shaped than the throat sweetbreads, which are elongated and somewhat sprawling in appearance. When they are cooked, however, there is little appreciable difference.

First, the sweetbreads, which must be exceedingly fresh, must be steeped in cold water, frequently changed, for about 3 hours so that all the blood and impurities will seep out. Some butchers sell sweetbreads already soaked, so that all you need do is just put them in cold water until you are ready to cook them.

The preliminary blanching is done by simply putting the sweetbreads into a large saucepan, covering them amply with cold water and bringing this very, very gently to the boil. Let it just boil 2 minutes. Take out the sweetbreads and plunge them immediately into cold water, pouring this off and renewing it so that the sweetbreads cool quickly. This first operation is to make the sweetbreads firm enough to handle.

You now trim off the horny parts and pipes and rough parts, taking care not to damage the thin membrane which covers the sweetbreads and without which they would fall to pieces during the second cooking.

At this stage it used to be considered necessary to lard or to *piquer* the sweetbreads with little strips of pork fat, but this operation is mostly dispensed with nowadays. Escoffier observes that 'neither studding nor larding enhances in any way whatsoever their quality or sightliness.'

What you do now, then, is to put the trimmed sweetbreads on a board or dish between two pieces of greaseproof paper; cover with another board or plate and on this put a weight. Leave for a minimum of 2 hours; the sweetbreads will then be pressed to an even thickness and they are ready for cooking in any way you please, and so long as they can be stored in a refrigerator or well-aired larder, they can be left until next day. The final stages of cooking are as described in the recipe below.

Lamb's sweetbreads (*ris d'agneau*) are prepared in much the same way but are used mainly as part of the garnish for a vol-au-vent *à la toulousaine, à la financière* and so on.

RIS DE VEAU À LA CRÈME AUX CHAMPIGNONS
VEAL SWEETBREADS WITH CREAM AND MUSHROOMS

So many ambitious sauces and garnishes can be served with sweetbreads and so few of them come up to expectations that I would never willingly order them in a restaurant. But once, at Barattero's at Lamastre in the Ardèche, Madame announced that there was *ris de veau à la crème* for dinner and that was that. One did not argue. The dish proved to be a very high-class one and I was grateful to be shown how good sweetbreads could really be. I cannot pretend that the recipe which follows is the Barattero one; I can only say that it is in the same manner, and that it is good.

Ingredients for two people are a pair of sweetbreads already prepared as above; 2 thin slices of back pork fat; an onion, 2 carrots, a couple of sprigs of parsley; white wine and water or mild clear veal or chicken stock. For the sauce, 2 oz. of mushrooms, butter, $\frac{1}{4}$ pint of thick cream. Fried bread for the garnish.

Wrap each prepared and pressed sweetbread in a slice of the larding fat and tie it with thin string. Slice the onion and carrots and put them in the bottom of a pan in which the sweetbreads will just fit and which will go in the oven. On top of the vegetables put the sweetbreads. Pour in a small glass of white wine, set the pan on the fire and cook until the wine gently bubbles. Add water just to cover the sweetbreads; season; bring the water to simmering point; cover the pan; transfer to a low oven and leave with the liquid just barely murmuring for 45 minutes to an hour. If you have good stock, the wine can be dispensed with and the sweetbreads covered straight away with the stock.

Wash and dry the mushrooms, quarter them, stalks included, then cut each quarter into little chunks. Fry them gently in a small piece of butter until the juices run. In more butter fry 2 thick slices of French bread, the outer crust trimmed off. Keep them warm.

Take the sweetbreads from the oven; untie the wrappings. Put them into a frying or sauté pan in which 1 oz. of butter is just barely bubbling; let them take colour on each side, but very gently. They must be the palest gold, but not brown. Add the mushrooms and 2 tablespoons of the liquid in which the sweetbreads have cooked. Pour in the cream, turn up the heat, shake and rotate the pan until the cream thickens. If it gets too solid add a little more liquid. Put the sweetbreads on top of the fried bread in the serving dish. Give the sauce another quick stir over the fire. Pour it round the sweetbreads and serve.

And now you see what I mean about sweetbreads being a trouble to prepare. Although, of course, half a dozen are not all that much more bother than two. If they are to be done at all, however, let them be done properly. As Madame Seignobos observes rather pointedly in an early twentieth-century book called *Comment on Forme une Cuisinière*, 'in certain backward countries, sweetbreads are cooked without a previous steeping and blanching; this faulty procedure deprives the sweetbread of the delicacy which is its principal merit.'

RIS DE VEAU À L'OSEILLE
VEAL SWEETBREADS WITH SORREL

This, says Madame Seignobos in *Comment on Forme une Cuisinière*, is a traditional dish of real old French cookery. The sweetbreads, prepared and cooked in a stock as above, are gently fried in butter; some of the cooking liquid is added and, when the sweetbreads are bronzed and glazed in their juice, you serve them on a purée of sorrel and you sprinkle over the juice to which you must add some more—*étranger* is the word Madame Seignobos uses—because that from the sweetbreads will be insufficient. The sweetbreads, she adds, must be 'united' with the sorrel only at the moment of service.

TÊTE DE VEAU VINAIGRETTE
CALF'S HEAD VINAIGRETTE

Calf's head is a dish which is not easily avoidable if you eat the set meals of small hotels and restaurants in France. When it is good, which is to say when it is served really tender and hot and you get a comparatively lean piece and the vinaigrette sauce has been well mixed, then it is quite good. More often, it is repellent. To cook it at home is a scarifying performance and this is what has to be done, presuming first that you have bought a half head from the butcher and that he has either boned and tied it, or else cloven it into about four manageable pieces.

The head is put to steep in cold water for a minimum of 2 hours, but overnight if you have the time. The brains should be scooped out and soaked separately. Then you put the head into fresh cold water, bring it to the boil, let it simmer 10 minutes, drain it, wipe off any scum that is sticking to the skin and remove any hairs that are still on the creature's snout.

You now bring a fresh saucepan of water to the boil, with onion and a couple of carrots; you put in the pieces of head, which must be covered by water, and again let it simmer for 10 to 15 minutes, removing all the scum that rises to the top. Then put in a tablespoon of salt, a dessertspoon of wine vinegar or lemon juice, a large bouquet of parsley and celery or tarragon and lastly 2 tablespoons of olive oil. Cover the saucepan and simmer very gently for 1½ hours. Having freed the brains of skin and blood, blanch them as explained in the recipe on page 359. Take out the pieces of head, remove the bone and serve very hot in a hot dish, with a cold vinaigrette sauce separately. This is made with chopped shallots, parsley, mustard, salt, pepper, olive oil, vinegar and capers, as explained in the recipe for beef salad on page 147, only in smaller quantities.

If the calf's head has to be kept waiting after it has cooked, take the pan from the fire but leave it covered with the lid, so that it does not get cold.

Some cooks consider it necessary to cook the head in the mixture known as a *blanc*, which is a sort of *court-bouillon* of water plus the flavouring vegetables, salt and herbs, to which 1 oz. of flour for 4 pints is added and stirred in when the water is boiling. The idea of this is to keep the meat white (a *blanc* is also used for certain vegetables, such as salsify) but it is really not strictly necessary, for the vinegar and the lemon juice, plus the olive oil on the top, are just as effective, and then you have the liquid as a basis for clear stock, for which it cannot be used if flour has been added.

Plats composés de Viandes diverses, Cassoulets, etc.

Composite meat dishes, cassoulets, etc.

SAUCE AU VIN DU MÉDOC

BEEF, RABBIT AND PORK OR HARE STEWED IN RED WINE

HERE is a dish which is something of a collector's piece. I did not have to search for the recipe because I did not know of its existence. It fell, in a most felicitous way, into my outstretched hands through the kindness of Miss Patricia Green, a highly enterprising young woman who has made a study of wine and wine production on the spot in the Médoc.

N

From Madame Bernard, the wife of a wine-grower of Cissac-Médoc, Miss Green obtained this recipe and passed it on to me exactly as it was given to her; and she told me that Madame Bernard knew as much as there was to know of the peasant cooking of the region. I should also perhaps add that the name of the dish is not a printer's error, nor does it mean you throw away the meat and only eat the sauce; for, although the meat is cooked so slowly for so long that it practically *is* sauce, it is not uncommon in country districts of France to hear a stew of this kind referred to as *la sauce*.

Here is the recipe, unaltered in any particular. You may think it needs an act of faith to try it but when you read the recipe carefully you see that it is not really so strange and wild as it seems at a first glance.

1 rabbit, 1½ lb. stewing beef, 1 hare or 1½ lb. lean pork, 6 shallots, 4 cloves of garlic, 1 bayleaf, small sprig of thyme, large bundle of parsley, 1 dessertspoon of flour, salt, sugar, 1 square of plain chocolate, 1 bottle red wine, equal quantity of water, 3 large carrots, pork dripping or oil.

This is essentially a peasant dish, '*la grosse cuisine de la campagne*,' and it should therefore be as rich and vulgarly hearty a savoury stew as possible when finished. It will be spoilt if the meat is cut into too delicate pieces or the carrots carefully sliced.

Heat the oil or, better still, pork dripping, in a large, thick saucepan which has a closely-fitting lid. Cut the shallots very finely, and slowly and gently brown them in the hot fat, adding the carrots carefully peeled but cut only in 2 or 3 pieces. Sprinkle generously with salt, and when well browned add the meat. For pork and beef, trim off gristle and excess fat and cut into rather large chunks. For hare and rabbit, dry the joints well before adding to the frying vegetables. Brown the meat well all over, then add the garlic finely sliced, and the herbs, sprinkle with flour and mix all well together. Now pour on a bottle of red wine and bring quickly to the boil and bubble vigorously for about 5 minutes, reduce the heat, add an equal quantity of water, stir well, add a teaspoon of sugar and 1 small square of plain chocolate. Put on the lid and simmer, just a murmur, for about 3 hours. Allow to get quite cold. On the second day simmer again for about 2 hours before serving. Taste before doing so and adjust seasoning; it may be a little sharp, in which case a sprinkle more sugar will usually put matters right.

The choice of meats, as you see, is left pretty well to individual taste (shin of beef cut from the bone and sparerib or hand of pork *on* the bone with its skin is what I use, plus a hare or rabbit if either happen to be available). A whole bottle of wine and an equal quantity of water seems a lot of liquid, and this question is one which frequently arises in French recipes of this type, because the French peasants and workmen reckon on filling out their meal with a great deal of bread soaked in the sauce; in fact, two-thirds of the quantities can be used, but less I think would deprive the dish of its character. If there is a lot of sauce left over, serve it with poached eggs as described for *œufs à l'huguenote* on page 190, or poured round a mousseline of potatoes (page 272).

As for the chocolate, of which rather less than an ounce is needed, it is not an uncommon ingredient in Italian and Spanish cookery, particularly in hare dishes, and is there as a sweetening and thickening for the sauce. Its use perhaps filtered down to the Bordelais through the channel of Basque and Béarnais cookery. And Bayonne, for generations one of the great chocolate manufacturing centres of France, is not far off.

CASSOULET DE TOULOUSE

On page 54 I have referred to Auguste Colombié and his cookery school in Paris for young ladies. Here is his recipe for the famous cassoulet of the Languedoc. Being a native of that province, he should know what he is talking about. His method, however, differs in several respects from that of other Languedoc cooks, but he shows how it can be made in quite a small quantity. It is, as he says, essentially a family dish, to be eaten at midday, and preferably on a Sunday or holiday, and if you insist on having a course to start with, it must be something very light; M. Colombié's suggestions are oysters when in season, or a few crisply fried small fish such as smelts. Here is his recipe:

CASSOULET COLOMBIÉ

BEANS WITH PORK, MUTTON, SAUSAGE AND GOOSE

'Three-quarters to a pound of white haricot beans, of the variety known as Soissons, or *flageolets* of Arpajon,[1] a garlic sausage, or a chitterling sausage weighing ½ lb., about ¾ lb. of preserved goose (I will discuss this later), 1 lb. of shoulder of mutton, 4 oz. of fat bacon or salt pork, 2 cloves of garlic, an onion stuck with 2 cloves, a little bouquet of parsley, a fresh tomato, a small quantity of breadcrumbs.

'Spread the beans *on the table*, so that you can see if there are any stones or grit to be discarded. Put them into a little cold water, and rub

[1] The districts of Soissons and Arpajon are both noted for the excellence of the beans grown there.

them between your hands to get rid of the dust. Change the water at least twice; not until it comes out quite clear are the beans properly clean.

'Put the beans into a small *marmite* or stock pot with 3½ pints of cold water. Bring to the boil, cover, remove from the fire, and leave them for about 40 minutes. The beans swell, go white, and throw off the oxide of potassium which they contain. The purpose of this operation is to make them more digestible and less flatulent.

'Throw away the water out of doors, *not down the sink*; its smell infects the kitchen for twenty-four hours. In the Languedoc the housewives keep this liquid in well-corked bottles and use it for removing obstinate stains on white and coloured linen.

'Return the beans to the pot with 2½ to 3 pints of tepid water and a little salt, and bring to the boil.

'In the meantime partly roast the mutton and soak the sausage in tepid water to rid it of dust. Add the meat and the sausage to the beans, plus the bouquet of parsley tied with a thread, the preserved goose, the tomato cut in half and the seeds removed, and the onion stuck with cloves. Cook extremely gently for 2 hours.

'Cut the salt pork or bacon into dice; crush the peeled garlic cloves. Dip a sturdy knife into very hot water and chop the salt pork or the bacon and garlic together. Add them to the beans. Cook for at least 1 more hour, preferably 2.

'Now carefully remove to a plate all the cooked meat. Transfer the beans to a deep earthenware or fireproof china dish, with just enough of their juice to moisten them; they should be milky white, and soft to the touch. Season them with pepper and sprinkle the top with breadcrumbs. Put the dish in a hot oven for 15 minutes.

'Cut up the mutton and put it in the centre of another dish with the preserved goose flanking it on one side and the sausage on the other. Serve the two dishes at the same time, with very hot plates.

'With this dish, drink a light red wine.'

I have quoted Colombié's recipe as he wrote it, but anyone who has experienced the dish in its native country, at Toulouse or Carcassonne, will know that it is more usual to find the meat and the sausages buried within the beans, and that it also includes the little squares of pork rind which make it so rich. Probably Colombié's version was the one current in his native town of Castres in the Tarn; as a matter of fact it is excellent, considerably less exacting both to cook and to eat than the Toulouse version; the manner of cooking the beans without a preliminary soaking works perfectly. And the preserved goose can be replaced, as it not un-commonly is nowadays by Languedoc housewives, with a larger piece of shoulder of lamb—2 lb. instead of 1 lb.—or with more sausages or with a small duck, partly roasted, then jointed. There should be enough for four people, but one never quite knows what other people's capacity for a cassoulet will be.

CASSOULET DE TOULOUSE À LA MÉNAGÈRE
BEANS WITH PORK, LAMB AND SAUSAGES

To cook the better known version of the cassoulet, in quantities for about eight to ten people, the ingredients would be 2 lb. of medium-sized white haricot beans (butter beans will not do), 1 lb. of Toulouse sausages (a coarse-cut type of pure pork sausage to be bought at Soho shops) or a garlic-flavoured boiling sausage of the kind now sold by most delicatessen shops, a pork sparerib or bladebone weighing about $2\frac{1}{2}$ lb., $1\frac{1}{2}$ lb. breast or shoulder of lamb (both joints boned), 8 to 10 oz. of salt pork or green bacon, an onion, a bouquet of herbs, garlic and seasonings, breadcrumbs.

Have the rind of the pork removed as thinly as possible. Remove also the rind from the salt pork. Cut these rinds into small squares and put them into the saucepan with the salt pork and beans, previously soaked. Add the onion and the bouquet of herbs, plus 2 flattened cloves of garlic, all tied with a thread. Cover with water and boil steadily for about $1\frac{1}{2}$ hours. In the meantime roast the pork and the boned lamb in a gentle oven. If Toulouse sausages are being used, cook them for 20 minutes in the baking dish with the meat. If a boiling sausage, cook it with the beans.

When the beans are all but cooked, drain them, reserving their liquid. Discard the onion and the bouquet. Put a layer of the beans, with all the little bits of rind, into a deep earthenware or fireproof china dish; on the top put the sausages cut into inch lengths, and the lamb and the two kinds of pork, also cut into pieces. Cover with the rest of the beans. Moisten with a good cupful of the reserved liquid. Spread a layer of breadcrumbs on the top. Put in a very low oven for $1\frac{1}{2}$ hours at least. There should be a fine golden crust on the top formed by the breadcrumbs, and underneath the beans should be very moist and creamy. So if you see during the second cooking that they are beginning to look dry, add some more liquid. Some cooks elaborate on this by stirring the crust, as soon as it has formed, into the beans, then adding another layer of bread-crumbs. This operation is repeated a second time, and only when the third crust has formed is the cassoulet ready to serve.

Naturally, anyone who finds Colombié's method with the beans more convenient or more satisfactory can cook and present this cassoulet in the same way—or a mixture of the two methods can be devised.

The cassoulet is a dish which may be infinitely varied so long as it is not made into a mockery with a sausage or two heated up with tinned beans, or with all sorts of bits of left-over chicken or goodness knows what thrown into it as if it were a dustbin. And the wise will heed M. Colombié's advice about eating the cassoulet at midday on a day when no great exertion is called for afterwards.

If you are visiting Toulouse, a lovely cassoulet is to be had at the Restaurant Richelieu-Michel in the rue Gabriel-Péri, but probably it will not be on the menu during the hot summer months.

BECKENOFF

PORK AND MUTTON BAKED WITH POTATOES

As its name implies, this is an oven-baked dish, a meat and potato stew of the kind which used to be sent to be baked in the local baker's oven. I would not recommend this as a party dish, but rather one to feed a large and hungry family on a cold day. The ingredients and method are reminiscent of the Lancashire hot pot and the Leicester medley pie, except that this dish, native to Alsace, contains the white wine of the country.

Ingredients are 1½ to 2 lb. each of lean pork and lamb or mutton. The cuts used vary, but if pork fillet or tenderloin is available, this is a good cut since it is lean and boneless but, failing that, buy sparerib, bladebone or hand of pork. For lamb, use middle neck or a half shoulder, not boned, but cut into sizeable pieces and excess fat trimmed off. The pork should also be sliced up, each fillet making four pieces, or if the shoulder cut or hand is used, sliced through the bone into pieces the size of a small chop. Other ingredients are about 2½ to 3 lb. of potatoes, 2 large onions, a bouquet of herbs and a small glass (8 tablespoons) each of dry white wine and clear meat stock, which can be made if necessary from the trimmings of your meat plus vegetables and seasonings, or even from a bouillon cube.

Peel and wash the potatoes, slice them evenly into rounds a bit thicker than a half-crown (do this on the mandoline if you have one). Arrange half of them in a layer in a large wide earthenware terrine or cocotte; on top put some sliced onion; sprinkle with salt and pepper. Arrange the meat neatly in layers. Season it. Bury the bouquet of bayleaves, parsley and several sprigs of thyme, all tied together with a thread, in the middle of the meat. Add seasoning, then the rest of the onions and sliced potatoes and a little more seasoning (I like to include a few crushed juniper berries with the salt and pepper, as the Alsatians do for their *choucroûte*).

Pour in the wine and the stock. Let it come to the bubble on top of the stove. Put a buttered paper or piece of foil over the top layer of potatoes to prevent them becoming dry, and put on the lid of the pan. Transfer to a low oven, Gas No. 3, 330 deg. F., for about $3\frac{1}{2}$ hours. By this time both meat and potatoes should be beautifully tender but not cooked to rags, and the stew can be served either direct from its own pot or arranged on a big, deep serving dish with some parsley sprinkled over the top.

If you use cider instead of wine for this dish, do not use an unlined iron pot in which there is a risk of the cider turning black.

Other vegetables won't be needed with this filling dish, but some sort of green salad afterwards would be welcome. The quantities given for the stew should be enough for six to eight people, and it can be reheated slowly without coming to harm, although it may need a little extra liquid for a second heating.

LA DAUBE VIENNOISE

'In my youth I saw the *daube viennoise*[1] being cooked. There was a family who, as Easter approached, would put a whole quarter of beef and some chickens into a great trough into which they poured abundant amounts of wine and spirits and spices. On Easter Sunday, all their friends were invited to eat the daube in ceremonial state; with it went the charming little wine of Saint-Prin.

'Today, a veal rump (this is the classic term) is served. It is presented whole upon a great dish, with its tail and kidneys nicely arranged upon a bed of big fat leeks.'

PAUL-LOUIS COUCHOUD.
Translated from an article on *La Bonne Table en Dauphiné*,
in the magazine *La France à Table*, undated but *circa* 1956

[1] This word refers to the town of Vienne on the Rhône, not to the Austrian capital.

Les Volailles et le Gibier

Poultry and game

The French housewife mixes chopped fresh pork or pure pork sausage meat with eggs and herbs to stuff a big fat fowl, she poaches it with vegetables and a bouquet of herbs and the result is that *poule au pot* which good King Henry of Navarre wished that all his subjects might eat on every Sunday of the year. Or perhaps that same housewife will cook her chicken without a stuffing and serve it with a dish of rice and a cream sauce; or if it is a plump young bird, she will roast it simply in butter and serve it on the familiar long oval dish with a tuft of watercress at each end and the buttery juices in a separate sauce-boat. The farmer's wife, faced with an old hen no longer of use for laying, will (if she has inherited her grandmother's recipes and has a proper sense of the fitness of things) bone the bird, stuff it richly with pork and veal and even, perhaps, truffles if it is for a special occasion, and simmer the bird with wine and a calf's foot to make a clear and savoury jelly, so that the old hen will be turned into a fine and handsome galantine fit for celebrations and feast days.

If she is in a hurry, the French cook will cut up a roasting chicken into joints, fry them gently in butter or oil, add stock or wine, perhaps vegetables and little cubes of salt pork as well, and the result will be the *poulet sauté* which, in a restaurant, will be glorified with some classic or regional label, or named after a minister or a famous writer or actress. *Parmentier* it will be if there are little bits of potato; *provençale* if there are tomatoes; *chasseur* or *forestière* if there are mushrooms; *Poincaré* if there are asparagus tips; *Mistral* if there are aubergines; *Célestine* if there are tomatoes and wine and mushrooms and cream all together. (Célestine was one of the Emperor Louis Napoleon's cooks, and he came from the Ardèche, but the dish became celebrated at a Lyon restaurant so whether Célestine invented it or not I do not know nor, I suppose, does anybody else.)

The old-fashioned *fricassée* is a sauté of chicken with a sauce thickened with egg yolks, not a dish of left-overs with a white sauce such as we understand it in English cookery; a *poulet à la crème* is another of these sauté chickens with a pure cream sauce, but for all their versatility I must confess that these cut-up chickens seldom appeal to me. However good and carefully cooked the dish, one nearly always finds that the chicken is a trifle dry, that it has lost some of its juices and its melting quality and, in fact, that it would very likely have been better had the bird been cooked whole and then jointed before serving. For this reason I rarely cook a sauté chicken and shall give only one or two examples of such recipes but it is, of course, a question which every cook must judge for himself.

The accomplished restaurant chef is apt to use chicken as a background to show off his skill in making fine cream sauces and *mousses* and aspic jellies; and when freshwater crayfish are to be had, perhaps he will serve you with a cockerel surrounded by a sauce or *coulis* of these crayfish, creamy and rose-coloured. You think it sounds outlandish. But it is delicate and poetical. You have a dish of plain rice to go with it and your wine will be a Meursault, a Montrachet, a Chablis or an Alsatian Traminer.

In Burgundy your cockerel will be served in a wine-dark sauce surrounded by little glazed button onions, mushrooms and cubes of salt pork, with a bottle of Chambertin to drink. Is it a little over-sung, this dish, I sometimes wonder? In Lyon there will be dark patches of truffles slipped in between the skin and the flesh of your poached *poularde de Bresse*. In Normandy the sauce will be compounded of thick white cream and Calvados. In Provence olives, tomatoes, oil, garlic and the aromatic herbs of the sun-baked hillsides will go into the pot with your chicken. In Touraine as well as in the modest Paris restaurant, ten to one it will be flavoured in some way or other with tarragon. Perhaps it is the best of all.

As for other domestic poultry and game, such things as ducklings, turkeys, geese and guinea fowl do not come one's way so often as to make it necessary to know a large variety of different recipes for cooking them.

The renowned *canard à la presse* and *canard à la rouennaise* require not only special implements but a special breed of duck, the Rouen duck being a cross between the common wild duck of the Seine estuary and a domestic duck. This duck is killed by strangulation, so that all its blood remains in the body; it has a strong gamey flavour which is something of an acquired taste, and it is really at its best plain spit-roasted. The *canard à la presse, au sang, à la rouennaise* and *à la Duclair*, in which the blood pressed from the half-roasted carcase of the animal constitutes a necessary part of the sauce for the dish, belong essentially to restaurant cooking. The Nantais ducks and ducklings more resemble our own domestic breeds and, when young, are best plain roasted; when elderly they can make, provided that they are painstakingly cooked, excellent farmhouse and country dishes, either with the traditional vegetables such as little turnips, young peas, olives or haricot beans, or with more fanciful garnishes such as bitter cherries or oranges for those who feel that something with a sweet-sour taste is needed to offset the richly-flavoured flesh of the mature duck.

Young game birds, pheasant, partridge and grouse (for which the nearest French equivalent is the *coq de bruyère*) are best roasted either on the spit, in the oven or in a heavy pot on top of the stove. The professional chefs, of course, like to do all sorts of elaborate and expensive dishes with them, usually involving truffles and *foie gras*.

Pâtés and terrines offer an excellent solution, perhaps the best, to people who have plenty of game at their disposal, while the deep freeze is kinder to game than to vegetables, meat or fish.

For people who have to buy their game, hare usually offers very remarkable value but it takes courage, I find, to cook it often, for the smell of a *civet* or of any other hare stew, as indeed of venison, is an over-powering, penetrating and lingering one; but every now and again it is well worth making the effort, for in some of the traditional recipes for cooking hare is to be found the very essence of old French country cookery and of the French genius for the gradual amalgamation of wine, vegetables and aromatic herbs with the flesh of the animal itself, all slowly, patiently simmered to form a richly flavoured, sumptuous whole.

Some of these old recipes call for ingredients which seem at first glance to be terribly discordant, and for methods which would make the school-trained cook recoil, so that their preparation may sometimes require an act of faith as well as one of courage. The cook with an adventurous spirit will not be daunted but, all the same, these dishes are quite a test of skill, taste and understanding.

POULET RÔTI AU BEURRE
CHICKEN ROASTED IN BUTTER

Stuff a plump 3 lb. roasting chicken (dressed and drawn weight) with a large lump of butter, about 2 oz., into which salt, freshly-milled pepper and, if possible, a little chopped fresh or dried tarragon have been incorporated. Place the chicken on its side in a baking tin and rub more butter plentifully over the exposed surface. Put in a fairly hot oven, Gas No. 6, 400 deg. F., and, after 20 minutes, turn the bird over. Add more butter. After 20 minutes more turn the bird again, and baste with the juices in the pan. In 1 hour altogether the chicken should be cooked and will be a most beautiful golden brown all over. The only sauce needed is supplied by the butter and the juices in the pan, which are poured off into a sauce-boat and served separately.

For a larger chicken, weighing say 4½ to 5 lbs. dressed and drawn, allow 30 minutes on each side at Gas No. 5, 375 deg. F., then about 30 minutes with the heat reduced to Gas No. 3, 330 deg. F.

POULET FARCI EN COCOTTE

POT-ROASTED CHICKEN WITH OLIVE STUFFING

Pot-roasting is a very easy way of cooking a chicken *provided* you have a suitable utensil. It should be deep enough to contain the bird, lying on its side, with the lid fitting tightly over the top; it should also be rather narrow, so it is all but filled by the bird, for if it is too big the butter or other fat in which the bird is cooking will be spread over too large an area and will dry up or burn. Also, of course, the pot must be a thick and heavy one in which the contents will not stick and in which an even temperature will be maintained throughout the cooking. A Le Creuset cast-iron cocotte of the type shown in the drawing on page 59 is suitable for pot-roasting. Le Creuset also produce a highly useful pot-roaster which goes by the name of *Doufeu*, meaning literally 'gentle-fire'.

To make an olive stuffing for a roasting chicken weighing 2¼ to 2½ lb. when drawn and dressed, stone and chop 20 black olives (about 2½ oz.) with 2 oz. of stale white bread weighed without **crust**, soaked in cold water and squeezed dry, a little piece of onion or garlic, a sprig or two of parsley; bind with a beaten egg and season with a little pepper and nutmeg but no salt. Stuff the bird and, if you have it ready in advance, keep it *out* of the refrigerator.

Heat 3 tablespoons of olive oil in the pot or saucepan, but don't let it get to the sizzling stage. Put in the chicken on its side. Leave it 5 minutes over gentle heat. Turn it over on to the other side, so that both thigh and one side of the breast of the bird are in contact with the oil. Cover the pan and cook for 1½ hours altogether, at a very low but steady pace, and turning the bird over twice more during the process, taking care not to damage the skin as you do so.

At the end of the cooking time the skin of the chicken is beautifully golden and crisp, and for once the legs will be cooked through as well as the breast. Remove it to the heated serving dish.

Have ready half a dozen medium-sized potatoes, boiled in their skins but kept slightly undercooked, peeled and cut into squares (or, when they are obtainable, whole small new potatoes). In the oil left from the cooking of the chicken and in the same pan, with the heat increased, brown the potatoes, turning them round and round with a fork; in 5 minutes at most they will be ready. Lift them out with a draining spoon, put them at one end of the dish with the chicken, sprinkle them with salt and parsley, and at the other end put a little bunch of watercress. The dish is ready. You have a complete and delicious main course —and only one pan to wash up.

I should add, perhaps, that the olive stuffing, although so good, is definitely rather odd. If the chicken is for guests with conventional tastes then it might be better to substitute a routine pork or herb stuffing.

POULET À L'ESTRAGON

CHICKEN WITH TARRAGON

Tarragon is a herb which has a quite remarkable affinity with chicken, and a *poulet à l'estragon*, made with fresh tarragon, is one of the great treats of the summer. There are any amount of different ways of cooking a tarragon-flavoured chicken dish: here is a particularly successful one.

For a plump roasting chicken weighing about 2 lb. when plucked and drawn, knead a good ounce of butter with a tablespoon of tarragon leaves, half a clove of garlic, salt and pepper. Put this inside the bird, which should be well coated with olive oil. Roast the bird lying on its side on a grid in a baking dish. Turn it over at half-time (45 minutes altogether in a pretty hot oven or an hour in a moderate oven should be sufficient; those who have a roomy grill might try grilling it, which takes about 20 minutes, and gives much more the impression of a spit-roasted bird, but it must be constantly watched and turned over very carefully, so that the legs are as well done as the breast).

When the bird is cooked, heat a small glass of brandy in a soup ladle, set light to it, pour it flaming over the chicken and rotate the dish so that the flames spread and continue to burn as long as possible. Return the bird to a low oven for 5 minutes, during which time the brandy sauce will mature and lose its raw flavour. At this moment you can, if you like, enrich the sauce with a few spoonfuls of thick cream and, at la Mère Michel's Paris restaurant, from where the recipe originally came, they add Madeira to the sauce. Good though this is, it seems to me a needless complication.

POULET SAUTÉ AUX OLIVES DE PROVENCE
CHICKEN COOKED IN OIL WITH OLIVES AND TOMATOES

For two people, buy a 1¾ to 2 lb. chicken split in two as for grilling. The success of all dishes in which the chicken is cut before cooking lies in having presentable portions. Nothing is more dismal than those *poulets sautés* and *fricassées de poulet*, in which all you get on your plate is an unidentifiable and bony little joint from which the dry flesh is detached only with great determination. Some skill is needed to joint a chicken into several pieces and, on the whole, it is more satisfactory to buy smaller chickens and simply split them, or have them split, in half.

Season the halves of chicken, rub them with lemon juice and insert a very small piece of garlic and a little sprig of thyme or basil under the skin of each piece. Dust with flour. In an ordinary heavy frying-pan heat a coffee-cup (after-dinner size) of olive oil. Make it fairly hot and put in the pieces of chicken skin side down. When they are golden on one side turn them over and, when both sides are seized, turn them over again, turn the heat low and cover the pan, removing the lid only from time to time to turn the chicken. After 20 minutes, transfer the chicken and nearly all the oil to a baking dish and put in a very low oven, covered, while the sauce is made.

For this have ready 4 large ripe tomatoes, skinned and chopped; 2 anchovy fillets roughly pounded with 2 cloves of garlic; a sprig each of thyme, marjoram and basil, dried if no fresh is available; a small glass of wine, white for preference but red if it is easier; and 4 oz. of stoned black olives.

First pour in the wine, detaching any brown pieces and juices which may have adhered to the pan. Let it bubble and reduce. Add the anchovy and garlic mixture, stir well in, then add the tomatoes and the herbs.

Simmer until the sauce is thick, add the olives, let them get hot and taste the sauce for seasoning.

Test the chicken by running a skewer through the thick part of the leg and, if the juices come out white, it is cooked. If still red, leave a little longer in the oven. For serving, arrange the chicken in a long dish *on top* of the very hot sauce.

A variation of this chicken dish is to cut all the flesh from a cooked bird (a boiling fowl could be used) into neat fillets, dip them in frying batter, fry them like fritters in very hot oil and serve them piled up in a dish with the same sauce made and served separately. This is called a *fritot de poulet*.

LA VOLAILLE DEMI-DEUIL
POACHED CHICKEN WITH TRUFFLES

This is the dish made famous by la Mère Fillioux of Lyon, whose restaurant is described on page 42. It is her own recipe and I quote it here because it is so beautifully simple. Even if such dishes cannot be made in England except at enormous expense, it is good to know how they were, and still are, cooked in the famous Lyon restaurants.

'Choose a fine chicken, preferably from the Louhans district, plump and tender and weighing about 2 lb. Slip thin slices of truffle under the skin of the bird. Fold it in a fine cloth and tie it lightly round with string. Put it into a pot containing a broth made from shin of veal, with leeks and carrots. Boil it for 15 minutes; then leave it for 20 more minutes in the *bouillon* and serve it with a pinch of coarse salt.'

But the secret . . . the secret, they say, is to cook fifteen chickens at a time . . . at least.

POULET AU GRATIN À LA SAVOYARDE
CHICKEN WITH CHEESE SAUCE

Put a small but plump 2½ lb. chicken, drawn and dressed weight, to roast in butter in the oven as described on page 394. While it is cooking, prepare a sauce from the following ingredients: 1½ oz. butter, 2 level tablespoons of flour, ¼ pint of stock made from the giblets of the bird and flavoured with herbs, onions, carrots and 4 tablespoons of white wine, ½ pint of thick fresh cream, 2 teaspoons of French mustard, a teaspoon of fresh or dried tarragon, 2 tablespoons of grated Gruyère cheese, salt and freshly-milled pepper.

Heat the butter in a thick pan, stir in the flour; when it is smooth add the hot strained stock; when this has amalgamated with the flour start adding the cream, a little at a time; when it has all been stirred in let it cook very gently for 5 minutes; now add seasonings, including plenty of pepper, the tarragon, the mustard and the cheese. Put the saucepan on a mat and leave on a very low flame, stirring from time to time, for 10 minutes, for the sauce to mature.

When the chicken is cooked, carve it into four pieces, put these in a gratin dish on top of a layer of the sauce, pour the rest on top, strew over a few fine breadcrumbs, add a little of the butter from the chicken and put on the top shelf of the hottest possible oven for 5 minutes. Finish under the grill for a minute or two and serve when the surface is golden and bubbling. Enough for two or four, according to what else is to be served.

Much of the success of the delicious sauce for this dish depends upon the mustard with which it is flavoured; Grey Poupon's *moutarde forte au vin blanc*, a yellow and strongly aromatic mustard, is one of the best for this purpose.

COQ AU VIN DE BOURGOGNE
COCKEREL STEWED IN RED WINE

Recipes for this famous dish vary a good deal and one meets with many bad imitations in which a boiling fowl is cooked to rags and then warmed up in some ready-made sauce vaguely flavoured with wine. There is also an idea that the sauce must be thickened with the blood of the animal to make a genuine *coq au vin*. This is not necessarily the case.

A typical Burgundian recipe, from the Cloche d'Or in Dijon, is as follows:

'Cut a cockerel into joints; in an earthenware saucepan melt a few pieces of streaky bacon, previously blanched; add some small onions and the pieces of chicken; when these have taken colour, pour off the fat. Set light to a glass of brandy, pour it over the chicken, then add a bottle of old red Burgundy and a little stock; season with salt and pepper; add 2 cloves of garlic, a bouquet of parsley and bay leaf. When it starts bubbling, close the pot hermetically and simmer gently. When cooked, remove the garlic and the bouquet, add a few mushrooms, and bind the sauce with *beurre manié*; cover, and let it bubble once more.'

This all sounds very easy but, in practice, it is difficult to get the sauce to the right consistency without spoiling the bird by overcooking; so one of two methods can be adopted. The first is to cook the bird whole and carve it for serving while the sauce is going through its final reduction and thickening. The second is to half prepare the sauce before cooking the bird, as follows:

Ingredients are a 2½ to 3 lb. cockerel or roasting chicken, ¾ bottle of inexpensive but sound red Burgundy or Beaujolais or Macon, ¼ lb. of salt pork or unsmoked bacon, 6 to 8 oz. of button mushrooms, 12 to 16 very small onions of the pickling type, a small glass of brandy, a carrot, an onion, herbs, garlic, seasonings, butter and oil, fried bread, a dessertspoon of flour.

(1) Have the chicken cut into four pieces.

(2) Make a little stock from the giblets of the bird, with an onion, carrot, bouquet of herbs and very little salt.

(3) Put the red wine into a large wide pan with a couple of bay-leaves, a sprig of thyme and a crushed clove of garlic. Add ¼ pint of the chicken stock. Simmer steadily for about 20 minutes until reduced to about half its original volume. During the last 5 minutes put in the mushrooms, washed and dried. Strain the wine, discard the herbs and garlic and keep the mushrooms aside. The seemingly large amount of wine is necessary to the dish on account of the reducing process, which in turn gives the sauce its characteristic flavour. Indeed, most recipes specify a whole bottle, but it is possible to manage with a little less.

(4) Cut the salt pork or bacon into little cubes. Put it in the rinsed-out pan with a good lump of butter and a few drops of oil. When the fat from the pork starts to run, put in the little onions and, as soon as they have taken colour, add the pieces of chicken, well seasoned with salt and pepper, and let them fry skin side downwards. When the skin has turned a nice golden colour, turn the pieces over, and cook another minute. Turn them over again. Heat the brandy in a little saucepan or soup ladle. Set light to it and pour it flaming over the chicken. Shake the pan and rotate it until the flames die down. Pour in the wine. Put a fresh bouquet of herbs and garlic in the centre. Cover the pan. Simmer gently for 40 minutes. Put in the mushrooms and cook 5 more minutes.

(5) Transfer the chicken, mushrooms, onions and pork or bacon cubes to a hot dish and keep warm in the oven.

(6) Have ready a number of triangles of bread, say 3 for each person, fried in butter, oil or beef dripping, and keep these also warm in the oven.

(7) Have ready a tablespoon of butter worked with a level dessertspoon of flour and divided into little pieces the size of a hazel nut. Add these to the sauce in the pan. Stir over a gentle flame until the flour and butter have melted into the sauce. In less than a minute it will be thickened. Just let it come to the boil (it is a fallacy that you must not

let a sauce thickened in this manner come to the boil, but it must only just do so) and it will take on a shiny, glazed appearance. Pour it over and round the chicken, arrange the fried bread round the edge of the dish and serve quickly.

Unorthodox though it may be, this method produces an excellent *coq au vin*.

LE POULET SAUTÉ DAUPHINOIS
CHICKEN COOKED WITH WHOLE GARLIC CLOVES

This recipe is given by Paul-Louis Couchoud, writing of the specialities of the Dauphiné in *La France à Table*.

'This is a simple dish but a difficult one to do well. With the chicken you must cook some cloves of garlic as large and as round as hazel nuts. They must be as saturated with the juices, as *rissolées*, and (this is of capital importance) as tender and sweet as new potatoes. To bring about this miracle, you must have heads of garlic from Provence, which have matured quickly and so have not had the time to become too impregnated with their special aroma.'

PETITS POUSSINS

To me these seem wretched little birds, poor in flavour and stringy in texture. They were evolved some time towards the end of the nineteenth century, in France, and were hailed as a great novelty—a one-man chicken. They are now, I fancy, more popular in England than across the Channel.

However, in a Strasbourg restaurant not long ago, I reluctantly took the management's advice and ordered their *petit poussin* speciality to follow the superb *foie gras*. The little birds were cooked *à la polonaise*, grilled whole, then coated with breadcrumbs, chopped parsley and hard-boiled egg, and browned crisp on the outside with melted butter. This is, perhaps, the best way of dealing with these baby birds, if you *have* to deal with them. Even so, there is little to recommend them.

LA POULE FARCIE EN DAUBE À LA BERRICHONNE
BONED STUFFED CHICKEN IN JELLY

Around Easter time and the early summer, when the old hens no longer useful for laying are killed off, different versions of this dish are made in many of the country districts of central France. It is a method of turning an old boiling fowl into a civilised and savoury dish.

Apart from a large boiling hen, the ingredients are ½ lb. each of minced pork and veal, and all the seasonings one would ordinarily use for a pâté, i.e. a little white wine and cognac, garlic, parsley, pepper, salt, an egg, perhaps pistachio nuts, a calf's foot and, if possible, a pint or so of veal stock, plus carrots and onions.

The poulterer or butcher must be persuaded to bone the bird for you; there are still many competent ones who will do this, and you never know till you ask.

Mix the pork and veal together, add the liver of the bird first stiffened in butter, then cut into little dice. Season with about 2 teaspoons of salt, pepper, a chopped clove of garlic, a tablespoon of chopped parsley, and about a dozen halved pistachio nuts if you have them. Add a coffee-cupful (after-dinner size) of white wine, a tablespoon of brandy and 1 whole beaten egg. Stuff the chicken with this mixture, reshape it as much as possible in its original form, tie round with string and secure the openings with little wooden skewers. Place on a bed of sliced onion and carrot in a deep oval pot which will go in the oven; put the calf's foot, divided into four, all round. Pour over the stock, fill up with water just to cover, add a bouquet of bayleaf, thyme and parsley, and cover with two layers of foil or greaseproof paper and the lid. Cook in a very slow oven, Gas No. 2, 310 deg. F., for 3 hours or a little over.

Remove the bird carefully; it is now advisable to continue cooking the liquid with the calf's foot for another hour at least in order that the jelly which it ultimately produces shall be really firm. Strain it into a bowl; leave to set. Remove the fat. Just melt the jelly; remove the strings from the bird and, in order to facilitate serving, carve into slices obliquely downwards as if you were cutting a sausage. If the leg bones have been left in, as they usually are, they will be soft enough to be carved right through with a good knife. Reshape the bird, put it in a deep serving dish, pour over the jelly and leave to set again.

Serve with a green salad or a potato salad; if you want to give a rather copious meal, it can serve as a first course in the same way as a pâté; otherwise as a main course.

POULE EN DAUBE

STUFFED CHICKEN IN JELLY

If you prefer, or are obliged, to cook the bird unboned, use the same stuffing but rather less of it (about 4 oz. each of pork and veal) and proceed in precisely the same way, cooking for 4 hours instead of 3.

Instead of **pouring the jelly** over the bird for serving, cut it into squares, arrange it all round the bird on a flat serving dish and carve as for any other cold chicken.

LA POULE AU POT À LA CRÈME NORMANDE
POACHED CHICKEN WITH BUTTER AND CREAM SAUCE

A boiling fowl, slowly simmered in water with vegetables and aromatic herbs, is served hot, cut into nice pieces, with the following sauce, made **at the** last moment when the dish is ready to serve.

In **a** heavy frying-pan or large sauté pan melt 3 oz. of unsalted butter, and when it is foaming (but it must not turn colour) pour in ½ pint of **thick** cream. In **a** few seconds the cream and butter will have amalgamated, thickened and started coating the wooden spoon with which **you** have been **stirring** and lifting the sauce. Taste for seasoning, add the smallest dusting of very finely chopped parsley and pour over the chicken. The process of thickening the cream takes hardly more than a minute, so long as a *wide* pan is used.

LA POULE AU POT DU BÉARNAIS

This is just one version of this celebrated method of cooking a good fat boiling chicken. A large deep saucepan or earthenware pot is essential, so that there is plenty of room for a variety of vegetables and a good covering of water, or the broth will boil away and its goodness be lost.

The chicken is stuffed with a mixture of the pounded liver of the bird, **a** good handful of breadcrumbs soaked in milk and squeezed dry and ¼ lb. of chopped fresh pork or sausage meat, and parsley and seasoning, into which you stir an egg or two. Brown the chicken all over in good dripping or butter, add carrots, a couple of turnips, an onion, a sliced leek, a piece of celery and salt and pepper. Pour in boiling water to cover the bird and the vegetables, and when the water comes to the boil again remove any scum which has risen to the top. Cover the pan and simmer very slowly for about 3 hours: 40 minutes or so before serving, the vegetables, which have been cooking in the pot and which, by now, are rather sodden and tasteless, can be removed and fresh ones added.

Serve the chicken with the vegetables all round and a *sauce vinaigrette à l'œuf* as described on page 122. The broth can either be served as a first course, or kept for another meal. In either case, a little rice can be boiled in it to give it body.

LA POULE AU RIZ À LA CRÈME

CHICKEN WITH RICE AND CREAM SAUCE

There are several ways of preparing this mild and soothing dish, which requires careful cooking and a well-made creamy sauce if it is to be presented at its best.

Supposing it is to be made with a boiling chicken weighing 4 to 5 lb., the other ingredients are ¼ lb. of fat unsmoked bacon or salt breast of pork, 2 onions, 3 or 4 carrots, a bouquet of herbs and garlic; if possible, approximately 4 pints of stock made from the giblets and a piece of knuckle of veal; and ¾ lb. of very good quality rice. And for the sauce, butter, flour, stock from the chicken, 8 oz. of cream, 2 egg yolks, lemon, with finely chopped parsley and tarragon to finish.

Line the bottom of a heavy oval pan with the bacon or salt pork cut in very thin slices. On top put the chicken, with its own fat or a piece of butter rolled in salt and pepper inside, and rubbed with lemon on the outside. Surround it with the sliced onions and carrots. Set it off on a moderate fire and let it cook gently about 10 to 15 minutes until the fat is running and a faint smell of frying comes from the pan; pour in the heated stock, of which there should be enough to cover completely the legs of the bird but not the breast; if there is not sufficient, make it up with water. (If you already have stock from a previously cooked chicken instead of having to make it specially, so much the better.) Put in a big bouquet of fresh parsley, bayleaves, a crushed clove of garlic and some sprigs of thyme or marjoram. Let the stock come to simmering point; add just a little salt. Cover the pot with buttered paper and a close-fitting lid. Transfer to a moderate oven, Gas No. 4, 355 deg. F., and allow about half an hour to the pound.

About 45 minutes before serving time, start on the rice, which is to be what the French call *riz au gras*, moist rather than fluffy, but still with all the grains separate. Having weighed out ¾ lb., measure it in a cup or glass and then calculate twice its volume in stock, which is to be taken from the pot in which the chicken is cooking. Put your rice into a big pan of boiling salted water and cook it about 7 minutes, boiling fairly fast. Drain it; hold the colander under the cold tap until the water which runs out is quite clear. Put the rice in a pot or pan which will go in the oven. Extract the required amount of stock from the chicken (at this moment turn the bird over in its liquid) and pour it over the rice. Bring to simmering point on top of the stove. Put a folded cloth on top, cover with the lid and put in the oven to finish cooking. It will be perfectly cooked, all the liquid absorbed, in about 25 minutes, but a little longer will do no harm.

For the sauce, melt 1 oz. of butter in a heavy saucepan, stir in 2 tablespoons of flour and about ½ pint of hot stock, which can have been taken from the chicken at the same time as that for the rice. Stir until you have a smooth, thickish sauce. Add your cream (single cream will be all right) and leave very gently cooking, stirring from time to time to prevent a skin forming. Season if necessary with salt; beat the egg yolks with a little lemon juice and stir them into the sauce. Keep another minute or two over the fire, add the chopped parsley and tarragon, dried when no fresh is available, and then put the saucepan into another one containing hot water, so that it does not boil again.

To serve, carve the bird, pour the sauce over the pieces, and serve the rice either separately or arranged all round the chicken. There will be ample rice and sauce for four people and probably enough chicken left over to make an *émincé* (see page 406) or other dish next day.

A young roasting chicken can be prepared in exactly the same way, except that it will need a good deal less cooking—not more than 15 minutes to the pound. The dish then becomes a *poularde*, instead of a *poule au riz*.

POULE À LA CRÈME ET À L'ESTRAGON
COLD CHICKEN WITH CREAM AND TARRAGON SAUCE

Tarragon, as I have already noted, is one of those flavours which, in western cooking, combine the most perfectly with chicken; and an old bird can be turned to very good account in the following way:

A boiling hen weighing 3 to 4 lb., onion, carrots, bouquet of herbs, butter, lemon. For the sauce, ¼ pint thick cream, the yolks of 4 large or 6 small eggs, chopped tarragon, if possible a little Madeira or white wine.

Put a lump of butter worked with pepper, salt and a few tarragon leaves inside the bird. Rub it all over with lemon. Put it in a saucepan with 3 carrots, an onion, a bouquet of bayleaf and parsley, a tablespoon of salt. Just barely cover with water or a light veal stock should it be available; bring very gently to simmering point and cook very slowly with the cover on the pan for approximately 35 minutes per pound from the time the water comes to simmering point.

Remove the bird from the liquid and, when cool enough to handle carve into nice large pieces; each side of the breast into two fillets, the legs divided in two, and the wings. Remove all skin, because on an old fowl it is thick and tough.

Measure 1 pint of the broth; mix with the well-beaten yolks of the eggs and the cream; cook very gently, stirring all the time, as for a custard, until the mixture is as thick as thick cream. Taste for seasoning, adding a little lemon juice and, if you like, a dessertspoon of Madeira or white wine. Stir in about a tablespoon of finely-chopped tarragon. Go on stirring the sauce until it has cooled a little. Pour it over the pieces of chicken arranged in a dish just deep enough for the sauce to cover the chicken completely. Arrange a little line of whole tarragon leaves, moistened with stock, along the centre of the dish, and serve cold. With it can be served the rice salad described on page 151.

For a special occasion, a plump and tender roasting chicken weighing about 3 lb. or a little more when plucked, drawn and dressed can be cooked in the same way but will need only an hour's gentle simmering at the most; so, to enrich the flavour of the resulting stock for the sauce, it is an improvement to add, when possible, about 4 tablespoons of a not too dry white wine or even of white vermouth. This should be put in right at the beginning of the cooking.

Now I know that many people find it difficult to get these cream and egg sauces to the right consistency. If they are cooked too fast they curdle, and the stirring of the sauce over a pan of hot water requires very great patience. A good solution is as follows: first, remember that the more thoroughly beaten the egg yolks, the less chance there is of their curdling. So, having attended to this matter, start your sauce off straight over the flame, but a gentle one of course. When it shows signs of starting to thicken, put your saucepan in another one, very much larger, containing hot water, barely at simmering point. You can now safely leave your sauce, giving it an occasional stir, for as long as half an hour, while it almost imperceptibly thickens; by this method the flavour is improved, too, for the sauce matures, as it were, and having heat all round it instead of merely under it, it thickens evenly and smoothly. And remember also that, for a cold dish, the sauce need not, and should not, be so thick as for a hot one, for like a custard it thickens as it cools.

ÉMINCÉS DE VOLAILLE AU GRATIN

CHICKEN WITH CREAM AND CHEESE SAUCE

This is an excellent dish to make from left-over cooked chicken or turkey. Ingredients for a dish for three or four people are about ¾ lb. of cooked chicken weighed when it has been taken from the bone and, for the sauce, 1½ oz. of butter, 2 heaped tablespoons of flour, ½ pint of milk, 4 tablespoons each of stock from the bird and cream or, if there is no stock, 8 tablespoons of cream. Seasonings include nutmeg as well as salt and freshly-milled pepper and 3 tablespoons of grated Parmesan or Gruyère plus a little extra, with breadcrumbs, for the final cooking of the dish.

Melt the butter in a thick saucepan, put in the flour, stir it round, off the fire, until it forms a smooth paste; add a little of the warmed milk. Return to the fire and stir while you add the rest of the milk. When the sauce is smooth and thick add the stock, cream and seasonings; there should be a good measure of pepper and nutmeg but only a very little salt until after the cheese has been added. It may then be necessary to add more. At this stage put the saucepan into another large one containing water and let it cook in this *bain-marie*, stirring frequently, for a good 20 minutes. Now add the cheese and stir again until it has amalgamated with the sauce. Remove all skin and sinew from the chicken; cut it into thin strips, as much of a size as possible.

Cover the bottom of a shallow gratin dish with a thin layer of the sauce. Put in the chicken. Cover it completely with the rest of the sauce. Sprinkle with breadcrumbs and grated cheese and cook for about 15 minutes in a moderate oven; and then transfer it to the grill for a minute or two, and serve it when the top is just beginning to blister into golden bubbles.

MAYONNAISE DE VOLAILLE

CHICKEN MAYONNAISE

This is made and garnished in the same way as the fish mayonnaise described on page 288.

When made in quantity with a chicken boiled especially for the purpose, a mayonnaise made with 2 or 3 egg yolks and ½ pint of olive oil will be needed. Preferably, the chicken should be sliced from the bones, skinned and mixed while still warm with half the mayonnaise. Pile it up into a pyramid in a shallow dish and leave the garnishing and the covering of the chicken with the remainder of the mayonnaise until just before serving.

The *sauce provençale* described on page 123 makes a good alternative to a straightforward mayonnaise. This is also a good way of using up left-over boiled or roast chicken, but to be really good there should be a fair proportion of both breast and leg meat.

FOIES DE VOLAILLE AU RIZ

CHICKEN LIVERS WITH RICE

Prepare a dish of *riz au gras* in the way described for *poule au riz*, page 404, using about ½ lb. of rice.

Slice ½ lb. of very carefully cleaned chicken livers into two or three pieces each. Season them and dust them with flour. Cook them gently a minute or two in foaming butter with an ounce or two of chopped cooked ham. Pour in 2 or 3 tablespoons of white wine or Madeira or white vermouth. Let it bubble and reduce. Add 3 tablespoons of the same stock which has been used for the rice. Cook another couple of minutes.

Turn out the rice on to a heated serving dish, and put the chicken livers in a mound on the top. Sprinkle with a little parsley. Enough for four as a first course.

DINDONNEAU FARCI AUX MARRONS, MODE D'ARTOIS
TURKEY STUFFED WITH CHESTNUTS AND APPLES

French cooks nearly always add pork or sausage meat to the chestnut stuffing for turkey. It helps lubricate the bird and improves the flat taste of chestnuts. In this northern French recipe apples are also added.

For an average turkey of about 12 lb. the proportions are 2 lb. of chestnuts, 1 lb. of sweet apples, 6 oz. of salted or fresh belly of pork, $\frac{1}{2}$ pint of milk, 2 shallots, parsley, an egg.

Make a crosswise incision across the rounded part of the chestnuts and roast them for 10 to 15 minutes in a moderate oven. Take out a few at a time and shell and skin them while still hot. Stew them in the milk, to which is added $\frac{1}{4}$ pint of water, until they are soft. This will take about half an hour. Cut the pork into small dice, and cook for 10 minutes in a little water. Peel and core the apples; stew them in a very little water until reduced to a purée. Mix with the pork and the drained and roughly broken-up chestnuts. Season with salt and pepper and the finely-chopped shallot and parsley, and bind with a beaten egg.

The stuffed turkey, liberally rubbed with butter, is roasted on its side, if possible, in a slow oven, covered with buttered paper or, nowadays, aluminium foil.

For a 12 lb. turkey cooked at Gas No. 3, 330 deg. F., the average cooking time is about $3\frac{1}{2}$ hours. Turn it over at half time. Do not attempt to cook a large turkey in a small oven at a high temperature, for it will dry up and the outside will burn.

For the sauce, a little white wine or Madeira can be added to the buttery juices in the pan, and the whole quickly boiled up in a small saucepan.

In France, a salad such as the beetroot and celery one on page 150, rather than vegetables, is usually served with the turkey.

If you prepare your chestnut and apple stuffing a day or two in advance, remember to take it out of the refrigerator some time before cooking the turkey. If it is icy cold when the bird is put into the oven it will be so long before the heat penetrates that it will not do its work of lubricating the bird.

LA PINTADE

GUINEA FOWL

The flavour of guinea fowl is mid-way between that of the chicken and the pheasant. It can be an excellent bird when well cooked but tends to be rather dry. So it is best cooked according to pheasant rather than chicken recipes. All the methods given for pheasant on pages 419–21 can be applied to guinea fowl, including, for an old bird, the one with rice, sausages and sweet peppers.

CANETON OU CANARD RÔTI AU FOUR

ROAST DUCK OR DUCKLING

A plain roast duck is one of the most excellent of dishes but one of the most difficult of all roasts to get quite right, for if the breast is properly cooked and still just pink inside, the legs are almost bound to be uneatably underdone. If the bird is only for rather small helpings for three or four people, this doesn't matter, for only the breast and wings are served, carved into elegant long pieces, the legs being kept and recooked for a second dish next day. But if the whole duck is to be eaten at one meal, then the legs must be properly cooked as well. In either case it seems preferable to me to roast the bird slowly, and during the process to get rid of at least some of the excess fat. For while chicken, turkey, veal and some beef cuts need extra basting fat, pork, duck and goose are best moistened with stock, wine or slightly salted water.

Suppose you have bought a full-grown 5 lb. duck which, when drawn and dressed, will weigh about 3 lb., start off then by making a stock as follows: put the giblets (but not the liver) in a small saucepan with, if possible, 2 or 3 tablespoons of white wine or vermouth; a small sliced onion, a little piece of carrot and a chopped unpeeled tomato. Let the wine bubble and reduce for a couple of minutes. Add a little salt and a bouquet of herbs including parsley, thyme and celery leaves. Cover with ¾ pint of water and simmer gently for an hour or so.

To cook the duck, turn on the oven low, to Gas No. 3, 330 deg. F. If the duck has been trussed with a wooden skewer thrust through the legs and its tail end rearing up in the air, remove the skewer so that the duck lies flat. Rub it all over with olive oil. Put it *on its side*, in the roasting tin, and leave it to cook uncovered for 30 minutes. Now pour from the tin all the fat which has run out. Turn the bird over on to its other side. Over it pour ½ pint of the strained stock, hot. Leave it another 30 minutes. Turn it breast upwards and cook another 10 minutes, for the skin of the breast to brown. Pour off the stock to serve separately as a sauce. There will not be much surplus fat to get rid of, because most of it has already been removed by the first operation of pouring it from the tin. Heat it quickly in a saucepan, adding what flavour you please, such as the finely pared, shredded and blanched rind of a Seville orange, a handful of stoned cherries, a few drops of orange or cherry-flavoured liqueur and so on. Alternatively, the duck could be stuffed with its liver as described in the recipe for *canard à la serviette*, and the sauce made in the same way.

Do not throw away the fat from the duck. It is valuable for frying bread, for sauté potatoes and so on.

A duck of this size should just about serve six people; but it must, although full grown, not be an elderly animal fit only for braising or stewing; and a duckling, which will weigh only about 2 lb. when plucked and drawn, needs only about 45 minutes' cooking by this slow-roasting system. But although this size bird is what is technically known as a duckling, full-grown young birds, weighing anything up to 6 lb. gross weight, are now commonly sold by English poulterers as ducklings. On the whole they are better value than the very small duckling or *caneton*.

CANARD AUX PETITS POIS
DUCK WITH GREEN PEAS

For a 5 lb. duck (weight before drawing and dressing), the other ingredients are 2 onions, 4 carrots, a little piece of turnip and a small stick of celery, 4 to 6 oz. of salt pork or streaky bacon, olive oil or butter, seasonings, bouquet of herbs, 3 lb. of very small new peas or a large tin of French or Belgian *petits pois extra fins*.

Buy the duck the day before it is to be cooked. Have it trussed flat, not rearing up like a heraldic animal as is customary for roasting ducks in this country. Rub it all over with coarse salt and leave in a big dish until next day.

Prepare a generous ½ pint of good stock by simmering the giblets of the duck, an onion, 2 carrots, a bouquet and the rind of the salt pork or bacon in water, with seasonings, for a good hour. Strain.

In a heavy oval braising pot heat a little olive oil or butter. Put in the salt pork or bacon cut into strips. Add 2 diced carrots, a finely-sliced onion and the little pieces of turnip and celery. When the fat from the salt pork or bacon is running, put in the duck from which the excess salt has been wiped with a soft cloth. Cover the pan and cook over low heat for 5 minutes until the vegetables are beginning to brown and the fat is running from the duck. It is an improvement to the finished dish if the duck is now removed from the pan and all the fat poured off. Put back the bird. Pour in the heated stock. Put in the bouquet of bayleaf, thyme and parsley. Add a little freshly-ground pepper but no salt. Cover the pan. Transfer to a preheated oven at Gas No. 3, 330 deg. F., and cook for an hour. Now pour all but a very little of the stock out of the pan into a bowl. Return the duck and the bacon, etc., to the oven and leave uncovered so that the skin of the bird can cook golden and crisp.

If fresh peas are being used, half cook them in salted water, strain them and put them round the duck to finish cooking. If tinned *petits pois* are to be used (it is impossible to use English tinned garden peas because, so far as I know, all of them have added green colouring matter, and this will quite ruin the appearance of the dish), strain off their liquid and put them, without further ado, into the pan with the duck.

By the time the duck and peas are ready, in about another 15 minutes, the gravy you have poured off should be fairly cool and the fat risen to the top. Pour this off. Quickly reheat the remaining clear gravy in a small saucepan, tasting it to see if the seasoning is right. Transfer duck, peas, bacon or pork and all the little pieces of vegetable to a sizzling hot serving dish. The gravy is to be served separately.

Readers may think all this represents rather a performance for a simple dish of duck and green peas. But, on second thoughts, they will probably realise that duck, which can be so good, is a fat bird and, if care is not taken with the cooking, may easily produce a greasy dish. In this recipe the overnight salting of the bird, the successive pouring off of the fat and clearing of the gravy will, if carefully attended to, produce a finished dish which is neither cloying nor too fatty. It is, after all, attention to these small extra details which makes the whole difference between a rough and ready dish and one which a Frenchman would call *soigné*.

CANARD AUX CÉLERIS
DUCK WITH CELERY

Cook your duck exactly as above and prepare a couple of heads of celery as described for celery stewed in butter on page 248. Keep them rather under-cooked and transfer them to the pan with the duck instead of the peas. Celery goes particularly well with duck.

CANARD AUX CERISES
DUCK WITH CHERRIES

For this dish, the proper cherries to use are the bitter, bright red morellos, the equivalent of the ones the French call *griottes*.

A 4 to 5 lb. duck is browned lightly in butter, in a *daubière* or braising pot, with 3 or 4 carrots, a small sliced onion, a bouquet of parsley, thyme and bayleaf, and a calf's foot split in two. Add a wineglass (6 oz.) of white wine and a pint of stock made from the giblets of the duck. Add seasoning, cover the pot and cook very gently either on top of the stove or in the oven for 1½ hours. Remove the duck and cook the rest of the contents for another 1½ hours. Strain the sauce into a bowl and, when it has set, remove all the fat. Stew ½ lb. of stoned morello cherries with a little sugar for a minute or two. Heat up the stock, clarify it if necessary (see page 72) and pour it into a square or oblong mould, terrine or tin, over the strained cherries.

To serve, surround the duck with the jelly, turned out of its mould and cut into squares, each with a cherry embedded in it. This is a simple version of the dish known to French chefs as *canard à la Montmorency*.

Tinned morello cherries can be used for garnishing the duck when fresh ones are unobtainable.

CANARD À LA SERVIETTE
BOILED DUCK

No doubt the idea of boiling a duck will cause raised eyebrows. All the same, it is an excellent method (the Welsh way of salting and boiling a duck is one of the very best of our native dishes) and provides an interesting alternative to roasting.

To cook the duck, first of all put a very large pan of water (I use a huge oval iron *daubière*) on to boil. Add a tablespoon of salt. While the water is coming to the boil, chop a few sprigs of fresh, washed parsley, and work it with 1 oz. of butter; to this add the liver of the duck, previously rinsed in warm water and also chopped. Season with salt and pepper. Stuff the bird with this mixture. If the poulterer has trussed the duck with a skewer through the legs, remove it because it is not necessary and only makes the animal more difficult to handle when it is cooked.

Wrap the duck in an old white napkin, cheesecloth or clean tea towel. Tie the ends like a sausage, and put a string also round the middle. Cook in the steadily boiling water for 50 minutes for a 4½ to 5 lb. duck (i.e. approximately 3 lb. when dressed and drawn). Remove from the saucepan and leave on a dish to cool a little before untying it. In the meantime prepare the following sauce: Melt a finely-chopped shallot in a little butter until it turns palest yellow. Pour in a small glass (4 tablespoons) of white or red wine or dry vermouth. Let it bubble. Add 2 tablespoons of reduced meat stock or stock from the duck giblets as explained below. Let this sauce reduce a little. Then, having unwrapped the duck, scoop out the liver stuffing with a spoon and stir it into the sauce. Now remove the saucepan from the fire and add to the sauce about 1½ oz. of butter cut into little pieces. Shake the pan until the butter has amalgamated with the sauce and thickened it but do not put the saucepan back on the fire again.

Serve the duck with a dish of pilaff rice cooked as follows: In a pan of boiling salted water cook 1½ teacups of long-grained Patna rice for 7 minutes. Drain it in a colander or sieve and then hold the sieve under running cold water until all the starch is washed away and the water runs out clear. Put the rice in an earthenware or other oven pot and pour over 2½ teacups of hot stock previously made, if you have none already available, from the giblets and neck of the duck plus vegetables, herbs and plenty of seasoning. Add a small lump of butter, about ½ oz., and stir it round in the rice. Now put a folded teacloth over the pot, then the lid, and cook in a moderate oven, Gas No. 4, 355 deg. F., for 25 minutes— all this arranged, of course, to coincide with the cooking of the duck. When you take the rice from the oven, the liquid will be absorbed and the rice will be swollen and perfectly cooked, shining and moist.

Now, as anyone can see, this dish is quite an arduous one to prepare because of the three separate operations involved. An alternative method is as follows: have your duck cold but give it an extra 20 minutes' cooking at a rather slower pace, because you will probably want to serve the legs as well as the breast, and at 50 minutes they are not sufficiently done for cold eating. The rice cooked in the duck stock and served with the liver sauce, which is quite delicious hot but not so good cold, can be served as a hot first course for another meal. The cold duck—and on the whole I think duck is at its best cold—can be accompanied by a green salad and followed by a hot sweet dish, such as an open apple tart. The first course could be a hot and creamy vegetable soup, a *gratin* of fish such as the one described on page 291 or perhaps the courgette soufflé on page 202.

OIE RÔTIE AUX POMMES DE TERRE, MODE DU PÉRIGORD
ROAST GOOSE WITH POTATOES

To roast a goose successfully a capacious, deep roasting tin is necessary to catch the large amount of fat which flows from the bird during cooking.

As there are plenty of potatoes to go with it, the goose need not necessarily be stuffed for this recipe; indeed, in spite of tradition, I think myself that a goose tends to be better without a stuffing, but a chestnut and apple mixture like the one described for the turkey recipe on page 408 can be cooked separately in a terrine to be served with the goose. It is preferable, though, to substitute veal for pork when the stuffing is for a goose.

The goose is covered with buttered paper or foil and is cooked standing on a grid placed in the baking tin. This is important. If the goose is put straight into the tin it will stew in its fat and be greasy. After the first hour, take it from the oven and pour off most of the fat in the tin. Put in 2 to 3 lb. of partly cooked potatoes cut into quarters, all the same size. By the time the goose is cooked the potatoes should be tender and deliciously flavoured with the fat from the bird. Ten minutes before serving add to the potatoes 4 or 5 hard-boiled eggs cut in quarters, which will also become golden and slightly crackling from the goose fat. Arrange the potatoes and eggs, drained of excess fat, all round the goose on the serving dish, and put a bunch of watercress at each end.

Cooking time is 2½ to 3 hours in a rather low oven, Gas No. 3, 330 deg. F., turned down to very low for the last hour, with the paper removed so that the skin becomes crisp and golden.

Good though the above method is, I cannot help agreeing with the author of one of my favourite French cookery books, *Clarisse, ou la Vieille Cuisinière*, that the goose, being to other poultry what pork is to butcher's meat, is at its best served cold, like all very fat meats. And nowadays many people have sensibly come round to the idea of cooking their Christmas bird the day before and thereby avoiding some at least of the last minute confusion and anxiety. By the time a large bird is carved and served it is usually tepid anyway, and a properly cooled bird is altogether more desirable.

Be sure to save the fat from the goose. It is valuable for many dishes.

As for the liver, there is little use in English cooks indulging in fantasies about *pâté de foie gras* or similar delicacies, for the liver of an English goose will weigh at the most about 4 oz., whereas those of the specially fattened geese of Alsace and the Périgord often weigh as much as 2 lb. or more. The dish of *foies de volaille au riz*, described on page 407, provides a good way of using up both goose and turkey livers.

L'ALICOT *or* ABATIS D'OIE EN RAGOÛT

GOOSE GIBLET STEW

A rich and savoury stew can be made from the goose giblets. This recipe is from south-western France.

Slice 2 or 3 large onions. Fry them very gently in a little goose fat. When they are pale golden, put in all the giblets except the liver, and a 6 oz. slice of salt pork or gammon. Let them take colour, add 3 or 4 sliced carrots, 3 large tomatoes, plenty of garlic, salt, pepper and a big bouquet of herbs.

Pour over ½ pint of heated stock. Bring to simmering point; cover the pot; cook in a very low oven for 2½ to 3 hours. Serve with boiled white haricot beans, augmented if you like with a well-spiced, coarsely cut sausage of the type sold in delicatessen shops as Spanish sausage.

PIGEONS EN ESTOUFFADE

STEWED PIGEONS

Our own wild wood-pigeons are rather different birds from the plump and tender little creatures of the *volière* or pigeon-run, which are those intended to be used in the majority of French recipes in which the pigeons or *pigeonneaux* (squabs) are roasted like game-birds or grilled *à la crapaudine*—in other words, spatchcocked. Not all cooks who adapt French recipes to English use quite realise this. Escoffier did, though, and gave us some admirable little pigeon dishes, published in *Le Carnet d'Épicure*. Here is one of them:

'Two or three young pigeons, dressed and drawn but not trussed, are to be lightly browned in butter and transferred to a terrine or other small heavy pot. Into the butter in which the pigeons have browned, pour a little glass of cognac and one of white wine; let this boil a few seconds and pour it over the pigeons. Surround the birds with a few little onions and mushrooms, also previously cooked in butter. Season with salt and pepper, add a few spoonfuls of good veal stock, cover the pigeons with a few little pieces of lean bacon first cooked in butter until the fat has run; seal the pot hermetically and cook in a gentle oven for 50 minutes.'

The time, as you see, is for young pigeons. Older and larger ones will take an extra 30 to 40 minutes.

In fact, this excellent method for pigeons is very much that of an *estouffade* or daube of beef, and any of the recipes for those dishes given in the meat chapter can be very successfully adapted to pigeons; red wine instead of white can be used; olives, black or green, make an excellent garnish; a tomato or two can be added to flavour the juice; and, above all, bear in mind that pigeons are dry birds, so that fats and juices are essential to their successful cooking.

For two pigeons, the quantities of other ingredients I use for Escoffier's dish are 3 to 4 oz. of bacon, 6 small onions, 4 oz. mushrooms, 4 table-spoons of red wine, 2 of brandy or *marc* and 4 of water or stock. The oven temperature should be very moderate—Gas No. 3, 330 deg. F.

PERDREAU RÔTI AU FOUR
ROAST PARTRIDGE

It is generally agreed that when young and in good condition, partridge are best presented in their most simple form—plain roasted with their own gravy as a sauce.

Work a little salt and pepper into a good lump of butter; put it inside the bird. Tie a wide, thin strip of larding fat (back pork fat) round the breast. If you can lay hands on some vine leaves, wrap one or two round the partridge. Lay the bird on its side in a small roasting tin. Put it in a preheated oven at a fairly high temperature. Gas No. 7, 420 deg. F., and after 10 minutes turn the bird over; lower the heat to Gas No. 5, 375 deg. F. After the next 10 minutes, turn the bird breast uppermost. Cook another 5 to 15 minutes making 25 to 35 minutes in all, depending upon the weight of the partridge, which may vary from 10 to 14 oz. Each time the oven is opened to turn the bird, pour a little hot melted butter over it; this butter, with any juices which have come from the bird during cooking, is subsequently poured off and served separately as a sauce. The bird is placed on a piece of bread fried golden in butter, and is to be eaten without delay.

It is worth noting that in French cookery it is fresh pork fat and not bacon which is tied round all birds for roasting. Bacon not only tends to curl away from the bird while it is cooking, but it spoils the flavour of the juices which are to be served as a sauce.

SALADE DE PERDREAUX À LA VENDÉENNE
PARTRIDGE SALAD

'When the first partridges are shot in the early morning, send them down to the house. As soon as they are received they should be plucked, drawn and trussed, and roasted without delay.

'Once roasted, carve into joints, put them in a bowl, season them while warm with salt, pepper, vinegar, olive oil and a tablespoon of rum, and take them straight down to the cellar to cool. The gravy from the roasting, in a separate bowl, also goes to cool.

'At lunchtime, put some lettuce hearts into the bowl, add the gravy, from which every particle of fat has been removed, 2 hard-boiled eggs cut into rounds, and a little more seasoning. This is an exquisite salad; the flesh of the partridges does not taste of rum but merely has a slightly enhanced gamy flavour, and the marinading after roasting has made it as tender as a partridge hung for 2 days.'

Recipe from BENJAMIN RENAUDET'S *Les Secrets de la Bonne Table*

PERDREAU AUX CHOUX À LA MODE DE BRETAGNE
PARTRIDGE WITH CABBAGE AND SAUSAGES

Now here is a useful lesson in ingenuity. By some chance you find yourself with two partridges, one a fine young roasting bird, the other, alas, well past its prime. To make the best use of both, try this recipe adapted from Édouard Nignon's *Les Plaisirs de la Table*.

First blanch 2 fine white cabbages in boiling salted water. Drain them, separate the leaves, cut out all hard stalks and the centres, rearrange the leaves to form one whole cabbage and, in the centre of it, lay your old bird, first gently coloured in butter. Close the leaves over the partridge, wrap up the cabbage in 1 or 2 large rashers of bacon, put it in a casserole and surround it with 1 lb. of streaky bacon cut in large chunks. Add a couple of pork sausages of the coarsely cut variety for boiling, to be found in delicatessen shops. Pour over a light meat stock to come half-way up the cabbage. Cover the pan and simmer very gently, preferably in the oven, for 4 hours. Half an hour before serving, remove the casserole from the oven and put it over the gentlest possible heat on top of the stove, turn the oven up and roast your young bird, as described on page 416. When it is ready, transfer the cabbage to a serving dish and remove the bacon wrapping and the old partridge, replacing it with the roasted one. Surround the whole with the sausages cut in slices and the chunks of bacon and serve very hot.

In this way two people may enjoy the one young bird, for half each will be sufficient and the cabbage will also be deliciously flavoured with partridge. Next day or the day after you can eat the old bird in a salad, with hard-boiled eggs, lettuce hearts or celery, and mayonnaise or a vinaigrette dressing.

PERDRIX À L'AUVERGNATE
PARTRIDGES STEWED IN WHITE WINE

For four stewing partridges, the other ingredients are 2 oz. of butter, 4 oz. of salt pork or mild streaky bacon, 5 tablespoons of brandy, 8 of

o

white wine, 4 of clear veal or other meat or game stock, a little bouquet of bayleaf, parsley, thyme and a crushed clove of garlic.

If salt pork is being used, steep it for 1 hour in water. Cut it in small cubes. Put it with 1 oz. of the butter in an earthenware or other heavy pan just large enough to hold the four birds. When the fat from the pork or bacon runs, put in the birds, breast downwards. (If they have been trussed for roasting by the poulterer, take out the wooden skewer before cooking them; it only makes the birds more difficult to fit into the pot and is a nuisance when it comes to serving them.) After 2 or 3 minutes pour in the warmed brandy; set light to it. Shake the pan so that the flames spread. When these die down, put in the white wine, warmed if you are cooking in an earthenware pan. Let it bubble a minute; add the stock and the bouquet. Cover the pan with paper or foil and a well-fitting lid. Transfer to a slow oven, Gas No. 3, 330 deg. F., and cook for 1½ to 1¾ hours. Pour off all the liquid into a wide pan, and keep the birds hot in the serving dish. Reduce the liquid by fast boiling to about half its original volume. Off the fire, add the second ounce of butter and shake the pan until the butter has melted and given the sauce a slightly glazed appearance. Pour it over the partridges. Serve at the same time a purée of brown lentils or of celeriac and potatoes.

Young partridges are excellent cooked in the same way, but according to size take only 30 to 40 minutes or so in the oven. If you have no stock use water instead but do not use a bouillon cube. It would falsify the flavour of the birds.

FAISAN EN PAPILLOTES
PHEASANT IN PAPER CASES

Roast a small young bird, weighing between 14 and 16 oz. when plucked and dressed, for 17 to 20 minutes in a hot oven, Gas No. 7, 420 deg. F. The bird should be cooked on its side rather than breast uppermost, and turned round two or three times, being very liberally basted with butter.

Meanwhile to prepare the *papillotes* fold sheets of greaseproof paper measuring roughly 20 inches by 10 inches in two, so that you have a 10-inch square, and cut these into a rough heart shape, with the point at the open end (see the drawing on page 78). Open them out and butter the inside of the paper copiously. This is essential, as the butter and its own juices will be the only sauce for the pheasant.

Carve the pheasant in half lengthways; lay each piece in the middle of one half of the buttered paper. Season lightly with salt, pepper and a few drops of white wine, Madeira, or concentrated meat or game stock, and pour over all the butter and juices from the roasting pan. Lay a slice of unsmoked bacon over each half-pheasant, fold over the paper, then twist down the edges all round so that no juices can possibly escape. Put the *papillotes* on a baking sheet and let them cook 12 to 15 minutes in a moderate oven, Gas No. 4 or 5, 355 to 380 deg. F.

Serve as they are, so that each person unfolds his own half-pheasant in its buttery juice, and be sure that the plates are very hot.

FAISAN EN COCOTTE
PHEASANT STEWED IN BUTTER

Melt 1 oz. of butter with 2 oz. of diced streaky salt or fresh pork, in a small, deep *cocotte* or other pan in which the pheasant will just fit; put in the bird; let it take colour on both sides. If you have a little brandy, Calvados or other spirit to spare, pour a small glass of it over the pheasant at this stage. Let it boil fiercely for a few seconds. Cover the pan; simmer gently for 40 to 45 minutes, turning the bird over at half-time. Remove it to the serving dish and, to the juices in the pan, add a claret glass (about 4 oz.) of white wine. Let it bubble and reduce, and when it has thickened slightly, pour into a sauce-boat.

As a vegetable, serve celery cooked as described on page 248.

A young but full-grown pheasant will weigh approximately 1¾ lb. when drawn and dressed. The times to be reckoned for cooking it are about the same as for a chicken of the same weight.

FAISAN À LA CAUCHOISE
PHEASANT WITH CREAM, CALVADOS AND APPLE

Cook a tender roasting pheasant in butter in a heavy iron or earthenware *cocotte* on top of the stove, turning it over once or twice so that each side is nicely browned. It will take about 40 to 45 minutes to cook. Carve it, transfer it to the serving dish and keep it warm. Pour off the juices into a shallow pan; let them bubble; pour in a small glass of warmed Calvados (or brandy, *marc* or whisky), set light to it, shake the pan and when the flames have burnt out add a good measure, 8 to 10 oz., of thick cream. Shake the pan, lifting and stirring the cream until it thickens. Season with a very little salt and pepper. Pour the sauce over the pheasant. Serve separately a little dish of diced sweet apple, previously fried golden in butter and kept warm in the oven: 2 apples will be sufficient for one pheasant.

This is, I think, the best of the many versions of pheasant with apples and Calvados, usually called *faisan normand.*

FAISAN À LA CHOUCROUTE

PHEASANT WITH PICKLED CABBAGE

There are so many recipes for *la vraie choucroute alsacienne* and *à la mode Lorraine*, and they vary so much, that the question of how long the *choucroute* is cooked, and whether in butter, goose or pork fat, and of what seasonings to add, is obviously very largely a matter of taste. My own feelings in the matter are that it should be cooked a relatively short time and served before it has acquired that brown, greasy, matted look which it gets from being cooked for hours in an oven. Seasonings must include juniper berries and, if possible, white wine; if I have pork or goose fat I use it, but otherwise butter; and a final glass of Kirsch ought to be more commonly added than it is: it makes the whole difference to the flavour and the digestibility of the dish.

So for 2 lb. of *choucroute* the other ingredients are 3 oz. of butter or rather less of pork or goose fat, a finely-chopped onion, 10 crushed juniper berries, $\frac{1}{2}$ pint of light stock and a small glass of dry white wine, or $\frac{3}{4}$ pint stock without the wine, a grated raw potato and a little glass of Alsatian or Swiss Kirsch.

Melt the butter or fat in a heavy pot; put in the onion; when it starts to sizzle add the well-washed and drained *choucroute* and the juniper berries; stir and lift the *choucroute* with a wooden fork, keeping the flame low, for 15 minutes; add the white wine and a little of the stock; keep the mixture over low heat for $1\frac{1}{2}$ hours, adding more stock from time to time, but there should never be so much liquid that the *choucroute* is floating in it. Season with freshly-milled pepper and a little salt. Stir in the grated potato and cook another 15 minutes; just before serving add 4 to 6 tablespoons of Kirsch. Turn on to a hot dish in a mound, on top of which you put the pheasant, either roasted, or cooked in butter in a *cocotte*, as explained on page 419, and garnish all round with slices of lightly-fried smoked bacon.

Even if you only have a few smoked Frankfurter sausages or some grilled gammon and potatoes boiled in their skins instead of the pheasant, this is still an admirable dish.

Miniature bottles of Kirsch from the Strasbourg firm of Dolfi and the Colmar firm of Jacobert can be bought at many wine merchants, but if you haven't got Kirsch, or don't want to go to the expense, just use gin instead. It does the trick quite well.

If you have any *choucroute* left over, it makes a good soup. Simmer a large cupful for another hour or so with a pint of light stock or water. Sieve, and finish the purée with a little thick fresh cream. Add a few little cubes of smoked sausage, or serve with fried croûtons.

FAISAN AU RIZ BASQUAIS

PHEASANT WITH SPICED RICE

A highly seasoned and highly colourful dish, which makes a most cheering sight on a chilly winter evening.

A large pheasant weighing 2 to 2½ lb., 4 Spanish or Basque sausages (chorizos) or ¾ lb. of the type of coarsely-cut boiling sausage sold in delicatessen shops, 6 to 8 oz. streaky bacon, a carrot, an onion, a bouquet of herbs plus a small strip of orange peel, a clove of garlic, pork, goose or duck dripping for frying, 1 lb. of ripe tomatoes, 3 or 4 sweet red peppers or the contents of a 4 oz. tin of Spanish sweet peppers or *pimientos* in oil, ¾ lb. rice, veal stock or water, paprika pepper.

Melt 2 tablespoons of the dripping (failing either pork, goose or duck dripping, olive oil will do) in a heavy saucepan large enough to hold the pheasant. Brown the sliced onion and carrot, then the pheasant, turning it over two or three times, so that it colours evenly. Cover with half-stock and half-water, or all water. Put in the bacon in one piece, the bouquet and the garlic; cover the pan. Simmer gently for 20 minutes before adding the sausages. Cook another 20 minutes if the pheasant is a roasting one, 1¼ to 1½ hours if an old bird, but in this case add the sausages only 20 minutes before the end.

Put the rice into a large saucepan of boiling salted water and boil for 10 to 12 minutes. Strain it very carefully. Put it, with a little more dripping, into the top half of a double saucepan. Pour over it, through a strainer, a ladle of the stock from the pheasant. Put a folded tea-cloth on top, then the lid of the saucepan, and steam for about 20 minutes, until the rice is tender.

In the meantime prepare the following tomato and sweet pepper mixture. Skin and chop the tomatoes, remove the seeds and cores of the peppers, wash them and cut them in strips. If tinned ones are being used, drain off the liquid and rinse them before slicing them. Heat another tablespoon of dripping in a small saucepan or frying-pan, put in the tomatoes and sweet peppers and cook fairly briskly for about 10 minutes. Season with salt, pepper and a dessertspoon of paprika, which is the nearest approach we can get here to the coarsely-ground red pepper called *piment basquais*, which they use in the Basque country. This tomato and pepper mixture must be thick but not a purée.

To serve, turn the rice on to a heated dish. Extract the sausages and the bacon from the saucepan. Cut each sausage into three slices, remove the rind from the bacon, cut into squares. The pheasant may be either carved and arranged in the centre of the rice, or brought to table whole and then carved. The sausages and bacon are arranged round the pheasant, and the tomato and sweet pepper mixture in a ring round the rice.

A chicken may be cooked in the same way, allowing 45 minutes for an average-size roaster, 2 to 3 hours' very slow cooking for a boiler.

The Spanish sausages can be bought in Soho shops and in quite a few delicatessens.

BÉCASSE RÔTIE

ROAST WOODCOCK

Nearly all French cooks and gourmets consider that a good roast woodcock is one of the most refined and exquisite morsels one can offer to honoured guests. I can't say I altogether share this opinion; I wouldn't, for instance, rate woodcock higher than grouse or partridge.

Woodcock should be well hung but, at the same time, they should not be kept so long that the skin breaks when you pluck them, for they are then likely to have a repellently high flavour.

They are roasted without being drawn or decapitated but with the gizzard removed and a piece of back pork fat tied over the breast, for about 18 to 20 minutes in a hot oven.

For each woodcock have ready a little slice of fresh, crisp hot toast. When the birds are cooked extract the entrails; mash these up with salt, pepper, lemon juice and a few drops of cognac; reheat this mixture in a little saucepan for a few seconds and then spread them on the toast. Serve each bird on top of its slice of toast, with quarters of lemon round the dish.

Snipe (*bécassines*) are cooked in the same way, but as they are so small they can be roasted under the grill, not too close to the flame.

PLUVIERS À L'AUVERGNATE

PLOVERS IN WHITE WINE

Little golden plovers are excellent cooked in the same manner as the partridges *à l'auvergnate*, described on page 417, but there is no necessity to add stock, and they are best cooked in a hot oven, Gas No. 7, 420 deg. F., for 12 to 15 minutes.

CANARD SAUVAGE À LA NAVARRAISE

WILD DUCK WITH SWEET PEPPER AND WHITE WINE

From the giblets of a wild duck (mallard) plus carrot, onion, herbs, a glass of white wine, a spoonful of Madeira, a little water and, if possible, a piece of dried sweet red pepper—not the burning chilli pepper—make about ½ pint of stock, strain it and reduce by fast boiling to ⅓ pint.

Prepare the following mixture: 2 shallots finely chopped, a carrot cut into small dice, ¼ lb. of gammon diced, half a fresh sweet pepper, all seeds and core removed, cut into little pieces, Melt this mixture in goose or pork fat or olive oil. When the shallots have taken colour put in the duck and let it gently brown. Warm a ladle of brandy, set light to it; pour it flaming over the duck. When the flames have died down add the hot stock. Cover the pan, transfer to a medium oven, Gas No. 4, 355 deg. F., and cook for 35 to 40 minutes. Serve with its own sauce, triangles of fried bread and a green salad.

This recipe can be adapted for pigeons or stewing partridges, which will, however, need much longer and much slower cooking.

When fresh sweet peppers are not to be come by, use tinned Spanish ones, which are very good.

SARCELLE RÔTIE AU FOUR
ROAST TEAL

Put a lump of butter inside the teal, which should be wrapped in a thin slice of back pork fat. Roast it on a grid in a baking tin right at the top of the oven, turned to its highest temperature. Turn the teal over after 10 minutes and baste with a little warmed port mixed with a little orange juice. In 15 to 20 minutes, according to whether you like it well done or underdone, it will be ready.

GRIVES AUX OLIVES CASSÉES
THRUSHES WITH CRACKED OLIVES

The cooking of thrushes can only be of academic interest to English readers but, in many parts of France, particularly in Provence and the Basses Alpes, thrushes and thrush pâtés are great specialities. I have chosen this particular recipe chiefly because of Prosper Montagné's interesting note about the olives:

'Have some fine well-hung thrushes; pluck, singe, gut and truss them, wrap them in thin slices of smoked streaky bacon. Brown them in butter, in a shallow earthenware pan (*poëlon*); when they have taken colour, add some tomatoes, a large onion, a clove of garlic, a sprig of parsley, all finely chopped, with a sprig of fennel, salt and pepper and, the most important, a good saucerful of *olives cassées*.

'*Olives cassées* are a speciality of Provence, more especially of the region between Avignon and Arles, which means St. Rémy, Maillane, Les Baux and Tarascon. They are prepared as follows: Take 2 or 3 kilos (4 to 6½ lb.) of fine green olives. Choose the almost round ones, the pointed variety being kept for the preparation known as *à la picholine*, which is almost the only method known for green olives outside the olive-producing area. Crack the olives on a chopping board, without breaking the stones. Put them into an earthenware jar filled with water; the olives must not be closely packed but must swim at their ease. Change the water every day for 6 to 8 days, and when the olives have lost all their bitter taste change the water for the last time, adding 8 to 10 oz. of melted salt and a big bouquet of fennel.

'These olives keep only a maximum of 2 to 3 months. Usually they are prepared in the second fortnight of October and eaten until Christmas.'

PROSPER MONTAGNÉ: *Le Trésor de la Cuisine du Bassin Mediterranéen*

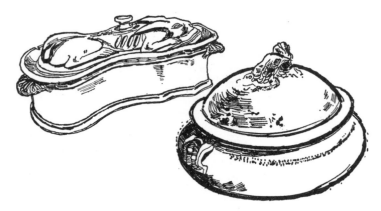

LE CIVET DE L IÈVRE DE DIANE DE CHÂTEAUMORAND
HARE STEWED IN RED WINE

This is a dish which is said to have come from the Abbey of St. Sulpice in the Valromey in Bresse. The noble lady after whom it is called was the rich and beautiful Marquise de Valromey, who married her brother-in-law, the Marquis de Valromey, after her first husband had divorced her to enter holy orders. Diane de Châteaumorand, it seems, was much addicted to hunting and coursing and was well versed in the art of game cookery:

'Put your skinned and cleaned hare, cut into pieces, in a big bowl and pour over it a glass of wine vinegar, half a glassful of olive oil, salt, pepper, a little bunch of thyme and a sliced onion. Keep aside the liver and the blood. Turn the hare several times in its marinade and leave it at least 12 hours before cooking it.

'Chop together an onion and a little under 1 oz. of fresh pork fat; put these ingredients together with 2 oz. of fresh butter into an earthenware or iron pot. Add the pieces of hare. Let them cook 20 minutes; sprinkle over them 1 oz. of flour; stir and simmer for 25 minutes. Add a soup ladle of beef stock and the same quantity of good red wine. Season with pepper and salt and cook another 35 minutes.

'Pound the liver to a fine paste; add the strained marinade; stir in the blood of the hare. Put through a fine sieve: 5 minutes before serving time add this mixture to the hare. Allow just to come to the boil. Taste the sauce; if it is insipid, add a few drops of vinegar. Finally, add a spoonful of olive oil. The *civet* can be made the day before it is to be eaten; it is all the better for being heated up. Its succulence depends upon the quality of the hare and the quantity of blood saved. The colour of the dish should be that of good chocolate cooked in water.'

This recipe is given in *La Table au Pays de Brillat-Savarin*, by Lucien Tendret, who also gives instructions (see recipe below) for a saddle of hare baked in cream. The two recipes can be usefully combined, using the saddle only for the cream dish and all the rest for Diane de Châteaumorand's *civet*; but if you do as Tendret suggests and make it the day before it is to be eaten, do not add the thickening of the animal's liver and blood until serving time. As a matter of fact, the addition of these ingredients gives the sauce a pretty powerful flavour which is not to everyone's taste, and the sauce being thick enough before the blood and liver are added, the dish *can* be served just as it is. If you choose to serve it in this way, then it becomes simply a stew rather than a *civet*.

The amounts of oil and wine vinegar for the marinade are about 3 and 6 oz. respectively, and of stock and wine for the cooking, 4 to 5 oz. each. Do not forget the final addition of the spoonful of olive oil.

RÂBLE DE LIÈVRE À LA CRÈME

SADDLE OF HARE BAKED IN CREAM

The *râble* is, correctly speaking, the back or saddle of the hare only; when it includes the hind legs it is called a *train de lièvre*.

Put the saddle of hare in an oval earthenware pot. Cover it with super-excellent cream (*excellentissime* is the word Tendret uses), add 2 spoonfuls of finely-chopped shallot and half a claret glass of red wine vinegar. Cook gently for 1¼ hours, frequently basting the meat with the cream which surrounds it; do not worry if the sauce takes on a sinister aspect and appears to be separating; it will put itself to rights, so wait until it is done; add salt but no pepper.

'You find this recipe astonishing?' adds Tendret. 'Try it and do not argue.'

Not everyone will have the faith which Lucien Tendret asks of his readers. So perhaps I had better say that he is quite right about the cream sauce: it *does* right itself. For the rest, the best way to proceed is as follows: Put the saddle from a young hare (don't forget to remove the membrane, as explained in the following recipe) into a long, narrow terrine or other fireproof dish. Add the chopped shallots, ½ pint of double cream and 2 tablespoons of wine vinegar—half a claret glass as specified by Tendret being too much for my taste. Cover the dish and cook in a low oven, Gas No. 1, 290 deg. F., for an hour. There is no need for basting and, if you don't look at the sauce, you won't see any sinister happenings. Now uncover the dish, stir a little salt and pepper into the sauce and spoon some of it over the saddle. Leave uncovered for another 15 minutes. Now transfer the saddle to a hot serving dish. Pour the sauce off into a wide shallow pan. Bring it to the boil, stir and lift it. It will soon start to thicken and turn a beautiful pale coffee colour. It is a great improvement to add at this stage a tablespoon of red-currant jelly, stirring it well in until it has amalgamated with the cream. Carve your saddle, pour the sauce round and serve it, preferably with a purée of chestnuts or of celeriac and potatoes.

These quantities and the timing are for a fairly small saddle, weighing not more than 1½ lb. The difficulty really is the dish to cook it in, for if this is too wide the cream will not cover the saddle. I have a beautiful old French terrine specially made for the cooking of a saddle of hare (it is in the drawing on page 424); I have also used for the purpose a boat-shaped fireproof fish dish, covering it with several sheets of foil. But failing some such dish, it is perhaps wiser not to attempt this particular recipe, unless of course you are prepared to lavish a lot of extra cream on it, but to try instead the following dish. The method is different but the result is very similar.

RÂBLE DE LIÈVRE À LA CRÈME À L'ALSACIENNE
SADDLE OF HARE WITH CREAM SAUCE AND NOODLES

Carefully remove the membrane or iridescent skin covering the saddle (in this case the back only) of a young hare. Wrap it completely in thin slices of pork fat or fat bacon. Roast it in a moderate oven, Gas No. 5, 375 to

380 deg. F., for approximately 30 minutes. Unwrap it, carve it into long fillets ready for serving, reconstitute into its original shape and keep hot in the serving dish. To the juices in the roasting pan, from which the excess fat has been poured off, add ¼ pint of thick cream and heat quickly on the top of the stove until the cream thickens. Pour over the hare and serve quickly.

For convenience' sake, roast the saddle in a grill pan with a handle, so that you can tip it, rotate and manipulate it with one hand while, with a wooden spoon in the other, you stir and scrape up the sauce as the cream thickens. But don't forget to have a thick cloth ready, because the handle of the pan will be pretty hot.

In Alsace boiled noodles are often served as an accompaniment to this and other meat and game dishes. Another alternative is the *pflütten* or potato and semolina gnocchi described on page 210, but without cheese, and poached as in the second method. But since neither of these accompaniments are very suitable for single-handed cooking, the more usual purée of chestnuts, celeriac or lentils, kept hot in a *bain-marie*, would do instead.

A saddle of young hare serves two or three people, or four if the rest of the meal is rather copious.

RÔTI DE LIÈVRE À LA BETTERAVE

ROAST SADDLE OF HARE WITH BEETROOT

This excellent recipe was given by Dr. Édouard de Pomiane, most spirited and interesting of contemporary French cookery writers, in the magazine *Cuisine et Vins de France*:

'Having obtained or killed a hare, you leave it to hang for three days, provided it is not battered by shot. Should it have rather large wounds, it is risky to leave it to hang.

'Skin and gut the hare. Separate the saddle (*râble*) which consists of the back and hind legs. Keep the fore legs and the liver, etc., to make a stew the next day. With a sharp knife remove the membrane covering the meat. Lard the flesh with strips of bacon. Place the saddle in an earthen baking dish in which some more strips of bacon have already heated in the oven so that their fat has seeped out. Return to a very hot oven for 20 minutes if you like your hare *saignant*, 35 if you prefer it well cooked. As soon as it starts to take colour, baste it continuously with cream. Season with salt and pepper. The cream will separate into butter. No matter. Proceed. Five minutes before the end of the cooking pour into the dish a half tumbler of boiling water. Baste with this cream and water mixture. In this way a sauce is obtained but it is not smooth. The roast is ready.

'Remove it from the oven. Pour the sauce into a saucepan. It will be fairly abundant. Bind it, over a *very low* flame, with thick cream mixed with a *suspicion* of flour. Let it boil just once. Keep it hot.

'While the hare was roasting, you have chopped finely 1½ to 1¾ lb. of cooked beetroot. You have reheated it with butter, salt, pepper, and have acidulated it very slightly with vinegar. All is ready. Carve the hare into slices. Arrange on a very hot dish, reconstituting the slices into their original shape. Make a ring all round with the beetroot. Moisten the hare only (not the beetroot) with a little of the sauce. Serve the rest separately.

'If the idea of the beetroot alarms you, prepare the hare without it. You would, however, be wrong.'

When cooking a bought hare the provenance of which is uncertain, it is advisable, I think, to cook it rather more gently and for a little longer, or it may be tough: 45 minutes at Gas No. 5, 375 to 380 deg. F., is safer than 35 at a greater temperature. The amount of cream needed is about ½ pint altogether. Another point is that the saddle, in England, is usually understood to be the back only, minus the hind legs. It depends rather on how many people are to be served. The back only is sufficient for three or four at the most. With the hind legs, it is enough for six or seven.

RÂBLE DE LIÈVRE À LA PIRON

SADDLE OF HARE MARINATED IN EAU DE VIE DE MARC

I will give only a brief résumé of this recipe; it is a lovely dish but one which is very extravagant for an English kitchen.

A saddle of hare, piquéd with pork fat, is to be marinated for two or three days with shallots, garlic, celery, thyme, bayleaves and *eau de vie de marc*. Roast the saddle so that the meat is still just pink; surround it with peeled and seeded grapes, white and black; pour in some warmed *marc* and set light to it. Just before serving pour round the juices which have come from the saddle during the roasting and to which have been added a spoonful of *poivrade* sauce and one of thick cream.

The recipe comes from Henri Racouchot, pre-war proprietor of the Restaurant des Trois Faisans in Dijon. *Eau de vie de marc*, distilled from the grape skins after the juice has been pressed for the wine, is made in every wine district of France; that of Burgundy is particularly reputed.

Poivrade sauce is made on a basis of the brown sauce known as

Espagnole, with the addition of some very much reduced stock or essence made from the trimmings of the hare or whatever game it is to accompany, plus a small proportion of the marinade and a plentiful seasoning of freshly-milled pepper.

FILETS DE LIÈVRE CHASSEUR
FILLETS OF HARE WITH MUSHROOMS AND CREAM

A saddle of hare, 4 or 5 shallots, 2 oz. of ham, ¼ lb. of mushrooms, 2 oz. cream, a glass of white wine, flour, a cup of stock, juniper berries, lemon.

Cut the flesh from the saddle of hare into fillets; season them with salt and pepper, a little lemon juice squeezed over them and about 8 pounded juniper berries.

In butter, brown the chopped shallots, the ham cut into strips, and the fillets of hare, dusted with flour; pour over the white wine. Cook 5 minutes, then add the cleaned mushrooms, whole, and the stock. Simmer 15 minutes. Heat the cream to boiling point, in a separate pan; add it to the hare, stir, add seasoning if necessary. Strew breadcrumbs on the top, add a little butter and put in a moderate oven for a few minutes. This will be enough for only three people; for a bigger dish use as well fillets from the back legs, putting them to cook a few minutes before those from the saddle.

ESTOUFFADE DE CERF AU VIN ROUGE
VENISON STEWED IN RED WINE

Buy about 2 lb. of shoulder or flank of venison in one piece. Tie it in a sausage shape and put it to marinate, in a glazed earthenware or china bowl, with 4 tablespoons each of port and wine vinegar, and 1 tablespoon of olive oil. Leave for 24 hours, then take out the meat, wipe it dry, roll it in flour and put it in a small oval earthenware dish in which it will just about fit. On top put a layer of sliced onions and then cover completely with thin slices of fat bacon. Pour over the marinade, add a seasoning of salt and pepper, cover with greaseproof paper and the lid of the dish and cook in a very slow oven, Gas No. 2, 310 deg. F., for 4 to 4½ hours.

Serve in a very hot dish with very hot plates, for nothing gets colder or congeals more rapidly than venison. Red-currant or rowan jelly, or any sweet-sour pickled fruit goes well with venison, and an excellent accompaniment is the purée of celeriac and potatoes described on page 248.

CÔTELETTES DE CHEVREUIL À L'ARDENNAISE

VENISON CUTLETS BAKED IN THE OVEN

In France it is *chevreuil* or roe-deer rather than the red deer or *cerf* which is cooked in small pieces such as cutlets, steaks or *noisettes*, and bought venison from the deep freeze is usually best stewed as in the above recipe. But if you happen to be given a joint, this method of dealing with the cutlets is a good one.

Have 6 to 8 neck cutlets of venison trimmed of fat and the bones laid bare as for lamb cutlets. Cook them exactly as for *côtes de veau à l'arden-naise* (page 374) but give them anything up to 30 minutes longer in the oven. Cutlets from the young roe-deer would, of course, require considerably less time. When they are tender pour off the sauce and keep the cutlets hot in the oven while you put the sauce into a wide, shallow pan and reduce it a little by fast boiling. At this moment you can add, if you like, a spoonful of red-currant jelly and the juice of half a bitter orange. Pour the sauce boiling over the venison cutlets and be sure to have your plates very hot.

Vegetables to go with venison, as well as a purée of celeriac and potatoes, are a purée of chestnuts (page 264), lentils *à la maître d'hôtel* (page 262) or a sauté of carrots and potatoes (page 247).

LE MARCASSIN

YOUNG WILD BOAR

Edmond Richardin, in *L'Art du Bien Manger*, 1913, gives the following interesting recipe for wild boar:

'In mild winters in the Pyrenees, when the snows do not reach the wooded zones, troops of wild boars feed there on acorns and beech nuts which have fallen in the autumn under cover of the forest. The flesh of wild boar killed at this period, and prepared with artistry, is not without delicacy.

'The haunch of the young boar, skinned and with the sinews removed, is threaded with lardoons. Then it is put into a marinade composed of $\frac{1}{2}$ litre of vinegar, a bottle of old red wine, thyme, parsley, wild marjoram, 5 bayleaves, some sliced onions, 3 cloves of garlic, 4 shallots, 2 sliced carrots, a plentiful amount of salt and pepper. Leave to steep for 4 days.

'Take the haunch from the marinade, drain and dry it; let it take colour in very hot fat in a braising pan; remove it; prepare a *roux* by adding 4 tablespoons of flour to the same fat, then gradually adding some of the marinade strained through a tammy cloth. Replace the meat and cook gently for 1 hour. Moisten with the remaining marinade, add a glass of old cognac and seasoning, and cook over a gentle fire for another $1\frac{1}{2}$ hours. Serve after having poured excess fat off the sauce.'

Wild boar is not uncommon in France. A number of Paris restaurants serve it during the winter, nearly always accompanied by a creamy chestnut purée. In Sardinia and in Italy I have also eaten this rather attractive game dish, and admirers of Norman Douglas will remember the splendid recipe he gives in *Birds and Beasts of the Greek Anthology*.

A joint of fresh pork may be prepared and cooked in a very similar way to that explained by Richardin, and tastes remarkably like the game it is intended to imitate. The recipe is on page 364.

Les Restes

The left-overs

'*L'Art d'accommoder les restes*,' says the *Larousse Gastronomique*, with some severity, 'is not to be considered as the summit of culinary achievement.' On the contrary, the writer of the article on *les restes* is of the opinion that any household where there is customarily an abundance of left-overs is badly run. Either the food has been carelessly bought or badly cooked.

However, Larousse makes a clear distinction between food left over through bad management and that intentionally cooked in large enough quantities to serve two or three meals. There are surely, though, other kinds of left-overs, and perfectly legitimate ones.

Without allowing economy to get out of hand to the point of hoarding things which should have been consigned to the dustbin in the first place, there are bones and trimmings from joints, small quantities of meat left on a chicken carcase, enough cold salmon or other fish to make a little dish for two people, the end of a ham or a piece of gammon, or a little rich sauce from a beef and wine stew.

The requisites of dishes made from such things are, as I see the matter, as follows. They should be cheap, quick and easy to cook, and the result should be as attractive as if all the ingredients had been chosen especially for that dish. These conditions preclude the buying of a lot of extra ingredients, the opening of jars of this and tins of that, which in their turn become left-overs; nine times out of ten a dish made in such a way is not only a false economy but a messy concoction, full of ingredients without point or purpose.

Next, and perhaps most important of all, use your little odds and ends of left-overs while they are still fresh; don't hoard them in the larder or refrigerator until they are dried up and stale.

Lastly, when it comes to heating up already cooked food, leave the frying-pan out of it as much as possible and, instead of frizzling the food in fat, heat it as slowly as possible in stock in a covered pan.

Here is a brief list of recipes in this book in which left-overs can be used, and some suggestions as to the best purpose to which trimmings and oddments can be put.

White fish: Mayonnaise de poisson, page 288.

In a creamy cheese sauce as for the skate dish, page 291.

Salmon: Mayonnaise de poisson, page 288.

Mousse made as for the ham mousse, page 235.

Mussels, prawns and other shell fish: Riz pilaff as for the mussel dish on page 320. Mussel omelette, page 196.

Stock from mussels: L'œuf du pêcheur, page 189.

Boiled beef: Bœuf en salade, page 147.

Roast beef: Best cold with a potato or other vegetable salad.

Juice or sauce from beef stews: Œufs pochés à l'huguenote, page 190. With *pommes mousseline façon provençale*, page 272.

Lamb, mutton, pork and veal: With pilaff rice cooked as for the mussel dish on page 320. In salad as for the beef salad, page 147. In stuffed cabbage as on page 252.

Bones and trimmings: For stock or to enrich the haricot bean and lentil dishes described in the chapter on vegetables.

Pork rinds and bones and veal bones: To enrich stews and stocks, especially those destined for jelly.

Ham and tongue: Ham mousse, page 235. Ham with cream sauce, pages 231-3.

Sausages: In *omelette campagnarde*, page 196.

Kidneys: In omelettes, with pilaff rice, with poached eggs.

Chicken, turkey: Mayonnaise de volaille, page 407. *Émincés de volaille*, page 406. In salad as for beef salad, page 147. In pilaff. In stuffing for *paupiettes de veau*, page 376.

Chicken and turkey carcases: In stock for celery soup, page 172. Carrot soup, page 168.

Goose: Rillettes d'oie, page 222. In pilaff.

Duck carcase: For stock for *potage de cèpes*, page 171, or beetroot consommé, page 380.

Game: As above, and in pilaff.

Potatoes: Sauté à la lyonnaise, page 273.

Choucroute: Soup, page 420.

Rice: In vegetable and fish soups. In stuffing for sweet peppers, page 269, or in tomatoes cooked in the same way.

Very small quantities of chicken, meat or fish: Saucisses de pommes de terre, page 274. Stuffed cabbage, page 252.

I think that any cook, however inexperienced, who cares to start from these few basic ideas, will very soon be able to devise his own dishes using up left-overs to the best advantage.

Les Desserts

Sweet dishes

PLEASE do not look in this chapter for anything but the simplest of creams and pastries, soufflés, ices and fruit dishes. Elaborate *pâtisserie* and confectionery require practical experience and knowledge of an art quite distinct from that of normal household cookery.

A French housewife, unless either she or her cook is particularly adept at pastry and cakes, is able to order what she requires in this line from that local *pâtissier* whom she knows to be most skilful and to use only the finest ingredients; she knows that she can rely upon not being let down, and it is no disgrace in France—rather the reverse—to say that you have ordered your *gâteau* or *tarte aux fraises* or *savarin aux fruits* from *chez* this or that celebrated *pâtissier*. Here in England, of course, we cannot do that, or at least only in the rarest of cases, for good and conscientious pastry shops are exceedingly few and far between. I know of one or two which have acquired a quite unmerited reputation simply because of the colossal prices they charge. Indeed, the ingredients of good pastries, cakes and *petits fours* are very expensive, but if one is paying, let us say, fourteen shillings a pound for those little biscuits called *florentines*, then it is a disillusion to find that the chocolate coating has been made with a cheap and nasty kind of *couverture*, or that a fifteen-shilling layer cake has been filled with cream made from custard powder or dried egg.

The remedy is to stick to sweet dishes which are simple and can be made at home. Personally, I prefer old-fashioned creams and compôtes and homely fruit tarts to all the shining and glorious confections of the pastry shops, and a straightforward cream ice made with what one knows to be the purest of ingredients is preferable (although the finish may not be very professional looking) to an ice *gâteau*, sporting five different flavours and a multitude of whirls and twirls and glacé cherries, of which the ingredients are to most people a mystery. Mercifully, perhaps, for if you know what they are, it is unlikely you will buy them.

So most of my sweet recipes are those of very simple French household cooking, *recettes de bonne femme*, as they say, which is not to imply that they are carelessly concocted or coarsely flavoured but just very straight-forward in conception and very restrained in decoration.

In fact, at routine French family meals, fresh fruit after the cheese mostly takes the place of a sweet course but, for more ceremonial occasions, a fruit tart, a soufflé or a cream of some sort usually appears. Fresh double cream served with sugar is considered more of a sweet in its own right than as an accompaniment to other dishes; and there are numerous little cream cheese confections which are served with sugar and perhaps a fruit purée for dessert. And if you habitually eat the kind of food already described in this book you will not need anything but very light and simple sweet dishes. Heavy puddings and rich cakes would be out of place, as well as being very fattening.

I have not, in this volume, included a separate chapter on preserves, for we have all our English recipes for jams and jellies which are probably most suited to the variety of fruits which are obtainable here; but in this chapter are a few recipes for lesser known preserves, such as peach jam and a high-class red-currant jelly. Incidentally, the famous white- and red-currant preserves of Bar-le-Duc are scarcely for home cooking, for each single currant is pierced by hand with a quill so that, thrown into boili g syrup, they absorb the sugar and when the jam cools the currants swell out again like little bubbles. (This at least used to be the procedure but perhaps by now a mechanical process has been devised for the piercing of the fruit.) The making of *marrons glacés* has also become very much a commercial affair, for no less than sixteen separate processes are involved before the candied chestnuts are ready for sale. No wonder they are a luxury.

But it would be wrong to give the impression that the art of home preserving is not still practised in France, for if you visit French country houses and farms during the months of July, August and September, you find, at least in those where tradition still prevails, that the careful housewife is busy turning the season's fruits into conserves, jams, liqueurs and cordials, so that all through the winter there will be greengages, mirabelles, peaches, apricots and dark purple plums for tarts and pastries, and little glasses of fruit brandies to offer to the *curé* and the neighbours and to the unexpected visitor.

Fruit growing and preserving on a commercial scale is, of course, an important industry in France. In the east the little golden mirabelles, the purple quetsches and the bitter cherries are distilled into the famous *eaux de vie*, or *alcools blancs*, of Alsace and Lorraine; in the Dordogne the plums make a powerful and strongly flavoured prune liqueur and greengages are preserved in *eau de vie* to be served in little glasses as a digestive; walnuts are made into an oil for salads and into a liqueur called *brou de noix*; big, dark imperial plums are dried on slates or bamboo slats and become the *pruneaux de Tours* or of Bordeaux which, packed in wide glass jars, find their way into the luxury shops all over the world at Christmas time. Then there are the crystallised apricots and plums and figs of Provence, and the world-famous *marrons glacés* of the Ardèche, and those soft, melting, stoned and stuffed *prunes d'Agen* from the Garonne which make such a lovely sweetmeat. And, throughout the districts of the Loire, the Dordogne, the Lot and the Périgord, and in Alsace and Lorraine, there will hardly be a celebration, a wedding feast or a festival at which the dessert does not include some sort of plum or mirabelle tart, made with fresh or dried plums or jam according to the season.

In the Orléans region there is the beautiful cornelian-coloured quince paste called *cotignac*, which comes packed in little cylinder-shaped chip boxes, in Toulouse the beguiling crystallised violets, in Aix-en-Provence the exquisitely melting little almond cakes called *calissons d'Aix*. And even in the most unexpected places in France one may find that there is a first-class baker or confectioner. Once, somewhere in some little ugly town in Alsace, I remember an abominable dinner consisting of a packet *pot-au-feu* (yes) and an unspeakably greasy *choucroute*; uncomfortable beds, cold water, deafening noise. But when our coffee came in the morning, and it certainly was welcome, it was accompanied by what I think were the best *croissants* I have ever eaten and some mirabelle jam so perfect as to be a revelation of what jam can be.

LES ABRICOTS

APRICOTS

The beautiful, aromatically-scented little golden fruit which is the apricot is one which I bracket with the fig as being the most elusive and most rare to find in perfect condition. To the fortunate it occurs every now and again to bite into the sweet purple flesh of a fig as it is ready to crack through its bright green skin or to pick the perfect ripe apricot warm from the sun. Then one sniffs and eats and is thankful that one should have been so favoured by Providence. There were just such apricots, I remember, in a garden at St. Rémy, in Provence. The meal in the hotel had been indifferent and the wine one of those pink Provençal ones which one drinks because one is very thirsty after a dusty drive. But the apricots made up for everything. And there was one summer in the Béarnais when there were two of the country's products which seemed, day after long summer day, to be always perfect. They were the potatoes and the apricots.

When the apricots are less than perfect (and how can they be otherwise when they reach our markets from so far away, from South Africa and Spain, from Italy and Provence?) then they can be cooked and still made quite delicious. But my recipes are for very easy homely dishes, for to me they seem to suit apricots better than the elaborate confections dabbed about with cream which so many cooks are inspired to concoct the minute they set eyes on this beautiful golden fruit. In fact, I cannot remember ever having seen, in France, the elaborate apricot *gâteaux* so popular here, although I suppose perhaps they do exist.

ABRICOTS AU FOUR

BAKED APRICOTS

Wipe the fruit with a soft damp cloth, make an incision along the natural division with a fruit knife and arrange them in a pyramid in a baking dish. For 2 lb. of fruit add 6 tablespoons of vanilla sugar (see page 100), or of ordinary white sugar plus a vanilla pod. It is astonishing how the vanilla flavour enhances that of the apricots. Moisten with 6 tablespoons of water, although if the fruit is very ripe less will be needed. Bake uncovered in a low oven for about one hour, until the apricots are soft. They should, however, retain their shape and the cooking time depends a good deal upon the condition of the fruit. Serve them hot, with slices of bread steeped in milk, then in beaten egg, fried in butter, and sprinkled with sugar.

For more extravagant occasions, 2 or 3 tablespoons of Alsatian or Swiss Kirsch can replace some of the water. This fruit alcohol is one which goes remarkably well with apricots, but a little goes a long way.

CROÛTES AUX ABRICOTS
APRICOT CROÛTONS

Spread plenty of butter on fairly thin slices of day-old bread. Arrange them on a well-buttered baking sheet. On each slice put 3 apricot halves, stones removed. Fill the cavities with vanilla sugar or plain white sugar, and press the fruit well down into the bread. Bake at a rather slow temperature, Gas No. 3, 330 deg. F, but near the top of the oven. In about 40 minutes the bread will be crisp, the apricots soft and with a nice coating of almost caramelised sugar. Serve them straight away.

COMPOTE D'ABRICOTS
APRICOT COMPOTE

For 2 lb. of apricots put about ¼ lb. of white sugar, a vanilla pod and about ½ pint of water into a saucepan. When the sugar has dissolved, put in the apricots, halved and stoned. Poach them gently and don't let them get too soft. Remove them from the liquid and reduce this to a fairly thick syrup by fast boiling. Take out the vanilla pod, pour the syrup over the apricots and serve them very cold with cream if you like, but for me it detracts from the flavour of the apricots.

ANANAS AU KIRSCH
PINEAPPLE WITH KIRSCH

This must be one of the best known of all French fruit dishes. Banal though it may sound, it is one which always pleases, and especially when it comes at the end of a meal which has been composed of rather rich food.

If you have bought a pineapple with a fine and well-shaped tuft of leaves, one decorative way of serving it is as follows: cut off the leaf end quite straight and with a good margin of the fruit adhering to it, so that it will stand level on a dish. Slice and peel the rest of the fruit, and cut out the centre cores if they are very hard. (It is easy to do this with an apple corer.) Arrange them in a circle on a flat round or oval dish. Sprinkle them with soft white sugar and a little Alsatian or Swiss Kirsch; about 2 tablespoons to a fair-sized pineapple is enough.

In the centre of the dish stand the top slice with the leaves.

BANANES BARONNET
BANANAS WITH KIRSCH AND CREAM

Usually I only find bananas acceptable when they are fried as a vegetable, or cooked in butter and rum for a sweet, but it must be admitted that the Kirsch in this recipe of Edmond Richardin's works wonders with the raw fruit.

Cut your bananas into rounds, sprinkle them with white sugar, add a coffee-spoon of matured Kirsch and a tablespoon of thick fresh cream for each banana. Mix carefully so that each round is well coated with the delicious mixture.

MARRONS AU KIRSCH
CHESTNUTS WITH KIRSCH

Shelled and skinned chestnuts (see page 263) are simmered gently in water with a little sugar and a vanilla pod until they are quite tender, but the greatest care must be taken to see that they do not break up. Leave them to cool in their syrup, then put half a dozen or so into a wine-glass for each person, with a very little of the syrup. Pour a couple of tablespoons of Alsatian or Swiss Kirsch into each.

Alternatively, serve the French tinned chestnuts in syrup in the same fashion. Either way, this is a dessert for the very rich or the very extravagant.

MELON AUX FRAISES DES BOIS
MELON STUFFED WITH WILD STRAWBERRIES

Cut a slice off the thick end of a Cantaloup, Charentais or Cavaillon melon and keep it aside. Remove the seeds and scoop out the flesh, taking care not to damage the skin. Cut the flesh into cubes and mix with ¾ lb. to 1 lb. of wild or wood strawberries. Add a little sugar and 2 or 3 tablespoons of port. Return the mixture to the melon, put back the top slice, surround the melon with plenty of cracked ice and leave for several hours before serving. Do not put it in the refrigerator, as the powerful aroma of melon penetrates all other foodstuffs.

An alternative filling to wild strawberries and port is a mixture of raspberries and Kirsch or Grand Marnier.

PUDDING AUX MÛRES

MULBERRY PUDDING

I quote this recipe from Madame Seignobos[1] because in composition it has a good deal of resemblance to our own Summer Pudding, and anyone lucky enough to have a mulberry tree in his garden may like to try it:

'Cook 2¼ lb. of mulberries in a syrup composed of 1 lb. of sugar and ¾ pint of water, then sieve them.

'In a round china vessel arrange slices of stale crumb of bread in several superimposed layers, pour the mulberry purée over and leave in the cellar to cool.

'When the bread has imbibed all the syrup, which is to say after 24 hours, turn it out on to a *compotier* and mask the pudding with a vanilla-flavoured cream.'

PÊCHES AU VIN BLANC

PEACHES IN WHITE WINE

The best peaches for this dish are the yellow-fleshed variety.

Dip the fruit in boiling water so that the skins can easily be peeled off. Slice them straight into big wine-glasses, sprinkle with sugar and pour a tablespoon or two of white wine into each glass. Don't prepare them too long ahead or the fruit will go mushy.

POMMES AU BEURRE

APPLES COOKED IN BUTTER

I have never very greatly appreciated cooked apple dishes, but from the French I learned two valuable lessons about them. First, choose hard sweet apples whenever possible instead of the sour cooking variety which are used for English apple dishes. And secondly, if the apples are to be eaten hot, cook them in butter instead of in water. The scent of apples cooking in butter is alone more than worth the small extra expense.

For 2 lb., then, of peeled and cored sweet apples, evenly and rather thinly sliced, melt 2 oz. of butter in a frying-pan. Put in your apples, add 3 or 4 tablespoons of soft white sugar (vanilla-flavoured if you like) and cook gently until the apples are pale golden and transparent. Turn the slices over very gently, so as not to break them, and, if they are very

[1] *Comment on Forme une Cuisinière.*

closely packed, shake the pan rather than stir the apples. Serve them hot; and I doubt if many people will find cream necessary. The delicate butter taste is enough.

POMMES À LA NORMANDE
APPLES WITH CALVADOS

Over the apples cooked as above pour a small glass of warmed Calvados; set light to it and shake the pan until the flames die down.

LES BOURDAINES
APPLES BAKED IN PASTRY

The Anjou version of the apple dumpling.

Fine large eating apples are peeled and cored, and the cavities filled with plum or quince jam. They are then wrapped in an ordinary tart pastry, the edges well pressed together, each dumpling brushed with milk or cream and baked in a low to moderate oven for about 1 hour.

An alternative to ordinary tart pastry is the *pâte sablée* or crumbly pastry described for the apple tart on page 452. But for 6 apples use twice the quantity of ingredients, divide the pastry into 6 equal pieces and roll each out to a square upon which you place the prepared apple. Fill it with the jam and draw the edges of the pastry up towards the top. Be sure to moisten all the joins with cold water so that the pastry does not burst in the baking. Place them on a baking sheet and cook them at Gas No. 3, 330 deg. F. for just over an hour. *Les bourdaines* make a dish of great charm for children.

POIRES ÉTUVÉES AU VIN ROUGE
PEARS BAKED IN RED WINE

A method of making the most cast iron of cooking pears very delicious. It is especially suitable for those households where there is a solid fuel cooker of the Aga or Esse type.

Peel the pears, leaving the stalks on. Put them in a tall fireproof dish, or earthenware crock. Add about 3 oz. of sugar per pound of pears. Half cover with red wine. Fill to the top with water. Bake in a very slow oven for anything between 5 and 7 hours, until the pears are quite tender and the juice greatly reduced. From time to time, as the wine diminishes, turn the pears over.

A big dish of these pears, almost mahogany-coloured by the time they are ready, served cold in their remaining juice with cream or creamed rice separately, makes a lovely sweet. The best way to present them is to pile them up in a pyramid, stalks uppermost, in a shallow bowl or a *compotier* on a pedestal.

POIRES SAVOIE

PEARS COOKED WITH CREAM

For this you need slightly unripe dessert pears. Peel 2 lb. of them, slice them into quarters or eighths and cut out the cores. Melt a small piece of butter, about ½ oz., in a shallow flameproof dish, in which the pears should fit as nearly as possible in one layer only. Put in the pears and add 4 to 6 tablespoons of white sugar and a piece of vanilla pod. Simmer very gently until the pears are soft, which will take 5 to 10 minutes if the pears are nearly ripe, 20 to 25 if they are hard. Pour in 4 to 6 tablespoons of thick cream and cook another minute or two, shaking the pan until the cream thickens. Transfer to a moderate oven for a few minutes until a golden skin has formed on the surface.

Serve hot, preferably in the dish in which they have cooked.

PRUNES AU FOUR

BAKED PLUMS

Fresh, slightly unripe plums are cooked in the oven in the same way as the apricots described on page 437, but usually they need less water, more sugar, and they will cook rather more quickly; all these factors, however, depend upon the variety, the size and comparative ripeness of the plums used. It is an excellent method of dealing with almost any sort of plums but, best of all, for large ones, purple, yellow or green.

CRÈME FOUETTÉE

WHIPPED CREAM

This is simply the old recipe for *crème Chantilly*—sweetened and flavoured whipped cream. This version comes from the celebrated *Cuisinier Royal*, 1828 edition.

'Into a tureen put some good cream and a proportionate quantity of powdered sugar, a pinch of gum arabic, a little orange flower water; whip all with a whisk made of peeled osier twigs; when the mixture is well swollen, leave it a moment and then take it up, bit by bit, with a skimmer, arranging it in a pyramid on a dish. Garnish round the base with little fillets of candied lemon or green orange peel and serve.'

The proportion of sugar to whipped cream should always be very small, just enough to slightly sweeten it, for the sugar melts in the cream, turns it grainy and watery and spoils its appearance. Personally, I do not bother about the gum arabic. One seldom needs to make whipped cream so long in advance that it needs stiffening.

CRÈME AUX FRAISES

STRAWBERRY CREAM

Hull ¾ lb. of strawberries and sieve them to a pulp, reserving half a dozen. Whisk ½ pint of double cream, fold in one stiffly whisked egg white, then the strawberry pulp. Add a little caster sugar, about 2 or 3 tablespoons. Arrange the cream piled up in a shallow bowl; stir in the reserved whole strawberries before serving. Enough for four people.

This is a most exquisite cream which can also be made with raspberries or, most beautiful of all, *fraises des bois*. The recipe comes from a dictionary of French cooking of the period of the Second Empire.

LES CRÉMETS

In its extreme simplicity this sweet, native to Anjou and Saumur, is one of the most delicious in all French cookery; although in fact that is the wrong term to use, since there is no cooking involved—just a lot of fresh cream and some egg whites.

For three or four people, whip ½ pint of fresh double cream until it is stiff. Fold in 2 egg whites beaten as for a soufflé. Have ready a square of fresh new muslin placed in a little mould pierced with holes. (There are special glazed earthenware or metal moulds sold in France for this purpose. One or two London shops sell them, but a small tin mould in which you make some holes with a tin opener will do, or even a large tumbler-shaped carton.) Turn your cream into this and fold over the corners. Stand the mould on some sort of trivet or stand over a plate, so that the cream can drain. Leave in a cold larder until the next day. Turn out the cream on to a plate; cover it completely with fresh plain unwhipped cream. Serve with plenty of soft white sugar and in the season with strawberries, raspberries or wild strawberries.

[1] See the list of shops selling French kitchen utensils, page 69.

In the winter you can serve, instead of fresh fruit, quince or raspberry jelly. But also the *crémets* can quite well be served on their own, perhaps with a glass of one of the lovely soft fruity white wines of Vouvray, Saumur or Sancerre.

FROMAGE À LA CRÈME

Another version of the many sweet cream cheese dishes current in French home cookery.

Buy ½ lb. of *unsalted* cream cheese, tasting it to make sure it *is* unsalted. If you cannot get it, use home-made milk cheese. The French cream cheeses called Isigny and Chambourcy can be used, but they are, of course, more expensive than the English ones. Turn the cream cheese into a bowl and mash it with a fork or, if it is the very grainy kind, press it through a sieve so that it is quite smooth. Add a tablespoon of caster sugar. Incorporate 3 stiffly beaten whites, as you would for a soufflé. Turn into a fresh muslin cloth or napkin; it should now go into a little rush basket or mould[1] pierced with holes, or a shallow tin 2 inches deep and approximately 4½ inches in diameter, pierced with holes. Leave in the refrigerator for 2 hours or so. To serve, turn out on to a plate, pour thick fresh cream over, about ¼ pint for this amount, and serve caster sugar separately. Plenty for four.

On no account must this lovely sweet, or indeed any of these cream cheese dishes, be despoiled of their cool cream and white beauty by the addition of any trimming or irrelevant decoration. In the season, however, a mound of fresh strawberries or raspberries, or an uncooked purée of either, can accompany the cream cheese; and another good combination is a bowl of pears which have been stewed in red wine, as described on page 441.

FROMAGE DE FONTAINEBLEAU

Fontainebleau is a very light and fluffy fresh cream cheese, which has now become a well-known commercial product, being sold in French dairies and restaurants enfolded in a little white cloth and served in individual portions in cartons or metal containers: and being prepared in large quantities by special machinery in a factory it attains a greater degree of aeration than can be achieved in the ordinary household. On the other hand, prepared at home it does not sink so quickly, is a fraction of the cost and tastes rather better. In the house where I stayed in Paris in my student days, we used to have it served in one large bowl

[1] See foregoing recipe

from which we all helped ourselves to pretty big quantities. The consumption of cream in that establishment must have been huge by present-day standards.

For ample helpings for four people, the ingredients are ½ pint of double cream, about 2 oz. of very fresh milk (in those days in France both cream and milk were unpasteurised), about a dessertspoon of caster sugar or vanilla sugar, if available.

Pour the fresh cream into a bowl, cover it, leave it in a cool place but not in the refrigerator, for 3 or 4 days, according to the weather. If it is insufficiently ripened it will be insipid but, on the other hand, it must not have the slightest hint of a cheesy taste. The day it is to be eaten, buy the fresh milk. Sprinkle the sugar over the cream and start to whip it with a loop whisk or a fork. As it gets stiffer, add the milk a little at a time. Don't whip it too stiff, or it will lose its lightness and turn to a buttery mass. Simply pile it up in a bowl or into little glasses and you will find that it keeps its shape. But if you want to make it fluffier, fold in a stiffly whipped egg white or two.

Serve it by itself, with caster sugar separately. When they were in season, we used to have fresh raspberries, or raspberries and red-currants mixed, or wild strawberries with our *Fontainebleau.*

MOUSSE AU CHOCOLAT À L'ORANGE
CHOCOLATE AND ORANGE MOUSSE

Nearly everyone knows and appreciates the old and reliable formula for a chocolate mousse—4 yolks beaten into 4 oz. of melted bitter chocolate, and the 4 whipped whites folded in. Here is a slightly different version, its faint orange flavour giving it originality.

Break 4 oz. of good quality bitter chocolate into squares and put in a fireproof dish in a low oven. When the chocolate is soft, after a few minutes, take it from the oven, stir in 4 well-beaten yolks, then 1 oz. of softened butter, then the juice of 1 orange. Use a Seville orange when in season; its aromatic flavour comes through better than that of the sweet orange.

Beat the 4 egg whites as for a soufflé and fold them into the chocolate mixture. Pour into little pots, glasses or coffee-cups. This quantity will fill 6. Put in the refrigerator or a cool larder until ready to serve.

Should you have some orange liqueur such as Grand Marnier or Curaçao, add a spoonful in place of the same amount of the orange juice.

SORBETIÈRES AND ICE-CREAM APPARATUS

The confection of sorbets and ice creams in refrigerator trays is only partially satisfactory. Timing is difficult to gauge, and, frozen statically, the cream mixture does not expand. The old hand-cranked ice tub or sorbetière can still be bought at big department stores and a few kitchen supply shops. Although efficient it devours ice and freezing salt and is mighty hard going to work. Electrically operated sorbetières, American, Canadian and French, are on the market. They are expensive, still require ice and freezing salt, although in smaller proportions than the hand-operated machine, and are really for restaurants or for largescale household use. For the small household about the best bet at present is the ARPI, a French device in the shape of a metal box with spaddles. This goes into the ice compartment— provided the depth allows— of a domestic refrigerator. Plugged into an outside socket, the flex does not impede the closing of the refrigerator door. The refrigerator is turned to maximum freezing point and the freezing of an ice cream or sorbet takes anything from one to two hours. The machine shuts itself off when the job is done. You remove the spaddles and the lid to which they are attached, replacing it with a plastic cover supplied for the purpose. You then leave the ice until you are ready to turn it out.

The ARPI costs about £9. 10. Dimensions are: depth $3\frac{1}{2}$ ins. width $5\frac{1}{8}$ ins, length $11\frac{3}{4}$ ins. capacity 2 pints. For stockists enquire from the importers,Messrs. Clarbat. 302 Barrington Rd., London S.W.9. All the recipes given in this book, although for refrigerator ices, can be applied to the ARPI apparatus, and to hand-turned or electrically operated sorbetières.

GLACE AU CITRON

LEMON ICE

$\frac{3}{4}$ pint of thin cream, the yolks of 4 small or 3 large eggs, 3 to 4 oz. of soft white sugar, the juice and grated peel of 1 large lemon.

Grate the peel of the lemon into the cream. Add the very well beaten egg yolks and the sugar. Stir over low heat until the mixture is the consistency of a thin custard. Remove from the fire, strain through a fine sieve and stir until cool. Add the strained juice of half the lemon. Freeze in the ice-tray of the refrigerator, turned to its maximum freezing temperature, for $2\frac{1}{2}$ to 3 hours. Have the tray covered with foil, and turn the cream sides to middle once or twice during freezing. For four.

GLACE MOKA

COFFEE ICE CREAM

A luxury ice cream, with a mild but true coffee flavour and a very fine texture.

First put $\frac{1}{4}$ lb. of freshly roasted coffee beans in a marble mortar. Do not crush them but simply bruise them with the pestle, so that the beans are cracked rather than broken up. Put them in a saucepan with a pint of single cream, the yolks of 3 eggs well beaten, a strip of lemon peel and 3 oz. of pale brown sugar (*cassonade*). Cook this mixture over very gentle heat, stirring constantly until it thickens. Take from the fire and go on stirring until it is cool. Strain through a fine sieve. When this cream is quite cold and thick, into it fold $\frac{1}{4}$ pint of double cream lightly whipped with a tablespoon of white sugar. Turn into a pint-sized freezing tray, cover with foil, and place in the ice-making compartment of the refrigerator, which should already be turned to maximum freezing point. Freeze for 3 hours; after the first hour stir the ice cream, turning sides to middle. Turn out whole on to a flat dish and cut into four portions.

The coffee beans can be used again for a second batch of ice cream; and a less expensive basic mixture using a pint of milk and 5 egg yolks still makes a very excellent ice. Always use a light roast of coffee.

GLACE À L'ABRICOT

APRICOT ICE

Make a custard with $\frac{1}{2}$ pint of thin cream or, for the sake of economy, milk, 2 oz. of sugar, a piece of lemon peel or a vanilla pod, and the yolks of 2 eggs.

Cook 1 lb. of fresh apricots with 2 oz. of sugar and $\frac{1}{4}$ pint of water until they are soft. Stone and sieve them.

Mix the apricot pulp with the cooled custard, from which you have extracted the lemon peel or vanilla pod. Squeeze in a little lemon juice and, immediately before freezing, fold in $\frac{1}{4}$ pint of lightly whipped thick cream. Freeze in the ice-trays of the refrigerator, at maximum freezing point, for about $2\frac{1}{2}$ hours, stirring once or twice during the process. Keep the trays covered with foil. Makes 6 to 8 helpings.

The sweetness or otherwise of apricots varies a good deal. Some may need more sugar, others less.

GLACE À LA FRAMBOISE

RASPBERRY ICE CREAM

Sieve ¾ lb. of fresh raspberries. Make a custard with just under ½ pint of milk or, preferably, thin cream, the yolks of 3 eggs, and 3 to 4 oz. of sugar, depending upon the sweetness or otherwise of the fruit. Early in the season, raspberries tend to need extra sweetening. When this is quite cold, mix it with the raspberry pulp. Fold in ¼ pint of thick, lightly whipped cream and freeze and serve as for the coffee ice on page 446. Ample for four.

Soft fruit such as raspberries and strawberries should never be *cooked* for creams and ices, and whether the pulp is mixed with a cooked custard or a syrup, this should always be left until quite cold before the two are stirred together. The fruit should be carefully picked over before sieving and any berries which look the slightest bit mouldy discarded, for even one bad one is liable to spoil the taste of the whole mixture.

A variation of this ice is to use ½ lb. of raspberries and ¼ lb. of red-currants, which considerably intensifies the flavour. In this case, use an extra ounce of sugar in the custard.

GLACE AU MELON DE L'ÎLE ST JACQUES

MELON ICE CREAM

Choose a large, handsome Charentais or Cantaloup melon. Cut a neat slice off the stalk end and put it aside. Remove the seeds and the fibrous centre, then carefully scoop out all the flesh without damaging the shell of the melon. Put the flesh in a saucepan with 4 to 6 oz. of soft white sugar, the exact amount depending on the size of the melon. Cook for 2 or 3 minutes until it is soft enough to sieve. Beat the yolks of 4 eggs until they are light and foamy. Blend with the fruit purée and cook over a low flame until thickened to the consistency of a thin custard. For safety this can be done in a double saucepan but it takes longer than if the saucepan is put over a direct flame. Very thorough whisking of the egg yolks diminishes the risk of curdling. When the mixture is quite cold, add a little glass of Kirsch and the juice of half a lemon. Then fold in ½ pint of whipped cream. Leave in a covered bowl in the refrigerator.

Three hours before dinner turn the refrigerator to its maximum freezing point; turn the prepared cream into the ice-trays, cover them with foil; freeze for 3 hours, stirring after the first hour and again after the second. To serve, fill the melon shell with the ice, closing it up with the top slice, and bring to table on one of those old-fashioned *compotiers* on a pedestal, or on a flat round dish lined with green leaves.

The melon ice has a strange, almost magic flavour and that is why I have called it after that French Caribbean island so unforgettably conjured out of the ocean, only to be once more submerged, by Patrick Leigh Fermor in *The Violins of St. Jacques*.

OMELETTE SOUFFLÉE AUX LIQUEURS

In a certain country inn in the village of Inxent, in northern France, although the house, the dining-room and the service are very modest, the cooking is famous both because of the excellence of the materials employed and the skill and simplicity with which the dishes are chosen and presented. There is very little choice. You will probably start with a trout, killed on the spot and cooked *au bleu*, served with melted butter so white and creamy that it practically *is* cream. Almost certainly the next course will be a chicken, plump, tender, roasted a delicate gold in butter, so full of flavour, the cooking so perfectly timed that you begin to wonder if you have ever really eaten a roast chicken before. Then there will be a dish of vegetables, perhaps *haricots verts*, again quite plainly cooked, with their exquisite savour absolutely intact. What on earth could you eat after three such sumptuously simple dishes? Imagine the ridiculous anti-climax of a showy pastry, an elaborate *gâteau*, a decorated ice cream. But the ladies who run that inn know what they are about: their last dish is invariably a *soufflé omelette aux liqueurs*, brought to table frothing and spilling over the dish, an aroma of fresh eggs, sizzling butter and mellow liqueur sharpening your senses once more so that you are able to enjoy your last course as much as you did your first.

Ingredients are 3 eggs, 2 heaped tablespoons of caster sugar, the grated rind of 1 orange, 2 tablespoons of Kirsch, Grand Marnier, Curaçao, apricot brandy, or almost any liqueur you please.

Separate the eggs and beat the yolks very thoroughly with the sugar, grated orange rind and liqueur. For an ordinary omelette the eggs are only lightly beaten; for soufflé omelettes they must be well beaten. Whip the whites until they stand in peaks. Amalgamate the two, quickly and more thoroughly than for a soufflé.

Heat a 10-inch omelette pan and have hot plates and a hot omelette dish in readiness. Put a nut of butter into the hot omelette pan. Quickly pour in the egg mixture and give the pan a shake. The outer surface next to the pan will brown at once and the rest puff up, and it will be cooked in about 1 minute, but to get it a little hotter the omelette pan

P

may be placed in a hot oven for about half a minute. Then take your omelette pan in one hand and the hot dish in the other, and holding the pan close to the dish, slide the omelette out, folding it over once as you do so.

This is an omelette for two people; do not attempt to make more than this in one pan. For four people double the quantities and make two omelettes.

SOUFFLÉ À LA VANILLE
VANILLA SOUFFLÉ

Make a basic soufflé mixture with 1½ oz. butter, 2 level tablespoons of flour and ½ pint of milk which has been heated with a vanilla pod and 3 oz. of soft white sugar; cook the sauce until it is very smooth and a little reduced. Remove the vanilla pod. Add the very well beaten yolks of 4 eggs, and remove the sauce from the fire. When the time comes to make the soufflé, whip the whites of 5 eggs until they stand in peaks. Fold them into the main mixture, turn into a 2-pint soufflé dish, make deep cross-cuts in the soufflé so that it is divided into four, place on a baking sheet and cook in a preheated moderate oven, Gas No. 4, 355 deg. F., for approximately 25 to 30 minutes. The places where the cuts were made should by this time have burst open. If they have not the soufflé is not yet ready. Shut the oven door gently and wait a few minutes before looking again.

This is quite a delicate soufflé in its own right, but the mixture can also be used as a basis for other flavours such as grated orange or lemon peel, or a sherry glass of liqueur substituted for an equal quantity of the milk and which should be added to the mixture at the same time as the egg yolks. This quantity makes enough for four.

For the beating and folding in of egg whites for a soufflé see pages 199 and 200.

SOUFFLÉ AUX ABRICOTS
APRICOT SOUFFLÉ

Dried apricots are used for this soufflé, which is made with no basic soufflé mixture and with a large proportion of egg whites. A flour and milk mixture falsifies the taste of the apricots, and as the prepared apricot purée is very thick it takes the extra whites to aerate it.

Put ½ lb. of the best dried apricots to soak in water to cover them: 2 hours is enough but, if more convenient, they can be left overnight.

Cook them uncovered in a very slow oven for about an hour until they are soft enough to put through a food mill. The improvement in the flavour of the apricots when they are oven-cooked rather than stewed is considerable. Drain off all the liquid before sieving them, as it will not be required. Into the warm purée stir 2 tablespoons of caster sugar, the well-beaten yolks of 2 eggs and 2 tablespoons of thick cream. When the mixture is cold, beat the whites of 5 eggs until they stand in peaks. Fold them into the apricot mixture very thoroughly but as lightly and quickly as possible. Turn into a 1¼-pint size soufflé dish, which should be put on a baking sheet in the centre of a preheated oven at Gas No. 4, 355 deg. F.: 25 minutes is approximately the right cooking time but, as everybody who has ever cooked a soufflé will know, it is scarcely possible to give exact timing to the minute.

You can, if you like, serve fresh cream with this soufflé, which, although not a large one, should be enough for four.

SOUFFLÉ AU CHOCOLAT
CHOCOLATE SOUFFLÉ

A chocolate soufflé is made on a somewhat different system from other soufflés, the melted chocolate itself being so thick that no other basic mixture is required. Also it cooks very quickly and equally quickly becomes dry, so careful timing is necessary, for to be good a chocolate soufflé must be creamy in the middle.

Melt 4 oz. of bitter chocolate in the oven with 2 or 3 tablespoons of water, rum or brandy. Stir it smooth, add 2 tablespoons of sugar and the very well beaten yolks of 4 eggs, then fold in the beaten whites of 6. Turn into a 2-pint buttered soufflé dish and cook with the dish standing on a baking sheet in a preheated hot oven, Gas No. 6, 400 deg. F., for approximately 18 minutes. Enough for four people.

This is a soufflé which is improved by fresh cream served separately.

TARTES AUX FRUITS À L'ALSACIENNE
OPEN FRUIT TARTS IN THE ALSATIAN WAY

Flat, open fruit tarts are made with the same pastries as for the onion tart, the cheese tart and the *quiches* on pages 205–7, with a little sugar worked in with the dough. The fruit, sweet apples, quetsch or mirabelle plums or any suitable fruit in season, is first partly cooked with a little sugar and water. If apples are being used peel and slice them into thin, even-sized pieces; if plums or apricots, cut them in half and stone them. For an 8-inch tart tin allow 1½ to 2 lb. of fruit, original weight, of any of these fruit.

The pastry is filled with the fruit, only a little of the juice being used. Cook as for the savoury tarts, but 5 minutes before taking them from the oven, pour in a mixture of 1 egg beaten with a few tablespoons of thick cream.

GALETTE AUX FRUITS

OPEN FRUIT PIE WITH YEAST PASTRY

A *galette* takes many forms. It can be a flat pastry, a cake special to Twelfth Night celebrations, a preparation of thinly sliced potatoes browned on both sides in a frying-pan or a variety of *petit four*.

This *galette* is made with a yeast dough and covered with previously cooked fruit, plums, apples, quinces, apricots, whatever happens to be in season. It is always much liked as a pudding course but it is rather filling so is perhaps best served when the rest of the meal has been rather light.

Ingredients for the dough are 5 oz. plain flour, ½ oz. baker's yeast, 1½ oz. butter, 1 egg, salt.

Soften the butter and beat it thoroughly but lightly into the flour; add a good pinch of salt, the whole egg and the yeast dissolved to a paste in a very little tepid water. Mix with your hands until all ingredients are well amalgamated, add a little more water if necessary, knead into a bun shape, put on a floured plate, make a deep crosswise incision on the top, cover with a cloth and leave to rise somewhere warm, such as the airing cupboard or near the boiler, for 2 hours.

In the meantime, prepare the fruit; for plums or apricots, make a cut along the natural division of the fruit, allowing 1½ lb. Put them in a slow oven with about 6 oz. of sugar and not more than a tablespoon of water, and bake them until soft enough for the stones to be extracted. For apples, use the same quantity, peel, core and slice them, cook them very gently in a frying-pan with butter (this makes a huge difference to the final flavour), sugar and a little water, and watch out that they don't get too much cooked and so lose their shape.

When the dough has risen, and in 2 hours it should have doubled in volume, work it again for a minute or so, sprinkling it with flour to make it drier and cooler to handle. Form it again into a bun, and place it in the centre of a lightly-oiled flan case or tart tin about 8 inches in diameter. Press it out with your hands until it covers the whole case. Spread the fruit on top, arranging it neatly in circles and filling the pastry amply but not using too much juice, which would overflow. Put the flan tin on a baking sheet; cook in a preheated oven at Gas No. 4 or 5, 360 to 380 deg. F., for 35 to 40 minutes. During the last 10 minutes, strew extra sugar on the top. Leave to settle a few minutes after taking from the oven. It is best served hot.

An added refinement is to pour on top of the fruit, 5 minutes before the end of the cooking time, a mixture of 2 oz. of cream and a well-beaten yolk of egg, and let it just barely set.

Those inexperienced with yeast cookery need not be alarmed; nothing is easier than to make this dough once you have done it two or three times, and the combination of the juicy fruit seeping into the bread-like paste is particularly good. But, of course, if preferred, an undercrust of simple pastry will do instead of the yeast dough.

LA TARTE AUX POMMES NORMANDE

OPEN APPLE TART

Cook 1½ lb. of sweet apples as for *pommes au beurre*. Make a *pâte sablée* or crumbly pastry by rubbing 3 oz. of butter into 6 oz. of plain flour, a quarter-teaspoon of salt and 3 teaspoons of white sugar. Moisten with 2 to 4 tablespoons of ice-cold water. If it is still too dry, add a little more, but the less water you use the more crumbly and light your pastry will be.

Simply shape the pastry into a ball and immediately, without leaving it to rest or even rolling it out, spread it with your hands into a lightly buttered 8-inch flan tin. Brush the edges with thin cream or milk; arrange the apples, without the juice, in overlapping circles, keeping a nicely-shaped piece for the centre. Bake, with the tin on a baking sheet, in a preheated hot oven at Gas No. 6, 400 deg. F., for 30 to 35 minutes, turning the tin round once during the cooking. Take it from the oven, pour in the buttery juices, which have been reheated, give another sprinkling of sugar and return to the oven for barely a minute.

Although it is at its best hot, this pastry will not go sodden even when it is cold.

PAVÉ AUX MARRONS

CHESTNUT AND CHOCOLATE CAKE

An excellent and comparatively simple chestnut sweet which is half pudding, half cake.

Shell and skin 1 lb. of chestnuts as described on page 263. Cover them with half milk and half water and simmer them very gently until they are very soft, which will take about an hour. Drain off the liquid. Sieve the chestnuts. To the resulting purée add a syrup made from 3 oz. of white sugar and 2 or 3 tablespoons of water, then 2 oz. of softened butter. When this mixture is thoroughly amalgamated, turn it into a rectangular mould of ¾ pint or 1 pint capacity. (An ice-tray from the refrigerator is a good substitute if you have no small loaf tin.) This should first be very lightly brushed with oil. (Sweet almond oil, to be bought from chemists, is ideal). Leave until next day in the refrigerator or larder. To turn it out, run a knife round the edges and ease out the cake.

Cover it with the following mixture: break up 3 oz. of plain chocolate and melt it on a fireproof plate in the oven, with 4 or 5 lumps of sugar and 2 or 3 tablespoons of water. Stir it smooth; add 1 oz. of butter. Let it cool a little, then with a palette knife cover the whole cake with the chocolate, smoothing it with a knife dipped in water. Leave it to set before serving. Ample for four.

GÂTEAU MOKA

COFFEE CAKE

This is the simplest sort of old-fashioned plain cake, saved from dryness by a coffee-cream filling, and admirable to serve with creams and ices.

To make the cake, beat 3 oz. of vanilla sugar with 3 yolks of eggs until the mixture is very creamy. Add 3 oz. of flour and then fold in the stiffly-whipped whites of the eggs. Turn into a lightly buttered oblong cake tin (1½-pint capacity) and bake in a moderate oven, Gas No. 4, 355 to 360 deg. F., for 30 minutes. Turn the cake out upside down on to a cake rack a few minutes after taking it from the oven.

To make the cream filling, work 3 oz. of butter with the yolk of an egg; add 3 oz. of sieved icing sugar; when the cream is smooth stir in a dessertspoon of very strong black coffee (nowadays the most convenient method is to use soluble coffee powder mixed to a thin paste).

Slice the cake into three or four layers. Spread each liberally with the coffee cream and reshape the cake. Press lightly as you put each layer back, so that the slices will stick together. Leave for some hours before serving.

GÂTEAU AU CHOCOLAT

CHOCOLATE CAKE

This is a cake which can also be eaten as a pudding, and is neither expensive nor difficult to make.

¼ lb. bitter chocolate, ¼ lb. caster sugar, 2 tablespoons of flour, 3 eggs, 3 oz. butter.

Melt the chocolate in the oven; mix it with the softened butter, flour, sugar and beaten egg yolks. Fold in the stiffly-beaten whites. Turn into a buttered 6-inch cake tin or 1¼-pint loaf tin and cook in a preheated moderate oven, Gas No. 4, 355 deg. F., for 35 minutes. There will be a thin crust on top of the cake but if you test it with a skewer the inside will appear insufficiently cooked, which in fact is correct, as it gets firmer as it cools.

As soon as it is cool enough to handle, turn upside down on to a cake rack. When cool, the cake can either be iced with the same mixture as described for the chestnut and chocolate cake on page 453, or covered with lightly-whipped cream.

The quantities given make a small cake, but it is somewhat solid and goes quite a long way.

GÂTEAU AU CHOCOLAT ET AUX AMANDES
CHOCOLATE AND ALMOND CAKE

¼ lb. of bitter chocolate, 3 oz. each of butter, caster sugar and ground almonds, 3 eggs, 1 tablespoon each of rum or brandy and black coffee.

Break the chocolate into small pieces; put them with the rum and coffee to melt in a cool oven. Stir the mixture well, put it with the butter, sugar and ground almonds in a saucepan and stir over a low fire for a few minutes until all the ingredients are blended smoothly together. Off the fire, stir in the well-beaten egg yolks, and then fold in the stiffly-whipped whites. Turn into a lightly-buttered shallow sponge-cake tin, of 7 to 8 inches diameter, or a tart tin with a removable base (see page 69). Stand the tin on a baking sheet and cook in a very low oven, Gas No. 1, 290 deg. F., for about 45 minutes. This cake, owing to the total absence of flour, is rather fragile, so turn it out, when it is cool, with the utmost caution. It can either be served as it is, or covered with lightly whipped and sweetened cream. It is a cake which is equally good for dessert or for tea-time.

CRÊPES DENTELLES

Here is a nice dish for children, rather different from the ordinary pancakes. Ingredients are 2 large eggs, their weight (which will be 4 to 5 oz.) in butter, flour and sugar, and about ¼ pint of milk, a tablespoon of rum, salt.

Stir the eggs, flour, sugar, a pinch of salt and the just melted butter all together until quite smooth. Gradually add the tepid milk and stir until you have a batter of about the consistency of thick cream.

Grease a heavy iron pan very, very lightly with butter, heat it and make very small pancakes with scarcely more than one tablespoon of the batter at a time. If you have a large pan, two or three little pancakes can be made at the same time, for the batter should be just stiff enough not to run in the pan unless it is tilted. Turn the pancakes over in the usual way and, when they are done on both sides, lift them out with a palette knife. They are nicest eaten with melted butter and sugar.

These quantities make twenty to thirty small pancakes, so they can be halved. The rum, little though it is, makes quite a difference to the flavour as well as to the crispness of the batter, but if you prefer to omit it, flavour the mixture instead with grated lemon or orange peel.

It makes little difference, with this batter, whether the pancakes are made at once or if it is left to stand. And the amount of butter used for cooking them should be infinitesimal.

GELÉE DE GROSEILLES

RED-CURRANT JELLY

This system of making red-currant jelly was given by Eliza Acton in her *Modern Cookery*, published in 1845. She says that it is a Norman receipt. It is the one I always use and find it makes, as Eliza Acton says, 'superlative' jelly. I was preparing the fruit for it one day when a friend from Paris arrived upon the scene. 'What on earth,' she said, 'are you doing wasting your time taking all the stalks off? At home we put the whole lot in the pan. It all goes through the cloth; the stalks don't affect it at all.' In every other detail, she told me, the system she used was the same as Miss Acton's. Ever since, I have followed her advice. So weigh your ripe red-currants and put them into the preserving pan, stalks and all, with an equal weight of sugar. Then proceed as follows, according to Miss Acton.

'Boil these together quickly for exactly 8 minutes, keep them stirred all the time and clean off the scum—which will be very abundant—as it rises; then turn the preserve into a very clean sieve, and put into small jars the jelly which runs through it and which will be delicious in flavour and of the brightest colour. It should be carried immediately, when this is practicable, to an extremely cool but not a damp place and left there until perfectly cold. In Normandy, where the fruit is of richer quality than in England, this preserve is boiled only 2 minutes and is both firm and beautifully transparent.'

MARMELADE DE COINGS
QUINCE MARMALADE

It was from *marmelo*, the Portuguese name for quince, that the word marmalade came into the French and the English languages.

There are as many different recipes for quince marmalade as there are for orange marmalade. The theory is always much the same; the skin and the pips are used to make a foundation syrup which will jelly, and in which the sliced fruit is cooked.

The following recipe makes a very richly-flavoured preserve, for my taste a good deal superior to orange marmalade.

Rub the whole fruit with a cloth to remove the down; put it in a preserving pan and cover completely with cold water. Simmer until the fruit is soft enough to pierce with a thin skewer; don't let it cook until the skins break. Extract the fruit, and when cool enough to handle, peel, slice and core it. Return the cores and the skins to the same water in which the fruit has cooked, and boil until reduced by about a third, when the juice will have just begun to take on the characteristic cornelian colour of quince jelly.

Strain this through a cloth. Weigh the sliced fruit; add its equivalent in white sugar. Put the sugar and fruit, together with the strained juice, back into the preserving pan and boil gently until the fruit is soft and translucent and the juice sets to jelly. The best way of ascertaining that the juice will set is to watch until it starts coating the back of the spoon, and slides off with a gentle plop when the spoon is shaken. Skim off any scum that has risen to the surface before turning off the flame. Put into warmed jam jars, cover with a round of paper dipped in brandy and tie down when cool.

PÂTE DE COINGS
QUINCE PASTE

Here is the easiest country method of making thick quince paste. Rub the quinces with a cloth to remove the down. Put them, whole and unpeeled, into a big, tall earthenware crock or jar, without any water. Leave them, covered, in a low oven until they are soft but not breaking up. When they are cool enough to handle, slice them, without peeling them, into a bowl, discarding the cores and any bruised or hard pieces. Put the sliced fruit through the food mill. Weigh it. Add an equal quantity of white sugar. Boil in a preserving pan, stirring nearly all the time until the paste begins to candy and come away from the bottom as well as the sides of the pan. Take care to use a long-handled wooden

Q

spoon for stirring, and to wrap your hand in a cloth, for the boiling paste erupts and spits. Continue stirring after the heat has been turned off until boiling has ceased. With a big soup ladle, fill shallow rectangular earthenware or tin dishes with the paste. Leave to get quite cold. Next day put these moulds into the lowest possible oven of a solid fuel cooker, or into the plate drawer of a gas or electric stove, while the oven is on, for several hours, until the paste has dried out and is quite firm. Turn out the slabs of paste, wrap them in greaseproof paper and store them in tins in a dry larder.

This paste is cut into squares or lozenges to serve as a dessert or as a sweetmeat for the children.

If you have no suitable utensil for the initial cooking of the fruit in the oven, it can be softened in a steamer over a big saucepan of boiling water.

MARMELADE DE PÊCHES (1)

PEACH JAM

Peach jams are a speciality of Apt, the centre of the fruit-preserving industry of Provence, but this is a household rather than a commercial recipe. White and yellow peaches are equally good for this jam.

Immerse the fruit in boiling water for a minute and then gently skin them. Extract the stones by pressing firmly with your finger on the stalk end. Cut the peaches in halves. Weigh them. For each pound weigh ¾ lb. of preserving or loaf sugar, and measure ⅛ pint of water. Put sugar and water into a preserving pan and bring to the boil. Put in the peaches, and when the sugar has once more come to the boil turn the flame low, and leave them very gently cooking, only just moving, for ¼ hour. Remove from the fire and leave until next day, when the jam is to be boiled as before, very gently, for ½ hour. If the syrup sets when poured on a plate the jam is cooked. If it is still too thin, remove the fruit, pack it carefully in jars, and continue cooking the syrup until it does set. Skim it when cool, pour it over the fruit, to fill the jars; tie down when cold. A dozen average-size peaches will make sufficient preserve to fill two 1 lb. jars.

This method makes a rather extravagant but very delicious preserve. Unfortunately it tends to form a skin of mould within a very short time, but this does not affect the rest of the jam, some of which I have kept for nearly a year, even in a damp house. As an alternative, here is a second method, less extravagant and just as good in its way, although sweeter and more of a true jam than the above.

MARMELADE DE PÊCHES (2)

PEACH JAM

Prepare the peaches as above; when they are skinned, stoned and halved weigh them and put them with an equal weight of loaf sugar in a china bowl. Leave for several hours, or overnight. Put them in a preserving pan without water and bring slowly to the boil. Boil until the syrup sets when tested on a plate. Put into pots and seal while warm.

PRUNES À L'EAU DE VIE

PLUMS IN BRANDY

A recipe from the Dordogne. Small purple plums or greengages (*Reines-Claudes*) can be used for this preserve, which is served mainly as a kind of dessert and liqueur combined—3 or 4 of the plums or greengages in a small thick wine-glass, with a little of the brandy in which they have been preserved.

Buy the fruit slightly under-ripe. Leave the stalks on and pierce each plum through to the stone with a skewer in three or four places, and leave in a bowl of cold water until all are ready. Bring a pan of water to the boil, put in the greengages and, as soon as the water comes up to a fast boil again, remove the fruit with a perforated spoon to a large china bowl. For each pound of fruit, measure a pound of white sugar and a wine-glass (somewhat under $\frac{1}{4}$ pint) of water. Boil together to the pearl stage (i.e. until the syrup is bubbling with little beads), throw in the fruit, leave until it comes to the boil again, then immediately return it to the bowl and pour the syrup over the fruit.

Leave for 24 hours and next day pour off the syrup, bring it to the boil, put in the fruit, bring it once more to the boil, and again put the fruit in the bowl and pour the syrup over, having carefully skimmed it.

After another 24 hours remove the fruit to large glass or stone jars. Boil the syrup until it has thickened somewhat. Filter through a cloth and, when cold, mix with it half a bottle of brandy or pure white spirit to every 3 lb. of fruit used. Stopper the jars, or tie down with several layers of paper, and leave it for at least a month before opening it.

Unlikely though it may sound, vodka can be used instead of brandy, and because it is a colourless spirit produces a preserve of better appearance than does brandy coloured with caramel. If you like a preserve with a more powerful flavour of spirits use a half-bottle to every two pounds of fruit instead of to every three.

Cookery books

'Which is the best cookery book? The one you like best, and which gives you that confidence that cannot be called forth to order, but which is instinctively felt. For myself I like those books which are not too complicated and which suggest ideas rather than being minutely detailed handbooks—I also like the kind of cookery book which evokes the good meals of the old inns, for reconstitution of the past is a delicate pleasure of which one should not be deprived. I do not by any means dislike the cookery book imbued with a certain fantasy, with initiative and with daring ideas; but this characteristic must not be exaggerated. Mere freakishness is no passport to glory. It is not even to be recommended.'
PIERRE DE PRESSAC: *Considérations sur la Cuisine*, 1931.

THERE are people who hold that cookery books are unnecessary. These people are usually those who innocently believe cookery to be a matter of a little imagination, common sense, and taste for food, qualities which are, of course, of enormous importance to a cook; but, as Maurice des Ombiaux says, 'Let us not make any mistake, the taste which one has for good living, however lively it may be, cannot take the place of the technical knowledge, the long habit, the constant practice of the difficult and complicated profession of cookery.'

One certainly cannot learn the technical details of cookery entirely from books; but if the cooks, celebrated and obscure, of the past had believed that written recipes were unnecessary, we should now be in a sad plight indeed. The culinary wisdom and skill of several centuries of practitioners, both professional and amateur, are distilled into the cookery books we now inherit. Speaking for myself, I can only say that, after years of study of many of the books I have listed below—and they represent only a microscopic cross-section of those which have been published during the past two hundred years in France alone—and after many years of constant practical work in the kitchen, I am, I think, just beginning to have some small glimmerings of what the art of cookery really means, of its development in the historical sense and of the causes and effects of things concerned with cookery, and I do not think that any cook, professional or amateur, could honestly claim that he owed nothing to any cookery book. So I have included in my bibliography the titles and authors of many of the great classic French works, particularly those of the nineteenth century, for although they may not be directly relevant to the subject of regional and provincial cookery, they are, indirectly, of the greatest importance. The influence of men like Carême who, it might be said, invented or at least brought to a hitherto unknown peak of perfection the elaborate cooking known as *haute cuisine*, of Urbain Dubois and Jules Gouffé, of Escoffier and of Prosper Montagné, can scarcely be over-estimated. The kind of cookery these men practised may now be out of date but, without it, European cookery would, whether for better or for worse, be something quite other than it is. And in the cases of Escoffier and Montagné, it is a point of considerable interest that, while both of them preached in the highest places of gastronomy of their time, neither of them ever forgot or came to despise the homely cookery of their native provinces which were, respectively, Provence and the Languedoc. Montagné, indeed, did much to popularise the regional cookery of the Languedoc, where for generations his ancestors had been inn-keepers and restaurateurs. Escoffier's *Ma Cuisine*, a book for housewives as well as for professionals, contains recipes for many of the famous country dishes of Provence, a part of Escoffier's work which is often overlooked, at any rate in England, for the book has never, so far as I know, been translated into English.[1] It was published only a year before Escoffier's death in 1935, at the age of 89.

In contrast to these great names, the authors of many of the little volumes dealing with regional cookery are unknown in the world of professional gastronomy. Many of these books are by amateurs. Some of the authors were men of letters who made collections of the recipes of their native provinces as a relaxation from their normal work; often, from the point of view of details, the recipes in these books leave much to be desired, but what they may lack in precision they make up for in their appeal to the imagination and in the feeling they give us of a domestic life now vanished or, at any rate, vanishing. I do not think there is one of these books, entirely lacking in pretension though they are, which does not provide us with some precious piece of culinary wisdom without which we should be the poorer. To posterity these historians of family life and of household cookery in France have rendered services beyond price.

[1] An English translation, retaining the French title, has recently (1965) been published by Hamlyn.

Bibliography

THIS bibliography is arranged in chronological order under the following headings: French cookery and other books of the eighteenth, nineteenth and twentieth centuries; English translations of French cookery books; English cookery and other books referred to in the text of this volume; Periodicals, French and English; Guide books, French and English; Bibliographies.

FRENCH: EIGHTEENTH CENTURY

Les Dons de Comus. Marin, à Paris, chez la Veuve Pissot, 1742 (first published 1739).

La Cuisinière Bourgeoise. Menon, à Paris, chez Guillyn, Quai des Augustins, 1746. This book was continuously reprinted and widely plagiarised during the two hundred years following its original publication.

Le Ménage des Champs et le Jardinier Français. Louis Liger, à Paris, chez Michel David, 1711.

FRENCH: NINETEENTH CENTURY

Almanach des Gourmands. Grimod de la Reynière. Paris, chez Maradan, 8 vols., 1803–1812.

Le Cuisinier Royal. Viard et Fouret, Paris, Dupont, Corbet, 13th edition, 1828. This book first appeared in 1806 with the title *Le Cuisinier Impérial.* For the 9th edition, 1817, 'Impérial' was changed to 'Royal'; for the 22nd edition, 1853, the title was again changed, this time to *Cuisinier National.* In 1854 it once more became the *Cuisinier Impérial.*

La Nouvelle Cuisinière Bourgeoise. Par l'Auteur du Parfait Cuisinier. 3rd edition, 1816.

La Cuisinière de la Campagne et de la Ville ou la Nouvelle Cuisine Économique. L. E. Audot, 84th edition. Mise au courant du Progrès annuel, Paris, Librairie Audot, 62 rue des Écoles, 1906. This book was first published in 1818 without the name of the author.

Le Cuisinier Parisien. B. Albert, Paris, Dufour et Cie, 3rd edition, 1825.

La Physiologie du Goût. Jean-Anthelme de Brillat-Savarin; first published in Paris by A. Sauteret et Cie, 1826.

Le Cuisinier Durand. Durand. Imprimerie P. Durand-Belle, Nîmes, 1830.

L'Art de la Cuisine Française aux XIXᵉ Siècle. A. Carême, Paris, l'Auteur, 5 vols., 1835. The two final volumes of this work were completed by Plumerey after Carême's death in his fiftieth year in 1833.

Néo-Physiologie du Goût par Ordre Alphabétique: Dictionnaire Général de la Cuisine Française Ancienne et Moderne ainsi que de l'Office et de la Pharmacie domestique. Paris, Henri Plon, Imprimeur-Éditeur, rue Garancière 10, 1886. In the preface of this work, the reader is told that the three collaborators are, firstly, 'a lady of good repute who has no children, who is no longer young, and who has not very much with which to occupy herself; secondly, her doctor, one of the cleverest of German medical men, who wishes, from philanthropic motives, to accord a system of hygiene with that of French cookery; thirdly, her cook, not the least intelligent of the three, who is tormented by the desire to speak the truth about the science which he professes.' Vicaire, however, says that the book was the work of M. Maurice Cousin, comte de Courchamps, a man whose reputation as a gourmet was very distinguished. The book was first published in 1839 and reappeared in 1853 and in 1866. A number of the recipes contained in it are claimed in the preface to be from unpublished papers of Grimod de la Reynière.

La Cuisinière des Cuisinières de la Ville et de la Campagne. Revue par Mozard, ex-chef d'office, 1840.

La Cuisinière du Haut-Rhin. Seconde édition, traduite de la 6e édition allemande, Mulhouse, 1842.

Science du Bien Vivre. Paul Ben et A.D., Paris, Martinon, 1844.

La Maison Rustique des Dames. Madame Millet-Robinet, 18th edition *circa* 1880, Paris, Librairie Agricole de la Maison Rustique (first published 1845).

Le Cuisinier Européen. Jules Breteuil, Paris, Garnier Frères, 1860.

Le Livre de Cuisine. Jules Gouffé, Ancien Officier de Bouche du Jockey-Club de Paris. Comprenant la cuisine de ménage et la grande cuisine. 4th edition, Paris, Librairie Hachette, 1877 (first published 1867).

Les 366 Menus de Baron Brisse. Baron Brisse, Paris, 2nd edition, Donnaud, 1875. First published *circa* 1867.

Grand Dictionnaire de Cuisine. Alexandre Dumas, Paris, Alphonse Lemerre, 1873.

La Bonne Cuisine Française, Manuel Guide pour la Ville et la Campagne. E. Dumont, Paris, Degorce-Cadot, 1889. First published 1873.

Les Hostelleries et Taverniers de Nancy. Jules Renauld, Nancy, Lucien Wiener, 1875.

Cuisine du Midi et du Nord. Revue, corrigée et augmentée par C. Durand, petit-fils de l'auteur. Paris, Garnier Frères, 1877. A revised edition (the 9th) of the original *Cuisinier Durand* of 1830.

Le Cuisinier à la Bonne Franquette. Mique Grandchamp, Annecy, Depollier et Cie, 1884.

100 Manières d'Accommoder et de Manger les Œufs. Alfred Suzanne, Paris, I. Frank. 1885.

La Cuisine de nos Pères. L'Art d'Accommoder le Gibier Suivant les Principes de Vatel et des Grands Officiers de Bouche. Paris, Librairie Illustrée, 1886.

L'Estomac de Paris. A. Coffignon, Paris, Librairie Illustrée, 1887.

L'École des Cuisinières. Urbain Dubois, Paris, E. Dentu, 6th edition, 1887.

La Cuisine de nos Pères. L'Art d'Accommoder le Poisson Suivant les Principes de Vatel et des Grand Officiers de Bouche. Paris, Librairie Illustrée, 1888.

Le Petit Cuisinier Moderne. G. Garlin (de Tonnerre), 1890.

La Vie Privée d'autrefois. Variétés Gastronomiques. Alfred Franklin, Paris, Librairie Plon, 1891.

Traité Pratique de L'Élevage du Porc et de la Charcuterie Suivi d'une Étude sur les Truffes et les Truffières. Par *Alf. Larbalétrier.* Aug. Valessert, Paris, Garnier Frères, 1891.

La Table au Pays de Brillat-Savarin. Lucien Tendret, Avocat à Belley, Chambéry, Librairie Dardel, 1934. First published 1892.

La Cuisine de Tous les Mois. Philéas Gilbert, Paris, Abel Goubaud, 1893. Gilbert was a celebrated teaching chef and was one of Escoffier's collaborators in the *Guide Culinaire.* He contributed articles on cookery to a fashion magazine and his book was addressed more to the readers of this magazine than to professionals. After the 1914 war, however, he realised that some of the content of this book was out of date and a revised edition was brought out, with new illustrations. A certain amount of detail necessary for housewives doing their own cooking, which had been omitted from the original edition, was included in the 2nd, 3rd and 4th editions.

La Cuisinière Provençale. Reboul, 1895. Chef de Cuisine, 14ème édition revue et augmentée d'un appendice. Marseille. Tacussel, 88 La Canebière. This book, first published in 1895, as *La Cuisinière du Midi,* is a valuable work of reference for students of Provençal cookery, although it is by no means exclusively confined to local recipes. It was not until after the appearance of the 6th edition that the author, upon the advice of the poet Mistral, incorporated Provençal translations of the names of dishes and technical terms into his work.

FRENCH: TWENTIETH CENTURY

Comment on Forme une Cuisinière: Petit Guide de la Maîtresse de Maison. Madame Seignobos. Compiled in part from articles which had appeared in *Mode Pratique.* Published by Librairie Hachette, Paris, in four parts. No date. Early twentieth century.

1e Partie: *Les Viandes de Boucherie.*

2e Partie: *Les Volailles, le Gibier, Salaisons de Porc, les Sauces et les Jus.*

3e Partie: *Les Potages, les Pâtes, les Œufs, les Légumes, les Poissons.*

4e Partie: *Les Conserves, les Sirops, les Entremets sucrés, les Pâtisseries.*

Les Secrets de la Bonne Table. 120 Recettes Recueillies dans les Provinces de France. B. Renaudet, Paris, Albin Michel. No date. Early twentieth century.

Le Guide Culinaire. Aide-mémoire de Cuisine Pratique. A. Escoffier avec la collaboration de Philéas Gilbert et Émile Fétu. Paris, E. Flammarion, 1921. 4th edition; first published 1902.

La Grande Cuisine Illustrée. Sélection Raisonnée de 1,500 Recettes de Cuisine Transcendante. Prosper Salles et Prosper Montagné, 1902. Imprimerie-Typo-Lithographique. Chêne, 40 rue Grimaldi, Monte Carlo.

Dictionnaire Encyclopédique de l'Épicerie et des Industries Annexes. A. Seigneurie, Édition Nouvelle, Paris. Bureau du Journal *l'Épicier,* 1904.

Le Cuisinier Landais et Les Bons Domestiques: Manuel des Jeunes Ménagères. À Dax, chez M. H. Labèque, propriétaire-éditeur, 11 rue des Carmes, 1904.

Le Manuel des Amphitryons. Au Début du XXe Siècle. Aug. Michel, Fabricant de Pâtés à Schiltigheim-Strasbourg. Paris, Aux Bureaux de l'Art Culinaire, Place Saint-Michel 4; 4th edition, 1904.

La Véritable Cuisine de Famille. 1,000 Recettes et 500 Menus. Par Tante Marie. Paris, A. Taride, Éditeur, 18-20 Boulevard Saint-Denis. Nouvelle édition.

La Cuisine à Nice. H. Heyraud, Nice, Léo Barma, *circa* 1907.

Gastronomie Pratique. Etudes Culinaires. Ali-Bab. Paris, Ernest Flammarion. 7th edition, 1928. Ali-Bab was the pen name of Henri Babinski. His book first appeared in 1907. By the time the 5th edition was published, the book had been extensively revised and enlarged. The 7th edition contains over 1,200 pages and the proportions and ingredients for every recipe are given, with the precision of a scientist writing a formula, down to the last gramme. It is a remarkable work by any standards; for an amateur cook it is a quite extraordinary achievement.

Cuisine Messine. Auricoste de Lazarque, Nancy, Sidot Frères; 4th edition, 1909. A most interesting collection of recipes mostly from the Metz district and other parts of Lorraine.

L'Art du Bien Manger. La Cuisine Française du XIVe au XXe Siècle. 2,000 Recettes Simples et Faciles. Edmond Richardin. Editions d'Art et de Littérature, Paris, 1913. 5e édition. Richardin, a native of Lorraine, was the proprietor of a celebrated restaurant in Nancy, the capital. His book is one of the most imaginative and interesting collections in the French language.

L'Alsace Gourmande. Poème Gastronomique, Suivi de Cent Quarante Recettes Alsaciennes. Georges Spetz. Revue Alsacienne, Strasbourg, 1914.

Les Bons Plats de France. Cuisine Régionale. Pampille, Paris, A. Fayard, 1919. Reprinted *circa* 1940 in the series Art Culinaire by Americ-Edit., Rio de Janeiro, Brazil. Pampille was the pen name of the late Madame Léon Daudet.

La Fleur de la Cuisine Française. Où l'on Trouve les Meilleures Recettes des Meilleurs Cuisiniers, Pâtissiers et Limonadiers de France, du XIIe au XIXe Siècle.

La Fleur de la Cuisine Française. Tome II. La Cuisine Moderne (1800-1921). *Les Meilleures Recettes des Grands Cuisiniers Français.*
Bertrand de Guégan 1920, 1921. An anthology, with notes by Bertrand de Guégan, of extracts and recipes from all the celebrated French cookery books from the years 1290 to 1920. A publication of the greatest possible interest and value.

Cuisine et Chasse de Bourgogne et d'Ailleurs. Charles Blandin, Dijon, Louis Damidot, 1921. 2 vols.

Clarisse, ou la Vieille Cuisinière. Éditions de l'Abeille d'Or, Paris, 1922. A most delightful little book, published anonymously.

Bien Manger pour Bien Vivre. Essai de Gastronomie Théorique. Édouard de Pomiane. Albin Michel, Paris, 22 rue Huyghens, 1922.

La Gourmandise à Bon Marché. Recettes simples et pratiques. Paul Bouillard, Propriétaire du 'Filet de Sole' de Bruxelles. Albin Michel, Paris, 22 rue Huyghens, 1925.

La Cuisine Berrichonne. Suivie de Chansons à Boire. Hugues Lapaire. À Paris, chez Helleu et Sergent, 1925.

Mets de Provence. Eugène Blancard, Grenoble. Successeur des Éditions J. Rey, 1926. A most interesting and authentic little collection of Provençal recipes.

Le Livre de Cuisine de Madame Saint-Ange. Madame E. Saint-Ange, Librairie Larousse, 1927. In my experience, this is to date far and away the most practical cookery book in the French language. It is a book of recipes of the very best and most carefully prepared kind of French household dishes. As such, it is directed at housewives rather than professionals but, in its impeccable precision of detail (six pages, for example, devoted to the proper method of beating egg whites) is much more valuable even than such classics as Escoffier's *Guide Culinaire* or Gilbert's *Cuisine de Tous les Mois.*

Les Secrets de la Cuisine Comtoise. Colligés ès Papiers Perdus des Abbayes de Baume et de Château-Chalon et de Quelques Autres plus Récents Éclaircis, Complétés et Mis en Lumière. Pierre Dupin, Professeur d'Histoire, 1927. Paris, Librairie E. Nourry, 62 rue des Écoles.

Les Plats Régionaux de France. Austin de Croze, Paris, Éditions Montaigne, 1928. A magnificent collection of recipes from every province of France.

107 Recettes ou Curiosités Culinaires. Recueillies par Paul Poiret, Président Honoraire du Club des 'Purs Cent.' Suivies de quelques pages de publicité gratuite par Sébastien Voirol. Henri Jonquières et Cie. À Paris, 21 rue Visconti, 1928. Poiret was the famous dress designer.

L'Art de Manger et son Histoire. Maurice des Ombiaux, Paris, Payot, 1928.

La Cuisine Lyonnaise. Mathieu Varille, Lyon, à la Librairie de Paul Masson, 1928.

Dissertations Gastronomiques. Ernest Verdier de la Maison Dorée. Paris, Noel et Chalvon, 1928. The Maison Dorée was a Paris restaurant celebrated during the period of the Second Empire and almost up to the end of the nineteenth century.

La Bonne Cuisine en Périgord. La Mazille. Flammarion, 1929. A lovely and evocative collection of recipes from south-western France.

Cuisine Juive, Ghettos Modernes, Gastronomie Juive. Édouard de Pomiane. Albin Michel, Paris, 22 rue Huyghens, 1929.

Cuisine et Pâtisserie de Russie, d'Alsace, de Roumanie et d'Orient. Suzanne Roukhomovsky. E. Flammarion, 1929.

Les Belles Recettes des Provinces Françaises. Les Sans-Filistes Gastronomes, Paris, Flammarion, 1929. A collection of prize-winning recipes from a radio competition.

Traité de Cuisine Bourgeoise Bordelaise. Alcide Bontou, Bordeaux, Féret et Fils; 6th edition, 1929.

Le Festin Occitan. Prosper Montagné. Éditions d'Art, Jordy, Cité de Carcassonne. Publication undated but my copy bears an inscription from the author to his friend and collaborator, Dr. Gottschalk, dated 1930.

Les Plaisirs de la Table. Édouard Nignon. Paris, chez l'auteur, 3 Place de la Madeleine, et chez Lapina, Éditeur, 75 rue Denfert-Rochereau, 1930.

Le Code de la Bonne Chère. 700 recettes simples. Édouard de Pomiane. Publiées sous les auspices de la Société Scientifique d'Hygiène Alimentaire. Paris, 1930.

La Gastronomie Africaine. Léon Isnard. Albin Michel, Éditeur, 22 rue Huyghens, Paris, 1930.

En Habillant l'Époque. Paul Poiret, *circa* 1930.

Le Trésor de la Cuisine du Bassin Mediterranén. Par 70 médecins de France. Révision et préface par Prosper Montagné. Offert par les Laboratoires du Dr. Zizine. No date—*circa* 1930.

Considérations sur la Cuisine. Pierre de Pressac. Paris, Gallimard, 1931.

Livre d'Or de la Gastronomie Française. Publication edited by Édouard Rouzier to mark the presentation of a number of dinners composed of the regional dishes of France at the Salon d'Automne of 1931. Similar presentations had been given at the Salons of 1924 and 1927, also organised by Édouard Rouzier, proprietor of the Rôtisserie Périgourdine in Paris.

Le Cuisinier Bourguignon. Nouveau Livre de Cuisine Pratique. Alfred Contour, Ancien Maître d'Hôtel de l'Hôtel du Chevreuil à Beaune. Louis Damidot. Dijon, 1931.

Cuisine Coloniale. Les Bonnes Recettes de Chloë Mondésir. Recueillies par A. Quérillac, Paris, Société d'Éditions Géographiques, Maritimes et Coloniales, 1931.

Une Vieille Tradition. La Cuisine en Poitou. Maurice Béguin. Archiviste des Deux-Sèvres. À la Librairie Saint-Denis, 15 Place du Temple, Niort, 1932.

Éloges de la Cuisine Française. Présentation de Sacha Guitry. Edouard Nignon. Paris, L'Edition d'Art, H. Piazza, 19 rue Bonaparte, 1933. Nignon was *chef des cuisines* at the famous restaurant Paillard in Paris, and before that at Claridges Hotel in London. His books are written in almost unbelievably bombastic language, but nevertheless contain some fine recipes and show a genuine devotion to his profession.

Ma Cuisine. A. Escoffier. Ernest Flammarion, 26 rue Racine, Paris, 1934.

Le Poisson d'Étang. Composé par l'Union Nationale des syndicats de l'Étang. Édité par le Comité National de l'Élevage, 41 rue Lafayette, Paris, *circa* 1934.

Vingt Plats qui Donnent la Goutte. Conseillés par la Pipérazine Midy, l'Anti-urique Type. Édouard de Pomiane. Éditions Paul Martial, Paris, pour le Pipérazine Midy, 1935.

Les Meilleures Recettes de ma Pauvre Mère, et Quelques Autres Encore. Pierre Huguenin. Publication du Comité de la Foire Gastronomique de Dijon. Dijon, Librairie Venot, 1936.

Les Viandes (Qualités et Catégories). H. Martel, Docteur-ès-Sciences, Directeur Honoraire des Services Vétérinaires de la ville de Paris et du Département de la Seine. Président de l'Académie de Médecine. Éditions Lajeunesse, 14 rue Brunel, Paris, 1937.

365 Menus, 365 Recettes. Précédés d'une Étude sur le Régime Alimentaire de

Chacun. Édouard de Pomiane. Editions Albin Michel, Paris, 22 rue Huyghens, 1938.

Larousse Gastronomique. Prosper Montagné, Maître Cuisinier, avec la collaboration du Docteur Gottschalk. Préface de A. Escoffier et de Philéas Gilbert. Librairie Larousse, Paris, 1938. A magnificent work of reference.

Les Meilleures Recettes Culinaires pour Poissons et Crustacés. Publié par le Comité Boulonnais de Propagande pour la consommation des produits de la Mer, 1938.

Les Poissons de Mer. J. Donies, Secrétaire de l'Enseignement Technique et Professionnel des Pêches Maritimes. Paris, Librairie Hachette. Undated. Pre-1939.

Gastronomie Nivernaise. Les Frères Drouillet, Moulins, Crépin-Leblond, 1939.

Dictionnaire Vilmorin des Plantes Potagères. Vilmorin-Andrieux, 4 Quai de la Mégisserie, Paris, 1946. Vilmorin-Andrieux are one of the largest and most famous seedsmen and nurserymen in France.

Six Cents Bonnes Recettes de Cuisine Bourgeoise. Pierre-Jacques Solandré, Paris, Librairie Garnier Frères; 4th edition, 1946.

À l'Infortune du Pot. La Meilleure Cuisine en 300 Recettes Simples et d'Actualité. Curnonsky, Prince élu des Gastronomes. Éditions de la Couronne, Paris, 1946.

L'Utilisation des Fruits. Henriette Babet-Charton. La Maison Rustique, 26 rue Jacob, Paris. 4th edition, 1947.

La Bonne Cuisine Méridionale de Tante Gracieuse. De Bordeaux à Menton. Les Éditions Provencia, Service des Ventes, Librairie du Petit Marseillais, 18 Place d'Armes, Toulon, 1947.

Histoire de l'Alimentation et de la Gastronomie depuis la Préhistoire jusqu'à nos Jours, 2 vols. Dr. Alfred Gottschalk, Paris, Éditions Hippocrate, Le François, 91 Boulevard Saint-Germain, 1948. A very fine and fairly detailed history of nutrition and cookery, chiefly that of France.

Cuisine Française et Africaine. Léon Isnard. Éditions Albin Michel, Paris, 22 rue Huyghens, 1949.

La Table et l'Amour. Nouveau Traité des Excitants Modernes. Curnonsky et André Saint-Georges. La Clé d'Or, Paris, 1950.

Vieux Pots, Saulces et Rosts Memorables. Essai Historique et Meilleures Recettes de la Cuisine Française. Charles Gay, Tours, Arrault et Cie, 1950. A rather pompous and tiresome book but well printed and sumptuously produced, with an interesting collection of illustrations.

Le Guide de la Charcuterie. Aide-Mémoire de Charcuterie Pratique. P. E. Laloue, 1954. En vente au Guide de la Charcuterie, 191 rue de l'Ermitage, Montreuil-sous-Bois (Seine). First published 1950.

Gastronomie Bourbonnaise. Roger Lallemand, Gannat, 1951.

Recettes et Paysages: (1) *Sud-Ouest et Pyrenées,* 1950. (2) *Sud-Est, Mediterranée,* 1951. (3) *Île de France, Val de Loire,* 1951. (4) *L'Est de la France, Champagne, Alsace, Lorraine, Bourgogne, Franche-Comté, Bresse,* 1952. (5) *Nord, Bretagne, Normandie, Pays de l'Ouest,* 1952. Paris, Publications Françaises, 13 rue de Grenelle. The recipes in these collections are mainly taken from other books, but the colour-photographs of food and cooked dishes are of unique quality.

La Véritable Cuisine Provençale et Niçoise. Jean-Noël Escudier. Éditions Gallia-Toulon, 1953.

Le Plus Doux des Péchés. Robert J. Courtine. Bourg. Éditions Touristiques et Littéraires, 1954.

L'Aventure est dans votre cuisine. Marie-Paule Pomaret et Hélène Cingria. Éditions Pierre Horay, 22B Passage Dauphine, Paris VI, 1954.

La Charcuterie à la Campagne. Henriette Babet-Charton. La Maison Rustique, 26 rue Jacob, Paris; 6th edition, 1954.

La Cuisine de Chez Nous: (1) *Le Bourbonnais.* (2) *Le Nivernais-Morvan.* Roger Lallemand. Imprimerie Régionale R. Gentil, Gannat (Allier), 1954, 1955.

Un Gastronome se Penche sur son Passé. Simon Arbellot, Paris, Éditions Colombier, 1955.

Les Sauces. Recettes et Conseils Pratiques. Collection Cuisine et Vins de France. Compagnie Parisienne d'Éditions techniques et commerciales, 94 Faubourg St. Honoré, 1957.

Manuel des Poissonniers. Édité par le Comité National Pour La Consommation du Poisson, 11 rue Anatole de la Forge, Paris, 1957.

ENGLISH TRANSLATIONS OF FRENCH COOKERY AND OTHER BOOKS

The French Family Cook. Being a complete system of French Cookery. Translated from the French. London. Printed for J. Bell, 148 Oxford Street, nearly opposite New Bond Street, 1793.

A Guide to Modern Cookery. G. A. Escoffier, with an introduction by Eugène Herbodeau. Heinemann, 1957. First published 1907. This translation of the *Guide Culinaire* is rather stilted and occasionally lapses into absurdity. All the same, and in spite of the fact that many of the recipes are now out of date, it remains a most valuable book of reference and, incidentally, provides some details of the eating habits of the time which, to us, already seem almost archaic. But, as Herbodeau very rightly says in his preface, 'There is a much greater difference between the recipes of Carême and those of Escoffier than between Escoffier's original recipes and our modern, less rich, adaptations.'

Clarisse, or The Old Cook. Translated from the French by Elise Vallée, with a preface by A. B. Walkley. London, Methuen & Co., 1926.

The New French Cooking. Paul Reboux. Translated by Elizabeth Lucas. Thornton Butterworth, 1927. Re-issued under the title *Food for the Rich*, by Blond, 1958.

French Cooking for Everywoman. Marcellys. Translated from *Les Recettes de Grandmère.* London, Country Life Ltd., 20 Tavistock Street, W.C.2, 1930.

L'Art Culinaire. Henri Pellaprat. First English translation *circa* 1930.

Good Fare: A Code of Cookery. Édouard de Pomiane. Translated by Blanche Bowes and edited by Doris Langley Moore, from *Le Code de la Bonne Chère.* Gerald Howe Ltd., 23 Soho Square, W.1, 1932.

Letters from Madame de Sévigné. Selected and translated by Violet Hammersley. London, Secker & Warburg, 1955. The letters in this edition run from 1648 to 1695.

Cooking in 10 Minutes: or the Adaptation to the Rhythm of our Time. Édouard de Pomiane. Translated by Peggie Benton. Bruno Cassirer, Oxford, 1948. Reprinted 1956.

Close to Colette. Maurice Goudeket, Secker & Warburg, 1956.

Fine Bouche: A History of the Restaurant in France. Pierre Andrieu. Translated from the French by Arthur L. Haywood. London, Cassell, 1956.

ENGLISH PUBLICATIONS REFERRED TO IN THE TEXT

The Modern Cook. By Mr. Vincent La Chapelle, Chief Cook to the Right Honourable The Earl of Chesterfield. London. Printed for the author and sold by Nicholas Prevost, at the Ship over-against Southampton Street, in the Strand. 3 vols. 1733. Dedicated to the Earl of Chesterfield. La Chapelle was subsequently Chef de Cuisine to the Prince of Orange and Nassau. His book was translated into French and published at The Hague in 1735 under the title *Le Cuisinier Moderne.* This version was dedicated to the Prince of Orange.

The Cook's Paradise, being William Verral's 'Complete System of Cookery'. Published in 1759. Reprint, with Thomas Gray's cookery notes in holograph, and Introduction and Appendices by R. L. Mégroz. London, 1948. The Sylvan Press, 24 Museum Street, W.C.1.

The Cook's Oracle. William Kitchiner, M.D. A new edition, London, 1829. Printed for Cadell & Co., Edinburgh; Simpkin & Marshall, and G. B. Whittaker, London; and John Cumming, Dublin. The preface to the 7th edition of this book is dated 1823.

The French Cook. A system of Fashionable and Economical Cookery for the Use of English Families. Louis Eustache Ude. Ci-devant cook to Louis XVI and the Earl of Sefton, and late steward to His Royal Highness the Duke of York. Ninth edition, enlarged. London, W. H. Ainsworth, 23 Old Bond Street, 1827.

Modern Cookery. Eliza Acton. Longmans, Green, 1855 edition. First published 1845. An important landmark in the history of English cookery books. Miss Acton seems to have been the first English author, preceding Mrs. Beeton by some fifteen years, to give minute detail and meticulous directions as regards quantities and timing in her recipes. She had also made a study of French cookery in France as well as making use of the instruction she received from French chefs in England. The book contains a number of authentic and interesting French recipes. It was much plagiarised by subsequent cookery writers, including Isabella Beeton. This ruthless, unacknowledged pillaging of her work was much resented by Miss Acton, as indeed it is by all authors who have experienced the same treatment, including Escoffier, who refers to it in the preface of *Le Guide Culinaire.*

A Ramble Through Normandy or Scenes, Characters and Incidents in a Sketching Excursion through Calvados. George M. Musgrave, M.A., London, David Bogue, Fleet Street, 1855.

Beeton's Book of Household Management. Edited by Mrs. Isabella Beeton, London, S. O. Beeton, 248 Strand, W.C.2, 1861.

Edible Mollusks of Great Britain and Ireland, with recipes for cooking them. M. S. Lovell, London, Reeve & Co., 1867.

The Book of Household Management. Mrs. Isabella Beeton. Entirely new edition. Revised, corrected, and greatly enlarged. Ward, Lock & Co., 1899.

A Little Tour in France. Henry James, London, William Heinemann, 1900.

Simple French Cooking for English Homes. Marcel Boulestin, London, William Heinemann, 1933. First published 1923.

A· Second Helping or More Dishes for English Homes. Marcel Boulestin, London, William Heinemann, 1925.

Birds and Beasts of the Greek Anthology. Norman Douglas. Chapman & Hall, 1928.

Journal, 1929. Arnold Bennett. London, Cassell & Co. Ltd., 1930.

French Dishes for English Tables: Soups and Potages, Hors-d'œuvre, Salads. J. Berjane (Comtesse de ——), London, Frederick Warne & Co. Ltd., 1931.

What Shall we have Today? Marcel Boulestin, London. First published 1931; William Heinemann, 1937, 2nd edition.

Having Crossed the Channel. Marcel Boulestin. William Heinemann, 1934.

Myself, My Two Countries. X. M. Boulestin. London, Cassell, 1936.

The Finer Cooking or Dishes for Parties. Marcel Boulestin, London, Cassell & Co., 1937.

Madame Bégué's Recipes of Old New Orleans Creole Cookery. Harmanson, 333 Royal Street, New Orleans. 2nd Edition, 1937.

Provence. Ford Madox Ford, London, George Allen & Unwin Ltd., 1938.

Return to Normandy. Vivian Rowe. Evans Bros., 1951.

The Sudden View. A Mexican Journey. Sybille Bedford, London, Victor Gollancz Ltd., 1953. Re-issued as *A Visit to Don Otavio*, Collins, 1960.

Alsace and its Wine Gardens. S. F. Hallgarten, London, André Deutsch, 1957.

By Request. An Autobiography. André L. Simon. The Wine & Food Society, 1957.

PERIODICALS

La Cuisine des Familles. Recueil Hebdomadaire de Recettes d'Actualité très clairement expliquées, très faciles à exécuter. Rédactrice en chef, Madame Jeanne Savarin, June 1905–June 1907. A number of the most distinguished chefs and gastronomes of the day contributed to this remarkable magazine, which cost 5 centimes a copy.

Le Carnet d'Épicure. Revue illustrée des Arts de la Table Littéraire, Philosophique et Gourmande, with English Translations of Escoffier's New Recipes. Editor-in-Chief, Th. Gringoire, 24 Johnson Street, Westminster. Monthly publication directed at professional chefs, restaurateurs and hôteliers. 1912–1914. Most of the well-known French chefs of the day, the majority of them working in England, contributed to this magazine, in the publication of which Escoffier was the leading spirit. It was 9d. a copy in England and Fr. 1.25 in France.

Les Feuillets Occitans. La Gastronomie Méridionale. Special number of this monthly publication devoted to the local cookery of the Languedoc, the Roussillon and the Pays d'Oc. Edited by Prosper Montagné, 1927.

La Table. Le Magazine de la Gastronomie Française. (1) Hiver 1931–1932. (2) Numéro 2. A sumptuous quarterly publication of which the Editor-in-Chief was Gaston Derys and Curnonsky the Literary Director. During its short life every distinguished gastronome in France appears to have contributed to this magazine. The price was Fr. 15.

The Wine and Food Society Quarterly. Edited by André L. Simon, President of the Wine and Food Society, 30 Grosvenor Gardens, London, S.W.1, 1934–1959.

La France à Table. Gastronomie et Tourisme. A magazine founded in 1934 by Curnonsky and the publisher Praget; it appeared every two months. Publication was suspended during the 1939–1945 war and resumed in 1949. Each number deals with tourism and regional cookery in one particular province of France. 11 rue Quentin-Bauchart, Paris 8ᵉ.

Cuisine et Vins de France. Monthly magazine founded by Curnonsky. January 1950–1959. 94 Faubourg Saint-Honoré (Place Beauvau), Paris 8ᵉ.

GUIDES

Guide Michelin. Yearly publication. Pneu Michelin, Services de Tourisme, 79 Boulevard Péreire, Paris 17.

Guide des Touristes Gastronomes. Réalisé sous la direction de Simon Arbellot, de l'Académie des Gastronomes. Kléber-Colombes. Yearly publication. Éditions Taride, 154 Boulevard St. Germain, Paris VIᵉ.

The Gourmet's Guide to Europe. Lieut.-Colonel Newnham-Davis and Algernon Bastard. Edited by the former; London, Grant Richards, 1903. This famous book by a celebrated gourmet of the day (Col. Newnham-Davis was a regular contributor on gastronomic subjects to the *Pall Mall* magazine) includes a chapter on eating in French provincial towns.

La France Gastronomique. Guide des merveilles culinaires et des bonnes auberges Françaises. Curnonsky et Marcel Rouff, Paris, F. Rouff, Éditeur, 148 Rue de Vaugirard.

L'Alsace. 1921.

L'Anjou. 1921.

Le Béarn. 1922.

Bordeaux, Le Bordelais et Les Landes. 1924.

La Bourgogne. 1923.

La Bretagne. 1923.

Le Périgord. 1923.

La Provence. 1923.

La Savoie. 1923.

La Touraine. 1922.

The Yellow Guides for Epicures. Paris. The Environs of Paris and Normandy. Curnonsky and Marcel Rouff. Thornton Butterworth Ltd., 15 Bedford Street, London, W.C.2, 1926.

What to Eat and Drink in France. Austin de Croze. (Translation by the author of *Le Trésor Gastronomique de France.*) London, Frederick Warne, 1931.

Le Trésor Gastronomique de France. Repertoire complet des specialités gourmandes des trente-deux provinces de France. Austin de Croze, Paris, Librairie Delagrave, 1933. First published 1929.

BIBLIOGRAPHIES

Bibliotheca Gastronomica. A Catalogue of Books and Documents on Gastronomy. Compiled and annotated by André L. Simon, President of the Wine and Food Society. London, The Wine and Food Society, 1953.

Bibliographie Gastronomique. G. Vicaire. First published 1890. Second edition published by Derek Verschoyle, Academic and Bibliographical Publications Ltd., London, 1954. Now distributed by André Deutsch, 12–14 Carlisle Street, London, W.1.

ADDITIONAL BOOK LIST

Traité Pratique de Panification Francaise et Parisienne. E. Dufour, boulanger, 1935. Fourth edition (revised and brought up to date)circa 1947. Published and sold by the author, Emile Dufour, Villeneuve-les-Bordes, Seine-et-Marne, France. Present edition (1957) printed by the S.G.I.C. 71 rue de Rennes, Paris. A valuable treatise, by a professional baker, on the constituents, the mixing, leavening, kneading, baking and sale of French household and fancy bread, croissants and brioches. Useful illustrations of bakery equipment and processes of bread mixing and baking.

A Book of Mediterranean Food. Elizabeth David. John Lehmann 1950. Penguin edition (revised) 1955. 2nd Penguin edition (re-revised) 1965. John Lehmann edition (revised as for 1955 Penguin edition) issued by Macdonald, 1958.

French Country Cooking. Elizabeth David. John Lehmann 1951. Penguin edition (revised) 1959. John Lehmann edition (revised) issued by Macdonald 1958.

Le Poisson dans la Cuisine Française. H-P Pellaprat Flammarion 1954.

La Cuisine Familiale. H-P Pellaprat. Flammarion. 1955. Pellaprat was one of the great teaching chefs of the 20th century. These two volumes are concerned with family and household cooking rather than with the *grande cuisine* for which Pellaprat is better known. Both books contain instructive and authentic illustrations.

Boulangerie d'Aujourdhui. Félix Urbain-Dubois, avec la collaboration de Louis Champeault, Professeur à l'École de Boulangerie des Grands Moulins de Paris. Éditions Joinville, 48 rue Monsieur le Prince, Paris 6ième. Third edition 1956. Explains the technical processes of French bread making, plain and fancy. Includes cake and pastry recipes and a few French regional bakery specialities. For the same subject see also Emile Dufour's book (1935) noted above.

Traditional Recipes of the Provinces of France. Edited by Curnonsky. W. H. Allen 1961.

Translation in one volume, and including the original colour photographs, of the regional recipes from *Recettes et Paysages de France* (see page 468).

Larousse Gastronomique. English translation and adaptation of Prosper Montagné's great work of reference. Paul Hamlyn 1962.

Some of the original text has been modified, cut, or replaced with new material. The new English colour photographs lack the authenticity of the French originals. On the whole however the transposition into English of this very complex work has been creditably accomplished.

Cooking with Pomiane. Translated and adapted by Peggie Benton from Dr. Edouard de Pomiane's *Radio Cuisine* books. Faber & Faber 1962.

Dr. de Pomiane's recipes have been admirably transposed into English usage and the spirit of his writing accurately conveyed by Peggie Benton. An entrancing book to read, and to cook from a highly instructive and successful one.

Meat at any Price. Translation and adaptation by Peggie Benton of *Viande à Tous Prix* by Ninette Lyon. Faber & Faber 1963. Recipes sketchy, but Mrs. Benton's explanations concerning the comparative French and English joints of meat and her notes on the cheaper cuts and ways of cooking them are valuable.

Mastering the Art of French Cooking. Simone Beck, Louisette Bertholle, Julia Child. Cassell & Co. 1963 (original American edition, Knopf 1961)

A very remarkable work indeed, dealing mainly with the finer French cooking. The techniques explained, and more authentically and fully explained than in any previous cookery book in the English language, are applicable to all French cooking of whatever category. The book is illustrated with instructive line drawings. An important reference book for every serious cook, amateur or professional.

La Cuisine Provençale de Tradition Populaire. René Jouveau. Éditions du Message Berne 1963.

The author of this very interesting book is the son of Maurice Jouveau, one of the successors of Frédéric Mistral as leader of the Félibrige writers of the Provençal revival movement.

René Jouveau has concerned himself mainly with the food and the cooking, the wines, the produce, and the traditional festival customs of the country people of Provence in the 19th century. In a sense the book could be described as the kitchen supplement to the work of the Félibrige writers, for René Jouveau has researched into the composition of almost every dish mentioned, and into the origins of every piece of ancient food lore recorded by Mistral and his circle of Provençal poets and writers.

Odeurs de Forêt et Fumets de Table. Charles Forot. Frontispice de Jean Chièze. Imprimerie Volle. Privas. 1963. Recollections of pre-1914 peasant and farmhouse cooking and gastronomy in the Vivarais and the Ardèche, with special reference to the works of Olivier de Serres, father of modern French horticulture and famous native son of the Ardèche. Some beautiful and unique recipes embodied in the text.

Cinq Mille Ans À Table. Georges et Germaine Blond. 483 pp. Publisher and printer not disclosed. Undated. Circa 1965. A luxuriously produced and well written although necessarily sketchy history of food and cookery with special reference to the origins and evolution of the famous dishes of France. Illustrated with scores of high quality black and white reproductions, imaginatively chosen, of contemporary paintings, engravings, drawings, book illustrations, tapestries, frescoes. Particularly interesting as an indication of the tremendous appeal to generations of French artists of cooking pots, kitchens, and all aspects of the pleasures of the table.

Index

R